Introducing Art

Teacher's Wraparound Edition

Glencoe
McGraw-Hill

New York, New York   Columbus, Ohio   Woodland Hills, California   Peoria, Illinois

About the Authors

Gene Mittler

Gene Mittler is one of the authors of Glencoe's middle school/junior high art series, *Introducing Art, Exploring Art,* and *Understanding Art.* He is also author of *Art in Focus,* a chronological approach to art for Glencoe's senior high program, and *Creating and Understanding Drawings.* He has taught at both the elementary and secondary levels and at Indiana University. He received an M.F.A. in sculpture from Bowling Green State University and a Ph.D. in art education from the Ohio State University. Dr. Mittler is currently Professor Emeritus at Texas Tech University.

Jean Morman Unsworth

Jean morman Unsworth, author, teacher, and consultant, is one of the authors of Glencoe's middle school/junior high book *Introducing Art.* Educated at the Art Institute of Chicago, University of Notre Dame, and the University of Georgia, she has taught elementary through graduate levels and was Professor of Fine Arts at Loyola University of Chicago until 1987. She initiated and designed Chicago Children's Museum and the Interdisciplinary Arts Masters program at Columbia College in Chicago. She now gives full time to writing and consulting.

Rosalind Ragans

Rosalind Ragans is one of the authors of Glencoe's middle school/junior high art series, *Introducing Art, Exploring Art,* and *Understanding Art.* She served as senior author on the elementary program *Art Connections* for the SRA division of McGraw-Hill, and wrote the multi-level, comprehensive *ArtTalk* text for Glencoe's senior high program. She received a B.F.A. at Hunter College, CUNY, New York, and earned a M.Ed. in Elementary Education at Georgia Southern College and Ph.D. in Art Education at the University of Georgia. Dr. Ragans was named National Educator of the Year for 1992.

Faye Scannell

Faye Scannell is an art specialist, lead art technology teacher, and teacher educator in the Bellevue, Washington Public Schools, the Bellevue Art Museum, and through Seattle Pacific University. She has written technology activities for Glencoe's , *Introducing Art, Exploring Art, Understanding Art,* and *ArtTalk.* She was educated at Kutztown State University of Pennsylvania, Lesley College, and several Washington universities. In 1993 she received the Art Educator of the Year Award from the Washington Art Education Association.

Glencoe/McGraw-Hill

A Division of The **McGraw·Hill** *Companies*

Send all inquiries to:
Glencoe/McGraw-Hill
21600 Oxnard Street, Suite 500
Woodland Hills, CA 91367

ISBN 0-02-662363-3 (Student Text)
ISBN 0-02-662364-1 (Teacher's Wraparound Edition)

Printed in the United States of America.

3 4 5 6 7 8 9   004/043   03 02 01 00 99

Table of Contents

New Directions in the Visual and Performing Arts

Teaching art goes well beyond the excitement of watching students analyze works of master artists or produce their own creations. You know that every child who identifies a work of a master artist, picks up a paint brush, or molds a lump of clay will do more. Students involved in a quality, comprehensive arts program will learn to convey ideas, feelings, and emotions. They will sharpen their ability to analyze, critique, and make informed judgments. Through a quality arts experience, all students benefit as they are encouraged to ask questions, to think, to learn, and to CREATE!

A quality, comprehensive art program enriches student's lives and allows for discovery and creative problem solving. It provides students with a broader perception of their environment and a greater understanding of historical and cultural perspectives. In the process, a quality art program cultivates learners who are able to make positive contributions to society.

Glencoe Addresses the New Directions

Glencoe addresses the new directions by providing three programs designed specifically for the middle school student. These comprehensive programs are structured around the belief that students learn best in a classroom that is engaging, meaningful, and focused on art as a core curriculum subject, one that is built on their everyday experiences and enriches their learning in all areas.

Providing a Comprehensive Art Program

▶ Each book in the series allows teachers to customize their lesson plans around a specific emphasis—the study of themes in art, art media and techniques, or the chronology and history of art.

▶ All programs in the series are similar in their presentation of historical and cultural boundaries particular to the study of art.

▶ Each text is sequentially developed in order that art can be taught as a core subject.

▶ Regular features throughout each text provide students the opportunity to see how art is integrated with other disciplines.

▶ All programs cover a wide range of media, techniques, processes, and artistic styles.

Integrating the Four Components

▶ **Artistic Perception** At the very center of arts instruction is the process of being able to talk about works of art and learning the basic skills and knowledge necessary to communicate in each art form. By learning the elements and principles of art, working with various media, and evaluating master artists' works, students develop an awareness of and appreciation for the presence of art both within the classroom and in their everyday experiences.

▶ **Creative Expression** Studio lessons and studio activities give students the opportunity to create works of art and use various media and techniques, including computers.

▶ **Historical and Cultural Context** Throughout the programs, works of art from various periods, styles, and cultural groups develop a broad base for students to celebrate cultural diversity and understand various global views.

▶ **Aesthetic Valuing** As students explore, theorize, and apply the principles of aesthetics and art criticism to their own artwork and the artwork of others, they formulate a lifelong appreciation and satisfying experience in the arts.

Linking the Performing Arts and Other Curriculum Areas

▶ Music, Dance, Theatre   The visual and performing arts are mutually reinforcing. Glencoe's art programs are designed to underscore that unity by presenting the exploration of art as it correlates to the performing arts. Students experience how the foundation of all areas of art are built upon corresponding concepts, whether those concepts are basic skills or cultural and historical contexts.

▶ Cross-Curriclum Connections   The art classroom provides an exciting opportunity to make connections between visual arts and other curriculum areas. Students learn how concepts in one subject area, in this case art, can enhance and increase their interest in and knowledge of other subject areas. Throughout Glencoe's middle school art programs, students make connections that translate across a wide range of curriculum areas—math, science, social studies, and language arts.

Addressing The National Standards for Arts Education

The National Standards for Arts Education provide guidelines that set benchmark stardards for grade-appropriate competency in the performing and visual arts. The Glencoe art programs are correlated to the National Standards (see Scope and Sequence on page TM8), and can help teachers design their lessons around the National Standards.

Expanding the Arts Through Technology

Advances in technology offer exciting opportunities to art teachers and students. Through videodiscs, CD-ROMS, and the Internet, students can sharpen their visual perception. With computer art programs, student push the limits of their creative expression beyond their expectations. New activities and resource components provided with the Glencoe art programs provide a range of technology options that encourage exploration of new possibilities both in art education and production.

Including Assessment Strategies

Throughout the Glencoe art programs, students are encouraged to keep sketchbooks and to develop a portfolio featuring their selected works of art. In addition, the frequent self-examination of completed artworks provides ongoing evaluation of each student's progress, fostering a sense of accomplishment and a commitment to high standards of art production, and preparing them for the transition to excellence in the work place.

Meeting the Needs of All Students

Believing that art is for all students, the Glencoe middle school art programs include activities and teaching strategies that help teachers adapt the art classroom to the specific needs of students. This inclusive approach reinforces the universal value of art education.

Glencoe answers the challenge to the new directions in art education with a 3-text middle school art series. This Series at a Glance displays a complete listing of chapters in the series.

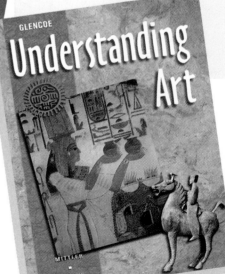

National Standards for the Visual Arts

The National Standards for Art Education represents, in part, the results of a 2-year effort by the Consortium of National Arts Education Associations to set standards for arts education in the United States. These six standards listed below are designed specifically for students in grades 5-8.

1. **Content Standard:** Understanding and applying media, techniques, and processes
   Achievement Standard:
   Students
   a. select media, techniques, and processes; analyze what makes them effective or not effective in communicating ideas; and reflect upon the effectiveness of their choices
   b. intentionally take advantage of the qualities and characteristics of art media, techniques, and processes to enhance communication of their experiences and ideas

2. **Content Standard:** Using knowledge of structures and functions
   Achievement Standard:
   Students
   a. generalize about the effects of visual structures and functions and reflect upon these effects in their own work
   b. employ organizational structures and analyze what makes them effective or not effective in the communication of ideas
   c. select and use the qualities of structures and functions of art to improve communication of their ideas

3. **Content Standard:** Choosing and evaluating a range of subject matter, symbols and ideas
   Achievement Standard:
   Students
   a. integrate visual, spatial, and temporal concepts with content to communicate intended meaning in their artworks
   b. use subjects, themes, and symbols that demonstrate knowledge of contexts, values, and aesthetics that communicate intended meaning in artworks

4. **Content Standard:** Understanding the visual arts in relation to history and cultures
   Achievement Standard:
   Students
   a. know and compare the characteristics of artworks in various eras and cultures
   b. describe and place a variety of art objects in historical and cultural contexts
   c. analyze, describe, and demonstrate how factors of time and place (such as climate, resources, ideas, and technology) influence visual characteristics that give meaning and value to a work of art

5. **Content Standard:** Reflecting upon and assessing the characteristics and merits of their work and the work of others
   Achievement Standard:
   Students
   a. compare multiple purposes for creating works of art
   b. analyze contemporary and historic meanings in specific artworks through cultural and aesthetic inquiry
   c. describe and compare a variety of individual responses to their own artworks and to artworks from various eras and cultures

6. **Content Standard:** Making connections between visual arts and other disciplines
   Achievement Standard:
   Students
   a. compare the characteristics of works in two or more art forms that share similar subject matter, historical periods, or cultural context
   b. describe ways in which the principles and subject matter of other disciplines taught in the school are interrelated with the visual arts

Reprinted by permission.

To identify how the lessons and activities in each chapter of *Introducing Art* meet these national standards, the Scope and Sequence on pages TM8–14 and each chapter opening page of the Teacher's Wraparound Edition displays the following abbreviated form for quick reference.

NATIONAL STANDARDS

This chapter addresses the following National Standards for the Visual Arts:

1.	(a, b)	**4.**	(a, b, c)
2.	(a, b, c)	**5.**	(a, b, c)
3.	(a, b)	**6.**	(a, b)

(R) = Chapter Review (CC) = Connections Feature (1), (2), (3) etc. = Lessons	Chapter 1 The Elements of Art	Chapter 2 The Principles of Art
NATIONAL STANDARDS FOR THE VISUAL ARTS	1. (a, b) 3. (a) 2. (a, b, c) 6. (b)	1. (a, b) 3. (a, b) 6. (b) 2. (a, b, c)
ARTISTIC PERCEPTION	Making a viewer (1) Studying uses of color in paintings (6) Perceiving color (CC) Thinking About Art (R)	Identifying movement in artworks (4) Identifying rhythm in artworks (4) Recognizing unity (6) Thinking About Art (R)
CREATIVE EXPRESSION	Experimenting with lines (2) Experimenting with color combinations (3) Mixing colors (4) Sketching a still life (5) Drawing a still life (6) Making rubbings for texture (7)	Sketching shapes with balance (1) Making a mask with formal balance (2) Studio Option (2) Painting a still life with emphasis (3) Creating a rhythmic drawing (4) Making a tessellation (5)
HISTORICAL/CULTURAL CONTEXT	Artist defined (1) Van Gogh's use of line (2) Hardin's art (3) Monet's use of color (4) Use of negative space (5) Texture in Guardian Figure (7)	Description of African mask (2) Community Connection (R)
AESTHETIC VALUING	Examining Your Work (4, 6)	Examining Your Work (2, 5) Identifying unity (6)
ELEMENTS AND PRINCIPLES OF ART	Using the artist's vocabulary (1) Line defined (2) Color defined (3) Properties of color (3) Combining colors (3) Shape, form, space defined (5) Texture defined (7)	Balance defined (1) Variety, harmony, emphasis, proportion defined (3) Movement, rhythm defined (4) Unity defined (6)
ART FORMS	Drawing (2, 5, 6) Painting (3, 5, 6, 7) Sculpture (5)	Drawing (2, 5) Painting (3) Sculpture (5)
MEDIA, TOOLS, TECHNIQUES, AND PROCESSES	Tools and processes for creating lines (2) Impressionist color techniques (4) Space techniques (5)	Making a viewer (1) Changing value and intensity (3) Mixing colors (4) Creating depth (5)
CURRICULUM AND PERFORMING ARTS CONNECTIONS	Science (CC, R) Computer Science (CC) Music (R)	Computer Science (5, CC) Math (CC) Language Arts (R)
CAREERS/PORTFOLIOS	Portfolio Ideas (p. 3) Portfolios (1, 2, 3, 5, 7)	Portfolio Ideas (p. 25) Portfolios (1, 3, 4, 6)

Chapter 3 Art Media and Techniques	Chapter 4 Looking at Art	Chapter 5 Art Through the Ages
1. (a, b) 3. (a, b) 6. (b) 2. (a, b, c) 4. (a, c)	1. (a, b) 2. (a, b, c) 3. (a) 6. (a, b)	1. (a, b) 3. (a, b) 5. (ε, c) 2. (a, b, c) 4. (a, b, c) 6. (ε, b)
Why artists draw (1) Perception defined (1) Thinking About Art (1)	Describing artworks (3) Point-of-view defined (4) Thinking About Art (R)	Thinking About Art (R)
Keeping a sketchbook (1) Making a gesture drawing (2) Experimenting with watercolors (3) Creating a portrait (4) Making a collage (7) Experimenting with art software (8)	Experimenting with non-objective art (3) Creating a realistic painting (4) Studio Option (4, 6) Creating an expressive word design (5) Creating an abstract figure (6)	Creating an Egyptian tomb painting (2) Making a relief sculpture (4) Making a stained glass window (5) Creating a diorama (6) Using abstraction in art (8)
History of painting media (3, 8) History of printmaking techniques (5)	History of non-objective art (3) Community Connection (CC)	Art of ancient Egypt, Greece, and Rome (1) Pericles and Exekias (1) Art of ancient India and Japan (3) History of Hinduism and Buddhism (3) African sculpture (4) Art of the Renaissance (5) Art of the 19/20th century (7)

Examining Your Work (2, 4, 7)
Planning a collage theme (7)
	Aesthetics and aesthetic views (1)
	Subject, composition, and
	   content defined (1)
	Art criticism (2)
	Describing, analyzing, interpreting, and
	   judging art described (2)
	Critiquing non-objective art (3)
		Examining Your Work (2, 4, 6, 8)
		Impressionists defined (7)
		Surrealists defined (7)
		Analyzing an abstract artwork (8)

Comparing portraits (4)	Elements and principles
	   as composition (2)
		Rules of Egyptian art (1)
		Elements and principles of art in Greek
		   vases (1)
		Symbol defined (2)
		Line perspective defined (6)
		Using color to create space (6)

Drawing (1, 2) Painting (3, 4) Printing (5) Sculpture (6) Computer Art (8)	Painting (1, 2, 3, 4, 5, 6, CC) Sculpture (3)	Sculpture (1, 2, 3, 4, 6) Pottery (1) Painting (2, 5, 7, 8) Painted screen (3) Architecture (5)
Art media defined (1) Drawing media (1, 2) Shading techniques (1) Gesture drawing defined (2) Paint defined (3) Painting media (3) Pigments, binders, and solvents defined (3) Printmaking (5) Sculpture (6) Collage defined (7) Computer art media (8)	Non-objective techniques (3) Expressive techniques (5) Abstract techniques (6)	Bust defined (1) Contour defined (2) Relief sculpture techniques (4) Architecture techniques (5)
Computer Science (7, 8, CC) Social Studies (CC) Music (R) Math (8, R)	Computer Science (5, CC) Technology (CC) Language Arts (R)	Computer Science (8, CC) History (CC) Music (R)
Portfolio Ideas (p. 41) Portfolios (1, 3, 5, 6, 8)	Portfolio Ideas (p. 63) Portfolios (1, 2, 3) Art Critic (2)	Portfolio Ideas (p. 81) Portfolios (1, 3, 5, 7)

(R) = Chapter Review (CC) = Connections Feature (1), (2), (3) etc. = Lessons	Chapter 6 Perceiving Nature	Chapter 7 Observing Animals
NATIONAL STANDARDS FOR THE VISUAL ARTS	1. (a, b) 3. (a) 5. (a, c) 2. (a, b, c) 4. (a) 6. (b)	1. (a, b) 3. (a, b) 5. (a, b, c) 2. (a, b, c) 4. (a, b, c) 6. (a, b)
ARTISTIC PERCEPTION	Landscape defined (1) Nature study defined (3) Point-of-view described (3, 4) Studying seasonal artworks (5)	Thinking About Art (R)
CREATIVE EXPRESSION	Making a stylized landscape (1) Creating a nature scene (1) Experimenting with point-of-view (3) Drawing from a bird's-eye view (4) Creating seasonal colors (5) Painting a seasonal event (6) Making a monoprint (7) Painting a storm (8)	Inventing a mascot (1) Creating a totem (2) Making a fish collage (3) Making a glue-line print (4) Practicing calligraphy (5) Making an animal sculpture (6) Creating an imaginary animal (7) Creating a fantasy creature (8)
HISTORICAL/CULTURAL CONTEXT	Leonardo da Vinci (3)	Prehistoric art (1) Australian aboriginal art (2) Early Chinese art (3) Modern Japanese art (3) Persian art (5)
AESTHETIC VALUING	Examining Your Work (2, 4, 6, 8) Expressive art (8)	Ritual art (1) Totem defined (2) Examining Your Work (2, 4, 6, 8)
ELEMENTS AND PRINCIPLES OF ART	Perspective in an artwork (1) Rhythm in an artwork (1, 2) Using elements and principles in an artwork (2) Size and placement in an artwork (5) Using color and shape in an artwork (6)	Using line (4) Line in illuminations (5) Identifying elements and principles in sculpture (6) Color in Expressionism (7)
ART FORMS	Painting (1, 2, 3, 4, 5, 6, 7) Assemblage (2) Drawing (3) Printmaking (7)	Sculpture (1, 6, 8) Painting (1, 5, 7) Pottery (3) Printmaking (4) Weaving (7)
MEDIA, TOOLS, TECHNIQUES, AND PROCESSES	Resist defined (6) Monoprint techniques (7)	Tools of early painters (1) Porcelain defined (2) Appliqué technique (3) Etching technique (4) Calligraphy defined (5) Tapestry defined (7) Overlapping technique (7) Folk art defined (8) Folk art media (8)
CURRICULUM AND PERFORMING ARTS CONNECTIONS	Computer Science (8, CC) Environmental Studies (CC) Music (R)	Computer Science (2, 8, CC) Creative Writing (8) History (CC) Science (R) Technology (R)
CAREERS/PORTFOLIOS	Portfolio Ideas (p. 103) Portfolios (1, 3, 5, 7)	Portfolio Ideas (p. 123) Portfolios (1, 3, 5, 7)

Chapter 8 Portraying People	Chapter 9 Visiting Places	Chapter 10 Examining Objects
1. (a, b) 3. (a) 5. (a, c) 2. (a, b, c) 4. (a, b, c) 6. (a, b)	1. (a, b) 3. (a, b) 5. (a, c) 2. (a, b, c) 4. (a, c) 6. (a, b)	1. (a, b) 3. (a, b) 5. (a, b) 2. (a, b, c) 4. (a, b, c) 6. (a, b)
Figure study defined (3) Thinking About Art (R)	Furniture design (2) Cities in art (5) Panorama defined (7) Thinking About Art (R)	Perceive defined (1) Nature studies described (1) Thinking About Art (R)
Making an expressive self-portrait (1) Creating an expressive face (2) Studio Options (2, 4, 8) Creating a figure study (3) Drawing a figure in action (4) Experimenting with abstract designs (5) Creating a clay portrait (6) Making a hero exhibit (7) Creating a mixed-media banner (8)	Drawing your room (1) Creating a piece of furniture (2) Making an architectural design (3) Creating a fanciful exterior (4) Drawing a building detail (5) Creating a mixed-media cityscape (6) Creating a panorama (7) Creating a seasonal panorama (8)	Viewing objects up close (1) Drawing a magical forest (2) Experimenting with form and value (3) Painting a watercolor still life (4) Creating an object design (5) Building a clay instrument (6) Studio Options (6) Creating a jewelry design (7) Creating a pendant (8)
Portraits as historical records (1) Painting in the 1500s (1) Japanese warrior masks (2) Renaissance sculpture (5) Michelangelo (5) African ancestor figures (5) Folk legends in art (7)	Vincent van Gogh (1) Homes of the past and present (3) Frank Lloyd Wright (3) Russian architecture of the 1500s (4) Victorian architecture (4) Louis H. Sullivan (5) John Sloan and the Eight (6)	Georgia O'Keeffe (1) Japanese still life (3) Persian applied art (5) Roman goldwork (5) Jewelry from the 1500s (7) Jewelry from the 1700s (7) Southwestern art (8)
Comparing artworks of different periods (1) Trompe-l'oeil defined (5) Public art defined (7) Memorial art defined (7) Examining Your Work (2, 4, 6, 8)	Painting of a room (1) Staged photograph of a room (1) Examining Your Work (2, 4, 6, 8)	Applied art described (5) Decorative arts described (7) Examining Your Work (2, 4, 6, 8)

Style defined (1)
Elements and principles used to
   suggest movement (3, 4)
	Using rhythm in architectural design (4)
	Organization of elements and principles
	   in an art work (5)
	Using color to suggest season (8)
		Using elements and principles
		   imaginatively (2)
		Using elements and principles
		   in still lifes (3)
		Using shape to create interest (8)

Painting (1, 3, 4) Sculpture (2, 5, 6, 7) Mixed media (8)	Painting (1, 2, 7) Photography (1) Architecture (3, 4, 5) Mixed media (6) Sculpture (6)	Painting (1, 3, 4) Drawing (1, 2) Sculpture (5) Jewelry making (5, 7, 8) Pottery (6) Pottery defined (6)
Portraiture defined (5) Embossed design described (6) Murals defined (7)	Staged photography defined (1) Architectural techniques defined (4) Cityscape defined (5) Seascape defined (7)	Still life described (3) Fluting defined (5) Slip defined (6) Kiln described (6)
Computer Science (6, CC) Social Studies (CC) Language Arts (R)	Computer Science (2, 8, CC) Social Studies (CC) Language Arts (R) Geography (R)	Computer Science (2, 4, CC) Music (CC) Language Arts (R) Family and Consumer Sciences (R)
Portfolio Ideas (p. 143) Portfolios (1, 3, 5, 7)	Portfolio Ideas (p. 163) Portfolios (1, 3, 5, 7) Architects (3)	Portfolio Ideas (p. 183) Portfolios (1, 3, 5, 7)

(R) = Chapter Review (CC) = Connections Feature (1), (2), (3) etc. = Lessons	Chapter 11 Recording Events	Chapter 12 Telling a Story
NATIONAL STANDARDS FOR THE VISUAL ARTS	1. (a, b) 3. (a, b) 5. (a, c) 2. (a, b, c) 4. (a, c) 6. (a, b)	1. (a, b) 3. (a, b) 5. (a, c) 2. (a, b, c) 4. (a, c) 6. (a, b)
ARTISTIC PERCEPTION	Visual reporting and recording (10) Check Your Understanding (1, 3, 5, 7) Reviewing Art Facts (R) Thinking About Art (R)	Visual stories (1, 2, 5) Using myths and legends in art (3) Thinking About Art (R)
CREATIVE EXPRESSION	Composing a photograph (1) Drawing a sporting event (2) Recording a historical event (3) Drawing a cartoon (4) Planning a mosaic (5) Creating a room in outer space (6) Planning a story board (7) Making a video documentary (8)	Designing a cartouche (1) Making a visual autobiography (2) Sketching a mythical beast (3) Creating a mythical creature (4) Painting a mural (6) Designing a letter (7) Creating a book cover (8)
HISTORICAL/CULTURAL CONTEXT	Artist as reporter (1) Artist as historian (3)	Chinese picture writing (1) Native American picture writing (1) Chinese mythical art (3) Hindu mythical art (3) Kachina defined (4) History of book illustration (5)
AESTHETIC VALUING	Examining Your Work (2, 4, 6, 8)	Examining Your Work (2, 4, 6, 8)
ELEMENTS AND PRINCIPLES OF ART	Using elements and principles to create movement (2)	Using color and pattern to create formal balance and rhythm (4)
ART FORMS	Photography (1, 5) Painting (1, 3) Drawing (2, 4) Mosaic (5) Sculpture (6) Motion pictures and videos (7)	Picture writing (1, 2) Mixed media (1) Drawing (3) Sculpture (3, 4) Painting (5, 6, 8) Textiles (5) Illumination (7)
MEDIA, TOOLS, TECHNIQUES, AND PROCESSES	Gouache defined (1) Caricature defined (4) Frieze defined (5) Kinetoscope defined (7) Motion picture media (7)	Pictograms described (1) Cartouche defined (1) Petroglyph defined (1) Fresco defined (5) Gold leaf (7) Font (8)
CURRICULUM AND PERFORMING ARTS CONNECTIONS	Computer Science (2, 6, CC) History (CC) Language Arts (R) Science (R)	Computer Science (2, 8, CC) Language Arts (CC, R) Technology (R)
CAREERS/PORTFOLIOS	Portfolio Ideas (p. 203) Portfolios (1, 3, 5, 7) Videographer (8)	Portfolio Ideas (p. 223) Portfolios (1, 3, 5, 7)

Chapter 13 Celebrations	Chapter 14 Creating Fantasy
1. (a, b)　　3. (a, b)　　5. (a, b, c) 2. (a, b, c)　4. (a, b, c)　6. (a, b)	1. (a, b)　　3. (a, b)　　5. (b) 2. (a, b, c)　4. (a, b)　　6. (a, b)
Interpreting celebrations (1, 3, 5, 7) Thinking About Art (R)	Juxtaposition described (3, 5)
Making a tricolor (1) Creating an event quilt (2) Studio Options (2, 6) Creating kinetic "festival" art (4) Making a hat (5) Collage of a family gathering (6) Creating an African design (7) Celebrating a role model (8)	Drawing in the Surrealist style (1) Creating a fantasy bird collage (2) Extending an image (3) Creating a puzzle picture (4) Creating an "impossible" city (5) Creating an "etching" of a strange place (6)
Artwork celebrating American Independence (1) Artwork celebrating Mexican Independence (1) Hopi celebrations (3) Chinese rite of passage object (5) African rite of passage object (5) Inuit art (7) Community Connection (R)	Surrealism defined (1) History of fantasy art (1) René Magritte (2) History of juxtaposition in painting (3)
Examining Your Work (2, 4, 6, 8)	Fantasy art defined (1) Surrealists described (1) Examining Your Work (2, 4, 6) Social protest art described (4)
Using variety in an artwork (2) Using repetition to create rhythm (4)	Examining Your Work (2, 4, 6)
Painting (1, 3, 4, 7) Textile (2) Mixed media (5, 6, 8)	Painting (1, 3, 4) Drawing (1, 6) Mixed media (2) Lithography (5)
Shadow puppet described (4) Kinetic art defined (4) Adenla defined (5)	Architectural rendering defined (5) Belvedere defined (5)
Computer Science (4, 8, CC) Performing Arts (CC) Social Studies (R)	Computer Science (6, CC) Language Arts (CC, R) Social Studies (R)
Portfolio Ideas (p. 243) Portfolios (1, 3, 5, 7)	Portfolio Ideas (p. 263) Portfolios (1, 3, 5)

(1), (2), (3) etc. = Lessons	Handbook
NATIONAL STANDARDS FOR THE VISUAL ARTS	1. (a, b) 3. (a, b) 5. (a, b, c) 2. (a, b, c) 4. (a, b, c) 6. (a, b)
ARTISTIC PERCEPTION	Contour drawing (3)
CREATIVE EXPRESSION	Making a color wheel (1) Creating a "clan" robe (2) Contour drawing (3)
HISTORICAL/CULTURAL CONTEXT	Artist profiles (pp. 292–297): Bearden, Hokusai, Leyster, Magritte, O'Keeffe, Phillips, Rivera, Steen, da Vinci.
AESTHETIC VALUING	Examining Your Work (1, 2, 3)
ELEMENTS AND PRINCIPLES OF ART	Color (1) Shape(1, 2,) Line (3) Balance (2)
ART FORMS	Painting (1) Computer Art (1, 2) Mixed media (2) Drawing (3)
MEDIA, TOOLS, TECHNIQUES, AND PROCESSES	Drawing tips (pp. 281–283) Painting tips (pp. 283–285) Printmaking tips (p. 285) Sculpting tips (pp. 285–288) Measuring (p. 288) Making a mat (pp. 289–290) Mounting a two-dimensional work (pp. 290–291) Working with tissue paper (p. 291) Working with glue (p. 291)
CURRICULUM AND PERFORMING ARTS CONNECTIONS	Art (p. 318) Communication (p.317) Dance (pp. 313, 314, 315, 316, 317) History (pp. 314, 316, 322) Language Arts (pp. 313, 318, 320, 321, 322, 323, 324, 325, 326) Music (pp. 314, 316, 318,319, 321, 322, 323, 325) Science (pp. 319, 321) Technology (pp. 313, 317) Theatre (pp. 319, 320, 324, 326) Voice (p. 317)

CAREERS/PORTFOLIOS	Career Spotlights (pp. 298–305):
	  Advertising Artist Industrial Designer
	  Architect Interior Designer
	  Art Director Landscape Architect
	  Art Teacher Museum Worker
	  Artist Photographer
	  Graphic Artist Textile Designer
	  Illustrator Web-site Designer

The Work Students Do

The *Introducing Art* student text introduces students to a theme-based program, laying the foundation for lifelong art appreciation and art production skills. From drawing and painting to architecture, graphic design, and photography, the 14 chapters interweave studio production with narrative lessons on the elements and principles of art, techniques, art history, and criticism.

CHAPTER OPENING Each chapter opens with a full-color motivational reproduction of a work of art related to the chapter's content. A brief introduction helps students focus on the chapter. Chapter objectives are listed as well as vocabulary terms that will be in the chapter.

CHAPTER 6

Perceiving Nature

Nature has many faces. You see its fury in the lashing rains of a fierce thunderstorm. You feel its kiss on a gentle spring day. You sense its majesty in a night-time sky aglitter with a billion stars.

Because of its ever-changing personality, nature has long been a favorite art subject. Examine the painting at the left. Which of nature's faces has this artist captured?

In this chapter you will learn about the ways in which artists have celebrated nature. You will see recent tributes and some from the past.

OBJECTIVES
After completing this chapter, you will be able to:
- Define the term *landscape*.
- Understand stylization.
- Explain what artists accomplish through nature studies.
- Experiment with two- and three-dimensional forms of self-expression.

WORDS YOU WILL LEARN
assemblage
landscape
monoprint
nature study
resist
study
stylized

PORTFOLIO IDEAS

A strong art portfolio contains samples of work created with a variety of media, techniques, and processes. Your entries might include preliminary sketches as well as finished works. By including self-reflections and written evaluations, you will learn more about yourself as an artist.

Figure 6–1 Notice how the artist used warm colors to help the viewer feel the heat of a July day. What principles of art did he use to show the motion of the hay cutters?
Thomas Hart Benton. *July Hay.* 1943.Oil and egg tempera on composition board. 96.5 × 67.9 cm (38 × 26½"). The Metropolitan Museum of Art, New York, New York. George A. Hearn Fund, 1943. © 1998 Thomas H. Benton & Rita P. Benton Testamentary Trusts/Licensed by VAGA, New York, NY

102

103

PORTFOLIO IDEAS With the increasing attention given to art portfolios as both a presentation and an assessment tool, each chapter begins with a suggestion of how students can use or adapt the activities within the chapter for their art portfolios.

NARRATIVE LESSONS Art concepts are presented and reinforced in accessible, easy-to-understand language, using relevant examples from art, from students' daily lives, or from history. Check Your Understanding provides a short review for each lesson.

STUDIO ACTIVITY Hands-on activities found in narrative lessons explore ways for students to quickly grasp ideas presented in the lessons. They are specifically designed to require minimal time and resources.

LESSON 3

Celebration Dances in Art

Does your school sponsor dances? Maybe a youth or social club in your community does. With few exceptions, such events in our society are leisure-time activities. Yet, in some cultures, dance plays a featured role in important celebrations.

In this lesson, you will explore two such celebrations. You will view artistic interpretations of dances that are part of these events.

A NATURE DANCE

Most of our dances are recreational. A few, however, have some special meaning. The opposite is true for the Hopi people of the American Southwest. In their culture, only a small number of dances are considered social events. The majority occupy an important place in rituals celebrating their people's oneness with nature.

One of these, the Green Corn Dance, is pictured in Figure 13–6. Examine this painting. Did you find your eye drawn to the sweeping curve formed by the ceremonial procession on the right side? The people in this line are the dancers. They are dressed in traditional clothing. Within the semi-circle is a second, smaller group that includes a drummer. Notice the dancers' upright posture. What does their body language suggest or tell about the *tempo*, or speed, of the music? Find the figure in the feathered headdress standing atop the **pueblo** (pweh-bloh), or *dried-clay dwelling*. Who do you think this person is?

A VICTORY DANCE

Some dances, like the one in Figure 13–6, are calm and dignified. Others are fast-paced and frenzied. How would you characterize the dance pictured in Figure 13–7? Without looking at the title, you can probably sense the joyous mood and high energy level of the dancers. The painting captures a part of a victory celebration in the artist's native island of Jamaica. Can you think of a dance or "ball" with a similar purpose in our own country?

Look closely at this painting. It is divided into three main sections. The top and bottom thirds of the picture plane are given over to musicians in brightly colored costumes. At the center are the dancers, framed against a field of vivid orange. Observe how the angled lines of their arms, legs, and bodies help convey a strong sense of urgent movement. Notice the array of bold colors that make up the buildings and plant life. What art principle has the artist used to control the many colors and shapes in this action-filled painting?

Check Your Understanding

1. What do most Hopi dances celebrate?
2. What event is the focus of the painting in Figure 13–7?

STUDIO ACTIVITY

Dance Gesture Drawing

Work with a group of about six classmates to learn and perform a popular dance step. The group is to repeat the same movements over and over. While they perform, the remainder of the class is to make individual gesture drawings of the event. Sketching rapidly in pencil, the students should try to capture the sense of movement, paying close attention to the angles of arms and legs. After completing their sketches, a second group of volunteers should perform the same step to allow the dancers to do their own gesture drawings.

portfolio

Write an evaluation of your gesture drawings. Did they capture movement? Were they in proportion? Put your critique in your portfolio with your drawings.

Figure 13–6 What do you think is the purpose of this dance? What role do the repetition of colors and forms and the use of vertical lines play in creating the painting's mood?
Fred Kabotie. *Pueblo Green Corn Dance, Hopi.* 1947. Oil on canvas. 75 × 64.8 cm (29⅜ × 25⅜"). The Thomas Gilcrease Institute of American History and Art, Tulsa, Oklahoma.

Figure 13–7 Would you describe this treatment as realistic? Has the artist used linear perspective or any of the other space-giving techniques described in Chapter 1?
Everald Brown. *Victory Dance.* 1976. Oil on canvas. 83.8 × 124.3 cm (33 × 49"). Organization of American States Museum, Washington, D.C. Collection of the Art Museum of the Americas.

Other Features of the Student Text:

Handbook includes Technique Tips, Artist Profiles, Career Spotlights, and Additional Studios.

Artsource®: Performing Arts Handbook highlights contemporary performing artists in music, dance, and theatre.

Artists and Their Works lists all artists and titles of their artworks and page references.

Glossary/Glosario defines each vocabulary term in English format, then separately in the Spanish Glosario.

STUDIO LESSONS Within each chapter, Studio Lessons are provided that build on previous narrative lessons and studio exercises. Each one gives students the opportunity to use various media and techniques. The lessons are illustrated by examples of fine art and include exemplary student artwork.

EXAMINING YOUR WORK This section guides students in applying the process of art criticism to their own works of art.

EXAMINING YOUR WORK

- Describe   List the materials used to create your animal. Describe the materials used for ears, eyes, and so on.
- Analyze   Describe the form you created. What surface texture did you use? What colors did you select?
- Interpret   What kind of mood or feeling does your creature express? Was your story funny or serious?
- Judge   Which aesthetic view would you use to describe your work? If you were to do this project again, what, if anything, would you change?

LESSON 8

Creating a Fantasy Creature

Look at the artwork in Figure 7–16. This is an example of folk art. **Folk art** is *art made by artists who have had no formal training.* The painting by Edward Hicks on page **140** is another example of folk art. In some cases, the name of the folk artist is not known.

The main medium in this example of folk art is bottle caps. The type used, called a crown cap, was first produced in 1891. Some bottlers today still use crown caps. These metal caps add an unusual surface texture to the giraffe. The work contains many other found objects as well. These include tree branches and a fur tail. All are attached to a metal body. How many different found media can you see?

Notice how the giraffe seems as though it is about to move. The diagonal slant of its legs and its neck help create that feeling.

WHAT YOU WILL LEARN

You will create a three-dimensional fantasy animal using recyclable materials and other found objects. Your creature will have a head, a body, legs, and a tail. Depending on the materials you collect, you may create other parts. These might include wings, ears, horns, spikes, hair, or fur. To add color, you will finish your creature by painting it or covering it with interesting buttons, fabric scraps, papers, foils, and so on. Give your creature a name. You will also write a story about its life and environment. Finally, present your creature to the class by telling your story.

WHAT YOU WILL NEED

- Assorted recyclable packing materials (yogurt cups, tubes, or other containers)
- White glue or masking tape
- Masking or transparent tape
- Newsprint for papier-mâché
- Cellulose wallpaper paste and water
- School tempera paints
- Assorted brushes
- Buttons, fabric scraps, pieces of broken toys, and other found materials
- Sheets of corrugated cardboard, poster board, or colored construction paper

Figure 7–16 What unusual material has the artist used to create this giraffe? What is the main principle of art in this sculpture?

Unknown American Artist. *Bottlecap Giraffe.* c. 1966. Carved and painted wood, bottlecaps, rubber, glass, animal hair and fur. 184.2 × 137.2 × 44.5 cm (72½ × 54 × 17½"). National Museum of American Art, Smithsonian Institution, Washington, D.C. Gift of Herbert Waide Hemphill, Jr. and museum purchase made possible by Ralph Cross Johnson.

138   Chapter 7   *Observing Animals*

Figure 7–17 Student work. Fantasy creatures.

WHAT YOU WILL DO

1. Collect a variety of recyclable packing materials. You might gather boxes, plastic containers, or tubes. Study these items. Practice placing them together to create the form of an imaginary creature. The form should include a head, a body, and legs.
2. When you have decided on an arrangement, attach the objects with masking tape. Apply papier-mâché strips to strengthen the joints and cover the body.
3. Choose colors of tempera paint. Decide whether your creature will have a smooth or rough surface texture. Apply the paint using brushes that will give the desired texture. Use large-bristled brushes for a rough texture. Use fine-bristled brushes for a smooth texture.
4. Add a tail, ears, eyes, and other parts. Use buttons, felt, trims, fabric, and other found objects. If you prefer, substitute pieces of cardboard, poster board, or colored construction paper.
5. Give your creature a name. Write a brief story about the creature and its environment. Present your fantasy creature to the class by reading your story aloud.

COMPUTER OPTION

Try This!   If your classroom computer has a 3-D modeling program, experiment with combining basic three-dimensional forms to make a fantasy animal. You might use a cube for the body and a cone for the neck. A sphere or ellipse might be the head. Use smaller versions of these shapes to make eyes, a nose, and so on. Adjust the lights to cast interesting shadows. Use the Render command to complete your creature.

Lesson 8   *Creating a Fantasy Creature*   **139**

Bibliography lists print and media resources for both the student and the teacher.

Index serves as a study aid and assists students in finding particular topics.

STUDENT ART
Exemplary student artwork of middle school/junior high students is displayed within the text to motivate your students.

COMPUTER OPTIONS
Where appropriate, technology alternatives for Studio Lessons are offered. They give students an opportunity to learn how to use the computer as an art tool, and how it can be used with traditional media and methods of creating art.

Integrating the Performing Arts

The **Artsource®: Performing Arts Handbook** is an exciting section in the *Introducing Art* Student Text. It features 14 artists or groups from the three fields of performing arts—dance, music, and theatre. The artists and groups are specifically chosen to correlate to the chapters in the book. *Introducing Art* provides this handbook as an opportunity for students to recognize and appreciate the connections that exist between the four arts disciplines. You are invited to use them as supplements to your lessons, or to have students work independently with the features as extension activities.

DANCE

Dance
Tandy Beal & Company

Tandy Beal is a dancer, choreographer, actress, comic, and dreamer. Born into a theatre family, she recalls her father's advice to struggling artists: "The most important thing about performing is that you must be truthful." Following his advice, her dance "Dust to Dust" explores the idea that although people look and act in ordinary ways, they can have a rich inner world of imagination. In a dramatic section of the piece, the dancers, wearing everyday clothing, tear through large sheets of paper that have projected images of themselves dressed as performers. The work ends when the dancers disappear, replaced by tall columns of sand and glitter falling lightly onto the stage.

Tandy Beal & Company. *"Dust to Dust."* Photo courtesy of Tandy Beal & Company.

■ DISCUSSION QUESTIONS

1. The photo on this page depicts a moment from the dance "Dust to Dust." Describe the positions of the dancers and the feelings you think they are expressing.
2. In thinking about the brief description of the dance, what do you think the choreographer was trying to show when she chose to replace the dancers with columns of sand and glitter? Discuss your ideas and give reasons to support them.
3. People can easily see the daily activities we do but cannot know what goes on in the world of our imagination. Discuss this idea and give examples from your own life.

■ CREATIVE EXPRESSION ACTIVITIES

Technology Using a camera, take close-up slides of different members of the class. Project these onto butcher paper in a darkened room and have people do simple movements, such as walking, skipping, jumping, and swaying in front of them so that the projections move back and forth from the paper to the people. Wear white for the best effect.

Language Arts Although people look ordinary and act ordinary in their daily lives, they can have a rich inner world of imagination. Write about this concept with regard to yourself.

MUSIC

Music
Chic Street Man

Chic Street Man is clever at communicating ideas through his music. He often combines storytelling in his compositions, as in *Rag Man.* He skillfully uses his guitar, his singing voice, and his speaking voice to tell the tale of a rag man, as seen through the eyes of a boy. This is a true story-song of an old man who used a horse and wagon to come into Chic's neighborhood looking for rags. The song is sung in a style derived from African cultural traditions, combining storytelling and poetry with music.

Chic Street Man. *Rag Man.* Photo by Neil Ricklen.

■ DISCUSSION QUESTIONS

1. Chic Street Man calls his *Rag Man* performance a "rap recitation." Why do you think he calls it that?
2. In *Rag Man* Chic weaves a story about a man who advertised his work by riding through the streets calling and singing to his potential customers. Do vendors still come to your neighborhood? If so, discuss what they sell and how they call to their customers.
3. Discuss how songs and music are used to advertise and sell products. Recall some songs that are memorable or are being currently used.

■ CREATIVE EXPRESSION ACTIVITIES

Language Arts Select three commercials using music or song that are memorable. Demonstrate and describe them, discuss the various music styles used, and suggest what type of audience the companies wish to reach.

Art/History/Culture Examine the artworks of African-American artists who, like their counterparts in music, have portrayed the historical, cultural, social, and political lives of their people. Look for the messages the artists convey, and describe how they communicated their messages through visual [...]

Theatre
Great Leap

For "Joanne Is My Middle Name," Nobuko Miyamoto went deep inside herself to dramatize the dilemma of being a third generation Japanese-American searching for a way to belong. She found the theme of trying to adapt her name and examined the trail of name changes. As a young girl, she connected with the magic of the arts through music, which in turn awakened her passion to dance and dramatically tell stories. This song/story begins with her childhood experiences of living in Japanese internment camps during World War II. It continues through her various rites of passage to the acceptance of her heritage and her name.

Nobuko Miyamoto and members of Great Leap. *"Joanne Is My Middle Name"* from *A Slice of Rice.*

■ DISCUSSION QUESTIONS

1. Many immigrants who come to this country change their names in order to fit into the American culture. Discuss the pros and cons of doing this.
2. Discuss the symbolic importance of names in relationship to our identity. What do names tell about us? Where did your name come from? Were you named after a relative or famous person? What do you feel that your name tells about you?
3. Make a list of the names of people in your class and what cultural heritage they represent. What are the advantages of having a name which in some way connects you to your heritage?

■ CREATIVE EXPRESSION ACTIVITIES

Language Arts Ask your parents how your name was chosen for you, and find out any interesting background related to your name and its original history. Write down this information, and then write your feelings about your name.

Theatre Assume the role of playwright and write a monologue or solo speech about an important event in your life. There should be a beginning, middle, climax, and conclusion with a clear emotional progression. Use the script for a classroom presentation.

THEATRE

Cross-Curriculum Links

Your visual arts classroom comes to life with a **Connections** feature. These self-contained pages weave the study of art with that of science, math, literature, social studies, health, and so on.

You will find the Connections feature at the end of each chapter, just before the chapter review page. Use it as a culminating activity that will deepen students' understanding of the links between what they learn in the art classroom with lessons and concepts from other curriculum areas. If your school encourages cross-disciplinary teaching, this feature is a worthwhile place to invite a teacher from the featured curriculum area to team teach with you.

SCIENCE

MATH

LANGUAGE ARTS

SOCIAL STUDIES

Support for the Art Teacher

The Teacher's Wraparound Edition provides complete lesson plans, teaching suggestions, supplemental information, cross-references, and more—all conveniently "wrapped" around every page of the reduced student text. Teachers will discover that the consistent, easy-to-follow lesson plan format gives a variety of teaching strategies to motivate students; to introduce, teach, and reinforce concepts; and alternative teaching strategies for adapting the program to your own teaching style and to the learning styles of your students.

CHAPTER OPENER

- Chapter Scan
- Resource cross-reference
- Artsource®: Performing Arts Handbook reference
- National Standards for the Visual Arts correlation
- Featured Artists
- Developing a Portfolio
- Strategies for introducing the Chapter
- National Museum of Women in the Arts reference

Organized with the Teacher in Mind

LESSON PLANS The teaching material follows a consistent, easy-to-use pattern. The complete lesson cycle—Focus, Teach, Assess, and Close—makes it easy for you to plan a lesson. As the core of the Teacher's Wraparound Edition, this lesson cycle provides you with complete suggestions for introducing each chapter and lesson and allows you to tailor the lesson to your own style and to the specific needs of your students.

FOCUS

- Suggested class time for each Studio Lesson
- A list of student objectives
- A convenient list of Supplies needed for the lesson
- Cross-references to supplemental blackline masters in the Teacher's Classroom Resources

TEACH

- A Motivator activity to involve students in the lesson
- A Vocabulary activity to help students build vocabulary skills
- Various activities related to the lesson's content, including Art Criticism, Art History, Cultural Diversity, Studio Skills, Cooperative Learning, and Aesthetics

ASSESS

- Assessment techniques, including strategies for reteaching students who have difficulty mastering the important lesson concepts.
- Extension activities designed for students who are able and willing to explore the content further

CLOSE

- An activity that brings closure to the lesson and recaps important concepts from the lesson

BOTTOM COLUMN ANNOTATIONS

BOTTOM COLUMN ANNOTATIONS Boxes at the bottom of the page give you additional information related to the content of the Student Text. This information supplements the core lesson plan by focusing on various areas of interest. The categories include:

More About. . .
Resources Beyond the Classroom
Curriculum Connections
Meeting Special Needs
Meeting Student Diversity
Technique Tips
Safety Tips
Developing a Portfolio
Technology Options
Internet Activities
Answers to Check Your Understanding

MAKING ART AVAILABLE FOR ALL STUDENTS

Teaching strategies in the Meeting Special Needs and Meeting Student Diversity boxes incorporate cultural perspectives, strategies for the physically and mentally disabled, and strategies for addressing different learning styles.

SPECIAL BOXED FEATURES
Stimulating and creative ideas to help you manage your classroom and help students recognize the presence of art all around them are available in three types of boxes set off from the lesson cycle.

Art in Everyday Life

Have students look around the classroom and notice how many different types of lines they see. Have them write on a sheet of paper examples of horizontal, vertical, diagonal, zigzag, and curved lines. Have them examine the lines around pictures hanging on the walls, lines in doors and windows, lines in clothing or objects on their desks. Have students take turns reading their lists aloud while volunteers write the various types of lines under appropriate headings on the board.

Sparking Creativity

Give students a sense of rhythm and movement in a creative way. Tell them: Rhythm in dance is found in the movements of the dancers. Try to see it and give it visual form. Ask one or two students to dance and have the class draw their movements rather than their bodies. Try a slow, graceful dance and then a rock rhythm. Compare students' drawings. Experiment with various tools and media and see how it will affect the rhythm of the designs.

Art on a Shoestring

Foam meat trays make excellent paint mixing trays. Sometimes store meat managers will sell some to you at a low cost if they know they are for school use.

STUDIO ACTIVITY Each activity in the Student Text has a corresponding box in the Teacher's Wraparound Edition that provides alternative ways for students to address the hands-on activity.

STUDIO ACTIVITY

Painting a Still Life with Emphasis

Help students find objects that have interest and meaning to them. Perhaps the collection could have a theme (sports equipment, percussion instruments, CD holders), or be whimsical in nature.

INTERNET ACTIVITY

Art on the Web You and your students are invited to take a trip through Glencoe's Fine Arts Site on the World Wide Web. Your class can explore *Studio Cyberspace*, full of art activities; *Glencoe Student Galleria*, a changing showcase of student artworks; links to lots of adventures through art museums, worldwide cultural treasures, and contact with other art teachers. You simply need a computer with a modem, an Internet hook-up, and curious minds. To reach the Glencoe Fine Arts page, type in the URL address exactly as shown:

http://www.glencoe.com/sec/art

Check the *Internet Activity Booklet* included with the *Introducing Art* program for more information.

INTERNET ACTIVITY Each Internet Activity box, found at the bottom of the Connections feature, offers ways for teachers to access and make use of Glencoe's new Fine Arts web site. Additionally, the feature offers strategies for implementing safe, educational Internet exploration in the classroom.

The Teacher's Resource Binder

A separate *Introducing Art* Teacher's Resource Binder provides you with a correlated supplemental resource for *Introducing Art*. It contains a wealth of additional handouts, teaching strategies, and resource material designed for more effective teaching. You can choose the materials that complement the skill level, time framework, and interest level of your class. The Teacher's Resource Binder is organized into chapters. In addition to chapter specific sections, the binder includes a section for resources and another that helps you integrate technology into your art classroom. The following types of teaching materials have been provided for each chapter.

- Reproducible Masters
- Cooperative Learning Activities
- Aesthetics/Art Criticism
- Art History
- Studios
- Appreciating Cultural Diversity
- Artist Profile
- Chapter Test

GLENCOE   TEACHER'S RESOURCE BINDER

Introducing Art

G62365.19

ISBN 0-02-662365-X

9 780026 623650

Glencoe
McGraw-Hill

Assessment

All subject areas recognize the importance of measuring individual student performance in attaining specified goals and objectives. A booklet titled *Portfolio and Assessment Techniques* is designed to address basic information used in portfolio assessment for visual art. Why is portfolio assessment important to use? Portfolio assessment provides

- Tangible evidence of anticipated student outcomes.
- Contextual information on student growth as an artist.
- An opportunity for students to reflect on their work, acknowledge their accomplishments, and evaluate personal artistic goals.
- Consistency and objectivity in the evaluation process for the instructor.

Fine Art Transparency Package

The ready-to-use overhead color transparency package contains 14 full-color Fine Art Transparencies, 14 Cross-Curriculum Transparencies, and 12 transparencies of student artwork. Accompanying the transparencies is an Instructor's Guide with background information and student activity sheets to assist the teacher in guiding discussion, all in a convenient 3-ring binder.

Fine Art Print Package

Twenty quality art masterpieces are printed on sturdy self-supporting stock to supplement the artwork appearing in the student text. The laminated prints are resistant to wear and are presented in a durable portfolio for convenient classroom use and storage. This package includes an Instructor's Guide with a page for teaching strategies and a student worksheet.

Media and Technology Support

National Gallery of Art Videodisc

This full-length video features 1,645 artworks from the National Gallery of Art collection, along with a tour of the gallery. Glencoe has published a separate *National Gallery of Art Correlation Bar Code Guide* for your convenience, including 300 artworks from the entire videodisc collection. Selected bar codes are reprinted in the Teacher's Wraparound Edition that correlate to lesson contents.

Artsource®: Performing Arts Package 1

This new performing arts package provides a multi-media resource for further exploration of artists and groups within the three performing arts areas—dance, music, and theatre. The units within the package supplement the *Artsource®: Performing Arts Handbook* in the Student Text, and include an Instructor's Guide that provides additional information about each artist and group and their performances. The media package includes both video and audiocassettes.

National Museum of Women in the Arts CD-ROM and Videodisc

This videodisc of 200 artworks from the collection of the National Museum of Women in the Arts includes a video introduction to the museum itself. The videodisc includes a 24-page bar code guide for all images. The CD-ROM provides multi-media access and activities for the 200 works, including an assessment tool to test students' knowledge of artist, time, location, media, and subject.

To assist with the planning and development of your individual course, this Pacing Chart is included in this section. These are only intended as suggested guidelines. Individual teachers will need to make necessary adjustments and modifications as required by their local, state, and national curriculum guidelines, and by the ability level and learning styles of their students.

			6 wk 30 days	9 wk 45 days	18 wk 90 days	36 wk 180 days
		Total Days				
Chapter 1 The Elements of Art						
Lesson 1	The Language of Art		½ day	½ day	1 day	1 day
Lesson 2	Line		½ day	½ day	1 day	1 day
Lesson 3	Color		1 day	½ day	1 day	2 days
Lesson 4	Mixing Colors		1 day	½ day	1 day	2 days
Lesson 5	Shape, Form, and Space		½ day	½ day	1 day	1 day
Lesson 6	Drawing a Still Life				2 days	2 days
Lesson 7	Texture		½ day	½ day	1 day	1 day
		Total	4 days	3 days	8 days	10 days
Chapter 2 The Principles of Art						
Lesson 1	The Language of Design		½ day	½ day	1 day	1 day
Lesson 2	Making a Mask with Formal Balance				2 days	3 days
Lesson 3	Variety, Harmony, Emphasis, and Proportion		½ day	½ day	1 day	1 day
Lesson 4	Movement and Rhythm		½ day	½ day	1 day	1 day
Lesson 5	Making a Tessellation				2 days	2 days
Lesson 6	Unity in Art		½ day	½ day	1 day	1 day
		Total	2 days	2 days	8 days	9 days
Chapter 3 Art Media and Techniques						
Lesson 1	Drawing		½ day	½ day	1 day	1 day
Lesson 2	Gesture Drawing		½ day		1 day	2 days
Lesson 3	Painting		½ day	½ day	1 day	1 day
Lesson 4	Creating a Portrait		½ day			2 days
Lesson 5	Printmaking			½ day	1 day	2 days
Lesson 6	Sculpture			½ day	1 day	2 days
Lesson 7	Making a Collage					3 days
Lesson 8	Computer Art			1 day	1 day	3 days
		Total	2 days	3 days	6 days	16 days
Chapter 4 Looking at Art						
Lesson 1	Aesthetics		½ day	1 day	1 day	1 day
Lesson 2	Art Criticism		1 day	1 day	1 day	2 days
Lesson 3	Critiquing Non-Objective Art		½ day	1 day	1 day	1 day
Lesson 4	Creating a Realistic Painting				2 days	3 days
Lesson 5	Creating an Expressive Word Design				1 day	2 days
Lesson 6	Creating an Abstract Figure				1 day	1 day
		Total	2 days	3 days	7 days	10 days
Chapter 5 Art Through the Ages						
Lesson 1	Art of Long Ago		½ day	½ day	1 day	1 day
Lesson 2	Egyptian Tomb Painting				1 day	2 days
Lesson 3	Eastern Art		½ day	½ day	1 day	1 day
Lesson 4	Making a Relief Sculpture				1 day	2 days
Lesson 5	Art of the Middle Ages and Renaissance		½ day	½ day	1 day	1 day
Lesson 6	Creating a Diorama				1 day	3 days
Lesson 7	Art of the Nineteenth and Twentieth Centuries		½ day	½ day	1 day	1 days
Lesson 8	Using Abstraction in Art			1 day	1 day	2 days
		Total	2 days	3 days	8 days	13 days
Chapter 6 Perceiving Nature						
Lesson 1	Landscape Art		½ day	½ day	1 day	1 day
Lesson 2	Creating a Nature Scene				2 days	2 days
Lesson 3	Nature Close Up			½ day		1 day
Lesson 4	Drawing from a Bird's-Eye View					2 days
Lesson 5	Art and the Seasons			½ day		1 day
Lesson 6	Painting a Seasonal Event					2 days
Lesson 7	The Power of Nature		½ day	½ day	1 day	1 day
Lesson 8	Painting a Storm		1 day	1 day	1 day	2 days
		Total	2 days	3 days	5 days	12 days
Chapter 7 Observing Animals						
Lesson 1	Animals in Earliest Art		½ day	½ day	1 day	1 day
Lesson 2	Creating a Totem			1 day		2 days
Lesson 3	Sea Creatures		½ day		1 day	1 day
Lesson 4	Making a Glue-Line Print				2 days	2 days
Lesson 5	Birds in Art		½ day			1 day
Lesson 6	Making an Animal Sculpture					4 days
Lesson 7	Fantasy Animals		½ day	½ day	1 day	1 day
Lesson 8	Creating a Fantasy Creature			2 days	3 days	4 days
		Total	2 days	4 days	8 days	16 days

Chapter 8 Portraying People

Lesson	Title				
Lesson 1	Portraits	½ day	1 day		1 day
Lesson 2	Creating an Expressive Face	1 day	1 day	1 day	2 days
Lesson 3	Figures in Action		½ day	1 day	1 day
Lesson 4	Drawing a Figure in Action			1 day	2 days
Lesson 5	Portraits in the Round	½ day	½ day	1 day	1 day
Lesson 6	Creating a Clay Portrait				3 days
Lesson 7	Heroes in Art		1 day	1 day	1 day
Lesson 8	Creating a Mixed-Media Banner				2 days
Total		2 days	4 days	5 days	13 days

Chapter 9 Visiting Places

Lesson	Title				
Lesson 1	Personal Places			1 day	1 day
Lesson 2	Furniture Design			2 days	2 days
Lesson 3	Architectural Design		1 day		1 day
Lesson 4	Creating a Fanciful Exterior		3 days		2 days
Lesson 5	Cityscapes	½ day			1 day
Lesson 6	Creating a Mixed-Media Cityscape	1 day			2 days
Lesson 7	The Outdoors	½ day		1 day	1 day
Lesson 8	Creating a Seasonal Panorama			2 days	2 days
Total		2 days	4 days	6 days	12 days

Chapter 10 Examining Objects

Lesson	Title				
Lesson 1	Objects in Nature	½ day	½ day	1 day	1 day
Lesson 2	Drawing a Magical Forest	1½ days	1½ days	2 days	2 days
Lesson 3	Grouping Objects		½ day	1 day	1 day
Lesson 4	Painting a Watercolor Still Life		1½ days	2 days	2 days
Lesson 5	Art Objects				1 day
Lesson 6	Building a Clay Musical Instrument				3 days
Lesson 7	Decorative Arts				1 day
Lesson 8	Creating a Pendant				2 days
Total		2 days	4 days	6 days	13 days

Chapter 11 Recording Events

Lesson	Title				
Lesson 1	The Media of Visual Reporting	½ day	1 day		1 day
Lesson 2	Drawing a Sporting Event in Action	1½ days	2 days		2 days
Lesson 3	The Artist as Historian			1 day	1 day
Lesson 4	Drawing a Cartoon			1 day	1 day
Lesson 5	Recording Exploration			1 day	1 day
Lesson 6	Creating a Room in Outer Space			3 days	3 days
Lesson 7	Advances in Visual Reporting				1 day
Lesson 8	Making A Video Documentary				2 days
Total		2 days	3 days	6 days	12 days

Chapter 12 Telling a Story

Lesson	Title				
Lesson 1	Picture Languages	½ day	½ day	½ day	½ day
Lesson 2	Making a Visual Autobiography	1½ days	1½ days	1½ days	1½ days
Lesson 3	Myths and Legends			½ day	½ day
Lesson 4	Creating a Mythical Creature			2½ days	2½ days
Lesson 5	Art Stories Larger than Life				½ day
Lesson 6	Painting a Mural About School Life				4 days
Lesson 7	Book Illustration				½ day
Lesson 8	Creating a Book Cover				2 days
Total		2 days	2 days	5 days	12 days

Chapter 13 Celebrations

Lesson	Title				
Lesson 1	Holiday Celebrations			1 day	1 day
Lesson 2	Creating an "Event" Quilt				10 days
Lesson 3	Celebration Dances in Art		½ day	1 day	1 day
Lesson 4	Creating Kinetic "Festival" Art		2½ days		2 days
Lesson 5	Celebrating Rites of Passage			1 day	1 day
Lesson 6	Collage of a Family Gathering			2 days	2 days
Lesson 7	Art that Celebrates Life	½ day		1 day	1 day
Lesson 8	Celebrating a Role Model	1½ days			2 days
Total		2 days	3 days	6 days	20 days

Chapter 14 Creating Fantasy

Lesson	Title				
Lesson 1	Dreams and Nightmares	½ day	½ day	1 day	1 day
Lesson 2	Creating a Fantasy Bird Collage	1½ days	1½ days	2 days	2 days
Lesson 3	Puzzling Paintings			1 day	1 day
Lesson 4	Creating Your Own Picture Puzzle			2 days	2 days
Lesson 5	Impossible Images			½ day	1 day
Lesson 6	Creating an "Etching" of a Strange Place		1 ½ days		3 days
Total		2 days	4 days	6 days	10 days

Handbook

			1 day	2 days

Safety in the Art Classroom

Art teachers and their students are often in contact with potentially harmful materials, although many may be totally unaware of the danger. Lead poisoning, cancer, nervous system disorders, anemia, silicosis, chemical pneumonia, asthma, dermatitis—all of these as well as others are recognized as industrial diseases caused by hazardous chemicals. However, many fail to recognize that these same diseases are found among artists, craftspeople, theater technicians, teachers, and students using art and craft materials without adequate precautions.

Although studies have been conducted and the findings published, many teachers remain unaware that toxic substances may be in some of the art materials they use routinely in their teaching. Other teachers, aware of the problem, feel that they are exercising adequate precautions by referring to the labels on the art products they use.

Labeling of Art Materials

The labeling of art materials continues to be limited in many ways. Ingredients that caused laboratory animals to perish within two weeks after a single dose was administered were identified as "acutely toxic" and must bear a warning label. However, if fewer than half the animals die, the product may be labeled "nontoxic." In addition, when products are imported or repackaged, the hazards may not be listed or properly described on the label.

Teachers should be aware of the fact that the Federal Hazardous Substances Act and other legislation introduced at the federal level, have not been entirely successful at rectifying problems of this kind. Some worrisome inadequacies persist.

Industry Safety Standards

Not to be overlooked is the fact that the art-materials industry has, for many years, supported voluntary safety standards. These standards have been developed with the cooperation and input of various manufacturers. The Arts and Crafts Materials Institute (ACMI) has for some time adhered to a voluntary program designed to ensure the safety of younger students working with art materials. Most art teachers are familiar with the two ACMI safety labels—AP indicating Approved Product, and CP specifying Certified Product. These labels certify that the products on which they are placed have been found to contain no ingredients in sufficient quantities to be toxic or harmful to users. In addition, products bearing a CP seal abide by certain quality standards pertaining to workmanship, working qualities, and color.

While the AP/CP seal applies to art products intended for use by younger students, a Certified Label (CL) is used to identify products considered to be more appropriate for older students and adults. The CL seal on a label indicates that the product's ingredients have been examined by toxicologists. The label lists any safety precautions required by law and by labeling standards developed by the American Society of Testing and Materials. Teachers are advised to read and adhere to the safety precautions listed on these labels.

Material Safety Data Sheets and Their Use

Teachers should realize that they may request a Material Safety Data Sheet (MSDS) from manufacturers pertaining to any art products they are unsure of. Among the items included on the MSDS are a listing of all the ingredients for which industrial standards exist, health-hazard information, fire-hazard data, and the chemicals with which the product might react dangerously.

In most school systems, central ordering procedures are—or should be—developed as a means of ensuring that all art materials entering the school are approved by appropriate authorities (for example, the Health Department or Board of Education). Requiring Material Safety Data Sheets from suppliers as a condition of purchase should eliminate many of the toxic materials that might otherwise be brought into the classrooms by unsuspecting teachers.

Protection from Exposure

Considerable protection from exposure to toxic materials can be achieved by promoting good hygiene in the classroom. Safe storage and proper labeling of art and craft supplies, keeping dust to a minimum by damp mopping rather than sweeping, and thorough cleanup after use of art and craft materials will help prevent toxic exposures. Personal hygiene also plays a role in the prevention of potentially harmful exposures. Students should refrain from eating or drinking while engaged in art projects, and they should wash their hands thoroughly when finished. Another general safety practice is to ensure proper ventilation in the art classroom so that contaminants may be diluted and eventually removed from the air. Exposure to hazardous dusts and fumes will be minimized if the instructor premixes dry materials with water (for example, tempera, wheat paste, and so forth) and fires ceramic products when students are away from the kiln area. If an art material has been transferred to an unlabeled container and its identity is unknown, it should be disposed of. For specific information on the proper disposal of art and craft materials, please contact your local county health department. (From the California Department of Education Program Advisory # CIL: 94[95-01].)

Safety Precautions for Students

In order for a chemical in an art material to harm a student, it must first come into contact with or enter the body. Teachers should be aware of the following three ways in which this can occur.

Skin Contact. Some chemicals such as those used in etching, or solvents like lacquer and paint thinners, can irritate the skin on contact and result in a variety of skin problems. Other chemicals, known as sensitizers, can cause skin allergies. Examples of these sensitizers include formaldehyde found in some color photography solutions, turpentine, epoxy glues and resins, nickel and chromium compounds, and many tropical woods.

However, the danger with regard to skin contact does not end here. Many toxic chemicals do not just damage the skin itself. They can also be absorbed through the skin into the bloodstream where they can affect other organs. Examples include methyl alcohol found in some shellacs, toluene found in lacquer thinners and silk screen inks, and glycol ethers found in photoetching materials.

Inhalation. Dusts, powders, vapors, gases, aerosols, and other airborne substances may be readily inhaled and, therefore, represent a health hazard. Examples include solvent vapors from paints, inks, and thinners; spray mists from air brush or aerosol spray cans; gases from photographic baths; pottery kiln firing; metal fumes from soldering, welding, and metal casting; and dusts from dyes and pigments, pottery glazes, and woodworking. Some of the chemicals in these materials can result in lung damage from inhalation while others can be absorbed into the bloodstream, where they can lead to a variety of problems including lead poisoning, nerve damage, and kidney damage.

Ingestion. Ingestion is of particular concern with younger students who are inclined to experiment and put things in their mouths. However, ingestion of hazardous substances can occur in the case of older students as well. These students can be affected if they eat, drink, or apply make-up in a classroom where art materials can contaminate these items.

Precautions in Selecting and Using Art Materials

Although some products on the market are labeled as "nontoxic," they should not be purchased for use by students in grades K-6 unless assurance is obtained from the manufacturer. A major reason for this is that the product may have been tested for acute toxicity only. Chronic hazards, cancer-causing potential, and other sensitivities are not included in acute toxicity testing. The "nontoxic" label can thus be misleading, and products identified with such labels should not always be regarded as safe for use by children.

There are certain safety precautions that all teachers should take when selecting art materials for use in their classrooms. Included in these precautions are the following:

- Make certain that the materials obtained for younger students (age 12 or under) have an AP or CP seal of approval; materials secured for use by older students should have a CL seal.

- Incorporate into the art curriculum written information on the potential hazards of art materials and techniques; students should be tested on this information just as they are tested with regard to other aspects of curriculum content. Documentation of this type of instruction should be made and filed.

- Carefully supervise students in the classroom, making certain that safety rules are understood and observed. Teachers must also remember to obey these safety rules themselves in order to impress upon their students the seriousness of these regulations. Students should never be allowed to work in the classroom, during or after school hours, without direct teacher supervision.

- Avoid using solvents or products containing solvents in the art room. These include turpentine, lacquer, shellac, paint thinner, rubber cement and rubber cement thinner, permanent markers, and solvent-based inks such as silk-screen printing ink.

- Do not use acids, alkalies, or bleaches.

- Do not use aerosol spray cans in the classroom, since the inhalation of the spray mist can cause injury to lung tissue.

- Use dust-causing products with care in a well-ventilated area. This precaution applies to the use of pastels, chalks, plaster and clays in dry form, copper enamels, glazes, papier-mâché mixtures, and powdered tempera paints.

- Place kilns in a separate room, outdoors, or if this is not possible, in an out-of-the-way part of the room where students are not likely to come into contact with them when they are in operation. In addition, all kilns should have local exhaust ventilation.

- Remember that good ventilation is an absolute necessity whenever using any art or craft material.

- Be prepared for emergencies by having written emergency procedures prepared, posted, and explained to students. This includes fire drill procedures and the use of fire extinguishers.

- Report all accidents, even minor ones such as a small cut. Illnesses suspected of being related to art materials should be reported in writing to the school principal or other designated authority at once so that an investigation can be conducted and corrective action determined.

A 1992 bulletin from the Consumer Product Safety Commission stated that art materials with any warning labels whatever are not suitable for use by students in grade 6 and under. These students cannot be expected to understand the hazards of toxic substances or to carry out precautions effectively or consistently. A teacher must "childproof" the art room to prevent either intentional or unintentional access to toxic materials or dangerous machinery.

At the beginning of each school year or new term, teachers are urged to determine if any of their students are asthmatic, visually impaired, hearing impaired, or on prescribed medication. If asthmatic students are enrolled in the art class, they should not be exposed to dusts, fumes, or vapors because of their breathing difficulties. Visually impaired students understandably operate very close to their artwork and, as a consequence, are more likely to inhale harmful dusts, vapors, and fumes. Students with hearing impairments should not be exposed to activities requiring loud hammering or noisy machinery, because this can aggravate their condition. If students are found to be on medication, the teacher should seek their physician's advice regarding the potentially harmful interaction between their prescribed medicine and the art materials they might use in class.

Similar precautions are recommended in situations involving students who are physically handicapped in other ways or who may be learning disabled or emotionally disturbed. These students are at an even greater risk from toxic materials and require special care and attention. In some instances, they might not be able to use the same materials and processes as other students. Careful evaluation is needed in each case to determine what special precautions might be necessary.

Clearly, the need to direct time and effort to safeguarding the health and safety of students in the art classroom is essential. Art teachers, aware of their responsibilities in this regard, recognize that assistance may be needed. In order to properly inform and train their students, teachers need specially tailored hazard communication (HAZCOM) training. The curriculum must include formal health and safety training at levels far above the basic information required by the law. This is not only proper, it provides an opportunity for the school to develop training materials for which there is a demand.

Steps to Incorporate Training into Your Program

First find out which law applies to you. There are state and federal HAZCOM laws and they differ somewhat in their requirements. Ask your employer, but do not stop there! Call your Department of Labor's Occupational Safety and Health Department to be absolutely sure whose jurisdiction you are under. Ask for a copy of the law and any additional free materials they may have.

Learning the Rules

1. Spend a few moments looking at the HAZCOM file. If you do not know where this file is kept, ask your school administrator. OSHA requires employers to include the file's location in HAZCOM training.
2. Look at the condition of the file. OSHA requires that it is organized and easy to read. Included in the file should be:
   a. A written program telling how the school will comply (including names of parties responsible for each compliance activity).
   b. A survey of all the potentially toxic substances in the school and their locations.
   c. An organized collection of material safety data sheets (MSDSs) on these substances.
   d. A record of training sessions, which usually includes dates of training, lists of participants, qualifications of trainers, results of quizzes given, and so on.
3. Check your classroom/shop.
   a. Are there any containers that do not have the following information:
      • identity of the substance (must be the same as on the MSDS)
      • hazard warnings, if needed
      • name and address of the manufacturer (required for transport)
   b. If children grade 6 and under ever have access to your classroom/shop, be sure there are no materials with warnings on them of any kind, no sharp tools, and no hazardous equipment. Look under sinks, in drawers, and so on. Children's classrooms, like homes, must be childproofed.
   c. Be sure you have a dilution ventilation system separate from the ventilation in the rest of the school if you work with solvents or solvent-containing products, black-and-white photo developing, resin casting, or any other process requiring it.
   d. Be sure you have local ventilation systems (e.g. spray booth and flexible ducts) for any process that puts substances into the air, such as spraying, air brushing, machine sawing, sanding, soldering, welding, mixing clay or glazes, and so on.

REMEMBER: No amount of training will make up for teaching without the proper safety equipment. **If you cannot demonstrate a process with all proper precautions, safety equipment, and ventilation, eliminate the project from the curriculum.** Don't ever let students see you violate safety rules or the law.

More information on safety in the art environment is available from:

Arts, Crafts, and Theater Safety (ACTS)
181 Thompson Street #23
New York, New York 10012–2586
(212) 777-0062
http://www.caseweb.com/acts/

Introducing Art

ABOUT THE PROGRAM

Introducing Art has a thematic focus. It presents a wide range of artworks and styles and groups them by the themes that served as inspiration for the works.

People, places, animals, and nature. Artists have used these themes as subjects for their art since the beginning of man. Animals and stick people appeared on the walls of caves more than twelve thousand years ago. They remain today as a visual link to our forebears.

Celebrations and events are commemorated in paintings, sculpture, and photographs. Fantasy is a powerful stimulus for the creative process. These and other themes in *Introducing Art* will bring creative inspiration to the classroom.

ABOUT THE COVER ILLUSTRATION

St. Basil's Cathedral. Begun in 1554 by Ivan the Terrible from the plans of architects Barma and Postmik. Completed in 1679. Red Square, Moscow. Images © 1996 Photodisc, Inc.

St. Basil's Cathedral, now a museum in Moscow, appears on the cover. Its colorful onion domes and patterned exterior are testament to the fact that even public buildings can be whimsical creations of an inspired artist.

Introducing Art

Gene Mittler, Ph.D.
Professor Emeritus
Texas Tech University

Rosalind Ragans, Ph.D.
Associate Professor Emerita
Georgia Southern University

Jean Morman Unsworth, M.F.A.
Professor of Fine Arts Emerita
Loyola University of Chicago

Faye Scannell
Specialist, Technology
Bellevue, Washington Public Schools

Glencoe McGraw-Hill

New York, New York   Columbus, Ohio   Woodland Hills, California   Peoria, Illinois

ABOUT THE AUTHORS

Gene Mittler

Gene Mittler is one of the authors of Glencoe's middle school/junior high art series, *Introducing Art, Exploring Art,* and *Understanding Art.* He is also author of *Art in Focus,* a chronological approach to art for Glencoe's senior high program, and *Creating and Understanding Drawings.* He has taught at both the elementary and secondary levels and at Indiana University. He received an M.F.A. in sculpture from Bowling Green State University and a Ph.D. in art education from the Ohio State University. Dr. Mittler is currently Professor Emeritus at Texas Tech University.

Jean Morman Unsworth

Jean Morman Unsworth, author, teacher, and consultant, is one of the authors of Glencoe's middle school/junior-high book *Introducing Art.* Educated at the Art Institute of Chicago, University of Notre Dame, and the University of Georgia, she has taught elementary through graduate levels and was Professor of Fine Arts at Loyola University of Chicago until 1987. She initiated and designed Chicago Children's Museum and the Interdisciplinary Arts Masters program at Columbia College in Chicago. She now gives full time to writing and consulting.

Rosalind Ragans

Rosalind Ragans is one of the authors of Glencoe's middle school/junior high art series, *Introducing Art, Exploring Art,* and *Understanding Art.* She served as senior author on the elementary program *Art Connections* for the SRA division of McGraw-Hill, and wrote the multi-level, comprehensive *ArtTalk* text for Glencoe's senior high program. She received a B.F.A. at Hunter College, CUNY, New York, and earned a M.Ed. in Elementary Education at Georgia Southern College and Ph.D. in Art Education at the University of Georgia. Dr. Ragans was named National Art Educator of the Year for 1992.

Faye Scannell

Faye Scannell is an art specialist, lead art technology teacher, and teacher educator in the Bellevue, Washington Public Schools, the Bellevue Art Museum, and through Seattle Pacific University. She has written technology activities for Glencoe's *Introducing Art, Exploring Art, Understanding Art,* and *ArtTalk.* She was educated at Kutztown State University of Pennsylvania, Lesley College, and several Washington universities. In 1993 she received the Art Educator of the Year Award from the Washington Art Education Association.

ABOUT ARTSOURCE®

The materials provided in the Performing Arts Handbook are excerpted from *Artsource®: The Music Center Study Guide to the Performing Arts,* a project of the Music Center Education Division. The Music Center of Los Angeles County, the largest performing arts center in the western United States, established the Music Center Education Division in 1979 to provide opportunities for lifelong learning in the arts, and especially to bring the performing and visual arts into the classroom. The Education Division believes the arts enhance the quality of life for all people, but are crucial to the development of every child.

Glencoe/McGraw-Hill

A Division of The **McGraw·Hill** Companies

Send all inquiries to:
Glencoe/McGraw-Hill
21600 Oxnard Street, Suite 500
Woodland Hills, CA 91367

ISBN 0-02-662363-3 (Student Text)
ISBN 0-02-662364-1 (Teacher's Wraparound Edition)

Printed in the United States of America.

3 4 5 6 7 8 9   004/043   03 02 01 00 99

EDITORIAL CONSULTANTS

Claire B. Clements, Ph.D.
Specialist, Special Needs
Associate Professor and Community Education
    Director at the Program on Human Development
    and Disability
The University of Georgia
Athens, Georgia

Robert D. Clements, Ph.D.
Specialist, Special Needs
Professor Emeritus of Art
The University of Georgia
Athens, Georgia

Cris Guenter, Ed.D.
Specialist, Portfolio and Assessment
Professor, Fine Arts/Curriculum and Instruction
California State University, Chico
Chico, California

Dede Tisone-Bartels, M.A.
Specialist, Curriculum Connections
Crittenden Middle School
Mountain View, California

Kathleen Laya
Educational Publishing and Curriculum Consultant
Wilmette, Illinois

CONTRIBUTORS/REVIEWERS

Max A. Butler
Fine Arts Instructor
Cedar Valley Middle School
Austin, TX

Gail F. Enkey
Art Teacher
Chiaravalle Montessori School
Evanston, IL

Stacey Hendrickson
Art Instructor
Gates Intermediate School
Scituate, MA

Joy Jones
Art Teacher
Chisholm Trail Middle School
Round Rock, TX

Cathy J. Kiser
Art Teacher
Jesse Stuart Middle School
Louisville, KY

Barbara A. Perez
Art Teacher
St. Athanasius School
Evanston, IL

Irene Wettermark Porter
Visual Arts Teacher
Hayes Middle School
Birmingham AL

Teri Power
Art Specialist & G&T Coordinator
East Elementary School
New Richmond, WI

Margaret Powers
Art Teacher
McAdory Elementary School
McCalla, AL

Wandra Merritt Sanders
Art Teacher
Hyde Park Elementary
Jacksonville, FL

Beverly N. Silletto
Art Teacher
Southern Middle School
Louisville, KY

Sylvia L. Thompson
Art Instructor
Cammack Middle School
Huntington, WV

PERFORMING ARTS HANDBOOK CONTRIBUTORS

Joan Boyett
Executive Director
Music Center Education Division
The Music Center of Los Angeles County

Melinda Williams
Concept Originator and Project Director

Susan Cambigue-Tracey
Project Coordinator

Arts Discipline Writers:
    Dance—Susan Cambigue-Tracey
    Music—Rosemarie Cook-Glover
    Theatre—Barbara Leonard

STUDIO LESSON CONSULTANTS

The authors wish to express their gratitude to the following art teachers who participated in field testing the Studio Lessons with their students.

Debra Belvin
Bearden Middle School
Knoxville, TN

Jeff Bender
Park Plaza Middle School
Evansville, IN

Ashley S. Benkwith
McAdory High School
McCalla, AL

Barbara Bugg
Westport Middle School
Louisville, KY

Gail F. Enkey
Chiaravalle Montessori School
Evanston, IL

Miranda Grubisich
Weber Middle School
Port Washington, NY

Stacey Hendrickson
Gates Intermediate School
Scituate, MA

Joy Jones
Chisholm Trail Middle School
Round Rock, TX

Natalie Jones
Oak Hill Middle School
Evansville, IN

Cathy J. Kiser
Jesse Stuart Middle School
Louisville, KY

Audrey Komroy
Akron Central School
Akron, NY

Pamela Layman
Bardstown Middle School
Bardstown, KY

Charles L. Osten
Whittle Springs Middle School
Knoxville, KY

Catherine K. Pate
Sneed Middle School
Florence, SC

Barbara A. Perez
St. Athanasias Grammar School
Evanston, IL

Irene Wettermark Porter
Hayes Middle School
Birmingham, AL

Margaret Powers
McAdory Elementary School
McCalla, AL

Mary Rokitka
Medina High School
Medina, NY

Gloria Santilli
Winman Junior High School
Warwick, RI

Faye Scannell
Cherry Crest Elementary
Bellevue, WA

Beverly N. Silletto
Southern Middle School
Louisville, KY

Lisa Solomon
Medina High School
Medina, NY

Sylvia L. Thompson
Cammack Middle School
Huntington, WV

Curtis R. Uebelhor
Perry Heights Middle School
Evansville, IN

TABLE OF CONTENTS ILLUSTRATION CREDITS

Lisa Pomerantz/Deborah Wolfe, Ltd.

STUDENT CONTRIBUTORS

The following students contributed exemplary work for the Studio Lesson pages:

Fig. 1–13, Dustin Keaton, Bardstown Middle School, Bardstown, KY; Fig. 1–19, Keyanda Brown, Bardstown Middle School, Bardstown, KY; Fig. 2–5, David Burkes, Plaza Park Middle School, Evansville, IN; Figure 2–13, Crystal Latham, McAdory Middle School, McCalla, AL; Fig. 3–7, Jack Nondorf, St. Athanasius School, Evanston, IL; Fig. 3–11. Cathleen Cramer, St. Athanasius School, Evanston, IL; Fig. 3–17, Nancy Gardner, Whittle Springs Middle School, Knoxville, TN; Fig. 4–9, Kathryn Ross, Cammack Middle School, Huntington, WV; Fig. 4–11, Mandy Grisham, Plaza Park Middle School, Evansville, IN; Fig. 4–13, Florian Kimpel, Plaza Park Middle School, Evansville, IN; Fig. 4–13, Jing Liu, Plaza Park Middle School, Evansville, IN; Fig. 5–6, Kate Morrison, St. Athanasius School, Evanston, IL; Fig. 5–10, Katie Harr, St. Athanasius School, Evanston, IL; Fig. 5–16, Andrew Zangerle, Medina High School, Medina, NY; Fig. 5–16, Jason A. Weeks, Medina High School, Medina, NY; Fig. 5–20, Caitlin Bradley, Oak Hill Middle School, Evansville, IN; Fig. 6–5, Emilia Hofmeister, St. Athanasius School, Evanston, IL; Fig. 6–9, Abby Taylor, St. Athanasius School, Evanston, IL; Fig. 6–13, Katie Miskel, Gates Intermediate School, Scituate, MA; Fig. 6–17, Kate Feeney, Cherry Crest Elementary, Bellevue, WA; Fig. 7–5, Caitlyn Lillo, Chisholm Trail Middle School, Round Rock, TX; Fig. 7–9, Deborah Laranjeira, Chisholm Trail Middle School, Round Rock, TX; Fig. 7–13, Alex Dorsey, Southern Middle School, Louisville, KY; Fig. 7–17, Brandie Rawlinson, Perry Heights Middle School, Evansville, IN; Fig. 7–17, Darrell Ray Morris, Perry Heights Middle School, Evansville, IN; Fig. 8–5, Jennifer Sturgill, Jesse Stuart Middle School, Louisville, KY; Fig. 8–9, LaToya Jackson, Southern Middle School, Louisville, KY; Fig. 8–13, Jimmy Crouch, Jesse Stuart Middle School, Louisville, KY; Fig. 8–17, Paul Bolling, Southern Middle School, Louisville, KY; Fig. 9–5, Bradley Camp, Westport Middle School, Louisville, KY; Fig. 9–10, Lorin Wilkie, Perry Heights Middle School, Evansville, IN; Fig. 9–14, Ai-ling Chang, Westport Middle School, Louisville, KY; Fig. 9-18, Rie Fujii, Bearden Middle School, Knoxville, TN; Fig. 10–5, Lisa Marie Rivera, Bearden Middle School, Knoxville, TN; Fig. 10–9, Susan Peng, Cammack Middle School, Huntington, WV; Fig. 10–13, Ashley Revell, Sneed Middle School, Florence, SC; Fig. 10–17, Stephen Schleh, Cherry Crest Elementary, Bellevue, WA; Fig. 11–5, Michael Kennedy, McAdory Middle School, McCalla, AL; Fig. 11–9, Joshua R. Reynolds, Whittle Springs Middle School, Knoxville, TN; Fig. 11–13, Nicholas Dutton, McAdory Elementary, McCalla, AL; Fig. 11–16, J. T. Helms, Sneed Middle School, Florence, SC; Fig. 12–5, LaToya Jackson, Southern Middle School, Louisville, KY; Fig. 12–8, Laura Jeanne Post, Chiaravalle Montessori School, Evanston, IL; Fig. 12–13, 9th grade art students, Beacon School, Port Washington, NY; Fig. 12–17, Matt Carlisle, Whittle Springs Middle School, Knoxville, TN; Fig. 13–5, Jessica Abbs, Keena Burgess, Ericka Chadsey, Sarah Chaffee, Lauren Cierniak, Danelle Edwards, Steven Frey (Director), Bill Gibson, Dawn Graham, Andrea Halbach, Iwona Klapa, Annette Koszuta, Rochelle Leiker, Sarah Linneman, Christina Lucciano, Susan Morris, Nickole von Ohlen, Jennifer Ormsby, Jamie Palfi, Scottie Rovito, Andrea Sagerman, Melissa Stone, Laurie Summers, Katie Tordy, Beth Tripi, Lauren Whelan, Fallan Winter, Akron Central School, Akron, NY; Fig. 13–9, Tina Sheppard, Hayes Middle School, Birmingham, AL; Fig. 13–13, Julia Bess Good, Chiaravalle Montessori School, Evanston, IL; Fig. 13–17, Dante Rhodes, Hayes Middle School, Birmingham, AL; Fig. 14–5, Brandie Rawlinson, Perry Heights Middle School, Evansville, IN; Fig. 14–9, Paul Goderis, St. Athanasius School, Evanston, IL; Fig. 14–13, Brittney Sohn, Whittle Springs Middle School, Knoxville, TN; Fig. S–1, Sarah Rosenfeld, Cherry Crest Elementary, Bellevue, WA; Fig. S–2, Sean Kebely, Clay Cuttitte, Kyle Kashiwagi, Matt Colville, Ryan Anderson, Lauren Marrs, Jessie Allen, Andrea Wilkerson, Sarah Rosenfeld, Cherry Crest Elementary, Bellevue, WA; page 278, Lindsay Dillon, Medina Elementary, Bellevue, WA.

CONTENTS

Credit line on page 48.

Credit line on page 76.

Credit line on page 138.

Credit line on page 153.

Credit line on page 254.

Credit line on page 228.

HANDBOOK

STUDIO LESSONS BY MEDIA

The Elements of Art

Resources

- 1-10 Chapter Test, TRB page 15
- Transparency CC-1, *Kouros* by Isamu Noguchi
- Transparency 1, *Inter-Urban Motor Man* by Eve Drewelowe
- Fine Art Print 1, *Landscape with Mountain Lake* by Ernst Ludwig Kirschner
- Fine Art Print 2, *Houses in Murnau* by Wassily Kandinski

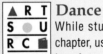

Dance While studying this chapter, use Performing Arts Handbook page 313 to show how Tandy Beal manipulates the elements of dance when she choreographs her dances.

NATIONAL STANDARDS

This chapter addresses the following National Standards for the Visual Arts:

1. (a, b)	**3.** (a)
2. (a, b, c)	**6.** (b)

Figure 1–1 Notice the colors, lines, and shapes the artist used to create these figures. What has she done to make them come alive as dancers?

Miriam Schapiro. *Pas de Deux*. 1986. Acrylic & fabric on canvas. 228.6 × 243.8 cm (90 × 96"). © Miriam Schapiro. Private collection. Courtesy Steinbaum Krauss Gallery, New York, New York.

2

FEATURED ARTISTS

Deborah Butterfield	Helen Hardin	Victor Vasareli
Alexander Calder	Roy Lichtenstein	Vincent van Gogh
Paul Cézanne	Henry Moore	
Richard Estes	Claude Monet	
Janet Fish	Miriam Schapiro	

The Elements of Art

Most people look at a blank surface and see nothing. The artist looks at the same surface and sees an exciting challenge. This is the challenge to create.

Study the painting at the left. Here are some questions the artist asked herself as she created the work: What colors and shapes will I use? How will those colors and shapes be arranged? Is my goal to suggest a feeling or to capture a lifelike image?

In this book, you will learn more about these and other questions artists ask themselves. You will also learn how you can use these questions yourself to better understand art.

PORTFOLIO IDEAS

You may be asked to keep your art projects in a portfolio. A **portfolio** is *a carefully selected collection of artwork kept by students and professional artists.* Keeping a portfolio will give you the opportunity to

- hold your artwork in one place and in good condition.
- show that you can apply art concepts, techniques, and skills.
- demonstrate your growth as an artist.

OBJECTIVES

After completing this chapter, you will be able to:

- Name and describe the elements of art.
- Describe the different types of line.
- Identify the properties of color.
- Experiment with various elements to understand their role in making art.

WORDS YOU WILL LEARN

artist
color
elements of art
form
hue
intensity
line
line quality
negative space
portfolio
shape
space
still life
texture
value

■ Chapter Overview

In this chapter, students will be encouraged to look at their world through the eyes of an artist. Everyone can participate in the artist's vision and expression of an idea or a feeling. To truly understand an artist's expression, however, we must understand the language of art, which is made up of the six visual elements of color, line, shape, form, space, and texture.

As students study this chapter, encourage them to find the elements of art in the world around them.

■ Chapter Motivator

Before students begin the chapter, encourage them to talk about and describe works of art that they have enjoyed or that they remember well. Ask them to give details about the work and explain why they liked it. Lead students to discover that different works have different elements that stand out in the viewer's mind. Tell them they will learn more about those elements in this chapter.

■ Examining the Artwork

Have students study the work on the opposite page. Ask them to discuss their initial responses. What do they notice most? Why?

National Museum of Women in the Arts

You may wish to use the National Museum of Women in the Arts videodisc and/or CD-ROM. The videodisc features a bar code guide, and the interactive CD-ROM provides stimulating activities.

DEVELOPING A PORTFOLIO

Types of Portfolios There are two main types of portfolio assessment: Authentic Portfolio (Process Portfolio) and Performance Portfolio (Showcase Portfolio). Authentic Portfolio provides evidence of student learning over time and includes self-reflection. Performance Portfolio features a formal presentation of the student's most outstanding works without reflective comments.

If using portfolios, consider what you expect from the portfolios. If you are emphasizing types of processes, you may want students to use Authentic Portfolios. If you are looking for finished products, you may prefer Performance Portfolios. For specific ideas and guidelines, refer to the booklet, *Portfolio and Assessment Techniques,* that accompanies the *Introducing Art* program.

The Language of Art

• • • • • • • • • • • • • •

F O C U S

☑ OBJECTIVES

After completing this lesson, students will be able to:
- Define what an artist is.
- Name the elements of art: line, color, shape, form, space, and texture.

☑ SUPPLIES
- Construction paper to make viewfinder and bulletin board
- Scissors
- Paper, pencil for sketchbook

Resources

- ◼ 1-1 What Is Art?
  TRB page 3
  (aesthetics/art criticism)
- ◼ Artist Profile,
  Paul Cézanne, TRB
  page 4

• • • • • • • • • • • • • •

T E A C H

◼ Motivator

Ask students what their idea of an artist is. Lead them to understand that artists are not very different from themselves. Ask students to discuss what they are studying in other subjects and how an artist could use that knowledge, too.

◼ Vocabulary

Write the six elements of art terms on the board. Ask students to read these terms out loud. Then ask students to define the word *elements*.

Have you ever heard a person described as "wearing many hats"? Saying a person wears many hats means he or she is good at a number of things. An **artist**—*a person who uses imagination and skill to communicate ideas in visual form*—wears many hats. Among the hats artists wear is one labeled "scientist." Wearing this hat, artists experiment with the effects of light on objects. Wearing the mathematician's hat, they carefully measure distances between objects. Wearing the hat of writer, they tell stories and record events.

In this book, you will learn about the different ways in which artists have used these skills over the centuries. You will also meet specific artists and learn about their creations.

THE ARTIST'S LANGUAGE

Like other professionals, artists "speak" a language all their own. Just as the mathematician uses numbers, so the artist uses *line*.

Much in the way musicians communicate through notes and sounds, artists speak in *color* and *shape*. The writer relies on words, sentences, and paragraphs, the artist on *form*, *space*, and *texture*.

These six terms—line, color, shape, form, space, and texture—make up the artist's vocabulary. The terms are grouped together under the heading **elements of art**. These are *the basic visual symbols an artist uses to create works of art*. An artist's success depends on how well he or she uses these elements.

Using the Artist's Vocabulary

When you look at an artwork, it is not always clear where one element ends and another begins. Study the artworks in Figures 1–2 and 1–3. You do not see the elements of form and color in the first or the element of line in the second. Instead, you see the works as a whole. As you examine each, your eye

Figure 1–2 Does the artist use a single color to show an object? Do the objects look real? What does this artwork "say" to you?

Paul Cézanne. *The Basket of Apples.* c. 1895. Oil on canvas. 65.5 cm × 81.3 cm (25¾ × 32"). Art Institute of Chicago, Chicago, Illinois. Helen Birch Bartlett Memorial Collection.

4 Chapter 1 *The Elements of Art*

more about • • •

The Skills of Art The Egyptians used their remarkable mathematical skills to build the Pyramids. The Greeks devised the Golden Rectangle, the basis of proportion for their temples and sculptures of human figures. Renaissance artists dissected cadavers to study human anatomy. One artist, Leone Battista Alberti, wrote a treatise in 1435 that helped to develop the mathematics of perspective. Today, artists need skills and knowledge in many fields in order to express ideas and work in the varied media of the arts.

"reads" all the elements together. In fact, it is the careful blending of elements that allows you to see an artwork as the artist meant it to be seen. Taken together, the elements in Figure 1–2 "add up" to a basket of apples and a bottle. The lines in Figure 1–3 cleverly suggest a familiar farm animal. Can you identify it?

"Reading" the Artist's Vocabulary

Think back to when you first learned to read. You did not start with a book. Rather, you began by reading a word at a time. This is how you will learn the vocabulary of art. You will learn about the elements of art one at a time.

Each of the remaining lessons in this chapter treats one or more elements. In later chapters, you will learn about other terms that are central to the practice and study of art.

 Check Your Understanding

1. Define *artist*.
2. Name the six elements of art.

 STUDIO ACTIVITY

Making a Viewer

To learn how a clock works, you might take it apart and study the pieces. The same is true of a work of art. By studying the elements, or "pieces," you learn what makes the work "tick." One tool that can help you sharpen your awareness of the elements of art is a viewfinder. You can easily make a viewfinder by following the directions in Technique Tip **8** on page **283.** Make a viewfinder and use it to focus on familiar objects in your community, such as a tree or a building. Keep a sketchbook in which you record your findings. As you learn more about the elements of art later in this chapter, return to these drawings.

 P O R T F O L I O

Select your best sketch, and date and sign it. Write a short evaluation on the back of the sketch and put it in your portfolio.

STUDIO ACTIVITY

Making a Viewer

Encourage students to experiment with their viewfinders for a few minutes before they study a particular object. Ask them to discuss how the viewfinder affects their ability to focus on a familiar object.

■ **Cooperative Learning**

Have students work in small groups to plan and make a bulletin board on what an artist sees.

After students have used their viewfinders and made their sketchbook images, invite volunteers to share some of their sketches for the bulletin board. Assign teams to select and arrange materials for the bulletin board and to create an artful title and border. Critique the finished board together.

• • • • • • • • • • • • • •

ASSESS

■ **Self-Assessment**

Have students complete the Check Your Understanding questions on this page. Answers are provided below.

■ **Reteaching**

Have students study Figure 1-2 and discuss what the artist was trying to communicate.

■ **Enrichment**

Have students work in small groups to discuss the following statement: "Imagination is more important than knowledge." (Albert Einstein). Invite students to share their reactions and to give reasons for their opinions.

Figure 1–3   **What are some of the questions you think the artist asked himself while he was creating this work?**

Alexander Calder. *Sow.* 1928. Wire. 19.5 × 43.2 × 7.6 cm (7⅔ × 17 × 3″). The Museum of Modern Art, New York, New York. Gift of the artist. © 1997 Artists Rights Society (ARS), New York/ADAGP, Paris

Lesson 1   *The Language of Art*   **5**

• • • • • • • • • • • • • •

CLOSE

Ask each student to name the elements of art.

Answers to ✔ CHECK YOUR UNDERSTANDING

1. An artist is a person who uses imagination and skill to communicate ideas in visual form.

2. The six elements of art are line, color, shape, form, space, and texture.

It might be said that all art begins with a line. You see lines everywhere in your daily life. As you ride in a car along a highway, the edges of the road straight ahead of you form two lines that meet in the distance. The edge of each wall of your classroom is a line. So are the curves that make up the letter *s*.

To the artist, a **line** is *the path of a dot through space.* In this lesson, you will learn about different kinds of lines. You will see how these lines can be used to suggest specific feelings and ideas.

KINDS OF LINE

By definition, every line goes somewhere. A line may "travel" up, down, or across. It may move at an angle, or it may curve back on itself. Each type of line carries a different message to the viewer.

There are five main kinds of line. These include:

Horizontal

Horizontal lines run from side to side. Lines of this type seem to be at rest. They may suggest peace and quiet. Think of the line of a calm lake where the water meets the sky (Figure 1–4).

Figure 1–4 **Horizontal line.**

Vertical

Vertical lines run up and down. They never lean. Lines of this type seem to be standing at attention. Artists use vertical lines to show strength and permanence. Picture the soaring lines of a skyscraper (Figure 1–5).

Figure 1–5 **Vertical line.**

Diagonal

Diagonal lines are straight lines that slant. Lines of this type suggest a sense of movement and excitement. They seem to be rising or falling. Diagonal lines are used to give a sense of movement.

Curved

Curved lines are lines that change direction little by little. Wiggly lines are made up of two or more curves. Spirals and circles also begin with curved lines. Like diagonals, curved lines express movement, but in a more graceful way.

Figure 1–6 **Curved line.**

6   Chapter 1   *The Elements of Art*

more about • • •

Experimenting with Lines Vincent van Gogh (1853–1890) was a Dutch painter whose work reflected the strong emotions of his own life. He is called a Post-Impressionist, because he followed the Impressionists but moved away from their concern for accurate representation of light conditions and used color and line to express feeling. Van Gogh used chalk, pen, reed pen, and ink on paper to create *View in the Park at Arles* (Figure 1-8). He and other Post-Impressionists experimented with a variety of tools to achieve strong emotion through line quality.

Zigzag

Zigzag lines are formed by joining together several diagonals that move in different directions. The diagonals form sharp angles that make lines change direction suddenly. Zigzag lines create confusion. They suggest action or nervous excitement (Figure 1–7).

Figure 1–7   **Zigzag line.**

LINE QUALITY

Think about the crease in a pair of freshly ironed trousers. Would you describe this "line" as smooth or rough? How about a line made with chalk? Smoothness, roughness, thickness, and thinness each represent a different **line quality.** This quality is *the unique character of any line.*

How a line appears depends on several factors. These include:

- *The tool used.* A crayon produces a slightly ragged line. A paintbrush dipped in ink produces a line that narrows and trails off.
- *The pressure of the artist's hand.* Pressing down on a tool creates a thicker line.

 STUDIO ACTIVITY

Experimenting with Lines

Gather a variety of art tools. These might include pencil, marker, brush and ink, chalk, and crayon. Practice using the tools to draw lines. Notice the quality of line each tool produces. Try drawing lines that express different feelings. These might include joy, fear, anger, and excitement. Share your lines with classmates.

P O R T F O L I O
Label the lines with the names of the feelings they express. Then store your experiment in your portfolio.

Using less pressure creates a thinner line. How would you describe the quality of the lines in Figure 1-8? Are the lines smooth or rough? Are they thick or thin?

✔ Check Your Understanding

1. Name the five directions a line can take.
2. Tell how each of the line types can make a viewer feel or react.
3. What is line quality?

Figure 1–8   **How many different kinds of lines has the artist used? Describe the quality of these lines.**

Vincent van Gogh. *Corner of a Park at Arles (Tree in a Meadow).* 1889. Reed pen and black ink over charcoal. 49.3 × 61.3 cm (19⅜ × 24″). Art Institute of Chicago, Chicago, Illinois. Gift of Tiffany and Margaret Blake, 1945.3

Lesson 2   *Line*   **7**

■ Studio Skills

Ask students to carry a sketchbook and find interesting lines in things they see every day, such as lines in bushes, trees, building details, traffic signs, and so on. Have students keep a line awareness log showing their continuing awareness of line quality and direction in the world around them.

■ Aesthetics

Help students discuss Figure 1-1 on page 2 at the beginning of the chapter. What kinds of lines can they find? Do the lines help communicate feelings or movement? After the discussion, ask students to write a short paragraph describing how the artist used lines to help create movement or strong feeling.

• • • • • • • • • • • • • •
ASSESS

■ Self-Assessment

Have students complete the Check Your Understanding questions on this page. Answers are provided below.

■ Reteaching

Work with small groups of students to review the five kinds of lines. Ask students to describe different line qualities.

■ Enrichment

Encourage students to examine the ways lines are used in textbooks. Have students bring in and discuss examples of type, boxes, borders, and other uses of lines in their books.

• • • • • • • • • • • • • •
CLOSE

Divide students into groups, assigning each group a kind of line. Ask each group to list as many things as they can find in the room that have that type of line. Allow five minutes, then ask groups to share their lists.

Answers to ✔ CHECK YOUR UNDERSTANDING

1. A line can be **horizontal,** running from side to side; **vertical,** running up and down; **diagonal,** running on a slant; **curved,** changing direction little by little; or **zigzag,** combining diagonal lines that move in different directions.

2. Horizontal lines suggest peace and quiet. Vertical lines show strength and permanence. Diagonal lines suggest movement. Curved lines express graceful movement. Zigzag lines create confusion. They suggest action or nervous excitement.

3. Line quality is the unique character of any line.

Color

• • • • • • • • • • • • •

F O C U S

☑ OBJECTIVES

After completing this lesson, students will be able to:

- Define color.
- Identify the three main properties of color: hue, value, and intensity.
- Define and identify monochromatic, analogous, and complementary color schemes.

☑ SUPPLIES

- Clear plastic page protectors
- Colored cellophanes and/or gels
- Scissors, transparent tape
- Overhead projector

Resource
■ 1-5 Scavenger Hunt, TRB page 8 (cooperative learning)

• • • • • • • • • • • • •

T E A C H

■ Motivator

Invite students to imagine what their world would be like without color. Explore ways in which color affects their moods and feelings about their clothes, their rooms, and other aspects of their daily lives.

Imagine a world without color. Like lines, color surrounds us. It is in the reds and purples of the sky at sunset. It is in the lush green of a well-tended lawn. Our moods even have "color." We describe someone who is angry as "seeing red." A happy, carefree person is said to be "in the pink."

In this lesson, you will learn about the way color is used in art. In the next lesson, you will practice using color yourself.

PROPERTIES OF COLOR

Have you ever tried to find a pair of matching socks on a dark winter morning? It is not easy. Without light, all colors look the same. Scientists and artists have long understood this. Both know that **color** is *what the eye sees when light is reflected off an object.*

Some artists use color boldly. Others use it softly. To get these results, artists need to understand the three main properties of color. These are hue, value, and intensity.

Hue

Hue is *a color's name.* Orange, green, and violet are all hues. The relationship among hues is shown in the color wheel in Figure 1–9. Three of the hues in the wheel—red, yellow, and blue—are known as the primary, or pure, hues. *Primary* means "first." They are called

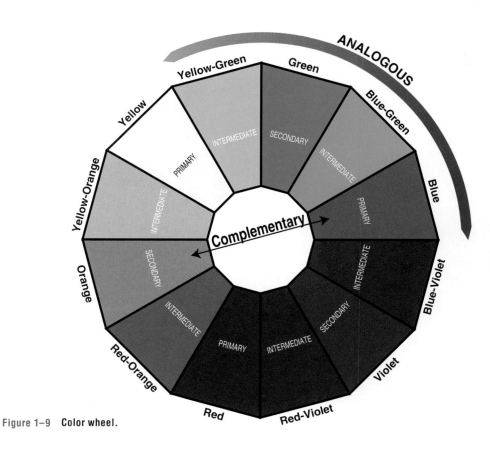

Figure 1–9   Color wheel.

TECHNOLOGY OPTIONS

National Gallery of Art Videodisc   Use the following images to show how color is used by artists.

Wassily Kandinsky *Improvisation 31 (Sea Battle)*	**Piet Mondrian** *Lozenge in Red, Yellow, and Blue*	**Auguste Renoir** *A Girl with a Watering Can*
Search Frame 2247	Search Frame 2255	Search Frame 1300

Use Glencoe's *National Gallery of Art Correlation Bar Code Guide* to locate more artworks.

Figure 1–10 What color questions do you think the artist asked herself? How did she portray the figures in this painting?

Helen Hardin. *Robed Journey of the Rainbow Clan*. 1976. Acrylic. 47 × 76.2 cm (18½ × 30").
© 1996 Helen Hardin, © 1999 Cradoc Bagshaw.

this because these three are mixed to create all the other hues. Mixing the two primary colors of yellow and blue gives green, a *secondary* color. Mixing a primary color like red with a secondary color like orange gives red-orange, an *intermediate* color. Look at the painting in Figure 1–10. The artist has overlapped hues to capture all the colors of the rainbow. Match the hues in the painting with those on the color wheel. Has the artist used any primary hues? Which secondary hues has she used? Which intermediate hues has she used?

Value

A second property of color, **value,** is *the lightness or darkness of a hue.* You can change a hue's value by mixing in white or black. When white is added to a hue, the resulting color is said to be a *tint.* When black is added, the result is called a *shade.* Pink is a tint of red. Maroon is a dark shade of red. These and other values of red appear in the "value scale" in Figure 1–11a.

SHADE   **TINT**

Figure 1–11a   **Value scale.**

Lesson 3   *Color*   **9**

HIGH INTENSITY   LOW INTENSITY

Figure 1–11b   Intensity scale.

■ Art Criticism

Ask students to examine the Helen Hardin painting. Have them name all the colors in it. Then ask students what effect the artist's choice of colors has on the viewer. What mood or feelings do the colors create? How would the result be different if the artist had used different colors? Why?

■ Studio Skills

Have students design a simple outline for a school flag or banner. Then have them reproduce the banner five times. On the first version, have students use only black and white to color their banner. On the second, only primary colors, and on the third, only complementary colors. For the fourth banner, students should use intermediate colors. On the final version, invite students to use colors from all parts of the color wheel. Display all the banners and encourage students to discuss their color choices and designs.

Intensity

Some colors appear lively and brilliant. Others look murky or dull. The difference is called the color's **intensity.** This is the *brightness or dullness of a hue.* A strong, bright hue is said to be "high-intensity." Pure green is such a hue. A faint, dull hue is said to be "low-intensity." Olive green is a hue that fits this description. The intensity scale in Figure 1–11b shows some intensities of green.

One way of lowering a hue's intensity is by mixing it with its *complementary,* or opposite, hue on the color wheel. Look once again at the color wheel on page **8.** Find the hues at either end of the double-headed arrow. If you mix these hues, you get a neutral color such as gray or brown. The same is true if you mix any other complementary hues.

COMBINING COLORS

You may have heard the term *loud* used to describe outfits of clothing. The term also refers to a combination of colors that clash. Art, like clothing, makes use of color combinations, or *schemes.* Different color schemes give different effects. Some color schemes are quiet. Others are exciting.

The following are some common color schemes used by trained artists:

Monochromatic

A monochromatic (**mah**-noh-kroh-**mat**-ik) color scheme uses different tints or shades of a single hue. Such a combination can help bring together the parts of a work.

Monochromatic color schemes must be used with caution, however, because they can produce a dull, uninteresting effect. See an example of a monochromatic color scheme in Figure 1–11c.

Analogous

An analogous (uh-**nal**-uh-gus) color scheme uses hues that are side by side on the color wheel and share a hue. (See Figure 1–11d.) Analogous color schemes relate objects in a work. Look at the color wheel shown in Figure 1–9 on page **8** and find the colors analogous to yellow. What hues would be included in an analogous color scheme based on red?

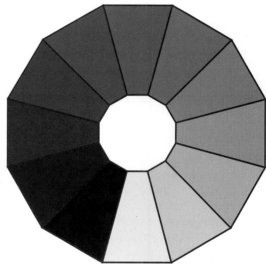

Figure 1–11c   Monochromatic color scheme.

MEETING SPECIAL NEEDS

Identifying Colors Correctly   Some students may not be able to identify colors correctly. If you feel the condition is not just a subjective misdetermination, you might have the school nurse check or mention it to the parents to determine if the student might have color-blindness. The inability to distinguish blue and green hues is the most common kind of color-blindness, and the condition affects more males than females.

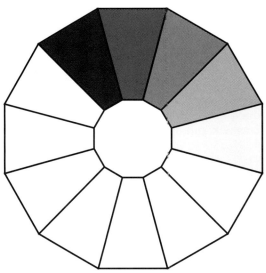

Figure 1–11d **Analogous color scheme.**

Complementary

As its name suggests, the complementary color scheme (Figure 1–11e) uses opposite hues on the color wheel. It makes for the most striking color combinations. As with monochromatic colors, care must be taken when combining complementary colors. Placing high-intensity complementary colors close together in an artwork can create an unusual flickering effect.

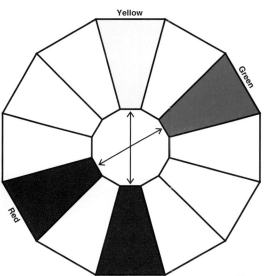

Figure 1–11e **Complementary color schemes.**

Experimenting with Color Combinations

Gather sheets of colored cellophane. Cut circles or other shapes from each sheet. Experiment with different color combinations by overlapping the shapes in a clear plastic folder. Secure the edges of the folder. Then hold it up to the light. In your sketchbook, note combinations that are especially pleasing to your eye. Repeat the experiment, this time overlapping more colors. Try more than one layer of a single color to deepen it. Last, try making combinations of *warm colors*—red, yellow, and orange—and of *cool colors*—blue, green, and violet. Think about scenes in which you might be likely to use a warm color scheme. How might you use a cool color scheme?

 P O R T F O L I O

On a separate piece of paper, list the color combinations that made your favorite warm color and your favorite cool color. Put this paper in your portfolio for use in an upcoming project.

 ## Check Your Understanding

1. Define the term *hue.*
2. What are the three properties of color?
3. Where do you find complementary colors on the color wheel?

Experimenting with Color Combinations

To prepare for the studio activity, place the supply of materials on a table, or distribute quantities of them on desks arranged in groups. Begin by demonstrating the effect of overlays of color on the overhead. As students experiment for themselves, encourage them to talk about the effects they achieve and their reactions to them.

• • • • • • • • • • • •
A S S E S S

■ **Self-Assessment**

Have students complete the Check Your Understanding questions on this page. Answers are provided below.

■ **Reteaching**

Work with small groups of students to review the concepts of primary, secondary, and intermediate colors.

Have students work in pairs to collect and identify different color schemes used in magazine or catalog pictures.

■ **Enrichment**

Let students work with partners to identify and analyze some of the color schemes used in some of the art reproduced in this book. Ask each pair of students to discuss what they found and what effect the various color schemes achieved.

• • • • • • • • • • • •
C L O S E

Review with students the differences between value and intensity. Discuss the differences between monochromatic, analogous, and complementary color schemes.

Answers to ✔CHECK YOUR UNDERSTANDING

1. Hue is a color's name. Orange, red, and green, for example, are all hues.
2. The three properties of color are **hue, value,** and **intensity.** The hue is the color's name, the value is the lightness or darkness of a hue, and the intensity is the brightness or dullness of a hue.
3. Complementary colors are found directly opposite each other on the color wheel.

(pages 12–13)

Lesson Time: 45 minutes

FOCUS

☑ OBJECTIVES

After completing this lesson, students will be able to:
- Understand color mixing.
- Be able to mix pure hues, tints, and varied intensities.
- Use brushes and paint.
- Mix colors to paint an artwork.

☑ SUPPLIES

- White drawing paper
- Tempera paints: two primaries and white
- Wash or bristle brush
- Cups for water
- Paper towels
- Plastic plates to use as palettes

Resource

■ Fine Art Print 2, *Houses in Murnau* by Wassily Kandinski

TEACH

■ Motivator

Divide the class into three groups. Give each group two primaries. Explain that they will be able to paint all full intensity colors by using two primaries. The studio option completes the experience of color mixing by intentionally achieving neutral tones.

■ Vocabulary

Have students review the terms from Lesson 3: *hue, value, intensity, primary, secondary, complementary, analogous, monochromatic.*

LESSON 4
Mixing Colors

Artists look at the world around them and see far more than a blue sky and green grass. Claude Monet was called an *Impressionist* painter because he looked at the landscape at different times of day and saw every color of the rainbow. At dawn he found purples, pinks, and blues in the farmer's wheat stacks. At noon these stacks appeared to be blazing oranges and yellows. He painted "impressions" of the wheat stack in Figure 1–12 by laying strokes of many colors on his canvas. As we look at his paintings, our eyes "mix" the strokes of color together. Look for the brush strokes in the haystack and elsewhere.

WHAT YOU WILL LEARN

You will discover colors by mixing tempera paints. You will use two *primary* colors and white. Each time you add a stroke of one of these colors and blend it on your paper, you can make a new color. When you have filled your paper, you will have a rich painting. Try to mix as many variations of your two colors as possible.

Figure 1–12 **What kind of color scheme has the artist used in this painting? How would you describe the intensity of the colors?**

Claude Monet. *Stack of Wheat.* 1891. Oil on canvas. 65.6 × 92 cm (25¼ × 36"). Art Institute of Chicago, Chicago, Illinois. Restricted gift of the Searle Family Trust; Major Acquisitions Centennial Endowment; through prior acquisitions of the Mr. and Mrs. Martin A. Ryerson and Potter Palmer Collections; through prior bequest of Jerome Friedman, 1983.29

TECHNIQUE TIP ▼

Using Brushes and Paint   As students paint, encourage blending to achieve new colors and moving around the paper as they mix, filling all of it. Suggest rinsing the brush and drying or blotting it occasionally with a rag or paper towel to get a fresh color start. Discourage using water unless the paint is dry. Colors will look thin and washed out.

When students are finished, have them thoroughly wash the brushes and store them bristles up. Have students close paint jars tightly to prevent the paint from drying out.

WHAT YOU WILL NEED

- White drawing paper, 9 x 12 inches (23 x 30 cm)
- Tempera paints—two primary colors and white
- Wash or bristle brush
- Cup of water, paper towels

WHAT YOU WILL DO

1. On a plastic plate, take spoonfuls of two primary colors and white tempera paint. Your teacher will divide the class into three groups and give red and yellow to one, red and blue to another, and yellow and blue to the third.
2. Wet your brush, squeeze the water out of it with your fingers, and dip it into one primary color. Paint an area on your paper. Rinse your brush and dry it with the towel before you start using a new color.
3. Dip into the second primary and begin blending the two colors on your paper until you get the *secondary color*—green or orange or purple.
4. Continue adding more of each primary color as you fill your paper, trying to make new colors each time. Blend the colors into each other.
5. When you have mixed many new colors, begin adding white to all of your colors to get *tints*.

EXAMINING YOUR WORK

- **Describe** Point out on your painting the secondary color you mixed and the many variations you blended. Locate the tints you made by mixing white with your colors.
- **Analyze** Discuss the experience of discovering new colors. What happened when you blended the colors longer with your brush?

Figure 1–13 **Student works. Mixing primary colors.**

STUDIO OPTIONS

Try This!

■ Add the third primary to your palette and mix the three colors right on the palette. You will find that you get a neutral brown. Do another painting in all neutral tones, adding more of each of your colors as you paint. You have now changed the *intensity* of your colors.

■ Make a class color wheel by arranging groups of paintings on a bulletin board. One painting from each group will give you all the colors of the color wheel. Put a neutral painting in the center.

Lesson 4 *Mixing Colors* **13**

CURRICULUM CONNECTIONS

Language Arts Encourage students to read the book *O the Red Rose Tree* by Patricia Beatty (New York: Morrow Junior Books, 1972), or you may want to read the story aloud to them. In this story of the 1890s, four girls try to find seven shades of red for an elderly friend who wants to make a special quilt. Though the right quilting materials are very hard to find, the girls are determined to keep a promise and find all the reds.

Discuss with students the importance colorful quilts and similar items can have. Invite students to write a poem or short story about a favorite quilt, blanket, or similar item they may have used as a young child. In their writing, students should describe why color was an important feature.

13

Shape, Form, and Space

☑ OBJECTIVES

After completing this lesson, students will be able to:
- Explain the difference between shape and form.
- Distinguish between geometric and free-form shapes or forms.
- Define space and negative space.
- Identify at least three techniques used to suggest space in two-dimensional art.

☑ SUPPLIES

- White drawing paper
- Pencils for sketching
- Several classroom objects including books

Resource

⬛ 1-6 Shaping a Culture, TRB page 9 (cultural diversity)

• • • • • • • • • • • • • •
TEACH

⬛ Motivator

Divide the class into pairs. Ask each pair to trace the outline of a book on a piece of paper. Then have them measure the height and width of their outlines. Explain that these outlined drawings have two dimensions, height and width. Then have students measure the third dimension of their books. Ask students to discuss the difference between two-dimensional and three-dimensional objects.

Here is a riddle. What do *you,* a stop sign, and a rubber ball have in common? You all exist in—and are set off by—space. This is true of all objects. Some objects are recognizable because of their shape or form alone. Even without seeing the letters or red color, you could identify a stop sign. You would recognize its octagonal shape. Even in the dark, you could identify a rubber ball. You would feel its round form.

Shape, form, and space are closely related. In this lesson, you will learn about these elements and their special place in art.

SHAPE

To an artist, a **shape** is *an area clearly set off by one or more of the other five visual elements of art.* Shapes exist in two dimensions. They have length and width but not depth. Shapes are flat.

All shapes are one of two types:

- **Geometric Shapes.** Geometric shapes are precise, mathematical shapes. They look as though they were made with a ruler, compass, or other special tool. The square, circle, and triangle are among the most common geometric shapes. The rectangle and oval are others. Geometric shapes are mostly, though not always, made by people. Examine the painting in Figure 1–14. Which geometric shapes has the artist used? How many of each of these shapes can you find in the work?

- **Free-form** or **Organic Shapes.** Free-form shapes are not regular or even. Such shapes are found throughout nature.

Figure 1–14   The title of this work mentions a free-form shape from music. Can you find this shape?

Roy Lichtenstein. *Modern Painting with Clef.* 1967. Oil and synthetic polymer and pencil on canvas. 252.4 × 458.2 (100⅛ × 180⅜"). Hirschhorn Museum and Sculpture Garden, Smithsonian Institution, Washington, D.C. Gift of Joseph H. Hirshhorn, 1972.

14   Chapter 1   *The Elements of Art*

TECHNOLOGY OPTIONS

National Gallery of Art Videodisc   Use the following images to show artists' use of shape, form, and space.

Helen Frankenthaler
Wales

Search Frame 2329

Alberto Giacometti
The City Square

Search Frame 2575

Marino Marini
Horseman

Search Frame 2569

Use Glencoe's *National Gallery of Art Correlation Bar Code Guide* to locate more artworks.

The outline of a lake is a free-form shape. So is the outline of your hand. The artwork in Figure 1–3 on page **5** is made up of a number of free-form shapes. How many different shapes can you find?

FORM

Like shapes, forms have height and width. Unlike shapes, they also have a third dimension: depth. **Form** is *an element of art that refers to an object with three dimensions.* When you hold a book in your hand, you are experiencing its form in three dimensions: height, width, and depth.

Forms are grouped as geometric or free-form, much as shapes are. An aluminum can is an example of the geometric form called *cylinder.* Rocks and clouds, by contrast, are free-form. So is the stack of wheat in Figure 1–12 on page **12.**

In art, a close relationship exists between shapes and forms. A two-dimensional circle and three-dimensional sphere have the same round outline. A two-dimensional square can be "stretched" into a third dimension to become a cube. These and other shape-form relations are shown in Figure 1–15.

SPACE

All objects take up space. **Space** is *the distance or area between, around, above, below, and within things.* Space is empty until shapes or forms fill it.

In some works of art, space is real. In others, it is only suggested. Compare the artworks in Figures 1–16 and 1–17 on pages **16–17.** The first is an example of sculpture. It exists in three dimensions. If you were viewing this work in person, you could walk around it. You could enter its space and appreciate its form.

The second work of art is a painting. The scene looks very realistic and lifelike. If you tried to move forward into it, however, you would bump into a flat surface.

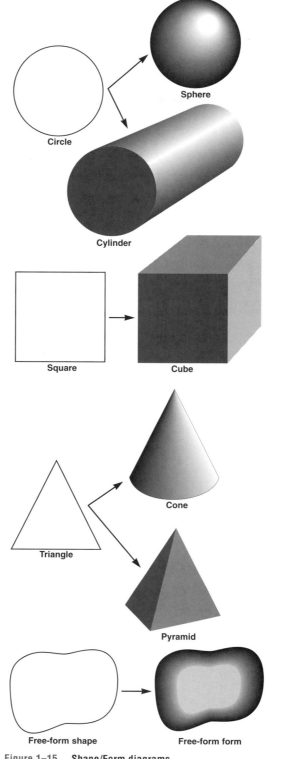

Figure 1–15   Shape/Form diagrams.

Lesson 5   *Shape, Form, and Space*   **15**

■ Vocabulary

List the new terms found in this lesson. Ask pairs of students to take one term, letter it on a strip of paper, and draw an example of its meaning. Design a bulletin board with these strips.

■ Aesthetics

Have students compare the Lichtenstein painting in this lesson with the Helen Hardin in Lesson 3 and the Claude Monet in Lesson 4. Ask: How does each artist use color and shape? Note that Monet almost loses the shape in his brush strokes, while Lichtenstein defines his shapes with strong contrasts. Monet is searching for color; Helen Hardin's shapes and colors are used as symbols. Lichtenstein is simplifying shapes as design. Ask students to write a short paragraph about the use of color and shape in one of these paintings.

■ Cooperative Learning

Divide students into small groups. Ask each group to find and identify objects in the classroom that represent the geometric shapes and forms shown in Figure 1-15. Allow the groups five to ten minutes to find as many examples as they can, then share with the class their list of identified objects.

Art in Everyday Life

Ask students to think about ways in which we perceive dimension as we watch television. Encourage them to discuss other forms of entertainment that involve "3D."

more about •••

Perspective   The Romans were using perspective in their paintings in ancient times. Remains of wall paintings in Pompeii show remarkable examples. But, from about A.D. 400 to about A.D 1000, all painting was flat, often with backgrounds of blue or gold. The Renaissance, beginning in the fifteenth century, was a period of rediscovery of Greek and Roman knowledge and art. An Italian architect, Filippo Brunilleschi, studied the ancient Roman buildings and drawings, and in the early 1400s he reinvented linear perspective.

■ **Cooperative Learning**

Have students work in groups to find magazine photographs showing the receding lines of perspective. Those with cameras can take pictures down the hallway or down streets to illustrate perspective. Have each group use tracing paper overlaid on the photographs and trace the perspective lines. Also, try using a washable marker directly on the window glass to draw an outside view down a street. Direct students to close one eye and focus on a line. Ask groups to share their resulting drawings to see how the eye sees space.

■ **Art Criticism**

As students study and discuss *Paris Street Scene* by Richard Estes, ask them to point to specific techniques the artist has used to achieve a feeling of depth and space. Encourage students to find additional examples of such techniques in other reproductions in this book.

■ **Studio Skills**

Students often feel clumsy in their first attempts at using linear perspective in their own drawings. Help them practice this skill by sketching a familiar classroom object, preferably one with a cubic form. Show them how to draw slanted parallel lines first by observing the example of a cube in Figure 1-15. As students get the hang of sketching cubes, they can apply the same understanding of dimension to other objects they draw.

Space Techniques in Two-Dimensional Art

The artist who painted the street scene in Figure 1–17 used several techniques to capture the feeling of deep space. Artists have developed a number of such techniques. These include the following:

- **Linear perspective.** The lines of buildings, roads, and similar objects are slanted. This makes them appear to come together or meet in the distance.
- **Size.** Distant objects are made smaller than objects that are close up.
- **Overlapping.** Nearer shapes and forms overlap, or partly cover, those meant to appear farther away.
- **Placement.** Distant objects are placed higher up in the picture. Closer ones are placed lower down.

- **Intensity and Value.** The colors of objects meant to appear in the distance are lower in intensity than objects meant to appear nearer. They are also lighter in value.
- **Detail.** More detail is added to closer objects and less detail is added to those in the distance.

Which of these techniques was used in Figure 1–17? What other steps has the artist taken to make forms seem to stand out in space?

Negative Space

When it comes to the element of space, there is one question every artist must answer. That is the question of how much negative space to build into a work. **Negative space** is the *empty spaces between the shapes or forms in two- and three-dimensional art.*

Figure 1–16 What makes this work a form rather than a shape? Has the artist used real or suggested space?

Henry Moore. *Reclining Figure.* 1939. Elmwood. 94 × 200.7 × 76.2 cm (37 × 79 × 30"). Detroit Institute of the Arts, Detroit, Michigan. Founders Society Purchase with funds from the Dexter M. Ferry, Jr. Trustee Corporation.

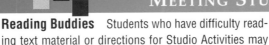

How the artist answers the question about negative space will affect the viewer's reaction to the work. Look back at the artwork in Figure 1–3 on page **5**. There is far more negative space than form to this work. The abundance of negative space gives it a light, airy feel. Contrast this with the negative space in Figure 1–16. This sculpture seems heavier and more compact because there is less negative space.

Little negative space in a painting or drawing makes the work look busy. A lot of negative space can express calm, peace, or even loneliness.

 Check Your Understanding

1. What is shape?
2. Define *form*. What forms are closely related to the circle?
3. Identify and describe at least three techniques artists use to suggest space in two-dimensional art.

STUDIO ACTIVITY

Sketching a Still Life

Look back at the painting of apples in Figure 1–2 on page **4**. This work is an example of a type of art called *still life*. A **still life** is *a painting or drawing of non-living objects*. What nonliving objects besides fruit did the artist choose for this still life? What techniques did he use to achieve a sense of space?

Plan a still life of your own by gathering several familiar objects. Use books, pencils, and other materials found in the classroom. Arrange these on a table. Study the arrangement from different angles. Make pencil sketches from several different views. Be sure to use techniques such as overlapping to capture a feeling of space.

 P O R T F O L I O

Save your best sketch for Lesson 6. Put it in your portfolio.

Figure 1–17 **What techniques has the artist used to give a feeling of space?**

Richard Estes. *Paris Street Scene.* 1972. Oil on canvas. 101.6 × 152.4 cm (40 × 60"). Virginia Museum of Fine Art, Richmond, Virginia. Gift of Sydney and Frances Lewis. © 1998 Richard Estes/Licensed by VAGA, New York, NY/Courtesy Marlborough Gallery, NY

 STUDIO ACTIVITY

Sketching a Still Life

Encourage students to walk around their still life arrangement to see it from all sides. Point out that viewing the materials from a standing position and from a seated position changes the shapes. Tell them to start their sketches with the forms in the foreground and then draw those behind them as they overlap.

ASSESS

■ **Self-Assessment**

Have students complete the Check Your Understanding questions on this page. Answers are provided below.

■ **Reteaching**

Ask students to review Figure 1-15, then explain the difference between shape and form.

■ **Enrichment**

Have students work in pairs or small groups to compare and contrast Figures 1-14 and 1-17. Ask: What similarities and differences do you see between these two paintings? What kinds of lines are used in each? What types of shapes do you find in each (geometric or organic)? Which painting do you prefer? Why? Have each group write a short summary of their responses.

CLOSE

Have students describe the use of shape, form, and space in one of the reproductions shown in this lesson.

Answers to ✔ **CHECK YOUR UNDERSTANDING**

1. Shape is an area clearly set off by one or more of the other five visual elements of art. Shape exists in two dimensions, length and width. Shapes can be geometric or free-form.
2. Form is an element of art that refers to an object with three dimensions. Forms can be geometric or free-form. Forms closely related to the circle are spheres and cylinders.
3. The techniques include the following (any three or more) and the descriptions should be accurate: linear perspective, size, overlapping, placement, intensity, detail.

Lesson Time: 90 minutes

☑ OBJECTIVES

After completing this lesson, the student will be able to:

• Use color properties to define objects and space.

• Use space techniques to arrange objects in a composition.

☑ SUPPLIES

• Pencils, sketch paper, erasers

• White or colored drawing paper

• Oil pastels

Resource

▪ 1-7 Be Still!, TRB page 10 (art history)

• • • • • • • • • • • • • •
TEACH

▪ Motivator

Direct students' attention to the painting by Janet Fish. Ask students to notice all the interesting colors and shapes she found in ordinary objects.

Have students look at their still-life sketches and find highlights and shadows. You might place a lamp near the still-life arrangement in order to create shadow effects. Ask students to draw very lightly with pencil and then begin building oil pastel color lightly. This will allow them to combine colors within shapes. Have students fill in the entire paper with color.

▪ Vocabulary

The term *still life* was not used until the 1600s, in Holland.

18

LESSON 6
Drawing a Still Life

Ordinary objects can become exciting shapes and forms when an artist sees them. Janet Fish arranged these glasses in front of a window and painted *Spring Evening* (Figure 1–18). Look at all the colors and shapes she found in the reflections. Notice how she used lines, colors, shapes, forms, and space to provide realism.

WHAT YOU WILL LEARN

Select the best of the still-life sketches you did in Lesson 5. Do an oil pastel drawing of it. You will use the space techniques you learned in Lesson 5 as you draw the objects and choose oil pastel colors. Look back at page **12** and study the way Claude Monet mixed colors in his painting *Stack of Wheat*.

Figure 1–18 Notice how the artist has overlapped the objects in this still life to show distance. Which objects are farthest from the viewer?

Janet Fish. *Spring Evening*. 1977. Oil on canvas. 111.8 × 162.6 cm (44 × 64″). Rose Art Museum, Brandeis University, Waltham, Massachusetts. Herbert W. Plimpton Collection.

18   Chapter 1   *The Elements of Art*

TECHNIQUE TIP

Using Oil Pastels   Instruct students on how to use oil pastels. Tell them that oil pastels are sticks of pigment held together with an oily binder. If they press down firmly as they draw with oil pastels, students will produce a brilliant-colored line. A lighter stroke produces a fuzzy, softer line. Students can use the brilliant colors to fill in shapes and blend a variety of color combinations with oil pastels.

One way to create a unique tint of a hue is to fill a shape with a soft layer of a hue and then color over the hue with a heavy layer of white. Encourage students to experiment with oil pastels to discover other effects on their own.

WHAT YOU WILL NEED

- Pencil, sketch paper, eraser
- White or colored drawing paper, 12 x 18 inches (30 x 46 cm)
- Oil pastels

WHAT YOU WILL DO

1. Study your sketches and choose the one you like best. Notice that drawings from different angles will show different arrangements of the same objects.
2. On your drawing paper, draw the objects lightly with pencil.
3. Begin applying colors lightly with the oil pastels, building up color as you go. Look for reflections, shadows, and changes in color on your objects.

EXAMINING YOUR WORK

- **Describe**   Point out the ways in which you used size, overlapping, and placement in your drawing. Show the way you used intensity and value in coloring your objects in the foreground and background.
- **Explain**   Tell what effect you were trying to create as you chose which colors to use. How did you use color to set off the objects in the foreground?

4. Choose background colors that will set off the objects in the foreground.
5. Fill the entire surface of your paper with color.

Figure 1–19   **Student work. A still life.**

Try This!

STUDIO OPTION

■ Look down a street in your neighborhood or outside your school. Can you see the street appear to narrow in the distance as it does in *Paris Street Scene*, Figure 1–17 on page **17**? Do a sketch of the street. Notice that the buildings in the distance seem smaller. Try closing one eye to see the narrowing lines of the street.

Lesson 6   *Drawing a Still Life*   **19**

CURRICULUM CONNECTIONS

Science   Ask students to think about ways in which they used size, overlapping, and placement in their drawings. Have them find pictures of the wild growth on the "floor" of a forest or rainforest. What is the relationship of tall plants to short ones? Of vines to bushes? Of trees to ground cover? Have students discuss the natural overlapping and positioning of plant life on the forest floor and analyze how nature uses color, shape, line, and form to create its own "still life."

■ Aesthetics

Have students compare the objects in still-life paintings from the 17th and 18th centuries with those of the mid- to late-twentieth century. Pop art brought commercial products in as subjects. Andy Warhol painted Brillo boxes and Campbell soup cans and soft drink bottles. Early still-life paintings showed the artist's skill in painting fur, metal, lace, and other detailed surfaces.

■ Studio Skills

Encourage students to experiment with the oil pastels to blend colors. Oil pastels are much softer than crayons and can be blended much more easily. Fingers can be used to rub colors together.

ASSESS

■ Self-Assessment

Have students use Examining Your Work on this page to evaluate the still life created in this lesson. Responses may be written or oral.

■ Reteaching

Display the still-life drawings and discuss the use of space and color in them. Ask students to find examples of the techniques of showing space.

■ Enrichment

Arrange glass tumblers and bottles on the window sill. Ask students to note how sunlight reflects on and shines through them. Explain that some glassware, like cut glass and crystal, are specialized art forms. Ask students to research how cut glass is made.

CLOSE

Have students summarize how they used color properties to define objects and space in their still lifes.

Texture

His beard was *rough as sandpaper.* The lake was smooth as glass. You have probably read and maybe even written descriptions like these. The descriptions are effective because they bring to mind the sense of touch. They remind us of familiar textures. As an art element, **texture** is *how things feel, or look as though they might feel if touched.*

Like space, texture in art can be *tactile,* texture that can be touched, or *visual.* In this lesson, you will learn about the double role of texture as an element.

TEXTURE

Imagine the smoothness of mashed potatoes, the brittleness of a wheat cracker. Our sense of touch is always alert to the things around us. It helps us identify them and enjoy their feel. It also helps us avoid unpleasant touch sensations. Such an unpleasant sensation is suggested by the sentence that opens this lesson.

Artists take advantage of our experience with textures to enrich their works. How an artist uses texture depends on whether he or she is working in two or three dimensions.

Tactile Texture

Sculptors, you may recall, work in real space. They also work in real texture. Refer back to the sculpture in Figure 1–16, page **16.** How do you think this work would feel to the touch? Contrast that sensation to the one you might get touching the work in Figure 1–20. This sculpture of a horse is life-size. It is made of mud and tree branches. What words would you use to describe its texture? What do you think it would be like to ride this horse?

Sometimes artists use texture to capture visual designs in three dimensions. The sculpture in Figure 1–21 is such a work. Have you ever touched a raised design in fabric? Do you think the "clothing" worn by this guardian would feel smooth or rough to the touch?

Visual Texture

Artists are aware that we experience texture not only through our sense of touch, but also through our sense of *vision.* Look back at the painting in Figure 1–18 on page **18.** The glassware has been painted in a very lifelike fashion. Each facet, or cut design in the glass,

Figure 1–20 Would you expect to see a horse that looks like this one? What materials has the artist used for texture?

Deborah Butterfield. *Horse.* 1977. Mud and sticks. Life-size. Zolla/Lieberman Gallery, Chicago, Illinois.

20 Chapter 1 *The Elements of Art*

more about • • •

Lifelike Texture Early Greek painters are believed to have painted very lifelike textures. One painting of grapes was said to be so realistic that birds came and pecked at it. Another artist showed his painting and was asked to remove the drape covering it. That was the painting! When oil paint was invented in the 1400s, artists could blend until they achieved remarkably realistic textural surfaces, like gleaming metal and glistening fruit. Today, lifelike texture is seen in Audrey Flack's paintings of women's faces and Andrew Wyeth's paintings of people and outdoor scenes.

looks real enough to touch. Yet, a viewer touching the surface would feel no such facets. The surface instead would feel flat. It would also feel slightly grainy rather than smooth. This is because the work was done on canvas, a coarse material.

This painting makes use of *visual texture*. We "feel" the texture with our eyes. Look back at the realistic street scene in Figure 1–17 on page **17**. How many different textures has the artist recorded? Which of these would feel smooth?

Figure 1–21 Describe the use of color and texture in this work. Notice the work's title and size. Why might the artist have made the sculpture so large?

Thailand. *Guardian Figure.*

STUDIO ACTIVITY

Making Rubbings for Texture

Explore your classroom and the school grounds for objects with uneven, hard textures. These might include coarse stones and grainy wood. Gather several different surfaces. Place a sheet of drawing paper over each. If possible, secure the paper with masking tape. Using the side of an unwrapped crayon, do a rubbing of each surface. Press down just hard enough to capture the texture.

Use the best of your rubbings as the basis for a still life. Refer to the sketch you did in Lesson 6. For this still life, however, cut the shape of each object from one of your rubbings. Try several arrangements of visual textures before you glue the pieces in place. Decide whether you need areas of solid color. If so, add these.

P O R T F O L I O

Compare this still life with the sketch you did for Lesson 6. Write a paragraph telling whether you were successful in using your previous sketch as a basis for this Studio Activity. Put this paragraph in your portfolio with the still life.

✔ Check Your Understanding

1. What is texture?
2. Which of our senses experience texture?
3. What are the two kinds of texture used in art?

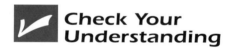

Answers to ✔ CHECK YOUR UNDERSTANDING

1. **Texture** is the element of art that refers to the way things feel, or look as though they might feel if touched.
2. Our sense of touch and our sense of sight experience texture.

3. Two kinds of texture are tactile and visual.

STUDIO ACTIVITY

Making Rubbings for Texture

Encourage students to use textures found at hand (sidewalk cement, bricks, etc.). After they fasten paper to a surface, they should rub evenly, then gradually intensify the color.

When each student has ten or twelve rubbings, they can begin their compositions. Caution students to use scissors carefully.

■ Cultural Diversity

Discuss with students their perceptions of the texture in Figures 1-20 and 1-21. Then, encourage students to share their knowledge of how artists from other cultures make use of and express texture in their artwork. If possible, bring in books showing a variety of works from different cultures and different periods.

• • • • • • • • • • •
A S S E S S

■ Self-Assessment

Have students complete the Check Your Understanding questions on this page. Answers are provided below.

■ Reteaching

Review with students the difference between tactile texture and visual texture. Have students give examples of each.

■ Enrichment

Ask student volunteers to research trompe l'oeil painting and its use of texture.

• • • • • • • • • • •
C L O S E

Ask students to explain the double role of texture as an element of art.

CONNECTIONS *Science*

After completing this feature, students will be able to:

- Explain how the eye perceives color.
- Describe how Vasarely used color in his artwork.

Teaching the Connection

- Have students read the feature on this page.
- Ask volunteers to share what they know about color. What are the colors of the spectrum? *(Red, orange, yellow, green, blue, violet.)* Which are the primary colors? *(Red, yellow, and blue.)* What colors are in the range between violet and red? *(Examples include magenta, fuchsia, berry.)* What is the name of the condition that affects a person's ability to distinguish colors? *(Color blindness.)* Why is color such an important element of art? *(Answers will vary.)*
- Tell students that Victor Vasarely (b. 1908) was a Hungarian artist known for his geometric paintings. Although his early works were complicated patterns in black and white, he soon began adding sharp color contrasts. Vasarely created illusions of depth and motion through his patterns of similar geometric shapes.

Answers to Making the Connection

- ✔ Vasarely also used line, shape, and space.
- ✔ Rods allow night vision, and cones sense color. They are located in the retina.
- ✔ Student responses will vary.

Victor Vasarely. *Paz-Ket*. 1969. Oil on canvas. No measurement available. Museo de Bellas Artes, Bilbao/Bridgeman Art Library. © 1997 Artists Rights Society (ARS), New York, NY

How Does the Eye Perceive Color?

Have you ever told a friend, "I like that blue sweater" only to find that your friend thought the sweater was green? Why did you and your friend see two different colors?

The way you perceive color depends on the way your brain responds to the signals from your eyes. When your eyes focus on an object, such as an orange basketball, you are actually seeing the light reflected from the ball. When light enters the eye, it lands on the retina. The retina contains rods and cones, which are cells that detect light. The rods allow you to see at night, and the cones sense color.

Light travels as electromagnetic waves. Each color in the spectrum is part of a range of wavelengths. The term *blue*, for example, refers to a series of colors. Your friend's sweater may not have been blue or green. Instead, it may have been turquoise or aquamarine, which are in the range of colors between blue and green.

Color is one of the six elements of art. Victor Vasarely used color as an important element in *Paz-Ket*. The placement of the dots in the work affects the way our eyes perceive the colors.

MAKING THE CONNECTION

- ✔ Besides color, what other elements of art did Vasarely use in this work?
- ✔ What is the purpose of rods and cones in the eye? In what part of the eye are they located?
- ✔ Learn more about the eye. Draw a picture of an eye and label its parts.

INTERNET ACTIVITY

Visit Glencoe's Fine Arts Web Site for students at:

http://www.glencoe.com/sec/art/students

INTERNET ACTIVITY

Art on the Web You and your students are invited to take a trip through Glencoe's Fine Arts Site on the World Wide Web. Your class can explore *Studio Cyberspace*, full of art activities; *Glencoe Student Galleria*, a changing showcase of student artworks; links to lots of adventures through art museums, worldwide cultural treasures, and contact with other art teachers and classrooms. To reach the Glencoe Fine Arts page, type in the URL address exactly as shown:

http://www.glencoe.com/sec/art

There you will also find a rich array of teacher resources waiting for you. Check the *Internet Activity Booklet* included with the *Introducing Art* program for more information.

REVIEW

 BUILDING VOCABULARY

Number a sheet of paper from 1 to 10. After each number, write the term from the box that matches each description below.

color	shape
elements of art	space
form	still life
line	texture
negative space	value

1. The path of a dot through space.
2. A painting or drawing of nonliving objects.
3. The basic visual symbols an artist uses to create works of art.
4. An area clearly set off by one or more of the other five visual elements of art.
5. The lightness or darkness of a hue.
6. The distance or area between, around, above, below, and within things.
7. An element of art that refers to an object with three dimensions.
8. Empty spaces between the shapes or forms in two- and three-dimensional art.
9. What the eye sees when light is reflected off an object.
10. How things feel, or look as though they might feel if touched.

 REVIEWING ART FACTS

Number a sheet of paper from 11 to 15. Answer each question in a complete sentence.

11. What emotion or feeling is suggested by horizontal lines? What feeling do diagonal lines communicate to the viewer?
12. What is the relationship between primary and secondary colors?
13. Under what circumstances might an artist choose to use complementary colors in a work?
14. In what ways are shape and form alike? In what ways are they different?
15. Name and explain three techniques artists use to achieve a feeling of deep space.

 THINKING ABOUT ART

On a sheet of paper, answer each question in a sentence or two.

1. **Analyze.** Imagine that you were asked to design the cover for a book about a basketball legend. What kind of color scheme would you choose for the cover? What kind of lines would you use for the illustration? Explain your choices.
2. **Interpret.** In this chapter, you learned about techniques for giving depth to forms in works of art. Yet, some artists—cartoonists, for example—purposely do not work at achieving depth. Why do you think this is so?

MAKING ART CONNECTIONS

1. **Science.** Artists, as you learned, sometimes "wear the hat" of scientist. Using an encyclopedia or on-line research tool, look up *optics*. Explain what this science is, and what contributions scientists have made through the ages. Conclude by explaining the role of optics in art.

2. **Music.** Music, like art, suggests moods and sensations. Think about the way sound captures certain sensations. Fast music, for example, can be "lively." Then make a three-column chart. Head the first column *Color,* the second *Line,* the third *Sound.* Choose at least three moods or sensations. For each, write the type of color, line, and sound it captures.

ANSWERS TO CHAPTER 1 REVIEW

■ **Building Vocabulary**

1. line
2. still life
3. elements of art
4. shape
5. value
6. space
7. form
8. negative space
9. color
10. texture

■ **Reviewing Art Facts**

11. Horizontal lines suggest peace and quiet. Diagonal lines suggest movement.
12. Primary colors are those from which all others are mixed. Secondary colors are made from two primaries.
13. He or she might do so to create a striking effect.
14. They are alike in that both can be geometric or free-form. They are different in that shapes are two-dimensional, while forms are three-dimensional.
15. Answers will vary. Possibilities include: linear perspective—the slanting of objects to make them appear to meet in the distance; size—making distant objects smaller and close-up objects larger; overlapping—having nearer shapes and forms partly cover those meant to appear farther away; placement—putting distant objects higher up in the picture, closer ones lower down; intensity and value—making the colors of objects meant to appear in the distance lower in intensity and darker than objects meant to appear nearer; detail—adding more detail to nearer objects, less to farther objects.

? THINKING ABOUT ART

1. Answers will vary. Some might suggest bright, bold warm colors to signal fast-paced action and diagonal lines to indicate tension and movement.

2. Students should recognize that the choice to add or not add depth is a function of style. Cartoon characters, because they are whimsical, do not have to exhibit depth or other suggestions of realism.

23

The Principles of Art

(pages 24–39)

Resources

- 2-9 Chapter Test, TRB page 31
- Transparency CC-2, *Liberty* by Robert Indiana
- Transparency 2, *Stone Cutter* by Diego Rivera
- Fine Art Print 3, *Still Life with Watermelon, Pears, and Grapes* by Lily Martin Spencer
- Fine Art Print 4, *Broadway* by William Conger

 Music

While studying this chapter, use Performing Arts Handbook page 314 to teach how George Gershwin used variation in his compositions.

NATIONAL STANDARDS

This chapter addresses the following National Standards for the Visual Arts:

1. (a, b)   3. (a, b)
2. (a, b, c) 6. (b)

Figure 2–1 How would you describe the overall "feeling" or "mood" of this painting? Notice the role line plays in creating this feeling. What other factors contribute?

Zanbur the Spy. Mughal period, reign of Akbar (1556–1605) c. 1561–76. Tempera on cotton cloth mounted on paper. 74 × 57.2 cm (28⅛ × 22½"). The Metropolitan Museum of Art, New York, New York. Rogers Art, 1923.

FEATURED ARTISTS

Charles Demuth
M. C. Escher
Sondra Freckelton
Katsushika Hokusai
Ramon José Lopez
Bridget Riley

James Rosenquist
Miriam Schapiro
Joseph M. W. Turner
Yaware People

The Principles of Art

To solve a jigsaw puzzle, you need to fit the pieces together just so. Only when you follow the puzzle maker's plan can you fit the pieces together properly and see the whole picture.

The same is true of looking at works of art. Every artwork is based on an overall plan, or design. The puzzle "pieces" are the elements of art. Only by understanding how the artist has organized these pieces can you fully appreciate works like the one at the left.

In this chapter you will learn about the rules artists use to plan their works. You will learn how to use these rules yourself to see the "whole picture."

PORTFOLIO IDEAS

You will often begin an artwork in a sketchbook. A **sketchbook** is *a pad of drawing paper on which artists sketch, write notes, and refine ideas for their work.* Sketchbook ideas can become plans for finished artwork that will go into your portfolio.

OBJECTIVES

After completing this chapter, you will be able to:
- Define the term *principles of art.*
- Explain the three kinds of balance.
- Tell how artists use the principles of variety, harmony, emphasis, proportion, movement, and rhythm.
- Explain how a work achieves unity.
- Practice organizing elements and principles in original works of art.

WORDS YOU WILL LEARN

balance
emphasis
harmony
movement
picture plane
principles of art
proportion
rhythm
sketchbook
unity
variety

25

DEVELOPING A PORTFOLIO

Keeping a Sketchbook If available, share your sketchbook and professional portfolio with your students. Explain to them that both of these items can help aspiring artists evaluate their artistic growth over time. Students can use the sketchbook to create preliminary sketches, write notes, and refine ideas.

Tell students that a sketchbook is similar to a journal. It is a place to start new ideas, improve ones they have already started, and make notes for future artworks. For more information, refer to the booklet, *Portfolio and Assessment Techniques* that accompanies the *Introducing Art* program.

The Language of Design

LESSON 1

The Language of Design

(pages 26–27)

☑ OBJECTIVES

After completing this lesson, students will be able to:
- Define the term *principle of art.*
- Tell how artists use the principle of balance.
- Explain the three kinds of balance.

☑ SUPPLIES
- Pencils and sketchpads

Resource

■ 2-1 Keeping Your Balance, TRB page 21 (cooperative learning)

■ Motivator

Ask a student to demonstrate being off balance. Then ask three students, as a group, to demonstrate being off balance. Lead a discussion of why balance is important or meaningful. Have students brainstorm ways in which we use or value balance, such as the bass and treble on the stereo, balancing a check book, and so on.

■ Vocabulary

Introduce the terms *formal* balance, *informal* balance, and *radial* balance. Use simple diagrams to illustrate each concept. Ask student volunteers to draw additional examples on the board.

26

Have you ever tried to learn another language? To do so, you need to know more than vocabulary. You also need to know the rules of grammar. These rules govern how words go together.

The language of art has its own set of rules. These rules are called **principles of art.** They are *guidelines that govern the way artists organize the elements of art.* In all there are seven such principles. They are: balance, variety, harmony, emphasis, proportion, movement, and rhythm. In this lesson, you will meet the first of these principles, balance.

THE PRINCIPLE OF BALANCE

You have probably lost your balance at one time or another. Maybe it was when you were riding your bicycle.

In art, as in life, balance is important. To an artist, **balance** is *a principle of art concerned with arranging the elements so that no one part of the work overpowers, or seems heavier than, any other part.* Artists speak of three types of balance:

- **Formal balance.** In art that has formal balance, one half of a work is a mirror image of the other half. Formal balance can give a feeling of dignity to a work of art. Notice the decorated screen in Figure 2–2. With your finger, trace a vertical line that divides the work in half and compare the two halves. Notice how they are alike. Can you find other examples of formal balance within this same work?

Figure 2–2
Imagine that the panel on the right is not there. What would happen to the balance in this work?

Ramon José Lopez. *Santa Maria y Jesus.* Altar screen (reredo). 1981. Hand-adzed pine painted with natural pigments. 2.4 × 2.7 m (8 × 9'). Collection of the artist.

26   Chapter 2   *The Principles of Art*

- **Informal balance.** Imagine yourself on a seesaw with a much heavier person. To balance the two sides, you might ask the heavier person to move closer to the center. In art, the problem of balance is solved through the use of color and other elements. A small, brightly colored shape or form in one area of a work will balance a larger, dull one elsewhere. The two shapes carry the same "visual weight." Works of this type are said to have informal balance. Look at the painting in Figure 2–3. What single large form is your eye drawn to? What smaller, brighter forms command the same attention?

- **Radial balance.** In art with radial balance, shapes or forms are arranged around a central point. Snowflakes exhibit radial balance. So do bicycle tires. For an example of radial balance in art, look again at Figure 2–2. Notice the half circles at the top of each panel. See how the gold-colored teardrop shapes in each seem to extend outward from an invisible point.

STUDIO ACTIVITY

Sketching Shapes with Balance

Look around your home, school, and community for objects with formal, informal, and radial balance. Be creative in your search. With pencil and a sketch pad, make sketches of at least three items. Share your sketches with classmates. Challenge them to identify the type of balance in each sketch.

 P O R T F O L I O

Label and date your sketches of formal, informal, and radial balance. Put the sketches in your portfolio for future reference.

✔ Check Your Understanding

1. Define *principles of art*.
2. List the principles of art.
3. Describe the three kinds of balance.

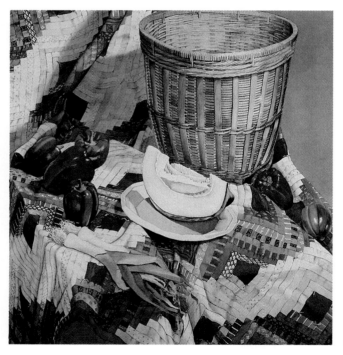

Figure 2–3 Where does your eye travel first in this painting? Where does it look next? Why is this so?

Sondra Freckelton. *Winter Melon with Quilt and Basket.* 1977. Watercolor on paper. 117.5 × 112 cm (46⅛ × 44⅛"). Virginia Museum of Fine Arts, Richmond, Virginia. Gift of Sydney and Frances Lewis.

Lesson 1   *The Language of Design*   **27**

■ **Cooperative Learning**

Divide the class into groups and assign a kind of balance to each group. Have them arrange themselves into a composition in their kind of balance. When the groups have decided on their arrangement, ask one group at a time to present their composition. Discuss how the groups achieved their balance.

■ **Cultural Diversity**

Ask students to find, in artifacts from their own family background or other cultural backgrounds, examples of formal, informal, or radial balance. Many ethnic art forms will be excellent examples of this. Plan a display labeling each item's ethnic culture, its location, and the family whose treasure it is. Discuss the kind of balance in each. (Note: Be sure students have family permission to bring in personal possessions.)

● ● ● ● ● ● ● ● ● ● ● ● ● ●

ASSESS

■ **Self-Assessment**

Have students complete the Check Your Understanding questions on this page. Answers are provided below.

■ **Reteaching**

Ask students to write briefly about their sketches of formal, informal, and radial balance. Look for comments on the method of identification.

■ **Enrichment**

Have students work with compasses and other tools of mathematics to design examples of all three kinds of balance. Discuss the connections between mathematics and art.

● ● ● ● ● ● ● ● ● ● ● ● ● ●

CLOSE

Ask students: How is the language of art similar to other languages? *(Each has rules and principles to follow.)*

LESSON 2

Making a Mask with Formal Balance

(pages 28–29)

LESSON TIME: 4 hours

• • • • • • • • • • • • • •
FOCUS

☑ OBJECTIVES

After completing this lesson, students will be able to:
- Work neatly and with craftsmanship in the process of papier mâché.
- Design and make a mask using formal balance and geometric form.

☑ SUPPLIES

- Pencils and paper for sketching
- Newspapers to cover desks and to make masks.
- Cellulose wallpaper paste, jars for mixing, plastic cups
- Masking tape, scissors
- Tempera paint or school acrylic, brushes; polymer gloss medium (optional)
- Decorative materials such as feathers and ribbon

Resource

■ 2-2 Out of Africa, TRB page 22 (cultural diversity)

• • • • • • • • • • • • • •
TEACH

■ Motivator

Show the Yaware mask and any other photographs of masks you can bring to class. Note the many different geometric forms used by various groups. Begin the project with sketches, but these will be only a start. The real form will develop from experimentation.

28

 LESSON 2

Making a Mask with Formal Balance

Think about masks you have seen or worn. Like the one in Figure 2–4, these masks probably exhibited formal balance. It is the nature of masks to do so. This is because the faces they are meant to cover also have formal balance.

The mask shown in Figure 2–4 was created by the Yaware people of Africa. It was carved from wood that was polished to a high sheen. Notice the assortment of shapes and forms the artist has used for the facial features. Some of these are geometric. Others are free-form. Can you find examples of each type in the work?

WHAT YOU WILL LEARN

You will design a mask using formal balance. The mask will be created using papier-mâché (**pay**-puhr muh-**shay**). This is a sculpting technique using newspaper and liquid paste. You will add interest to your work by using geometric shapes for facial features and decorations. (Note: For additional information on working with papier-mâché, see Technique Tip **20** on page **287**.)

WHAT YOU WILL NEED

- Pencil and sketch paper
- Newspaper
- Scissors
- Masking tape
- Dish for paste
- Cellulose wallpaper paste
- Water
- Tempera or school acrylic paint and brushes
- Polymer gloss medium (optional)
- Found objects, such as feathers and ribbon

Figure 2–4 How many geometric shapes do you find in this Yaware mask? How many free-form shapes do you see?

Africa. Yaware People. *Face Mask.* Early twentieth century. Wood. 50.8 × 22.8 cm (20 × 9"). Private collection.

28   Chapter 2   *The Principles of Art*

TECHNIQUE TIP

Working with Papier Mâché   Have students dip strips of newspaper into the cup of paste one at a time, and apply them to the mask. Encourage smoothing each piece as it is laid on. You will need at least three layers around the frame and on all details of the face. Masks can be allowed to dry and worked on a second day. When all the papier mâché is finished, allow the masks to dry for a few days before painting them.

Cellulose wallpaper paste will not sour, as wheat paste does. Do not empty cups back into the jars, however.

WHAT YOU WILL DO

1. Do several pencil sketches of mask designs. Let your imagination guide you. Each design should have formal balance. The facial features and any other details are to be geometric shapes. Choose your best sketch.
2. Cover your desk with layers of newspaper.
3. Fold two sheets of full-size newspaper lengthwise down to two inches. Fit it around your face and attach the ends with masking tape. Lay the oval shape on your desk. This will be the frame of your mask.
4. Crumple up sheets of newspaper and fill the center of your frame with them. Then place a final sheet of newspaper over the filled-in frame, gluing its edges to the frame.
5. Begin cutting small pieces of newspaper. Fold them to make the facial feature shapes on your best sketch. Attach them to the mask with tape to make raised three-dimensional details. Add more forms around the frame if you choose.
6. Tear strips of newspaper (with the grain) about 2 inches wide and 6 inches long. Dip one strip at a time into the bowl of paste. Run it lightly between your fingers to remove the extra paste. Lay each strip on the mask. Work from the frame into the center. Overlap the strips to cover all parts of your mask. Smooth out the edges of the strips where they overlap.
7. When your mask is finished, allow it to dry thoroughly. This will take several days.

EXAMINING YOUR WORK

- **Describe** Point to the different facial features of your mask. Identify the colors you used in your mask. What shapes did you use?
- **Analyze** How have you created balance in your mask design?

8. When your mask is dry, transfer the geometric face features and other details from your sketch to your mask. Paint the mask. The painted design, like the mask itself, should show formal balance. If you want your mask to have a high luster, apply the polymer gloss. Allow the mask to dry again, then add feathers, ribbons, or other materials as you choose.

Figure 2–5 **Student work. Mask with formal balance.**

STUDIO OPTION

- Use a plastic gallon milk bottle to make a mask. The bottle's handle can be the nose. Add other features using cut paper, yarn, and any other materials you can find.

Lesson 2 *Making a Mask with Formal Balance* **29**

CURRICULUM CONNECTIONS

Social Studies Have students read the book *Masks Tell Stories* by Carol Gelber (Brookfield, Conn.: Millbrook, 1993), *Joshua's Masai Mask* by Dakari Hru (New York: Lee and Low, 1993), or another book of your choice about how masks are used and how they can seem to transform the wearer. Have students design a mask based on the material they have read. You may also want to ask students to find out more about how masks are used in a particular culture and report back to the class.

Variety, Harmony, Emphasis, and Proportion

(pages 30–31)

Variety, Harmony, Emphasis, and Proportion

"Variety is the spice of life." Are you familiar with this saying? It means that a break from humdrum routines makes life more interesting.

This wise saying applies not only to life but also to art. In this lesson, you will learn how variety and three other principles—harmony, emphasis, and proportion—add interest to artworks.

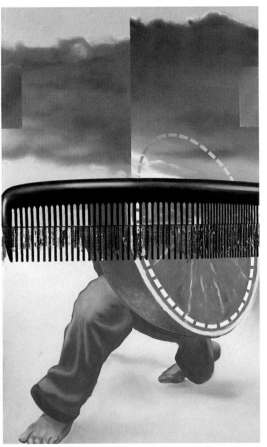

Figure 2–6 Notice the work's title. What statement might the artist be making about morning routines? What clues are provided by the running feet of the figure in pajamas, the orange, and the comb?

 James Rosenquist. *Early in the Morning*. 1963. Oil on canvas. 241.3 × 142.2 cm (95 × 56"). Virginia Museum of Fine Arts, Richmond, Virginia. Gift of Sydney and Frances Lewis.

THE PRINCIPLE OF VARIETY

Think about your favorite TV show. Suppose you were forced to watch this show for hours. In time, you would become bored. You might even grow to dislike the program.

Like TV viewing habits, art needs variety. In art, **variety** is *combining one or more elements of art to create interest.* A splash of brilliant color will add zest to a painting that has mostly dull tones. A free-form shape adds pep to a work done with mostly geometric shapes. Study the unusual painting in Figure 2–6. How many different textures can you find? What else has the artist done to add variety?

THE PRINCIPLE OF HARMONY

Just as you can have too little of a good thing, you can also have too much. In art, an excess of variety can be offset by using the principle of harmony. **Harmony** means *combining the elements of art to accent their similarities.* Look again at the painting in Figure 2–6. This time, study its **picture plane.** This is *the flat surface of a painting or drawing.* Find the horizontal line that divides the upper and lower halves of the picture plane. It runs through the center of the comb. Do you recall from Chapter 1, Lesson 2, the effect horizontal lines have on the viewer? What other lines has the artist used to bring harmony and order to this active painting?

30   Chapter 2   *The Principles of Art*

THE PRINCIPLE OF EMPHASIS

To attract a viewer's attention to an important part of a work, artists use emphasis. **Emphasis** is *making an element or an object in a work stand out.* One way artists create emphasis is through contrast. Examine the sculpture in Figure 2–7. Notice how the artist uses contrasting bold colors to draw the viewer's eye into and around the dancing figures. What object or element is emphasized in the work in Figure 2–6?

THE PRINCIPLE OF PROPORTION

As an art principle, **proportion** is *how parts of a work relate to each other and to the whole.* One might say that the proportion or amount of red in a painting is greater than the proportion or amount of the other colors. A large shape in a picture filled with smaller shapes would stand out because of the different proportions in size. Look once more at the sculpture in Figure 2–7. Notice how the larger-than-life size of the figures adds to their importance and interest.

STUDIO ACTIVITY

Painting a Still Life with Emphasis

Arrange several everyday objects on a table or other flat surface. Plan a painting in which you give emphasis to one of the objects. You will do this by using one or more of the elements of art. Use acrylic paints to complete your picture. Share your still life with classmates, challenging them to identify the way or ways you achieved emphasis.

PORTFOLIO

Sign, date, and title your artwork. Put it in your portfolio.

✔ Check Your Understanding

1. Name two ways artists can achieve *variety* in their work.
2. How do artists achieve *harmony*?
3. Explain the principle of *proportion*.

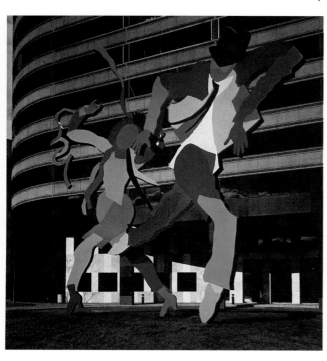

Figure 2–7 Why do you suppose the artist chose to make the dancing partners so large? Why do you think she chose the colors she did?

Miriam Schapiro. *Anna and David.* 1987. Painted stainless steel and aluminum. 10.6 × 9.4 × .23 m (35′ × 31′ × 9″). Steinbaum-Krauss Gallery, New York, New York.

Lesson 3 *Variety, Harmony, Emphasis, and Proportion* **31**

Answers to ✔ CHECK YOUR UNDERSTANDING

1. Artists can achieve variety by varying colors and textures (or any of the elements).
2. Harmony means blending elements of art in a pleasing way. Artists achieve this by using any and all of the elements—color, line, shape, texture, space, and form.
3. Proportion means the size relationships of one part to the whole, and of one part to another.

STUDIO ACTIVITY

Painting a Still Life with Emphasis

Help students find objects that have interest and meaning to them. Perhaps the collection could have a theme (sports equipment, percussion instruments, CD holders), or be whimsical in nature.

■ Vocabulary

These four terms have many applications. Ask students to look each of them up in Roget's *Thesaurus* and discuss the synonyms they find. Discuss these terms as they apply to relations between friends and families.

● ● ● ● ● ● ● ● ●
ASSESS

■ Self-Assessment

Have students complete the Check Your Understanding questions on this page. Answers are provided below.

■ Reteaching

Ask students to work in pairs to identify ways in which the artist achieved variety, harmony, emphasis, and proportion in one of the two artworks in this lesson.

■ Enrichment

Look at architecture for its application of the principles learned in this lesson. Help students find variety and harmony in materials, shapes, and details. A building's façade may be its point of emphasis. Proportion can relate to its placement on a site as well as the relation of its parts. Have students critique nearby buildings.

● ● ● ● ● ● ● ● ●
CLOSE

Ask students to choose one of the works in this lesson and describe how it uses the principles learned in lessons 1 and 3.

31

Movement and Rhythm

Have you ever heard a book described as a "page turner"? This label is given to books with exciting stories. The writer's skill takes you beyond the mere words on the page. It permits you to see vivid, fast-paced action as though it were happening before your eyes.

The same may be said for some skillfully done works of art. Through the careful use of elements such as line, shape, and color, the artist captures movement.

In this lesson, you will learn about movement as a principle of art. You will also learn about a companion principle, rhythm.

THE PRINCIPLE OF MOVEMENT

When you meet a person for the first time, what feature do you notice first? Experts tell us that we look at a person's eyes. Then our gaze moves outward to take in the shape of the person's face. All of this happens in less than a second!

Figure 2–8 Imagine that this work is a "freeze frame" from a motion picture. What do you think will happen in the next instant?

Katsushika Hokusai. *Fishing Boats at Choshi in Shoshu.* c. 1833. Woodblock print. 18.9 × 25.8 cm (7½ × 10½"). The Art Institute of Chicago, Chicago, Illinois. The Kate Buckingham Fund, 1983.583

32   Chapter 2   *The Principles of Art*

• • • • • • • • • • •
FOCUS

☑ OBJECTIVES
After completing this lesson, students will be able to:
• Define *movement* and *rhythm* in art.
• Explain how artists use rhythm and movement in their work.

☑ SUPPLIES
• White drawing paper
• Pencils, rulers, markers, crayons, colored pencils

Resource
■ 2-4 Pop and Op, TRB page 25 (art history)

• • • • • • • • • • •
TEACH

Motivator
Ask a student to think of a rhythmic sequence and tap it on his or her desk. The others will identify it as **123**, **123** or **1234**, **1234**, and so on. Listen to music and find the rhythmic pattern.

Vocabulary
Distinguish between *rhythm* meaning repetition and *movement* meaning action or the path of the eye through a work. Ask students to brainstorm simple examples of each.

MEETING SPECIAL NEEDS

Rhythm in Music   Students with hearing impairment may be helped by listening to musical selections using an earpiece or headphones, so that the volume can be turned as loud as personally needed by the student. A wooden floor that vibrates to the beat of the music can help students with hearing impairments feel the rhythm. Painting to music is a rewarding activity for students with disabilities, because the requirement for visually accurate representation is minimal or non-existent.

Figure 2–9 This painting was created by a member of a group of artists who called their work "Op art." *Op* is short for a word meaning "eye." Why do you suppose they called their work by this name?

Bridget Riley. *Current.* 1964. Synthetic polymer paint on composition board. 148.1 × 149.3 cm (58¾ × 58⅞"). The Museum of Modern Art, New York, New York. Philip Johnson Fund.

Although you may not be aware of it, the same thing happens when you look at a work of art. Your eyes focus on one part. Then they move to the next. This visual journey takes place thanks to **movement.** This is *the principle of art that leads the viewer to sense action in a work, or it can be the path the viewer's eye follows through the work.*

Artists create movement through a blending of elements. Look at the artwork in Figure 2–8. Notice how the fishing boats seem to toss and rock. See how the giant waves churn and foam as they swell and curl high above the boats. What elements of art are used to create this sense of motion?

Artworks do not need recognizable subjects to communicate a sense of motion. Study the painting in Figure 2–9. Notice how the curves in this work seem to dance and shimmer. It is as though the painting were alive!

THE PRINCIPLE OF RHYTHM

Do you have a favorite recording artist? If you do, chances are you are a fan of the

person's or group's rhythm. Rhythm is the beat we feel and hear when we listen to music.

In art, **rhythm** is *the repetition of an element of art to make a work seem active.* Look again at the painting in Figure 2–9. The artist achieves rhythm by carefully spacing the curves at equal distances from one another. What kind of rhythm do you detect in Figure 2–8?

 Check Your Understanding

1. What is movement in art?
2. Define *rhythm* in art.
3. How do artists create movement and rhythm?

● ● ● ● ● ● ● ● ● ● ● ● ● ● ●
F O C U S

☑ OBJECTIVES

After completing this lesson, students will be able to:

• Design a motif to be used in a tessellation.

☑ SUPPLIES

• Scissors, transparent tape, rulers

• 3-inch squares of oak tag (use old file folders) cut on a paper cutter

• Pencils, colored markers

• White or colored drawing paper

Resources

◼ 2-5 Read This Message, TRB page 26 (studio)

◼ 2-6 The Very Principle!, TRB page 28 (art criticism)

◼ 2-7 Artist Profile, M.C. Escher, TRB page 29.

● ● ● ● ● ● ● ● ● ● ● ● ● ● ●
T E A C H

◼ Motivator

Hand out the oak-tag squares. Have students cut a shape from one side, cutting no farther than half way into the square. Position the piece by sliding it to the opposite side and taping it in the corresponding position. Do this same procedure on the remaining two sides of the square, resulting in a puzzle-like shape. Allow students to cut more than one until they are satisfied.

34

Making a Tessellation

A term often tied to rhythm in art is *pattern*. Patterns, as you know, are made up of repeating shapes or forms. In some patterns, the same shape or form repeats over and over. In others, it varies.

The interesting artwork shown in Figure 2–10 contains an example of a type of pattern called *tessellation*. This is a pattern of shapes that fit together in a way that leaves no space in between. The term comes from the Latin word *tessella*, meaning "tile." Perhaps you have seen floors surfaced with tiles. Look closely at Figure 2–10. On the right side of the work, white birds fly over a small town surrounded by farmlands and a river. On the left side, black birds fly over a mirror image of the same scene. Together, the two flocks form a tessellation. The white birds serve as background for the black birds, and the black birds become a background for the white birds.

WHAT YOU WILL LEARN

You will design a *motif* (moh-**teef**), or basic shape, to be used in a tessellation. You will repeat the motif to fill an entire page. Using your imagination, you will add details to your motif. These details will change the shape into a fantasy creature. You will complete your design by using colored markers.

WHAT YOU WILL NEED

• Scissors
• Squares of 3-inch (7.7-cm) oak tag
• Transparent tape
• Ruler
• Sketch paper
• Pencil
• Drawing or construction paper, 12 x 18 inches (30 x 46 cm)
• Colored markers

WHAT YOU WILL DO

1. Cut a shape from one side of an oak tag square. Carefully tape the shape to the opposite side of the square in the same position (see Figure 2–11).

2. Cut a shape from a third side. Tape it to its opposite side. You will have a shape that looks something like a jigsaw puzzle piece. This is called a template. Turn the shape you have created. Examine it from different sides and angles. Picture fantasy creatures that might be formed by adding details. Draw around the template on sketch paper, and record some of your

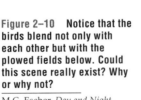

Figure 2–10 Notice that the birds blend not only with each other but with the plowed fields below. Could this scene really exist? Why or why not?

M.C. Escher. *Day and Night.* 1938. Woodcut in black and gray printed from two blocks. 39.1 × 67.7 cm (15⅜ × 26⅜"). © 1996 Cordon Art, Baarn, Holland. All rights reserved.

TECHNOLOGY OPTIONS

National Gallery of Art Videodisc Use the following images to show how artists create movement and rhythm in their works.

Eugène Delacroix
Arabs Skirmishing in the Mountains

Search Frame 1130

Henri Matisse
Large Composition with Masks

Search Frame 2211

Auguste Renoir
Girl with a Hoop

Search Frame 1320

Use Glencoe's *National Gallery of Art Correlation Bar Code Guide* to locate more artworks.

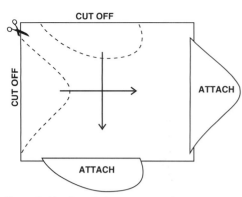

Figure 2–11 **Cut off shape and attach to opposite side.**

- **Describe** Explain how you made your motif.
- **Analyze** Tell what details you added to make a fantasy creature.

ideas in pencil. You may have to experiment with several squares until you have a shape you like.

3. Place your template so that it lines up with the upper left-hand corner of the paper. Using a pencil, carefully draw around all edges. Move the shape to the right. The cutout on the left side of the cardboard should line up with the bulge on the right of the first shape drawn. Draw around it again until you have completed one row.

4. Move the template underneath the first shape you made. (See Figure 2–12). Draw around the edges with the pencil. Continue in this fashion until you have completed a second row. Keep making rows until you have covered the entire paper.

5. Refer to the sketches you made. Choose details for your fantasy creature. Transfer these features to each of the motifs with colored markers.

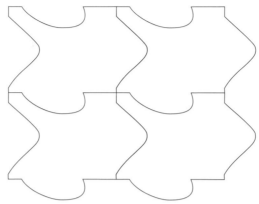

Figure 2–12 **A design using tessellation.**

Figure 2–13 **Student work. A tessellation.**

COMPUTER OPTION

Try This!

■ Select the Rectangle or Hexagon shape tool and no-fill color. Draw an open square, rectangle, or hexagon. Choose the Pencil tool and draw a varied line from the top corner of one side, ending at the bottom corner of the same side. Use the Lasso selection tool to select the side. Make a copy and paste the copy on the opposite side of the shape. This makes a slide translation. Erase the unneeded lines with the Eraser tool. Beginning on a third side, make a second slide translation using the same steps. Title and save. Add details, texture, and color to describe the real or imaginary object. Retitle and save. Choose the Lasso selection tool to select, copy, paste, and arrange multiple copies next to each other like pieces of a puzzle. Retitle, save, and print.

Lesson 5 *Making a Tessellation*   **35**

— *more about* • • • —

Tessellations Maurits Cornelis Escher, known as M.C. Escher, (1898–1972) was born in Leewarden, Holland. He studied at the School of Architecture and Ornamental Design in Haarlem, where he learned graphic techniques. Years spent in Italy and many study-travel tours exposed him to the rich patterns and designs of history. However, his own inventions went far beyond the uniform designs he saw. His unique tessellations are now printed on scarves, ties, and many other items.

Art in Everyday Life

Ask students to find more examples of tile patterns in school, at the mall, at home. Invite them to research mosques, temples, and churches to find other exquisite patterns.

■ **Art History**

Discuss mathematics in recent design history. Have students research Hard Edge and Minimal artists, whose work is often pure geometry; or Cubism, based on basic geometric shapes.

• • • • • • • •
ASSESS

■ **Evaluation**

Have students use Examining Your Work to evaluate their tessellations.

■ **Reteaching**

Review the concept of tessellations and how repetitive patterns can be used to make art.

■ **Enrichment**

Have students find books about M.C. Escher and enjoy his tessellations and his remarkable and imaginative drawings.

Also, there are books on making tessellations that demonstrate tessellating triangles, hexagons, and other shapes. Encourage students to pursue this form of design further, with or without the help of a computer.

• • • • • • • •
CLOSE

Display the tessellations. Talk about the importance of accurate rendering in such artwork.

• • • • • • • • • • • • • •
FOCUS

☑️ **OBJECTIVES**

After completing this lesson, students will be able to:

• Define unity and all the principles of art.

• Look for these principles in a work of art.

☑️ **SUPPLIES**

• 30 to 40 foot length of thick cord

Resource

■ 2-8 A Unity "Score Card", TRB page 30 (reproducible master)

• • • • • • • • • • • • • •
TEACH

■ **Motivator**

As a way of demonstrating unity, ask students to stand in a group and take hold of the cord. First ask them to let the cord wind around and through the group in a random way. Feel the chaos. Then "orchestrate" the group to create shapes and movement with the cord and evaluate the unity in their designs.

Spend time on the Turner painting. Go back to other works in this chapter and discuss unity in them. Use this as an opportunity to review the elements and principles of art. Look for each of them in the works of art.

■ **Vocabulary**

Ask students to find related forms of the word *unity* and write their definitions. Lead students to see the common root word, meaning "one."

 LESSON 6

Unity in Art

You have probably witnessed the pluses of teamwork. When members of the school basketball team play as one, they usually win. When members of the marching band are "in sync," they put on a great performance.

This idea of acting as one is important in art, too. When you look at a successful work of art, you do not see parts. You see a well-designed whole that has **unity.** This is *the arrangement of elements and principles of art to create a feeling of completeness or wholeness.*

UNITY

You have probably had toys or other possessions that were broken. Sometimes, a broken object can be glued back together so that the cracks are invisible. In an artwork with unity, the "cracks" are likewise invisible. You cannot point to unity as you can an element or principle. You can sense it, however. You can also sense its absence.

Examine the painting in Figure 2–14. This powerful work shows a fierce storm. Much of the picture is given over to a sweeping

Figure 2–14 How would you describe the feeling conveyed by this painting? What principles of art have been used to create this feeling?

Joseph M. W. Turner. *Valley of Aosta: Snowstorm, Avalanche, and Thunderstorm.* 1836–37. Oil on canvas. 92.2 × 123 cm (36⅓ × 48"). Art Institute of Chicago, Chicago, Illinois. Frederick T. Haskell Collection, 1947.513

36   Chapter 2   *The Principles of Art*

RESOURCES BEYOND THE CLASSROOM

Media Supply Houses   Students rarely need to obtain art supplies beyond the minimum—tempera paints, inexpensive brushes. Yet, by introducing them to media supply houses, you can help them feel more confident in understanding and using various media, in analyzing cost, and understanding the care of materials and supplies. Visits to such sources can also stimulate the imagination.

Some examples are crafts and hobby shops and bead shops. Fabric stores are equally interesting, as are architectural supply stores, print shops, school specialty supply houses, photo shops, and even hardware stores and sheet metal suppliers.

curve of wind and snow. Can you find the people in this picture? Their tiny forms, along with that of a small animal, appear huddled in the lower right corner. The artist achieves unity in this work in the following ways. He:

- uses *proportion* to contrast the vast fury of the storm with the small people.
- captures vivid *movement* through the careful use of line and color.
- adds excitement and suspense through informal *balance*.
- draws the viewer's eye from one part of the work to another through *variety* in shape, form, and color.

Look back at the painting that opened this chapter on page **24**. What arrangement of principles and elements did the artist use to achieve unity?

Recognizing Unity

One way of recognizing unity in an artwork is by using a checklist like the one in Figure 2–15. For each element used, you would make a check mark in the box under the principle or principles the artist has used to organize each element.

STUDIO ACTIVITY

Identifying Unity

Copy the checklist in Figure 2–15 onto a blank sheet of paper. Look back at Figure 2–8 on page **32**. Go through the checklist one element at a time. For each element found, identify the principle or principles used. Remember that not all artworks use all elements and principles. When you have finished, share and compare your checklist with those of classmates.

 P O R T F O L I O

Put the list in your portfolio. Make another copy of the checklist to keep in your portfolio. Use it to analyze your own artworks.

✔ Check Your Understanding

1. Define *unity*.
2. Explain how an understanding of unity is important to an understanding of art.

DESIGN CHART	PRINCIPLES OF ART					
	Balance	Variety	Harmony	Emphasis	Proportion	Movement/Rhythm
ELEMENTS OF ART Line						
Color						
Shape						
Form						
Space						
Texture						

UNITY

Figure 2–15 **Unity checklist.**

Joseph Mallord William Turner (1775–1851) began painting in the Academic tradition of English landscapes, but his fascination with nature—he once had himself tied to the mast of a sailing ship during a storm on the English Channel so that he could experience the violence of the winds and rain—brought him to break from defined shapes and paint in pure color. Many of his paintings are almost abstractions. Turner opened the way to the Impressionists of the later nineteenth century. Invite students to find out more about Turner and his influence on his contemporaries.

• • • • • • • • • • • • • •
A S S E S S

■ **Self-Assessment**

Have students complete the Check Your Understanding questions on this page. Answers are provided below.

■ **Reteaching**

Ask students to identify the principles of art and point to some examples of each from artwork in Chapter 1 or 2.

■ **Enrichment**

This is a good time for a "field trip" to a museum or art exhibit. If a real field trip is not possible, set up a display with the transparencies and the prints accompanying this text. Ask individuals to be a museum docent and take the class through part of the print display. Ask the docents to comment on the work and ask other students about it.

• • • • • • • • • • • • • •
C L O S E

Review the concept of unity as it applies to life situations and to artworks.

Answers to ✔ CHECK YOUR UNDERSTANDING

1. Unity is the arrangement of elements and principles of art to create a feeling of completeness or wholeness.

2. In an artwork with unity, you do not see parts. You see a well-defined whole. Understanding the elements of art and the principles of art helps to evaluate how and whether the artist has achieved a unified whole.

Everyday Uses of Math

☑ OBJECTIVES

After completing this feature, students will be able to:

- Identify some everyday uses of math.
- Explain how math skills are used in art.

Teaching the Connection

- Have students read the feature on this page.
- Ask volunteers to share what they know about math. Which math skills do you commonly use outside of school? *(Answers will vary.)* What are some specific branches of mathematics? *(Examples include algebra, geometry, trigonometry, calculus.)* For what careers would math skills be useful? *(Answers will vary but could include almost any career.)*
- Tell students that Demuth's *The Figure 5 in Gold* was inspired by a poem called *The Great Figure* by William Carlos Williams. The painting is an abstract representation of the poem. It shows a dark, rainy night in which the No. 5 fire truck clangs through city streets.

Answers to the Connection

- ✔ Balance—centering the figure 5; harmony—repeating the figure; emphasis—drawing attention to the figure; proportion—making the figure larger than the other parts of the work; rhythm—forming a pattern with the figures.
- ✔ Measurement and division—to determine the sizes of the figures.
- ✔ Possible answers include counting money, calculating a restaurant tip, and balancing a checkbook.

Are you a "math person?" Maybe you consider yourself a "word person" or a "computer person" instead. Do you sometimes wonder why you need to memorize multiplication tables or learn division? Whether you enjoy math or not, you will use math principles often in life—probably more often than you think.

If you have ever figured out the sales tax when you purchased a CD or school supplies, you used math. You need math skills to divide a square of chocolate cake into four equal pieces. Doubling or halving a muffin recipe is another everyday use of math.

Although you may not realize it, art also requires the use of math skills. Some of the principles of art, including balance and proportion, are based on math skills. You also use math to perform certain tasks in art. To make a grid for enlarging, for example, you need to measure, count, and divide. (See Technique Tip **5** on page **281**.)

In Charles Demuth's *The Figure 5 in Gold*, the most obvious reference to math is simply the number five. However, the artist also needed math skills to create the numeral in diminishing sizes.

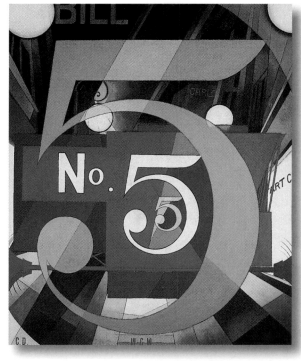

Charles Demuth. *The Figure 5 in Gold.* Oil on composition board. 91.4 × 75.6 cm (36 × 29¾"). The Metropolitan Museum of Art, New York, New York. Alfred Stieglitz Collection, 1949.

MAKING THE CONNECTION

- ✔ Which principles of art did Charles Demuth use in *The Figure 5 in Gold*? Explain your answer.
- ✔ What math skills do you think Demuth needed to create this work? Explain your answer.
- ✔ Besides those mentioned, what are some other everyday uses of math?

INTERNET ACTIVITY

Visit Glencoe's Fine Arts Web Site for students at:

http://www.glencoe.com/sec/art/students

38 *Chapter 2 Connections*

INTERNET ACTIVITY

Glencoe Student Galleria This very special on-line gallery showcases the work of student artists who have produced exemplary models of art. Introduce your students to this site and let them examine the art of other students. You might ask them to examine these works using the steps of art criticism from the student text.

Don't forget to check the *Galleria Archives* for a glimpse of past featured art. Find out how you can submit artworks made by your students in the *Teacher Resources* area of Glencoe's Fine Arts Site. Find us at **http://www.glencoe.com/sec/art**

REVIEW

◆ BUILDING VOCABULARY

Number a sheet of paper from 1 to 10. After each number, write the term from the box that matches each description below.

balance	principles of art
emphasis	proportion
harmony	rhythm
movement	unity
picture plane	variety

1. How parts of a work relate to each other and to the whole.
2. Combining one or more elements of art to create interest.
3. The arrangement of elements and principles of art to create a feeling of completeness or wholeness.
4. The principle of art that leads the viewer to sense action in a work, or it can be the path the viewer's eye follows through the work.
5. Making an element or an object in a work stand out.
6. A principle of art concerned with arranging the elements so that no one part of the work overpowers, or seems heavier than, any other part.
7. Guidelines that govern the way artists organize the elements of art.
8. The repetition of an element of art to make a work seem active.
9. The flat surface of a painting or drawing.
10. Combining the elements of art to accent their similarities.

◆ REVIEWING ART FACTS

Number a sheet of paper from 11 to 15. Answer each question in a complete sentence.

11. What kind of balance does a hubcap have?
12. What happens when there is too much harmony in a work of art? What can be done to correct this problem?
13. What are some ways of achieving proportion in an artwork?
14. What principle might be used to organize a work of art that contains a motif?
15. What is a tessellation?

THINKING ABOUT ART

On a sheet of paper, answer each question in a sentence or two.

1. **Extend.** Suppose you were creating a painting of a crowd scene and wanted one figure to stand out. What art principles might you use to achieve this goal? Explain your answers.
2. **Compare and contrast.** How are the principles of movement and rhythm similar? In what ways are they different?

MAKING ART CONNECTIONS

1. **Language Arts.** Emphasis occurs in literature as well as art. In stories, for example, words are *italicized* to show they receive stress or emphasis. In plays, emphasis is achieved through stage directions—commands to the actor that appear after a part name. With a group of classmates, write a short story or play in which words or lines are emphasized. Read or perform your creation in front of the class.
2. **Community Connection.** Locate examples of formal and radial balance in your community. Search both for examples that are made by people and those arising in nature. Devote a page of your journal to your research. Share and compare your findings with classmates.

Chapter 2 Review **39**

■ Building Vocabulary

1. proportion
2. variety
3. unity
4. movement
5. emphasis
6. balance
7. principles of art
8. rhythm
9. picture plane
10. harmony

■ Reviewing Art Facts

11. It would have radial balance.
12. The work can become boring or monotonous. This problem can be remedied by using variety, emphasis, or proportion.
13. It can be achieved by varying the size of objects or the amounts of color used in different objects.
14. The principle would be rhythm.
15. It is a pattern of shapes that fit together in a way that leaves no space in between.

THINKING ABOUT ART

1. Two possibilities are emphasis and proportion. Emphasis: You could make the figure stand out by making his or her clothes a different color from those of other crowd members. Proportion: You could have the person appear taller than other crowd members or draw the scene in such a way that the person is in the foreground.

2. Both help convey a sense of action in an artwork. Movement achieves this effect usually through line. Rhythm, on the other hand, achieves a sense of action through the repetition of an object or element.

Art Media and Techniques

(pages 40–61)

Resources

- 3-11 Chapter Test, TRB page 50
- Transparency CC-3, *Tlinglit Effigy Pipe Bowl*
- Transparency 3, *Anemones in a Blue Vase* by Emil Nolde
- Fine Art Print 5, *Mother with Child* by Elizabeth Catlett
- Fine Art Print 6, *Personal Appearance* by Miriam Schapiro
- Artist Profile: Napachie Pootoogook, TRB page 35

A R T
S O U
R C E
ARTSOURCE

Music
While studying this chapter, use Performing Arts Handbook page 315 to show how the Ballet Folklorico uses media in their dance.

NATIONAL STANDARDS

This chapter addresses the following National Standards for the Visual Arts:

1. (a, b)   **4.** (a, c)
2. (a, b, c)   **6.** (b)
3. (a, b)

40

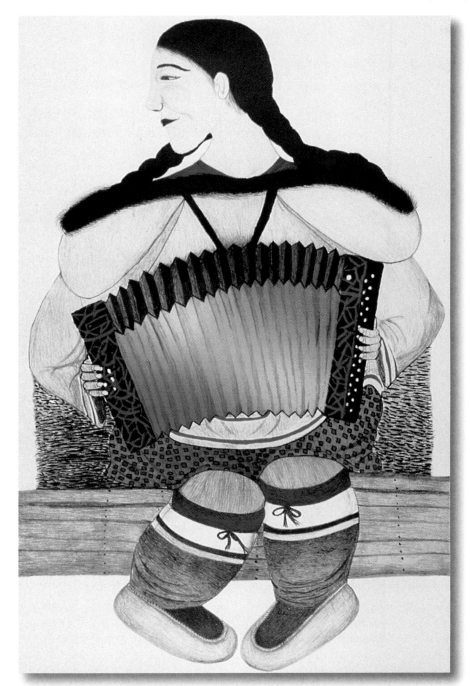

Figure 3–1   This is a lithograph, an artwork made by a printing method. Notice the colors and textures.

Napachie Pootoogook. *My New Accordion.* 1989. Lithograph on wove, rag paper. 112.4 × 79.9 cm (44¼ × 31⅜″). Dorset Fine Arts, Toronto, Ontario, Canada.

FEATURED ARTISTS

Romare Bearden	Gustav Klimt	Napachie Pootoogook
Mary Cassatt	Jeanette Leroy	John Wilson
Honoré Daumier	Shiko Munakata	
Francisco Goya	Emil Nolde	
Rhoda Grossman	Erol Otis	

Art Media and Techniques

Every musical instrument has its own voice, or characteristic. You can identify a guitar by its twang, a tuba by its deep grumble.

Like musical instruments, art materials have different characteristics. Examine the artwork in Figure 3–1. Can you tell which technique was used to create the work?

In this chapter, you will learn about the tools and materials artists use. You will learn to appreciate the special characteristics of each.

PORTFOLIO IDEAS

Each entry in your portfolio should be marked clearly for identification. Make sure each piece includes:

- Your name and the date of the artwork
- The assignment
- Your comments or self-reflection
- Any additional information requested by your teacher

OBJECTIVES

After completing this chapter, you will be able to:

- Define the term *medium of art.*
- Identify the different kinds of media used in drawing, painting, printmaking, and sculpture.
- Experiment with various art media.
- Use mixed media to create an original work of art.

WORDS YOU WILL LEARN

art medium
binder
gesture drawing
intaglio
perception
pigment
portrait
printmaking
sculpture
solvent

■ Chapter Overview

In this chapter, students will begin to explore the characteristics of various art media—the tools of the artist. They will learn about the media used in drawing, painting, printmaking, and sculpture and have an opportunity to experiment with a variety of art media to create their own artwork.

■ Chapter Motivator

Ask students to discuss the tools people need for their particular jobs. Have students collaborate on a word association web: carpenter—hammer; electrician—switches; piano tuner—tuning fork; and so on. Lead students to think about and discuss what they already know about the tools of the artist. Explain to students that with an abundance of new and traditional tools and technology, artists can expand their vision and their ability to create works of art.

■ Examining the Artwork

Explain to students that Napachie Pootoogook is an Inuit artist. Here she has shown a woman playing an accordian. Her medium was lithography, a printmaking technique in which the image is drawn on limestone, zinc, or aluminum with a special grease crayon. When the ink is applied, the greasy area alone holds the ink. Then the image is transferred to paper. How many colors can students see? What principle is predominant? *(balance)*

National Museum of Women in the Arts

You may wish to use the National Museum of Women in the Arts videodisc and/or CD-ROM. The videodisc features a bar code guide, and the interactive CD-ROM provides stimulating activities.

DEVELOPING A PORTFOLIO

Written Summaries Art assessment involves more than providing a single correct answer. It is an evaluation technique that challenges students to think critically. Through this process, students increase their perceptual and analytical skills. Students, however, need to know how to support their opinions, based on reasonable rationales.

When assessing student responses, focus on the quality of the content rather than just the written expression. You may want to develop a rubric, a guide for scoring an assignment. For more information on developing a rubric, refer to the booklet, *Portfolio and Assessment Techniques,* that accompanies the *Introducing Art* program.

Drawing

☑ OBJECTIVES

After completing this lesson, students will be able to:

• Define *perception.*
• Recognize blending and cross-hatching as methods of achieving depth in drawing.
• Draw with their eyes on the object.

☑ SUPPLIES

• Newsprint or drawing paper
• Pencils or crayons
• Objects to draw

Resource

⌕ ■ 3-1 Napachie Pootoogook, page 35 (artist profile)

■ Motivator

Discuss the importance of drawing for every person. Perceptual drawing can be done by everyone. Emphasize looking at the object while drawing. This is a means of getting "right brain" control of the drawing. The hand will follow the path of the eye. Reassure students that this takes much practice.

■ Vocabulary

Encourage students to brainstorm other words they may know that have an irregular plural form like medium, media *(stadium, stadia; datum, data; and so on).* Have students research the word history of *medium.*

To most people, a pencil is a writing tool. To artists, it is a key. As an art medium, this familiar object opens the door to endless creative possibilities. An **art medium** is *a material used to create a work of art.* When we speak of more than one medium, we use the word *media.* Artists rely on a wide variety of media in their work, such as pencils, paints, charcoal, and pastels.

In this lesson, you will learn about media used in drawing. In later lessons, you will learn about media used to create other kinds of art.

Figure 3–2 **What drawing medium was used for this sketch? How would you describe the characteristics of this art tool?**

Gustav Klimt. *Sleeping Boy.* 1905–07. Graphite pencil on cream wove paper. 55 × 35 cm (21¾ × 13¾") The Detroit Institute of Arts, Detroit, Michigan. Founders Society Purchase, John S. Newberry Fund.

42 Chapter 3 *Art Media and Techniques*

WHY ARTISTS DRAW

In baseball, a pitcher takes warm-up throws before facing a batter. Musicians warm up before a performance. Artists follow a similar approach by drawing. Drawing "limbers" up the artist's eye. It helps develop visual **perception** (pur-**sep**-shun). This is *an awareness of the elements of an environment by means of the senses.* Perception is more than looking at an object. It is really "seeing" the object. It is studying how shapes, forms, lines, and colors blend to form the whole.

Some drawings are used to plan paintings or other large projects. Figure 3–2 shows this type of drawing, or "study." Other drawings are done as finished works of art. Such a drawing appears in Figure 3–3.

DRAWING MEDIA

Do you recall scribbling with a crayon when you were small? You didn't realize it at the time, but you were using a drawing medium. Crayons, colored markers, pencils, pens, and chalk are all drawing media.

Each drawing medium has its own characteristics. Chalk and crayon, for example, produce rough lines. Pens, by contrast, make smooth lines. Figure 3–4 shows lines made with three different drawing media. Notice the line quality of each.

SHADING TECHNIQUES

Look once more at the drawing in Figure 3–3. The scarf in this picture looks so real you can almost feel the texture in the fabric. The artist accomplishes this through shading. *Shading* is the use of light and shadow to give a feeling of depth and texture. There are four main shading techniques:

• **Hatching.** This is drawing thin lines all running in the same direction.
• **Crosshatching.** This is drawing crisscrossing lines.

TECHNIQUE TIP ▼

Build Confidence Let this lesson be the beginning of daily drawing, just a few minutes at a time, to strengthen students' skill and confidence. Begin by having students take off one shoe, inspect it carefully, and feel its edges and patterns with their fingers. Then have them place their shoe near the paper and begin to draw. Tell them to let their eye "crawl" along each edge as their hand draws that edge. Encourage flowing lines rather than short broken ones. Postpone blending and crosshatching until students have done many drawings.

Figure 3–3 Notice the attention to detail in this pencil drawing. What art principles have been used to organize the work?

Jeanette Leroy. *Scarf on a Coat Rack.* 1976. Pencil on paper. 55.9 × 38.1 cm (22 × 15″). The National Museum of Women in the Arts, Washington, D.C. Gift of Wallace and Wilhelmina Holladay.

- **Blending.** This is changing color value little by little.
- **Stippling.** This is creating dark values by means of a dot pattern.

Which of these shading techniques was used in Figure 3–3? Which was used in Figure 3–1 on page **40**?

✔ Check Your Understanding

1. What is *perception?* Why is developing perception important?
2. Name four drawing tools.
3. Demonstrate the four shading techniques.

STUDIO ACTIVITY

Keeping a Sketchbook

One way in which artists develop perception is by keeping a *sketchbook.* Many artists carry a sketchbook everywhere they go. They use it to record interesting scenes and objects.

Begin a sketchbook of your own. Choose a notebook that is easy to carry and has unlined paper. Use your sketchbook to sharpen your drawing skills and perception. The more you draw, the better you will "see" objects.

P O R T F O L I O

Put your best sketch in your portfolio. Remember to date, sign, and write a self-reflection.

Pencil

Oil pastel

Colored Marker

Figure 3–4 Drawing Media.

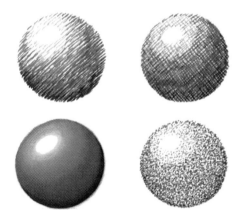

Figure 3–5 Shading Techniques.

■ Art Criticism

Display student drawings of their shoes. Encourage positive critique—looking for what is good, finding the problems (lack of proportion, detail, etc.) not to belittle, but rather to sharpen perception and prepare for the next drawing. It is essential that students develop this kind of attitude toward learning from their work.

Art on a Shoestring

Check with local printers, paper distributors, and similar suppliers to see if they would be willing to donate paper products to the school, especially overruns, unclaimed orders, and so on.

• • • • • • • • • • • •
ASSESS

■ Self-Assessment

Have students complete the Check Your Understanding questions on this page. Answers are provided below.

■ Reteaching

Ask students to quiz each other on the kinds of drawing media they are familiar with. Then have students review the four kinds of shading techniques. Ask volunteers to demonstrate each.

■ Enrichment

Ask students to research the sketches of James Thurber. Thurber's doodles and whimsical drawings often served as the core ideas for his humorous stories. Encourage students to explore similar ways in which a sketchbook could be useful to an artist or a writer.

• • • • • • • • • • • •
CLOSE

Have students define visual perception and explain how drawing and sketching can help to develop one's perception.

Answers to ✔ CHECK YOUR UNDERSTANDING

1. Perception is an awareness of the elements of an environment by means of the senses. It is important to develop one's perception in order to fully "see" an object.
2. Answers will vary. Possibilities include: pencils, crayons, colored pencils, chalk, pens, and colored markers.

3. Students should demonstrate hatching, crosshatching, blending, and stippling.

LESSON 2

Gesture Drawing

(pages 44–45)

LESSON TIME: 2 hours

• • • • • • • • • • • • • •
FOCUS

☑ OBJECTIVES

After completing this lesson, students will be able to:

• Draw figures using several different drawing media.
• Capture the form and actions of a subject.

☑ SUPPLIES

• Sheets of white paper
• Pencils, charcoal sticks, crayons, markers, chalk
• Drawing boards if possible (so students can position themselves around the model)

• • • • • • • • • • • • • •
TEACH

■ Motivator

You will probably find students who are afraid to draw figures. Tell them not to expect their first drawings to be perfect. This takes practice and careful looking. It is important to teach students the value of trying and failing. Explain that they will learn from each effort. Tell students that their drawing styles will be as uniquely their own as their handwriting.

■ Vocabulary

Ask students to discuss the meaning and history of the word *gesture*. Help them discover that gestures emphasize an idea, a feeling, or a movement.

 LESSON 2

Gesture Drawing

Examine the drawing of the figures in Figure 3–6. From an art standpoint, the most important thing about the work is not *who* it shows, but *what* it shows. This drawing is of the human form. Capturing the human form has been a goal of artists through the ages. Notice the loose, scribbly quality of most of the lines. The artist used a technique called **gesture drawing.** This means *moving a drawing medium quickly and freely over a surface to capture the form and actions of a subject.* In gesture drawing you draw with your whole arm, not just your hand. Some gesture drawings are merely quick scribbles. Others are done with greater precision and care. How would you describe the lines the artist has used in Figure 3–6? What parts of the subjects have been recorded with the most care?

WHAT YOU WILL LEARN

You will make several quick gesture drawings of a classmate using several different drawing media. Focus on the form and action of the subject, not on one part, like the foot or face. You will not be concerned with capturing the model's likeness, but rather the feeling of motion. You will then make a large, slower sketch of a seated figure. Emphasize one area of the figure using shading. (For more information on gesture drawing, see Technique Tip **1** on page **281.**)

Figure 3–6 Do you think the artist captured the appearance of the human forms? Where is line used to show details?

Honoré Daumier. *Family Scene.* c. 1867–70. Pen and black ink, and brush and gray wash, on ivory wove paper (discolored cream). 21.6 × 20.5 cm (8½ × 8"). Art Institute of Chicago, Chicago, Illinois. Helen Regenstein Collection, 1965.633

44 Chapter 3 *Art Media and Techniques*

MEETING SPECIAL NEEDS

Flexible Expectations Some students with limited mental capacity may not be able to conceive of the human figure in action as a continuous gesture. They may be able to conceive of it as sticks or sausages linked together, or as a circle, perhaps with stick arms and legs, or as simply a scribble. Allow for such variations in your expectations. Students with neurological/orthopedic disabilities may be able to draw with a finger in white salt spread evenly onto a piece of black paper to suggest the figure's motion.

WHAT YOU WILL NEED

- Assorted drawing media, such as sticks of charcoal, soft graphite, unwrapped crayons, and markers
- Sheets of white paper, 12 x 18 inches (30 x 46 cm)
- Sharpened pencil

WHAT YOU WILL DO

1. You and your classmates will take turns modeling. Models should pretend to be frozen in the middle of an activity. This may be an everyday action, such as jogging, lifting, or dancing. Throwing a ball is another possibility.
2. Make at least four gesture drawings. Use a different medium for each drawing. Make your figures at least eight or ten inches tall. Begin by drawing the head. Sketch loose, free lines. Draw quickly to capture the overall form of the subject. Build up the shape of the figure little by little.

EXAMINING YOUR WORK

- **Describe.** Did you include all the body parts in each of your rapid gesture drawings? Identify the medium used for each drawing.
- **Analyze.** Point to and describe the different kinds of lines in your gesture drawings. Is the area you chose to emphasize clearly identified with shading?

3. Switching to the pencil, make a slower gesture drawing of a seated model. Fill an entire sheet of paper. Select one area of the figure to emphasize as the artist has done in Figure 3–6. You might select a hand, sleeve, or shoe. Emphasize this area with details and shading.
4. Display your finished pencil drawing along with those of classmates. Compare the detail emphasized in the different drawings.

Figure 3–7 Student work. Gesture drawings.

 Try This!

STUDIO OPTION

■ Have three volunteers pose, changing poses every 45 seconds. Do one gesture drawing of each person. Use rough, scribbly lines to capture the poses. Remember to draw quickly. Drawing quickly helps you warm up.

Lesson 2 *Gesture Drawing* **45**

CURRICULUM CONNECTIONS

Language Arts Have students work in groups of three or four to write a short skit or scene about an event at school or in the community. The only requirement is that the skit must rely mostly on **gestures,** rather than words, to communicate the actions and feelings of the actors. Invite students to practice or rehearse their ideas as they write out the scene, assigning a role to each person in the group, then perform their skit for the class.

As students plan their skits, work with each group to provide ideas about effective gestures that convey meaning with physical movement and expression rather than words.

■ Aesthetics

Explain that artists draw figures in many styles, some quite accurate anatomically, others abstract or exaggerated. Find other examples of figures in drawings and paintings in the text and discuss the artists' approaches to interpreting the figures they have drawn.

■ Art Criticism

Invite students to study the effects of various media on the drawings. Students should develop a sensitivity to media so that they can make an informed choice when they begin a drawing. Encourage shading and use of hatching, crosshatching, or stippling to show volume and shadows.

• • • • • • • • • • ASSESS

■ Self-Assessment

Have students use Examining Your Work to evaluate their gesture drawings.

■ Reteaching

Have students do frequent sketches from posed models to build confidence. Review what students learned about the media they used. Ask for words to describe the quality of each.

■ Enrichment

Display posters with figures done by many different artists. Enjoy with your students the marvelous variety of styles and the flexibility and grace of the human body. Discuss the inspiration for such gesture drawings, such as watching a basketball game or viewing a ballet. Have students think about other activities as inspiration for figure movements.

• • • • • • • • • • CLOSE

Have students explain why they chose the media they did.

45

LESSON 3

Painting

(pages 46–47)

• • • • • • • • • • • • • • •

F O C U S

☑ OBJECTIVES

After completing this lesson, students will be able to:

• Define the three main parts of paint.

• Understand the difference between oil-based and water-soluble paints.

• Make a painting with watercolors on paper, experimenting with varying amounts of water.

☑ SUPPLIES

• Watercolor sets, large brush and small brush for each student

• Watercolor paper

• Trays or boards for paper

• Cups for water; sponges; paper towels

• Pencils

Resources

■ 3-2 Expressing Themselves, TRB page 36 (art history)

■ 3-3 Brush This Off, TRB page 37 (appreciating cultural diversity)

• • • • • • • • • • • • • • •

T E A C H

■ Motivator

Ask students what their previous experiences with paints have been. In earlier grades, what kinds of painting media did they use? Which ones did they enjoy? Why? List on the board the kinds of paints the students name.

■ Vocabulary

Review definitions of *pigment*, *binder*, and *solvent*.

46

LESSON 3

Painting

Many people, when they hear the term *art*, think of paintings. This is not unreasonable when you consider that the first artists were painters. They produced their "artworks" on the walls of caves some 15,000 years ago. They made paint from crushed rocks mixed with animal fat or blood.

Since that time, many new painting media have appeared. In this lesson, you will learn about some of these.

PAINT

Although paints have changed over the centuries, the way of making them has not. Like paints used by early cave artists, those today contain three main parts:

• **Pigment.** Pigment is *a finely ground powder that gives paint its color.* The pigment that cave artists relied on came from minerals in rocks. Through the mid-1800s, artists continued to grind their own pigments.

Figure 3–8 Notice this artist's attention to detail. What shading technique did he use?

John Wilson. *My Brother.* 1942. Oil on panel. 30.5 × 27 cm (12 × 10⅝"). Smith College Museum of Art, Northhampton, Massachusetts. Purchased 1943.

46   Chapter 3   *Art Media and Techniques*

TECHNOLOGY OPTIONS

National Gallery of Art Videodisc   Use the following images to show examples of various painting styles.

William M. Harnett *My Gems*	Wassily Kandinsky *Improvisation 31 (Sea Battle)*	George Inness *The Lackawanna Valley*
Search Frame 1972	Search Frame 2249	Search Frame 1951

Use Glencoe's *National Gallery of Art Correlation Bar Code Guide* to locate more artworks.

Figure 3–9 When watercolors are applied to wet paper, the colors flow and blend.

Emil Nolde. *Self-Portrait.* 1917. Watercolor, reed pen, and black ink. 21 × 16.8 cm (8½ × 6½"). The Detroit Institute of Arts, Detroit, Michigan. Bequest of John S. Newberry.

- **Binder.** A binder is *a liquid that holds together the grains of pigment.* The binder allows the pigment to stick to the surface. The liquid parts of eggs have long been used as a paint binder.
- **Solvent.** A painter may also choose to use a **solvent** when working with paints. This is *a liquid used to control the thickness or thinness of the paint.* Solvents are also used to clean paintbrushes and other applicators.

PAINTING MEDIA

As with drawing media, there are many different kinds of paint. Each has its own personality. Some paints that artists use are oil-based. Others are made with plain water.

Oil-Based Paint

First used in the 1400s, oil paint remains a popular medium today. True to its name,

Experimenting with Watercolor

Using a primary hue of watercolor, draw several shapes on a dry sheet of watercolor paper. Repeat the process, this time using paper that has been brushed thoroughly on both sides with water. Share and compare your results with those of classmates.

 PORTFOLIO

Note the properties of watercolor on a piece of paper. Put this in your portfolio with your painting.

oil paint uses linseed oil as its binder. Its solvent is turpentine.

One advantage of oil paint is that it dries slowly. This allows the artist to blend colors right on the canvas. The work in Figure 3–8 is an oil painting. Notice how smoothly the colors blend together.

Water-Based Paint

The most popular of water-based painting media, watercolor takes its name from its solvent, water. The binder is gum arabic. Watercolors give a transparent quality to paintings. Compare the watercolor in Figure 3–9 with the oil painting in Figure 3–8. What differences do you see?

Tempera, another water-based paint, comes in both powder and liquid form. Because tempera is not oil-based, it dries more quickly than oil paint. It is also more opaque than watercolor.

✔ Check Your Understanding

1. What are the three main parts of paint?
2. What is the difference between oil paint and tempera?

Lesson 3 *Painting* **47**

LESSON 4

Creating a Portrait

(pages 48–49)

LESSON TIME: 90 minutes

• • • • • • • • • • • •
FOCUS

☑ OBJECTIVES

After completing this lesson, students will be able to:

• Draw a portrait of another student.
• Add shading and highlighting using oil pastels to create an expressive portrait.

☑ SUPPLIES

• Pencil and sketch paper
• Mirrors
• White paper
• Black colored marker
• Oil pastels
• Watercolors; brushes
• Cups for water; paper towels

Resource

• ■ 3-4 Critiquing Portraits, TRB page 39 (art criticism)

• • • • • • • • • • • •
TEACH

■ Motivator

Ask students to explore their faces with their fingers. Then have them use mirrors to draw and paint a life-size face, neck, and shoulder image on paper using watercolors. (Help them mix red, yellow, and blue watercolors in the cover of the paint box until a neutral brown is achieved. Note that, just as in the Nolde portrait in Lesson 3, exact color is not necessary.)

■ Vocabulary

Have students create a word portrait of the model before they begin drawing. Ask how a word portrait is different from an artist's portrait.

48

Creating a Portrait

Look once more at the paintings in Figures 3–8 and 3–9 on pages **46** and **47**. Both are examples of a type of artwork called *portrait*. A **portrait** is *a visual representation of a person at rest.* Compare these two portraits with the one in Figure 3–10. This artwork was done with oil pastels. This is a medium with properties of both drawing and painting media. Notice the delicate lines and soft tones in this work. See also how the artist used dark values to shade some areas of the subject and light values to highlight others.

WHAT YOU WILL LEARN

You and a partner will take turns serving as model and artist. As artist, you will create a portrait of the other person's face. You will make certain to place each feature of the face in its proper place. You will add shading and highlighting using oil pastels, as in Figure 3–10. Your portrait will express a mood or feeling, as do the portraits in Figures 3–8 and 3–9. To do this, you will have to capture the model's expression, which might be happy or sad, angry or bored.

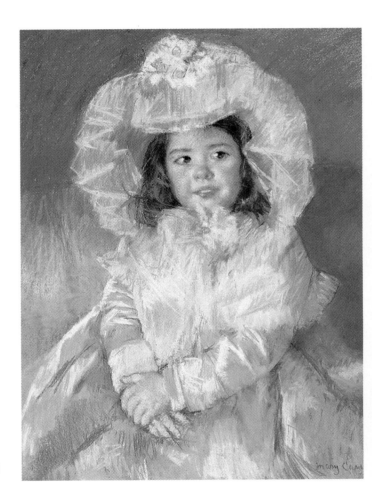

Figure 3–10 What mood or feeling has the artist captured? What shading technique has she used to create depth?

Mary Cassatt. *Margot in Blue.* 1902. Pastel. 61 × 50 cm (24 × 19⅞″). The Walters Art Gallery, Baltimore, Maryland.

48 Chapter 3 *Art Media and Techniques*

MEETING STUDENT DIVERSITY

Painting Partners Help students understand the personal nature of portrait drawing. As partners, students should develop a relationship of trust and acceptance of each other as unique and valuable human beings. Encourage them to discover interesting and positive characteristics about each other, going beyond outward, physical features.

As students work together, encourage each pair to spend a few minutes talking and getting to know each other better. You may want to give students a list of interview questions to ask each other before they begin, such as "What do you like to do after school?" "What is your favorite sport/TV program/book/animal?" and so on.

WHAT YOU WILL NEED

- Pencil and sketch paper
- Sheet of white paper, 9 x 12 inches (23 x 30 cm)
- Black colored marker
- Oil pastels

WHAT YOU WILL DO

1. Have your model sit facing you head-on. This means that you are looking squarely at the person's face. Ask the model to express a mood with his or her facial expression. Make several quick gesture drawings of the person's face. Add eyes, nose, mouth, ears, and hair, making certain each is in its proper place. Your goal is not to create an exact likeness. Rather, it is to capture the shape of the person's head and facial features. You are also to capture a mood or feeling as seen in your model's expression.
2. Transfer the best of your drawings to the sheet of paper.
3. Using the black marker, go over the outline of the head and facial features. Work quickly, as you did in the gesture drawings. The lines should have a sketchy quality, as in Figure 3–9 on page **47**.
4. Decide which areas of your portrait you will shade. Decide which you will highlight. Use a dark value of a single color of pastel for the shaded areas. Use a light value of the same color for highlighted areas.
5. Display your completed work along with those of classmates. Challenge students to identify the mood or feeling your portrait expresses.

EXAMINING YOUR WORK

- **Describe** Identify the type of artwork you created. Did you include all of the facial features? Were these in the proper places on your portrait?
- **Analyze** What value did you use to shade areas of the portrait? What value did you use to highlight areas?

Figure 3–11 **Student work. A portrait.**

Try This! STUDIO OPTIONS

■ Do a second portrait based on the same sketch. This time, substitute watercolors for the oil pastels. Moisten cakes of watercolor with a few drops of water. This will soften them. Use a fairly large brush to apply the paint. Compare the results of your two portraits.

■ Do a gesture drawing of a familiar object using oil pastels. Add shading as you did in your portrait. Reinforce some of the lines to add emphasis.

Lesson 4 *Creating a Portrait* **49**

■ Art History

Explain that artists have painted portraits in many ways, some aiming at exact representation, others exaggerating to express emotion. Look at Franz Hals's portrait, Figure 8-3 on page 145. A Dutch painter who wanted to capture the expressions of his subjects, Hals often showed them smiling. Renaissance painters before him posed their subjects very formally.

■ Studio Skills

Review with students techniques for using oil pastels. (See Technique Tip 3 on page 281.)

Sparking Creativity

Invite students to add zest to their portraits by giving a unique mood or expression to their portrait. Remind them that a particular emphasis is one way to achieve interest in their subject.

ASSESS

■ Self-Assessment

Have students use Examining Your Work to evaluate their work.

■ Reteaching

Ask students to discuss their portraits and how they captured the model's expression.

■ Enrichment

Challenge students to find out about the Smithsonian Institution's National Portrait Gallery in Washington, D.C. This gallery contains portraits of hundreds of significant American citizens.

CLOSE

Have students share their opinions of the strengths of the portraits they painted.

Printmaking

••••••••••••

FOCUS

☑OBJECTIVES

After completing this lesson, students will be able to:
*   Define *relief* and *intaglio* printmaking.
*   Make and print a relief plate.

☑SUPPLIES

*   Cardboard cut to 4 × 5-inch pieces
*   String, glue, scissors, spoons
*   Two or more 4-inch brayers
*   Waterbase black block-printing ink and spatula
*   Two or more palettes (water resistant surfaces)
*   8½ × 11-inch bond paper
*   Newspaper, paper towels

Resources

*   ■ 3-5 Collagram, TRB page 41 (studio)
*   ■ 3-6 Hands Off, TRB page 43 (studio)
*   ■ 3-7 Cut! Print!, TRB page 45 (appreciating cultural diversity)

••••••••••••

TEACH

■ Motivator

Show students some rubber stamps if you have them. Demonstrate to show that the image is reversed when it is printed. If students choose to cut their initials for their design, they must glue them in reverse order. Smooth string (not fuzzy yarn) can be added to the design to make lines. When ready, the design should be glued with strong school glue and allowed to dry before printing.

50

What comes to mind when you hear the word *printing?* You may think of writing in block letters. You may think of the process used to create books, newspapers, and magazines. To an artist, printing, or **printmaking,** is *transferring an image from an inked surface to create a work of art.* As in commercial printing, the artist uses a printing press of sorts. As in forming letters, the artist creates by hand the image to be printed.

PRINTMAKING BASICS

While prints may be made with many different media, all use the same basic tools. These are:

*   **A printing plate.** This is a surface on which the print is made. The plate carries the mirror image of the finished print. Letters and numbers must be made backward on the plate.

*   **Ink.** Ink is applied to the plate. It is responsible for the image appearing on the print.
*   **Brayer.** The brayer is a roller with a handle. It is used to "ink"—or apply ink to—the plate.

Editions

Usually, more than one print is made from a single plate. Together, all the prints made from a plate form an *edition.* Each print in an edition is signed and numbered by the artist. The number is made up of two numerals with a slash (/) between them. The first number tells which print you are viewing. The second tells how many prints are in the edition. The number 4/50 means "the fourth print in an edition of fifty." How would you read 13/25?

Figure 3–12   What principle of art has been used to organize this work?

Shiko Munakata. *Floral Hunting Scene.* 1954. Woodcut, printed in black and dark grey. 131.8 × 159.7 cm (51⅞ × 62⅞"). The Museum of Modern Art, New York, New York. Gift of the Felix and Helen Juda Foundation.

50   Chapter 3   *Art Media and Techniques*

TECHNIQUE TIP

Setting Up a Printing Station   Cover a table with newspaper. Set out two or more palettes and brayers for students to take turns inking their plates. Place a stack of newspapers near each palette. A student will lay the plate on this stack, roll the brayer on the palette until ink is evenly distributed on the brayer, and then roll the brayer on the plate. The student then takes the plate to a newspaper-covered desk. The plate is laid on the desk, a sheet of paper is laid evenly on top, and pressure is applied all over the block area. The paper is pulled up and a print appears.

Figure 3–13 How does this intaglio print differ from the woodcut in Figure 3–12?

Francisco de Goya. *Capricho n. 43: The Sleep of Reason Produces Monsters.* 1796–98, published 1799. Etching and aquatint. 21.5 × 15 cm (8½ × 6″). Courtesy of The Hispanic Society of America, New York, New York.

PRINTMAKING TECHNIQUES

Imagine touching your finger to a stamp pad and then pressing your finger on paper. In doing so, you would make a *relief* (ruh-**leef**) print. This is an image raised from a background that is inked and printed. The raised ridges on your finger would pick up the ink and then transfer your "fingerprint" to the paper. Relief printing is one of the oldest forms of printmaking. It dates back nearly 2,000 years.

A popular medium used in relief printing is wood. The artist cuts away the areas of the surface not meant to hold ink. Figure 3–12 shows a woodblock print, or *woodcut.*

Figure 3–13 shows the result of another printing process. This process is known as **intaglio** (in-**tahl**-yoh). It is *a printmaking technique in which the image to be printed is cut or scratched into a surface.* In a way, intaglio is the reverse of relief printing. The image on the plate is transferred when paper is forced into grooves that hold the ink. Study the intaglio print in Figure 3–13. Notice the many fine lines.

✔ Check Your Understanding

1. Define the term *printmaking.*
2. What are the three tools in printmaking?

Lesson 5 *Printmaking* **51**

STUDIO ACTIVITY

Making a Relief Block Print

Printing needs careful preparation and cooperation. Explain the procedure before beginning the inking. Desks and hands must stay clean. If used newspaper is removed each time, the area will be ready for each new inking. Put about a tablespoon of ink on the palette; add more as needed. Wash brayers with water when finished, checking the edges and handle for ink traces.

■ Art Criticism

Display the student prints and discuss the designs in terms of the principles of art learned in Chapter 2. Look for balance, harmony, variety, emphasis, and proportion. Find rhythm in repetition and movement. Critique prints for unity, neatness, and craftsmanship.

•••••••••••••••
ASSESS

■ Self-Assessment

Have students complete the Check Your Understanding questions on this page. Answers are provided below.

■ Reteaching

Ask students to explain the differences between relief and intaglio printmaking.

■ Enrichment

The term *print* has a different meaning when referring to commercially printed reproductions or posters. Ask students to research commercial printing processes. Have them also explore other printmaking techniques, such as lithography and serigraphy.

•••••••••••••••
CLOSE

Have students describe the process used in making a relief block print.

Answers to ✔ CHECK YOUR UNDERSTANDING

1. Printmaking is a process of transferring an inked image from one prepared surface to another.

2. The three tools in printmaking are:
   • **printing plate,** the surface on which the print is made
   • **ink,** which is applied to the plate with a brayer
   • **brayer,** a roller used to apply ink to the plate.

Have you ever built a house of cards? Maybe you have made a project out of modeling clay. Both activities borrow processes from the art of sculpture. **Sculpture** is *a three-dimensional work of art*. Artists who work in sculpture are called sculptors.

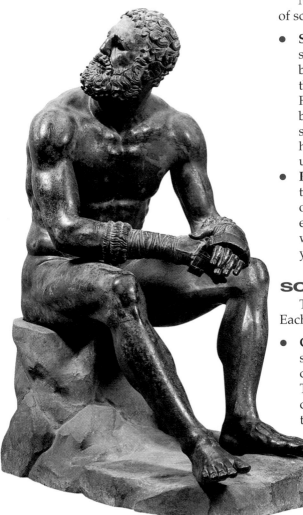

Figure 3–14 What sculpting process and medium was used for this sculpture? What has the artist done to make this boxer look like a real person?

The Pugalist. c. 50 B.C. Bronze. Museo Nazional Romano delle Ferme, Rome, Italy. Scala/Art Resource, NY

THE MEDIA OF SCULPTURE

Like other artists, sculptors use a wide variety of media in their work. One sculpting medium you may have worked with is modeling clay. Various woods and metals are other sculpting media. What medium was used for the sculpture in Figure 3–14?

No matter what medium is used, a work of sculpture will be one of two types:

• **Sculpture in the round.** This is a type of sculpture that is surrounded *on all sides* by space. Another name for sculpture in the round is *freestanding sculpture*. Like Figure 3–14, sculptures in the round can be statues of people. Not all freestanding sculptures have recognizable subjects, however. Examine the sculpture in Figure 1–16 on page **16.**

• **Relief sculpture.** This is a type of sculpture in which forms extend into space on *one* side only. Figure 3–15 shows an example of relief sculpture. If you could walk around to the back of this sculpture, you would find that it is flat.

SCULPTING TECHNIQUES

There are four basic sculpting processes. Each gives a different result. These are:

• **Carving.** In this process, the sculptor starts with a block of material. He or she cuts or chips away pieces of the block. The relief sculpture in Figure 3–15 was created by carving. What medium did the sculptor use?

TECHNOLOGY OPTIONS

National Gallery of Art Videodisc   Use the following images to show additional sculptural styles.

Jean-Baptiste Carpeaux *Neapolitan Fisherboy*	Jean-Antoine Houdon *Louise Brongniart*	Tilman Riemenschneider *Saint Burchard of Würzburg*
Search Frame 2514	Search Frame 2485	Search Frame 2437

Use Glencoe's *National Gallery of Art Correlation Bar Code Guide* to locate more artworks.

- **Casting.** In this process, the sculptor starts by making a mold. He or she then pours in a melted-down metal or other liquid that later hardens. Bronze, the medium used in Figure 3–14, is a common metal used for casting. It is an alloy made of copper and tin. In recent years, sculptors have begun experimenting with different casting media. There is even a 9-foot statue completed in 1996 that is cast from chocolate!
- **Modeling.** Modeling is building up and shaping a soft material to create a sculpture. Fresh plaster can also be used for modeling.
- **Assembling.** Also known as *constructing,* assembling is a process in which pieces of material are glued or joined together. As in modeling, assembled sculptures are built up. A house of cards, for example, is made by assembling.

Check Your Understanding

1. Name three media used in sculpture.
2. What is the difference between sculpture in the round and relief sculpture?
3. Name four processes for making sculpture.

Figure 3–15   What kind of balance has the artist used? What sculpting medium was used?

King Prasenajit Visits the Buddha. Early second century B.C. Hard, reddish sandstone. 48 × 52.7 × 9 cm (19 × 20¾ × 3½"). Freer Gallery of Art, Smithsonian Institution, Washington, D.C.

Experimenting with Assembling

One way in which artists join the pieces of an assembled sculpture is through *slotting.* This is cutting slits in cardboard or similar media and then fitting the pieces together.

Gather sheets of scrap cardboard. These may come from a discarded carton or box. Cut the sheets into rectangles of varying sizes. Experiment with fitting together the pieces by slotting. Slot together at least ten rectangles. When you have created an interesting design, paint your sculpture. Use a large brush and school tempera. Title your work and display it along with those of classmates.

PORTFOLIO

Take a photograph of your sculpture. In self-reflection, write what you learned about the slotting process and how it might be used in another project.

Lesson 6   *Sculpture*   **53**

■ Vocabulary

Review terms for sculpture: *in the round, relief, carving, modeling, constructing,* and *sculptor.* Review the term for three-dimensional work—*form.*

■ Art Criticism

Ask students to work in pairs to apply the four stages of art criticism to their own sculptures: describing, analyzing, interpreting, and judging them.

■ Art History

Sculpture has been an important art form through the ages. Ask students to research particular forms of sculpture—portrait, religious, mythological, war memorial, and so on. Have them locate the time and place in which they were created and the ideas they were meant to represent.

ASSESS

■ Self-Assessment

Have students complete the Check Your Understanding questions on this page. Answers are provided below.

■ Reteaching

Have students explain how a sculpture is different from a painting.

■ Enrichment

Encourage students to discuss and explore some contemporary sculpting media used in free-standing or relief sculpture, such as holograms.

CLOSE

Ask volunteers to give examples of different media used in the four sculpting techniques.

Answers to ✔ CHECK YOUR UNDERSTANDING

1. Answers will vary. Some possibilities include clay, wood, metal, stone, and plaster.
2. Art that you can walk around and see from all sides is called sculpture in the round. Relief sculpture has forms that extend into space on one side only.
3. Four processes of making sculpture are carving, casting, modeling, and assembling (or constructing).

LESSON 7

Making a Collage

(pages 54–55)

LESSON TIME: 3 days

• • • • • • • • • • • • • •

FOCUS

☑ OBJECTIVES

After completing this lesson, students will be able to:
• Define the term *collage.*
• Produce a collage that applies the principles of art.

☑ SUPPLIES

• A variety of old magazines
• Pencils and sketch paper
• White paper
• Crayons or markers
• Scissors, glue
• Assorted colors of construction paper
• Sheets of oaktag

• • • • • • • • • • • • • •

TEACH

■ Motivator

Explore with students the Bearden collage to see how he selected images and combined them to express his idea. Make magazines available to students for cutting. Ask them to select a theme and find several photos that fit it. If students have trouble thinking of a theme, encourage them to brainstorm ideas that have meaning to them. Encourage drawing to add to their theme.

■ Vocabulary

Remind students that the word *collage* is derived from the French word for paste. Point out that there are many art terms that come from French, for example, *papier-mâché,* a French word meaning *chewed paper.* Ask volunteers to identify other art terms from the French.

54

LESSON 7
Making a Collage

Artists are always on the lookout for new ways of creating. One such way is shown in Figure 3–16. This work is a *collage* (kuh-**lahzh**). Based on a French word meaning "to glue," a *collage* is an artwork arranged from cut or torn materials that are pasted to a surface. The group of artists who came up with this idea lived and worked in the early 1900s.

Study Figure 3–16. The work contains a rich assortment of objects and materials. These include photographs of African masks and one of a cat. What other familiar images can you find? Notice how the artist used rectangular patches of colored paper to create a window.

WHAT YOU WILL LEARN

You will make a collage out of colored paper that exhibits a variety of shapes and hues. You will use images and, if you like, words clipped from magazines. Your collage will express a theme. The addition of original crayon drawings will help you carry out your theme.

WHAT YOU WILL NEED
• Discarded magazines
• Pencil and sketch paper
• Sheets of white paper, 9 x 12 inches (23 x 30 cm)
• Crayons or markers
• Scissors
• Sheets of construction paper in assorted colors
• Sheet of oaktag, 12 x 18 inches (30 x 46 cm)
• Glue

Figure 3–16 **What kinds of shapes has the artist used? How many visual textures do you count? How has the artist introduced variety?**

Romare Bearden. *Saturday Morning.* 1969. 111.8 × 142.2 cm (44 × 56"). Collage. © 1998 Romare Bearden Foundation/ Licensed by VAGA, New York, NY

54   Chapter 3   *Art Media and Techniques*

more about • • •

Collage as Art   Romare Bearden (1911–1988) is a renowned African American artist. His paintings and collages reflect the experience of Black Americans in a way that shows their struggles and their dignity. His work is unique in its ability to unify many diverse elements.

Another innovative artist is Robert Rauschenberg, born in Texas in 1925. Rauschenberg introduced assemblage by combining three-dimensional objects with painted or collaged canvases. He also used photographic images silkscreened onto canvas. Locate examples of his work to show students.

WHAT YOU WILL DO

1. Decide on a theme for your collage. Some possibilities include sports, animals, nature, or cities. Browse through old magazines. Be on the alert for photos, illustrations, and words that go along with your theme. Carefully remove the pages containing these images.

2. Think of other words or images that support your theme. Make sketches of these images. Transfer your best sketches to white paper. Complete these drawings using crayon or marker.

3. Cut around the images you have selected or created. Arrange these on the oaktag in an interesting way. You may want to alternate your original drawings with your magazine clippings.

4. Next, cut shapes from construction paper. These are to fill the spaces between your images. They are also to serve as background. Add these around and under the images on the oaktag.

EXAMINING YOUR WORK

- **Describe** Identify the images you chose or created for your collage. Explain how these images emphasize your theme.
- **Analyze** Did you use a variety of shapes and hues in your collage? In what way is harmony demonstrated in your work?

5. When you are satisfied with your design, begin gluing the pieces. Start with the construction paper shapes. Work carefully so as not to disturb the unglued portions of your design. Use the glue *sparingly*. If any glue oozes out from under the pieces, carefully remove it with a slightly damp tissue.

6. When your collage is dry, display it along with those of your classmates. Challenge classmates to identify your theme.

Figure 3–17   Student work. A collage.

Try This! COMPUTER OPTION

■ Find clip art that expresses the theme of your choice. Add original computer creations of your own that support your theme. With the Rectangle, Circle, or Polygon tool, create closed shapes of different sizes.

From the Textures menu, choose different textures to fill these shapes. Choose designs such as brick and fabric for contrast. Fill the shapes. Arrange these under the images using the Order command. Save your work for your portfolio.

Lesson 7   *Making a Collage*   **55**

ASSESS

■ **Self-Assessment**

Have students use Examining Your Work to evaluate their collages.

■ **Reteaching**

Discuss with your students their feelings about the process of making a collage. Did it free them to take chances on new ideas? This is an important learning experience, one which the arts can teach well.

■ **Enrichment**

Ask students to research the Dada movement, which began in Zurich, Switzerland, in 1916. These artists used "chance" in making their collages and doing performances. They wrote poetry by throwing words on the floor. They were reacting to World War I by saying in their art that the world was not acting rationally in killing millions of people.

CLOSE

Have students explain how the images in their collages communicate their theme.

RESOURCES BEYOND THE CLASSROOM

Art Museums Art museums have much more to offer than just guided tours. In addition to providing brochures, maps, and newsletters about the collection, museum shops often sell inexpensive postcards and slides featuring art reproductions. Museums also offer high quality reproductions of museum pieces that can be purchased, or, occasionally, borrowed. Major museums such as the Metropolitan Museum of Art in New York City and the National Gallery of Art in Washington, D.C., provide more in-depth literature and catalogs that describe and depict all or part of their collections. Other resources include museum "lending libraries," where films, videos, and multimedia presentations of art are available to schools.

Computer Art

Throughout history, advances in technology have shaped the way artists create. The 1930s, for example, saw the arrival of paints made with plastic binders. These paints extended the media choices of painters. They were also less messy than oil paints because they used water as a solvent.

More recent advances have brought about other far-reaching changes in the way art can be created. In this lesson, you will learn about an advance that has touched off a new revolution in art. That advance is the digital computer.

THE MEDIA OF COMPUTER ART

Before the mid-1800s, painters had to grind pigments by hand. The appearance of paint in tubes changed all that. It made the painter's life easier.

In a very real sense, the same may be said of computers. They have made—and will continue to make—certain art tasks easier.

Computer Art Programs

Do you have a computer in your classroom? Maybe you have one at home. If you have

Figure 3–18   What is happening in this picture? What statement might the artist be making about computer art?

Rhoda Grossman. *Self-Portrait After Escher.* 1992. Electronic. Salzman International, San Francisco, California.

56   Chapter 3   *Art Media and Techniques*

┌ *more about* • • • ┐

Computer as Art Medium   The introduction of the computer as an art medium initially generated the same concerns in the art world as did the introduction of photography. Many critics discredited the art. However, as critics became familiar with the tools and unique qualities of the computer, they saw that computer art could be judged by the same criteria as other art. While technology makes many common tasks easier, the artist still makes aesthetic choices and decides which tasks are best completed with each art tool.

56

worked with computers—and even if you have not—you are probably aware that they do a number of different jobs. Each job is done by a separate program, or *application.* As is true of other computer applications, art images are stored as files in the computer's memory. Once saved, they may be opened and reworked.

Most computer art applications are one of two main types:

- **Paint programs.** In paint programs, images are stored as *bitmaps,* which are series of tiny dots. The advantage is the ability to edit pixel by pixel. In general, paint programs are capable of producing more lifelike pictures than those done in draw programs. Figures 3–18 and 3–19 were made using paint programs.

- **Draw programs.** In draw programs, images are stored as a series of lines and curves. Each line or curve results from a mathematical formula and is known as an *object.* An advantage of drawing programs over painting programs is that objects can be "resized"—shrunk or enlarged—without distortion. Figure 3–20 on the next page shows an image, or "group of objects," created in a drawing program.

In the last decade, the lines between paint and draw programs have begun blurring. Many paint programs nowadays do jobs that were once done only by a draw program, and vice versa.

Figure 3–19   How does this self-portrait and the one on the facing page differ from the ones in Figures 3–8 and 3–9 on pages 46–47?

Erol Otis. *Self-Portrait.* 1991. Electronic. Courtesy of the artist.

Lesson 8   *Computer Art*   **57**

■ **Vocabulary**

To further explain the terms and tools listed in Figure 3-21, share with students the following:

- **Brush tool** paints with current fill color. Menus allow choice of color, shape, and size.
- **Pencil tool** draws in a single pixel line. It can be used for editing with the Zoom-In tool.
- **Eraser** erases marks under the tool. Sizes can be changed. In many programs, you can conveniently double click to erase "visible" screen. You can erase to a white page or fill color. Some programs use a different icon.
- **Paint Bucket** pours the Fill color and/or texture into a space.
- **Rectangle shape tool** captures rectangular or square shapes. When an object is selected it looks as if it has "marching ants" around the perimeter.
- **Selection tool** for a Draw or object-oriented program puts "handles," or four small squares, at the corner points. These can be used to alter the image. Clicking in the center and dragging moves the object.

Figure 3–20 The image in the upper-left was made from the 298 separate "objects" shown in the lower-right. Do you recognize this familiar image?

Tools of the Computer Artist

In computer art, there are tools and there are *tools*. The physical tools that the computer artist actually handles are called *hardware*. Hardware includes the equipment, such as the monitor, keyboard, and printer, used in computer graphics.

The most important real tool of the computer artist is the mouse. This is the familiar pointing and clicking device. The mouse is used mainly to make selections from menus. These are lists of commands appearing in a bar at the top of the screen. The mouse may also be used as a drawing or painting device.

Tool	Description	Type of Program
🔍 Zoom tool	Magnifies a part of a painting or drawing.	Paint or Draw
🖌 or ✏ Brush tool	Paints lines of different thicknesses.	Paint
✒ Pencil tool	Draws lines and curves.	Paint only
◢ Eraser tool	Changes one color to another.	Paint
🪣 Fill tool	Adds color, gradients, patterns to closed objects or shapes.	Paint or Draw
⬚ Rectangle shape tool	Creates rectangles and squares.	Paint or Draw
➤ Selection tool	Selects.	Draw
⬚ Selection tool	Selects a rectangular space around an object.	Paint
◯ Lasso Selection tool	Selects only the object.	Paint
◯ Ellipse or Round Shape tool	Draws ovals and circles.	Paint or Draw

Figure 3–21 Common on-screen tools.

more about • • •

Technology   Many artists and illustrators use computer art applications to quickly combine images and make multiple copies in varying sizes faster than with other art techniques. The computer offers artists advantages over conventional techniques because it can quickly make two-dimensional objects look three-dimensional. Some art applications provide tools or menus to add textures that change the surface quality of the image to imitate textured surfaces of different kinds. Have students experiment with simple draw programs. Encourage them to explore the applications and techniques and in paint programs.

Some other real tools used by professional computer artists include the following:

- **Stylus and graphics tablet.** In simplest terms, a stylus and graphics tablet are electronic answers to the pencil and paper. In recent years, these tools have been improved. The stylus now responds to pressure from the hand, much like a real pencil, pen, or brush. The woman in Figure 3–18 on page **56** is shown using a stylus and graphics tablet.
- **Scanner.** A scanner is a device that "reads" a printed image. It then translates the image into a language the computer—and the computer artist—can use. The work in Figure 3–19 began with a photograph that the artist scanned into his computer.

On-Screen Tools

A second category of tools computer artists work with is "on-screen" tools. These mimic the hand-held tools used by conventional artists. On-screen tools include pencils, pens, assorted brushes, and even erasers.

The set of on-screen tools varies from program to program. The table in Figure 3–21 shows some common tool icons and the type of program in which each is found. It also shows the icon, or picture symbol, commonly used to indicate each.

Check Your Understanding

1. What is the difference between a painting program and a drawing program?
2. Name three real tools and three on-screen tools.

STUDIO ACTIVITY

Experimenting with Art Software

There is an old saying that "experience is the best teacher." You are about to prove the truth of this saying, especially if you have never created computer art.

Begin by opening a new file. Do this by clicking "File" at the left of the menu bar and selecting "New." Using the Ellipse tool, draw an oval. Beginning at one edge, draw a second oval about twice the size of the first. Switch to the Rectangle tool. Create a tall, slender rectangle somewhere on the page. The rectangle should be about the same height as that of the large oval at its highest point. Switch to the Arrow Selection tool. Select or draw a "marquee" around the rectangle. A dotted line will appear around the shape. Click Edit, then Copy, then Paste. A second rectangle identical to the first will appear at the upper left corner of the screen. Drag the rectangle to a position under the left side of the large oval and just touching it. Re-select the original rectangle and move it to a corresponding position on the right side of the large oval. Perhaps now you will recognize the image you have created as an animal. Add details, such as a tail, using the Pencil or Brush tool. Complete your animal by adding color using the Fill tool.

PORTFOLIO

Save and print your animal. Put the printout in your portfolio with an evaluation of what you did to create the animal.

Lesson 8 *Computer Art* **59**

STUDIO ACTIVITY

Experimenting with Art Software

While some students may be familiar with graphics packages or scanners, most students will not. Encourage all students to use an available Paint or Draw application to explore the tools and menus. If color printing is not an option, complete the drawing in black and white, print, and then apply color with pencils, pens or paints.

ASSESS

■ Self-Assessment

Have students complete the Check Your Understanding questions on this page. Answers are provided below.

■ Reteaching

Ask students to review ways to use the computer to create art.

■ Enrichment

Invite a computer teacher or architectural draftsperson to demonstrate a high-end graphics program. Encourage students to experience firsthand the advantages and disadvantages of using such programs to create art.

CLOSE

Have students define and discuss the two types of computer art applications.

Answers to ✔ CHECK YOUR UNDERSTANDING

1. In paint programs, images are stored as bitmaps, a series of tiny dots. In draw programs, images are stored as a series of lines and curves. Objects created in draw programs can be resized without distortion.

2. Real tools include the monitor, the keyboard, the mouse, a stylus and graphics tablet, a scanner, and the computer itself. On-screen tools include pencils, pens, brushes, and erasers.

The Mass Production of Books

Gutenberg Bible. c. 1455. Vellum. The Huntington Library, San Marino, California/Superstock.

☞ OBJECTIVES

After completing this feature, students will be able to:

- Compare book production before and after the invention of movable type.
- Explain how the invention of movable type made it possible for more people to learn to read.

Teaching the Connection

- Have students read the feature on this page.
- Ask volunteers to share what they know about book production. What is the style of lettering for printed material called? *(Typeface or font.)* What skills might a book illustrator of today need that one of ancient times did not need? *(Design skills, computer skills.)*
- Tell students that Gutenberg's invention of movable type was quickly adopted by printers throughout Europe. As books became more widely available, their tremendous impact became clear. The mass production of books greatly contributed to the spread of new ideas about religion, politics, and philosophy.

Answers to Making the Connection

- ☞ They seem to be purely decorative because they do not seem to be illustrating a story.
- ☞ Using a brush or pen dipped in ink, a scribe copied the words to create a duplicate.
- ☞ Books could be printed efficiently and inexpensively. More books became available and were affordable to more people.

Look carefully at this page in your textbook. Now compare it with the same page in the textbook of the person sitting next to you. Do you notice any differences? Most likely, the two pages look identical. This textbook, like other modern books, was mass produced. This means that thousands were manufactured at the same time.

The mass production of books would not have been possible without the invention of movable type. Before 1450, every book was written by hand. To create a duplicate, a scribe copied the words using a brush or pen dipped in ink. Copying books took a great deal of time. Consequently, books were not widely available. Without books, the majority of people did not learn how to read.

All that changed, however, when Johannes Gutenberg invented movable type. This invention made it possible to print books efficiently and inexpensively. Books then became available to a larger number of people. With more affordable books, more people learned how to read.

The first book to be printed using movable type was the Gutenberg Bible. Although the illustrations were hand painted, the text was mass produced.

MAKING THE CONNECTION

- ☞ What do you think is the purpose of the illustrations on this page from the Gutenberg Bible? Explain your answer.
- ☞ Explain how books were created before the invention of movable type.
- ☞ How did the invention of movable type make it possible for more people to learn to read?

INTERNET ACTIVITY

Visit Glencoe's Fine Arts Web Site for students at:

http://www.glencoe.com/sec/art/students

60   *Chapter 3 Connections*

INTERNET ACTIVITY

Safe Passage on the Net   You may have concerns about how to supervise students while on-line to keep them on track and in safe areas as they explore the resources provided on Glencoe's Fine Arts Site. Guide students' first experiences by directing them to the *Glencoe Student Galleria* or to the activities in *Studio Cyberspace*. The information contained here is confined to materials and activities designed or reviewed by Glencoe's Internet Development Staff. These areas will keep students occupied on specific tasks without the need to search undirected through the Internet for activities. You will find additional guidelines for Internet use in the *Internet Activity Booklet* included in the *Introducing Art* program.

Find us at **http://www.glencoe.com/sec/art**

REVIEW

BUILDING VOCABULARY

Number a sheet of paper from 1 to 10. After each number, write the term from the box that matches each description below.

art medium	pigment
binder	portrait
gesture drawing	printmaking
intaglio	sculpture
perception	solvent

1. Transferring an image from an inked surface to create a work of art.
2. A liquid that holds together the grains of pigment.
3. A printmaking technique in which the image to be printed is cut or scratched into a surface.
4. An awareness of the elements of an environment by means of the senses.
5. A visual representation of a person at rest.
6. A three-dimensional work of art.
7. A material used to create a work of art.
8. A finely ground powder that gives paint its color.
9. Moving a drawing medium quickly and freely over a surface to capture the form and actions of a subject.
10. A liquid used to control the thickness or thinness of the paint.

REVIEWING ART FACTS

Number a sheet of paper from 11 to 20. Answer each question in a complete sentence.

11. What are three ways in which artists use the art of drawing?
12. Name and describe four shading techniques.
13. What is the binder in oil paint? What is one advantage of using this medium?
14. What is a water-soluble paint?
15. What are the three tools common to printmaking? Name two techniques of printmaking.
16. How does the use of space in sculpting differ from its use in other areas of art?
17. What is relief sculpture?
18. Name and describe four methods of sculpting.
19. Explain the difference between computer painting and drawing programs.
20. Identify three pieces of hardware used in computer art.

THINKING ABOUT ART

1. **Analyze.** In this chapter, you learned how various art media have changed through the ages. What needs of the artist do you suppose brought about some of these changes? What role did changing technology play?
2. **Compare and contrast.** Imagine that you are planning a painting. What factors might lead you to select a water-soluble paint over an oil paint? What might prompt you to make the opposite choice?

MAKING ART CONNECTIONS

1. **Music.** Preview and then bring to class a recording that reveals the characteristics of different musical instruments. Possibilities include Prokofiev's *Peter and the Wolf* and Britten's *The Young Person's Guide to the Orchestra*. Play the music for classmates. Identify the characteristics of each instrument's sound.

2. **Mathematics.** Computer drawing objects, as you learned in Lesson 8, are based on mathematical formulas. Interview a teacher in your school's computer science or math department about other advances in computer art that draw on mathematics. Share your findings with classmates in an oral report.

THINKING ABOUT ART

1. Answers will vary. Students might mention artists' need to create art for technological media such as television, video games, and other electronic media.

2. Select water-soluble paints for a transparent effect, quick drying, and easy cleanup. Select oil paint for easy blending, longer working time, and richer color.

■ Building Vocabulary

1. printmaking
2. binder
3. intaglio
4. perception
5. portrait
6. sculpture
7. art medium
8. pigment
9. gesture drawing
10. solvent

■ Reviewing Art Facts

11. Drawing limbers up the artist's eye, develops perception, and serves as a plan for a finished artwork.
12. Hatching—thin lines running in the same direction; cross-hatching—crisscrossing lines; blending—changing color value gradually; stippling—using dot patterns.
13. Linseed oil. Oil paint dries slowly and blends smoothly.
14. A water-soluble paint is one in which water is the solvent.
15. Tools: printing plate, ink brayer. Techniques: relief prints and intaglio.
16. Sculpture is three-dimensional and occupies space.
17. Relief sculpture forms extend into space on one side only.
18. Carving—chips away pieces; casting—a liquid is poured into a mold; modeling—shaping a soft material; assembling—pieces are joined together.
19. In paint programs, images are stored as bitmaps; in draw programs, images are stored as lines and curves.
20. Hardware includes monitor, mouse, keyboard, scanner, stylus and graphics tablet, and the computer itself.

Looking at Art

(pages 62–79)

Resources

- 4-9 Chapter Test, TRB page 68
- Transparency CC-4, *Kastūra* by Frank Stella
- Transparency 4, *Two Children at the Seashore* by Mary Cassatt
- Fine Art Print 7, *The Three Umbrellas* by Raoul Dufy
- Fine Art Print 8, *The Challenge* by David Alfaro Siquieros

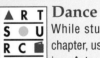

Dance
While studying this chapter, use Performing Arts Handbook page 316 to learn how the AMAN Folk Ensemble researches how time and place affect artistic expression.

NATIONAL STANDARDS

This chapter addresses the following National Standards for the Visual Arts:

1. (a, b)   3. (a)
2. (a, b, c) 6. (a, b)

Figure 4–1 Look at this painting closely. If you see only a vase of flowers, move closer.

Jan Davidsz de Heem. *Vase of Flowers.* c. 1660. Oil on canvas. 69.6 × 56.5 cm (27⅜ × 22¼″). National Gallery of Art, Washington, D.C. Andrew W. Mellon Fund.

62

FEATURED ARTISTS

Arthur G. Dove	Pieter de Hooch
Albrecht Dürer	Edward Hopper
Naum Gabo	Henri Matisse
Jan Davidsz de Heem	Pablo Picasso
Winslow Homer	Jan Vermeer

Looking at Art

To understand some poems and stories, you need to look beyond the mere words on the page. You need to "read between the lines." Only by doing so are you able to see the true meaning.

The same may be said of art. Consider the painting at the left. On the surface, this simply looks like a vase of flowers. However, did you notice the lizard looking hungrily at a spider, the ants exploring an open pod, or the snail making its way across the shelf? What has the artist done to draw the viewer's attention to these details?

In this chapter, you will learn how to ask—and answer—questions like this one. You will learn how to "read" between the lines and make discoveries that will change the way you see and respond to art.

PORTFOLIO IDEAS

Include some form of written self-reflection with your portfolio entry. In self-reflection, you have the opportunity to critique your own works. You tell what you learned from the assignment. You can also express feelings about the work by telling whether you think it succeeds, and what you liked or didn't like about doing the project.

OBJECTIVES

After completing this chapter, you will be able to:

- Explain how subject, composition, and content relate to works of art.
- Define *aesthetics*.
- Identify the four steps of art criticism.
- Discuss the different ways in which critics judge works of art.

WORDS YOU WILL LEARN

abstract
aesthetics
aesthetic view
art critic
composition
content
credit line
non-objective
point of view
subject

63

■ Chapter Overview

In this chapter, students will explore ways of looking at art that will encourage them to ask and answer questions about why a piece of artwork is successful. By understanding the nature of aesthetics and art criticism, students can better evaluate and understand the art of others as well as their own works.

■ Chapter Motivator

Ask students to discuss a toy or other object that, when they first saw it, they were not interested in. Yet, after closer inspection, they found they really liked it. Have students explain what changed their minds. Perhaps they noted details they hadn't noticed at first. Help students see that, by looking past the obvious, we can often find value we didn't know was there.

■ Examining the Artwork

Direct students' attention to de Heem's painting and ask them if they consider this to be a successful work of art. Do they think it is necessary to provide reasons for an art decision of this kind? Ask them to name some of these reasons. List these on the board. Write the word *aesthetics* on the board. Explain that this is the term used to describe the *act of making judgments about art and offering reasons to explain those judgments.* Ask students to discuss their judgments about de Heem's painting and their reasons for those judgments.

National Museum of Women in the Arts

You may wish to use the National Museum of Women in the Arts videodisc and/or CD-ROM. The videodisc features a bar code guide, and the interactive CD-ROM provides stimulating activities.

DEVELOPING A PORTFOLIO

Choosing a Project A portfolio should exhibit strong, confident examples of a student's work. Typically, evaluators would rather see fewer competent works than many that are mediocre. However, a diversity of artistic skill is also critical, so students must learn to balance both objectives. Encourage them to approach each assignment as a potential project for their portfolios, and as a method of isolating their strengths and weaknesses. For more information on choosing projects to include in portfolios, refer to the booklet, *Portfolio and Performance Assessment* that accompanies the *Introducing Art* program.

Aesthetics

Aesthetics

FOCUS

✓ OBJECTIVES

After completing this lesson, students will be able to:
- Define *aesthetics*.
- Identify the three aesthetic views of art: subject, composition, and content.

✓ SUPPLIES

- Old magazines
- White drawing paper
- Scissors, paste, pencils, markers

Resource

- 4-1 Debate, TRB page 55 (cooperative learning)

TEACH

■ Motivator

Begin this lesson by asking students if they can recall what is meant by *aesthetics*. Then ask them to identify the three ways by which a work of art can be measured. Have students give examples of subjects, compositions, and content in art found in the school and in other creative works such as books.

■ Vocabulary

Ask students to look up the term *aesthetics* in the dictionary and trace its word history (from the Greek *aisthetikos* meaning "sensitive").

Taste is a personal matter. What is music to one person might be noise to another. In art, differences in taste may be traced to **aesthetics** (es-**thet**-iks). This is *the study of the nature of beauty and art.* Aesthetics raises the question "What makes a work of art successful?"

Over the centuries, thinkers seeking answers to this question have come up with different "aesthetic views" of art. An **aesthetic view** is *an idea or school of thought on what is most important in a work of art.* Historically, the debate among scholars has centered on three competing aesthetic views. These are the *subject view,* the *composition view,* and the *content view.*

Figure 4–2 What is the subject of this work? What elements and principles of art has the artist used? What mood or feeling does the work communicate?

Pieter de Hooch. *A Woman Preparing Bread and Butter for a Boy.* 1660–63. Oil on canvas. 68.3 × 53 cm (26⅞ × 20⅞"). The J. Paul Getty Museum, Los Angeles, California.

64   Chapter 4   *Looking at Art*

SUBJECT VIEW

The subject view holds that a successful artwork is one whose subject looks convincing and lifelike. A work's **subject** is *an image viewers can easily identify.* The subject may be a person or people, as in Figure 4–2. It may be an object, such as a chair. It may even be an event, such as a holiday celebration. Look again at the painting in Figure 4–2. Notice how realistic the subject is. The work could almost be mistaken for a photograph. How do you think a scholar taking the subject view would evaluate this painting?

COMPOSITION VIEW

The second aesthetic view—the composition view—maintains that what counts most in an artwork is its **composition.** This is *the way the principles are used to organize the elements of art.* Supporters of the composition view attach the most importance to how the parts of a work fit together. They might look, for example, at the way balance is used to control shape or form. Such people would find much to applaud in the painting in Figure 4–3. Examine this work yourself.

Figure 4–3 Notice how this work communicates with the viewer even though it has no subject. What colors has the artist used? What shapes can you find?

Arthur Dove. *Fog Horns.* 1929. Oil on canvas. 45.5 × 66 cm (18 × 26"). Colorado Springs Fine Arts Center, Colorado Springs, Colorado.

---

more about • • •

Arthur Dove   Dove was an American artist whose ambition was to simplify the forces of nature just as music had done with sound. He used colors, shapes, and lines to represent those forces in his paintings. Ask students when they first realized that Dove's painting was an effort to express the sounds of fog horns. He was quite familiar with fog horns, which are used in misty coastal areas to warn ships of danger or approaching vessels. For years, Dove lived on a 42-foot boat, wandering from port to port along the East coast.

During the last years of his life, the artist lived in an abandoned post office on Long Island, still actively painting. Though partially paralyzed by a stroke in 1946, he stubbornly continued to paint with his wife's help.

Figure 4–4 **Examine the body language of the people in this painting. What mood is conveyed? What role does color play?**

Pablo Picasso. *The Tragedy.* 1903. Oil on wood. 105 × 69 cm (41½ × 27⅛"). National Gallery of Art, Washington, D.C. Chester Dale Collection.

Notice that it lacks any recognizable subject matter. The artist has relied instead on the elements of color and shape to spark visual interest. What art principle has been used to organize these elements?

CONTENT VIEW

The third and final view states that the most important single ingredient of any artwork is its **content.** This is *the message, idea,*

STUDIO ACTIVITY

Analyzing an Illustration

Browse through old unwanted magazines. Clip out illustrations for advertisements and action photographs that you find interesting. Avoid ordinary head shots and the like. Paste one clipping to the top of a large sheet of paper. Divide the area beneath into three columns. Head one column *Subject,* one *Composition,* and one *Content.* List details and properties of the image in each column.

P O R T F O L I O

Select one of the artworks in your portfolio. Write a critique of it using all three of the aesthetic views. Put your critique in your portfolio.

or feeling expressed by a work of art. Scholars who hold the *content* view place the greatest value on a work's expressive qualities. A painting like the one in Figure 4–4 would earn high marks from people who hold this view. Notice the downward glances and forlorn expressions. Observe how the man's body language—his arms folded tightly about him—seems to shut out the world around him. You can almost feel this family's pain. Note the work's title. Do you find yourself wondering about the tragedy that befell them?

Check Your Understanding

1. What is aesthetics?
2. What are the three commonly held aesthetic views?

Lesson 1 *Aesthetics* **65**

STUDIO ACTIVITY

Analyzing an Illustration

As students begin this Studio Activity, encourage them to work in pairs or small groups. Ask them to challenge each other to explain their reasons for listing the details they did in each column. As they talk through their reasoning, students will be practicing important thinking and verbalizing skills necessary in analyzing and evaluating artwork.

■ Aesthetics

Have students study the artworks reproduced in this lesson. Have them work in pairs to identify and describe the subject matter, composition, and content of each work of art. Help those students who may have trouble differentiating between subject matter and content. Call on volunteers to share their ideas.

ASSESS

■ Self-Assessment

Have students complete the Check Your Understanding questions on this page. Answers are provided below.

■ Reteaching

Work with small groups of students to review the meaning of aesthetics and the three aesthetic views discussed in the lesson.

■ Enrichment

Ask students to find out more about the artists whose work is shown in this lesson. Their lives span many different cultures and historical periods. Invite students to write a summary of the times and cultural background of each.

CLOSE

Have students restate the three aesthetic views.

Answers to ✔CHECK YOUR UNDERSTANDING

1. Aesthetics is the study of the nature of beauty and art.
2. The three views are **subject view, composition view,** and **content view.** The **subject** view holds that if the subject of a work looks convincing and lifelike, the work is successful. The **composition** view holds that the way the principles of art are used to organize the elements of art is the most important aspect of a work of art. The **content** view states that the most important ingredient for a successful work of art is its content—the message, idea, or feeling expressed by the work of art.

Art Criticism

☑ **OBJECTIVES**

After completing this lesson students will be able to:

• Define *art criticism.*

• Name and explain the four types of art criticism questions.

☑ **SUPPLIES**

• Paper and pencil

• White paper, 12 × 18 inches

• Mixing trays; water

• Watercolors, brushes

Resource

■ 4-2 Reading a Credit Line, TRB page 57 (reproducible master)

■ **Motivator**

Tell students that in this lesson they will learn that art criticism is a process strategy that will enable them to focus their attention on each of these aesthetic views in artworks created in a realistic style.

Do you enjoy solving mysteries? Maybe you are a fan of brainteasers. In either case, having all the facts at hand is critical to finding a solution. So is arranging the facts in a logical fashion.

These statements apply not only to "whodunits" and puzzles. They also apply to artworks. In getting to the "bottom" of a work of art, you need to follow a series of ordered steps. In this lesson, you will learn about these steps and about the solutions they yield. You will also learn how to apply these steps to your own works of art.

THE ART CRITIC

As an amateur detective, you use evidence and clues to crack a case. In a sense, art critics do the same. An **art critic** is *a person whose job is studying, understanding, and judging works of art.* In getting this job done, critics will use all three aesthetic views.

When studying a work of art, the critic uses a four-step process. These steps are *describing, analyzing, interpreting,* and *judging.* The first three of these steps, as you will see, correspond to the three aesthetic views.

Figure 4–5 **Does this work succeed because it is lifelike, because of its composition, or because of the mood it expresses?**

Winslow Homer. *Crossing the Pasture.* c. 1872. Oil on canvas. 66.4 × 96.9 cm (26⅛ × 38¼"). Amon Carter Museum, Fort Worth, Texas.

66   Chapter 4   *Looking at Art*

TECHNOLOGY OPTIONS

National Gallery of Art Videodisc   Use the following images to show other artworks on which to practice the steps of art criticism.

Martin Johnson Heade
Cattleya Orchid and Three Brazilian Hummingbirds

Search Frame 1946

Georgia O'Keeffe
Shell

Search Frame 3009

Helen Frankenthaler
Wales

Search Frame 2327

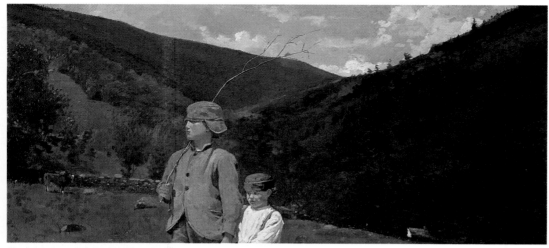

Figure 4–6a What would you say is the subject of this painting?

Winslow Homer. *Crossing the Pasture*. Detail. c. 1872. Oil on canvas. 66.4 × 96.9 cm (26⅛ × 38⅛"). Amon Carter Museum, Fort Worth, Texas.

It is important that students realize that each of the first three art-criticism questions focuses on one of the ways of measuring a work's success. In this way a pluralistic approach to aesthetics is accommodated by the art-criticism operations of description, analysis, interpretation, and judgment. Point out that a positive judgment for a work of art can be made in terms of subject matter, composition, *or* content.

■ **Art Criticism**

Provide time for students to prepare written descriptions of the painting by Winslow Homer. Then ask them to present and discuss their descriptions. Follow the same procedure with the remaining art-criticism questions. Here are guidelines for student responses:

- In the descriptions, make certain that students note the presence of the bull.
- Analysis should reveal the artist's concern for composition. Dabs of bright color that define the wildflowers and highlight the bull, trees, rocks, and house help unify the scene. The light value of the smaller boy's shirt helps draw the viewer's attention to him.
- During interpretation, students should be able to detect a sense of alertness in the taller boy's protective stance. The other boy shelters himself close to his side. Ask students if they can identify the subject of his concern. A bull, either the one in the left background or another one out of view may be a danger to the boys.
- Have students express their judgments about the painting and tell why they responded as they did.

Describing

In describing a work, the critic asks the question "What do I see when I look at this work?" The work's *subject* is the focus of this step. Carefully list all the things you see in the work. Look at the credit line to find out what medium the artist has used and how large the artwork is.

Examine the work shown in Figure 4–5.

- How many figures do you see in the picture?
- What object are they both holding? What does the taller boy have over his shoulder?
- What animals do you see in the background?
- How would you describe the surroundings?

In answering these questions, you will be *describing* the subjects of this artwork.

Analyzing

In analyzing a work, the critic asks, "How is work of art organized? How are the elements and principles of art used?" The work's *composition* is the focus of this step.

Again, look at the detail of the painting in Figure 4–6a.

- What forms appear at the center of the composition? Why does the artist place the boys in the center, close to the viewer?
- Can you find any intense or bright colors in this picture?
- Where is the lightest value? What purpose does it serve?
- Notice the diagonal lines formed by the stick in the taller boy's hand and by the downward slope of the hill on the right. These lines converge on, and emphasize, the face of the taller boy. Can you find a third diagonal line that does the same?
- Can you find a more gently sloping diagonal that points to the face of the smaller boy?
- What colors has the artist used? What textures has he included?
- How has the artist used emphasis to make the subjects stand out?
- What role does proportion play in this artwork?

These questions and their answers are examples of the critic's analysis of the composition in the painting *Crossing the Pasture*.

Lesson 2 *Art Criticism* **67**

MEETING SPECIAL NEEDS

Critiquing Artwork Students with disabilities involving speech, hearing, and vision will probably require adaptive consideration when the class views and discusses art prints. Of course, those with visual impairments should be seated close to the artwork, and a good light should fall on the artwork. Likewise, those with hearing impairments should be seated up close to the teacher in order to hear the discussion leader. Be patient with students with speech disabilities; do not interrupt students who stutter. Encourage them to give in-depth answers by saying, "What makes you think that?" Even students with no language can participate by holding the art print up for viewing by the entire class.

■ **Cooperative Learning**

Divide students into small groups and have them work as a unit to apply the art-criticism questions to Figure 4-2 on page 64. Remind the groups that they do not have to agree, particularly in their interpretations and judgments. When they have completed the process, have a spokesperson for each group share their ideas and explain the various judgments within each group.

Students can learn a great deal about works of art through this kind of collaborative information exchange. Discussions of this kind help in expanding art vocabulary and overcome the dearth of linguistic tools that often hamper student efforts to respond to works of art.

■ **Art History**

After students begin to look at art more critically, their curiosity may be aroused and they may begin to ask such questions as, "Who painted this work?" "When was it done?" "Where was it done?" Explain that these are art-history questions that require research to answer. Appoint two teams of two or three students each to research the lives and careers of both Pieter de Hooch (Figure 4-2) and Winslow Homer (Figure 4-5) and present their findings in class.

┌─────────────────────────┐
Art in Everyday Life

Encourage students to be on the lookout for articles about art in newspapers and periodicals. Have them bring in clippings as they find them and post them on a bulletin board under the heading "Art in the News."
└─────────────────────────┘

Interpreting

In interpreting a work, the critic asks, "What is the artist saying to me? What moods, feelings, or ideas are expressed?" The work's *content* is the focus of this step. Look closely at Figure 4–6b.

- What emotion is communicated by the look and body language of the taller boy? Would you say that he stands tall and appears sure of himself?
- Contrast these observations with the facial expression and posture of the smaller boy.
- Why has the artist placed the boys against a darker, textured background?

Does this focus your attention on their faces and facial expressions? What do you think the artist has accomplished by drawing the viewer's eyes to the boys' expressions and body language?

- What visual clue can you find in the distance off to the left that might explain the boys' behavior?

Interpretation can be the most challenging step in art criticism. It is challenging because you must use your imagination. Do not be afraid to make an interpretation that is different from someone else's. Your interpretation will depend on what you have experienced in life.

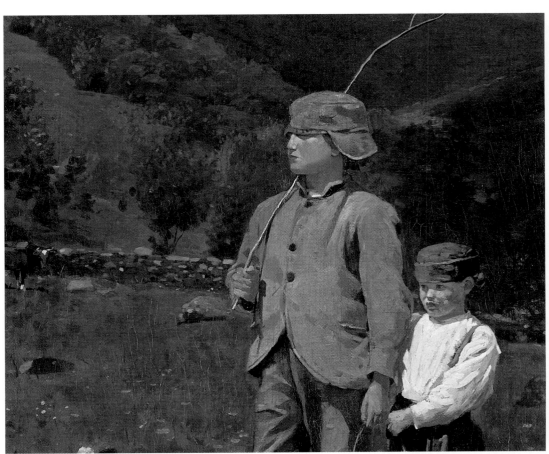

Figure 4–6b Notice the feelings conveyed by the boys' expressions. How does this information help you understand the story the painting tells?

Winslow Homer. *Crossing the Pasture.* Detail. c. 1872. Oil on canvas. 66.4 × 96.9 cm (26⅛ × 38⅛"). Amon Carter Museum, Fort Worth, Texas.

68   Chapter 4   *Looking at Art*

CURRICULUM CONNECTIONS

Social Studies   Painters often provide an important glimpse into the life and cultures of the past. The works of Pieter de Hooch (1629–1684) are often described as "portraits" of his native Holland. From his work we have learned about the daily life of the prosperous Dutch citizens of his time. He painted what other artists overlooked—the customs and daily routines of ordinary people.

The works of Winslow Homer (1836–1910) also reflect time and place. His early paintings record rural American scenes of the time—school rooms, croquet games, husking bees. His illustrations of Civil War battlefield scenes portrayed the cruel images of war. Eventually Homer focused on the role of the sea in late nineteenth century America.

Judging

In judging a work, the critic asks, "Is the work successful?" This step depends on the answers to the questions asked during the first three steps. A work may be judged successful on the basis of its subject, composition, content, or some combination of the three. How do you think an art critic would judge the painting in Figure 4–5? Using what you have learned, how would you judge it?

If you have been an alert art sleuth up to this stage, you might have homed in on the story this painting tells. A part of it is revealed in the detail from the work in Figure 4–6b.

The slightly comical narrative centers on two boys, probably brothers. The two are seen crossing a field—taking a shortcut, maybe, after having just completed the morning's milking. Suddenly, each becomes aware of a real and present danger. Did you notice the bull in the background? The two boys certainly did! The younger boy's fear is obvious as he clings to his companion. The older boy, armed with a switch, proceeds fearlessly—or so he would like his younger brother to believe.

Once you have described, analyzed, and interpreted this painting, you will be able to decide for yourself whether or not it is successful. Do you find, now that you have gone through the three steps of art criticism, that you have made a judgment about whether Homer's *Crossing the Pasture* is a successful work of art? What is your opinion?

 ## Check Your Understanding

1. What is art criticism?
2. Name the four steps used by art critics. Explain what is done at each step.

STUDIO ACTIVITY

Reading a Credit Line

Look again at the painting in Figure 4–5 on page **66.** You can learn a lot about this work by examining the subject. You can also pick up an important clue by noting its title, *Crossing the Pasture.*

This information and much else appears in the painting's credit line. A **credit line** is *a listing of important facts about an artwork.* Appearing under or near a work, a credit line has six parts. It begins with the artist's name and the title of the artwork. The year the work was created and the art medium or media appear next. After that comes the size of the artwork. The last piece of information is the name of the museum, gallery, or other place in which the work is located. Referring to the credit line of Figure 4–5, you would learn that the work was painted by Winslow Homer in about 1872. The *"c."* before the date means "about." What medium did the artist use?

Every artwork in this book has a credit line. Use the credit lines in Figures 4–1, 4–2, and 4–3 to answer the following:

- Which of the works was painted by artist Pieter de Hooch?
- Which work was painted around 1600?
- What is the name of the artist who painted *Fog Horns?*
- Which of the works is housed in the National Gallery of Art?

 P O R T F O L I O

Write a credit line for the next artwork you complete. Put it in your portfolio with your work.

STUDIO ACTIVITY

Reading a Credit Line

Direct students' attention to the credit line for Figure 4-5. As students discuss the elements in a credit line, ask them to think about why such information is important and how it can be used. Invite them to investigate other credit lines in the book.

ASSESS

■ Self-Assessment

Have students complete the Check Your Understanding questions on this page. Answers are provided below.

■ Reteaching

Have students work in pairs to practice applying the four steps of art criticism to a work of art.

■ Enrichment

Ask students to write a critical review of a program they have seen on TV. Be sure students use the four steps used by art critics.

CLOSE

Have students retrace the steps used in art criticism.

Answers to ✔CHECK YOUR UNDERSTANDING

1. Art criticism is a process of studying works of art to determine if they are successful or not.
2. The steps in art criticism are: description, analysis, interpretation, and judgment. In the description, the critic asks, "What do I see, and what elements of art are predominant?" In the analysis, the critic looks at the composition of the art, asking "How are the principles of art used to organize the elements of art?" In interpreting the art, the critic focuses on the content, asking "What moods, feelings, or ideas are expressed?" In judging the work, the critic asks "Is the work successful?" The answer depends on the answers found in the first three steps.

Critiquing Non-Objective Art

• • • • • • • • • • • • •

FOCUS

☑ OBJECTIVES

After completing this lesson
students will be able to:

• Identify non-objective art.
• Apply the art-criticism
  questions to critique non-
  objective works of art.
• Create a non-objective sound
  design.

☑ SUPPLIES

• Markers and watercolors;
  brushes
• Mixing trays
• Containers of water
• White drawing paper

Resource

■ 4-3 In the Eye of the
  Beholder, TRB page 58
  (appreciating cultural
  diversity)

• • • • • • • • • • • • •

TEACH

■ Motivator

Begin this lesson by briefly reviewing the three ways of measuring success in works of art
and explaining that this lesson will
focus on the second of these:
dealing with composition. Explain
that in order for a work to be
judged successful in terms of
composition it must have **unity.**
Ask them to explain what this
term means to them. Write the
word *unity* on the board. Remind
students that if an artwork has
unity, the different parts in the
work *look* as if they belong
together.

Describing a work of art, you have
learned, means identifying what you see.
Sometimes this is easier said than done. Examine the artwork on this page. Compare it
with the painting in Figure 4–3 on page **64.**
How would you describe these works? What
do you see when you look at each?

In this lesson, you will learn how to apply
the steps of art criticism to works without recognizable subjects.

NON-OBJECTIVE ART

Artists do not work in isolation. Each generation builds on and refines the ideas of the
one that came before. At times, throughout
history, this process has led to startling
changes. It has provided new answers to the
question "What is art?"

One such major breakthrough came in the
early 1900s. For several decades, artists had
been experimenting with distorting shapes

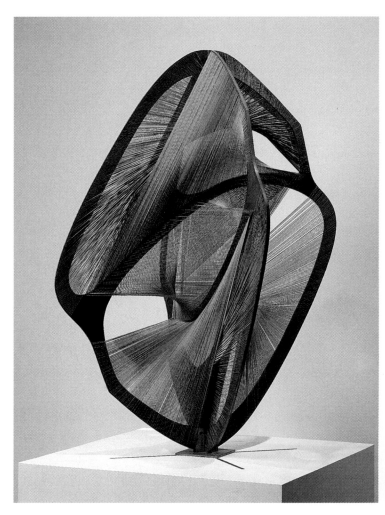

Figure 4–7 **What elements
and principles of art would
you point out during an
analysis of this work. How
is repetition used in this
sculpture?**

Naum Gabo. *Linear Construction
No. 4.* 1962. Bronze, stainless
steel, piano wire. 128.3 × 63.5 ×
63.5 cm (50½ × 25 × 25"). The
Detroit Institute of Arts, Detroit,
Michigan. Gift of W. Hawkins
Ferry.

70   Chapter 4   *Looking at Art*

MEETING STUDENT DIVERSITY

Diverse Discussions   Everyone's opinion is important. Here are suggestions for conducting successful art-
criticism discussions:

• Maintain order. Have students raise their hands to
  speak.
• Resist lecturing.
• Ask students to think and express ideas clearly.

• Demonstrate that *you too are thinking.*
• Avoid efforts at achieving consensus. Students must
  realize that art is open to different interpretations and
  judgments.
• Accept diverse ideas.
• Encourage students to use the steps of art criticism as
  an objective way to evaluate art.

and forms. This new group took matters a step further. They abandoned subject matter altogether. They created non-objective works of art. **Non-objective** means *having no readily identifiable subjects or objects.*

Critiquing a Non-Objective Artwork

In studying non-objective works of art, critics apply the same four-step process outlined in the previous lesson. The main difference comes at the description step. To see this, look again at the sculpture in Figure 4–7. There is no identifiable subject. Even the title provides little help. In *describing* this work, a critic would, therefore, concentrate first on identifying the elements of art in it. He or she would take note of the different lines and forms that are used. Because the work is a sculpture that exists in three dimensions, the critic would pay special attention to the element of space. How would you describe the sculptor's use of space? How would you describe his use of negative space?

Now it is your turn to be a critic. Using the skills you have learned, try applying each of the following art-criticism steps to this artwork:

- **Describing.** How would you describe this sculpture? How many varieties of line have been used? What kinds of geometric or free-form shapes are visible? Is there any color used? Where are negative spaces apparent?
- **Analyzing.** How would you analyze this sculpture? What principle or principles of art have been used to organize the elements of art?
- **Interpreting.** What ideas, moods, and feelings are suggested by this work? Does the sculpture express an idea of some kind?
- **Judging.** Would you say that this work is successful? Does it have unity? What factors contribute to its success or lack of success?

Experimenting with Non-Objective Art

Look once again at the painting in Figure 4–3 on page **64.** This time, notice the title. The artist has created the sensation of sound in this painting. He has done this by carefully arranging colors and shapes. As you gaze at this painting, listen for the deep, muffled song of distant fog horns.

Now try to achieve a similar effect yourself. First choose a familiar sound. It might be the sound of traffic on a busy street. It might be a barking dog or the hum of machinery. Select shapes, lines, and colors that express this sound. Create a visual version of this sound using colored markers and watercolors. Use the markers first. Then blend watercolor hues into your design.

 P O R T F O L I O

For your portfolio, write an explanation of the sound you selected and describe how you created a visual version of this sound.

 Check Your Understanding

1. What is meant by non-objective art?
2. When examining a non-objective artwork, what is identified during the description step?

Have students think about ways to represent sounds in a non-objective painting. Ask how a picture suggesting the rumble of thunder would differ from one representing the whisper of a soft summer breeze. What colors, lines, and shapes would they use to suggest each sound? Discuss sounds that they might wish to express and list them on the board. (Examples: a fire bell, the crashing waves of the sea, a bird call, footsteps crunching in the snow, an ambulance siren.) Demonstrate how they could use a combination of crayon and watercolor to reproduce various sounds.

• • • • • • • • • • • • • •
ASSESS

■ Self-Assessment

Have students complete the Check Your Understanding questions on this page. Answers are provided below.

■ Reteaching

Review with students what non-objective art is. Have students point to some examples in the book.

■ Enrichment

Invite students to research the work of Pablo Picasso. Ask students to choose one of his works of art and write a brief critique of it, using the steps discussed in this lesson.

• • • • • • • • • • • • • •
CLOSE

Ask students to summarize the steps used to critique non-objective art.

Answers to ✔ CHECK YOUR UNDERSTANDING

1. Non-objective art is a term used to describe works with no readily identified subjects or objects.

2. When examining non-objective works of art, the elements of art are identified during description and the principles during analysis.

LESSON 4

Creating a
Realistic
Painting

(pages 72–73)

Lesson Time: 3 hours

• • • • • • • • • • • • •
FOCUS

☑ **OBJECTIVES**

After completing this lesson,
students will be able to:
- Draw a window and the scene
  viewed through the window in
  a realistic style using oil
  pastels.
- Understand the viewer's point
  of view.
- Evaluate and judge their
  drawings in terms of their
  realistic treatment of subject
  matter.

☑ **SUPPLIES**

- Sketch paper and pencils.
- Oil pastels
- White drawing paper

> **Resource**
>
> ■ 4-4 Get Real!,
>   TRB page 60 (art history)

• • • • • • • • • • • • •
TEACH

■ **Vocabulary**

Tell students that Hopper's
paintings are often praised because they succeed in expressing
moods. Ask them what the term
mood refers to. Explain that mood
is a term that refers to *a state of
feelings at a particular time.* Ask
students to write a sentence using
the word *mood.* (Example: The
sunny morning put me in a cheerful mood.) Have them read their
sentences and discuss the different moods identified.

 LESSON 4

Creating a Realistic Painting

The emptiness and gloom of a nation
fallen on hard times would seem like a
strange theme for art. Yet, it is precisely this
theme that runs through the works of American artist Edward Hopper. Hopper lived
through a period called the Great Depression.
This was a time when there was very little
money. Many people in the United States and
abroad were left without jobs or homes. Hopper's paintings accurately capture the mood
of the era. They show lonely, often desperate
people in shabby, rundown rooms.

Figure 4–8 shows one of Hopper's best-
known paintings. Notice the **point of view.**
This is *the angle from which the viewer sees the
scene in an artwork.* Typical of Hopper's work,
we do not see the people in this picture head-
on. Instead, we are given a glimpse of them
through a window.

WHAT YOU WILL LEARN

In this lesson you will use oil pastels to
create your own Hopper "window." Like Figure 4–8, your painting will have a realistic
subject. You point of view, like Hopper's, will
be outside, looking into a lighted room
through a window. It will be nighttime. The
room will have no people. The furniture and
other contents will overlap to indicate space.
These objects will be drawn to show the
mood or personality of the person living or
working in this room.

WHAT YOU WILL NEED

- Pencil and sheets of sketch paper
- Oil pastels
- White drawing paper, 12 x 18 inches
  (30 x 46 cm)

Figure 4–8 Notice the title of the painting. What do you think it means? Why do
you think these people sit idly around the counter of an all-night diner?

Edward Hopper. *Night Hawks.* 1942. Oil on canvas. 84.1 × 152.4 cm (33 × 60″). The Art
Institute of Chicago, Chicago, Illinois. Friends of American Art Collection, 1942.51

72   Chapter 4   *Looking at Art*

---

more about • • •

Edward Hopper   Hopper (1882–1967) was a twentieth
century American painter who worked mainly in New York.
He gained widespread recognition as a realistic painter of
the American scene. However, he once said, "I don't think
I ever tried to paint the American scene; I'm trying to paint
myself." Discuss with students what they think the artist

meant by this statement. If he were indeed trying to paint
himself, what does *Night Hawks* tell us about him? Hopper was a shy, reserved man who preferred a public image
of an uneducated and backward artist working in a realistic tradition. His paintings, however, reveal the artist's own
sensitive, strongly felt emotions.

WHAT YOU WILL DO

1. Begin by looking closely at the building across from the all-night diner in Figure 4–8. Study the row of dark windows on the second floor. Try to picture the kinds of rooms behind those windows. Decide whether they are fancy apartments, drab hotel rooms, offices, or something else. Think about the outside of the building. What material is it made of?

2. Imagine that the lights were turned on inside one of the rooms. Make several sketches of what your mind "sees." Draw a window frame like the one in Figure 4–8, only larger. As you sketch, continue to imagine the contents of the room. You might include wallpaper, carpeting, and other furniture. As you work, ask yourself, "What kind of person lives or works here?" Decide what clues you can provide in your drawing to tell viewers something about the mood or personality of this person.

3. Transfer your best drawing to the white drawing paper. Work lightly in pencil. Make the outside wall of the building look like brick, stone, or wood.

4. Color your picture using oil pastels. Select colors that will give your room a "personality" to match that of its imaginary occupant.

5. Like Hopper, avoid small, unnecessary details. Lay one color over another to create textures. Overlap shapes and forms to suggest space inside the room.

6. Display your finished drawing in a horizontal row along with those of classmates.

EXAMINING YOUR WORK

- **Describe** Are the objects inside the room easy to identify? What texture did you use for the outside of your building?
- **Analyze** Did you show the different values for objects inside the lighted room compared to those in the darkness outside? Did you overlap shapes and forms to suggest space?
- **Interpret** Does your drawing offer clues about the mood or personality of the person who might live or work in the room?
- **Judge** Do you think your drawing is successful? Does it present the subject matter in a realistic way?

Figure 4–9 **Student work. Hopper windows.**

Try This! STUDIO OPTION

■ Create another version of your Hopper window. This scene is to be set during the day and is to reflect a mood opposite the one in your first drawing. This time the point of view will be looking through the window to the outside. Use pastels for the window frame and watercolors for the landscape out of doors.

Lesson 4 *Creating a Realistic Painting* **73**

TECHNIQUE TIP

Achieving Texture and Dimension Review with students the guidelines for using oil pastels (see Handbook page 281). Then give them ample time and opportunity to experiment with this medium to create texture and dimension. Remind them to lay one color over another to build a sense of texture.

To create dimension and a sense of space within the scene they are painting, students should overlap the various shapes and forms. For example, a chair at an angle in front of a table suggests depth and space. Point out techniques used in other paintings within the text to give students additional models to emulate.

■ Aesthetics

Ask students if they think the subject matter in Hopper's painting should be an important consideration when judging it. Do they feel that this work could also be judged in terms of its composition and content? Remind students that many artworks can be judged using all three aesthetic views.

■ Studio Skills

Have students speculate about the rooms behind the windows in *Night Hawks*. Discuss the furniture and other objects that might be in those rooms and how these might reflect the mood of the occupant. Encourage students to brainstorm ideas, then develop their ideas in sketches. Provide time for them to experiment with the oil pastels before beginning work on their finished drawings.

ASSESS

■ Self-Assessment

Have students use Examining Your Work to evaluate their realistic paintings.

■ Reteaching

Review with students the four steps in art criticism.

■ Enrichment

Assign volunteers to find a reproduction of Hopper's *Room in New York* (1932, University of Nebraska Art Galleries, Lincoln, Nebraska). Have students compare the mood of that painting with the moods found in some of theirs. How were the various moods achieved?

CLOSE

Have students summarize why they think Hopper's *Night Hawks* is or is not a successful painting.

LESSON TIME: 90 minutes

• • • • • • • • • • • • • •
FOCUS

☑OBJECTIVES

After completing this lesson, students will be able to:

• Create a design using the letters of an expressive word and a background of color bands that all together imply the emotion conveyed by that particular word.

• Describe, analyze, interpret, and judge their design in terms of its success in expressing an emotion.

☑SUPPLIES

• Sheets of sketch paper and pencils

• Sheets of white drawing paper

• Tempera or acrylic paint, mixing trays, brushes

• Water and paper towels

Resources

■ 4-5 More Mood, TRB page 62 (studio)

■ 4-6 In the Mood, TRB page 64 (art history)

• • • • • • • • • • • • • •
TEACH

■ Motivator

Have students examine the engraving by Albrecht Dürer and ask them to describe what they see. Is the feeling or mood of this artwork easily understood? What elements and principles has the artist used to stress that feeling or mood?

74

Creating an Expressive Word Design

Have you ever had one of those days in which nothing seemed to go right? Maybe, like the young woman in Figure 4–10, you felt "blue." Study this fine-art print. Notice that the artist has not shown us much of the woman's face. We are still able to "read" her mood by observing her body language. What details of the woman's posture help us identify how she is feeling? What other moods can you identify from the way a person sits or stands?

WHAT YOU WILL LEARN

The artist has taken one approach to capturing a particular mood or feeling. In this lesson, you will take another approach. You will communicate the mood of your choice through a word, written in large block letters, rather than an image. You will use variety of shapes and colors to create a background that emphasizes the emotion suggested by this word.

Figure 4–10 What does the subject's body language reveal about her mood?

Albrecht Dürer. *Melencholia 1.* 1514. Engraving. 24.1 × 18.6 cm (9½ × 7⁵⁄₁₆″). The Metropolitan Museum of Art, New York, New York. Harris Brisbane Dick Fund, 1943.

74   Chapter 4   *Looking at Art*

RESOURCES BEYOND THE CLASSROOM

Local Manufacturers and Printers   Tour a local manufacturer of art supplies where students might learn how paint or ink is made, how fabric is woven, or how wood is milled. Such tours can alert students to potential hazards of the materials they use and show them appropriate safety procedures.

If feasible, arrange a tour of a local printer. Ask to see the printing process used: relief, offset, and/or gravure; or possibly screen process, collotype, or flexographic printing. Encourage students to ask lots of questions and to take notes. Ask to have each step demonstrated and find out which processes are used for the fine arts.

WHAT YOU WILL NEED

- Pencil and sketch paper
- White drawing paper, 9 x 12 inches (23 x 30 cm)
- Tempera paint
- Mixing trays
- Brushes
- Water

WHAT YOU WILL DO

1. With classmates, brainstorm words naming moods and emotions. Possibilities include *happy, tired, worried, angry,* and *bored.*

2. Choose one of the words. On sketch paper, write the word out in large block letters. Experiment with different letter designs that communicate the mood you have chosen. You might, for example, use rounded, overlapping letters for an upbeat mood. Letters with straight edges and sharp points might communicate a negative mood, such as anger. Letters may be all capitals or upper and lower case but should fill the page.

3. Transfer your best design to the sheet of drawing paper. Still working in pencil, create a background design. This is to have the form of thick and thin bands extending horizontally or vertically from one edge of the paper to the other. As with the shape of the letters, the bands should reflect the word you are using. Zigzag lines might be used for the word tense. Curved lines signal a more peaceful mood.

4. Select a color scheme that emphasizes the emotion or feeling of your word. Again, think about the expressive nature of

- **Describe** Is the word you selected easily read? Did you use large block letters to write this word?
- **Analyze** Did you create a background made up of bands of color? Did these colors contrast with one another to create variety?
- **Interpret** Does your design reflect the mood or feeling of the word? Do the shapes and colors help emphasize that emotion?
- **Judge** Does your design communicate an emotion with letters, shapes, and colors? Is this a successful work of art?

color. Boldly contrasting hues, intensities, and values might be used to express tension. Hues, intensities, and values that are harmonious could express peace.

5. Paint the background bands in the colors you have selected. Do not paint the letters themselves.

Figure 4–11 Student work. An expressive word.

COMPUTER OPTION

Try This!

■ Choose a word related to a mood or feeling. Select the Text tool and type the word. From the Font menu, choose a typeface that reflects the mood of your choice. For example, use a playful font, such as Hobo, for an upbeat mood. Select the entire word, and drag the corner of the surrounding box to enlarge the word. Fill the entire screen. Fill your word with a color or preset pattern that helps communicate the mood you have chosen.

Lesson 5 *Creating an Expressive Word Design* **75**

■ Art Criticism

Divide the class into three groups of art critics with differing aesthetic points of view. One group feels that subject is the primary concern, another that composition is the determining factor, and the third that content is most important. Have each group critique Figure 4-10 using the art-criticism questions of description, analysis, interpretation, and judgment.

■ Studio Skills

Demonstrate ways to create simplified block letters. The letters must be thick and large and may overlap slightly, but where this occurs, erase overlapping lines. Show students how to create different kinds of horizontal and vertical bands that vary in width to go behind the letters.

ASSESS

■ Self-Assessment

Have students use Examining Your Work to evaluate their art.

■ Reteaching

Work with students to identify moods in art and type designs.

■ Enrichment

Ask students to find examples of expressive word designs found in print advertising. Have them display the examples with an exhibit of the students' designs.

CLOSE

Have students critique each other's expressive word designs.

MEETING SPECIAL NEEDS

Overcoming the Odds People with disabilities have to consciously and proactively work to overcome conditions and frequently display the strength of character that goes along with hopefulness and overcoming. People with some disabilities, such as athletes who use wheelchairs and prosthetic limbs, visibly show to the world inspiring examples of the attributes of overcoming and hopefulness. In the students' designs, encourage them to show not just the positive elements, but also somehow represent, perhaps abstractly, the negative elements against which their hope is pitted.

LESSON 6

Creating an Abstract Figure

LESSON 6

Creating an Abstract Figure

(pages 76–77)

Lesson Time: 90 minutes

. . . .
FOCUS

☑OBJECTIVES

After completing this lesson, students will be able to:

- Define *abstract art*.
- Create a simplified abstract shape using a single, continuous line.
- Describe, analyze, and interpret their designs and judge them on the basis of composition.

☑SUPPLIES

- Pencils and sheets of sketch paper
- Pieces of colored yarn or heavy cord about 60 inches long
- Liquid starch, wax paper, plastic mixing bowls

Resources

- ◾ 4-7 Henri Matisse, TRB page 66 (artist profile)
- ◾ 4-8 anyone lived, TRB page 67 (art criticism)

. . . .
TEACH

◾ Motivator

Bring in several examples of paintings by Henri Matisse. Ask students to express their opinions of his style. What elements and principles seemed to appeal to him? Explain that he used shape and color to express joy and beauty. Direct attention to Figure 4-12. Point out that in an effort to eliminate detail, Matisse often distorted the shapes in his works.

76

Non-objective art, as you learned in Lesson 3, began in the early 1900s. By avoiding subject matter, non-objective artists created a new means of self-expression. Since that time, other artists have taken a more middle-of-the-road approach to subject matter. They have produced art that is **abstract.** This means *having a recognizable subject that is shown in an unrealistic manner.*

The work in Figure 4–12 is an example of abstract art. Its subject is a character from Greek mythology. His name is Icarus. According to legend, Icarus tried to fly using wings held together with wax. Ignoring warnings, Icarus flew too close to the sun. The wax melted, and the youth fell to his death. Study this work of art. Can you recognize it as a falling figure?

Figure 4–12   How would you describe the use of negative space in this work? Why do you think the artist chose to make the figure abstract?

Henri Matisse. *Icarus.* Plate VIII from *Jazz.* 1947. Pochoir, printed in color. Each single page: 21.1 × 32.6 cm (8⅓ × 12⅝"). The Museum of Modern Art, New York, New York. The Louis E. Stern Collection.

76   Chapter 4   *Looking at Art*

CURRICULUM CONNECTIONS

Language Arts   For centuries, artists and writers alike have reinterpreted and retold the stories from Greek mythology. Tell students that myths are traditional stories that are usually about a superhuman being. Myths often try to explain why things are the way they are in the natural world. It is possible that your students may be studying ancient Greek culture in their social studies classes. Invite them to share what they know of Icarus, Daedalus, and other mythological figures. Encourage students to explore other Greek myths. See *Mythology* by Edith Hamilton (Boston: Little Brown, 1942) or *A Book of Myths* by Thomas Bulfinch (New York: Macmillan, 1942).

WHAT YOU WILL LEARN

Using your imagination, you will create a simplified abstract shape. The shape will be of a falling figure. The image will be made with a single, continuous line. You will use a length of colored yarn to form the line. The same thickness of the line throughout will add harmony to your work.

WHAT YOU WILL NEED

- Pencil and sketch paper, 12 x 18 inches (30 x 46 cm)
- Waxed paper
- Transparent or masking tape
- Yarn, about 60 inches (152 cm) in length
- Large bowl
- White glue, thinned with water

WHAT YOU WILL DO

1. Study Figure 4–12. Notice the way the artist has captured the sense of a figure falling through space. Trace your finger around the outline of the abstract shape of this figure.
2. Complete several drawings of your own version of the falling Icarus. As in Figure 4–12, your work should be abstract. Use a single continuous pencil line to create your figures.
3. Transfer your best drawing to a sheet of sketch paper. Make a heavy line using pencil. Cover the drawing completely with a sheet of waxed paper that is smaller than the page. Secure the waxed paper in place with tape. The drawing should be clearly visible through the waxed paper.
4. Draw a line of white glue over the pencil line. Carefully lay the yarn on the line of glue. Allow time for the yarn to dry.

EXAMINING YOUR WORK

- **Describe**   Is your work easily recognized as an abstract figure?
- **Analyze**   Did you use one continuous line to create the abstract shape? Did the use of a line with the same thickness throughout add harmony to your design?
- **Interpret**   Does your figure appear to be falling through space?
- **Judge**   Using composition to measure accomplishment, is your work a success? Why or why not?

5. Once the glue is thoroughly dry, the yarn will be stiff and hold its shape. Carefully lift the shape off the waxed paper. Use thread to suspend your Icarus figure from a clothesline or the ceiling of the classroom.

Figure 4–13   **Student work. Abstract figures.**

 Try This!

STUDIO OPTIONS

■ To add color to the shape of your figure, cut and glue on pieces of colored tissue paper.

■ To make a more three-dimensional form, create basic body shapes first. Cut out several of the same body shapes from analogous colors of construction paper. Overlap them to create a sense of movement. Glue them together using small "spacers" cut from cardboard. Arrange a display with the work of other students.

Lesson 6   *Creating an Abstract Figure*   **77**

TECHNIQUE TIP

Working with Glue and Yarn   Show students how yarn can be used to outline the shape of an abstract figure. Explain that when the yarn is laid in glue and allowed to stiffen, it will hold its shape. Students can place a large pencil sketch beneath a sheet of wax paper and draw a glue line on the paper of the desired shape. For a more three-dimensional appearance, place wadded newspaper at different positions under the pencil sketch and wax paper to create an uneven surface.

■ Aesthetics

Tell students to imagine they are describing Matisse's cutout to a friend over the telephone. Would they spend as much time identifying the elements of art as they would the subject? What does this tell them about how they might go about judging this artwork?

■ Cultural Diversity

Ask students to locate and read myths from other cultures, such as African, Norse, Chinese, or Native American. If possible, have students also locate artworks that deal with mythological characters or creatures from those cultures.

■ Art History

Appoint a team of students to find and bring to class a picture of Matisse's cutout *La Negresse* in the National Gallery. How does this work, inspired by the American entertainer, Josephine Baker, compare with *Icarus?* Ask students if they think cutouts like these are historically important. Why or why not?

• • • • • • • • • • • • • • •
ASSESS

■ Self-Assessment

Have students use Examining Your Work to evaluate their art.

■ Reteaching

Ask students to explain what makes Matisse's image of Icarus abstract.

■ Enrichment

You may want to ask students to refer to Bruegel's *Fall of Icarus* in Chapter 12 (Figure 12-19, Connections page 240). Ask: How has each artist treated his subject matter? Have students write a brief comparison of the two pieces.

• • • • • • • • • • • • • • •
CLOSE

Have students review the concept of abstraction.

CONNECTIONS   *Technology*

Exploring Space

OBJECTIVES

After completing this feature, students will be able to:

- Explain how we can learn about seventeenth-century astronomy by studying Vermeer's painting.
- Describe some scientific advancements made in the field of astronomy in the twentieth century.

Teaching the Connection

- Have students read the feature on this page.
- Ask volunteers to share what they know about astronomy. What are the names of the nine planets? *(Earth, Jupiter, Venus, Mercury, Mars, Pluto, Neptune, Saturn, Uranus.)* What Polish astronomer discovered that the planets revolve around the sun? *(Nicolaus Copernicus.)*
- Tell students that Jan Vermeer (1632–1675) is considered one of the greatest Dutch painters in history. Although only 35 of his paintings exist today, he is considered a master of composition. Most of his works, including *The Astronomer,* are interior scenes of Dutch life.

Answers to Making the Connection

- He is looking at a globe and a book. A measuring device and a chart are also in the room.
- Seventeenth-century astronomers used charts and globes. They did not have the sophisticated equipment astronomers use today.
- Johannes Kepler formulated the laws of planetary motion. Sir Isaac Newton developed the laws of universal gravitation and motion. Galileo discovered the four largest satellites of Jupiter.

Exploring Space

Jan Vermeer van Delft. *The Astronomer.* 1668. Oil on canvas. 51.5 × 45.5 cm (20¼ × 18″). The Louvre, Paris, France. Erich Lessing/Art Resource, NY.

Since the dawn of time, people have dreamed of exploring space. They looked to the heavens and questioned what was out there. Did other civilizations exist somewhere in the universe?

In the seventeenth century, when Jan Vermeer painted *The Astronomer,* major breakthroughs provided clues into the solar system. One important development was the telescope. Galileo, an Italian astronomer, developed a telescope that magnified objects by 20 times. Using this telescope, Galileo saw that the surface of the moon was made of mountains and craters.

It was 300 years later, however, before people were actually able to reach the moon. In the middle of the twentieth century, advances in technology finally provided the means necessary for space travel. In 1969, astronaut Neil Armstrong landed on the moon. He took "one small step for man, one giant leap for mankind."

Today, scientists send satellites into space to orbit the Earth. These satellites observe, measure, and record information that would be impossible to obtain from Earth. Weather satellites, for example, provide data that helps forecasters predict weather conditions around the world.

MAKING THE CONNECTION

- What clues tell you that the subject of Vermeer's painting is an astronomer?
- By studying this painting, what can you learn about astronomy in the seventeenth century?
- Find out more about astronomy. Besides the telescope, what other developments occurred during the 1600s?

INTERNET ACTIVITY

Visit Glencoe's Fine Arts Web Site for students at:

http://www.glencoe.com/sec/art/students

INTERNET ACTIVITY

Curriculum Links   Explore World Wide Web links related to the content of each chapter in this book. These pre-selected links can be found under *Curriculum Links* in the *Teacher Resources* section of Glencoe's Fine Arts Site. Find the chapter you are studying in the Table of Contents and click on one of the highlighted or underlined "hot links" that will transport you to an appropriate, previewed site guaranteed to expand your students' experience. Many of these sites offer views of extensive art collections from museums and art galleries. Cultural connections will link students to Internet sites around the world. They can learn first-hand about art, artists, and art history. Find us at **http://www.glencoe.com/sec/art**

CHAPTER 4
REVIEW

 BUILDING VOCABULARY

Number a sheet of paper from 1 to 10. After each number, write the term from the box that matches each description below.

abstract	content
aesthetics	credit line
aesthetic view	non-objective
art critic	point of view
composition	subject

1. The message, idea, or feeling expressed by a work of art.
2. A person whose job is studying, understanding, and judging works of art.
3. Art with a recognizable subject that is shown in an unrealistic manner.
4. Art with no readily identifiable subjects or objects.
5. An image viewers can easily identify.
6. The way the principles are used to organize the elements of art.
7. The study of the nature of beauty and art.
8. A listing of important facts about an artwork.
9. The angle from which the viewer sees the scene in an artwork.
10. An idea or school of thought on what is most important in a work of art.

 REVIEWING ART FACTS

Number a sheet of paper from 11 to 15. Answer each question in a complete sentence.

11. Why do students of art usually accept more than one aesthetic view?
12. What are the four steps of art criticism?
13. What kinds of art criticism questions join an art element with an art principle?
14. Why is it impossible to measure the success of a non-objective artwork in terms of subject?
15. When examining a non-objective artwork, what is identified during description?

 THINKING ABOUT ART

1. **Interpretation.** Imagine that two critics are examining the same work of art. Each comes up with a different interpretation. What reasons can you think of that might explain this?
2. **Extend.** Do you think a critic could ever change his or her mind about an artwork's success or lack of success? Why or why not?
3. **Extend.** Which of the art-criticism questions do you find the most difficult to ask? Which is hardest to answer? Explain your answers.

MAKING ART CONNECTIONS

1. **Language Arts.** Review the artworks in this chapter. Select one that might be a good illustration for a short story or poem. Write the story or poem.
2. **Community Connection.** Find a work of art in your community. You might choose a public statue or other well-known work. Apply the four art-criticism steps to the work. Write your report on the work in a way that could be understood by readers who know nothing about art or art criticism. Use the classroom computer to publish your report. Share the report with family members and friends.

Chapter 4 Review **79**

Art Through the Ages

(pages 80–81)

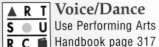
Resources

- 5-12 Chapter Test, TRB page 87
- Transparency CC-5, Temple at Angkor Wat
- Transparency TR-5, *Janitor* by Duane Hanson
- Fine Art Print 9, *Theresa, Countess Kinsky* by Marie-Louise Elisabeth Vigée-Lebrun

Voice/Dance
Use Performing Arts Handbook page 317 to learn how Tandy Beal and Bobby McFerrin use an interactive creative process called improvisation.

NATIONAL STANDARDS

This chapter addresses the following National Standards for the Visual Arts:

1. (a, b)	**4.** (a, b, c)
2. (a, b, c)	**5.** (a, c)
3. (a, b)	**6.** (a, b)

80

Figure 5–1   **Notice the way in which the artist interacts with the viewer. What mood is expressed by this work?**

Judith Leyster. *Self-portrait.* c. 1630. Oil on canvas. 74.6 × 65.7 cm (29⅜ × 25⅞"). National Gallery of Art, Washington, D.C. Gift of Mr. and Mrs. Robert Woods Bliss.

FEATURED ARTISTS

Exekias	Claude Monet
Orazio Gentileschi	Elizabeth Murray
Judith Leyster	Maruyama Okyo
Helen Lundeberg	Jan Steen

CHAPTER 5

Art Through the Ages

In art, background information is important. Look at the painting at the left. The work shows the artist turning from her self-portrait to look at the viewer. By looking at the credit line, you learn that it is a self-portrait. Take a closer look at the credit line, however. Notice not only the questions it answers—who painted the work and when—but also the ones it raises: Is this painting similar to others done around the same time? What other works did this artist produce?

In this chapter you will learn how to ask and answer such questions. You will learn how the time and place in which artists worked have a strong effect on the style and content of their artworks.

PORTFOLIO IDEAS

A strong art portfolio reflects what you learn about art history as well as art techniques. Make sure to include written entries that demonstrate your ability to describe an artwork from the art historian's point of view—by telling who created the work, and when and where it was created. Show that you understand how time and place influence an artist.

OBJECTIVES

After completing this chapter, you will be able to:
- Explain why art history is important.
- Recognize the changes and similarities among artworks through the ages.
- Understand the goals of different cultures and art movements.
- Create works of art of different cultures and times.

WORDS YOU WILL LEARN

applied art
architecture
art historians
art movement
bust
contours
diorama
fine art
hieroglyphic
painted screen
Renaissance
symbol

■ Chapter Overview

Having a general understanding of art history is fundamental to students' appreciation of art. In this chapter, students will look at the effects of time and place on artists and their works. They will begin to see the changes and similarities among artworks, cultures, and movements through the ages.

■ Chapter Motivator

Tell students that in this chapter they will have an opportunity to get a behind-the-scenes view of art—the story behind much of the art created over many centuries and all over the world. As they take this journey, encourage students to ask questions about art, artists, and their time and place.

■ Examining the Artwork

Have students try to guess what kind of personality Judith Leyster had based on how she looks in her self-portrait. Point out how she interacts with the viewer.

National Museum of Women in the Arts

You may wish to use the National Museum of Women in the Arts videodisc and/or CD-ROM. The videodisc features a bar code guide, and the interactive CD-ROM provides stimulating activities.

81

DEVELOPING A PORTFOLIO

Parental Review Periodically, you may wish to have parents review the student portfolio entries. This not only gives the student additional feedback and reinforcement, but it also helps communicate the purpose and scope of the art class. Here are some questions for parents to consider as they review their child's portfolio:
- What was the goal of the work reviewed?

- What was the student trying to do or say?
- Why did the student make the decisions he or she did?
- Why did the student choose to include this entry?
  Invite parents to share with you their comments. For more information, see *Portfolio and Assessment Techniques,* the booklet that accompanies this program.

LESSON 1

Art of Long Ago

No artist works completely alone. Artists of each age, rather, study and learn from works created in ages past. The same may be said of **art historians.** These are *people who study art of different ages and cultures.* Like art critics, art historians examine and analyze art. Unlike critics, art historians are not content to look only at artworks. Their job is to look *beyond* them. They record milestones in art and changes in the way artists work.

In this chapter, you will journey back through the ages. You will learn about some of these milestones and changes. Your journey will begin with a look at art of earlier times.

ART OF ANCIENT EGYPT

Have you ever followed a brook or stream to its source? If we follow the long, twisting "stream" of art history to its source, we end up on the banks of an actual river. That river is the Nile. The time is 5,000 years ago. The place is Egypt. There, in the cradle of Western civilization, powerful kings called *pharaohs* ruled. Farming and trade thrived. So did art.

Rules of the Egyptian Artist

The Egyptians built mighty temples and monuments. It was with an eye toward decorating these structures that much of their art was created. Study the relief carving in Figure 5–2. This work probably once graced a pharaoh's tomb. The subject is the Egyptian

Figure 5–2   Look at the subject of this sculpture. What does it reveal about the Egyptians' system of beliefs?

Egyptian. *Thoth, God of Learning and Patron of Scribes.* Egyptian. 26th Dynasty, 663–525 B.C. (Late period). Slate relief. 36.5 × 12 × 1 cm (14⅜ × 4¾ × 7⁄₁₆"). Dallas Museum of Art, Dallas, Texas. Gift of Elsa von Seggern.

FOCUS

☑ OBJECTIVES

After completing this lesson, students will be able to:

• Understand the work of an art historian.
• Describe the styles of ancient Roman and Greek art.
• Differentiate between fine art and applied art.
• Design and draw a bottle shape that depicts a contemporary event.

☑ SUPPLIES

• Pencils and sketch paper
• White drawing paper
• Markers, oil pastels

Resources

- 5-1 Rivers of Life, TRB page 73 (appreciating cultural diversity)
- 5-2 Fine or Applied?, TRB page 75 (art criticism)

TEACH

■ Motivator

Write the word *civilization* on the board and ask students what this means. Tell students that civilization is a stage of development in which people gather to form towns, conduct trade, and generally try to make life safer and more productive. Some historians believe that civilization and recorded history began between 4000 and 3000 B.C. in several areas including the Near East, India, and China. Have students find these locations on a map.

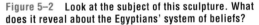

CURRICULUM CONNECTIONS

Social Studies   Have students find Egypt on a world map. Ask them what they think of when they think of Egypt. (Many will mention the pyramids.) Explain that the pyramids are just one aspect of the ancient Egyptian culture. Building these huge structures required the efforts of 100,000 men for thirty years. Workers labored to stack 2.3 million blocks of stone to heights of 480 feet (146.3 m). The stone blocks, each averaging 2.5 tons, were fitted precisely together and covered with a smooth layer of polished white limestone. Ask students if they know why the pyramids were built *(to house the dead bodies of the pharaoh, the queen, and their immediate family, the most important people in Egyptian society.)*

god of learning. The figure has a human body and the head of a bird, specifically an ibis. This long-beaked creature was one of many animals the Egyptians worshiped. They believed the ibis possessed special powers.

Did you notice anything unusual about the way the figure is shown? Some body parts, including the head and arms, appear as they would if they were viewed from the side. Others, such as the shoulders, are shown as if they are seen from the front. This odd mix-and-match might seem at first to be a mistake. In fact, it is common to Egyptian art. It reflects certain strict rules Egyptian artists were forced to follow. The rules required that each body part be shown from its most familiar angle. What parts besides those mentioned above are shown as side views? Which are treated as views from the front?

ART OF ANCIENT GREECE

While Egypt was still at its peak, another great empire took root some 500 miles to the north. This was Greece. Greece reached its peak during the fourth and fifth centuries B.C. This was a time known as the Golden Age. It was called the Golden Age because it produced great writers and thinkers. It produced great political leaders. It also produced great artists.

Greek Vases

One of the most powerful leaders and influential thinkers of the Golden Age was a man named Pericles (**pehr**-ih-kleez). Pericles loved beauty and preached its importance. The aesthetic ideals Pericles held sacred may be seen in everything the Greeks created. Beauty can be found in the perfectly proportioned temples of the period. It is reflected in the idealized sculptures of gods and athletes. It also appears in carefully designed vases such as the one in Figure 5–3.

Examine this art object. Vases like this are examples of **applied art.** This is *art made to be useful as well as visually pleasing.* Applied art is usually seen in contrast with **fine art,** or *art made*

Figure 5–3   Notice how line has been used to suggest movement. What art principles have been used to organize this vase painting?

Greek. Exekias. *Quadriga Wheeling Right.* Slip-decorated earthenware. 46.2 cm (18⅛"). Toledo Museum of Art, Toledo, Ohio.

to be enjoyed visually, not used. In this program, you will see many examples of each type of art.

Like other Greek vases, this one is remarkable for the beauty of its form. It is equally noteworthy for the quality of the painting that decorates it. The painting was done by Exekias (ex-**zee**-kee-uhs), the most famous of Greek vase painters. It shows a chariot led by a team of four spirited horses. Notice the air of excitement in the work. What art elements contribute to this feeling? What principles of art are used to organize them?

Lesson 1   *Art of Long Ago*   **83**

■ Cultural Diversity

Explain to students that the painted vessels of ancient Greece are generally called vases, but they were intended to hold more than just flowers. The Greeks designed each vase to serve a specific purpose, creating shapes to fill every possible need, from large storage jars to delicate drinking cups. Ask students to research the design and purpose of vases and similar vessels in other cultures. Bring in photocopies of examples from China, Australia, Native American cultures, and African cultures. One source on ancient Native American clay pots is the Caldecott Honor Book *When Clay Sings* by Baylor and Bahti [New York: Macmillan (Alladin) 1972].

■ Art History

Point out the locations of Greece and Rome on a map. Tell students that the Western world owes a debt of gratitude to the ancient Greeks and Romans. The Greeks made the first recorded contribution to Western philosophy, science, and art. The Romans' interest in engineering, law, and government built on the Greeks' contribution. Ask students to discuss how such areas of interest and expertise could influence artists and their works.

Art Criticism

Ask students to explain how any examination of a Greek vase painting is really an examination of two works at the same time. Would it be possible to judge one of these works a success and the other a failure? If so, how would they judge the complete work of art? Students should recognize that a thorough critique of a Greek vase must take into account the vase itself as well as the painting on it.

ART OF ANCIENT ROME

Despite its greatness, Greece suffered from fighting within the empire. As a nation divided, it was doomed. After 1,300 years of almost continuous strife, Greece fell. The people who conquered it were the Romans.

Although Greek power came to an end as Rome grew in strength, Greek influence continued on. The Romans admired Greek art. Following their conquest of Greece in 146 B.C., they shipped many Greek art treasures to their homeland. They also hired many Greek artists to work for them.

Roman Portrait Sculpture

Roman artists were skilled at creating life-like sculptures. Like the Greeks, they made statues of important people such as rulers.

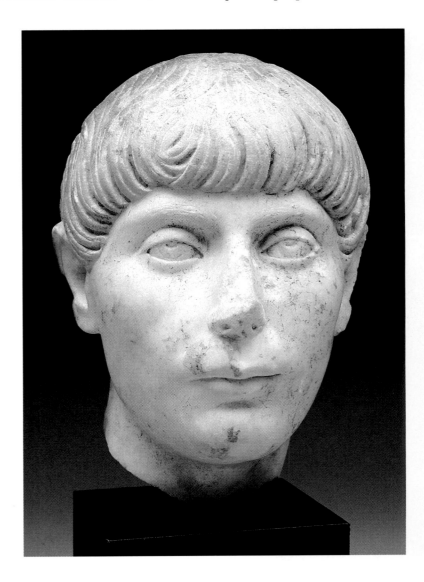

Figure 5–4 This face looks like one you might see on the street today. What quality of the work accounts for this?

Roman. *Head of a Young Man.* A.D. 100–130. Marble. 22.5 × 16.5 cm (8⅞ × 6½"). Dallas Museum of Art, Dallas, Texas. Anonymous gift in memory of Edward Marcus.

─ *more about* ● ● ● ─

Greek Vase Painting   Unfortunately, no examples of Greek painting still exist. However, we can get an idea of what they may have looked like by examining images found on Greek vases that *have* survived.

Early Greek vase paintings of people and the Greek gods were little more than stick figures. The style evolved until the figures became more lifelike and lively. The style of these vase paintings also changed from the **black figure** to the more elegant and detailed **red figure** style.

For more information about how archaeologists use ancient pottery to learn about the past, have students read *Fired Up! Making Pottery in Ancient Times* (Minneapolis: Lerner, 1993).

Unlike the Greeks, who always showed the entire figure in their sculptures, Roman artists instead focused on heads and busts. A **bust** is *a sculpture that shows a person's head, shoulders, and upper chest.*

Many wealthy Romans had busts made of themselves and their families. These were placed in the subject's home. One such portrait sculpture appears in Figure 5–4. It is a marble head of a young man. Clearly, the artist made no effort to flatter the sitter. Rather, the sculpture captures in great detail the likeness of a real person, blemishes and all. Inspect this work. In what ways is it similar to other portrait sculptures you have seen? In what ways is it different? Would a critic taking the content view praise this work? Why or why not?

Check Your Understanding

1. What is the job of an art historian?
2. Why did Egyptian artists always show the human figure in the same unusual way?
3. When did ancient Greece reach its peak? When and by whom was it conquered?
4. How did Roman sculptures of people differ from Greek sculptures of people?
5. What is the difference between applied art and fine art?

STUDIO ACTIVITY

Making a Bottle Decoration

In its day, the vase in Figure 5–3 was admired not only for its beauty. It was also prized for the practical purpose it served—storing water.

Look again at Figure 5–3, specifically at the painting on the vase. This painting portrays a chariot race, a sporting event of the period. Think of a sporting event of your own time. Then select a familiar vase shape on which to record this event. One possibility would be the type of bottle in which commercial sports drinks are sold. Make a pencil drawing of your bottle shape. Your drawing should be large enough to fill a 9 x 12-inch (23 x 30-cm) sheet of white drawing paper. Decorate this shape with a picture of the present-day event you have chosen. Design your picture to fit the bottle shape. Complete your drawing with markers or oil pastels. Choose a color scheme similar to that used in the Greek vase painting.

PORTFOLIO

Imagine how your vase would have been used in ancient Greek history. Write a short paragraph telling why it was made and where it would have been kept. Keep your written description with your vase in your portfolio.

STUDIO ACTIVITY

Making a Bottle Decoration

Before students choose an event to depict on their bottle design, ask them to imagine that their bottle design will go into a time capsule to be viewed in the year A.D. 3000. Ask: What do you want to share about today's culture?

ASSESS

■ **Self-Assessment**

Have students complete the Check Your Understanding questions on this page. Answers are provided below.

■ **Reteaching**

Ask students to give examples of the differences between fine art and applied art.

■ **Enrichment**

Invite students to respond to a classmate's comment that Greek vase paintings lacked interest and excitement. Ask them what they would point to in Exekias's artwork, for example, to convince others that Greek vase paintings are worthy of close examination.

CLOSE

Have students explain what an art historian would want to know about their bottle design.

Answers to ✔CHECK YOUR UNDERSTANDING

1. An art historian studies art of different ages and cultures.
2. Ancient Egyptian artists were required to follow certain strict rules in portraying the human form.
3. The ancient Greek civilization reached its peak during the fourth and fifth centuries. It was conquered by the Romans in 146 B.C.
4. Greek artists of people always showed the entire figure, but Roman artists often created portrait heads and busts.
5. Applied art is art made to be useful as well as visually pleasing. Fine art is art made to be enjoyed visually, not used.

☑ OBJECTIVES

After completing this lesson, students will be able to:

• Design and create an Egyptian tomb painting.

• Describe, analyze, interpret, and judge their own paintings.

☑ SUPPLIES

• Pencils, sketch paper
• White drawing paper
• Fine-tipped black marker
• Tempera paints; mixing tray
• Medium and fine brushes
• Paper towels
• Colored construction paper
• Scissors, glue; crayons

Resource

■ 5-3 Reading Pictures, TRB page 76 (reproducible master)

• • • • • • • • • • • • •
TEACH

■ Motivator

Bring in or create a simple example of pictographic writing to share with students. Ask them to try writing a few sentences using mostly simple pictures. Have them try to read each other's sentences. Point out that the ancient Egyptians also used symbols and pictures in their writing, called hieroglyphics.

86

LESSON 2
Egyptian Tomb Painting

Look back at the Egyptian relief sculpture in Figure 5–2 on page **82.** This work teaches us about the ancient Egyptian system of beliefs. The same may be said of the painting in Figure 5–5. The work is from the tomb of an Egyptian pharaoh named Sethi. He is the figure pictured on the right. With him is the goddess Hathor. According to Egyptian myth, Hathor was the goddess of the sky. She was also queen of heaven. It appears that Hathor is about to take the pharaoh's hand, as if to lead him somewhere. Where might she be preparing to lead the fallen pharaoh?

Look more closely at this painting. Did you notice the abstract shapes in the rounded boxes? They appear in the picture above the head of Sethi. These are examples of **hieroglyphic** (hy-ruh-**glif**-ik). This is *an early form of picture writing.* Perhaps these "words" identified the object that the goddess is handing to the pharaoh.

Figure 5–5   Notice the use of balance and texture in this work. What makes you think these figures are important?

Egyptian. *The Goddess Hathor Places the Magic Collar on Sethos I.* Thebes, 19th Dynasty. c. 1303–1290 B.C. Painted bas-relief. 226.5 cm (89⅛"). The Louvre, Paris, France.

86   Chapter 5   *Art Through the Ages*

WHAT YOU WILL LEARN

In this lesson, you will design and create an Egyptian tomb painting. The subject will be a well-known figure from American or world history. In portraying this figure, you will try to show his or her character. You will also follow the rules of Egyptian art. You will use a repeating pattern for the figure's clothing, as in Figure 5–5. In the background, you will include hieroglyphics. These will be made up of objects that help define the person's identity. You will complete your tomb painting using tempera paints.

WHAT YOU WILL NEED

• Pencil and sheets of sketch paper
• White drawing paper, 12 x 18 inches (30 x 46 cm)
• Fine-tipped black marker
• Tempera paints
• Mixing tray
• Medium and fine brushes
• Paper towels

---

more about • • •

Egyptian Pyramids   The Egyptians thought the huge pyramids they built would protect the mummified bodies of their dead rulers for all time. However, they were wrong. The fortress-like tombs were often quickly broken into and robbed of their treasures. In fact, a written account exists of eight tomb robbers who were caught, tried, and found guilty. They were imprisoned until the pharaoh chose a suitable punishment; their ultimate fate is unknown. When King Tutankhamen's tomb was discovered undisturbed in 1922, it was a rare find indeed. The tomb had remained intact for more than thirty-two centuries.

WHAT YOU WILL DO

1. With a partner, brainstorm possible historical figures as subjects for your tomb painting. Choose a person you know a lot about. Think about objects and visual symbols that help define the person's identity. A **symbol** is *an image used to stand for a quality or idea.* If you chose George Washington, for example, your symbols might include an ax and a cherry tree. Jot down notes about your subject and symbols.
2. Study the figures in Figure 5–5. Notice the position of the head, shoulders, chest, arms, legs, and feet. Make pencil sketches of your subject. Follow the same formula the ancient Egyptian artist used.
3. Transfer your best sketch to the drawing paper. Make your figure large enough to fill the page. In the background, draw boxes with rounded corners. These are to contain your hieroglyphics. In the boxes, draw abstract visual symbols based on the notes you made.
4. Complete your painting by mixing tints and shades of tempera paint. Apply the colors to your figure and background objects. Carefully color the motifs in your pattern.
5. Switch to fine-tipped black marker. Lightly retrace the **contours,** or *outlines and surface ridges,* of important shapes, including body parts. Create a pattern on your subject's clothing.
6. When your painting is dry, display it alongside those of fellow students. Challenge classmates to identify the subject of your work.

EXAMINING YOUR WORK

- ...**ibe** Is your painting based on a figure ......story? Did you include symbols that would help your viewer pinpoint the person's identity?
- **Analyze** Did you follow the rules of Egyptian art for representing human body parts? Did you use a repeating pattern to decorate the person's clothing?
- **Interpret** Did you capture the character of your figure? Were classmates able to identify your person?
- **Judge** Do you consider your painting successful? Why or why not?

Figure 5–6 **Student work. Egyptian tomb painting.**

Try This! ## STUDIO OPTION

■ Make a clay carving of your tomb design. Begin with a ball of modeling clay roughly the size of a grapefruit. Flatten the ball with your hand. Using a large wooden dowel or rolling pin, roll the lump into an oblong measuring approximately 6 x 8 inches. With a modeling tool or popsicle stick, carve the outline of your figure into the clay surface. Wipe the tool from time to time with a damp cloth to remove any excess clay. Add hieroglyphics and other background details. When the clay slab is dry, fire it with your teacher's help.

Lesson 2 *Egyptian Tomb Painting* **87**

MEETING STUDENT DIVERSITY

Individual Differences Students will bring a diverse mix of prior knowledge to their brainstorming activities. You may want to team students who are less able or less knowledgeable with those who are more so. As students exchange ideas and information about historical figures, have them ask each other specific, detailed questions about the person. Encourage them to consider a wide variety of historical figures, both men and women, from different fields of endeavor. You may want to discourage too many sports figures. Guide students to use easily available reference materials to check facts and gather additional information about their subjects.

■ Studio Skills

To demonstrate rules of Egyptian art, have students draw and cut from colored construction paper 15 simple shapes representing the following:

Seen from the front: upper body
Seen in profile: head, lower body, and *two each* of upper legs, lower legs, upper arms, lower arms, hands, and feet. Have students cut the shapes to create a figure that will fill a 12 × 18-inch sheet of construction paper. Show how these 15 shapes can be assembled in different ways to show movement by bending the arms at the elbows and the legs at the knees. Once the shapes have been glued in place, students may use a combination of crayon and smaller bits of construction paper to add details. If eyes are added, they must be shown as if viewed from the front.

■ Cultural Diversity

Explain to students that the Egyptians mummified their dead and carefully entombed them in preparation for an afterlife. Other cultures throughout history have used embalming and other burial processes to treat the dead. Have students discuss burial customs from their own cultures or others.

• • • • • • • • • • • • • •
ASSESS

■ Self-Assessment

Have students use Examining Your Work to evaluate their art.

■ Reteaching

In pairs have students identify the subjects of each other's work.

■ Enrichment

Have students find out what items and artifacts were typically buried in Egyptian tombs. (Food, clothing, jewelry, and treasures.)

• • • • • • • • • • • • • •
CLOSE

Guide students in a summary of the ancient Egyptian figure painting style.

LESSON 3

Eastern Art

✓ OBJECTIVES

After completing this lesson, students will be able to:

• Appreciate the artistic traditions of ancient Asian civilizations.

• Define *Hinduism* and *Buddhism*.

• Create a drawing of an image from memory.

✓ SUPPLIES

• Drawing paper

• Pencils, colored pencils, oil pastels

Resource

■ 5-4 Message in the Sand, TRB page 77 (studio)

• • • • • • • • • • • • • •

TEACH

■ Motivator

Ask students to think of a river they have seen or learned about. What is the river like? How do people use it or benefit from it? Point out that rivers have always played an important part in the development of civilization. For example, fertile river valleys were productive farmland. Rivers provided a means of transportation. Have students discuss other ways that rivers have affected civilization.

No tour of the ancient art world would be complete without a swing through Asia. Here, halfway around the globe from the great temples and pyramids of Egypt, other mighty empires rose and fell. Each left behind an artistic tradition as rich as those of the Greeks and Romans.

In this lesson, you will read about two of those cultures. You will also view some of the art treasures they left behind.

ART OF ANCIENT INDIA

In the mid-1800s, railroad workers digging in the Indus River valley of present-day Pakistan made a remarkable discovery. They unearthed bits and pieces of a lost city. Archaeologists later pieced together this ancient puzzle. Their explorations revealed that the city was once the center of a river civilization that had existed some 4,500 years earlier. It had achieved a splendor at least as great as that of ancient Egypt.

Like the Egyptians, the people of the Indus River valley worshiped animals and the forces of nature. These beliefs were later combined with others to form the foundation of one of the world's great religions. That religion is Hinduism (**hin**-doo-iz-uhm). Today, this faith has 700 million followers.

Sculpture

Among the gifts passed down by the Indus River valley civilization was a knowledge of bronze casting. This sculpting method was used by later inhabitants of the region to create the work in Figure 5–7. The subject of this sculpture is Hanuman, king of the monkeys. According to Hindu myth, Hanuman helped the god Rama rescue Rama's wife from a demon's evil clutches.

Like other characters in Hindu legend, Hanuman represents a human virtue (**vur**-chew). A *virtue* is a positive quality, in this case loyalty.

Figure 5–7 Notice that the creature has the body of a human but a monkey's head and tail. What does Hanuman's posture tell you about his character?

Indian, Tamil Nadu. *Standing Hanuman.* Chola Period. Eleventh century. Bronze. 64.5 cm (25⅜"). The Metropolitan Museum of Art, New York, New York. Purchase, funds and bequests from various donors.

88   Chapter 5   *Art Through the Ages*

CURRICULUM CONNECTIONS

Social Studies   All of the early civilizations began in river valleys, where the soil was fertile and the water supply abundant. Among the first of these was Sumer, located in the lower part of the Tigris-Euphrates Valley (now Iraq). Tiny Sumerian farming villages had formed in the valley by about 5000 B.C.; by about 3500 B.C., many villages had grown to the size of small cities. The Sumerians developed the first known system of written language, called cuneiform writing. They also invented the potter's wheel and produced decorative pottery. They designed and made beautiful jewelry, metalware, musical instruments, and glass items.

ART OF ANCIENT JAPAN

The civilization of the Indus River valley is among the earliest on record. Evidence of an even older culture has been found on the island nation of Japan. This culture is believed to have sprung to life around 5000 B.C.

As with Indian art, the art of ancient Japan was inspired by religion. Interestingly, one of the religions that shaped much of early Japanese art began in India and then came to Japan through China in A.D. 552. That religion is Buddhism (**boo**-diz-uhm). Buddhism was an outgrowth of Hinduism. It emphasizes physical and spiritual discipline as the means for reaching a state of inner peace.

Screen Painting

One common form of Japanese artistic expression is shown in Figure 5–8. Each object is a **painted screen**. This is *an art object used as a wall or room divider.* Do you recall the name for art that is both useful and pleasing to the eye?

Look carefully at these screens. They show two creatures, one real and one mythical. Both have symbolic value. The tiger was believed to chase evil. The dragon was thought to bring luck.

STUDIO ACTIVITY

Creating a Japanese Drawing

Before creating artworks, Japanese artists would silently and carefully study their subject.

Bring an object of nature, such as a leaf, stone, or seed pod to class. Silently study the object from different angles. Examine its lines, form, texture, and color. Place the object out of sight. Using black or colored pencils, create the image of the object that remains in your mind.

P O R T F O L I O

For your portfolio, write a short paragraph explaining whether you were successful at creating an image of the object from your memory of it.

✔ Check Your Understanding

1. How was the Indus River valley civilization discovered?
2. For what is this civilization most remembered?

Figure 5–8 The artist painted the subjects of these works realistically. What would defenders of each of the three aesthetic views have to say about these paintings?

Maruyama Okyo. *Tiger and Dragon Screens.* 1781. Edo Period. Ink and colors on paper. Each 168 × 188 cm (66¼ × 70″). Detroit Institute of Arts, Detroit, Michigan. Founders Society Purchase with funds from various contributors.

Lesson 3   *Eastern Art*   **89**

LESSON TIME: 3 hours

• • • • • • • • • • • • • •
FOCUS

☑ OBJECTIVES

After completing this lesson, students will be able to:

• Design and create an abstract sculpture modeled after a Kota figure.

• Describe, analyze, interpret, and judge their figures.

☑ SUPPLIES

• Large and small pieces of cardboard

• Pencils; scissors; white glue

• Several rolls of aluminum foil

• Transparent or masking tape

Resources

■ 5-5 Mountains in the Mist, TRB page 79 (studio)

■ 5-6 You, the Critic, TRB page 81 (art criticism)

• • • • • • • • • • • • • •
TEACH

■ Motivator

Ask students to examine the Kota figure and identify its different parts, pointing out the large oval shape representing the head and the open, diamond shape suggesting a body or legs. Tell them that the shapes at the top and sides of the head may represent a headdress, although some claim these shapes were intended to be wings. Ask students to identify how the figure is balanced. They should note that the figure is symmetrically balanced in terms of its overall shape and surface decorations.

90

LESSON 4

Making a Relief Sculpture

Examine the work in Figure 5–9. It is the product of another culture that has a long tradition. That culture is the Kota of central Africa. Unlike other peoples you have learned about, little is known about the Kota and other cultures of early Africa. In fact, much of the early art of these groups no longer exists. Many of their creations were crafted from wood. Often these were destroyed by the damp climate of the region.

The Kota sculpture in the picture is an abstract figure. Works like this were placed over a container. Inside the container were the remains of an honored ancestor. The original purpose of the sculptures remains a mystery. One popular view is that the works were meant to drive away evil spirits. What are some other possibilities?

WHAT YOU WILL LEARN

You will create an abstract sculpture modeled after the Kota figure in Figure 5–9. Like that sculpture, your work will have formal balance. It will be decorated with a pattern of lines made from glue. These will suggest facial features and add tactile texture.

WHAT YOU WILL NEED

• One large piece of cardboard, about 12 x 8 inches (30 x 20 cm), and several smaller pieces

• Pencil

• Scissors

• White glue

• Heavy twine

• Aluminum foil

• Transparent or masking tape

Figure 5–9 At one time the creations of African artists went unappreciated in the Western world. This is because they lacked realism. Have standards in art changed? If so, how?

African. Gabon, Kota. *Reliquary Figure.* Nineteenth-twentieth century. Wood, brass, copper, iron. 73.3 cm (28⅞"). The Metropolitan Museum of Art, New York, New York. Purchase 1983.

90   Chapter 5   *Art Through the Ages*

---

more about • • •

African Art   Because African artists made use of the abundant supply of wood, shells, and natural fibers, much of their art is perishable. In fact, much of the African art in museums today dates from only the nineteenth and twentieth centuries. The Kota figure shown is from an area that is now Gabon, on the west coast of Africa. Gabon has a hot, humid climate, with nearly 100 inches of rainfall yearly. Its dense forests are its greatest natural resource, with ebony, mahogany, and okoumé trees. Gabon has few metals. The Kota figure has brass and copper sheets flattened over carved wood. Ask: What does this use of rare metals tell us about the importance attached to such figures? *(Such works must be especially important.)*

WHAT YOU WILL DO

1. Carefully study the Kota figure illustrated in Figure 5–8. Examine the tactile textures in the work. Notice the use of formal balance. On the large piece of cardboard, complete an outline drawing in pencil of a similar figure. Like the one pictured, your figure should be abstract.

2. Cut out your figure. With the pencil, add facial features and decorative lines. Squeeze white glue over the pencil lines. Lay twine over glue lines. Allow the glue to dry before proceeding to the next step.

3. Lay the prepared figure on a sheet of aluminum foil. Place a dull pencil point on the foil about one-half inch from the outer edge of the figure. Following the contour of the figure, make a light outline one-half inch larger.

4. Using the indented outline as a guide, cut out the foil copy of your figure. Beginning on one side, fold the foil over the edge of the cardboard. Gently smooth it down and press it into place.

5. Press the foil securely around the raised glue lines. Use the blunt end of a brush, dull pencil, or your fingers to make these lines stand out clearly. Be careful not to tear the foil.

6. When completed, the foil should be bent under all edges of the figure and smoothed flat everywhere except over the glue lines. Secure the foil to the cardboard with tape.

7. Use the same blunt tool to apply texture—dots and lines.

 Try This! STUDIO OPTIONS

■ Accent the decorations on the foil surface of your Kota figure. Do this by painting on a coat of black ink. You may have to apply several coats to penetrate all areas. When the ink has dried, lightly rub steel wool over the design. The raised areas will return to their original metallic finish. The other areas will remain black.

■ Use the steps outlined in this lesson to create an abstract figure of your own design. Before sketching a design for your figure, decide on its purpose. Ask yourself what mood the completed work will express.

 EXAMINING YOUR WORK

- **Describe** Does your figure include all the shapes identified in the original?
- **Analyze** Does your figure have formal balance? Does it show features of the face and decorations as patterns of line on the surface of the sculpture? Do these lines give your work an interesting texture?
- **Interpret** Do you think your figure looks as though it, too, could chase away evil spirits?
- **Judge** Suppose you were to make another Kota figure. What would you do differently to make it better?

Figure 5–10 **Student work. Relief sculpture.**

Lesson 4 *Making a Relief Sculpture* **91**

Discuss with students why it is necessary to understand the culture from which it comes before one can understand a particular example of African art. Students should realize that Africa is composed of peoples of many different cultures, and that each is unique.

■ Studio Skills

Demonstrate how to complete a symmetrical drawing of the Kota figure on the large piece of cardboard. Some students may need help in cutting the figure out. Show how to use pencil lines for facial features and how to apply white glue and twine over the lines. Demonstrate how to apply the aluminum foil, pressing firmly around the twine.

● ● ● ● ● ● ● ● ●
ASSESS

■ Self-Assessment

Have students use Examining Your Work to evaluate their art.

■ Reteaching

In pairs, have students write three analysis questions about their figures.

■ Enrichment

In most African art, the head is large in comparison to the body to show its importance as the center of reason and wisdom. Ask students to find other examples of African art that have this same characteristic.

● ● ● ● ● ● ● ● ●
CLOSE

Have students explain how their figure is similar to the Kota original.

SAFETY TIP ⚠️

Using Scissors Cutting through thick cardboard can be hazardous. Remind students to be very careful when using any cutting tools such as scissors and knives. They should pick up the tool only by the handle, never by the blade. If handing the tool to another person, students should offer the handle.

Have students hold the cardboard away from them as they make their cuts. Tell them to make sure no one is standing nearby. Demonstrate safe cutting procedures and help any student who may be frustrated. Provide sharp scissors. Dull ones can fail to cut materials cleanly and can slip, causing accidents.

Art of the Middle Ages and Renaissance

☑ **OBJECTIVES**

After completing this lesson, students will be able to:

• Understand what the terms *Middle Ages* and *Renaissance* mean.
• Define architecture.
• Make a stained-glass window using butcher paper and colored tissue.

☑ **SUPPLIES**

• Black butcher paper
• Colored cellophane or tissue paper
• Scissors

Resources

■ 5-7 Centuries of Change, TRB page 82 (cooperative learning)
■ 5-8 Orazio Gentileschi TRB page 83, (artist profile)
■ 5-9 Art of the Floating World, TRB page 84 (appreciating cultural diversity)

• • • • • • • • • • • • •
T E A C H

■ **Motivator**

Begin the lesson by asking students to imagine what it must have been like in western Europe after Rome lost its power. What feelings might people experience when hearing that invaders from the north were fast approaching? Explain that fear of the unknown caused people to destroy grand temples in order to use the stone to build fortresses.

Empires, as you have learned, come and go. Rome was no exception. In the fifth century, this great empire suffered the fate that had earlier claimed Egypt, Greece, and the Indus River valley civilization.

The period following Rome's collapse was one of chaos. Today we know this time in history as the Middle Ages. It lasted some 1,000 years.

ART OF THE MIDDLE AGES

After Rome fell, some of its great temples and palaces were torn down. The stone was carried off and used to build fortresses. These were built to keep invaders out. In time, structures of this type led to a new form of architecture. **Architecture** is *the art of planning and creating buildings*.

Castle Building

You probably recognize the structure in Figure 5–11. It is a castle. This is a fortlike dwelling with high walls and towers. Many castles were further protected by moats and drawbridges.

Figure 5–11 The architect of this castle avoided windows because the walls would not support them. What other factors might have led to a lack of windows?

View of castle, Alcazar, Segovia, Spain. Eleventh-fifteenth centuries. SEF/ Art Resource, N.Y.

92 Chapter 5 *Art Through the Ages*

Figure 5–12 The cathedral has graceful, upwardly soaring lines and large windows.

Beauvais Cathedral, West Facade. Beauvais, France.

Guards stationed in the towers would sound the alarm when enemies approached.

Study the castle in Figure 5–11. Do you think the architect's main concern was safety or comfort?

Cathedral Building

Just before Rome fell, Christianity spread throughout much of Europe. During the Middle Ages, the Church remained the single strongest force.

By around 1300, a new type of building began to appear. This type of structure is shown in Figure 5–12. It was a special type of church known as a *cathedral* (kuh-**thee**-druhl).

Compare the cathedral in this picture with the castle in Figure 5–11. The cathedral has graceful, upwardly soaring lines.

ART OF THE RENAISSANCE

After ten centuries of slumber, Europe awoke in the 1400s to a period of unparalleled

---

TECHNOLOGY OPTIONS

National Gallery of Art Videodisc   Use the following images to show examples of realistic art.

Botticelli	Pieter Bruegel, the Elder	Jacques-Louis David
The Adoration of the Magi	*Landscape with the Penitance of Saint Jerome*	*Napoleon in His Study*
Search Frame 152	Search Frame 2779	Search Frame 1100–04

Use Glencoe's *National Gallery of Art Correlation Bar Code Guide* to locate more artworks.

growth. Trade and knowledge spread. New discoveries were made in science. Artists and scholars developed an interest in the art and literature of ancient Greece and Rome. This period is known today as the **Renaissance** (**ren**-uh-sahns), which means *period of rebirth.*

Renaissance Painting

The Renaissance was a time of great discoveries in art as well. Painters achieved a level of realism never before imagined by using perspective to give depth and shading to provide three-dimensionality.

This realism is evident in the painting in Figure 5–13. The work was done sometime after the Renaissance. Notice the attention to detail. Every fold in the woman's clothing is faithfully recorded. So is the glint in her eye. Look at her expression. What do you suppose she is thinking about as she pauses from playing her violin?

 ## Check Your Understanding

1. What is meant by the term *Middle Ages?*
2. What was the main source of power in Europe during this era?
3. What changes occurred in art during the Renaissance?

  ## STUDIO ACTIVITY

Making a Stained-Glass Window

Cathedrals like the one in Figure 5–12 were fitted with *stained-glass* windows. These were made of colored glass pieces held together with lead strips. Because of these windows, the insides of the cathedrals were bathed in softly tinted light.

Cut black butcher paper into a circle about 12 inches in diameter. Fold the circle in half three times until you have a cone shape. Cut out geometric and simple shapes from the two folded sides. Vary the sizes of the cuts. Open the circle. Cover each opening with a patch of colored cellophane. Cut the patches so that each slightly overlaps the shape it is meant to cover. Secure the cellophane patches with transparent tape. Place your finished work on a windowsill.

 P O R T F O L I O

When your stained-glass window is complete, write a short paragraph explaining how you made your choices of colors and shapes. Keep your description and your artwork together in your portfolio.

Figure 5–13 Observe the striking use of value in this painting. How does it add to the lifelike quality of the work?

Orazio Gentileschi. *Young Woman with a Violin.* c. 1612. Oil on canvas. 83.5 × 98 cm (32¾ × 38⅛"). Detroit Institute of Arts, Detroit, Michigan. Gift of Mrs. Edsel B. Ford.

Lesson 5 *Art of the Middle Ages and Renaissance* **93**

• • • • • • • • • • • • • • • •

FOCUS

☑ OBJECTIVES

After completing this lesson, students will be able to:

• Create a diorama of a realistic scene.

• Describe, analyze, interpret, and judge their diorama in terms of its success in showing depth.

☑ SUPPLIES

• Pencils and sketch paper
• Cardboard cartons
• White glue
• Large supply of found objects
• Tempera paints, brushes, mixing trays, paint cloths
• Chalk or markers
• Colored construction paper
• Several rolls of plastic wrap

• • • • • • • • • • • • • • • •

TEACH

■ Motivator

Draw a large rectangle on the board. Ask students how two circles drawn in that rectangle could be made to look as if they are at different distances in space. Have them draw the circles in the rectangle. Their drawings should show how differences in size, overlapping, and placement (higher or lower) can suggest depth. Then ask them how changes in hue, intensity, and value can also add to the illusion of space. Have them draw and color another series of circles in the rectangle, this time using changes in color to suggest depth (brighter and darker circles appear closer than duller, lighter ones).

 LESSON 6

Creating a Diorama

The Renaissance, you have learned, was a time of bold new discoveries. One of these was a technique called *linear perspective.* This technique aided painters in their quest for realism. In linear perspective, the horizontal lines of objects are slanted. This makes them appear to extend back into space. As Figure 5–14 shows, the lines meet at an imaginary point called the *vanishing point.*

The painting in Figure 5–15 uses linear perspective. Examine this lifelike work. Find the slanted lines in the vine-covered lattice-work above the dancers. Try extending these lines with your finger. At what point in the painting do they come together? Where else in the work has the artist used slanted lines? What other techniques has he relied upon to create a sense of depth?

WHAT YOU WILL LEARN

Linear perspective is used to lend a feeling of space to two-dimensional works. In this lesson, you will create a three-dimensional

Figure 5–14 **Diagram showing linear perspective.**

work of art that uses both real and suggested space. You will use a variety of items to create a **diorama** (dy-uh-**ram**-uh). This is *a scenic representation in which miniature sculptures and other objects are displayed against a painted backdrop.* You will create a sense of deep space through changes in hue, intensity, and value.

WHAT YOU WILL NEED

• Pencil and sketch paper
• Cardboard box, lid discarded

Figure 5–15 **This painting was done a generation after the Renaissance. It, nevertheless, owes a debt to the genius of that period.**

Jan Steen. *The Dancing Couple.* 1663. Oil on canvas. 102.5 × 142.5 cm (40⅜ × 56⅛″). National Gallery of Art, Washington, D.C. Widener Collection.

94   Chapter 5   *Art Through the Ages*

RESOURCES BEYOND THE CLASSROOM

Festivals and Fairs Festivals and fairs let budding artists explore the arts of other countries and other times. Ethnic and religious festivals, such as Greek Orthodox fairs, Native American powwows, and Hispanic-American festivals, show how different cultures create and use art. Some festivals may celebrate the Chinese New Year, while others may host a St. Patrick's Day parade. These events allow students to see artists and craftspeople at work. Other kinds of fairs are also becoming popular, in particular medieval or Renaissance festivals, modeled on societies of centuries ago. Authentic foods, crafts, and leisure activities are all re-created at these events.

- Construction paper in a variety of colors
- White glue
- Chalk or markers
- Tempera paints
- Mixing tray
- Brushes, paper towels
- A variety of found objects

WHAT YOU WILL DO

1. Complete several pencil sketches of an imaginary scene. Include buildings, trees, and other objects. Select a point of view that suggests depth. One possibility might be a view looking down a city street.
2. Turn the box on its side. On the outside of the box, use colored construction paper to decorate the bottom, sides, back, and top. Glue the paper in place. Allow time for the glue to dry.
3. Select your best sketch. Using chalk or markers, transfer the scene to the back wall of the box. Sketch the lines of buildings along the sides of the box. The lines of objects should mirror the natural lines of the box.
4. Choose hues of tempera paint that reflect the colors of objects in your scene. You might use brown for buildings, gray for pavements. Mix duller intensities and lighter values of these hues. These will be used to show objects in the distance. Use a fine brush to add details, such as doors and windows.
5. Use found materials to form free-standing houses, trees, and other objects in your sketch. Gravel might be used for a stone fence, for example. Bark might be used for tree trunks. To give a sense of deep space,

EXAMINING YOUR WORK

- **Describe** What have you included in your diorama?
- **Analyze** Did you use changes in hue, intensity, and value to create the feeling of deep space? Did you use placement of objects to help carry out this feeling?
- **Interpret** Would anyone looking at your diorama think it is much deeper than it actually is?
- **Judge** Does your diorama succeed in using real and suggested space?

glue larger, more colorful objects in the foreground. Smaller, less colorful objects should be placed farther back.
6. Display your finished work.

Figure 5–16   **Student work. A diorama.**

STUDIO OPTION

■ Do a realistic painting of the scene in your diorama. Your painting should use linear perspective to suggest depth.

Refer to Figure 5–14 to help you plan this project. Use size, overlapping, and values and intensities of hues to help create a feeling of space.

■ Studio Skills

Help students brainstorm ideas for scenes for their dioramas. For example, an underwater scene might include fish, shells, seaweed, stones, shipwrecks, treasure chests. Point out that the more objects they include the better, since it will give them more opportunities to use overlapping and changes in color and size to suggest space.

For additional review of linear perspective and other space techniques, see Chapter 1.

Art on a Shoestring

Encourage students to be imaginative in identifying found objects to include in their dioramas. The items can be extremely simple and common. It is the composition of the items that requires creative thought.

ASSESS

■ Self-Assessment

Have students use Examining Your Work to evaluate their art.

■ Reteaching

Ask pairs of students to identify each other's scene and point of view in their dioramas.

■ Enrichment

Ask students to consider creating a diorama for a social studies unit they may be studying. Remind them to create a sense of deep space and point of view.

CLOSE

Have students explain how they were able to achieve depth in their dioramas.

MEETING SPECIAL NEEDS

Renaissance Perspective Some students with mental retardation and those who have never had sight may not be able to grasp the notion of vanishing-point perspective. It was many centuries before Renaissance artists developed vanishing-point perspective. If the idea that depth can be shown by slanting the horizontal lines of forms diagonally toward one or two points on the horizon is too difficult for some students to grasp, other ways to show depth can be shown. These include using overlapping, placing figures in the background higher on the picture plane, and making distant forms lighter, grayer, and bluer.

Art of the Nineteenth and Twentieth Centuries

• • • • • • • • • • • • • •
FOCUS

☑ OBJECTIVES

After completing this lesson, students will be able to:

- Define *art movement.*
- Understand the goals of the Impressionists and of the Surrealists.
- Create an Impressionist painting.

☑ SUPPLIES

- Pencils and sketch paper
- White drawing paper
- Tempera or acrylic paints
- Brushes; mixing trays; paint cloths

Resource

- ■ 5-10 Trends and Movements, TRB page 85 (art history)

• • • • • • • • • • • • • •
TEACH

■ Motivator

Tell students to follow your signal and look at the Monet painting. After five seconds, have them close their books and describe what they saw. Have them do the same with the Lundeberg painting. Ask them which painting captures what and how the eye actually sees. Did they notice that the blurred effects of the Monet painting captures the effects of bright sunlight? Did the Lundeberg painting cause any confusion?

Seen against the long tapestry of art history, the last hundred years is but a stitch. Yet, during this century, more changes have taken place in art than in all the centuries before.

In this lesson, you will learn about some of the changes that have occurred since the late 1800s.

Figure 5–17 Compare this painting with the one in Figure 5–15. In what way is this nature scene more "realistic" than the painting of the dancers?

Claude Monet. *Poplars on the Bank of the Epte River.* 1891. Oil on canvas. 100.3 × 65.2 cm (39½ × 25¹¹⁄₁₆"). Philadelphia Museum of Art, Philadelphia, Pennsylvania. Bequest of Anne Thomson in memory of her father, Frank Thomson, and her mother, Mary Elizabeth Clarke Thomson.

96   Chapter 5   *Art Through the Ages*

ART OF THE NINETEENTH CENTURY

In the centuries following the Renaissance, the pursuit of realism continued. Artists produced pictures that showed solid figures moving naturally in space. They created works in which sunlight poured through windows, glinting off glass goblets and other shiny surfaces. Their brushes captured the look and feel of warm skin, cold metal, and soft velvet.

Toward the end of the 1800s, the search for realism took a new direction. One group of French painters in particular "saw the light." They left their dark studios and went to paint outdoors. They worked feverishly, using all their energies to capture the fleeting effects of sunlight on objects. This group became known, at first jokingly, as the *Impressionists.*

Painting

The leader of this **art movement**—*a trend formed when a group of artists band together*—was an artist named Claude Monet (**klohd moh-nay**). Monet's goal was to record what the eye saw at any given moment. Have you ever noticed how, on a cloudy day, the sun "goes in" and "comes out" again without warning? It was this "reality" that Monet set out to capture.

The work in Figure 5–17 is one of his paintings. Viewed up close, it looks like a hastily done collection of paint dabs and dashes. When seen from a distance, however, the painting takes on an almost shimmering quality. The dabs and dashes are now brilliant flecks of color and blend together to form a stand of slender trees by the banks of a river. You can almost feel the gentle breeze rustling through the leaves on the trees and rippling the glassy surface of the water.

CURRICULUM ❯ CONNECTIONS

Language Arts   For another approach to understanding the Impressionists, share the book *Linnea in Monet's Garden* by Bjork Anderson with the class. Students will enjoy visiting Claude Monet's garden in Giverny along with Linnea in the book. As they accompany Linnea through his house and garden, and stand on the bridge over his lily pond, students, like Linnea, will have a greater appreciation of what it means to be an Impressionist.

Figure 5–18 What statement might the artist be making about the passage of time? What clues are provided by the object in the hand of each figure?

Helen Lundeberg. *Double Portrait of the Artist in Time*. 1935. Oil on Masonite. 121.3 × 101.6 cm (47¾ × 40′). National Museum of American Art, Smithsonian Institution. Washington, D.C.

ART OF THE TWENTIETH CENTURY

You have learned that the Impressionists were seeking new ways to capture realistic appearances in their art. However, the search for realism was nothing new. Roman sculptors and Renaissance painters sought the same goal. Strands in the fabric of art history, it seems, loop back on themselves.

One strand that came full circle in the twentieth century is the use of symbolism in art. You learned about symbolism in the lessons on Egyptian art earlier in this chapter. A heavy reliance on symbols became a feature of a twentieth-century art movement known as *Surrealism.*

Painting

In their works, the Surrealists tapped into the mysterious world of dreams. In this nighttime "world," symbols often play important roles. Consider the curious painting

STUDIO ACTIVITY

Creating an Impressionist Painting

Select an outdoor scene in your community. Complete a rough line drawing of your scene on a sheet of 9 x 12-inch (23 x 30-cm) white drawing paper. Load a fine-tipped brush with tempera paint. Apply color in quick dabs of the brush. Blur contours and details to re-create the appearance of sunlight on the subject. Use colors that will indicate a certain time of day. Select a color scheme that will convey a particular mood.

PORTFOLIO

For your portfolio, write a short paragraph explaining whether you were successful at communicating a mood with the blurred images.

in Figure 5–18. Notice the work's title. You will probably have no trouble finding the two "portraits" of the artist. One—the artist as a child—appears in the lower half of the picture. The other—the adult artist—appears in the picture on the wall. The long, unnatural shadow cast upward by the child's image helps tie the two portraits together.

Yet, like most Surrealist paintings, this one asks more questions than it answers. What, for example, is the meaning of the clock? What are we to make of the empty container in the painting within a painting? Some critics have detected a sense of sadness or longing in this painting. What feeling does the work communicate to you?

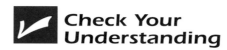

Check Your Understanding

1. What was the aim of the Impressionists? What was the goal of the Surrealists?
2. What is an art movement?

Lesson 7 *Art of the Nineteenth and Twentieth Centuries* **97**

Aesthetics

Ask students to point out the differences between the paintings by Monet and Lundeberg. Then ask them what they have in common. Although they appear to have more differences than similarities, both works are described as realistic. Ask students how this can be explained.

Art History

Explain to students that when the artworks of the Impressionists were first exhibited, and for many years thereafter, art critics and the public rejected these works. To most viewers, their work looked unfinished. Critics thought the works looked more like sketches than fully developed compositions. Today the art of the Impressionists is among the most admired in history.

ASSESS

Self-Assessment

Have students complete the Check Your Understanding questions on this page. Answers are provided below.

Reteaching

Have student partners choose to describe the Impressionistic or Surrealistic style of painting.

Enrichment

Instruct students to visit the library to find reproductions of twentieth century paintings done in styles *other than* Surrealism. Have them bring examples to class and discuss them. Point out that the twentieth century is characterized by diversity. Some artists have relied on a realistic style, while others have moved in the direction of abstraction and nonobjective art.

CLOSE

Ask students to describe the qualities of Impressionism found in their own Impressionistic scene.

LESSON TIME: 2 hours

• • • • • • • • • • • • • •
FOCUS

☑️OBJECTIVES

After completing this lesson, students will be able to:

• Draw and paint an abstract or simplified image representing their aspirations for the future.

• Describe, analyze, interpret, and judge their abstract painting.

☑️SUPPLIES

• Pencils, sketch paper
• Sheets of illustration board
• Tempera or acrylic paints
• Brushes, mixing trays, paint cloths
• Rulers or straight edge
• Scissors; white glue

Resource
■ 5-11 Lives of the Artists, TRB page 86 (art history)

• • • • • • • • • • • • • •
TEACH

■ Motivator

Ask students to examine the painting by Elizabeth Murray in Figure 5-19. Can they identify the objects depicted in this painting? Call attention to the title, *Painter's Progress*. What meaning do they attach to this title? How does the artist exhibit her progress as a painter? *(She does so with the painting itself.)* Tell students that Murray's work identifies her *aspirations* to succeed as a painter, and she presents her work to show her progress.

98

Using Abstraction in Art

While some artists today have borrowed ideas and techniques of the past, others have moved in new directions. One such ground-breaking direction is reflected in the painting in Figure 5–19. This work is an example of abstraction in art. As you read in Chapter 4, *abstract* means having a recognizable subject that is shown in an unrealistic or simplified manner. Abstract art straddles the fence between representational—or realistic—art and non-objective art.

Examine the painting in Figure 5–19. You will probably recognize the fragmented objects in this brightly colored work. The main one is a painter's palette. Protruding from it is an assortment of brushes. Why has the artist chosen to shatter these familiar images? What do the picture's content and title reveal about the changes you read about in the previous lesson?

WHAT YOU WILL LEARN

In this studio lesson, you will create your own abstract painting. Through abstraction, you will express your goals and hopes for the future. Your finished work will exhibit a variety of brilliantly colored, angular shapes. As in Figure 5–19, these will be joined together to make a visually pleasing whole.

WHAT YOU WILL NEED

• Pencil and sketch paper
• Two sheets of illustration board, one measuring 12 x 18 inches (30 x 46 cm) and the other 18 x 24 inches (46 x 61 cm)

Figure 5–19 Notice how the artist has used the art elements of shape and color. How are variety and harmony demonstrated in this painting?

Elizabeth Murray. *Painter's Progress.* 1981. Oil on canvas in 19 parts. 294.5 × 236.2 cm (9'8" × 7'9"). Museum of Modern Art, New York, New York. Acquired through the Bernhill Fund and gift of Agnes Gund.

98   Chapter 5   *Art Through the Ages*

— *more about* • • • —

Careers and Aspirations   Many students may not have a clear idea of their future goals at this stage of their lives. Urge them not to struggle too much with making choices for this Studio Lesson. Rather, encourage them to think of activities and subjects that interest or motivate them. For example, a student who enjoys math problems might choose images of a calculator, ruler, and protrac-

tor. A student who aspires to write about sports might choose images of sports equipment or newspaper headlines. For additional ideas, direct students to career books in the library. For information about careers in art, see *Careers for Artistic Types* by Andrew Kaplan (Brookfield, Conn.: Millbrook, 1991).

- Tempera or acrylic paints
- Brushes
- Mixing tray
- Paint cloth
- Ruler or other straight edge
- Scissors
- White glue

WHAT YOU WILL DO

1. Everyone has dreams and goals. Some people dream of becoming astronauts, others doctors or writers. What is your own life goal? Begin this studio lesson by answering that question. Think of symbols or objects connected with your goal. Draw several sketches of these images. Then abstract, or simplify, the images by eliminating all unnecessary details.
2. Transfer your best sketch to the sheet of illustration board. Fill the board completely with your drawing.
3. Using tempera or acrylic paints, paint your subject. Include a background area as the artist has done in Figure 5–19. Use bright hues.
4. When your work is dry, turn it over. With a ruler or other straight edge, draw straight lines at angles to one another. Include enough lines to divide the painting into at least 15 large and small angular shapes.
5. Use scissors to cut out your shapes. As you work, turn each piece over so its painted side is facing up. Carefully fit the cut-out pieces together so that you know where each one goes.
6. Center the rearranged shapes on the sheet of illustration board. Overlap some

EXAMINING YOUR WORK

- **Describe**   Did you select images that identify a particular dream or goal? Did you simplify the images?
- **Analyze**   Did you use a variety of brightly colored hues? Does your work contain large and small angular shapes?
- **Interpret**   Do you think other people could interpret the images in your picture? Would they be able to recognize the idea the images represent?
- **Judge**   Do you think the shapes in your composition are joined in a way so as to create a pleasing whole?

pieces. Leave narrow spaces between others. Move the shapes around until you are satisfied with the arrangement. Then glue the pieces in place. Title your work.

Figure 5–20   **Student work. Abstraction in art.**

COMPUTER OPTION

■ Think of a familiar object, plant, or animal. Choose the Straight Line tool and draw the object using only straight lines. Vary the line thickness. Add color with the Bucket tool to some of the spaces. Give your work a title. Save and print.

Open a new page. Draw a second version with only the Straight line tool, but this time, rearrange

and move the lines farther apart. Add color to some of the spaces. Retitle, save, and print.

Open a new page. Draw a third edition. This time, look carefully at your second attempt. Create a pleasing design by rearranging the thick and thin straight lines, then add color. Retitle, save, and print. Display all three abstractions together.

Lesson 8   *Using Abstraction in Art*   **99**

Students should have fun with the possibilities offered in this Studio Lesson. Encourage them to look around for unusual items or unconventional ideas that convey their goals and interests. Have them experiment with atypical colors or shapes that express their personalities as well as their interests.

■ Art Criticism

Tell students that Murray's painting makes effective use of contrast. Explain that contrast is a technique in which differences between objects are stressed. A tall person contrasts with a short one, a dark patch of sky contrasts with a light one. Ask students to point out two ways Murray uses contrast in her painting. (*Contrast of red and green; curved painted shapes and angular cut-out shapes.*)

ASSESS

■ Self-Assessment

Have students use Examining Your Work to evaluate their work.

■ Reteaching

Have pairs of students interpret the images found in each other's work.

■ Enrichment

Encourage students to create another abstract painting, but this time choose images that symbolize their personality and character traits. Have students critique each other's use of color and shape to create contrast and a visually pleasing whole.

CLOSE

Have students look for and identify another example of abstract art in the book.

MEETING STUDENT DIVERSITY

Adapting Materials   Some students may not be able to easily cut through the illustration board. If you have students with disabilities, or if enough illustration board is not available for each student to use two pieces, this studio can be done with other materials. The original painting can be

created on white drawing paper. It is easy to draw lines on the back of the painting and then cut out the shapes. The shapes can then be mounted on illustration board, if it is available, or the pieces can be mounted on a larger piece of colored construction paper or white drawing paper.

CONNECTIONS *History*

OBJECTIVES

After completing this feature, the student will be able to:

- Explain why silk remained a valuable trade item for centuries.
- Describe how the secret of silk production spread throughout the world.

Teaching the Connection

- Have students read the feature on this page.
- Ask volunteers to share what they know about silk. What are examples of products made from silk? *(Examples include clothing, accessories, linens.)* What are other examples of fine fabrics? *(Examples include velvet, satin, angora.)* Why do you think the artist who created this temple hanging chose to use silk? *(Silk gives the piece an elegant look. It may have been created for a special occasion or an important person.)*
- Tell students that the Tibetan Temple Hanging was created for religious celebrations. The silk panel contains appliqué and brocade work. The temple hanging shows several Buddhas surrounded by lotus blossoms and other Buddhist symbols.

Answers to Making the Connection

- Silk is a fine fabric that gives a rich, lustrous look to the textile art.
- Because silk was produced only in China, it was difficult to obtain and became a valuable trade item.
- They smuggled silkworms and four Chinese girls out of China. The girls taught them how to produce silk.

Central Tibet. Temple Hanging. Detail. 1940. Appliqué with cut silk, brocade, and pearls. 1.2 × 13.1 m (4 × 43′). Los Angeles County Museum of Art, Los Angeles, California. Gift of Mr. and Mrs. James Coburn.

The Secret of Silk

Have you ever heard the expression "as smooth as silk?" Silk is a valuable fiber used to make fine fabrics. It is produced by the silkworm. Silk is sometimes also used in decorative textiles, such as the *Tibetan Temple Hanging* on this page.

The origin of silk dates back to the twenty-seventh century B.C. The silkworm moth was originally found only in China. For thousands of years, the people of China kept the silk-producing process a secret. Because silk was difficult to obtain, it became a valuable trade item.

Although silk fabric was traded to other countries, it was produced only in China. In about A.D. 300, however, a group of people from Japan smuggled silkworms out of China. They brought the silkworms and four young Chinese women back to Japan to teach them how to produce silk.

About 200 years later, a Roman emperor sent two monks to China to smuggle silkworm eggs. The monks hid the eggs in their hollow walking canes. With the secret revealed, silk production spread throughout Asia and the West.

MAKING THE CONNECTION

- How do you think silk fabric enhances this textile art?
- Explain why silk was a valuable trade item.
- How did the people of Japan learn the Chinese secret of silk production?

INTERNET ACTIVITY

Visit Glencoe's Fine Arts Web Site for students at:

http://www.glencoe.com/sec/art/students

100 *Chapter 5 Connections*

INTERNET ACTIVITY

On-Line and Multimedia Resources Visit the Teacher Resources area to find lists of helpful *On-Line and Multimedia Art Resources.* Here you can click on World Wide Web links to find out about art media and reference materials, image libraries, and art-history resources. Locate distributors of computer art software, art-related CD-ROMS, and art media and supplies you can use in your art classroom. You may even have your own favorite resources that you would like to add. Simply click on the *Contact Us* button to send us information about resources you think would be useful to other art teachers. We welcome your feedback on this and other resources of our site. Find us at **http://www.glencoe.com/sec/art**

REVIEW

■ BUILDING VOCABULARY

Number a sheet of paper from 1 to 12. After each number, write the term from the box that matches each description below.

applied art	diorama
architecture	fine art
art historians	hieroglyphic
art movement	painted screen
bust	Renaissance
contours	symbol

1. Art made to be enjoyed visually, not used.
2. People who study art of different ages and cultures.
3. An image used to stand for a quality or idea.
4. An early form of picture writing.
5. The art of planning and creating buildings.
6. A sculpture that shows a person's head, shoulders, and upper chest.
7. Period of rebirth.
8. Art made to be useful as well as visually pleasing.
9. Outlines and surface ridges.
10. An art object used as a wall or room divider.
11. A trend formed when a group of artists band together.
12. A scenic representation in which miniature sculptures and other objects are displayed against a painted backdrop.

■ REVIEWING ART FACTS

Number a sheet of paper from 13 to 17. Answer each question in a complete sentence or two.

13. What are the rules of Egyptian art for showing the human body?
14. Name a difference and a similarity between the way the Greeks and Romans showed the human figure.
15. What religious beliefs guided the art of the Indus River valley? What beliefs guided the art of ancient Japan?
16. What methods did Renaissance painters use to achieve realism in their works?
17. Compare and contrast the goals of the Impressionists and the goals of the Surrealists.

THINKING ABOUT ART

On a sheet of paper, answer each question in a sentence or two.

1. **Interpret.** Select any three artworks that you learned about in this chapter. Tell why each would appeal to an art critic taking the composition view.
2. **Compare and contrast.** The chapter covers two types of architecture from the Middle Ages. What are the most important differences between the two?

MAKING ART CONNECTIONS

1. **Music.** Like art, music has undergone changes over the centuries. Investigate this idea. Working with a group, research the following "movements" in the history of music: Romanticism, Expressionism, Neo-Classicism. For each, identify when the movement occurred and the names of the principal composers. Share your findings with classmates in an oral report. If possible, include short recorded passages of representative compositions.

2. **Community Connection.** Learn about the pointed arch. This was one of the architectural breakthroughs that permitted the building of cathedrals during the Middle Ages. Share your findings with family members and friends. If possible, include drawings, photos, or descriptions of churches or other structures in your community that use pointed arches.

Chapter 5 Review **101**

■ Building Vocabulary

1. fine art
2. art historians
3. symbol
4. hieroglyphic
5. architecture
6. bust
7. Renaissance
8. applied art
9. contours
10. painted screen
11. art movement
12. diorama

■ Reviewing Art Facts

13. The rules of Egyptian art require all major body parts to be shown from their most familiar angle.
14. The Greeks and Romans both made statues of important people and rulers. The Greeks showed the whole figure in their sculptures, whereas the Romans focused on heads and busts.
15. People of the ancient Indus River valley worshiped animals and nature; those beliefs influenced their art. Buddhism influenced the art of Japan.
16. Renaissance painters used linear perspective and lifelike expression to achieve realism in their art.
17. The Impressionists sought to record what the eye saw at any given moment. The Surrealists relied on symbolism and dreamlike images.

? THINKING ABOUT ART

1. Answers will vary, but students should give reasons for their views.

2. Student responses will vary. Castles were built for protection. They were flat and squat with high walls, towers, moats, and drawbridges. Cathedrals were built as headquarters for bishops. Cathedrals were tall and graceful.

Perceiving Nature

(pages 102–121)

Resources

- 6-11 Chapter Test, TRB page 103
- Transparency CC-6, *Krishna Lifts Mount Govardhan*
- Transparency 6, *Autumn Oak and Beech*, by C.W. Jeffries
- Fine Art Print 10, *The Cottage Door* by Thomas Gainsborough

 Music
While studying this chapter, use Performing Arts Handbook page 318 to learn how musician and songwriter Paul Tracey looks to nature to raise people's awareness and perception of the beauty and delicate balance in nature.

NATIONAL STANDARDS

This chapter addresses the following National Standards for the Visual Arts:

1. (a, b)	**4.** (a)
2. (a, b, c)	**5.** (a, c)
3. (a)	**6.** (b)

Figure 6–1 Notice how the artist used warm colors to help the viewer feel the heat of a July day. What principles of art did he use to show the motion of the hay cutters?

Thomas Hart Benton. *July Hay*. 1943. Oil and egg tempera on composition board. 96.5 × 67.9 cm (38 × 26¾"). The Metropolitan Museum of Art, New York, New York. George A. Hearn Fund, 1943. © 1998 Thomas H. Benton & Rita P. Benton Testamentary Trusts/Licensed by VAGA, New York, NY

102

FEATURED ARTISTS

Thomas Hart Benton	Frank Johnston	Frederick Varley
Pieter Bruegel	Leonardo da Vinci	Andrew Wyeth
Charles Burchfield	Joan Miró	
Albrecht Dürer	Joseph Pickett	
Carmen Lomas Garza	Tom Thompson	
Katsushika Hokusai	José Antonio Velasquez	

Perceiving Nature

Nature has many faces. You see its fury in the lashing rains of a fierce thunderstorm. You feel its kiss on a gentle spring day. You sense its majesty in a nighttime sky aglitter with a billion stars.

Because of its ever-changing personality, nature has long been a favorite art subject. Examine the painting at the left. Which of nature's faces has this artist captured?

In this chapter you will learn about the ways in which artists have celebrated nature. You will see recent tributes and some from the past.

PORTFOLIO IDEAS

A strong art portfolio contains samples of work created with a variety of media, techniques, and processes. Your entries might include preliminary sketches as well as finished works. By including self-reflections and written evaluations, you will learn more about yourself as an artist.

OBJECTIVES

After completing this chapter, you will be able to:

- Define the term *landscape.*
- Understand stylization.
- Explain what artists accomplish through nature studies.
- Experiment with two- and three-dimensional forms of self-expression.

WORDS YOU WILL LEARN

assemblage
landscape
monoprint
nature study
resist
study
stylized

■ Chapter Overview

Artists continually try to capture the beauty and mystique of the natural world. In this chapter, students will look at nature from an artist's point of view.

■ Chapter Motivator

Ask students to think of a favorite activity or event spent outdoors—perhaps a family picnic, a hike in the woods, a special soccer game, watching the sun set, or some other regular or occasional outdoor happening. Have them close their eyes and visualize an image of that event. What aspect of nature contributed to their enjoyment of that event? In general, what do they enjoy about nature?

Explain that nature has long been the focus of artists, and that in this chapter, students will explore ways of their own to capture images of nature special to them.

■ Examining the Artwork

Tell students that Thomas Hart Benton was a member of the Regionalist movement. These painters strove to paint the American scene in a clear, simple way so that it could be understood and enjoyed by all. Here Benton shows the summer season, when hay is being cut.

National Museum of Women in the Arts

You may wish to use the National Museum of Women in the Arts videodisc and/or CD-ROM. The videodisc features a bar code guide, and the interactive CD-ROM provides stimulating activities.

103

DEVELOPING A PORTFOLIO

Establishing Expectations Knowing what can go into a portfolio helps both the teacher and student. Written observations, verbal responses, records, sketches, and final products are recognized as the basic contributions.

Try to include students in the development of what is expected in the portfolio. Asking questions like, "What do you think would be useful for me to see in your art portfolio?" immediately involves them in the learning and helps them see the rationale for the assignments they do. It also sets a pattern for self-reflection. For other ideas, refer to the booklet, *Portfolio and Assessment Techniques* that accompanies the *Introducing Art* program.

☑ OBJECTIVES

After completing the lesson, students will be able to:
- Define landscape art.
- Understand what it means for a work to be done in a *stylized* way.
- Draw a stylized landscape.

☑ SUPPLIES

- Pencils and sheets of sketching paper
- White construction or watercolor paper
- Watercolors, brushes, and water containers
- Markers and colored pencils

Resources

- ■ 6-1 This Tears It, TRB page 91 (studio)
- ■ 6-2 Take It Outside! TRB page 91 (cooperative learning)

T E A C H

■ Motivator

Have students cover the title of Figure 6-1 and imagine where and what type of place it represents. Ask students to describe this place and record their responses. Then, have them view Figure 6-3 and ask them to respond to the same question, adding new words to the list. Now, tell students they have just won a vacation to the "paradise" of their dreams. Ask students to make a list of words that describe this place.

■ Vocabulary

Discuss the meaning of *landscape* with students. Compare *landscape* with *cityscape* (refer to Chapter 9, Lesson 6). Ask students what a *moonscape* would be.

How many products have you seen that carry the words *all natural* on their labels? This phrase has become commonplace in today's society. It represents people's desire to live in a healthy way and to appreciate nature. Artists have valued and represented nature throughout the years. Their works have long paid tribute to nature's beauty and its bounty.

LANDSCAPES

What do you see when you look out the nearest window? Do you see buildings, streetlights, and cars? Maybe you see plants, trees, and hills. If your answer leans more toward the second description, you are looking at a landscape. In art, the word **landscape** refers to *a drawing or painting of mountains, trees, or other natural scenery.* Artists have been creating landscapes for more than one thousand years.

The possible subjects for a landscape are limitless. So are the ways in which artists have chosen to represent nature scenes. The landscapes in Figures 6–2 and 6–3 show two examples that have some similarities and some differences.

Perspective in a Landscape

Examine the painting in Figure 6–2. It shows a hilly Pennsylvania town in the early 1900s. What do you see first when you look at this painting? Is your eye attracted to the large building on the hill? What do you notice next? The train, the river, or the little buildings in the foreground? Notice that the artist has made these buildings smaller than those in the distance. Why might the artist have created this visual puzzle? Perhaps he wanted to give more importance to the flag blowing proudly in the wind.

Figure 6–2 Besides the perspective, what other unusual landscape features can you find in this picture? Can you identify the season of the year?

Joseph Pickett. *Manchester Valley.* 1914–18. Oil with sand on canvas. 115.6 × 154 cm (45½ × 60⅝"). The Museum of Modern Art, New York, New York. Gift of Abby Aldrich Rockefeller.

TECHNOLOGY OPTIONS

National Gallery of Art Videodisc Use the following images to show additional landscape artworks.

Paul Cézanne *Landscape near Paris*	Paul Gauguin *Haystacks in Brittany*	Thomas Gainsborough *Landscape with a Bridge*
Search Frame 1432	Search Frame 1540	Search Frame 1621

Use Glencoe's *Correlation Bar Code Guide to the National Gallery of Art* to locate more art works.

Rhythm in a Landscape

Compare the painting in Figure 6–2 with the one in Figure 6–3. The two landscapes were painted about the same time. Like the work on the opposite page, this one shows a cheerful scene from nature. It even includes some of the same features, such as trees.

However, that is where the similarity ends. Whereas the landscape in Figure 6–2 portrays a city setting, the one in Figure 6–3 records a rural scene. The work, moreover, follows a careful design. Notice the row after row of evenly spaced seedlings in the bottom half of the picture. Notice how the artist overlapped the shapes to give depth to the scene.

 ### Check Your Understanding

1. What is a landscape?
2. What similarities can you find between this painting and the one on the facing page? What differences can you find?

Figure 6–3 Notice the use of repetition in this painting. What other principle of art has Miró used to give this artwork a lively feeling?

Joan Miró. *Vines and Olive Trees, Tarragona.* 1919. Oil on canvas. 72.5 × 90.5 cm (28½ × 35⅝"). The Metropolitan Museum of Art, New York, New York. The Jacque and Natasha Gelman Collection. © Artists Rights Society (ARS), New York/ ADAGP, Paris.

Lesson 1 *Landscape Art* **105**

A Stylized Landscape

Look again at the plants, trees, and plowed fields in the landscape on this page. These objects have been represented in a highly **stylized** way. This means *simplified* or *exaggerated.* Some artists choose to stylize their works because it allows them to picture nature in a unique, personal way.

Select a park or other familiar nature scene in your community. On a sheet of drawing paper, sketch the trees, flowers, and other landscape features. Make your view stylized by simplifying or exaggerating the shapes of these objects. Complete your stylized landscape with markers.

 PORTFOLIO

Write a description of how you stylized the objects in your landscape. Evaluate the success of your efforts and put this evaluation in your portfolio with your work.

STUDIO ACTIVITY

A Stylized Landscape

Instruct students to choose his/her own style of representing this scene. The view should have some recognizable features. Have students make several sketches and explore different media to discover textures and effects they want to use.

■ Art Criticism

Have students use the four steps of art criticism to critique Pickett's and Miró's paintings. Then have them compare the paintings. Is each painting successful? Why or why not?

■ Cultural Diversity

Divide the class into small groups. Assign each group a culture of the early 1900's to research. Areas of study:
- geography, including topography, climate, crops, industry
- culture, including music, art, literature, dance
- significant events and people

• • • • • • • • • •
ASSESS

■ Self-Assessment

Have students complete the Check Your Understanding questions on this page. Answers are provided below.

■ Reteaching

Have students explain what is stylized about their landscapes.

■ Enrichment

Bring in, if you can, additional examples of Gauguin's and Miró's work. Invite students to draw a landscape imitating the style of each.

• • • • • • • • • •
CLOSE

Ask students to define a stylized landscape.

105

• • • • • • • • • • • • • •
FOCUS

☑ OBJECTIVES

After completing this lesson, students will be able to:
• Create an *assemblage*.
• Describe, analyze, interpret, and judge their work.

☑ SUPPLIES

• Pencil and sheets of sketching paper
• Collection of small natural objects
• White construction paper or poster board
• Oil pastels, markers
• White glue

Resource

▪ 6-3 In Their Nature, TRB page 94 (cultural diversity)

• • • • • • • • • • • • • •
TEACH

▪ Motivator

Ask students if they have ever walked along a path so many times that they felt they could go there with their eyes closed. Have students recall a familiar landscape scene and identify details about the scene others might not notice. Explain that artists like to use that special, overlooked detail as the focus of a painting.

▪ Vocabulary

Explain the term *assemblage*. Point out that the word comes from *assemble*. Help students understand the three-dimensional qualities of an assemblage.

106

 LESSON 2

Creating a Nature Scene

Have you ever taken a route so many times that you felt you could travel it with your eyes closed? Such a path appears in the work in Figure 6–4. It leads to a village in the artist's native Honduras. Notice how plants, trees, and the stone fence bordering the path are painted rhythmically as repeated shapes and textures. Despite being stylized, the work invites the viewer in for a stroll toward the town. Look carefully. The painting is organized so as to lead your eye to the center of interest. Can you identify that center of interest? What elements and principles of art are used to help draw your eye to it?

WHAT YOU WILL LEARN

You will make a nature scene of a familiar place that you know well or have recently visited. You will begin by collecting small natural objects to make an **assemblage** (ah-sem-**blahzh**). This means *a three-dimensional artwork consisting of many pieces assembled together.* You will also use markers and oil pastels to draw other objects and details. To do this, you will organize your work to create a center of interest. You will emphasize the most important part of the scene using lines, shapes, colors, and textures.

Figure 6–4   Notice how the textures are created in this painting. What principle of art has the artist used to draw your eye to the center of interest?

Jose Antonio Velasquez. *San Antonio de Oriente.* 1957. Oil on canvas. 66 × 94 cm (26 × 37″). Collection of the Art Museum of the Americas, Organization of American States, Washington, D.C.

106   Chapter 6   *Perceiving Nature*

MEETING STUDENT DIVERSITY

Diverse Learners   Making an assemblage is a good way to build self-esteem and self-confidence in students whose style of learning is more kinesthetic, or for those who may not view themselves as particularly talented artists. Encourage students to be creative in their search for natural objects, and make practical suggestions for tactile, textured objects that are easily collected. Augment what the students collect with a variety of easy-to-get objects like seeds, leaves, twigs, and so on.

As students gather their found natural objects, be sure they do not pick any protected species of wildflower or take anything from private property without prior permission.

WHAT YOU WILL NEED

- Pencil and sheets of sketch paper
- White construction paper or poster board, 12 x 18 inches
- Collection of small natural objects
- Oil pastels
- Markers
- White glue

WHAT YOU WILL DO

1. Visit a park or other local area that might make a good subject for a landscape. Carry a sketch pad with you. Make several sketches. Include important features such as plants, trees, houses, and hills. Show these as simple, flat shapes. Plan the picture to emphasize a particular object or area as the center of interest.
2. Before leaving the area, collect small objects in a plastic bag. Possibilities include small twigs, pebbles, sand, bark, leaves, or dried grass. Avoid objects that are likely to wilt or change in a few days, such as fresh flowers or insects.
3. Transfer your best sketch onto construction paper or poster board. Using oil pastels or markers, begin adding color. Apply hues that match the colors of the natural objects you plan to use.
4. Decide which areas of your composition you will decorate with the objects you collected. Choose objects whose natural textures suit the subject matter. You might use sand for a path. Attach the objects with white glue. Make sure all areas of the composition are covered.

EXAMINING YOUR WORK

- **Describe**   Identify the objects and shapes in your landscape scene. Describe the setting.
- **Analyze**   Explain how you organized your picture to create a center of interest. Which object or area did you emphasize? Where did you use tactile and visual textures?
- **Interpret**   Decide what feeling or mood your work communicates to viewers. Find out if viewers can identify the place your picture describes.
- **Judge**   Tell whether you feel your work succeeds. Explain your answer.

5. Step back and review the organization of your work. Make sure the elements of art emphasize one part of the picture. If you like, use drawing media to add buildings, animals, or human figures to the scene.
6. When the glue is dry, display your work.

Figure 6–5 **Student work. A nature scene.**

Try This! STUDIO OPTIONS

■ Plan another assemblage. This time, create an imaginary landscape. Use a larger sheet of poster board or work with a small group to produce four separate panels that will fit together.

■ With a group, make a nature diorama. Combine found natural objects and drawings. Include forms of plant life and, if you prefer, animal life. These are to be sculpted to scale from materials such as modeling clay, wire, wood, and cotton.

Lesson 2   *Creating a Nature Scene*   **107**

more about • • •

Naïve or Folk Art Velasquez tried several careers before he began to paint in 1933. These professions included mayor of San Antonio de Oriente, which is the subject of his painting in Figure 6-4, and barber in the Pan American School of Agriculture. Velasquez is considered to be a Naïve or folk artist because he is not interested in representing a realistic image but is more interested in communicating an idea or feeling. Naïve artists appear to lack the knowledge or interest in using accurate proportion, perspective, shading, and other visual elements that make an artwork look realistic. Their work provides an invaluable visual history of everyday life.

■ **Aesthetics**

Velasquez was a self-taught painter whose drawings weren't as realistic as those of other painters. Ask students how important realism is to the success of the painting and why.

■ **Cultural Diversity**

José Antonio Velasquez was born in Caridad, Honduras, and made this painting in 1957. As a class, research Honduras using a variety of sources to find out the size, location, climate, geography, crops/products, and history as well as other Honduran artists of the time. Include information on occupations, housing, and living conditions.

■ **Studio Skills**

Students should sort the assembled objects to make them easier to use. Then have students make a few preliminary sketches to plan the composition so that it emphasizes a center of interest. Encourage students to add color first to the poster board spaces, then use a thick, non-toxic white glue to attach materials.

• • • • • • • • • • • • • • •
ASSESS

■ **Self-Assessment**

Have students use Examining Your Work to evaluate their art.

■ **Reteaching**

Ask students to work in pairs to explain to each other the center of interest in their assemblages.

■ **Enrichment**

Invite students to research the lush vegetation and topography of Honduras or another tropical country. Have them create an assemblage from that location.

• • • • • • • • • • • • • • •
CLOSE

Have students share their assemblages and explain their center of interest.

Nature Close Up

• • • • • • • • • • • • •
FOCUS

☑OBJECTIVES

After completing this lesson, students will be able to:
• Define *study* and *nature study* as they relate to art.
• Use an unusual point of view to draw a familiar object.

☑SUPPLIES

• Pencils and sheets of sketch paper
• Sheets of watercolor or drawing paper
• Watercolors, brushes, water containers, paper towels

Resource

■ 6-4 Miniatures,
   TRB page 95 (art history)

• • • • • • • • • • • • •
TEACH

■ Motivator

Put a sample of soil on a sheet of paper. Have students predict what they could expect to find in the soil. Use a pencil to separate small sticks, stones, and to observe all other soil ingredients. What did they discover in closely examining the soil that they did not expect to find?

■ Vocabulary

Review the meaning of *point of view*. Then clarify the meaning of *study* as a noun, and *nature study*.

Have you ever looked at a familiar object under a microscope or magnifying glass? Maybe you have seen the "rivers" that crisscross the surface of human skin. Perhaps you discovered that grains of table salt, far from shapeless forms, are perfect cubes!

When seen up close, the world reveals many surprises. Artists have long known this. Many have recorded insect's-eye views of nature. In this lesson, you will see some of these.

NATURE STUDIES

As noted in Chapter 3, the art of drawing serves several purposes. One of these is to help artists improve perception—how they "see" objects. Another is to make studies. A **study** is *a drawing used to plan a painting or other large project.* The artwork in Figure 6–6 was created with both purposes in mind. The work is an example of a **nature study.** This is *a drawing used to help artists sharpen their perception of natural objects.*

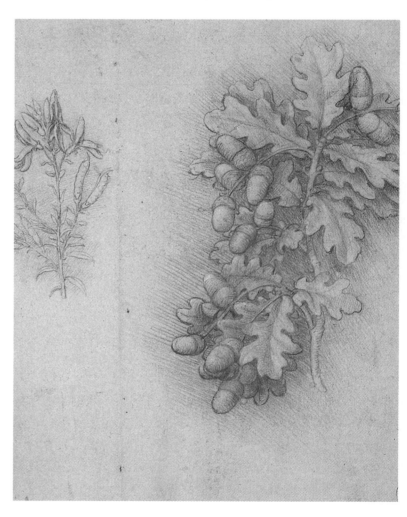

Figure 6–6 Which of the works on these two pages is more realistic? What role do you think art materials played in this difference?

Leonardo da Vinci. *Oak Leafs and a Spray of Greenwood.* c. 1506–08. Red conte pencil. 18.8 × 15.4 cm (7½ × 6"). The Royal Collection © Her Majesty Queen Elizabeth II.

108 Chapter 6 *Perceiving Nature*

◆ *CURRICULUM* ▷ *CONNECTIONS* ◆

Science Ask a biology teacher or other science teacher to allow your class to take a closer look at a drop of pond water, grains of table salt, a slice of onion, or some other small item with the aid of a microscope. First have students write down a description of the sample item, using the unaided eye. Next, ask the science teacher to demonstrate the proper and safe use of the microscope and allow each student to investigate the item with the aid of the lens. (If necessary, ask the science teacher to help students identify what they see.) Have students write about what they see using the microscope. What details do they see that they could not see before? Have students discuss the differences in point of view.

Figure 6–7 How many different plants do you count in this painting? How many of these forms do you recognize?

Albrecht Dürer. *The Great Piece of Turf.* c. 1503. Watercolor on paper. 41.3 × 31.8 cm (16¼ × 12½"). The Bridgeman Art Library, London. Albertina Graphic Collection, Vienna, Austria.

The artist who made this drawing is Leonardo da Vinci. Leonardo had many talents. He was an architect, a musician, and an inventor. As an artist, he filled many sketchbooks with drawings like the one on this page. He often included detailed written descriptions of what he saw. Study Figure 6–6. Do you recognize the objects hanging between the leaves of the branches? Leonardo called them "oak nuts." You probably know them better as *acorns*. Notice how the artist has created three dimensions working with pencil. How many different textures can you find in the work?

A Painting of Nature Up Close

Not all studies of nature are drawings. The work in Figure 6–7 is a painting. It was done around the same time as Leonardo's nature study. Like Figure 6–6, it shows a close-up view of plant life.

STUDIO ACTIVITY

Experimenting with Point of View

One interesting aspect of the painting in Figure 6–7 is its *point of view*. As noted in Chapter 4, point of view is the angle from which the viewer sees the scene in an artwork. The point of view of this painting is ground level. We see the images as an ant or other insect might see them.

Choose a familiar object, such as a chair in your home or classroom. Using pencil, sketch this object from an unfamiliar point of view. You may want to lie on the floor and draw the object looking up at it. Use shading and other techniques you have learned about to make your subject look three-dimensional.

PORTFOLIO

Write a description of a problem you had in drawing your object from an unusual point of view. Tell how you solved it. Attach this evaluation to your work and put it in your portfolio.

Study this painting. In it, the artist focuses mainly on the shapes and patterns of the leaves. He uses different values of green and yellow to capture lines and details. How does he create a sense of depth in this painting? What aesthetic view would you use to judge this work? (See Chapter 4, pages **64–65** for a review of the aesthetic views.)

✔ Check Your Understanding

1. What is a study? What is a nature study?
2. What were some of Leonardo da Vinci's talents besides art?
3. What is the point of view of the painting in Figure 6–7?

■ Art Criticism

Have students describe both works. Ask them to decide if one work shows more texture and represents nature more effectively. What is the message or artists' intent in making the drawing and the painting?

■ Art History

In small groups, have students research the Renaissance. List important historical events, famous people in the arts, popular literature, dance forms, music, and other artists and their works.

Sparking Creativity

For the Studio Activity, nudge students to choose an unexpected familiar object. For example, did they ever take a close look at the door, from the point of view of the floor? Students can add a little whimsy to this activity with a creative spark.

ASSESS

■ Self-Assessment

Have students complete the Check Your Understanding questions on this page. Answers are provided below.

■ Reteaching

Ask students to work in pairs to discuss the point of view they used in their sketches.

■ Enrichment

Invite students to research the life of Leonardo da Vinci in more detail. Have students share what they discover, for example, about his roles in science, medicine, architecture, and art.

CLOSE

Ask students to define *nature study* and *point of view.*

• • • • • • • • • • • •
FOCUS

☑ OBJECTIVES

After completing this lesson, students will be able to:

• Draw a nature scene using a bird's-eye point of view.
• Use chalk and oil pastels to express feeling in their work.
• Describe, analyze, interpret, and judge their work.

☑ SUPPLIES

• Pencil and sketching paper
• Light-colored construction paper
• Chalk, oil pastels
• Fixative or acrylic polymer medium

Resource

■ 6-5 Please Repeat That, TRB page 96 (art history)

• • • • • • • • • • • •
TEACH

■ Motivator

Ask students if they have ever wanted to climb to a high place to get a better view of the world. Tell them that such a view is called a "bird's-eye view." Ask students if Wyeth's painting in Figure 6-8 is effective in showing a "bird's-eye view."

■ Vocabulary

Explain that *organic* refers to nature. Organic lines or shapes would be those lines or shapes that represent and describe natural shapes and forms.

110

LESSON 4

Drawing from a Bird's-Eye View

The painting in Figure 6–7 on page **109**, as you have learned, was done from an interesting point of view. So is the one in Figure 6–8. Look carefully at this work. Like those in the previous lesson, this one provides a close-up view of nature. In this case, the subject is a tree. The point of view is from high among the branches. There is much more to the work, however. Did you notice the lone human figure in the painting? He is easy to spot because of his red cap, which stands out vividly against the mostly brown earth tones. He is a hunter. You won't find his prey—a bird—in the picture. That is because the bird sits in the branches, gazing down at the hunter. You are seeing the scene through the bird's eyes!

WHAT YOU WILL LEARN

In this lesson, you will picture a familiar scene as a bird might view it. Depending on where you live, the scene may be in the country or city. You will include natural objects, such as mountains, fields, rivers, and streams, or objects made by people, such as buildings, streets, and trucks. After sketching the scene in chalk, you will add color by blending oil

Figure 6–8 Notice the attention to detail in this work. How many different visual textures can you find?

Andrew Wyeth. *The Hunter.* 1943. Tempera on Masonite. 83.8 × 86 cm (33 × 33⅞"). Toledo Museum of Art, Toledo, Ohio. Elizabeth C. Mau Bequest Fund.

110   Chapter 6   *Perceiving Nature*

RESOURCES BEYOND THE CLASSROOM

Shadowing   Students can learn about art careers by "shadowing" adults who work in art-related fields. The adults allow students to follow—shadow—them in the workplace for a few hours. When appropriate, students can actually participate; for instance, help arrange the background for a display case. An alternative is a "lunch-buddy" program, where students are paired up with adults in art-related fields. At lunchtime, the adults eat with their assigned student in the school cafeteria. Students get a chance for one-on-one discussions of art careers, and adults have the opportunity to mentor a young person. Lunch-buddy programs work best when "buddies" meet frequently throughout the year.

pastels. Use colors that give your picture a certain mood or feeling. As in Figure 6–8, your work will make use of different textures to achieve variety.

WHAT YOU WILL NEED

- Pencil and sketch paper
- Any light color of construction paper, 12 x 18 inches (30 x 46 cm)
- Chalk
- Oil pastels

1. Select the place you will draw. Complete several sketches of this location from a bird's-eye view. Include natural or other objects found in the setting.
2. Decide which is your best sketch. Redraw it lightly in chalk on construction paper. Use a pencil eraser to remove any unwanted lines.
3. Choose hues of oil pastels that fit your subject. Blend some colors. Include

EXAMINING YOUR WORK

- **Describe**   Tell what your work shows. Point to natural objects or those objects in the work that were made by people.
- **Analyze**   Identify the hues in your work. Which hues were created by blending oil pastels? Explain how you added variety using different textures.
- **Interpret**   Tell what mood your drawing captures. Did you record a stressful moment, as in Figure 6–8?
- **Judge**   Tell whether you are satisfied with your drawing. Identify areas of the work that especially pleased you. Address what you would do differently next time.

different textures, as in Figure 6–8, to add variety to your work. Color in all of the areas of your picture.

Figure 6–9   Student work. A bird's eye view.

STUDIO OPTIONS

■ Draw a view of the same location as though you were a worm. Use a combination of media such as oil pastels and watercolors.

■ Using pencil, draw Figure 6–8 from the hunter's point of view. Decide what the hunter is looking at. Use crayons or markers to capture some of the same tones the artist did.

Lesson 4   *Drawing from a Bird's-Eye View*   **111**

SAFETY TIP

Using Fixatives in the Classroom   Be sure to stress safety if you allow students to spray or brush their artwork with any kind of fixative in the classroom. Fumes from sprays can be toxic. (Acrylic polymers are not toxic.) Check the labels on all supplies to be certain they are safe for school use. Before applying fixatives, make sure the room is well ventilated. If you plan to spray every student's work, do it outdoors or in batches over several hours if possible.

■ Aesthetics

Have students compare and contrast Wyeth's painting with Thomas Hart Benton's painting on page 102, Figure 6-1. Discuss differences in subject matter, painting style, techniques, organization, and the year each was painted. Ask: How is the mood or message different? Which painting would you buy? Explain why.

■ Art History

Tell students that *The Hunters* was painted in 1968 when Andrew Wyeth was very popular. Ask students to research what music and movies were popular and who were the other artists of that time.

■ Cooperative Learning

Students may have difficulty imagining a familiar scene from a bird's-eye point of view. Encourage students to work in small groups to come up with a list of ideas to draw from. Then have them fine tune their choice and proceed with the studio lesson.

ASSESS

■ Self-Assessment

Have students use Examining Your Work to evaluate their bird's-eye view drawing.

■ Reteaching

Ask students to explain how they attempted to achieve texture and mood in their drawings.

■ Enrichment

Invite students to find out about the Wyeths and share that information with the class, bringing in examples of their work. Have a one-day Wyeth festival to discuss the variety and scope of this family's talent.

CLOSE

Have students differentiate the natural and manufactured objects in their drawings, and explain the mood they tried to achieve.

111

LESSON 5

Art and the Seasons

☑ OBJECTIVES

After completing this lesson, students will be able to:

• Understand that certain images and colors are linked to different seasons.

• Complete a chalk drawing using hues and details to represent a landscape during a season of the year.

☑ SUPPLIES

• Pencil and sketching paper
• Colored construction paper
• Chalk for paper
• Fixative

Resources

■ 6-6 Pieter Bruegel the Elder, TRB page 97 (artist profile)
■ 6-7 Celebrating Seasons, TRB page 98 (cooperative learning)

■ Motivator

Have students look closely at the winter landscape in Figure 6-11. From the details, can they identify the time and place where it was painted? Have students make a list of all the tasks they observe people doing in the painting. How was everyday life then different from today?

■ Vocabulary

Have students look up the word *season*. What parts of speech is this word? *(Noun and verb.)*

112

The seasons showcase nature's many faces. Think of the changing leaves in autumn. Think of winter, with its icy chill. Imagine the beauty of spring with its new buds and shoots.

The seasons and their colors have appealed to artists throughout the ages. Many artists have used their art to share special views of one season or another.

A WORK SHOWING AUTUMN

From falling stars to rainbows to picture-perfect sunsets, nature stages many remarkable shows. One spectacular view is depicted in the painting in Figure 6–10. Study this work. It was done early in the twentieth century by a Canadian artist. The painting records the changing of the leaves in autumn. Have you ever heard autumn colors described as *fiery?* It is precisely this aspect of the leaves that the artist has captured. See how the sweeping brushstrokes and bright hues combine almost to suggest flames. As you study the painting, in which direction is your eye drawn? What principles have been used to organize the work?

A WORK SHOWING WINTER

Another seasonal event recorded by an artist is shown in Figure 6–11. The artist has offered a glimpse not only of an event but of

Figure 6–10 Where is this landscape set? What aspects of scenery has the artist included to define this setting?

Tom Thompson. *Autumn Foliage.* 1916. Oil on wood. 26.7 × 21.5 cm (10½ × 8½"). National Gallery of Canada, Ottawa.

112   Chapter 6 *Perceiving Nature*

CURRICULUM CONNECTIONS

Music Locate a tape or CD of Vivaldi's concertos *The Four Seasons*. Before you play the music for students, ask them to get paper and pencil out to take notes. As you play segments of the music, invite students to imagine what season the music seems to suggest. Explain that they may or may not "hear" all four seasons, but encourage them to describe any seasonal images that do come to mind. In their word descriptions, students should use colorful, vivid language to create a seasonal word picture.

a season. This winter scene has been preserved for over four centuries.

Examine the work. It shows a party of hunters and their dogs. They are returning home after a cold outing in the woods. A trio of birds huddle in the bare branches of the trees above the hunters. Still farther overhead is a bleak sky that promises more snow. Yet, the scene is not gloomy. In fact, it is almost cheerful. Down below the hunters, on a frozen lake, townspeople merrily skate.

Notice the suggestion of distance in the painting. The artist has used several of the techniques for capturing space covered on page **16** in Chapter 1. Two of these are *size* and *placement*. Observe how the trees in the background are smaller and placed higher up in the picture plane than the hunters are. What other techniques for suggesting space can you find?

Check Your Understanding

1. What images and colors are linked with different seasons?
2. Which of these colors and images appear in the two works in this lesson?

STUDIO ACTIVITY

Creating Seasonal Colors

Look once more at Figure 6–10. The objects in the work—leaves and branches, a lake, and the sky—are clearly recognizable. The work also captures the mood of autumn. Imagine that the artist had painted the same landscape in the dead of winter. What colors do you suppose he would have chosen?

Here is your chance to find out. Do a rough pencil sketch of a similar scene on a sheet of white construction paper. Your landscape does not have to be identical to the one in Figure 6–10. Complete your drawing using colored chalk. Select hues to emphasize the season and the mood.

PORTFOLIO

Share your work with classmates. Take turns critiquing each other's work. Take notes on the comments made about your landscape and put them in your portfolio with the work.

Figure 6–11 **This work by Pieter Bruegel shows winter activities in the 1500s. How has the artist used color to portray a winter landscape?**

Pieter Bruegel. *Return of the Hunters.* 1565. Oil on wood. 117 × 162 cm (46 × 63¾″). Kunsthistorisches Museum, Vienna, Austria. Erich Lessing/Art Resource, NY

Lesson 5   *Art and the Seasons*   **113**

LESSON TIME: 120 minutes

• • • • • • • • • • • • • •
FOCUS

☑ OBJECTIVES

After completing this lesson, students will be able to:

• Create a visual record of their home during a specific season of the year.
• Describe, analyze, interpret, and judge their work.

☑ SUPPLIES

• Pencil and sketch paper
• White drawing or construction paper
• Markers, oil pastels
• Watercolors, brushes, water containers, and paper towels

Resources

• 6-8 Landscape Gardening, TRB page 99 (reproducible master)
• 6-9 In Any Kind of Weather, TRB page 100 (aesthetics/art criticism)

• • • • • • • • • • • • • •
TEACH

■ Motivator

Ask students to think about what their homes and neighborhoods look like in different seasons. Ask students which senses (sight, smell, taste, sound, or touch) help them to instantly recall a significant vision.

114

Painting a Seasonal Event

Examine the painting in Figure 6–12. The subject of this work is a family sharing dessert after dark. Look closely at the scene. It shows a front porch where brothers and sisters, parents, and grandparents are enjoying cold watermelon on a hot summer night. Flowers are blooming, a quarter moon shines high in the sky, and the family has gathered at the end of the day. How has the artist used color to show it is nighttime? How has she used value? Do you think her recollection of summer nights is a pleasant one?

WHAT YOU WILL LEARN

You will create a visual record of where you live right now. Your record will depict your home at a season of the year that holds special meaning for you. You will include objects, details, and colors that provide clues as to the time of year. Choose a point of view for your picture, perhaps a view like the one in Figure 6–12. Plan the composition of your work to communicate your feelings. Use repeated lines, shapes, and colors to create harmony.

Figure 6–12   Notice how the artist has used color and shape in this scene. What principles of art has she used?

Carmen Lomas Garza. *Sandia/Watermelon*. 1986. Gouache. 50.8 × 71.1 cm (20 × 28″).
© 1986 Carmen Lomas Garza. Private collection.

114   Chapter 6   *Perceiving Nature*

---

more about • • •

Carmen Lomas Garza   Some people write about their day-to-day experiences. Carmen Lomas Garza tells her life story through her paintings. By age 13, Garza knew that she wanted to be an artist. She decided to use art as a way to express her pride in her Mexican heritage and to inform people about this culture. "I felt I had to start with my earliest recollections…."

She creates *monitos*, or little people paintings. The paintings show scenes of everyday life. They also recount special events and Mexican celebrations such as hitting a *piñata* at a birthday party.

WHAT YOU WILL NEED

- Pencil and sketch paper
- White drawing or construction paper, 12 x 18 inches (30 x 46 cm)
- Markers
- Oil pastels, watercolors
- Brushes, water
- Paper towels

WHAT YOU WILL DO

1. Complete several sketches showing your home and surrounding area at a particular time of year. Include details and objects that provide clues as to the season. Organize the composition to emphasize a mood or feeling.
2. Transfer your sketch to drawing or construction paper. Outline important objects—animals, people, houses, and so on—with a fine-tipped black marker. Repeat lines and shapes to create a sense of harmony.
3. Choose hues of oil pastels that communicate the season and mood of the picture. Use these to color the outlined objects. Repeat colors to increase a sense of harmony.
4. Switch to watercolors. Using a medium brush, paint over the oil pastels and blank areas to cover the remaining spaces. Work freely over the entire surface. The oil pastels, which are oily, will act as a **resist.** This is *an art medium, such as crayon, that serves as a protective coating*. The pastels will prevent the watercolors from reaching the paper.

EXAMINING YOUR WORK

- **Describe** Identify the objects in your picture. Point out your home and other interesting features of your neighborhood. Describe the point of view you used.
- **Analyze** Explain how your work is organized. Identify how you used the elements of line, shape, and color to create harmony.
- **Interpret** Explain the mood of your work. Can classmates correctly identify the season you have captured?
- **Judge** Decide if your work succeeds in communicating a special seasonal event. What would you change if you were to do it again?

Figure 6–13 **Student work. Winter holiday season.**

![Try This!]

STUDIO OPTIONS

■ Working with several classmates, plan and make a mural. The work should detail a special historical event in your school or community, such as Founder's Day. Research the history of the event. Complete the mural on a sheet of wrapping or butcher's paper using the media of your choice.

■ Make a memory collage of a favorite seasonal event. Think of images that bring to mind the sounds, smells, and tastes of that event. Include photographs and pictures from magazines and newspapers. Add original drawings that help convey this memory.

Lesson 6 *Painting a Seasonal Event* **115**

■ Aesthetics

Ask students how Garza's scene differs from Breugel's landscape. Does the fact that Garza's painting is more stylized rather than realistic make it a better or poorer painting? Do both artists communicate the same message in their paintings? Does Garza successfully communicate her reason for painting this scene? Ask students to explain their opinions.

■ Cultural Diversity

Every artist is influenced by his or her culture. Have small groups research other American folk artists who have painted in the past century and share their findings with the class. They should include information on where these artists lived, their cultural backgrounds, other occupations, if any, and what kinds of themes or ideas they painted.

ASSESS

■ Self-Assessment

Have students use Examining Your Work to evaluate their art.

■ Reteaching

Ask students to explain how oil pastels act as a resist.

■ Enrichment

Have students explore the theme of home or season in poetry. Ask them to bring in some selections to read aloud.

CLOSE

Have students explain the season and mood of their art and the principles used to organize it.

Using Oil Pastels Explore making different textures and patterns with oil pastels by blending colors and using a variety of lines and shapes. Compare the results of outlining some objects with pen to other shapes and forms that are just filled in with color. Demonstrate the resist process by using water color to cover remaining paper spaces between the oil pastels. Show students how to protect oil pastels from smearing as they work by laying a sheet of paper under their hand. It also helps to work from the top of the paper to the bottom if possible.

• • • • • • • • • • • • • • •
FOCUS

☑ OBJECTIVES

After completing this lesson, students will be able to:

• Recognize how the use of expressive color schemes and diagonal lines can communicate nature's power.

• Define and create a monoprint.

☑ SUPPLIES

• 12 × 18-inch construction paper in light colors

• Oil pastels or crayons in dark colors

• Liquid starch

• White powdered tempera

• • • • • • • • • • • • • • •
TEACH

■ Motivator

Have a group of students demonstrate the position of their bodies as they struggle and strain against a powerful imaginary wind. Point out the diagonal body lines. Ask students to list all the different ways the artists show the action of the wind in Figures 6-14 and 6-15.

■ Vocabulary

Have students look up the combining form *mono-* in the dictionary, then list some words that begin with *mono-*.

LESSON 7

The Power of Nature

"March comes in like a lion and goes out like a lamb." You have probably heard this saying. It describes two of nature's personalities. The second of them is nature's gentle side. This can be seen on a mild spring day when there is sunshine, a soft breeze, and the season's first flowers.

The first—nature's rough and sometimes frightening side—is another personality. With floods, earthquakes, and tornadoes, we experience the power of nature. In the lesson, you will see and learn about artworks that relate to nature's power.

CAPTURING A STORM IN A PAINTING

Sometimes nature's fury makes the headlines. The threat of a hurricane sends coastal residents packing. A blizzard dumping three feet of snow closes schools for days.

Weather conditions command the attention of the news media and artists. The painting in Figure 6–14 shows the raw power of nature. Look closely at this work. You can almost feel the force of the wind that tears at the struggling tree in the foreground. You can almost hear the sound of the foaming waves crashing against the rocks.

Figure 6–14   In what direction is the wind blowing in this picture? How do you know this?

Frederick Varley. *Stormy Weather, Georgian Bay.* 1920. Oil on canvas. 132.6 × 162.8 cm (52⅛ × 64″). National Gallery of Canada, Ottawa.

116   Chapter 6   *Perceiving Nature*

Expressive Color Schemes

The creator of the painting in Figure 6–14 achieved this powerful effect using a cool color scheme. The limited use of color in this painting emphasizes the idea that the wind is everywhere. There is no escape or shelter from it. Its fierce gusts overpower the trees, land, the water, and even the sky. What basic hues are used in this painting? Where do you find light values of those hues? Where are darker values used?

CAPTURING A STORM IN A PRINT

You will find a similar theme running through Figure 6–15. This work is a wood-block print. Notice the work's title. Ejiri is a place in the artist's homeland of Japan. Examine the use of line and color in the work. In what ways is this "view" of the wind similar to the one in Figure 6–14? What differences can you find between the two works?

 Check Your Understanding

1. What type of color schemes show nature's seasons?
2. What is a monoprint? Why can only a single image be created using this printmaking technique?

 STUDIO ACTIVITY

Making a Monoprint

You are about to make a **monoprint**. This is *a print made by applying ink or paint to a plate and then transferring the image by hand-rubbing.*

Begin by drawing a simple landscape in crayon on a sheet of gray or pale blue construction paper. Use mostly dark values of the colors you choose.

Place a drop of liquid starch the size of half a dollar on a table top. Sprinkle a small amount of white powdered tempera onto the starch. With one bare hand, mix the starch and paint. Spread the mixture out until it is the size of your drawing. Make diagonal lines and swirls in the paint with your hand. Wash and dry your hands. Carefully lay your drawing face-down on the "plate" you have created. Press all over the surface with your other hand. Lift your print by pulling it up from one side. Lay it on newspapers to dry.

 P O R T F O L I O

Examine your monoprint. Evaluate the success of your technique on a sheet of paper and put it in your portfolio with the print.

Figure 6–15 How would you have been able to identify a gust of wind as the subject of this painting without the aid of the title?

Katsushika Hokusai. *A Gust of Wind at Ejiri,* from the series *The Thirty-Six Views of Fuji.* 1831–33. Wood block print. 24.5 × 37.5 cm (9⅝ × 14¾"). The Metropolitan Museum of Art, New York, New York. Rogers Fund, 1936.

Lesson 7 *The Power of Nature* **117**

 STUDIO ACTIVITY

Making a Monoprint

Emphasize that using color heavily assures that shapes will not disappear later under the monoprint. Demonstrate the printing process. Remind students to use only one hand to mix the starch and paints. Have them explore different kinds of action lines with the side or palm of their hand. Since the printing process removes most of the fingerpaint, more starch and tempera need to be added for the next student, and it cleans up very easily.

Art in Everyday Life

Observing the power of nature is a good way for students to see and appreciate the art and beauty that is all around them. Discuss ways that nature can inspire us as artists.

ASSESS

■ Self-Assessment

Have students complete the Check Your Understanding questions on this page. Answers are provided below.

■ Reteaching

Have students practice using cool colors and diagonal lines to create a stormy scene.

■ Enrichment

Invite students to research how severe weather systems and hurricanes are tracked. Have students discuss how artists might be inspired by such images.

CLOSE

Have students evaluate the monoprint technique.

Answers to ✔CHECK YOUR UNDERSTANDING

1. Dark, monochromatic color schemes can be used to communicate the power of nature.

2. A monoprint is a print made by applying ink or paint to a plate and then transferring the image by hand-rubbing. This printing technique produces only a single image because the plate can be used only once. This is because the transferred image absorbs all the ink.

☑OBJECTIVES

After completing this lesson, students will be able to:

- Identify the kinds of lines, colors, and brushstrokes that create movement.
- Plan an informally balanced composition that includes repeating lines, shapes, and colors.
- Paint a stormy scene mixing a single hue plus white and black.
- Describe, analyze, interpret, and judge their work.

☑SUPPLIES

- Pencil and sketch paper
- Dark colored posterboard or construction paper
- Tempera paints: black, white, and other hues
- Paper plates or painting palettes
- Brushes, water containers, paper towels

Resource

■ 6-8 Storm Front, TRB page 101 (cultural diversity)

. . . .
TEACH

■ Motivator

Have students identify the feelings and moods they associate with dramatic weather changes and storms. Have students identify the lines and brushstrokes that help to create movement in the painting.

118

Painting a Storm

Have you ever had days when things just didn't seem to go right? So, it seems, does nature. Such a day is the subject of Figure 6–16. The work pictures a bleak, rainy afternoon. Unlike the works you studied in the previous lesson, there is no fury in the storm depicted here—just gloom. Notice the churning gray clouds overhead. See the rippling puddles underfoot of anyone unlucky enough to be out on such a day. The monochromatic tones of clouds and buildings make you glad to be inside, where it is safe and dry. That is, in fact, where you are as you look at this scene. Did you notice the blurred lines on the window at the left? The distortion is caused by the rain on your own window—the one you are gazing through. Can you find the single raindrop that has beaded on the glass?

WHAT YOU WILL LEARN

You will paint an expressive bad-weather scene. You will begin by selecting a season,

Figure 6–16   The artist uses slanted lines to represent the falling rain. What type of line does he use to capture the clouds? What type of color scheme does he use?

Charles Burchfield. *Night of the Equinox*. 1917–55. Watercolor, brush, and ink, gouache and charcoal on paper. 102 × 132.5 cm (40⅛ × 52³⁄₁₆"). National Museum of American Art, Washington, D.C. Gift of the Sara Roby Foundation/Art Resource, NY

118   Chapter 6   *Perceiving Nature*

MEETING SPECIAL NEEDS

Behavior Disorders   Painting a stormy scene provides an excellent opportunity to communicate troubling emotions through the veiled language of art. Some students with behavior disorders may show evidence of problems in their actions and in their artwork. Classroom teachers may be among the first to see cues in an emotionally upset child's artwork, suggesting a corroboration of an unhappy or upsetting life situation. Of course, untrained people should certainly not attempt to diagnose from artwork, but artwork can provide specialists with corroborating clues to conditions.

time of day, and place. You will include trees, plants, and objects that help to describe the setting and the weather conditions. You will use tints and shades of a single hue of tempera paint. Various tints and shades of blue, for example, might be used to suggest a landscape with falling snow. You will use a variety of lines to help express movement.

WHAT YOU WILL NEED
- Pencil and sketch paper
- Poster board or heavy construction paper, 12 x 18 inches (30 x 46 cm)
- Tempera paint
- Paper plate
- Brushes
- Water container
- Paper towels

WHAT YOU WILL DO
1. With classmates, brainstorm examples of bad weather. Jot down specific images that come to mind. Choose a particular image. Decide on the time of year and place.
2. Working by yourself, complete several sketches of your foul-weather scene. Sketch plants, trees, and other objects quickly. Use a variety of lines that suggest movement, as in Figure 6–16. Repeat some of the lines to create rhythm.
3. Transfer your scene onto poster board or construction paper. Choose a color of tempera that best fits your scene. On the paper plate, mix white and black tempera with the color you selected to create different tints and shades. Paint your scene. As you work, keep mood and color uppermost in your mind.

EXAMINING YOUR WORK
- **Describe** Identify the season in your painting. Identify the time of day and place.
- **Analyze** Explain how you organized your work. Identify the different tints and shades you used. Where did you repeat lines or shapes to show movement?
- **Interpret** Tell what mood or feeling your work communicates. What is the title of your painting? Does it capture this mood or feeling?
- **Judge** State whether your artwork is successful. What details help make your painting expressive?

4. Paint all of the spaces. Switch to a small brush with fine bristles to paint small shapes and details. Use black or white tempera to outline any important areas.
5. Choose a title for your work that reflects the mood and weather. See if other students can identify the season, time of day, and place in your painting.

Figure 6–17   **Student work. Rain in spring.**

Try This!

COMPUTER OPTION

■ Use your program's Shape and Fill tools to create a simple landscape. Shapes should be flat. Choose dark shades of colors. If the software you are using has a Blend or Smear brush, select and use it. Paint objects with diagonal lines. Make some lines longer than others. Describe the effect you have achieved.

CURRICULUM CONNECTIONS

Language Arts Weather and the forces of nature have mesmerized humans for millennia. Like other kinds of artists, poets have always had a fascination with nature. You may want to read some of the following poems to students, or encourage them to find others to read and illustrate on their own.

"Rainy Day" by Henry Wadsworth Longfellow

"Dust of Snow" by Robert Frost
"Bitter Cold, Living in the Village" by Po Chü-i
"Autumn" by Emily Dickinson
"The Sky" by e.e. cummings
"Night Clouds" by Amy Lowell
"Winter" by Nikki Giovanni
"Fog" by Carl Sandburg

■ **Cooperative Learning**

Divide the class into groups of three. Have each group collect old newspaper and magazine articles and photos related to severe weather. Have them share their findings with the whole class.

■ **Art Criticism**

Have students describe and analyze Burchfield's painting in Figure 6-16. Ask: What is the feeling or mood of the painting, and which elements convey that mood or feeling?

■ **Studio Skills**

Review mixing tints and shades by adding white and black to the hues. Have students use different brushes and strokes to represent the kinds of lines and weather conditions in their painting, and use pure hues or black or white to outline any important shapes or features.

ASSESS

■ **Self-Assessment**

Have students use Examining Your Work to evaluate their stormy weather scenes.

■ **Reteaching**

Ask pairs of students to identify the season and the mood in each other's work.

■ **Enrichment**

Tell students that Charles Burchfield (1893–1967) lived much of his life along the southern shores of Lake Erie. Ask students to research the states that border this Great Lake. Based on this information, ask students whether Burchfield used real or imaginary images of nature in this painting.

CLOSE

Have students evaluate their paintings in terms of the concept "storm."

CONNECTIONS *Environment*

Frank Johnston. *Fire-Swept Algoma*. 1920. Oil on canvas. 127.5 × 167.5 cm (50⅛ × 66″). National Gallery of Canada, Ottawa.

OBJECTIVES

After completing this feature, students will be able to:
- Understand why forest preservation is essential.
- Explain how artwork, such as Johnston's painting, can help us understand the importance of forests.

Teaching the Connection

- Have students read the feature on this page.
- Ask volunteers to share what they know about preserving forests. Who was the first U.S. president to make forest conservation a top priority? *(Theodore Roosevelt.)* Name some national parks and forests. *(Examples include Grand Canyon, Yellowstone, Yosemite.)* What organizations promote forest and wildlife preservation? *(Sierra Club, National Audubon Society, National Wildlife Federation.)*
- Encourage students to discuss the meaning of the following quote from Chief Standing Bear. "The old Lakota was wise. He knew that man's heart away from nature becomes hard; he knew that lack of respect for growing, living things soon led to lack of respect for humans too. So he kept his youth close to its softening influence."

Answers to Making the Connection

- ✔ Forests are essential to human life. Trees and other plants absorb carbon dioxide and give off oxygen.
- ✔ Fire can cause great devastation to forests.
- ✔ Johnston used a stark, grim style to paint the total destruction caused by a forest fire.

Why Do We Need to Preserve Forests?

Have you ever been camping in the woods? Do you enjoy eating a picnic lunch in a park? Have you ever been hiking or biking on wooded trails? Forests are an important part of our natural environment.

Not only do forests provide recreational areas, but they are also essential to human life. Trees and other plants absorb carbon dioxide in the air. In turn, they give off the oxygen we need to breathe. In addition, forests prevent soil erosion and provide a place for animals to live.

In pioneer times, American settlers thought that the Earth's natural resources were unlimited. They cut down many of the huge forests that once covered the eastern United States. They used the wood for lumber and cleared the land in order to build homes and create farmlands. Many forests have also been destroyed by fire. The majority of forest fires are started by carelessness. In Frank Johnston's painting, we see the tragic effects of a forest fire.

Today, we realize the importance of forests and other natural resources. Many conservation efforts have been made, including the establishment of national parks and forests.

MAKING THE CONNECTION

✔ Why are forests so important?
✔ What message do you think Frank Johnston was trying to convey in *Fire-Swept Algoma*?
✔ What techniques did the artist use to convey his message?

INTERNET ACTIVITY

Visit Glencoe's Fine Arts Web Site for students at:

http://www.glencoe.com/sec/art/students

INTERNET ACTIVITY

Meet the Masters Using our Internet activities, have small groups of students find out about an artist such as: Michelangelo, da Vinci, Monet, Renoir, or van Gogh. Students will experience the lifestyle, locale, influences, techniques, and artworks of this artist. Locate the step-by-step guidelines and worksheets for this activity in *Studio Cyberspace*. You may print out the instructions, or use the scrolling frame on the monitor to follow each step. Each activity screen will provide students with high-lighted hot links which will take them to information on the World Wide Web to complete the activity. Find us at **http:www.glencoe.com/sec/art**

C H A P T E R 6

REVIEW

 BUILDING VOCABULARY

Number a sheet of paper from 1 to 7. After each number, write the term from the box that matches each description below.

assemblage resist
landscape   study
monoprint   stylized
nature study

1. A drawing or painting of mountains, trees, or other natural scenery.
2. An art medium, such as crayon, that serves as a protective coating.
3. A three-dimensional artwork consisting of many pieces assembled together.
4. Simplified or exaggerated.
5. A drawing used to plan a painting or other large project.
6. A drawing used to help artists sharpen their perception of natural objects.
7. A print made by applying ink or paint to a plate and then transferring the image by hand-rubbing.

REVIEWING ART FACTS

Number a sheet of paper from 8 to 12. Answer each question in a complete sentence.

8. Give two reasons why artists might stylize works of art.
9. What were Leonardo da Vinci's two purposes in creating the drawing in Figure 6–6?
10. What is point of view?
11. What are some hues associated with spring? What colors are associated with winter?
12. What season is shown in Figure 6–12? How did the artist convey this time of year?

 THINKING ABOUT ART

On a sheet of paper, answer each question in a sentence or two.

1. **Analyze.** How did the artist of Figure 6–11 on page **113** prevent the scene from appearing lonely and gloomy?
2. **Compare and contrast.** The paintings in Figures 6–14 and 6–16 both make use of limited colors. Yet, the two works communicate different moods. How do you explain this?

MAKING ART CONNECTIONS

1. **Music.** Storms have been the subject not only of works of art. They have also been depicted in numerous musical compositions. Speak with a music teacher in your school or community to learn about musical works that "describe" storms. Two such works are Moussorgsky's *Night on Bald Mountain* and the "Cloudburst" movement of Grofe's *Grand Canyon Suite*. If you can, listen to one or more of these compositions. Share them with classmates, explaining how the works capture some of the images shown in the works in Lesson 7.

Chapter 6 Review **121**

ANSWERS TO CHAPTER 6 REVIEW

■ **Building Vocabulary**

1. landscape
2. resist
3. assemblage
4. stylized
5. study
6. nature study
7. monoprint

■ **Reviewing Art Facts**

8. This is done to fit the design rules of a specific culture and to personalize a work of art.
9. He did this to improve perception and as a study for a larger project.
10. The angle from which the viewer sees the scene in an artwork.
11. Spring colors include green and yellow. Winter colors include blue and white.
12. The season is summer. This is clear from the fact that the family is wearing summer clothes and eating watermelon.

? THINKING ABOUT ART

1. He managed this by including people, some of whom are engaged in a lively leisure-time activity.

2. The first of the two paintings is a pure landscape and depicts a fierce windstorm. The second has an urban or semi-urban setting. The point of view, moreover, is from indoors, where it is safe and warm.

121

Observing Animals

(pages 122–142)

Resources

- 7-12 Chapter Test, TRB page 120
- Transparency CC-7, *Howling Coyote*
- Transparency 7, *Bactrian Camel*
- Fine Art Print 11, *Daniel in the Lions' Den* by Peter Paul Rubens

Theatre/ Music

While studying this chapter, use Performing Arts Handbook page 319 to raise our sense of connection with animals through Minden's musical story about whales.

NATIONAL STANDARDS

This chapter addresses the following National Standards for the Visual Arts:

1. (a, b)   4. (a, b, c,)
2. (a, b, c,)   5. (a, b, c,)
3. (a, b)   6. (a, b)

Figure 7–1   How many different animals can you find in this picture? Would you expect to see these animals together? What message might the artist be sending by grouping the creatures in this manner?

Bev Doolittle. *The Sacred Circle*. 1991. Watercolor. 58.4 × 58.4 cm (23 × 23″) Courtesy of The Greenwich Workshop, Inc., Shelton, Connecticut.

122

FEATURED ARTISTS

Habib Allah
Constantin Brancusi
Bev Doolittle
Martin Johnson Heade
Edward Hicks

Charles Leonard
Franz Marc
Ayako Miyawaki
Spider Nabunu

CHAPTER 7

Observing Animals

Animal shapes are part of our earliest experiences as children. Our first toys include stuffed animals. Picture books of animals help us learn to read. Is it any wonder animals have long fascinated artists?

The painting on the facing page is made up of a group of nine artworks that Bev Doolittle did on the subject of animals and their environments. Notice how the art is placed so that the white areas in each artwork join to form the "sacred circle."

In this chapter, you will see the many different ways in which artists have shown animals in their work.

PORTFOLIO IDEAS

Make sure each entry remains separate and protected in your portfolio. You may want to separate artworks with a piece of tissue paper or newsprint. Mount and label photographs for clear identification. All entries should be easy to identify and see or read.

OBJECTIVES

After completing this chapter, you will be able to:
- Identify the way in which artists use the environment for subject matter.
- Explain the effects of culture and beliefs on art.
- Define the term *symbol,* and tell how symbols are used in art.
- Create art featuring real and imaginary animals.

WORDS YOU WILL LEARN

appliqué
calligraphy
environment
folk art
illumination
mascot
Old Stone Age
porcelain
symbol
tapestry
totem
trait

■ Chapter Overview
Understanding and appreciating the role of animals in the world of art is the focus of this chapter. Students will explore ancient artworks of animals as well as contemporary works. They will see how animals of the air, the land, and the sea have inspired artists, and they will tap their individual imaginations to create animal artworks of their own.

■ Chapter Motivator
Invite students to imagine that they could transform themselves into an animal. What creature would it be? Why? What characteristics does that animal have that are admirable or beautiful? Have students discuss any artworks of animals they have seen. Explain that in this chapter, students will observe animals in art.

■ Examining the Artwork
Point out to students that Bev Doolittle's *The Sacred Circle* is made up of nine separate paintings and that each is linked to its neighboring paintings by the use of the white areas.

National Museum of Women in the Arts
You may wish to use the National Museum of Women in the Arts videodisc and/or CD-ROM. The videodisc features a bar code guide, and the interactive CD-ROM provides stimulating activities.

123

DEVELOPING A PORTFOLIO

Presentation   When making decisions about the appearance of artworks in a portfolio, encourage students to pay attention to important concerns such as the mounting for paintings and using protective jackets for pastels and chalk drawings. Remind them to label individual pieces to avoid loss. Use slides for projects too large to include and show multiple viewpoints of three-dimensional artworks. When photographing a work of art, encourage the use of quality film and careful lighting, as it will enhance the finished slide. For more information, refer to the booklet, *Portfolio and Assessment Techniques* that accompanies this program.

Animals in Earliest Art

Does your family have a cat or dog? Maybe you own a bird or horse. Perhaps you know someone else who does. Animals, whether they are pets or roam wild, share our **environment,** or *surroundings.* Like other objects in the environment, animals have also long been a favorite subject of artists.

In the lessons to come, you will learn about different ways artists have portrayed animals. This lesson will focus on the role of animals in earliest art.

ANIMALS AS SUBJECTS

Using animals as art subjects is as old as art itself. For proof, look at the painting of a horse in Figure 7–2. This picture is on the wall of a cave in the Dordogne region of France. Two boys came upon the cave while playing ball. The boys made their discovery in 1941. The picture, however, is tens of thousands of years old. It dates back to the **Old Stone Age.** This is *the historical period that occurred between 30,000 and 10,000* B.C.

Experts regard this painting as one of the earliest artworks on record. Why did the first artists make pictures of animals? The experts have come up with likely answers to this question by looking closely at the role animals played in the environment of people long ago.

To people of the Old Stone Age, animals meant life. Their main source of food was the animals around them. They wore the animals' pelts, or furs, to protect them from the cold. For these reasons, a successful hunt was important and the paintings may have been used in a *ritual,* or ceremony, to bring luck.

Tools of the Early Painter

The environment of early artists not only answers the question of *why* they made cave paintings. It also answers the question of how. Like artists today, they started with pigment, which often came from clay. Iron deposits in the clay may account for the heavy presence of red, yellow, and brown. The pigment was then mixed with animal fat,

Figure 7–2 This prehistoric cave painting is sometimes called *The Chinese Horse.* Animals shaped like this one appear in later Chinese art.

Cave Painting. Lascaux, Dordogne, France. *Chinese Horse* (The Yellow Horse). c. 15,000–10,000 B.C.

124   Chapter 7 *Observing Animals*

CURRICULUM CONNECTIONS

Science   The Stone Age is the period of human culture in which people used stone, bone, wood, and ivory—rather than metal—to make tools. The period ended with the beginning of the Bronze Age, about 3500–3000 B.C. Stone Age art consisted of rock paintings, clay figures, pottery, and engravings and carvings of bone, stone, antlers, ivory, teeth, and shells. Paint pigments were four basic colors: black from charcoal, clay, and ground-up oxide of manganese; yellow and red from ocher (hydrated oxide of iron mixed with yellow clay), mashed berries and seeds, and animal blood; and white from clay and lime mud. Cave paintings and stone engravings still in existence provide scientific evidence about animals and humans during the Stone Age.

vegetable juice, or egg white as binders. The paint may have been brushed on with fingers, leaves, or animal hide. It may also have been blown onto the wall through a hollow reed.

EARLY ANIMAL SCULPTURES

After the Old Stone Age, animal art was not limited to painting. Some early artists worked in three dimensions. The miniature hippopotamus shown in Figure 7–3 comes from ancient Egypt. This sculpture is nearly 4,000 years old. It was found in the tomb of an important member of Egyptian society. The hippo was meant to protect the body after death. It is believed that this hippo was placed in the tomb as a good luck charm to protect the tomb from intruders.

There is another way in which the hippo in this artwork relates to its environment. The creature's head, back, and sides are decorated with features of the lotus plant. This plant grows in the marshes where hippos live. The sculptor painted a "record" of the hippo's environment on its body.

Check Your Understanding

1. Why may early cave dwellers have made pictures of the animals in their environment?
2. What clue to the environment of the hippopotamus is included in the Egyptian sculpture?

Figure 7–3 The artist has given clues to the hippo's environment by decorating its body with lotus plants. These grow in the marshes where hippos live.

Egyptian. Meir, Tomb of Senbi. *Figure of Hippopotamus.* Twelfth Dynasty (1991–1786 B.C.). Ceramics-Faience. 11 × 20 cm (4⅓ × 7⅚″). The Metropolitan Museum of Art, New York, New York. Gift of Edward S. Harkness, 1917.

Inventing a Mascot

Look again at the hippo in Figure 7–3. Its form is so appealing that it has become the mascot of Metropolitan Museum of Art in New York City. A **mascot** is *an animal or person used by a group as a sign of luck.* Your school sports teams may have mascots.

Make a mascot for your class or for yourself. Begin by thinking about popular animal sayings. *Sly as a fox* and *strong as a bull* are two such sayings. Decide on the **trait,** or *personal characteristic,* your mascot will show. Write the trait down on a sheet of paper. Next, study the shapes of animals in pictures found in books or magazines. Select an animal to draw. If possible, your choice should relate to the trait you wrote down. Notice the outline of the animal's body. Practice by making some rough sketches. Then, using markers, draw the shape of the animal on white paper. Add the head, legs, tail, and other details. Your mascot may be cartoon-like or realistic.

P O R T F O L I O

Write a short paragraph telling how you used the elements of art to draw your animal. Put it in your portfolio with your artwork.

Inventing a Mascot

Encourage students to study animals and to view other animal art and artists' techniques. Bring in books or show slides to provide animal models. Point out that mascots may be realistic but are often stylized or humorous. Encourage the students to use an imaginative approach.

■ Art History

For more details on art of the Stone Age, share with students portions of *The Beginnings of Art* by Philip Van Doren Stern (New York: Four Winds Press, 1973).

● ● ● ● ● ● ● ● ● ● ● ● A S S E S S

■ Self-Assessment

Have students complete the Check Your Understanding questions on this page. Answers are provided below.

■ Reteaching

In pairs, have students read their paragraphs telling how they used the elements of art in their drawings.

■ Enrichment

Students may enjoy researching team mascots used by various professional sports clubs or other organizations.

● ● ● ● ● ● ● ● ● ● ● ● C L O S E

Ask students to give examples of how Stone Age people created artwork.

Answers to ✔CHECK YOUR UNDERSTANDING

1. Animals were a very important part of their lives. They provided food and clothing. The paintings may also have been used in a ritual to bring luck in their hunting expeditions.

2. The top of the hippo is decorated with lotus plant leaves and flowers. The lotus plant is common to the marshy environment of the hippo.

LESSON TIME: 90 minutes

• • • • • • • • • • • •
FOCUS

☑ OBJECTIVES

After completing this lesson, students will be able to:

• Understand the importance of a totem to aboriginal people.
• Create a totem that relates to their character and personality.
• Describe, analyze, interpret, and judge their totems.

☑ SUPPLIES

• Sketch paper and pencils
• White drawing paper
• Oil pastels or crayons
• Watercolor paints, trays
• Large, soft brushes

Resources

■ 7-4 Animal Art, TRB page 110 (studio)
■ 7-5 The Stone Age Today, TRB page 112 (appreciating cultural diversity)

• • • • • • • • • • • •
TEACH

■ Motivator

Explain how a totem is different from a mascot. Point out that a totem serves as an emblem, or respected symbol.

■ Vocabulary

Have students look up synonyms for the word *aboriginal* (native, first, indigenous).

 LESSON 2

Creating a Totem

Study the painting in Figure 7–4. It shows a long-necked tortoise. It is the work of an Australian Aborigine (ab-uh-**rij**-ih-nee). The term *Aborigine* comes from two word parts. The first part, *ab*, means "from." The main part, *origine,* means "the beginning." Aborigines are so called because their ancestors were the first humans to settle a given area. The traditions of Australian Aboriginal art go back 50,000 years. This fact was proven by researchers who discovered and dated rock engravings and paintings similar to those being done today.

The tortoise in this picture was the artist's totem. The word **totem** means *an object that serves as an emblem or respected symbol.* This totem may have been used to protect the artist's family from harm.

Figure 7–4 Notice the artist's use of line in this picture. What has he done to give the work variety?

Spider Nabunu. *Long-Necked Tortoise.* 1956–1960. Bark painting. 57.2 × 43.2 cm (22½ × 17"). The Art Gallery of New South Wales, Sydney, Australia. Aboriginal and Torres Strait Islander Collection. Gift of Stuart Scougall.

WHAT YOU WILL LEARN

You will design and create a totem of your own. As in Figure 7–4, your totem will be an animal. Select as your totem an animal that you believe symbolizes the kind of person you think you are. Begin by drawing the outline of the animal of your choice. Then fill in the outline with a pattern. Next, color the lines of the pattern with oil pastels or crayons. Finally, use a contrasting color of watercolor paint to fill in the animal shape and complete your totem.

WHAT YOU WILL NEED

• Sketch paper and pencil
• White drawing paper, 12 x 18 inches (30 x 46 cm)
• Oil pastels or crayons
• Watercolor paints
• Large, soft brushes

WHAT YOU WILL DO

1. With a partner, brainstorm a list of animals that would make good subjects for a totem. Share your ideas with the class.
2. From all the ideas presented, choose an animal as the subject of your own totem. Select an animal that you believe symbolizes the kind of person you think you are. Study photographs of that animal and make several sketches. Focus mainly on the animal's outline. Choose your best drawing. Decide on a name for your totem. Write this name on the sketch you have chosen.

✎ *more about* • • •

Aboriginal Art   The Aborigines have inhabited Australia for over 40,000 years. Art was the core of their life, an expression of knowledge that gave them strength and power. Their arts and crafts were varied and rich and are carried on by their ancestors today. They carved wood and stone figures, then painted them. They also carved intricate designs on the surfaces of rocks, on wooden grave posts, spear handles, canoe paddles, and boomerangs. Their cave paintings and paintings on eucalyptus bark and on stone are world renowned. Their best known paintings include the white *wondjina,* or ancestor spirit figures. The artistic Aborigines were equally skilled in weaving beautiful baskets, bags, and mats out of twine made from fur, root fibers, bark, and hair.

3. Using a light pencil line, transfer your line drawing to a sheet of white paper. Fill the page, as the Aboriginal artist has done in Figure 7–4. Letter a name for your totem somewhere in your design.
4. Next, study the pattern of lines and dots the Aboriginal artist has used. Notice how this pattern adds texture to the painting. Think of a pattern that would go well with the animal you have selected. Practice making this pattern. Then fill in the animal's body using this pattern.

Figure 7–5   Student work. A totem.

EXAMINING YOUR WORK

- **Describe**   Explain what animal appears in your totem. Tell what name you chose for your totem and where it appears in the design.
- **Analyze**   Identify the pattern you used to fill the shape of your animal. Tell what colors of oil pastel you used and which colors of watercolor you selected. Explain whether the colors emphasize your pattern.
- **Interpret**   Write a brief paragraph explaining what this animal symbolizes. Explain why it makes a good totem.
- **Judge**   Tell whether you think your work is successful. Explain what you would do differently if you had a chance to do the project over again.

5. With oil pastels or crayons, go over all the lines in your picture. This includes the lines that make up your pattern. Use pressure to make the lines bold so the oil pastels will resist the watercolor.
6. Finally, select contrasting colors of watercolor paint. Choose colors that will make your design stand out and emphasize your pattern. Using a large brush, apply these colors to the entire surface of your paper. Do not worry about painting over the lines you made. The natural oils in the oil pastels or crayons will resist the paint.

Try This!

COMPUTER OPTION

■ Select the Pencil tool, Brush tool, or Shape tool of your program. Using the tool you chose, create several unfilled animal shapes. Select textures from the pattern menu to fill each shape, using a different pattern for each one. If your software has a Blend command, blend the textures. Identify which shapes and blends look like fur, feathers, or scales. Title and save your picture.

Lesson 2   *Creating a Totem*   **127**

127

The word *earth* has two meanings. It is the name of the planet we live on and also another word for "land." Yet, land accounts for only 30 percent of Earth's surface. The rest is given over to a mysterious world with its own special population, the world of water—the rivers, lakes, and oceans.

Like creatures of the land, the animals of this special environment have long held a fascination for artists.

EARLY ART OF SEA ANIMALS

Ancient Egypt, which you learned about in Lesson 1, was one of the first great civilizations to create many kinds of art. Another early people who invented numerous art forms were the Chinese.

The jar shown in Figure 7–6 is described as "blue-and-white ware." It is made of **porcelain** (**por**-suh-lihn), *a fine-grained, high-quality form of pottery.* Porcelain is very hard to work with because it is a very stiff clay. The Chinese perfected work in this medium during the 1300s. It was around that time that this jar was made.

The jar is notable not only for its craft. It is also important because of the design on its surface. The design shows a fish in its natural environment.

Notice the attention to detail shown in this jar. You can easily find the fish's mouth, eye, gills, and other body features. The fish is shown surrounded by water lilies and other water plants. The artist appears to have been quite familiar with these fresh-water plants.

Figure 7–6 **Notice how the shape of the flower petals has been repeated to create the full blossom. Where have lines been repeated to create other forms?**

China. Yuan Dynasty. *Blue and White Jar with a Design of Fishes and Water Plants.* Early 1300s. Porcelain with underglaze decoration. 29.8 × 34.9 cm (11¾ × 13¾"). The Brooklyn Museum, Brooklyn, New York. Gift of the Executors of Augustus S. Hutchins.

TECHNOLOGY OPTIONS

National Gallery of Art Videodisc   Use the following images to show additional works featuring sea creatures.

John Singleton Copley	Henri Matisse
Watson and the Shark	*Beasts of the Sea*
Search Frame 1768–1171	Search Frame 2203

Use Glencoe's *National Gallery of Art Correlation Bar Code Guide* to locate more artworks.

Figure 7–7   **Where has the artist used line in this work? Where has she used repetition to create harmony?**

Ayako Miyawaki. *Various Fish.* 1967. Cotton collage on burlap. 33 × 29.9 cm (13 × 11¾"). National Museum of Women in the Arts, Washington, D.C. Gift of the artist.

PRESENT-DAY ART OF SEA ANIMALS

Ancient Chinese ways of making art were shared with China's neighbors. One of those neighbors is the island nation of Japan. The artwork in Figure 7–7 was done by a Japanese artist not long ago. Her name is Ayako Miyawaki.

Many people, when they think of art, think of paintings. Artists, as you have learned, are forever looking for new ways of creating. The work of art in Figure 7–7 was created with fabrics and fibers. It is an example of a technique called **appliqué** (ap-lih-**kay**). This is *an art form in which cutout shapes are attached to a larger surface.* They can be stitched or glued in place.

Miyawaki cuts her fabrics freehand. In this artwork, she has carefully cut out fabrics to represent various kinds of fish. Observe how

STUDIO ACTIVITY

Making a Fish Collage

An art technique closely related to appliqué is collage. Using brightly colored construction paper, make a fish collage. Begin by locating pictures of fish in books or sporting magazines. Study the outlines of shellfish, such as lobsters, and finned fish. Practice drawing the outlines of these sea creatures on sketch paper. Save your drawings for use in the next lesson.

When you are satisfied with your results, try making cutouts from the construction paper. You may need two or three tries to get your work right. Glue your completed shapes on a background of white paper. If you wish, use colored pencils or markers and add lines to give texture and variety to the gills, fins, scales, and tails.

P O R T F O L I O

Write an evaluation of your work to keep in your portfolio along with your finished collage.

the shapes of the fish differ, and how their mouths, fins, and tails vary in shape. Look at the striped and plaid fabrics the artist has used. Can you tell where she has overlapped fabrics to add gills and eyes? The symbol in the lower right corner is the artist's signature. It appears in every one of her works.

Check Your Understanding

1. In what century and by whom was the technique for blue-and-white ware invented?
2. Explain the term *appliqué*.

■ Art History

European traders brought Chinese porcelain to Europe in the 1100s. By the late 1600s, there was a big demand for porcelain. In 1771, near Limoges, France, large deposits of kaolin, a pure white clay, were discovered. The French were then able to perfect a porcelain similar to that of the Chinese. Limoges soon became one of the largest porcelain centers in the world.

■ Cultural Diversity

The deep blue color for blue-and-white ware comes from the metal cobalt. The Mongols introduced cobalt to China. The Chinese called this "Mohammedan blue" because the cobalt was imported from Iraq, a country that followed the religion of Muhammad, Islam.

■ Aesthetics

Let students discuss their responses to Ayako Miyawaki's artwork, Figure 7-7. Ask: What colors has the artist used? How do the patterns and textures bring these sea creatures to life?

• • • • • • • • • • • • • •
ASSESS

■ Self-Assessment

Have students complete the Check Your Understanding questions on this page. Answers are provided below.

■ Reteaching

Ask students to explain the technique of appliqué.

■ Enrichment

Tell students to imagine they have been invited to travel with a famous oceanographer like Jacques Cousteau to explore the South Pacific Ocean. Have them draw the colorful sea creatures they would see on their journey.

• • • • • • • • • • • • • •
CLOSE

Have students explain why blue-and-white ware porcelain is a notable art form.

Answers to ✔ CHECK YOUR UNDERSTANDING

1. The Chinese are credited with perfecting the technique of making blue-and-white ware in the fourteenth century.

2. Appliqué is an art form in which cutout shapes are fastened to a larger surface to create a new design.

Making a Glue-Line Print

(pages 130–131)

LESSON TIME: 90 minutes

• • • • • • • • • • • • • •
FOCUS

☑ OBJECTIVES

After completing this lesson, students will be able to:

• Design and create a glue-line print of a fish.
• Describe, analyze, interpret, and judge their glue-line print.

☑ SUPPLIES

• Pencils and sketch paper
• White glue, scrap paper, toothpicks
• Medium weight cardboard
• Water-soluble printing inks
• Inking plate and soft brayer
• Sheets of kraft paper
• Oil pastels or colored pencils

Resource
■ 7-7 Animals of the World, TRB page 115, (reproducible master)

• • • • • • • • • • • • • •
TEACH

■ Motivator

Review with students the concept of etching. Remind them that an etching is an intaglio print made by scratching an image onto a specially treated copper plate. Explain that in this lesson, they will create another kind of print called a glue-line print.

■ Vocabulary

Go over the terms *intaglio* and *brayer* with students. Pass a sample of kraft paper around for students to see and feel.

130

Making a Glue-Line Print

What do you think of when you hear the word *tuna*? If you are like most people, you think of flakes of fish that come packed in a can. There is more to tuna than this, however. The print in Figure 7–8 shows a whole tuna. This sea creature is a member of the yellow-fin family. It swims in both the Atlantic and Pacific oceans.

WHAT YOU WILL LEARN

Look again at Figure 7–8. This work is an example of the type of print called an *etching*. The artist has added extra color to this print by painting the finished work.

In this studio lesson, you will create another type of print. This type, a glue-line print, uses ordinary white glue. Like Figure 7–8, your print will be of a fish. It will make heavy use of the element of line. You will add an undersea environment such as seaweed to your design.

WHAT YOU WILL NEED

• White glue
• Scrap paper
• Toothpick
• Pencil and sketch paper
• Sheet of medium-weight cardboard, 8½ x 11 inches (22 x 28 cm)
• Water-based printing inks
• Inking plate and soft brayer
• Sheets of kraft paper, 9 x 12 inches (23 x 30 cm)
• Oil pastels or colored pencils

Figure 7–8   Notice how the artist has used shading to give the fish its form. How has he used line?

Charles Leonard. *Yellow Fin Tuna.* 1996. Hand-colored etching. 38 × 56 cm (15 × 22″). Private collection.

130   Chapter 7   *Observing Animals*

TECHNIQUE TIP

About Glue-Line Prints   Before you begin this lesson, here are some additional suggestions:

• Since students are using water-soluble inks, they cannot use watercolor paints to hand-color their works.
• You can substitute tempera paint and a brush for the ink and brayer.

• Any non-porous material can be used for an inking plate—a floor tile, a flat plate.
• Remind students that the print will be the reverse of the plate.
• When they press the paper onto the plate, do not let them leave it too long or the paper will stick.

WHAT YOU WILL DO

1. Squeezing the white glue directly from its container, practice drawing lines on scrap paper. Use a large amount of glue to make a thick line. If it forms dots, use a toothpick to pull them together.
2. Refer to the saved fish sketches you made in the Studio Activity on page **129**. Using pencil, transfer one of the sketches onto the cardboard. This is to be your printing plate.
3. Sketch and then transfer an undersea environment to your plate.
4. Using the glue as in Step 1, "draw" over the lines on your printing plate with glue.
5. When the glue looks clear, it is completely dry and the plate is ready to print. Squeeze a small amount of ink onto the inking plate. Roll your brayer into the ink, first in one direction, then in the other. Be sure that the brayer is well coated and sticky with ink. Transfer the ink to your printing plate by rolling the brayer across your fish design in all directions.
6. Lay a piece of kraft paper on top of the printing plate. Using the palm of your hand, gently press the paper onto the plate.
7. Pull the kraft paper carefully off the plate. Put it in a place where it can dry without being disturbed. Make two more prints with fresh paper, re-inking the plate each time.
8. When the prints are dry, add color with oil pastels or colored pencils.

EXAMINING YOUR WORK

- **Describe**   What parts of the fish have you shown? What environmental features have you selected?
- **Analyze**   Explain how you used lines and patterns in your print. Tell why you chose the colors you used.
- **Interpret**   Does your edition of prints convey a feeling or mood? How would you describe this feeling or mood?
- **Judge**   Which aesthetic view would you use to judge your work? If you were to redo this project, what, if anything, would you change?

Figure 7–9   **Student work. A glue-line print.**

Try This! STUDIO OPTION

■ Draw an underwater creature using a glue line on dark construction paper. Let the glue dry. Use chalk to add color. Do a crayon rubbing for another version of your creature and its environment.

Lesson 4   *Making a Glue-Line Print*   **131**

■ Studio Skills

Caution students that it is difficult to get a good print the first time because the dry surface absorbs more ink than later prints. Also advise students to use their whole hand, including fingertips, to rub over the paper to print in between the glue lines.

• • • • • • • • • • • • • •
ASSESS

■ Self-Assessment

Have students use Examining Your Work to evaluate their art.

■ Reteaching

Ask students to explain the process they used to make their glue-line print.

■ Enrichment

After students have finished their prints, you may want to have them mount their work. As an interesting variation, have them mount the printing plate next to the print itself. Make an exhibition of the sea creature prints and invite a group of younger students to come see them.

• • • • • • • • • • • • • •
CLOSE

Have students critique each other's prints, noting especially the environmental features and whether lines and patterns were used successfully.

MEETING STUDENT DIVERSITY

Students with Reading Problems   This studio lesson requires students to follow written directions carefully and in order. For students who are slow readers or students who are not yet proficient in reading English, you may want to assign reading buddies. Ask the reading buddies to read each instruction to their partners. As students gain confidence, they can take turns reading the steps. If possible, demonstrate the process for students, using gestures and body language to help communicate what you are doing at each step.

LESSON 5
Birds in Art

• • • • • • • • • • • • • • •
FOCUS

☑ OBJECTIVES

After completing this lesson, students will be able to:
• Understand the history and purpose of illumination.
• Define and identify calligraphy.
• Practice calligraphy by drawing the outline of a bird.

☑ SUPPLIES

• Round watercolor brushes
• Black watercolor paint
• Sketch paper and pencils
• White drawing paper

Resource

■ 7-8 For the Birds, TRB page 116 (aesthetics)

• • • • • • • • • • • • • • •
TEACH

■ Motivator

Direct students' attention to Figure 7-10. Ask them to describe the setting shown. Encourage them to hunt for details. Explain that the purpose of miniature paintings was to "shed light on," or illuminate, a story or poem. Some illuminations explained a portion of a story, others nearly all of the story.

■ Vocabulary

Ask students to think of other words that are made by combining form of -graph or -graphy. What do those words mean? Encourage students to look at word parts to help unlock the meaning of unfamiliar words.

132

Have you ever wondered what it would be like to soar like a bird? If you have, you are not alone. Since earliest times, humans have dreamed of flying. This dream became a reality in 1903. That year the Wright Brothers conquered the air in the first "flying machine."

The desire to capture the grace and majesty of birds has not been limited to inventors. Artists, too, have long been inspired by the beauty of flight and of creatures that fly.

Figure 7–10 Notice that some birds appear higher in the picture. This was the artist's way of adding depth. What are some other ways of suggesting space?

Habib Allah. *Concourse of the Birds* from the Mantiq at-Tayr (Language of the Birds), by Attar. c. 1600. Colors, gold and some silver on paper. 25.4 × 11.4 cm (10 × 4½"). The Metropolitan Museum of Art, New York, New York. The Fletcher fund.

132   Chapter 7 *Observing Animals*

EARLY BIRD ILLUMINATION

You have probably heard the saying "A picture is worth a thousand words." Artists have understood the truth of this saying for more than eleven centuries. Since about A.D. 850, artists have been making pictures to illustrate books. The picture in Figure 7–10 is from ancient Persia. It is a type of *hand-painted book illustration* known as an **illumination.** The word *illuminate* means "to light up." These miniature paintings were so named because they "shed light on" the words, or made them easier to understand. Imagine that the book you are reading right now contained no pictures. Think how hard it would be to "see" the artworks from descriptions of them alone.

The illumination in Figure 7–10 tells a story. It is about thirty birds that set out on a long journey. Their goal is to find the king of birds.

Notice the many different types of birds in this picture. How many can you identify? What other animals are in the scene?

Illuminations and the Element of Line

Like most Persian paintings, this one makes strong use of the element of line. With your finger, trace the flowing curves that make up the birds, tree, and landscape. These lines suggest graceful movement. The tree is made to look as if it is growing beyond the picture's frame.

You may have noticed the curves in the two corner boxes. These are more than just decoration. They are an example of **calligraphy** (kuh-**lig**-ruh-fee). This word is from two Greek words meaning "beautiful" and "writing." Calligraphy is *the art of beautiful writing.* These curves are letters of the Persian alphabet. Notice that the thickness of these lines varies from curve to curve.

TECHNOLOGY OPTIONS

National Gallery of Art Videodisc   Use the following images to show additional works featuring birds in art.

Martin Johnson Heade
Cattleya Orchid and Three Brazilian Hummingbirds

Winslow Homer
Right and Left

Berthe Morisot
Girl in a Boat with Geese

Search Frame 1946

Search Frame 2038

Search Frame 1270

Use Glencoe's *National Gallery of Art Correlation Bar Code Guide* to locate more artworks.

RECENT BIRD ART

Although we think of birds as creatures of flight, the sky is only one environment in which birds live. The nature study in Figure 7–11 shows another. This is the Brazilian rain forest in South America. The brightly colored winged creatures in the work are hummingbirds. Hummingbirds are special because of their ability to fly backward and their great speed. They are also the smallest of all birds. Some are less than 3 inches (8 cm) long!

Here the artist has provided a close-up of three of these unusual birds in their natural environment. They hover near an orchid, a type of flower. The birds may have fed moments earlier on the flower's nectar. What principle of art has the artist used to draw the viewer's attention to the birds and flower?

Check Your Understanding

1. What is an illumination? For what were illuminations used?
2. In what way is a line of calligraphy different from lines of other kinds?
3. What is the environment of the birds in Figure 7–11?

STUDIO ACTIVITY

Practicing Calligraphy

Look again at the calligraphy in Figure 7–10. With practice, you can learn to make lines like these.

Select a round watercolor brush and dip the bristles in black watercolor paint. Move the brush slowly in the paint while twirling the handle. This will form the brush into a point. Grasp the brush near the metal part, above the bristles. Holding the brush straight up and down, touch the tip lightly to a sheet of sketch paper. Begin drawing a line slowly. The line should be thin. Press down slightly as you go. This will make the line thicker. Continue practicing, reloading the brush with paint as needed.

Once you feel comfortable making lines of different thickness, draw an outline of a bird on white paper. Work from a picture or from memory. Start at the beak. Make a single line that gets thicker as it rounds the curve of the body. Your finished bird should look graceful.

PORTFOLIO

Evaluate your calligraphy in a short paragraph. Put this in your portfolio with your artwork.

Figure 7–11 How many different textures and shapes can you find in this rich painting?

Martin Johnson Heade. *Cattleya Orchid and Three Brazilian Hummingbirds.* 1871. Oil on wood. 34.8 × 45.6 cm (13¾ × 18"). National Gallery of Art, Washington, D.C. Gift of Morris and Gwendolyn Cafritz Foundation.

Lesson 5 *Birds in Art* **133**

Making an Animal Sculpture

Around the time the Wright Brothers were experimenting with flight, a Romanian artist was doing the same. His name was Constantin Brancusi (**kon**-stan-teen bran-**koos**-ee). The sculpture shown in Figure 7–12 is the result of one of Brancusi's more successful experiments. Study the work. In it, the artist has captured the essence of a soaring bird. What elements of art contribute to this feeling? What principle has been used to arrange the elements of art?

☑ OBJECTIVES

After completing this lesson, students will be able to:
• Create an abstract sculpture of an animal at rest.
• Describe, analyze, interpret, and judge their artwork.

☑ SUPPLIES

• Pencils and sketch paper
• Muslin or other smooth cloths
• Clay; clay modeling tools

Resource

■ 7-9 What's My Medium?
TRB page 117 (aesthetics)

■ Motivator

Engage students in a discussion of their favorite animals. What does the animal look like when at rest? Ask students to discuss ways of observing animals to learn more about them. Explain that they will create a clay sculpture of an animal at rest. Like Brancusi, they should keep their image simple.

■ Vocabulary

Review with students the meaning of the word *abstract*. Ask them what makes the animal in Figure 7-12 abstract. (*Recognizable but not realistic image of a bird.*)

WHAT YOU WILL LEARN

Notice how Brancusi has simplified the bird into a solid form. Using the method of modeling, you will create an abstract sculpture of a real or imaginary creature at rest. You will begin by molding the basic form of this creature with clay. When the clay has turned leather hard, you will create a texture or polish the animal to give harmony to your sculpture.

WHAT YOU WILL NEED

● Pencil and sketch paper
● Wooden board
● Ball of clay (about the size of an orange)
● Clay modeling tools

WHAT YOU WILL DO

1. Look at Figure 7–12. Observe how the artist has simplified the shape of the bird. Draw several sketches of an animal at rest. Simplify the shape of your animal, keeping the legs, tail, and head close to the body. Choose your best sketch.

Figure 7–12 How would you describe the artist's use of line? What idea or feeling does this sculpture communicate?

Constantin Brancusi. *Bird in Space.* 1928. Bronze (unique cast). 137.2 × 21.6 × 16.5 cm (54 × 8½ × 6½″). Museum of Modern Art, New York, New York. Given anonymously.

134 Chapter 7 *Observing Animals*

TECHNIQUE TIP ▼

Working with Clay Before students start this Studio Lesson, refer them to the Technique Tip on page 285, Working with Clay.

For safety, place kilns in a separate room, or at least locate them in an out-of-the-way corner of the room.

Instruct students to stay well away from the kilns when the kilns are in operation. Make sure kilns have proper ventilation and follow the directions that accompany each particular model.

2. Knead your ball of clay on the board to rid it of air bubbles. Begin to form the ball into the general shape of the animal in your sketch. Use your fingers or clay modeling tools to make shallow indentations that indicate the position of the head, legs, and tail. Keep turning your sculpture as you work to make sure it looks good from all angles.

3. If you intend to fire the piece in a kiln, use a pencil to push holes into the bottom, when the clay is firm but not dry, to keep it from exploding in the kiln.

4. Finish your sculpture by using clay modeling tools to add texture to part or all of the surface. A comb or toothbrush pulled across the surface will create the look of fur. You can use the back of a spoon to polish the surface for a shiny look. This is called burnishing.

5. Display your finished work with that of your classmates to make an abstract zoo.

EXAMINING YOUR WORK

- **Describe**   What kind of a creature did you create? What surface texture did you use?
- **Analyze**   Name the most important element and principle of art you used in creating your animal. Tell how you used them to give your animal harmony.
- **Interpret**   Were you able to create the impression that your animal was at rest? Describe how you created this feeling.
- **Judge**   Which aesthetic view would you use to judge this work? Tell whether you think your work is successful.

Figure 7–13   **Student work. A creature at rest.**

Try This!   STUDIO OPTION

■ Do a second clay sculpture, this time creating an imaginary creature. Exaggerate the features of this animal, making it look fierce and active. Use many textures to provide a varied surface. Give your creature a name that fits its personality. Photograph this sculpture for your portfolio.

Lesson 6   *Making an Animal Sculpture*   **135**

Fantasy Animals

☑ OBJECTIVES

After completing this lesson, students will be able to:
- Recognize the use of symbols in art.
- Define *tapestry.*
- Understand that Expressionism is an art style in which artists express strong inner feelings.

☑ SUPPLIES

- Pencils and sketch paper
- Magazines and books with pictures of various animals
- White drawing paper
- Watercolors, brushes, trays

Resources

- ◼ 7-10 Franz Marc, TRB page 118 (artist profile)
- ◼ 7-11 Board Game, TRB page 119 (cooperative learning)

• • • • • • • • • • • • • •
T E A C H

◼ Motivator

Have students study Figure 7-14. Ask if they can identify the animal. Explain that myths and legends from many cultures feature such imaginary creatures.

◼ Vocabulary

Students may be unfamiliar with applied art forms such as tapestry. Tell them that a tapestry is usually a heavy cloth woven by hand or machine that has decorative designs or pictures woven into it.

Land, sea, and air are the only true environments of animals. Yet, artists sometimes turn to another special environment when creating animal art. This is the environment of the imagination.

Some imaginary animals in art are inspired by myths, legends, or beliefs. Others reflect an artist's personal style or tastes. Still others are made up of the body parts of many animals. You may have read Dr. Seuss books when you were small. If you did, you are probably familiar with such animals.

Figure 7–14 What techniques has the artist used to give a feeling of depth in this tapestry?

The Unicorn Tapestries, VII: The Unicorn in Captivity. c. 1500. Silk, wool, silver and silver-gilt threads. 3.7 × 2.5 m (12′ 1″ × 8′3″). The Metropolitan Museum of Art, New York, New York. Gift of John D. Rockefeller, Jr., The Cloisters Collection.

FANTASY ANIMALS FROM MYTH

The ancient Egyptians, you may recall, viewed animals as symbols. A **symbol** is *an image used to stand for a quality or an idea.* The hippopotamus was a symbol of strength.

Another animal symbol from long ago appears in Figure 7–14. You may recognize this fantasy animal as a unicorn. The name blends the word parts *uni,* meaning "one," and *corn,* meaning "horn." It comes from the single twisted horn on the creature's forehead. White in color, the unicorn was a symbol of purity. Its horn was thought to have many magical powers. One power was the ability to restore health to someone who has been poisoned.

Fantasy Animals in Applied Art

The artwork in which the unicorn appears is a **tapestry.** This is *a woven wall hanging with decorative designs or colorful scenes.* This tapestry was made during the Middle Ages. It was one of a series of seven. Together they recorded the legend of the hunt for the unicorn. In this tapestry, the unicorn has been captured. It rests on a bed of flowers deep in the forest.

The artist has placed the unicorn in the center of the scene. This emphasizes its importance in the story. The light color value of the animal makes it stand out from the colorful background of plants and flowers. Notice how the artist has used the fence to create a sense of depth. This technique is called *overlapping.* The front half of the fence overlaps, or covers, the unicorn's back legs. Where else is overlapping used in the work? What other techniques has the artist used to suggest depth?

FANTASY ANIMALS THAT REFLECT STYLE

In art and the surrounding world, colors are sometimes used as symbols. A person who

---

CURRICULUM ▶ CONNECTIONS

Social Studies   Examples of ancient tapestries are rare, though this textile art probably originated well before 3500 B.C. During the Middle Ages, tapestry flourished. Because many tapestries were woven of wool, they served not only as art but also as warm insulators on cold walls. The nobility often took their tapestries along when they traveled, and knights even hung them in their tents at jousts or on the battlefield. Symbols and scenes on the tapestries often had historic or religious meaning. Interest in tapestry declined during the Industrial Revolution, but its popularity has increased in the last fifty years with the renewed interest in crafts and weaving.

is scared is called "yellow." Someone who is sad is said to feel "blue." During the early 1900s, a group of artists in Europe developed a new way of making art, called *Expressionism*. It was called this because it expressed inner feelings. Color was very important to the Expressionists. It was especially important to one of their leaders, Franz Marc.

An Expressionist Fantasy Painting

Yellow Cow, the painting in Figure 7–15, is one of Marc's most famous. To Franz Marc, *yellow* meant "gentle" and "cheerful." This leaping cow is so cheerful it seems as though it is about to jump off the canvas. Trace the sweeping curve that starts at the cow's tail. It pulls your eye through the painting.

Check Your Understanding

1. What is a symbol?
2. What was the unicorn's color? What did that color symbolize?

STUDIO ACTIVITY

Creating an Imaginary Animal

As noted earlier, some fantasy animals are made by combining body parts from different animals. In this studio activity, you will create such an animal.

Begin by brainstorming animals famous for their unusual body parts. The giraffe, for example, has a long neck. The elephant has a trunk. Working independently, select body parts you want to use to create your creature. Make some rough sketches. Choose your best idea and draw your animal in pencil. Using watercolors, complete your fantasy animal. Select colors that suggest a mood. Use contrasting colors to create its environment. Name your creature.

P O R T F O L I O

Write down your ideas for animals with unusual body parts. Put the list in your portfolio, adding to it from time to time. Use the list as an idea bank for creating other fantasy animals.

Figure 7–15 What kinds of color has the artist used to communicate a message about the animal in this picture?

Franz Marc. *Yellow Cow.* 1911. Oil on canvas. 141 × 189 cm (55⅜ × 74½"). Solomon R. Guggenheim Museum, New York, New York.

Lesson 7 *Fantasy Animals* **137**

Answers to ✔ CHECK YOUR UNDERSTANDING

1. A symbol is an image used to stand for a quality or an idea.

2. The unicorn was white in color. White symbolized purity.

STUDIO ACTIVITY

Creating an Imaginary Animal

As an alternative, have students try using chalk on dark colors of construction paper, instead of using watercolors. The dark construction paper will reveal the texture of the chalk strokes.

■ Aesthetics

The Expressionist movement originated in Germany in the early 1900s. The Expressionists ignored the "rules" of contemporary art. They experimented with exaggeration, proportion, and color. Ask students to look at Figure 7-15. How has the artist experimented with color?

ASSESS

■ Self-Assessment

Have students complete the Check Your Understanding questions on this page. Answers are provided below.

■ Reteaching

Ask students to work in pairs to find and explain examples of symbols used by artists in this chapter.

■ Enrichment

One of the most historically significant tapestries still in existence is the Bayeux Tapestry (1000s–1100s). Have students find out what famous battle scene is depicted on this work and why the scene is important. *(Battle of Hastings in 1066, in which the Normans defeated England; William the Conqueror became king of England.)*

CLOSE

Have students explain how they used color to express mood.

Creating a Fantasy Creature

LESSON 8

Creating a Fantasy Creature

(pages 138–139)

LESSON TIME: 90 minutes

FOCUS

☑ OBJECTIVES

After completing this lesson, students will be able to:

- Create a three-dimensional animal using recyclable materials and found objects.
- Write a story about the creature's life and environment.
- Describe, analyze, interpret, and judge their fantasy creature.

☑ SUPPLIES

- Assorted recyclable materials (plastic and cardboard containers, lids, and so on)
- Buttons, fabric scraps, ribbon, broken toys, and other found materials
- White glue; masking tape
- Newsprint for papier-mâché
- Cellulose wallpaper paste and water
- Tempera paints, brushes
- Sheets of corrugated cardboard, poster board, or heavy construction paper

TEACH

■ Vocabulary

Ask students to think about expressions that share the word *folk*—folk art, folk music, folk tales, folk dance, folklore. Explain that these are all aspects of culture shared and usually handed down among the common people.

Look at the artwork in Figure 7–16. This is an example of folk art. **Folk art** is *art made by artists who have had no formal training*. The painting by Edward Hicks on page **140** is another example of folk art. In some cases, the name of the folk artist is not known.

Figure 7–16 **What unusual material has the artist used to create this giraffe? What is the main principle of art in this sculpture?**

Unknown American Artist. *Bottlecap Giraffe.* c. 1966. Carved and painted wood, bottlecaps, rubber, glass, animal hair and fur. 184.2 × 137.2 × 44.5 cm (72½ × 54 × 17½"). National Museum of American Art, Smithsonian Institution, Washington, D.C. Gift of Herbert Waide Hemphill, Jr. and museum purchase made possible by Ralph Cross Johnson.

138 Chapter 7 *Observing Animals*

The main medium in this example of folk art is bottle caps. The type used, called a crown cap, was first produced in 1891. Some bottlers today still use crown caps. These metal caps add an unusual surface texture to the giraffe. The work contains many other found objects as well. These include tree branches and a fur tail. All are attached to a metal body. How many different found media can you see?

Notice how the giraffe seems as though it is about to move. The diagonal slant of its legs and its neck help create that feeling.

WHAT YOU WILL LEARN

You will create a three-dimensional fantasy animal using recyclable materials and other found objects. Your creature will have a head, a body, legs, and a tail. Depending on the materials you collect, you may create other parts. These might include wings, ears, horns, spikes, hair, or fur. To add color, you will finish your creature by painting it or covering it with interesting buttons, fabric scraps, papers, foils, and so on. Give your creature a name. You will also write a story about its life and environment. Finally, present your creature to the class by telling your story.

WHAT YOU WILL NEED

- Assorted recyclable packing materials (yogurt cups, tubes, or other containers)
- White glue or masking tape
- Masking or transparent tape
- Newsprint for papier-mâché
- Cellulose wallpaper paste and water
- School tempera paints
- Assorted brushes
- Buttons, fabric scraps, pieces of broken toys, and other found materials
- Sheets of corrugated cardboard, poster board, or colored construction paper

CURRICULUM CONNECTIONS

Language Arts For additional opportunities to read about animals or view animals in art, you may want to refer students to some of the following books and magazines:

- "Animals in Art," in *Faces: The Magazine About People* (N. Y.: Cobblestone, Jan., 1995)
- *Aesop's Fables: A Classic Illustrated Edition* by Russell Ash and Bernard Highton (N.Y.: Chronicle Books, 1990)

- *Painting Animals Step by Step* by Barbara Luebke-Hill (Cincinnati: North Light Books, 1992)
- *Animals Observed: A Look at Animals in Art* (New York: Scribner's, 1993)

Figure 7–17   Student work. Fantasy creatures.

WHAT YOU WILL DO

1. Collect a variety of recyclable packing materials. You might gather boxes, plastic containers, or tubes. Study these items. Practice placing them together to create the form of an imaginary creature. The form should include a head, a body, and legs.
2. When you have decided on an arrangement, attach the objects with masking tape. Apply papier-mâché strips to strengthen the joints and cover the body.

EXAMINING YOUR WORK

- **Describe**   List the materials used to create your animal. Describe the materials used for ears, eyes, and so on.
- **Analyze**   Describe the form you created. What surface texture did you use? What colors did you select?
- **Interpret**   What kind of mood or feeling does your creature express? Was your story funny or serious?
- **Judge**   Which aesthetic view would you use to describe your work? If you were to do this project again, what, if anything, would you change?

3. Choose colors of tempera paint. Decide whether your creature will have a smooth or rough surface texture. Apply the paint using brushes that will give the desired texture. Use large-bristled brushes for a rough texture. Use fine-bristled brushes for a smooth texture.
4. Add a tail, ears, eyes, and other parts. Use buttons, felt, trims, fabric, and other found objects. If you prefer, substitute pieces of cardboard, poster board, or colored construction paper.
5. Give your creature a name. Write a brief story about the creature and its environment. Present your fantasy creature to the class by reading your story aloud.

Try This! COMPUTER OPTION

- If your classroom computer has a 3-D modeling program, experiment with combining basic three-dimensional forms to make a fantasy animal. You might use a cube for the body and a cone for the neck. A sphere or ellipse might be the head. Use smaller versions of these shapes to make eyes, a nose, and so on. Adjust the lights to cast interesting shadows. Use the Render command to complete your creature.

Lesson 8   *Creating a Fantasy Creature*   **139**

■ Art Criticism

Have students use the four steps of art criticism to discuss Figure 7-16. Discuss how the work is organized and what elements are most important. Is this art successful?

■ Studio Skills

As students work to construct their creatures, instruct them to spread the glue thinly so that the surfaces will stick quickly. They may need to tape the glued segments together until the glue has dried, or use ribbon or thread to string items together before fastening them.

■ Art History

Bottlecaps were perfected at the end of the 1800s and used all over the world. They were seen by artists as raw material for craft and art projects. Some turned them into flexible ropes by punching a hole in the center of each cap and stringing them on wire. The ropes were used to create baskets, miniature furniture, and other objects.

ASSESS

■ Self-Assessment

Have students use Examining Your Work to judge their work.

■ Reteaching

Have students describe how they achieved texture and dimension in their artwork.

■ Enrichment

The fantasy creature in Figure 7-16 was made by an American artist. Invite students to find examples of fantasy creatures created by artists of other cultures. Make photocopies to make an international display.

CLOSE

In a round-table discussion, have students explain how their fantasy creatures are examples of folk art.

RESOURCES BEYOND THE CLASSROOM

Illustrated Books   Children's picture books can provide excellent examples of the art of manuscript illumination. Just as medieval artists enhanced a manuscript with ornate images that explained the text, children's book illustrators also capture the essence of the story in their drawings and paintings. Exemplary children's book illustrations convey a sense of character, setting, action, and time. Although their choice of subject matter and other elements might be restricted, children's book artists often create masterpieces of art. Explore editions of *Aesop's Fables* and *Grimm's Fairy Tales*, as well as the Caldecott Medal books. Children's librarians can assist you with appropriate titles.

CONNECTIONS
History

OBJECTIVES

After completing the feature, students will be able to:

- Describe the historical contributions of William Penn.
- Identify the symbolism of the Native Americans and domesticated animals in the painting.

Teaching the Connection

- Have students read the feature on this page.
- Ask volunteers to share what they know about Pennsylvania. What is the nickname of Pennsylvania? *(The Keystone State.)* What is the state capital? *(Harrisburg.)* What river separates Pennsylvania from New Jersey? *(The Delaware River.)* What is the nickname of Philadelphia? *(The City of Brotherly Love.)* In Hicks's painting, what relationship is made between the animals and the group of Quakers and Native Americans? *(All have a calm demeanor.)*
- Tell students that Edward Hicks (1780–1849) is best known for his farm scenes and landscapes. In the artwork, all people and animals exist in peace, a charming visual representation of the Book of Isaiah, Chapter 11.

Answers to Making the Connection

- Peace on Earth.
- Lions, leopards, lambs, wolves, cows, bears, oxen, and humans are shown. These animals are usually natural enemies.
- Hicks was a Quaker minister; Quakers believe in pacifism.

Edward Hicks. *The Peaceable Kingdom.* c. 1837. Oil on canvas. 73.7 × 90.8 cm (29 × 35¾"). The Carnegie Museum of Art, Pittsburgh, Pennsylvania. Bequest of Charles J. Rosenbloom.

The Founding of Pennsylvania

The Liberty Bell. Independence Hall. Gettysburg Battlefield. What do these things have in common? They are all located in the state of Pennsylvania.

Pennsylvania was founded by William Penn, an English Quaker. The Quakers are a religious group. In 1681, King Charles II of England gave William Penn a territory in North America. The territory was a payment for a debt that the king owed to Penn's father. In 1682, William Penn sailed to America. The land that Penn owned was located between New Jersey and Maryland. The king named it Pennsylvania, which means Penn's Woods.

About 15,000 Native Americans were living in the area that became Pennsylvania. In October 1682, William Penn met with the Native Americans and made a treaty of friendship with them. This meeting is shown in *The Peaceable Kingdom.* Penn also founded the city of Philadelphia.

The Peaceable Kingdom was painted by Edward Hicks, who lived in Pennsylvania. Hicks was a pacifist, which means that he did not believe in violence. He believed that people could get what they wanted through peaceful means.

MAKING THE CONNECTION

- What is the overall theme of this painting?
- Identify the animals shown in this work. Why do you think Hicks grouped these particular animals together?
- Look for information about Edward Hicks. What influenced him to be a pacifist?

INTERNET ACTIVITY

Visit Glencoe's Fine Arts Web Site for students at:

http://www.glencoe.com/sec/art/students

140   *Chapter 7 Connections*

INTERNET ACTIVITY

Teacher Resources   You will find *Curriculum Links* filled with content-related web sites matched to each chapter of this text. Linking to *On-Line Classrooms* and *From the Classroom Of...* allows you to visit other sites that have been created by teachers and by art classrooms to share their explorations and experiences. Listings of national organizations and schedules of conferences will help you keep abreast of new teaching strategies and art-related information. Connections to more low-cost studio ideas and additional studio lessons are provided. This is also the place to submit student works for consideration in the *Glencoe Student Galleria*. Find us at **http://www.glencoe.com/sec/art**

REVIEW

 BUILDING VOCABULARY

Number a sheet of paper from 1 to 12. After each number, write the term from the box that matches each description below.

appliqué	Old Stone Age
calligraphy	porcelain
environment	symbol
folk art	tapestry
illumination	totem
mascot	trait

1. The historical period that occurred between 30,000 and 10,000 B.C.
2. Surroundings.
3. A fine-grained, high-quality form of pottery.
4. A woven wall hanging with decorative designs or colorful scenes.
5. An art form in which cutout shapes are attached to a larger surface.
6. Art made by artists who have had no formal training.
7. The art of beautiful writing.
8. An image used to stand for a quality or an idea.
9. A hand-painted book illustration.
10. An animal or person used by a group as a sign of luck.
11. Personal characteristic.
12. An object that serves as an emblem or respected symbol.

 REVIEWING ART FACTS

Number a sheet of paper from 13 to 22. Answer each question in a complete sentence.

13. What do experts believe was the purpose of the cave paintings?
14. Explain why experts believe a sculpture of a hippo was placed in the tomb of Soneb.
15. Name two ways in which an appliqué can be fastened to a background surface.
16. What type of print is *Yellowfin Tuna?* How are such prints made?
17. What art element was emphasized most in Persian painting?
18. What effects are achieved through the use of this element in the illumination in Figure 7–10?
19. What did the color yellow symbolize for Franz Marc?
20. What did the artist symbolize in the painting *The Peaceable Kingdom?*

 THINKING ABOUT ART

On a sheet of paper, answer each question in a sentence or two.

1. **Extend.**   Lesson 1 mentions one source of pigment available to cave dwellers. What other sources do you think these early artists used? What colors do you suppose these sources produced? What kinds of containers do you think the artists used to mix their paints? Explain your answers.
2. **Interpret.**   Choose one artwork from the chapter with symbolic meaning. Explain the symbol. Tell how it adds to your appreciation of the work.

┌─ **MAKING ART CONNECTIONS** ─┐

1. **Science.**   Learn about carbon-14 dating. This is a technique scientists have used to prove that cave paintings were really done thousands of years ago. Use an encyclopedia or on-line resource. Share your findings in a report.

2. **Technology.**   Use a still camera or video camera to record actions of a pet or other animal. Your video might show birds or fish. Share your photographs or video with your classmates. Discuss which images make the best art subjects and why.

■ **Building Vocabulary**

1. Stone Age
2. environment
3. porcelain
4. tapestry
5. appliqué
6. folk art
7. calligraphy
8. symbol
9. illumination
10. mascot
11. trait
12. totem

■ **Reviewing Art Facts**

13. They believe the paintings may have been used in a ritual to bring luck.
14. The hippo was probably meant to protect the body after death.
15. It can be stitched or glued into place.
16. It is an etching. An etching is made by inking an engraved surface.
17. The element of line.
18. The flowing curved lines suggest graceful movement.
19. The yellow symbolized gentleness and cheerfulness.
20. The artist symbolized peace.

? THINKING ABOUT ART

1. Responses will vary. Early artists probably used plant material, charcoal, clay, and other natural materials to make earthy colors as well as black and white. They may have mixed their paints in animal skins, wood pots, or clay pots.

2. Student responses will vary. Students should support their responses with specific details.

Portraying People

(pages 142–161)

Resources

■ 8-9 Chapter Test, TRB page 139
■ Transparency CC-8 *A Meeting*, by Marie Bashkirtseff
■ Transparency 8 *Señora Sabasa Garcia* by Francisco Goya
■ Fine Art Print 12, Seated Bodhisattva: *Guanyin*

Theatre
While studying this chapter, use Performing Arts Handbook page 320 to learn how The Chameleons portray the gamut of human experience through mime.

NATIONAL STANDARDS

This chapter addresses the following National Standards for the Visual Arts:

1. (a, b)   4. (a, b, c)
2. (a, b, c)   5. (a, c)
3. (a)   6. (a, b)

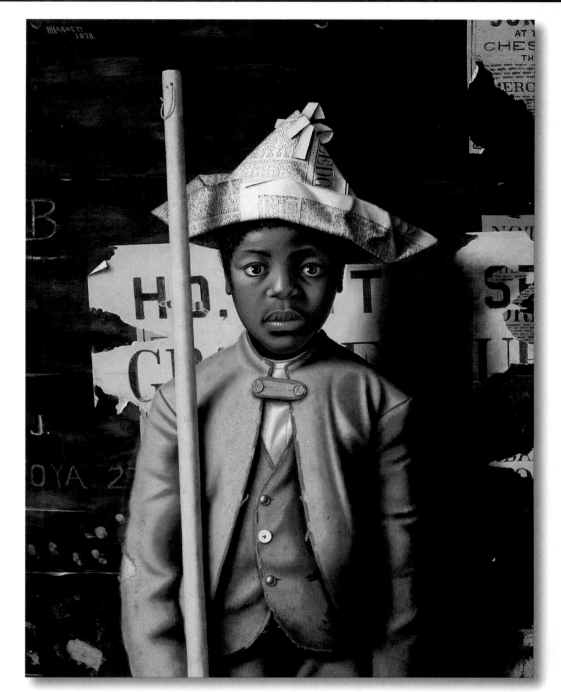

Figure 8–1 Notice the torn posters and handbills in the background of this painting. What do these objects seem to reveal about the subject in the foreground?

William M. Harnett. *Attention, Company!* 1878. Oil on canvas. 91 × 71 cm (36 × 28"). Amon Center Museum, Fort Worth, Texas.

FEATURED ARTISTS

Agnolo di Cosimo Bronzino
Franck Craig
Honoré Daumier
Arthur B. Davies
Jean Dubuffet

Frans Hals
William Michael Harnett
Michelangelo
Henry Moore
Jerry Pinkney

Portraying People

Like snowflakes, no two people are exactly alike. Each has his or her own likes, dislikes, thoughts, feelings, and dreams. It is this one-of-a-kind quality that has made people a favorite subject of artists.

Study the painting on the facing page. The subject of this work is a child playing soldier. Notice the youth's "rifle" and "military hat." What do these props suggest about the power of the child's imagination?

In this chapter, you will learn how to "read" works of art that depict people.

PORTFOLIO IDEAS

There are different ways to choose what to put into your portfolio. For example, you might select an artwork because

- it represents your best example of composition
- it demonstrates your growth in using a specific medium, or
- it shows the skill you exhibited in making an artwork.

OBJECTIVES

After completing this chapter, you will be able to:

- Explain what is meant by having a *style* in art.
- Identify differences in the way people have been portrayed in different ages and cultures.
- Complete artworks with people as subjects.

WORDS YOU WILL LEARN

ancestor figure
figure study
murals
portraiture
public art
self-portrait
style
trompe-l'oeil

■ Chapter Overview

Capturing the individuality of a person is the essence of the portrait. In this chapter, students will explore the various ways in which artists have tried to capture their subject's unique qualities. They will learn what it means to have a style in art. They will learn, too, that human subjects have been portrayed differently, depending on time, place, and cultural influences.

■ Chapter Motivator

Ask students to bring a snapshot of themselves from an earlier grade and a recent photo as well. Ask them to compare the two pictures How are the pictures similar? How are they different? If they were to draw a picture of themselves combining the best qualities of each photo, what would the drawing look like? What would the drawing reveal about their personal style? Tell students that in this chapter they will study ways in which artists have shown the human figure. They will also learn about the *styles* of art.

■ Examining the Artwork

Have students look at the boy in Harnett's painting. Ask why he might be wearing the folded-newspaper hat. What clue does the title give about the hat? What does the date indicate about the time the portrait was painted? How has Harnett captured the unique qualities of his subject?

143

National Museum of Women in the Arts

You may wish to use the National Museum of Women in the Arts videodisc and/or CD-ROM. The videodisc features a bar code guide, and the interactive CD-ROM provides stimulating activities.

DEVELOPING A PORTFOLIO

Organizing the Portfolio Providing students with an outline or checklist of the assignments that have been given in the grading period helps them keep track of what should be completed and can go into the portfolio. This outline can be posted, but students should have their own copies. They can easily record assignments themselves and reflect on where they are with the assignments as they check the list. Throughout the grading period it is a good idea to set aside time for students to update and reorganize their portfolios. Peer reviews and written reflection can occur at these times, too. Times for updates can be reinforced with a brief review of the established rubric for the portfolio.

143

Portraits

• • • • • • • • • • • •
FOCUS

☑ OBJECTIVES

After completing this lesson, students will be able to:
• Define *style.*
• Describe the artistic style known as Mannerism.

☑ SUPPLIES

• Pencils and sketch paper
• Mirrors
• White drawing paper
• Charcoal, white chalk

• • • • • • • • • • • •
TEACH

■ Motivator

Begin the lesson by asking students to describe their own personal style. Ask: How can you define a person's style? Explain that art styles are defined by the ways artists use the elements and principles of art to express themselves.

■ Vocabulary

Point out to students that the words *portrait* and *portray* come from a Latin word meaning "to draw." Ask students to discuss the ways a person can be portrayed: in a picture or painting, in a sculpture, in words, in a movie or play, and so on. Have students write a brief word portrait of themselves.

144

Ever since the first cave dwellers roamed the earth, the world's population has been steadily growing. So has the number of ways of portraying people in art. Each age has given rise to new art styles. A **style** is *an artist's personal way of using the elements and principles of art to express feelings and ideas.*

In this chapter, you will see examples of different styles artists have used to depict people through the ages.

PORTRAITS AS HISTORICAL RECORDS

Today, we know what our leaders and other celebrities look like. It wasn't always so.

Imagine for a moment that you live in an age before television, newspapers, and magazines. Such a time existed in the not-too-distant past. As recently as the early 1800s, people who wanted to see important figures had to rely largely on painted *portraits* of them.

Portrait from the 1500s

Figure 8–2 shows a portrait from the 1500s. As the credit line reveals, the subjects are a woman and her son. Look again at the credit line. The artist, you will notice, did not work alone. Like other successful portrait painters of the era, he had a "workshop" of assistants. The need for such helpers was prompted by two factors. One was a demand

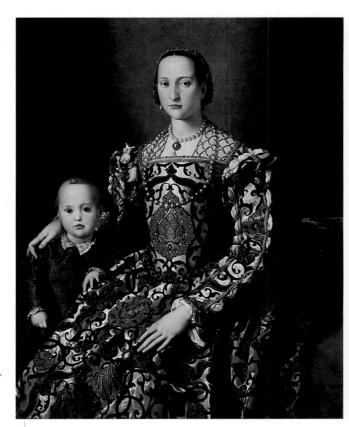

Figure 8–2 Compare this work with the Roman portrait sculpture on page 84 (Figure 5–4). Which of the works do you think is truer to life? Why?

Agnolo Bronzino. *Eleonora of Toledo and Her Son.* c. 1550. Oil on panel. 1.2 × 1 m (48 × 39⅜"). Detroit Institute of Arts, Detroit, Michigan. Gift of Mrs. Ralph Harmon Booth in memory of her husband Ralph Harmon Booth.

144   Chapter 8   *Portraying People*

Figure 8–3 Compare the use of light and shadow in this portrait and the one in Figure 8–2. Which painting uses light more effectively? Why do you feel as you do?

Franz Hals. *Portrait of an Elderly Lady.* 1633. Oil on canvas. 103 × 86.4 cm (40¼ × 34"). © 1997 Board of Trustees, National Gallery of Art, Washington, D.C. Andrew W. Mellon Collection.

for copies of portraits, which were often given as gifts. Another was a lack of technology for reproducing images. The full potential of the printing press, still in its infancy, had not yet been realized.

Turn your attention to the portrait itself. Look at the way the figures are dressed. What does this tell you about their social standing? Do you think they were rich or poor? Do you think the artist's main goal was to show these people as they really looked or as they preferred to be shown?

EXPRESSIVE PORTRAITS

The portrait in Figure 8–2 represents a style of art known as *Mannerism.* In its day, this term was used scornfully. It was applied to works that seemed overly stiff and formal.

Compare this painting with the one in Figure 8–3. This second work was done in the 1600s, almost a one hundred years after the

Making an Expressive Self-Portrait

The artist who made the painting in Figure 8–2 lived more than 300 years ago. We know what he looked like, however, because he made several self-portraits. A **self-portrait** is *a painting or drawing of an artist's own image.*

Now it is your turn. Begin a self-portrait by studying your face in a mirror. Using charcoal, draw a large oval to represent the outline of your face. Lightly add guidelines for your hairline and facial features. Try to capture your expression. Use white chalk to highlight eyes, cheeks, and so on. Complete your self-portrait by adding details and shading.

P O R T F O L I O

Write one paragraph describing the expression you were trying to capture in your portrait and whether you believe you were successful. Keep the paragraph with the drawing in your portfolio.

first. Notice the expression on the subject's face. Her eyes, which reflect the wisdom of her years, are boldly fixed on the viewer. Deep lines are etched in the woman's face. Even the firm grip of her hand on the arm of the chair seems to signal an inner strength and energy. What words would you use to describe this sitter's personality? What kinds of behavior would you expect from her?

✔ Check Your Understanding

1. What is style?
2. How did portrait painting change from the 1500s to the 1600s?

STUDIO ACTIVITY

Making an Expressive Self-Portrait

Tell students to reproduce a facial expression that will tell viewers something about their personality. Demonstrate the fundamentals of drawing a face: show how an imaginary horizontal line that roughly bisects the oval of the face would represent the plane of the eyes. Show approximate placement of features. Have students constantly refer to their "models" in the mirror.

■ Art History

Explain that *Mannerism* is a style of art that developed in Rome and Florence during the 1520s as a reaction to some of the goals of the Renaissance. The Renaissance reflected a period of peace and confidence that ended with the Protestant Reformation in 1517, and the Sack of Rome in 1527. These events led to feelings of tension and confusion, reflected in Mannerist art.

• • • • • • • • • • • • • •

ASSESS

■ Self-Assessment

Have students complete the Check Your Understanding questions on this page. Answers are provided below.

■ Reteaching

Have students compare artists' styles in Figures 8-2 and 8-3.

■ Enrichment

Ask a local portrait photographer to come in. Encourage students to ask questions about how a photographer can develop an artistic style.

• • • • • • • • • • • • • •

CLOSE

Ask students to describe the style they used in their portraits.

Answers to ✔ CHECK YOUR UNDERSTANDING

1. Style is an artist's personal way of using the elements and principles of art to express feelings and ideas.

2. In the 1500s, portrait painting appeared stiff and formal, and people were portrayed as they wanted to be shown, not as they really were. In the portraits of the 1600s, figures were shown with more realistic expression.

• • • • • • • • • • • • • •
FOCUS

☑ OBJECTIVES

After completing this lesson, students will be able to:
• Plan and create an expressive face from torn pieces of colored construction paper.
• Describe, analyze, interpret, and judge their pictures of expressive faces.

☑ SUPPLIES

• Pencils and sketch paper
• Black construction paper, large sheets and scraps of colored construction paper
• White glue or glue sticks
• Scraps of corrugated cardboard
• Scissors

• • • • • • • • • • • • • •
TEACH

■ Motivator

Direct attention to the Japanese mask in Figure 8-4 and ask students to express their opinions about it. On the board, compile a list of adjectives used by students to describe the mask. What do they think masks like this might be used for? Discuss the various occasions on which masks are used today. In addition to frightening or grotesque masks, what other types of masks can they name?

146

Creating an Expressive Face

Have you ever heard the expression "whistling in the dark?" It refers to efforts to look and sound brave in the face of danger. The iron mask in Figure 8–4 was created for much the same purpose. It was worn by a fifteenth-century Japanese warrior—making him look fierce and frightening to enemies— while adding to his own confidence in battle. Take a closer look at this art object. Notice the furrowed brow, the wide-open eyes, and the angry scowl. Does the expression on this mask succeed in frightening you?

WHAT YOU WILL LEARN

In this lesson, you will create a masklike, expressive face. You will use a variety of large and small shapes in contrasting colors torn from colored construction paper. These will be assembled and glued to a sheet of black construction paper. To make the face as expressive as possible, you will exaggerate and distort the features and use contrasting colors. Then arrange the shapes in layers to give your picture a bold, expressive look.

Figure 8–4 What expression do you "read" on this mask? What features give it such an expression?

Japan. *Mask.* 1716. Iron repoussè. 19.7 × 17.1 cm (7¾ × 6¾"). The Metropolitan Museum of Art, New York, New York. Rogers Fund, 1913.

146 Chapter 8 *Portraying People*

CURRICULUM ▶ CONNECTIONS

Social Studies As early as the thirteenth century, masks similar to the one illustrated in Figure 8-4 were worn in Japan during war. At that time, the Mongols under Kublai Khan took control of China. Hearing of Japan's wealth, Khan decided to extend his rule to Japan. Over 100,000 warriors and 3,500 warships were readied for the assault. Nature, however, played a decisive role. The invasion was launched in 1281, but a storm, which came to be known as "the Great Wind," scattered the ships of the Mongol invaders. Thousands of men perished or were captured as slaves. Yet so great was the danger that even today when a Japanese mother hears her child crying, she asks, "Do you think the Mongols are coming?"

WHAT YOU WILL NEED

- Pencil and sheets of sketch paper
- Colored construction paper 9 x 12 inches (23 x 30 cm)
- White glue or glue sticks
- Cardboard cut into ½-inch (1.3-cm) squares
- Scissors

WHAT YOU WILL DO

1. Begin by studying the Japanese mask in Figure 8–4. Note the way the artist distorted the features and expression of the face to make it appear more frightening.
2. Complete several sketches of faces, focusing on expressions. Experiment with different ways of exaggerating and distorting the facial features. Notice the different moods and feelings suggested by the sketches.
3. Using your best sketch as a guide, tear a wide oval or round shape from a piece of construction paper. *Do not use scissors for this task.* Glue the shape to a sheet of construction paper.
4. Tear other shapes from the construction paper to form the eyes, eyebrows, nose, and mouth. For each feature, tear out *six or more* shapes. Layer them from large to small. Keep in mind that the more shapes you use for a single feature, the more sculpted it will look. To make your work more expressive, distort the shapes. Be sure to use bright, contrasting colors.
5. Assemble the various features on the face shape. For each feature, glue the largest piece in place first. Continue stacking smaller shapes in this fashion. The result will be a layered effect.

EXAMINING YOUR WORK

- **Describe** Are all the features of the face included in your mask? Are these features distorted?
- **Analyze** Did you use a variety of large and small shapes? Point out places on your mask where contrasting colors are used.
- **Interpret** Would viewers agree that your mask is expressive? If asked to describe your mask with a single word, what word would you choose?
- **Judge** Do you think you succeeded in creating an expressive face? If you were to do another, what would you change to make the work more effective?

Figure 8–5 **Student work. Expressive face.**

Lesson 2 *Creating an Expressive Face* **147**

STUDIO OPTION

Try This!

- Cut and tear a number of different large and small geometric shapes from a sheet of white drawing paper. Using fine-tipped markers in complementary or analogous colors, create a variety of patterns on each of these shapes. Assemble these shapes on a sheet of colored construction paper to create a different kind of expressive face.

Figures in Action

One of the hardest parts of a barber's or hairstylist's job is working on a customer who won't sit still. Even the slightest movement presents a real challenge to the stylist's sure hand.

This observation holds true not only for haircutters but also for artists. For the artist, however, the challenge provided by the human body in motion is a *welcome* one. It is an opportunity to present people as they often appear—in the midst of one activity or another.

In this lesson, you will learn about artworks that show figures in action.

FIGURE STUDIES

As emphasized in Chapter 6, the Renaissance artist Leonardo da Vinci filled many sketchbooks with drawings. Among the sketches he made were hundreds upon hundreds of figure studies. A **figure study** is *a drawing that focuses on the human form.* Leonardo observed and faithfully recorded in great detail the workings of the arms and legs in motion.

The studies Leonardo made set the stage for generations of artists to follow. Take a moment to study the drawing in Figure 8–6. Notice the way in which this artist captures a messenger in flight.

Figure 8–6   Do you detect a sense of urgency? What kinds of lines has the artist used to convey this feeling?

Honoré Daumier. *The Young Courier.* Black chalk and gray wash on laid paper. 15.5 × 23.2 cm (6⅛ × 9⅛"). © 1997 Board of Trustees, National Gallery of Art, Washington D.C. The Rosenwald Collection.

148   Chapter 8   *Portraying People*

ACTION PAINTING

The recording of figures in action is not limited to drawing. Neither is it confined to works with highly representational subjects. For proof, look at the abstract painting in Figure 8–7.

The work shows the fluid movement of dancers. Notice how the dancing figures seem to blend into one another. The bright hues give the work a joyous quality. The work is so lively that some viewers have claimed they can hear the music.

 ## Check Your Understanding

1. What is a figure study?
2. Describe the body language of the figures in motion on these two pages.

Figure 8–7 **Notice the simple shapes the artist has used. What principle of art has he used to suggest movement?**

Arthur B. Davies. *Dances.* 1914–15. Oil on canvas. 2.1 × 3.51 m (7' × 11' 6"). Detroit Institute of Arts, Detroit, Michigan. Gift of Ralph Harmon Booth.

 ## STUDIO ACTIVITY

Creating a Figure Study

You and a partner are to take turns serving as model and artist. Each of you is to concentrate on capturing the other in action. Begin by posing your model as if he or she were frozen in an act of some kind. Possibilities include throwing a ball, sweeping the floor, or lifting an object off the floor. Moisten a 9 x 12-inch (23 x 30-cm) sheet of white drawing paper with water. Tint the paper with one or more colors of watercolor. While the paint is still wet, quickly draw the model using a black marker. Concentrate on capturing the major action lines of the body. Do not worry that the ink spreads and blurs.

Complete several such drawings. Arrange the works in order.

 P O R T F O L I O

On a piece of paper, note whether your efforts at capturing action improved with practice.

STUDIO ACTIVITY

Creating a Figure Study

Remind students to move their eyes continuously back and forth from the model to their drawing. Repeat variations of this exercise often, making sure that students date each drawing so that they can measure their progress.

■ **Aesthetics**

After they have had an opportunity to examine Figure 8-6, ask students to express their opinions about it and tell why they think as they do.

Art in Everyday Life

Remind students that action figures are all around them. Ask them to take closer notice of all the walkers and joggers they see everyday. If possible, students should try to capture such action in their sketchbooks.

• • • • • • • • • •
ASSESS

■ **Self-Assessment**

Have students complete the Check Your Understanding questions on this page. Answers are provided below.

■ **Reteaching**

Ask pairs of students to demonstrate body language.

■ **Enrichment**

Invite students to locate examples of Leonardo da Vinci's drawings, and bring in a copy of his self-portrait for discussion.

• • • • • • • • • •
CLOSE

Have students review their figure studies and explain their particular focus.

149

Answers to ✔CHECK YOUR UNDERSTANDING

1. A figure study is a drawing that focuses on the human form. Da Vinci observed and recorded in great detail the actions of muscles and muscle groups. He studied arms and legs in motion, and he examined and drew the minute differences between facial expressions like a frown and a scowl.

2. In Figure 8-6, the runner is leaning forward as he races to deliver his message. In Figure 8-7, the dancers are moving freely, arms open, bodies flexed.

LESSON TIME: 60 minutes

• • • • • • • • • • • • • •
FOCUS

☑ OBJECTIVES

After completing this lesson, students will be able to:

- Paint an abstract figure in action.
- Use a variety of lines, shapes, colors, and textures to add visual interest and a sense of movement to their work.
- Describe, analyze, interpret, and judge their abstract figures.

☑ SUPPLIES

- Pencils and sketch paper
- White drawing paper and black construction paper
- Black felt markers with medium points
- Tempera paints, brushes, mixing trays
- Scissors, white glue

• • • • • • • • • • • • • •
TEACH

■ Motivator

Instruct students to examine Jean Dubuffet's painting *The Reveler*, Figure 8-8. Ask them if the artist's technique of using small shapes reminds them of anything *(pieces of a puzzle)*. Ask them what this indicates *(puzzles appeal to children)*. Is there anything else that suggests children? *(manner in which the work is created appears to be childlike)*. Explain that Dubuffet admired children's drawings and tried to capture in his own work the freedom and joy he observed in those drawings.

150

LESSON 4
Drawing a Figure in Action

The action painting in Figure 8–7, as you saw, has an energetic quality. Its mood is achieved, moreover, through a union of free-flowing abstract shapes.

Both those comments apply equally to the work in Figure 8–8. Take a moment to examine this painting closely. Do the playful shapes in it remind you of the interlocking pieces of a jigsaw puzzle? If so, your thinking is in line with the artist's. All of his art was meant to be playful. Notice the work's title. The word *reveler* means merrymaker. Can you find the head, arms, and legs of this merrymaker?

WHAT YOU WILL LEARN

In this studio lesson, you will paint an abstract figure in action. You will not worry about making your subject look real. Instead, you will concentrate on using a variety of lines, shapes, bright colors, and textures to suggest a moving figure. These art elements will add up to a cheerful design.

WHAT YOU WILL NEED

- Pencil and sheets of sketch paper
- White drawing paper, 12 x 18 inches (30 x 45 cm)

Figure 8–8 **Notice the variety of lines and shapes in this painting. How has the artist tied these elements together to form a human figure?**

Jean Dubuffet. *The Reveler.* 1964. Oil on canvas. 195 × 130.2 cm (76¾ × 51¼"). Dallas Museum of Art, Dallas, Texas. Gift of Mr. and Mrs. James H. Clark.

150 Chapter 8 *Portraying People*

— *more about* • • • —

Innocence and Spontaneity Dubuffet was born in France in 1901 and moved to Paris at 17 to study painting. After six years, he set his art aside to run the family business. Eighteen years later, he returned to painting, arousing public anger with his abstract, childlike figures. Dubuffet was not the only artist fascinated with the innocence and spontaneity of childlike art. Two others were Paul Klee and Joan Miró. Bring in works by these artists to show to students. Ask students with younger siblings to bring in some of their drawings. Have students compare Klee and Miró's paintings to Dubuffet's. Then compare the works of all three to the children's drawings. Which ones are more successful in capturing the innocence and spontaneity of childhood?

- Black marker with a medium point
- Several brushes
- Tempera paints, mixing tray
- Scissors
- White glue
- Black construction paper

WHAT YOU WILL DO

1. Begin by looking again at Figure 8–8. Concentrate on the lines of the figure. Observe how the artist has used a variety of lines, shapes, colors, and textures, within the overall shape. See how these add action to the work's composition.
2. Complete several pencil sketches of a student model in an action pose. In your sketches, focus on capturing the lines of action in the figure. Draw only the outline of the figure.
3. Working lightly with a continuous pencil line, transfer your best sketch to the sheet of white drawing paper. Make your drawing large enough to fill most of the paper. Go over the pencil line with a black marker.
4. Still working with the marker, divide your figure into a variety of large and small shapes.
5. Switching to tempera and brush, paint the smaller shapes within the large figure shape. Select bright, cheerful colors that contrast with one another. You do not have to paint all the shapes. You may also want to add painted lines or lines made with the marker to some of the shapes. Notice that the artist has done this in Figure 8–8 to create different textures.
6. With scissors, cut out your drawing. Use white glue to mount the drawing on a sheet of black construction paper.

EXAMINING YOUR WORK

- **Describe** Can you easily identify the head, arms, and legs in your figure? Does the figure appear to be moving?
- **Analyze** Did you break up your figure with a variety of large and small shapes? Did you also use a variety of colors and textures?
- **Interpret** Do you think most viewers will recognize your work as an abstract figure in action?
- **Judge** What do you consider to be the best part of your composition?

Figure 8–9 Student work. Abstract figure in action.

Try This! STUDIO OPTION

- Complete another abstract figure in action. This time, use dark, somber colors. Mount your finished composition on a sheet of brightly colored construction paper. Compare it to your first painting. Which is more successful?

Lesson 4 *Drawing a Figure in Action* **151**

■ Aesthetics

Ask students if their opinions about Dubuffet's painting changed as they learned more about it. Do they think it is appropriate for an adult artist to employ a painting style based on the art of children? Why or why not?

■ Studio Skills

Remind students to concentrate exclusively on the outer edges of the model and to use a carefully drawn, continuous line to draw that contour. (See Technique Tip below.) Instruct them to avoid looking at their paper while drawing. Their eyes should move slowly around the contour of the figure as their pencil slowly records what they see. Students should complete several contour drawings, then choose their best one to reproduce on the white drawing paper. At this point, they can divide the figure into various shapes and add color and texture.

ASSESS

■ Self-Assessment

Have students use Examining Your Work to evaluate their art.

■ Reteaching

In pairs, have students discuss the varied use of line and color in Figure 8-8.

■ Enrichment

Gather and display examples of younger children's drawings of figures in action. Create a children's corner or gallery and have your students identify those pieces that have the most energy and movement. Ask: what techniques are common to those drawings that successfully show movement and visual interest?

CLOSE

Have students critique each other's work, noting particularly the ways they achieved a sense of movement.

TECHNIQUE TIP

Contour Drawing Remind students that contour drawing requires moving the eye and hand in tandem, looking constantly at the model and not at the paper. It is as though their drawing tool is moving along all the edges and ridges of the form itself. By practicing their contour drawing, students will improve their perceptual skills. Reinforce students' efforts, and tell them not to worry if their drawings appear awkward at first. For additional help in developing the skill of contour drawing, refer students to the Technique Tip on page **281** of the Handbook.

Portraits in the Round

• • • • • • • • • • •

FOCUS

☑ OBJECTIVES

After completing this lesson, students will be able to:

• Explain what *trompe-l'oeil* painting is.
• Explain what an *ancestor figure* is.
• Make an abstract wall design.

☑ SUPPLIES

• Pencils and sketch paper
• White drawing paper or colored construction paper
• Colored chalk or markers

Resource

■ 8-4 Three High Renaissance Masters, TRB page 130 (art history)

• • • • • • • • • • •

TEACH

■ Motivator

Begin by asking students to reexamine Harnett's *Attention, Company!* (Figure 8-1) on page 142. Ask students to point out realistic details.

■ Vocabulary

Explain that the French term *trompe-l'oeil* refers to a style that goes back to ancient Greece and Rome, when artists were judged on their ability to achieve a realistic image. In modern times, the style goes a step farther. An artist using the trompe-l'oeil style wants us to ask, "Is it a photograph or a painting?"

Are you familiar with the phrase *in the flesh?* It is a colorful way of saying "in person." This phrase also calls to mind a property of people that can never be fully captured in two-dimensional paintings or drawings. That is the three-dimensionality of the human form. What better way to show this property than in art that has three dimensions?

In this lesson and the next, you will explore another approach to **portraiture** (pohr-tray-chur)—*the art of making portraits*—that highlights this property. You will learn about and see examples of portraits "in the round."

SCULPTURE

Many artists through the ages have strived for realism in their works. Look back at the painting that opened this chapter on page **142.** The work, completed toward the end of the 1800s, exhibits an art style known as **trompe-l'oeil** (trohmp-**loy**). This is *a style of painting in which objects are depicted with photographically realistic detail.* The term is French for "trick the eye."

Renaissance Portrait Sculpture

The groundwork for this pursuit of realism was laid during the Renaissance. One of

Figure 8–10 Does this figure appear calm and relaxed? If not, how would you describe him?

Michelangelo. *Moses.* c. 1513–15. Marble. Approx. 244 cm (8′) high. San Pietro in Vincoli, Rome. Scala/Art Resource, NY

---

more about • • •

Michelangelo Although Michelangelo (1475–1564) is best known for his achievements as a sculptor and painter, he was also an architect and an impassioned poet. For most of his life, Michelangelo devoted himself to grand, large-scale works of art. His most famous project was painting the ceiling of the Sistine Chapel in the Vatican for Pope Julius II. It took nearly four years to complete.

Michelangelo had a strong personality and fierce pride. He was an intense competitor and a temperamental perfectionist. His rivalry with contemporaries was legendary, especially with Leonardo. He was even known to taunt the older man in public. In later years, Michelangelo mellowed, writing poetry and nurturing a few close friendships.

the giants of this period was the artist who produced the work in Figure 8–10. You probably know his name. It is Michelangelo. Although Michelangelo made many great paintings, he thought of himself first as a sculptor. His paintings and sculptures reflect an interest in realism that is similar to that of trompe-l'oil.

Study Figure 8–10. The subject is the Bible figure Moses. Michelangelo has brought the figure to rousing life through his careful attention to detail. Examine the left arm, for example. See how each muscle and vein stands out in vivid relief.

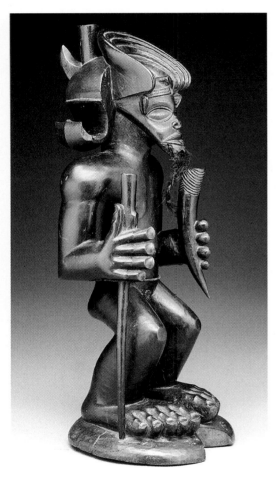

Figure 8–11 What clues can you find that this figure was a great leader and hunter?

Africa. Angola. Chokwe. *Chibinda (The Hunter), Ilunga Katele.* Mid-nineteenth century. Wood, hair, hide. Height: 40.6 cm (16"). Kimbell Art Museum, Fort Worth, Texas.

STUDIO ACTIVITY

Experimenting with Abstract Designs

Like most artists of early Africa, the Chokwe people relied heavily on abstraction. Notice the free-form curves that make up the headdress of the subject in Figure 8–11.

Make an abstract design for a wall in your room at home. Use shapes and lines that reflect your hobbies and interests.

PORTFOLIO

Ask two or three classmates to evaluate your abstract design. Were they able to identify the images you wanted to show with shapes and lines? Write down what, if anything, you might do differently if you were to repeat the activity. Put this critique in your portfolio with the artwork.

African Ancestor Figure

As with two-dimensional art, styles of portrait sculpture vary from culture to culture. The work in Figure 8–11 is typical of the style of art of the Chokwe (**choh**-kway) people of Africa. The work is an example of an **ancestor figure.** This is *an image carved in wood that was used as the resting place of a spirit.* This particular ancestor figure is based on an actual person—a great leader and hunter.

Examine this carving. Like most African figures, it was created for two reasons. One of these was respect for the dead. The other reason was a fear of angry spirits of the dead. Notice that each body part is carved with great care. What words would you use to describe the look and posture of this figure?

✔ Check Your Understanding

1. Which of the sculptures in this lesson served as an example for artists who created realistic art later on? Explain your answer.
2. What is an ancestor figure?

Lesson 5 *Portraits in the Round* **153**

■ **Art Criticism**

Ask students to identify some of the details that make Michelangelo's *Moses* (Figure 8-10) look lifelike. Then ask them to discuss the ancestor figure; what details tell the viewer that this figure is based on a real person? Which sculpture seems to portray more emotion? Does a portrait sculpture have to be completely realistic to be successful? Why or why not?

• • • • • • • • • • • • • • ASSESS

■ **Self-Assessment**

Have students complete the Check Your Understanding questions on this page. Answers are provided below.

■ **Reteaching**

Ask students to explain what trompe-l'oeil is.

■ **Enrichment**

Ask students to find several additional examples of still-life paintings by William Harnett and bring them to class. Ask students why the artist might have chosen to paint ordinary things.

For more information about trompe-l'oeil art, refer students to *Artistic Trickery, The Tradition of Trompe L'oeil Art* by Michael Capek (Minneapolis: Lerner Publications, 1995).

• • • • • • • • • • • • • • CLOSE

Have students discuss how the trompe l'oeil style relates to the pursuit of realism in art.

Answers to ✔ CHECK YOUR UNDERSTANDING

1. Michelangelo's *Moses* served as a model of realistic art. This sculpture comes to life through careful attention to detail. Each muscle and vein stands out in vivid relief. The sculpture is so realistic it almost fools the eye.

2. An ancestor figure is a carved image that was used as the resting place of a spirit. It was created out of respect for the dead and out of fear of angry spirits of the dead.

Creating a Clay Portrait

Style in art, as you have learned, can differ from place to place. As you are about to see, it can also change over *time*. Compare the portrait sculpture in Figure 8–12 with the one in Figure 5–4 on page **84**. Both works are portraits. Both were done in ancient Rome. Yet, the differences between the two are easy to see. The work on this page is more blocklike and less natural than the earlier sculpture on page **84**. What factors might explain these changes? What might they reveal about the changing goals of artists in ancient Rome?

WHAT YOU WILL LEARN

In this lesson, you will create a carved portrait. Your work, which will be made from clay, will be a relief sculpture. Your work need not look like any subject in particular, although you should try to make it lifelike. The features in your work will be in correct proportion to the face. Where possible, you will use tactile texture to make your portrait interesting to the eye and to the touch.

WHAT YOU WILL NEED

• Two wood strips to use as guides, each about ½ inch (1.3 cm) thick
• Board
• Clay
• Rolling pin
• Modeling tools
• Newspaper
• Sheet of plastic

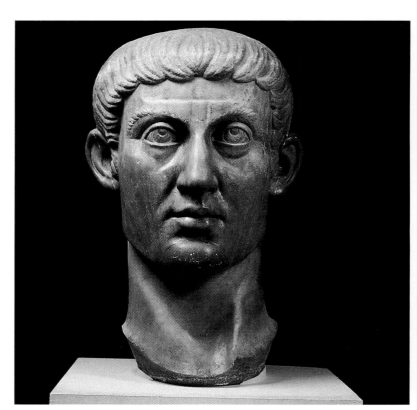

Figure 8–12   The subject was a great emperor of Rome. How would you describe the expression on the face of this figure?

Roman. *Portrait of the Emperor Constantine I.* c. A.D. 325. Marble. 95.3 cm (37½"). The Metropolitan Museum of Art, New York, New York. Bequest of Mark Clark Thompson, 1923.

154   Chapter 8   *Portraying People*

MEETING SPECIAL NEEDS

Accepting Appearance   To encourage students with disabilities to accept their appearances, show pictures of famous persons with distinctive features, such as Mikhail Gorbachev with his birthmark. Include famous persons with disabilities, for example, Ray Charles, Helen Keller, Steven Hawking, and Ludwig van Beethoven. Then encourage all students to include distinctive features in their artwork, for example, ears that protrude, freckles, glasses, and hearing aids.

WHAT YOU WILL DO

1. Wedge the clay. Place the wood strip guides on the board about 8 inches (20 cm) apart. Flatten the clay between the guide sticks with the palm of your hand. Use the rolling pin to roll out the clay.

2. With a modeling tool, lightly draw an oval shape in the clay. This is to represent your subject's face.

3. Add lightly etched guidelines to help you locate the position for each feature of the face. Form the nose by cutting its contour in the clay, then carefully pulling the form outward. Support the feature with a small ball of clay until it hardens enough to support itself. Cut and shape small pieces of clay to serve as pupils, eyelids, eyebrows, and lips. Attach each by crosshatching, adding slip to each piece to be joined.

4. Use modeling tools to add texture to hair and eyebrows.

5. Hold your relief with one hand, and with the other gently push the facial area out to form a more three-dimensional look.

6. Roll up a thick layer of newspaper pages. Cover this with a sheet of plastic. Gently lay your relief on top of this rolled-up bundle to give it a rounded appearance.

7. When your relief is completely dry, have your teacher help you fire it. Display the finished portrait.

EXAMINING YOUR WORK

- **Describe** Are all the features of your relief in correct proportion to the face? Have they been placed in the right locations?
- **Analyze** Did you make use of tactile texture in your relief?
- **Interpret** Do you feel that your portrait is lifelike?
- **Judge** How do you feel about your portrait? Are you satisfied with its appearance? What is its best feature?

Figure 8–13   Student work. Clay portrait.

 Try This!

COMPUTER OPTION

■ Create an *embossed*, or relief, design. Using a drawing program, begin by selecting the Rectangle tool and draw a rectangle 4 inches wide by 1 inch tall. Fill the rectangle with a medium shade of gray. Switch to the Text tool and set the type size to around 35 points and the color to black. Placing the cursor over the box you have drawn, type your name. Make two copies of your name, using the Duplicate or Copy and Paste commands. Fill one copy with the same shade of gray you used for your rectangle. The third should have a white fill. Use the Arrange command to layer the white and black copies behind the gray one. Move the white and black copies until only a small amount of each shows below and above the gray copy. Does your name look like a relief design?

Lesson 6   *Creating a Clay Portrait*   **155**

Heroes in Art

Every culture and generation has its heroes. Some heroes are living, breathing people. Firefighters, law enforcement officers, and doctors are but a few of these. Other heroes are lasting symbols of values we hold dear. The larger-than-life Paul Bunyan and his faithful companion, Babe the blue ox, are a pair of such folk heroes.

In this lesson, you will meet examples of each type of hero. You will also see ways in which these heroes have been celebrated and remembered in art.

PUBLIC ART

Are there statues in your city or community? Perhaps there is a statue of your city's founder in a local park or square. Such works are examples of **public art**. This is *art to be displayed in and enjoyed by a community.* Usually, public art is found outdoors. It may be in the form of statues, fountains, or murals. **Murals** are *large two-dimensional works painted on walls.*

Memorial Art

The work displayed in Figure 8–14 is a special type of public art. Called *memorial art,* its purpose is to help people remember the singular achievement or dedication of a group or individual. The group commemorated in this work were United States Marines. Some 6,000 of these brave fighters gave their lives in a single battle while fighting for democracy during World War II.

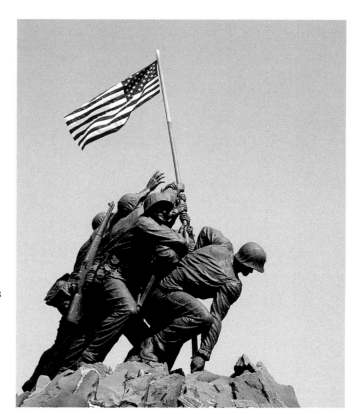

Figure 8–14   This artwork is displayed, appropriately, in Arlington National Cemetery outside Washington, D.C. Heroes of World War II and other campaigns are buried here.

Raising the Flag on Iwo Jima. Arlington Cemetery, Arlington, Virginia.

156   Chapter 8   *Portraying People*

FOCUS

☑ OBJECTIVES

After completing this lesson, students will be able to:
- Define *public art.*
- Define *mural.*
- Understand what heroes and folk heroes are.

☑ SUPPLIES
- Old newspapers and magazines
- Colored construction paper
- Markers
- White glue or glue sticks; scissors
- Poster board

Resources

- ■ 8-6 Community Hero Mural, TRB page 133 (cooperative learning)
- ■ 8-7 Making a Hero Mural, TRB page 135 (studio)
- ■ 8-8 Heroes All, TRB page 137 (appreciating cultural diversity)

TEACH

■ Motivator

Ask students to identify people they regard as heroes. Distinguish between real heroes and fictional ones. Next, discuss the qualities and actions common to *folk heroes.* Explain that folk heroes often take on a "larger than life" quality—their strengths and achievements are exaggerated and enlarged as the stories about them pass from generation to generation. Some folk heroes are based on real people; others are composites of people who may or may not have lived.

CURRICULUM CONNECTIONS

Music   Bring in and play for students recordings of folk songs that celebrate folk heroes. Here are some suggested titles (available on CD and/or cassette):
- *John Henry* Brad Kessler and B.B. King; Rabbit Ears Productions, 1993 (dist. by BMG Music, N.Y)
- *Folk Classics: Roots of American Folk Music,* Columbia, 1989

- *Folk Song America: 20th Century Revival,* vol. I & II, Smithsonian/SONY, 1991
- *American Folk Heroes,* Beanstalk Productions, 1986
- *Early American Heroes,* The Kingston Trio, Pair Records, 1984

HUMAN LEGENDS IN ART

Figure 8–15 shows a hero of a different sort. He is the folk legend John Henry. A mythical railroad worker of the 1800s, he has been the subject of countless songs and poems. John Henry symbolizes the "sweat and tears" of hardworking people during our nation's time of growth. In this painting, he raises two hammers above his head as he gazes out on future generations of settlers heading west. How has the artist captured the inner—and outer—strength of this hero? What meaning can you attach to the rainbow that appears in the distance? Notice how the muscles of the figure's forearms glisten. What sculpture from this chapter does this attention to detail call to mind?

Check Your Understanding

1. What is public art? What are murals?
2. What folk hero appears in Figure 8–15?

Figure 8–15 Notice that the artist has chosen not to show John Henry's face. Why do you suppose this is so?

Jerry Pinkney. *John Henry.* 1994. Pencil, colored pencils, and watercolor on paper. 32.4 × 40.6 cm (12¾ × 16"). From *John Henry* by Julius Lester, published by Dial Books, 1994.

STUDIO ACTIVITY

Making a Hero Exhibit

With several classmates, plan a "Heroes in the News" exhibition. Search newspapers and magazines for illustrations of heroes of the moment. Cut out the images. Work together to think of words that help convey the heroism of the people in the pictures. Write these words in decorative fashion on strips of colored construction paper. With white glue, paste the images and words to a sheet of poster board.

PORTFOLIO

Take photographs of the poster so that each member of your workgroup has a copy. Attach your photo to a self-reflection and put them into your portfolio.

STUDIO ACTIVITY

Making a Hero Exhibit

Have students create a **mural** of "Heroes in the News." Have groups of students work together to plan the mural for main corridor or other wall in the school.

■ Cultural Diversity

Have students report on one hero, telling about that person's heroic qualities and sharing any drawings they find as well. Suggested books:
- *Her Stories* by Virginia Hamilton (N.Y.: Blue Sky Press, 1995)
- *Hero Tales from Many Lands* ed. by Alice Hazeltine (N.Y.: Abingdon Press, 1961)
- *Larger Than Life* by Robert D. San Souci (N. Y.: Doubleday, 1991)

ASSESS

■ Self-Assessment

Have students complete the Check Your Understanding questions on this page. Answers are provided below.

■ Reteaching

Ask students to give examples of public art.

■ Enrichment

Ask students to identify local memorials and bring in pictures or drawings of them to create an exhibit of monuments honoring local heroes.

CLOSE

Have students summarize how heroes and folk heroes are celebrated in public art.

Answers to ✔CHECK YOUR UNDERSTANDING

1. **Public art** is art that is displayed in and enjoyed by a community. **Murals** are large two-dimensional works painted on walls.

2. John Henry is the folk hero depicted in Figure 8-15.

After completing this lesson, students will be able to:

• Create a mixed-media banner honoring a hero.

• Describe, analyze, interpret, and judge their banners.

☑ SUPPLIES

• Pencils and sketch paper
• Rulers, straight edges
• Butcher paper 18 x 24 inches
• Scissors
• Tissue paper in assorted colors
• White glue
• Pen, colored markers
• Sticks or dowels

• • • • • • • • • • • • • •

TEACH

■ Motivator

Direct students' attention to Figure 8-16. Tell them that Joan of Arc was a simple, quite religious French peasant girl born in about 1412. In a vision, she saw herself helping King Charles VII of France drive the English from France. She was successful in several battles, but Joan was captured in 1431 and burned at the stake. She became an admired folk heroine of legendary proportions.

■ Vocabulary

Ask students to recall what a *symbol* is. You may also want to review the word *texture* (see Chapter 1, Lesson 7). Have students explain the difference between visual texture and tactile (actual) texture.

158

LESSON 8

Creating a Mixed-Media Banner

In the previous lesson, you viewed art based on several heroes. Figure 8–16 contains yet another such work. Do you recognize the hero in this painting? It is Joan of Arc. Joan of Arc lived in France in the 1400s. She was not much older than you when she bravely led an army of French troops against the English.

Look closely at Figure 8–16. The picture is filled with figures and action. Even so, Joan is easily identified. She is mounted on a white charger and carries a huge banner.

WHAT YOU WILL LEARN

In this lesson, you will create your own banner honoring a hero. Your banner, which will use mixed media, may focus on a real-life or made-up hero. The work will be divided into three sections. In each section you will use different media to create images and symbols associated with your hero. Using different media will allow you to create a variety of visual textures. These in turn will add interest to your banner.

WHAT YOU WILL NEED

• Pencil and sheets of sketch paper
• Ruler or other straight edge
• Butcher paper, 18 x 24 inches (46 x 61 cm)
• Scissors
• Tissue paper in assorted colors
• White glue
• Pen
• Magazines
• Colored markers

Figure 8–16 Do you sense movement when you look at this artwork? What element of art contributes to this strong feeling?

Franck Craig. *"La Pucelle": Jeanne d'Arc Leads Her Army.* 1907. Oil on canvas. 190 × 341.5 cm (74¾ × 134⅜"). Musee d'Orsay, Paris, France. Erich Lessing/Art Resource, NY

158   Chapter 8   *Portraying People*

MEETING SPECIAL NEEDS

Being Heroic Heroic actions take place in everyday situations such as dealing with a disability or caring for a family member or friend with a disability. Students with disabilities show heroism by courageously dealing with life situations that do not challenge most people. When students with (and also without) disabilities are teased by classmates, it is heroic to do the right thing and point out that people shouldn't be picked on because of their looks or disabilities. Encourage students to accept others for what they can do and the special abilities they have.

WHAT YOU WILL DO

1. Select a hero. Sketch several designs for banners to honor your hero. Use straight or curved lines to divide each banner design into three sections.
2. In each of the three sections, create images or symbols that tell something about your hero. For example, a banner honoring Paul Bunyan might include trees, an ax, and a blue ox. Make your drawings large. Avoid small details.
3. Using a ruler or other straight edge, transfer your best banner design to a sheet of butcher paper. Fill the paper with your design. With scissors, trim away the portions of the paper beyond the banner's outline. Divide the banner into three sections with straight or curved pencil lines. Using your sketch as a model, lightly draw the images and symbols for each section.
4. Cut or tear shapes from sheets of colored tissue paper. Overlap and glue these down to complete one section. Define shapes and details with pen. Cut or tear pictures and words cut from magazines to complete another section. Complete the third section using colored markers. Make certain to fill each section of your banner with color. Take care not to cross the lines between sections
5. Place your banner on display. Ask classmates if they can identify your hero.

EXAMINING YOUR WORK

- **Describe** Identify the images and symbols in each of the three sections of your banner.
- **Analyze** Does your banner show a variety of visual textures? In which section of your banner do you think texture is best demonstrated?
- **Interpret** Could classmates identify the hero your banner honors? What image or symbol was most helpful to them in making this identification?
- **Judge** What is the best feature of your design? If you were to make another banner, what would you do to change it?

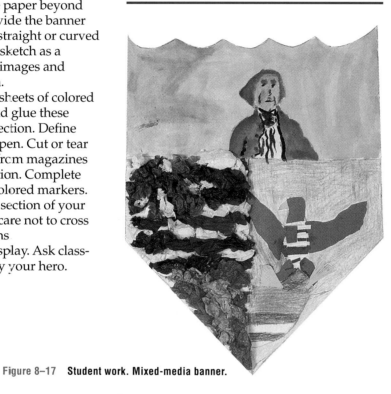

Figure 8–17 **Student work. Mixed-media banner.**

Try This! STUDIO OPTION

■ Make a small drawing of a banner with a different shape, and divide it into three sections. Lay a sheet of waxed paper over the drawing. Use the edge of a scissors to scrape crayon shavings onto the banner image, which can be seen appearing through the waxed paper. Use a different color for each of the three sections. Lay another sheet of waxed paper on top. With an adult's help, use a warm iron to melt the crayon shavings. Cut your banner shape out, and add loops for hanging.

Lesson 8 *Creating a Mixed-Media Banner* **159**

CURRICULUM CONNECTIONS

Social Studies The banner is a traditional part of American folk history and lore. Students may enjoy reading all or part of the book *The Bird, the Banner, and Uncle Sam: Images of America in Folk and Popular Art* by Elinor Lander Horwitz (Philadelphia: J. B. Lippincott, 1976). In the library, you can find additional books and resources about the history and use of banners in battle as well as in peacetime. Consult your school or public librarian for additional suggestions.

OBJECTIVES

After completing this feature, students will be able to:

- Describe some similarities among families.
- Explain the importance of the family in art.

Teaching the Connection

- Have students read the feature on this page.
- Ask volunteers to share what they know about families. What are some other functions of families? *(Examples include teach life skills, provide financial support, care for sick members.)* What is a blended family? *(A family that includes a stepparent, stepbrothers, or stepsisters.)* When aunts and uncles or grandparents live with other family members, what type of family is formed? *(Extended family.)* What type of family is depicted in Moore's sculpture? *(Nuclear family.)*
- Tell students that Henry Moore (1898–1986) was a British sculptor. He often created large sculptures of the human figure in a semiabstract style. Mother and child and family groups are themes commonly found in his work. Moore is also well known for his many sculptures of the reclining human figure.

Answers to Making the Connection

- Children are a shared responsibility.
- To provide for members' physical and emotional needs and to teach values, offer guidance, and encourage independence.
- Examples will vary.

The Family Unit

Henry Moore. *Family Group*. 1948–49. Bronze (cast 1950). 150.5 × 118 × 75.9 cm (59¼ × 46½ × 29⅞"). The Museum of Modern Art, New York, New York. A. Conger Goodyear Fund.

What kind of family do you have? Perhaps you live with your mother, father, and a brother or sister. Maybe you live with just one parent. You might live with a parent, stepparent, and stepbrothers or stepsisters. Families come in all shapes and sizes. They are the most common type of group in our society.

Although family structures vary, many similarities exist among families. Throughout history, the functions of families have remained the same. The most basic function is to provide for family members' physical needs. These needs include food, clothing, and shelter. Families also provide for members' emotional needs. They offer love, support, and security. Families have other important functions as well. They teach values, offer guidance, and encourage independence.

The family has always been a popular theme in art. Henry Moore explored this subject in *Family Group*. In his sculpture, Moore depicts a common family group—mother, father, and child.

MAKING THE CONNECTION

- Notice the position of the child in Henry Moore's sculpture. What message do you think the sculptor was trying to convey about this family group?
- What are some of the functions of families?
- Find other examples of artwork that depicts families. Compare the artists' messages. Do the families seem realistic or idealistic?

INTERNET ACTIVITY

Visit Glencoe's Fine Arts Web Site for students at:

http://www.glencoe.com/sec/art/students

INTERNET ACTIVITY

Studio Cyberspace You and your students will want to visit this area of Glencoe's Fine Arts World Wide Web Site often. It is the place where creative adventures begin. You will find well-planned, outcome-based activities designed to motivate students to find their way around cyberspace. They will answer questions, accomplish tasks, complete projects, and increase their knowledge about art and artists of the world. Students will find easy-to-follow instructions and clearly marked pathways to help them through their web experiences. Many choices await them in activities such as virtual field trips, studio tours, collages and crafts, applied arts experiences, and gallery-hopping adventures. Find us at **http://www.glencoe.com/sec/art**

C H A P T E R 8
REVIEW

 BUILDING VOCABULARY

Number a sheet of paper from 1 to 8. After each number, write the term from the box that best matches each description below.

ancestor figure   public art
figure study   self-portrait
murals   style
portraiture   trompe-l'oeil

1. Art to be displayed in and enjoyed by a community.
2. A drawing that focuses on the human form.
3. A style of painting in which objects are depicted with photographically realistic detail.
4. A painting or drawing of an artist's own image.
5. The art of making portraits.
6. An image carved in wood that was used as the resting place of a spirit.
7. Large two-dimensional works painted on walls.
8. An artist's personal way of using the elements and principles of art to express feelings and ideas.

 REVIEWING ART FACTS

Number a sheet of paper from 9 to 13. Answer each question in a complete sentence.

9. Why did portrait painters in the 1500s need assistants?
10. What features gave the Japanese mask a fierce look?
11. What types of lines are emphasized in the action figure drawings in this chapter? Why are they emphasized?
12. What are some of the ways in which Michelangelo made his figures lifelike?
13. What are two reasons why the Chokwe of Africa made figure carvings?

 THINKING ABOUT ART

On a sheet of paper, answer each question in a sentence or two.

1. **Synthesize.** Explain the following statement: Art styles change over time and from place to place. Restate this in your own words. Use examples from the chapter that illustrate the truth of this statement.
2. **Extend.** In what ways has technology changed the way in which artists show people in their works?
3. **Compare and contrast.** What are some similarities and differences among the two types of "hero art" discussed in the chapter?

MAKING ART CONNECTIONS

1. **Language Arts.** With the help of the school librarian, locate a book of poems that includes "The Ballad of John Henry." Practice reading the poem aloud. Share it with classmates as they look at Figure 8–15. Follow up with a discussion of the qualities of this fictional character that the artist pinpoints in his work.
2. **Community Connection.** With a group, brainstorm examples of public art in your own community. You might take a walking tour to look for examples. Keep on the alert not only for statues but also for decorations on buildings. Use the four steps of art criticism to write a short explanation of why each example you find is important. Print out copies of your comments on the classroom computer. Share these with family and community members.

Chapter 8 Review **161**

ANSWERS TO CHAPTER 8 REVIEW

■ **Building Vocabulary**

1. public art
2. figure study
3. trompe-l'oeil
4. self-portrait
5. portraiture
6. ancestor figure
7. murals
8. style

■ **Reviewing Art Facts**

9. Sitters wanted copies of portraits for gifts and there was no means of mass reproduction.
10. The fierce expression was due to the furrowed brow, the wide-open eyes, and the angry scowl.
11. Diagonal lines are emphasized. This is because they suggest tension and movement.
12. He recorded details, such as muscles and veins, faithfully. He also gave lifelike postures to his figures.
13. These include respect for the dead and a fear of angry spirits of the dead.

THINKING ABOUT ART

1. Answers will vary. An example of the first statement may be seen in changes in portrait sculpture in ancient Rome. An example of the second may be seen in the differences in the way figure sculpture is done in Japan and in countries in Europe and Africa.
2. Answers will vary. Students might note that the advent of television and modern print media have removed some of the importance once attached to portraiture.
3. A difference among the two types of hero art is that one celebrates real individuals, and the other, legendary heroes. A similarity between the two is that both highlight human virtues, such as courage.

161

Visiting Places

(pages 162–181)

Resources

- 9-9 Chapter Test, TRB page 152
- Transparency CC-9, *The Blind Girl* by Sir John Everett Millais
- Transparency TR-9, *Venice, the Quay of the Piazzetta* by Canaletto
- Fine Art Print 13, *The Dovecoat* by Francois Boucher
- Fine Art Print 14, *The Old Bridge* by Hubert Robert
- Fine Art Print 15, *The Farm* by Joan Miró

 Music
Use Performing Arts Handbook page 321 to learn how Danais and Ara Tokatlian research musical traditions.

NATIONAL STANDARDS

This chapter addresses the following National Standards for the Visual Arts:

1. (a, b)	**4.** (a, c)
2. (a, b, c)	**5.** (a, c)
3. (a, b)	**6.** (a, b)

Figure 9–1 What art element has the artist used to lead your eye into and around this nighttime street scene? What principle of art is used to organize this work?

Vincent van Gogh. *Cafe Terrace at Night.* 1888. Oil on canvas. 81 × 65.5 cm (31⅞ × 25¾″). Rijksmuseum Kroller-Muller, Otterlo, the Netherlands.

162

FEATURED ARTISTS

Fred Assa	Diego Rivera
Jean Baptiste Camille Corot	Charles Sheeler
Vincent van Gogh	Sandy Skoglund
David Hockney	John Sloan
Winslow Homer	Frank Lloyd Wright
Philip Johnson and Associates	Louis Le Vau, Jules Hardouin-Mansart

CHAPTER 9
Visiting Places

Do you have a favorite place? Many people do. Maybe it is an afterschool hangout, a park, or a shopping mall. Your favorite place might even be—or be in—another city or a country you have visited.

Artists, like the rest of us, have favorite places. One of these is recorded in the artwork on the facing page. What can you tell about this place by looking at the picture? How does the artist communicate his feelings for this place?

In this chapter, you will journey to some new places. You will also visit some familiar ones. You won't need a ticket or passport—just a good imagination and a knowledge of the elements and principles of art.

PORTFOLIO IDEAS

Find an artwork in this chapter that has a dramatic feeling. What elements of art did the artist use to create the artwork's expressive qualities? What principles of art were used? Create your own portfolio entry. Include your preliminary sketches and any notes you made to explain the techniques you used.

OBJECTIVES

After completing this chapter, you will be able to:

- Understand approaches artists have taken in using places as subjects for their work.
- Recognize how the idea of *home* has changed over time.
- Define *cityscape* and *seascape*.
- Create two- and three-dimensional works that show space.

WORDS YOU WILL LEARN

architects
cityscape
columns
The Eight
elevation
façade
panorama
Rococo
seascape
staged photograph

DEVELOPING A PORTFOLIO

Art Criticism Entries Whether students critique their own artwork, the work of another student, or the work of a famous artist, art-criticism entries kept in their portfolios provide excellent opportunities to demonstrate their knowledge of the elements and principles of art. It also allows them to share their personal views in a non-threatening, written format. Remind students that interpretation and judgment vary from person to person. There are no right or wrong answers, but students do need to provide facts to support their opinions. Encourage students to periodically review their art-criticism entries to determine whether they have seen any growth in their art knowledge.

LESSON 1

Personal Places

· · · · · · · · · · · · · ·

FOCUS

☑ OBJECTIVES

After completing this lesson, students will be able to:

• Explain why van Gogh's decision to paint his bedroom was so unusual.

• Explain that van Gogh used vivid colors and distortion to communicate his personal feelings about places.

• Define a *staged photograph* as an art medium.

☑ SUPPLIES

• Pencils and sketch paper

• White drawing paper

• Markers or oil pastels

Resources

■ 9-1 Interview with an Interior Designer, TRB page 143 (cooperative learning)

■ 9-2 Vincent van Gogh, TRB page 144 (artist profile)

■ 9-3 Dwelling Places, TRB page 145 (reproducible master)

· · · · · · · · · · · · · ·

TEACH

■ Motivator

Tell students to write these words down: "My own special place is …" Have them complete the thought in a detailed description of this special place. Ask how many students identified their bedrooms as their own special place. Discuss their reasons. Ask how many selected a place other than their bedrooms. What made those places special?

164

Rooms come in all sizes and shapes. Some are large and airy. Others are small and cramped. How would you describe your room at home? Regardless of your answer to that question, this much is clear: your room, whether or not it is shared, is one of a kind. It contains your personal things, and there is no other place exactly like it.

Perhaps it is this unique quality that has made rooms a popular subject for art.

PAINTING OF A ROOM

Possibly the first artist ever to make a picture of his room was Vincent van Gogh (van **goh**). You may have heard of him. Books, movies, and even a song have been devoted to his dark, troubled life. Before van Gogh, few artists thought a room without people could be a subject worthy of art. Yet, the artist found peace and safety in his simple room that he could find nowhere else. He wanted to express his personal feelings in his art.

Look closely at van Gogh's painting of his room in Figure 9–2. What do you think he was trying to say about this safe haven in a stormy world? What objects did he emphasize? Did you notice that the window shutters are closed? What meaning, if any, do you attach to this? Carefully study each of the items in the room. Do these items tell you anything about the artist's feelings or mood?

STAGED PHOTOGRAPH OF A ROOM

A room of a very different kind appears in Figure 9–3. This room is different from van Gogh's not only in its content but also in the medium the artist chose. This work is a

Figure 9–2   What personal "stamp" has the artist placed on his room? In what ways is this room similar to yours? How is it different?

Vincent van Gogh. *Bedroom at Arles.* 1888. Oil on canvas. 73.6 × 92.3 cm (29 × 36�5⁄₁₀"). The Art Institute of Chicago, Chicago, Illinois. Helen Birch Bartlett Memorial Collection.

MEETING SPECIAL NEEDS

Making the Most of It   Shy and self-conscious students, with and without disabilities, may be reluctant to verbally or visually share the details of their less-than ideal sleeping rooms at home. To overcome this, discuss how some famous people have had only a living room couch or pad on the floor, shared with others in a succession of different houses, with next-to-no possessions, to call "their room." Provide emotional assurance that "good people" have lived in such rooms and created productive lives and good artworks out of the experience. For students with orthopedic disabilities, discuss how personal spaces have been modified with safety bars and ramps.

staged photograph. Far from an ordinary snapshot, this is *a photographic composition that makes use of artificial images or processes.* In this case, Sandy Skoglund sculpted each of the goldfish from clay. She also painted the room to look like an underwater environment. Then she used models to pose while she photographed the room.

Examine the strange world the artist has created. Notice the title. Can you think of other creatures who, like goldfish, live in a "controlled environment"? Maybe you keep such creatures as pets. Imagine waking up in a room like this one!

 ## Check Your Understanding

1. Why did van Gogh choose to paint a picture of his room? What did he hope to communicate through his painting?
2. How did Sandy Skoglund create her staged photograph?

STUDIO ACTIVITY

Drawing Your Room

Look again at the painting in Figure 9–2. Notice that the artist was not concerned with realism. Here, as in other paintings, he used vivid colors to communicate how he felt about his subject.

Using markers or oil pastels, draw your room at home. Personalize your work, as van Gogh has done, by selecting colors that create a mood. Feel free to add "new" furniture and other details that reflect your personality. Does your finished drawing express your feelings about your room?

 P O R T F O L I O

Write a self-reflection on a piece of paper telling what techniques you used to picture your personality and whether you feel the technique was successful. Put this paper in your portfolio with the artwork.

Figure 9–3 How is the room in this staged photograph different from the painting in Figure 9–2? What kind of color scheme did the artist use?

Sandy Skoglund. *Revenge of the Goldfish.* 1981. Staged photograph. Lorence Monk Gallery, New York, New York.

■ **Aesthetics**

Ask students if they noted the unrealistic distortion in van Gogh's painting of his room. Did they think these distortions were intentional or the result of a lack of skill? Did this cause them to react unfavorably to the work? What quality in the artwork compensates for its lack of realism?

■ **Art Criticism**

Ask students: What techniques has van Gogh used to suggest space? How has the artist used diagonal lines to draw the viewer in? Ask students to identify with a single word the mood or feeling associated with this painting. Have them explain their choice. Tell students to make a judgment about the work's success or lack of success and give reasons for their judgment.

• • • • • • • • • • •
ASSESS

■ **Self-Assessment**

Have students complete the Check Your Understanding questions on this page. Answers are provided below.

■ **Reteaching**

In pairs, have students identify ways in which van Gogh expresses personal feelings about his room.

■ **Enrichment**

Have students create a variation of a staged photograph. Have them begin with an enlarged photo of the classroom (8 × 10 inches or larger, if possible). Then have them cut out drawn images to add to the photo to create a unique version of a familiar place.

• • • • • • • • • • •
CLOSE

Ask students to explain why rooms are a popular subject for artists.

165

• • • • • • • • • • • • • • •
FOCUS

☑ OBJECTIVES

After completing this lesson, students will be able to:

- Design a piece of furniture that fits in with the rest of the objects in *Spring Cleaning.*
- Describe, analyze, interpret, and judge their furniture design.

☑ SUPPLIES

- Pencils and sketch paper
- White drawing paper
- Tempera paints, brushes, trays
- Black markers

• • • • • • • • • • • • • • •
TEACH

■ Motivator

As students inspect the contents of the room in Figure 9-4, ask them to compare some of the items to items they might find in their own rooms. Have them imagine how they are alike or different from the person who lives in this room. Before the groups brainstorm other objects that might be in the room, have them write a character profile of the inhabitant.

■ Vocabulary

You may want to encourage students to look up the word **furniture** in an on-line or print encyclopedia and note some of the styles pictured. Have students describe some of the furniture pictured in Figure 9-4 and see if the pieces relate to any of the styles shown in the encyclopedia reference.

166

Furniture Design

What word comes to mind when you look at the room in Figure 9–4? The title, *Spring Cleaning,* may help you answer that question. The artist has recorded a room cluttered with toys, books, appliances, and other belongings. The subject is about to begin the task of throwing out possessions and other objects she no longer wants. Which choices would you make if this were your room? Which items would you throw out?

WHAT YOU WILL LEARN

The floor of the room in Figure 9–4 is already crowded. Nevertheless, in this lesson you will create a piece of furniture or "knick-knack" for this room that fits in with all the others. You will use tempera paints for this purpose. Your design will exhibit intense colors and patterns featuring bold lines and shapes. Your completed object will match the style of those in the painting.

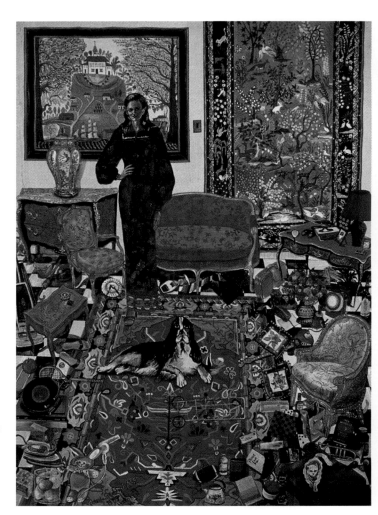

Figure 9–4   Does your room at home look anything like this one? What feeling toward this room and its contents is suggested by the title?

Fred Assa. *Spring Cleaning.* 1979. Oil on canvas. 122 × 91.4 cm (48 × 36″). Collection of the artist.

166   Chapter 9   *Visiting Places*

---

more about • • •

Furniture Styles   The history of furniture styles mirrors the social, political, and artistic movements that have evolved throughout the world. Each age and culture has made a contribution to the art of furniture design, from the ancient Egyptians and ancient Greeks to the European countries of the Renaissance and the developing industrial nations of the twentieth century. For centuries, artists and artisans (and, more recently, architects) hand-crafted richly designed furniture in a wide variety of styles— usually for those of high rank and position. Simple, sturdy pieces sufficed for humble household use. By the late 1900s, however, mass production of furniture made a wider variety of furniture styles and pieces available to the masses.

WHAT YOU WILL NEED

- Pencils and sketch paper
- White drawing paper, 9 x 12 inches (23 x 30 cm) or larger
- Tempera paints
- Brushes
- Mixing tray or paper plate
- Paint cloth
- Black marker

WHAT YOU WILL DO

1. Begin by inspecting the contents of the room in Figure 9–4. Notice the assortment of items the person living in this room has collected. What are the person's interests—her likes and dislikes? With a group, brainstorm other objects the occupant of this room might add to the collection shown.
2. Choose an object mentioned during the brainstorming session. Complete several sketches of it. Imitate as well as you can the style of the objects shown in the picture. Use a bold pattern of lines and shapes in each of your sketches.
3. Select your best sketch and transfer it to the white drawing paper. Fill the entire sheet with your drawing. Choose bright colors of tempera. Again, the intensity of the colors you select should be in keeping with the artist's. Paint your design. When it has dried, add textures and patterns with a black marker.
4. With classmates, plan a "furniture exhibit" that includes your newly designed piece. Place your completed paintings on a bulletin board, or arrange a display elsewhere in the classroom.

EXAMINING YOUR WORK

- **Describe** Is your design easily recognizable as a piece of furniture or other room object?
- **Analyze** Did you use bright colors to decorate your object? Did you add a pattern of bold lines and shapes?
- **Interpret** Would your object blend in with those in the painting? Where in the picture do you think it would be best placed?
- **Judge** Do you think your work is successful? On what grounds do you base this judgment?

Figure 9–5 **Student work. An invented lamp.**

Try This!

COMPUTER OPTION

■ Using the Pen, Pencil, or Shape tool, create an object that would fit in with those in Figure 9–4. Make sure you have completed a closed figure. Fill your object with a pre-programmed pattern or other interesting fill. Title and save your work to a disk.

Lesson 2 *Furniture Design* **167**

■ Aesthetics

Have students work in small groups to discuss *Spring Cleaning* in terms of the elements and principles of art. Ask each group to present a summary of the group's discussion to the class.

■ Art Criticism

After the students have finished their furniture designs, have them work in pairs to critique each other's work. As peer reviewers, remind them to look for positive attributes and to make their responses constructive.

Art in Everyday Life

Ask students to find magazine ads or catalog pages from stores selling furniture. Make a display to evaluate the many styles found. Discuss the importance of an aesthetic approach to furniture design.

ASSESS

■ Self-Assessment

Have students use Examining Your Work to evaluate their art.

■ Reteaching

Work with students to find additional pictures of furniture in home decorating magazines.

■ Enrichment

Have students cut out their furniture designs and glue them to posterboard props so that they will stand upright. Assemble all the students' furniture pieces to create a three-dimensional exhibition of their work.

CLOSE

Ask students to describe the style used in *Spring Cleaning* and tell how their furniture design fits that style.

CURRICULUM CONNECTIONS

Technical Arts Invite a technical arts teacher or woodworking expert to your class to talk about and demonstrate how furniture is made, or take your class to the wood workshop to see firsthand the procedures and equipment used. If possible, have the woodworker show how to make a simple piece of furniture like a stool, using conventional electrical tools. Have the expert explain the purpose of each tool and how to use it safely. Have students prepare questions in advance to find out information such as how decorative embellishments are achieved or how pieces are fastened together. Ask the expert to finish the demonstration with a discussion of styles.

• • • • • • • • • • • • • •

F O C U S

☑ OBJECTIVES

After completing this lesson, students will be able to:

• Understand what architects do.
• Define the Rococo style of art.
• Understand that home designs, like other forms of art, have a variety of styles.

☑ SUPPLIES

• Pencils and sketching paper
• Assortment of cardboard boxes
• Rulers
• White drawing paper

Resources

■ 9-4 Frame-Up,
TRB page 146 (studio)
■ 9-5 Questionnaire,
TRB page 148
(art criticism)

• • • • • • • • • • • • • •

T E A C H

■ Motivator

Tell students to assume that they are architects and have been asked to design a house or apartment building. What must they take into account when working on a design like this? Explain that architects must first make certain that their buildings are tailored to meet the practical purposes for which they are intended. A house, for example, must provide adequate space for the daily needs of the family. However, there is no reason why a design cannot be *both* functional and attractive.

LESSON 3

Architectural Design

Home. Think about that word. Where do you head when you "go home"? For some people, "home" is a cozy apartment. For others, it is a sprawling mansion. For still others, it is a shelter made of straw or fabric. These are just some of the forms that dwellings have taken since the earliest people set up housekeeping in caves.

In this lesson, you will expand your understanding of the place called *home.* You will also learn about some of the challenges of home design facing **architects**—*artists who plan and create buildings.*

A HOME OF THE PAST

Imagine that you are going to design a house for yourself, and money is no object. What sort of dwelling would you build? What kinds of features would you include inside? It was precisely these questions that faced a king who ruled France in the 1700s. This king, Louis XIV, had very lavish tastes. His answers to these questions, or at least part of them, appear in the photograph in Figure 9–6.

This is a single room in the house Louis had built for him. The building, the Palace at

Figure 9–6 Notice the detail of the painted ceilings. What feeling do you think you would get standing in this room?

Louis Le Vau and Jules Hardouin-Mansart. The Hall of Mirrors at the Palace at Versailles, France. 1646–1708. Erich Lessing / Art Resource, NY

Home Elevations   The home elevation drawings of some students with disabilities may be only a rectangle with two or three inner rectangles indicating windows and doors. Of course, always urge students to add details, yet be aware that some students' stages of visual conception or physical dexterity may be such that fine details might be omitted. Even the simplest type of representation can be discussed, and the student can share it with the class.

Versailles (vuhr-**sye**), was named for the Paris suburb where it was built. Study the room. It is interesting not only for what it reveals about the king. It is also interesting for the new art style it launched. That style was called **Rococo** (roh-**koh**-koh). This is *an art style of the 1700s that emphasized graceful movement, curving lines, and delicate colors.* Rococo architecture relied on the heavy use—sometimes overuse—of pattern. Notice how every surface is covered in one kind of rich decoration or another. What words would you use to describe this room?

A HOME OF THE TWENTIETH-CENTURY

It is hard for most people to imagine living in a place like the Palace at Versailles.

Figure 9–7 Notice the use of vertical and horizontal lines on the exterior of this building. What would you expect the inside of this house to look like?

Frank Lloyd Wright. *Falling Water House,* Bear Run, Pennsylvania. 1936. Copyright © 1997, The Frank Lloyd Wright Foundation, Scottsdale, Arizona.

STUDIO ACTIVITY

Making an Architectural Design

Collect a number of boxes of various sizes. Stack these to create a dwelling for a single family or many families. On a sheet of paper, draw the dwelling you have created. Your point of view should be from the front of the house. Add windows, doors, and other details. Share your architectural design with classmates.

P O R T F O L I O

Evaluate your drawing after discussing your design and those of other students. Write a brief evaluation, attach it to your drawing, and put your evaluation and design in your portfolio.

Compare the two buildings in Figures 9–6 and 9–7. What differences do you detect? Obviously, the house on this page has much simpler and cleaner lines. The most striking thing about it, though, is its location. It was built on a rocky ledge directly above a small waterfall. The house, designed by twentieth-century architect Frank Lloyd Wright, even earned a nickname based on its unusual setting: "Fallingwater."

Notice the way in which the house blends into its natural surroundings. Its horizontal lines echo the natural rock formations, its vertical ones the cascading water. Wright once commented, "A house should not be *on* a hill, it should be *of* a hill." What do you think the architect meant by these words? How is this idea reflected in the work of architecture on this page?

 ## Check Your Understanding

1. How is Rococo style captured in the Palace at Versailles?
2. How did the architect of "Fallingwater" make this structure feel like part of nature?

Lesson 3   *Architectural Design*   **169**

■ **Aesthetics**

Ask each student to identify on a sheet of paper a building in their community that they feel is both functional and attractive. Collect and list these on the board. Did the list include buildings serving a variety of different functions? Was one building mentioned more than others? If so, discuss reasons why this building proved to be so highly regarded.

• • • • • • • • • •
ASSESS

■ **Self-Assessment**

Have students complete the Check Your Understanding questions on this page. Answers are provided below.

■ **Reteaching**

Work with individual students to identify the particular features of the Rococo art style found in Figure 9-6.

■ **Enrichment**

Bring in books such as *Amazing Buildings* by Philip Wilkinson (N. Y.: Dorling Kindersley, 1993) or *Round Buildings, Square Buildings, and Buildings That Wiggle Like a Fish* by Philip Isaacson (N. Y.: Knopf, 1988). Show students the astonishing variety and scope of building design in different cultures and in different times. Invite students to pick an architectural achievement to research in more depth, such as the design of the Alhambra, the Moorish palace in Granada, Spain; or the Solomon R.Guggenheim Museum in New York. Ask students to share their research with the class.

• • • • • • • • • •
CLOSE

In pairs, have students discuss the challenges architects face in designing a home.

Answers to ✔ CHECK YOUR UNDERSTANDING

1. The Rococo style is evident in the heavy use of pattern and decoration. Every surface is covered in one kind of rich, curvilinear decoration or another.

2. The house was built on a rocky ledge directly above a small waterfall. It blends into its natural surroundings by means of horizontal lines echoing the natural rock formations, and vertical lines that seem to echo or repeat the lines of cascading water.

Creating a Fanciful Exterior

(pages 170–171)

Lesson Time: 3 hours

• • • • • • • • • • • • • •
FOCUS

☑ OBJECTIVES

After completing this lesson, students will be able to:
• Identify the building features found in Victorian style houses.
• Draw an elevation of a Victorian house.
• Describe, analyze, interpret, and judge their drawings.

☑ SUPPLIES

• Pencils and sketch paper
• Construction paper in assorted colors
• Oil pastels or crayons
• Scraps of construction paper
• White glue

Resources

• 9-6 The Naming of Parts, TRB page 149 (cooperative learning)

• • • • • • • • • • • • • •
TEACH

■ Motivator

Ask students to explain what a "fad" is. *(An interest or activity that is very popular, but only for a short time.)* Direct attention to Figure 9-8. What features of this house design are a fad?

170

Creating a Fanciful Exterior

If you thought gingerbread houses were the stuff of fairy tales, think again. The buildings in Figures 9–8 and 9–9 both look as though they might be made of gingerbread. Yet, both are real structures, made of hard materials. The house in Figure 9–8 represents a style of architecture popular in the 1800s. The building with the onion-shaped domes is even older. It was built in the city of Moscow in Russia during the 1500s. The structure was a cathedral and has now been made into a museum.

Figure 9–9 This is a cathedral in Russia. What art elements have been used to decorate this structure?
St. Basil's Cathedral, Moscow. 1551–60.

Figure 9–8 What kinds of shapes have been used to decorate this house?
Victorian "Painted Lady" (gingerbread house).

WHAT YOU WILL LEARN

You will make an elevation of a house like the one in Figure 9–8. An **elevation** is *a drawing of an outside view of a building.* Your elevation will show the **façade** (fuh-**sahd**). This is *the front of a building.* In your design, you will include a porch and other features of the house. You will use a combination of lines and shapes to decorate the surfaces. Finally, you will make a decorative border for your drawing with cut geometric shapes. These will follow a regular rhythm, which is explained in Chapter 2, page **33.**

---

more about • • •

St. Basil's Cathedral   As students can see from the photos of the buildings in this lesson, the spectrum of architectural styles is wide and diverse. St. Basil's Cathedral is an example of the *Byzantine* style of architecture. The Byzantine style is distinguished by its distinctive use of domes and by an interior design that often features beautiful colored marble, magnificent murals and frescoes, and stunning glass mosaic designs. St. Basil's was built in 1554 in the center of Moscow—in Red Square near the Kremlin. Each of its eight bulb-like domes is different, and all of the domes are painted in brilliant colors. Recently this old Russian church was converted into a museum.

WHAT YOU WILL NEED

- Pencil and sketch paper
- Assorted colors of construction paper, 12 x 18 inches (30 x 46 cm)
- Oil pastels or crayons
- Small sheet of paper or paper towel
- Scraps of construction paper
- White glue

WHAT YOU WILL DO

1. Study the house in the picture. Complete several quick sketches of a similar house. Begin with simple shapes such as squares, triangles, rectangles, and half circles. Use these to build arches, towers, and **columns.** These are *vertical posts that rise to support another structure.* Add a porch and a variety of window and door shapes.
2. Choose your best sketch. Using oil pastels, transfer your design to a sheet of construction paper. Begin with a light color of pastel. Use this to draw the lines and shapes of the house, doors, and windows. While you work, place a small sheet of paper or a paper towel under your hand. This will prevent the colors from smearing.
3. Add railings and decorative touches like the ones in Figure 9–8. Use different combinations of repeated lines—straight, zigzag, curved—and shapes to invent patterns, natural rhythms, and textures. Decorate every surface of the house.
4. After your drawing is complete, make a border for the picture. Use small squares of construction paper for this. Choose colors that complement your house

EXAMINING YOUR WORK

- **Describe**   Does your house have features and decorations like those in Figure 9–8?
- **Analyze**   Did you use a variety of patterns, textures, and details to decorate all the spaces of the house?
- **Interpret**   What part of the house looks the most important? What details contribute to this feeling?
- **Judge**   Compare your house with the one in Figure 9–8. Explain how they are alike and how they are different. Is your design successful?

design. For variety, you may want to cut some of the squares into triangles, circles, diamonds, or other shapes. Layer the shapes and colors to make a regular or alternating rhythm around the picture. Glue them down.

Figure 9–10   **Student work. A fanciful exterior.**

Lesson 4   *Creating a Fanciful Exterior*   **171**

STUDIO OPTIONS

Try This!

■ Paint a tempera "gingerbread" house elevation on newspaper. Use the lines of the text to guide your vertical and horizontal lines. Begin by sketching the outside lines and shapes of the house with a light color of tempera paint. Then mix a variety of tints and shades. Fill all the spaces with color and a variety of lines and shapes to make patterns, textures, and decorations.

■ Take photos of local homes. Make a display for the bulletin board. Your local historical society may have community resources such as a photo file of historic buildings in your community.

■ Art History

Explain that the kind of design in Figure 9-8 is called **Victorian.** The term is applied to a style of architecture that was popular during the reign of Queen Victoria in England, 1873–1901. Victoria was extremely influential and served as monarch longer than any other English ruler. The Victorian style emerged as a reaction to the dull, dark, and heavy classical Georgian style that preceded it.

■ Art Criticism

Have students describe and analyze the building designs in Figures 9-8 and 9-9. Which elements and principles of art play the most important role in each? What feeling or mood does each design communicate? Is each work successful? Why or why not?

• • • • • • • • • • • •
ASSESS

■ Self-Assessment

Have students use Examining Your Work to evaluate their art.

■ Reteaching

Using home design magazines, have students find different examples of elevation drawings.

■ Enrichment

Many old buildings are destroyed to make room for newer structures. Others are preserved as landmarks. Ask students to identify and research any historic landmark buildings in their community. What qualifies a building for landmark status? Why is it important to save old buildings?

• • • • • • • • • • • •
CLOSE

Have students explain how their decorative façades are similar in style to the building in Figure 9-8.

RESOURCES BEYOND THE CLASSROOM

Home Tours   Many communities sponsor tours of private homes in connection with real estate agents, architects, builders, and interior designers. Certain homes, designated "show homes," are specifically built and decorated to show off the talents of the people and companies involved, and to encourage community members to think about refurbishing their homes or buying new

ones. Other tours serve to celebrate and rediscover timeless design styles. Home tours are excellent opportunities for students to study architectural forms and building construction techniques more closely. These tours can also give students a clearer understanding of some art-related careers.

LESSON 5

Cityscapes

(pages 172–173)

Cityscapes

Cities have been around in one form or another for more than 7,000 years. Like rooms, however, they have begun to appear as subjects of art only recently. In this lesson, you will learn about various ways in which artists have viewed and portrayed cities. You will also learn about the contributions of architects to the changing face of cities.

THE CITY IN ART

Factories, traffic jams, and high-rise apartment buildings are all part of modern city life. They are also a theme in some cityscapes. A **cityscape** is *a drawing or painting focusing on large buildings and other objects found in cities.* As an art form, the cityscape dates back to the early 1700s.

At the beginning of the twentieth century, the focus of the cityscape began to shift. Many artists began concentrating on the less glamorous aspects of the inner city. Such a painting appears in Figure 9–11. On its surface, the painting is a realistic picture of an industrial scene. Included are plant buildings, loading docks, girders, pipes, and assorted heavy machinery. The painting does not stop there, however. Notice its organization. Observe the use of geometric forms and shapes. Count the many horizontals, verticals, and diagonals. Note the careful combination of light and dark values of a single hue. In what way can this painting be said to be greater than the sum of its parts?

Figure 9–11 Find the pipe running across the center of this carefully composed work. What other object follows a straight path, then veers off at the last instant? What other "echoes" of lines and shapes can you find?

Charles Sheeler. *City Interior.* 1936. Aqueous adhesive and oil on composition board. 56.2 × 68.4 cm (22 × 27″). Worcester Art Museum, Worcester, Massachusetts. Elizabeth M. Sawyer Fund in memory of Jonathan and Elizabeth M. Sawyer.

• • • • • • • • • • • • • • •
FOCUS

☑ OBJECTIVES

After completing this lesson, students will be able to:
• Define *cityscape.*
• Understand the contributions to modern-day architecture made by architects like Louis H. Sullivan.
• Draw a sketch of a building detail.

☑ SUPPLIES

• Viewfinders made by combining two L-shaped pieces cut from poster board
• Pencils and sketch paper
• Rulers or straight edges
• White drawing paper

Resource

■ 9-7 Post and Lintel, TRB page 150 (art history)

• • • • • • • • • • • • • • •
TEACH

■ Motivator

Instruct students to examine Figure 9-11. Ask if they think Sheeler included everything in the scene before him when he painted the picture. Would his painting have been more effective if he had made it wider or taller to include more of the scene? Is it important for an artist to decide just how much of a scene to include in a painting? Tell students that the artist must develop a "selective eye," that is, skill in deciding exactly what to put in or leave out of a picture.

TECHNOLOGY OPTIONS

National Gallery of Art Videodisc Use the following images to show additional examples of city buildings.

Canaletto
The Square of Saint Mark's

Search Frame 470–473

Auguste Renoir
Pont Neuf, Paris

Search Frame 1288

Maurice Utrillo
Street at Corté, Corsica

Search Frame 2163

Use Glencoe's *National Gallery of Art Correlation Bar Code Guide* to locate more artworks.

THE ART OF THE SKYSCRAPER

Ancient cities were located in spacious river valleys such as along the Nile in Egypt. They had plenty of room to spread out. This is not true of modern urban centers such as New York, London, and Tokyo. In the last hundred years, these overcrowded cities have had only one direction in which to go. That direction is up.

The solution to the problem of limited space was solved toward the close of the 1800s. The person credited with the solution was a pioneering Chicago architect. His name was Louis H. Sullivan. Sullivan hit upon the idea of a steel frame made of crisscrossing beams. To this day, Sullivan's steel "skeleton" is at the heart of every skyscraper. An example of this modern architectural wonder appears in Figure 9–12. What steps has the architect taken to make this structure less boxlike than other skyscrapers you may have seen?

✔ Check Your Understanding

1. What is a cityscape?
2. What was Louis H. Sullivan's contribution to modern-day architecture?

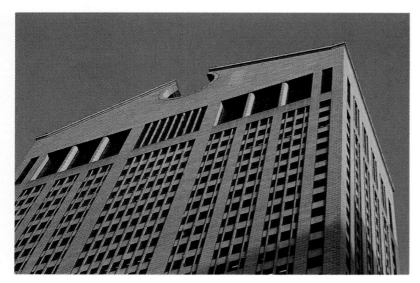

Figure 9–12 The top of this skyscraper borrows its design from a style of Rococo furniture. Do you recall what Rococo means?

Philip Johnson and Associates. AT&T Building, New York, New York.

Lesson 5 *Cityscapes* **173**

Answers to ✔ CHECK YOUR UNDERSTANDING

1. A cityscape is a drawing or painting focusing on large buildings and other objects found in cities.

2. Louis H. Sullivan developed the idea of using a steel frame made of crisscrossed beams to create the building's structure. To this day, Sullivan's steel skeleton is at the heart of every skyscraper.

STUDIO ACTIVITY

Drawing a Building Detail

Show slides of local buildings, and demonstrate how to use a viewfinder to identify an interesting portion of a building. Then show on the board how such a detail can be used as the basis for an interesting drawing, adding details, light and dark values, and textures.

■ Aesthetics

Ask students to identify a work in the book that they feel demonstrates the artist's use of a "selective eye." Discuss things the artist *might* have included in the work but chose to leave out. Are there any works in the book that students feel might have been more successful if the artist had been more selective? Have students explain.

• • • • • • • • • • • •
A S S E S S

■ Self-Assessment

Have students complete the Check Your Understanding questions on this page. Answers are provided below.

■ Reteaching

Ask students to explain how architects have solved the problem of limited space.

■ Enrichment

Overcrowding in cities is not a new phenomenon. What effects did overcrowding have in Europe in the 1700s, for example? Have students explore the history of the development of the city and the problems large, crowded cities have faced in the past and continue to deal with even today.

• • • • • • • • • • • •
C L O S E

Have students explain how architects like Louis Sullivan changed the "face" of modern cities.

☑ OBJECTIVES

After completing this lesson, students will be able to:

• Combine watercolor and construction paper shapes to create a mixed-media cityscape.

• Describe, analyze, interpret, and judge their pictures.

☑ SUPPLIES

• Pencils and sketch paper
• White drawing paper
• Watercolors, large brushes, trays
• Colored construction paper
• Crayons or oil pastels
• Rulers or straight edges
• Scissors, white glue

• • • • • • • • • • • • • •
TEACH

■ Motivator

Have students examine Figure 9-13. Ask: What is the season and time of day represented? Why are so few people on the city streets? What hints does the artist provide to suggest that the "real" action of the city is taking place elsewhere? Have students speculate on where the artist must have been to view this scene. How is space suggested? Point out the artist's use of size, color, and placement of building shapes to create the illusion of space. Tell students that they will use these same techniques in their own mixed-media cityscapes.

LESSON 6

Creating a Mixed-Media Cityscape

There is something magical about the sights and sounds of the big city. Some cities, even at night, seem to give off energy and electricity. One such place is the focus of Figure 9–13. Do you recognize this city? It is New York. One artist who fell under its spell was a painter named John Sloan. Sloan belonged to *a group of American realists who worked at the beginning of the twentieth century.* Because there were eight in the group, they referred to themselves simply as **The Eight.**

In their paintings, The Eight realistically recorded the images of everyday life in the big city. Look closely at the cityscape in Figure 9–13. At its center, an elevated commuter train roars around a curve partially hidden by a low-rise building. You can almost hear the screech of metal and clatter of wood as the train rushes toward you.

WHAT YOU WILL LEARN

You will create a city skyline. Your work will be made up of buildings cut from construction paper in a variety of hues. These will be set against a watercolor background suggesting day or night. To create a sense of space, you will place darker-colored buildings in the bottom foreground. These will overlap lighter-colored buildings placed higher in the picture plane.

Figure 9–13 Critics, scornful of the subject matter of The Eight's work, dubbed the group the *Ashcan School.* What other art movements have you learned about with similar stories?

John Sloan. *The City from Greenwich Village.* 1922. Oil on canvas. 66 × 85.7 cm (26 × 33¾"). National Gallery of Art, Washington, D.C. Gift of Helen Farr Sloan.

MEETING STUDENT DIVERSITY

Students of Diverse Backgrounds   You may find that many of your students have a firm understanding of and familiarity with a large metropolitan city. Others may be less experienced or familiar with the look and feel of the big city. For students with a rural or more suburban up-bringing, provide a "tour" through a real city, showing travel movies or slides of a large metropolis—up close and personal. Help all students get a feeling of the noise, the pulse, and the congestion of a large city before they begin to work on their mixed-media cityscapes. The more prior knowledge each student has, the more interesting and detailed his or her artwork will be.

WHAT YOU WILL NEED

- Pencil and sketch paper
- White drawing paper, 12 x 18 inches (30 x 46 cm)
- Water container
- Watercolor paints
- Large brush
- Paint cloth
- Sheets of thin paper, such as newsprint
- Crayons or oil pastels
- Ruler or other straight edge
- Scissors, white glue

WHAT YOU WILL DO

1. Complete several sketches of city skylines. Include overlapping buildings of different sizes and shapes. Add details such as windows and signs.
2. With the brush, cover the sheet of white drawing paper evenly with water. Decide whether your scene will take place at night or during the day. Depending on your choice, load a brush with a dark (for night) or light hue of watercolor paint. Add color to the wet paper. Do not worry that the color "bleeds," or runs. In fact, you may wish to use two or more colors, allowing them to mix together.
3. Set your watercolor painting aside to dry.
4. Referring to your sketches, cut out different building shapes from colored construction paper. Use a straight edge and scissors for this task. Cut larger buildings from the darker paper and smaller buildings from the lighter ones.

EXAMINING YOUR WORK

- **Describe** Does your picture look like a city skyline?
- **Analyze** Do the sizes, colors, and placement of your buildings create the feeling of space?
- **Interpret** Does the sky suggest a particular time of day?
- **Judge** Are you pleased with your picture? What do you like best about it?

5. Arrange your cut-out buildings on the dry watercolored sheet. About a third of the way down from the top of the sheet, start arranging the smaller, lighter-colored buildings. Place the darker buildings closer to the bottom of the sheet—in the "foreground." Do these last, so that they overlap the lighter buildings. When you are satisfied with the placement of your buildings, glue them down.
6. Draw windows, signs, and other details with oil pastels or crayons.

Figure 9–14 **Student work. A mixed-media cityscape.**

 Try This! STUDIO OPTION

■ Make a skyline *relief.* Do this by gluing building shapes in place so they project outward from the painted background. Use stacks of small pieces of cardboard to place building shapes at different levels.

Lesson 6 *Creating a Mixed-Media Cityscape* **175**

■ **Art Criticism**

Explain that when the artists of the so-called Ashcan School first exhibited their paintings in New York in 1908, they were laughed at by critics and the viewing public. Tell students to pretend they are art critics for a newspaper and they must write a newspaper review in which they express their view of the Ashcan artists' work. Is it serious art, worthy of merit, or is it unworthy of serious consideration as art? Tell students to use Sloan's painting to support one of those views.

■ **Studio Skills**

Make sure that students arrange their building shapes using the techniques of placement, overlapping, and color to suggest space. Stress the importance of details to give the buildings a more interesting and realistic appearance.

• • • • • • • • • • • • • • ASSESS

■ **Self-Assessment**

Have students use Examining Your Work to evaluate their art.

■ **Reteaching**

In pairs, have students compare techniques used to create the feeling of space in their work.

■ **Enrichment**

Four artists formed the nucleus of the Ashcan School. They were John Sloan, William Glackens, George Luks, and Everett Shinn. Have volunteers locate information about any of The Eight as well as examples of his work, and share their findings with the class. Discuss how the works of these artists are similar and how they differ.

• • • • • • • • • • • • • CLOSE

Have students explain how details in their cityscapes provide a realistic view of a big city.

CURRICULUM CONNECTIONS

Social Studies In 1871, the Great Chicago Fire destroyed much of the city. Devastating as it was, the disaster gave architects a challenge and an opportunity to create stronger, more durable structures. One architect, William Jenney, trained architects in his Chicago office, teaching them to try new ideas. He designed the first metal frame skyscraper, the Home Insurance Building in Chicago (1885). One young associate, Louis Sullivan, gained fame for his innovative crossbeam, steel-framed designs. Sullivan soon became the leader of the *Chicago School* style of architecture. He argued that "form follows function," and that good design embraces nature, society, and humanity. His philosophy and insight greatly influenced a young employee of his, Frank Lloyd Wright.

● ● ● ● ● ● ● ● ● ● ● ●

FOCUS

☑ OBJECTIVES

After completing this lesson, students will be able to:

- Define a panorama.
- Work with a group to create a panoramic view of a colorful, textured landscape.

☑ SUPPLIES

- Pencils
- White drawing paper
- Oil pastels (colored chalk, crayon, or tempera paint can also be used)

Resource

■ 9-8 East Meets West, TRB page 151 (appreciating cultural diversity)

● ● ● ● ● ● ● ● ● ● ● ●

TEACH

■ Motivator

Ask students to use their imaginations and describe the things they might see out the window of an automobile during a leisurely drive through the countryside. Have a student list these on the board. Did students include the road on which they were driving? Direct students' attention to Hockney's painting in Figure 9-15. Can they easily identify the road referred to in the title?

■ Vocabulary

Tell students that the word **panorama** comes from the Greek *pan-* meaning "across" and *-rama,* meaning "to see."

The Outdoors

The invention of the airplane in 1903 by the Wright Brothers changed the way people viewed their world. From the air, nothing on earth seemed as powerful or important as it did at eye level. Cars, buildings, and even entire cities looked like toys. Roads and rivers looked like small ribbons. Plowed fields became so many squares on an endless patchwork quilt.

As you will see, this new view of our world was to have a lasting impact on another world. That was the world of art.

LANDSCAPES

As noted in Chapter 6, successful *landscapes*—representations of scenes from nature—invite the viewer in. They tempt you with their shapes and colors.

A very different approach to landscape painting was taken by the artist responsible for Figure 9–15. This landscape, completed in 1980, does not invite you *into* it. Rather, it begs your eye to move *across* it. The painting will seem immediately familiar to players of certain "highway" video games. In this artwork, as in some of those games, you follow the line of a road that winds through the countryside. On your journey, you pass clumps of trees, tennis courts, and houses. What sets this painting apart is the ever-shifting point of view and brilliant analogous colors—purples, reds, oranges. The subject is a well-known stretch of road in southern California. The artist has attempted to capture not only how the scenery looks to him but also how it *feels.* Notice that you may start your trip at either the left edge or right edge of the painting. What differences do you detect when you view the work beginning from one side or the other?

SEASCAPES

Even before the invention of the airplane, artists were recording broad vistas and panoramas. A **panorama** is *a complete view of an area in all directions.* One popular panoramic subject is exhibited in Figure 9–16. This work is a **seascape,** *a drawing or painting of the ocean and objects found on or around it.*

Figure 9–15 Which images demand that you "slow down"? Which require that you "speed up"? What art elements or principles control your speed?

David Hockney. *Mulholland Drive: The Road to the Studio.* 1980. Acrylic on canvas. 218.4 × 617.2 cm (86 × 243″). Los Angeles County Museum of Art, Los Angeles, California. Purchased with the funds provided by the F. Patrick Burnes Bequest.

CURRICULUM CONNECTIONS

Science In the last few decades, photography and computer technology have had a significant impact on landscape and seascape art. Photographing wide expanses of land or sea has been enhanced with the aid of the wide-angle camera lens, aerial photography, and panoramic film. Artists can use such photographs to help them "see" more at a glance than they could see with the naked eye. Computer instruments, too, provide model images for artists to use. The Hubble telescope in space, for example, provides panoramas few ever dreamed about. Ask students to investigate other technological advances that provide artists real models of panoramic proportions.

This particular seascape was completed just four years before the Wright Brothers took to the sky. Examine the painting. Much of the work is given over to an endless expanse of blue-green water, its surface flecked with whitecaps. The centerpiece, of course, is a small boat. Did you notice that the craft's mast is missing? It and its lone occupant are in trouble as the boat bobs helplessly on the water. The danger is made greater by a school of sharks circling the boat. Did you notice the creatures' black fins jutting above the water? Look even more carefully, and you will also notice a ship on the horizon. Its sails are barely visible as gray shapes against the white of the clouds. The artist, it seems, has provided a faint ray of hope—or has he? It is up to you, the viewer, to decide how this drama unfolds. Will the ship rescue the man before it is too late? Are those on board even aware of his presence?

 ## Check Your Understanding

1. What is a panorama? Describe the panoramas in the two paintings on these pages.
2. Describe all the dangers facing the figure in the seascape on this page.

  # STUDIO ACTIVITY

Creating a Panorama

Working with a group of classmates, create a panoramic view of a colorful, highly textured landscape. A winding road should pass through the work, as in Figure 9–15. Begin by arranging sheets of 12 x 18-inch (30 x 46-cm) white drawing paper so that the tops align. There should be one sheet for each group member. One student is to draw a twisting, curving road across the entire surface of the pages combined. Each member is then to work on a single page. Divide your page into eight or more sections. With oil pastels, add and color in houses, fields, forests, and meadows. Use different hues and textures in each section. When finished, your part of the landscape will be joined with those of other group members.

PORTFOLIO

Take a photograph of the panorama you worked on. Add it to your portfolio with a written evaluation of the success of your portion and the way the parts combined to make a panorama.

Figure 9–16 **What do you feel poses the greatest threat to the man on the boat? What type of emotion do you "read" on the man's face?**

Winslow Homer. *The Gulf Stream*. 1899. Oil on canvas. 71.4 × 124.8 cm (28⅛ × 49⅛"). The Metropolitan Museum of Art, New York, New York. Catherine Lorillard Wolfe Collection, Wolfe Fund, 1906.

Lesson 7 *The Outdoors* **177**

■ Art Criticism

Use the following art-criticism questions to lead a discussion of Hockney's painting:

• What do you see below the road in this painting? What is above the road?
• How many different colors can you name? Can you find any straight lines? Where are most of these straight lines found? How is line used to unify this composition? How many different textures can you point out?
• Could Hockney's painting be said to show the passing of time? How so?
• Is Hockney's painting successful? Explain your reasoning.

ASSESS

■ Self-Assessment

Have students complete the Check Your Understanding questions on this page. Answers are provided below.

■ Reteaching

Ask students to discuss how they worked with their classmates to create their panorama.

■ Enrichment

Invite students to look back at Winslow Homer's *Crossing the Pasture* in Chapter 4, Lesson 2, page 66. Have them compare the two paintings. Reread the notes about Homer in the teacher's material on that page. Ask students if they think Homer's experience as a war artist influenced his work. Have them explain their thinking.

CLOSE

Have students evaluate their panoramas in terms of color and texture.

Answers to ✔ CHECK YOUR UNDERSTANDING

1. A panorama is a complete view of an area in all directions. Hockney's panorama captures the scenery and feel of a stretch of road in southern California. Homer's panorama shows an endless expanse of blue-green water, with a small boat in distress in the center. Sharks have encircled the boat, but another ship is visible in the far distance.

2. The dangers include drowning, starving, or being devoured by sharks.

Creating a Seasonal Panorama

FOCUS

☑ OBJECTIVES

After completing this lesson, students will be able to:
• Paint a panoramic landscape that shows a particular season.
• Describe, analyze, interpret, and judge their paintings.

☑ SUPPLIES

• Pencils and sketch paper
• White drawing paper
• Tempera paints, brushes, trays
• Black markers or india ink and pens (optional)

TEACH

■ Motivator

List the four seasons on the board. Under each, have students identify various weather conditions associated with each—hot, cold, balmy, rainy, windy, icy, and so on. Direct students' attention to Figure 9-17. Ask them if the artist succeeded in showing a particular time of the year and have them explain how he did this.

■ Vocabulary

As a review, ask students to identify the warm and cool colors. Ask them why these colors are referred to as warm and cool. In Corot's painting, how are the shadowed areas indicated? How are the sunlit areas shown?

178

You have examined panoramic views of land and of water. The painting in Figure 9–17 gives you two vistas in one. In the near distance, just below the hill on which the viewer is standing, is a city—Genoa, Italy. Beyond is a stretch of sea rippling and shimmering in the sunlight. Notice how the strong Mediterranean sun glints off the stark white houses. What do you think it would be like to visit this combined city-seascape in person? Do you think cooling breezes from the sea might counter the noonday heat?

In making this painting, the artist faced a challenge. That challenge was capturing the dazzling effects of bright sunlight and its reflected light on a clear summer day. In this lesson, you will face a similar challenge.

WHAT YOU WILL LEARN

You will paint a landscape that shows a particular season. You will begin by selecting hues, values, and intensities that suggest heat or cold, sunlight or shade. You will choose warm or cool hues and vary value and intensity depending on your purpose. For more on hue, value, and intensity, see pages **9–10** in Chapter 1.

WHAT YOU WILL NEED

• Pencils and sketch paper
• White drawing paper, 9 x 12 inches (23 x 30 cm) or larger
• Tempera paints
• Brushes
• Mixing tray
• Paint cloth

Figure 9–17 **Which part of the painting is your eye drawn to first? Why do you think this is?**

Jean Baptiste Camille Corot. *View of Genoa.* 1834. Oil on paper mounted on canvas. 29.5 x 41.7 cm (11⅝ x 16⅜"). Art Institute of Chicago, Chicago, Illinois. Mr. and Mrs. Martin A. Ryerson Collection, 1973.1017

178 Chapter 9 *Visiting Places*

CURRICULUM CONNECTIONS

Language Arts Landscapes and seascapes find their way into poetry and other forms of literature as well as into paintings. Locate one of the following anthologies that combines poetry and fine art. Read several selections to students and share the artwork that has been teamed with each. Ask students to respond to the combinations of literature and art.

• *An Illustrated Anthology of Poems for Young People: Talking to the Sun* selected and introduced by Kenneth Koch and Kate Farrell (N. Y.: Metropolitan Museum of Art and Henry Holt, 1985)
• *Celebrate America in Poetry and Art* edited by Nora Panzer, illustrated with fine art from the National Museum of American Art (N.Y.: Hyperion, 1994)

WHAT YOU WILL DO

1. Brainstorm with classmates to create a list of objects associated with landscapes, cityscapes, and seascapes. Name as many features as you can. Record the list in your sketchbook.
2. Choose one of the four seasons. Do not reveal to classmates the season you have chosen. Make several sketches of a panoramic outdoor scene that shows this season. Your panorama may be a landscape, seascape, or cityscape. Include at least four objects from the list you made. Tailor your choices to the season you have selected.
3. Transfer your best sketch to the white drawing paper. Paint your scene with colors that will help convey the season. Choose light values of high-intensity warm colors for warmer seasons. Choose

EXAMINING YOUR WORK

- **Describe**   Did you use at least four objects selected from the list you brainstormed? Can these objects be easily identified?
- **Analyze**   How did you use warm or cool colors to suggest heat or cold? How did you use light and dark values and bright and dull intensities to show sunlight and shadow?
- **Interpret**   How did your color choices contribute to the mood in your painting?
- **Judge**   Are you pleased with your picture? What is its best feature?

dark values of low-intensity cool colors for colder seasons.

4. Display your finished painting alongside those of classmates.

Figure 9–18   **Student work. A seasonal panorama.**

COMPUTER OPTION

Try This!

■ Select your program's Geometric shape tool. Create landscape objects—trees, hills, a shoreline—as angular abstract shapes. After deciding on a season for your painting, fill each shape with a single color.

Choose light values of high-intensity warm colors for warmer seasons. Choose dark values of low-intensity cool colors for colder seasons. Be sure to save your picture.

Lesson 8   *Creating a Seasonal Panorama*   **179**

TECHNIQUE TIP

Value and Intensity   Have students look at the colors, values and intensities in Figure 9-17, Corot's *View of Genoa*. Point out how the most intense colors are in the foreground and how the atmosphere between the viewer and the background makes the colors in the distance

less intense. Have students analyze the student work in Figure 9-18 using the four steps of art criticism. Ask what the student has done in this winter scene to convey the chill of a winter day. Focus students' attention on the use of white, low intensity colors, and light values.

CONNECTIONS *Social Studies*

After completing the feature, students will be able to:

- Explain how communities were first developed.
- Describe the civilization depicted in Diego Rivera's painting.

Teaching the Connection

- Have students read the feature on this page.
- Ask volunteers to share what they know about communities. What are some types of communities in which people live today? *(Urban, suburban, rural.)* What types of community programs are available in your area? *(Answers will vary.)* Besides the community where you live, what are some other communities to which you belong? *(Possible answers include school, church or synagogue, clubs, band, Scout troop.)* How does Rivera's painting portray a sense of community? *(The people are working together to accomplish a goal.)*

Answers to Making the Connection

- ✔ Student responses will vary.
- ✔ Farming provided a regular supply of food. People settled in communities because they no longer had to travel in search of food.
- ✔ Student responses will vary.

Diego Rivera. *Civilizacion Totomac (The Totomac Civilization)*. 1947.

The Development of Communities

In what type of community do you live? Perhaps you live in an apartment building in a large city. Maybe your home is a farm in a rural community.

Communities have existed for thousands of years. In ancient times, before civilizations developed, people moved often. They traveled from place to place in search of food. Then, in about 6500 B.C., farming was developed. With farming, people could count on a regular supply of food. This is when people began settling in permanent communities. They settled in areas near a water source, such as a river.

The first ancient civilizations developed in the Middle East, China, the Indus Valley in India, the island of Crete, and Central America. Although these civilizations were isolated from one another, they had many similarities. The people built cities and raised animals. They also developed systems of writing and created techniques for using metals and making pottery.

In the artwork on this page, Diego Rivera depicts the Totomac civilization. The Totomac are Native South Americans who lived in Mexico.

MAKING THE CONNECTION

- ✔ Look carefully at the artwork. Identify some of the tasks being performed by the Totomac.
- ✔ How did the discovery of farming lead to the development of communities?
- ✔ Draw a picture of the community in which you live. How is it different from the community shown in *Civilizacion Totomac?*

INTERNET ACTIVITY

Visit Glencoe's Fine Arts Web Site for students at:

http://www.glencoe.com/sec/art/students

INTERNET ACTIVITY

Community Outreach Make use of the Information Superhighway to transport your students beyond the classroom door and into your community. Your own school or district may have its own World Wide Web site. Offer to have some of your students contribute studio or computer art to that Home Page. Use the on-line search capabilities to locate art societies, local galleries, or artists in your community. Many cities and counties maintain community calendars or events schedules on their Home Page. There you might find opportunities to stage exhibitions of your students' artworks. Let members of the community know what your art classes are accomplishing, and what they can to do encourage growth in the arts. Find us at **http://www.glencoe.com/sec/art**

REVIEW

 BUILDING VOCABULARY

Number a sheet of paper from 1 to 10. After each number, write the term from the box that best matches each description below.

architects   façade
cityscape   panorama
columns   Rococo
The Eight   seascape
elevation   staged photograph

1. Vertical posts that rise to support another structure.
2. An art style of the 1700s that emphasized graceful movement, curving lines, and delicate colors.
3. The front of a building.
4. A complete view of an area in all directions.
5. A drawing or painting focusing on large buildings and other objects found in cities.
6. A drawing or painting of the ocean and objects found on or around it.
7. A group of American Realists who worked at the beginning of the twentieth century.
8. Artists who plan and create buildings.
9. A photographic composition that makes use of artificial images or processes.
10. A drawing of an outside view of a building.

 REVIEWING ART FACTS

Number a sheet of paper from 11 to 15. Answer each question in a complete sentence.

11. Why did van Gogh choose to paint a picture of his room?
12. What is the meaning of the title of Figure 9–4 on page **166**?
13. What is the name of the palace Louis XIV had built for him? What side of the king's personality does this palace reflect?
14. What change took place in the painting of cityscapes at the turn of the twentieth century?
15. What was the contribution of Louis H. Sullivan to the look of cities today?

 THINKING ABOUT ART

On a sheet of paper, answer each question in a sentence or two.

1. **Compare and contrast.**   In what way might a room and a city be similar in the eyes of an artist? How are they different?
2. **Explain.**   What style did The Eight use to show life in big cities?
3. **Interpret.**   What properties or qualities of the sea are reflected in the painting in Figure 9–16?

MAKING ART CONNECTIONS

1. **Language Arts.**   Imagine that you are a real estate agent. Your job is to describe homes that are for sale. Choose one of the dwellings in Figure 9–6, 9–7, or 9–8. Write a paragraph describing the structure. Identify the type of individual who might feel at home in the dwelling you have chosen. Explain how you came to this conclusion.

2. **Geography.**   Genoa, Italy—the city shown in Figure 9–17—has a celebrated past. Among other distinctions, the city was the birthplace of Christopher Columbus. A statue of the explorer even graces the town center. Using an encyclopedia or other resource, find out more about Genoa's past and present. What is the city most noted for today? Share your findings with the class in an illustrated oral report.

Chapter 9 Review   **181**

Building Vocabulary

1. columns
2. Rococo
3. façade
4. panorama
5. cityscape
6. seascape
7. The Eight
8. architects
9. staged photograph
10. elevation

Reviewing Art Facts

11. Van Gogh led a troubled life, and his room was a place where he felt safe.
12. The title, *Spring Cleaning*, is a reference to the clutter in the room shown. Spring is traditionally a time when people throw out objects that clutter their living space.
13. It is the Palace at Versailles. The palace, with its ornate design and expensive furnishings, reveals the king's lavish tastes.
14. The subject matter shifted away from grandeur and toward more realistic subjects, such as factories.
15. He designed the steel crossbeam "skeleton" used for the framework of modern skyscrapers.

 THINKING ABOUT ART

1. Both a room and a city have the potential to hold personal importance. An artist might record this importance of either place in a work of art. A difference between the two might lie in the way each is depicted. For example, a city might be represented in a panorama, whereas a room could not.

2. The Eight used realism in their artworks.
3. The sea wields enormous power. It can be brutal and unforgiving, as when its force is summoned into a tidal wave. It is these qualities of the sea that the work calls to mind.

Examining Objects

(pages 182–201)

Chapter Scan

Lessons

1 Objects in Nature
 2 Drawing a Magical Forest
3 Grouping Objects
 4 Painting a Watercolor Still Life
5 Art Objects
 6 Building a Clay Musical Instrument
7 Decorative Arts
 8 Creating a Pendant

Resources

- 10-8 Chapter Test, TRB page 166
- Transparency CC-10, *Lidded Jaguar Vessel*
- Transparency 10, *Covered Bowl with Floral Scrolls*
- Fine Art Print 16, *Watch* by Gerald Murphy

A R T
S O U **Music**
R C E While studying this
chapter, use Perform-
ing Arts Handbook
page 322 to appreciate how Chic
Street Man portrayed a man and
the objects that were an integral
part of his life.

NATIONAL STANDARDS

This chapter addresses
the following National Standards for the Visual Arts:
1. (a, b)   **4.** (a, b, c)
2. (a, b, c)   **5.** (a, b)
3. (a, b)   **6.** (a, b)

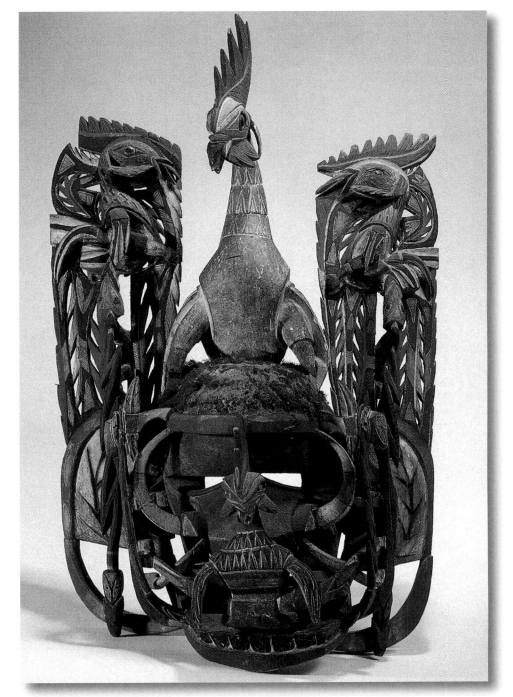

Figure 10–1 In what ways is this mask similar to others you have seen? What kind of balance does it have?

New Ireland. *Mask.* c. 1800. Wood and paint. 74.4 × 45.5 cm (29³⁄₁₀ × 17⁹⁄₁₀″). Galerie Ch. Ratton & G. Ladriere, Paris, France.

FEATURED ARTISTS

Everald Brown   Georgia O'Keeffe
Charles Demuth   Charles Sheeler
Suzuki Kiitsu   Paul Sierra
Lik'an

Examining Objects

Do you have a most prized possession? Maybe you know someone else who does. Some prized possessions are valuable items—a rare coin or stamp, for example. Others have a value that is clear only to their owner—a torn ticket stub, an old toy, a tarnished locket.

It is this second, hidden meaning of objects that makes them candidates for art subjects. In this chapter you will learn about ways in which artists have captured the inner beauty of everyday objects. You will also learn about works of art that are themselves considered *objects*. One of these is pictured at the left. Can you identify the "object" shown? What objects can you identify within the work?

PORTFOLIO IDEAS

From time to time, review your portfolio contents. If you have been using it to hold all of your notes, sketches, and finished artworks, you might want to review your selections and replace some of your entries. Remember, your goal is to present a portfolio of works that communicates your growth as an artist.

OBJECTIVES

After completing this chapter, you will be able to:
- Explain how artists perceive objects.
- Define the term *applied art*.
- Compare art objects from different cultures and times.
- Use a variety of media to create original art objects.

WORDS YOU WILL LEARN

applied art
jewelry
kiln
pendant
perceive
pottery
slip
vessel
watercolorist

■ Chapter Overview

All around us are common objects that have intrinsic beauty, if we learn to perceive that beauty as artists do. In this chapter, students will learn about artworks as objects—objects from different cultures and different times.

■ Chapter Motivator

Instruct students to think about common objects they see every day—athletic shoes, their backpack, a baseball cap, a teacher's desktop, a geranium on the window sill, and so on. Ask them to describe the object, listing as many details as possible. Were they able to provide lots of details? Explain that in this chapter, students will improve their skills as observers of familiar objects in order to see that even common, everyday things have special meaning and beauty.

■ Examining the Artwork

Instruct students to examine Figure 10-1, *Mask*. Explain that this artwork is from New Ireland, an island that is part of Papua New Guinea, an island country in the southwest Pacific. Masks like this were used in ritual ceremonies that marked important events such as birth, death, and initiation rites. The mask features likenesses of animals, much like the totem images discussed in Chapter 7, Lesson 2.

National Museum of Women in the Arts

You may wish to use the National Museum of Women in the Arts videodisc and/or CD-ROM. The videodisc features a bar code guide, and the interactive CD-ROM provides stimulating activities.

183

DEVELOPING A PORTFOLIO

Building A Storage System Artists have used folders, envelopes, binders, cases with zippers, and bags for organizing and storing their work. Actual physical construction of a portfolio case or folder can become a design assignment in itself. If you anticipate the type of assignments, including size, materials, and durability of the resulting artwork, you can establish some guidelines for the construction of a practical portfolio case. Then you can discuss the ways in which the work might be organized for storage within the classroom. This helps the students appreciate keeping the portfolios and is the beginning of establishing group expectations for the portfolios.

☑ OBJECTIVES

After completing this lesson, students will be able to:
• Define the word *perceive.*
• Explain why American artist Georgia O'Keeffe painted flowers on a large scale.
• Tell why the Chinese artist Lik'an chose to paint pictures of bamboo.

☑ SUPPLIES

• Pencils
• White drawing paper
• Magnifying glasses
• Collection of small ordinary objects familiar to students

Resources

■ 10-1 Say It With Flowers, TRB page 157 (art history)

■ Motivator

Make available a collection of small, ordinary objects and instruct each student to select one. Call on several students to describe the object they selected. Then ask them to examine the objects with a magnifying glass. Did the closer examination reveal details that were overlooked at first? Direct attention to the two artworks in this lesson. Point out that both works were done by artists who took time to find beauty in the kind of common objects we often take for granted.

184

Objects in Nature

Artists have a special way of looking at things. They look at the ordinary and see the *extraordinary.* They look at a rain-slicked fence in the countryside and see a study in color and form and texture. They look at a battered old shoe and see a wholeness—a unity—that goes beyond the scuffed leather and tattered laces.

Some artists are born with this ability to "see." Others are trained to **perceive**—to *become aware through the senses of the special nature of objects.* In this chapter, you will share several artists' one-of-a-kind visions of objects in the world around them. You will also sharpen your own ability to perceive.

NATURE STUDIES

"Stop and smell the roses." Are you familiar with this saying? It underscores the idea that there is much that is beautiful and exciting in nature, if only we take the time to notice it.

Artists have been seeking out and perceiving the beauty in nature throughout the ages. The works on these pages are the result of two stops to "smell the roses." The paintings were made at different times and in different places. Yet, a common link exists between them. Both record objects found in nature.

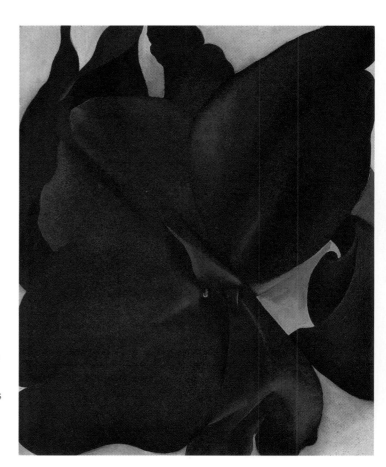

Figure 10–2   The artist explained that her goal was to startle viewers. Do you feel she succeeded? Why or why not?

Georgia O'Keeffe. *Red Cannas.* 1927. Oil on canvas. 91.8 × 76.5 cm (36⅛ × 30⅛"). Amon Carter Museum, Fort Worth, Texas. © 1997 The Georgia O'Keeffe Foundation/Artists Rights Society (ARS), New York, NY

184   Chapter 10   *Examining Objects*

---

more about • • •

Georgia O'Keeffe   This influential American artist (1887–1986) was born in Sun Prairie, Wisconsin. She studied art in Chicago and New York City, then taught art in Texas, where the natural terrain of the great Southwest first inspired her to paint objects common to the desert, the mountains, and the rugged land. Though she lived and worked in New York City for many years, O'Keeffe eventually settled in New Mexico. Many of her paintings are of rocks, flowers, and animal skulls. Encourage students to read more about this famous artist in such books as *Inspirations: Stories About Women Artists* by Leslie Sills (N. Y.: Whitman, 1989) or *Portraits of Women Artists for Children: Georgia O'Keeffe* by Robyn Montana Turner (N. Y.: Little, Brown, 1992).

An Object Up Close

The subject of the painting in Figure 10–2 is an object of a type you have seen. Did you immediately recognize it as a brightly colored tropical flower? If you did not, the reason may have to do with the way in which the artist represented it. Notice the size of the painting. Why would any artist choose to magnify an image of a flower many hundreds of times?

The answer rests with events of the period in which the artist, Georgia O'Keeffe, lived. O'Keeffe was active in the early 1900s. The world was changing fast. Tall buildings were going up in big cities such as New York, where O'Keeffe lived. Convinced that people had begun to overlook nature's wonders, O'Keeffe painted her subjects larger than life, just like the buildings.

An Object from Long Ago

The painting in Figure 10–3 focuses on a plant native to its artist's homeland. In this case, the plant is bamboo. The artist was from China. Look closely at this work. See the care given to each small leaf. The elegant lines call to mind *calligraphy* (kuh-**lig**-ruh-fee)—the art of beautiful writing. In fact, the artist was a noted calligrapher in his day. What quality of this work do you think prompted some viewers to call it a portrait of an actual plant?

STUDIO ACTIVITY

Viewing Objects Up Close

With a magnifying glass, study a common object. Choose something so ordinary and familiar that you never take the time to look at it closely. Possibilities include a shell, a leaf, or your thumbprint. Draw the object large enough to fill a sheet of 9 x 12-inch (23 x 30-cm) white drawing paper. Include every detail, every change of value, every line, and every texture.

PORTFOLIO

Write a paragraph describing the experience of perceiving an everyday object. Explore your feelings as you discovered the special nature of the object. Put the paragraph in your portfolio with your artwork.

✔ Check Your Understanding

1. Define the term *perceive*.
2. Why did Georgia O'Keeffe paint flowers on such a large scale?

Figure 10–3 This ink painting of an actual bamboo plant shows many of its characteristics. How has the artist made some leaves look near and others look farther away?

Lik'an. *Ink-Bamboo.* (Detail.) 1308. Handscroll, ink on paper. 37.5 × 237.5 cm (14¾" × 7′ 9″). The Nelson-Atkins Museum of Art, Kansas City, Missouri. Purchase: Nelson Trust.

Lesson 1 *Objects in Nature* **185**

■ Art Criticism

Divide the class into two groups, assigning each group one of the artworks in this lesson. Have students use the following questions to examine each work:
- How would you describe your work in a single, detailed sentence?
- Which work emphasizes line and value? Which emphasizes shape and color? How do both demonstrate variety and harmony?
- What ideas and feelings does the work communicate to you?
- Do you think this work is successful? Explain.

ASSESS

■ Self-Assessment

Have students complete the Check Your Understanding questions on this page. Answers are provided below.

■ Reteaching

Ask students to explain what senses they use when they try to *perceive*.

■ Enrichment

Arrange students in small groups and ask them to discuss this question: Is more skill required to paint a landscape with trees, fields, flowers, rivers, sky, and clouds than is required to paint subjects like bamboo or a single flower? Why or why not? Have groups find examples to support their conclusions and share the results of their discussion with the class.

CLOSE

Have students explain how one's senses can empower a person to detect the extraordinary nature of ordinary objects.

• • • • • • • • • • • • • •
FOCUS

☑OBJECTIVES

After completing this lesson, students will be able to:

• Create a picture of a forest of trees decorated in a rich pattern of lines and shapes with bright, warm hues.

• Use overlapping techniques to suggest space, and color to show contrast.

• Describe, analyze, interpret, and judge their finished pictures.

☑SUPPLIES

• Pencils and sketch paper
• White drawing paper
• Colored markers

Resource

■ 10-2 Almost Human, TRB page 158 (reproducible master)

• • • • • • • • • • • • • •
TEACH

■ Motivator

Have students examine the painting by Paul Sierra in Figure 10-4. Ask them if they think the trees and plants in the painting have been painted in a realistic way. What is there about them that is *not* realistic? Could he have been interested in something other than realism? What else could have interested him?

LESSON 2

Drawing a Magical Forest

Nearly everyone has read a story or seen a cartoon in which non-human objects—houses, trees, or animals—were given a magical feeling. The objects may have looked something like the plants in Figure 10–4. Examine this fanciful work. Notice the color scheme. Are reds, greens, and blues the colors that come to mind when you think of tropical plants? Use your imagination and ask yourself where these plants might be growing.

WHAT YOU WILL LEARN

In this lesson you will learn how, with imagination, ordinary objects can be presented in exciting new ways.

You will use colored markers to create a magical forest of colorful trees and shrubs. Your forest will contain no less than five trees. These will overlap to create a sense of space. The trunks and leaves of the trees will be filled with rich patterns of shapes and lines. These will be drawn with warm colors, as in Figure 10–4. Larger shapes in cool colors will be used for the background.

WHAT YOU WILL NEED

• Pencils and sketch paper
• White drawing paper, 9 x 12 inches (23 x 30 cm) or larger
• Colored markers

WHAT YOU WILL DO

1. Bring to class a small branch. This is to serve as a model for your tree drawing. Make sketches of the branch in several different positions. Each sketch is to represent a different tree in your forest. Include at least five different trees. One of these must lean to the side. Another

Figure 10–4   Notice how the artist has used contrasting shapes for variety. What other element of art is evident?

Paul Sierra. *The Color of Summer.* 1996. 127 × 152.4 cm (50 × 60″). Oscar Friedl Gallery, Chicago, Illinois.

186   Chapter 10   *Examining Objects*

MEETING SPECIAL NEEDS

Using Analogies   The ability to understand and use analogies is not just the essence of creative thought, it is also an excellent way to bring insight to students with visual disabilities. For example, "The plant's leaves are shaped like the blade of a knife, but they have a surface like an unmade bed's rumpled blankets," helps students understand similarities by linking a new description with objects they can feel. Engage the student with a visual disability in a dialogue about what the object might be like. Rather than making a line drawing, a student with a visual disability might use wire to create a three-dimensional outline of the essence of the form.

must extend off the top edge of the paper. Overlap the trees and place them to suggest depth.

2. When you are satisfied with your forest, transfer your sketch to the drawing paper in light pencil. Then go over each of the pencil lines with a black marker.

3. Use the colored markers to fill in the trunks and leaves of the trees with a pattern of shapes and lines. These are to be drawn in bright, warm hues.

4. Divide the background space into large shapes. Color in these areas with dark, cool colors, as in Figure 10–4.

EXAMINING YOUR WORK

- **Describe** Does your picture include at least five different trees?
- **Analyze** Are your trees placed to suggest depth? Were bright warm hues used to create a pattern of shapes and lines in the trees and shrubs? Do these contrast with the cooler colors of the background?
- **Interpret** Does your colorful version of a forest create a magical feeling?
- **Judge** Would you like others to judge your picture on the basis of subject, composition, or content? Why?

Figure 10–5 Student work. A magical forest.

Try This! **COMPUTER OPTION**

■ Arrange objects to show depth. Include changes in size, detail, color, placement on the picture plane, and overlapping. Create an imaginary scene for a story, play, or movie you have imagined, written, or heard about. Think of the kind of setting and objects you will need. Choose from a variety of tools and draw the basic features. Choose the Lasso tool to select, move, and arrange the shapes. Select some of the objects and change their size to larger or smaller if this option is available. Overlap shapes. Move smaller shapes higher on the picture plane. Think of the mood. Select from the Paint tools and add colors and special effects so colors fade in the distance. Title, save, and print.

Lesson 2 *Drawing a Magical Forest* **187**

■ **Studio Skills**

Demonstrate on the board how to use various views of a tree branch model to create a forest drawing. Make certain to include at least five trees, pointing out that one or more of these must run off the top of the paper. Tell them that space can be suggested by overlapping trees. Have students experiment creating small shapes and lines of the kind they will use in their trees and shrubs. Tell them to experiment with many different patterns.

Sparking Creativity

Remind students that their trees do not have to be realistic. Ask them to envision a goal, whether realistic or abstract. Their vision should include color used in imaginative, unexpected and creative ways.

• • • • • • • • • • • •
ASSESS

■ **Self-Assessment**

Have students use Examining Your Work to evaluate their art.

■ **Reteaching**

Ask pairs of students to review each other's work in terms of its "magical" or imaginative qualities.

■ **Enrichment**

Bring to class an illustration of a tree painting by Piet Mondrian. Have students compare and contrast this work with that of Sierra.

• • • • • • • • • • • •
CLOSE

Ask students to tell how their magical forest drawings successfully present ordinary objects in exciting new ways.

CURRICULUM CONNECTIONS

Botany Trees are a common and conspicuous part of our existence—graceful, useful, and important to our lives. Have students take a tree tour of their neighborhood. Have them collect samples of various species and compile a directory of trees in the area. Demonstrate how to press and mount the leaves between sheets of paper. Then, using a simple tree guidebook available at the library, have students identify each species with the common as well as scientific name. Point out that in North America, there are over 750 species of trees. How many can they find? Ask students to study the characteristics of each leaf in detail and to compare the patterns and variations in shape, color, and line. What differences and similarities do they perceive?

Grouping Objects

☑ OBJECTIVES

After completing this lesson, students will be able to:

• Define *still life* as an art form.
• Compare and contrast a Western and an Eastern still life.
• Understand how to use graduated changes in value to achieve a three-dimensional appearance.

☑ SUPPLIES

• Several common objects such as fruit, eggs, jars, bottles
• Large, square sticks of charcoal
• White drawing paper
• Tissues

Resource

■ 10-3 An "I" Object, TRB page 159 (studio)

■ Vocabulary

Explain that artists often choose to paint **still lifes,** pictures of ordinary objects, because they are mainly interested in **composition.** (See Chapters 1 and 2 for a review of composition.) Such works are meant to be quietly pleasing rather than loudly dramatic or shocking. Point out how Charles Sheeler's painting, for example, is a thoughtful arrangement of a few rounded objects.

Have you ever been warned that "you can't mix apples and oranges"? Artists have been ignoring this piece of advice for well over 2,000 years. Their works have mixed apples, oranges, and countless other fruits and objects. In this lesson, you will look at two such mixtures. After careful examination, you may decide that the whole *can* be greater than the sum of its parts.

OBJECTS IN STILL LIFES

An important scholar once noted that there are no new ideas, just new combinations of old ones. This statement certainly applies to the works of art called *still lifes.* These are paintings or drawings of *inanimate,* or unmoving, objects.

The objects depicted in still lifes are familiar. What is unfamiliar is their combination—their arrangement. Each still life presents its subject matter in a new, startling way.

A Western Still Life

As a Western art form, the still life is one of the oldest. Descriptions of realistic paintings of grouped objects appear in Greek writings dating back to about 2400 B.C.

A painting fitting this description is shown in Figure 10–6. This still life, however,

Figure 10–6   Compare this still life with the one in Figure 1–2 on page 4. What similarities do you detect? What differences?

Charles Sheeler. *Suspended Forms.* 1922. Charcoal, black and brown chalk, watercolor. 48.2 × 38.7 cm (19 × 15¼"). The Saint Louis Art Museum, St. Louis, Missouri. Bequest of Marie Setz Hertslet, 123:1972

188   Chapter 10   *Examining Objects*

TECHNOLOGY OPTIONS

National Gallery of Art Videodisc   Use the following images to show additional still lifes with grouped objects.

Georges Braque	John Frederick Peto	Pablo Picasso
Still Life: The Table	*The Old Violin*	*Juggler with Still Life*
Search Frame 2171	Search Frame 1978	Search Frame 2281

Use Glencoe's *National Gallery of Art Correlation Bar Code Guide* to locate more artworks.

Figure 10–7 **Notice the arrangement of the objects in this still life.**

Suzuki Kiitsu. *Seashells and Plums.* Japanese. Edo Period. Nineteenth century. Color on silk. 34.6 × 29.2 cm (13⅝ × 11½"). Los Angeles County Museum of Art, Los Angeles, California. Etsuko and Joe Price Collection.

was completed in the twentieth century. Its artist, moreover, was American. Examine the work. It is a detailed, lifelike painting of several ordinary objects. Notice their placement. Would you say they have been arranged haphazardly or with care? Find the single horizontal line in the picture. What does this line represent? In what way does it add a welcome contrast to the design?

An Eastern Still Life

Like the artworks you learned about in Lesson 1, the two on these pages are separated by time and place. The still life in Figure 10–7 was completed more than a century before the one in Figure 10–6. The artist who made this second painting was from Japan. The work, in fact, gives us a sense of traditional Japanese design. It also provides an insight into Japanese culture.

Experimenting with Form and Value

Look again at Figure 10–6. The artist has created a sense of three-dimensional form mainly through *value*. By changing little by little from dark to light values, he makes the objects appear solid and round.

Experiment with this method yourself. Arrange several objects, such as apples, eggs, and jars, on a tabletop. Step back and study this arrangement carefully. Then draw the composition with charcoal. Show gradual changes of value.

P O R T F O L I O

In a short paragraph, evaluate the result of the shading technique you achieved with charcoal. Tell whether this medium was more or less effective than others you have used for shading.

Examine the contents of the painting. These are summed up neatly in the title. What do the first of these items, the shells, reveal about Japan's geography? Look next at the still life's composition. How would you describe the arrangement of the objects? How similar is this arrangement to the one in Figure 10–6? As you study this work, it becomes clear that the artist's goal was to create an elegant, balanced design. Do you think he has succeeded?

✔ Check Your Understanding

1. What is a still life?
2. In what ways are the still lifes on these pages similar? How are they different?

Lesson 3 *Grouping Objects* **189**

Experimenting with Form and Value

Supervise students as they arrange their objects. Tell them to fill the paper with their drawing. Demonstrate how the charcoal can be smudged with a piece of tissue to create gradual changes in value. Areas that appear to be too dark can be lightened using a soft or kneaded eraser.

■ Art Criticism

Have students describe each of the still lifes shown. Tell them that their descriptions should include mention of the elements of art noted in each work. Ask why the artists chose not to include background detail. Have them analyze both works by identifying the principles of art used to organize the elements.

• • • • • • • • • • • ASSESS

■ Self-Assessment

Have students complete the Check Your Understanding questions on this page. Answers are provided below.

■ Reteaching

In pairs, have students find and discuss other still-life paintings in this book.

■ Enrichment

While still in his teens, Suzuki Kiitsu was accepted as a student by the famous painter Sakai Hoitsu. Hoitsu made certain that Kiitsu's studies included poetry and the tea ceremony. Ask students to discuss how such a broad education might be helpful to an artist's success.

• • • • • • • • • CLOSE

Have students describe the organization they used in their still lifes.

Answers to ✔ CHECK YOUR UNDERSTANDING

1. A **still life** is a painting or drawing of inanimate, familiar objects.

2. Kiitsu and Sheeler both painted still-life objects to look three-dimensional. They both have little background detail. The subject matter of each is different.

• • • • • • • • • • • • • •
FOCUS

☑ OBJECTIVES

After completing this lesson, students will be able to:
- Create a watercolor of two vegetables and a bottle or jar.
- Describe, analyze, interpret, and judge their work.

☑ SUPPLIES

- Pencils
- White drawing paper
- Watercolors, large flat brushes, mixing trays, paint cloths
- Wooden skewers
- Flat containers with india ink
- Vegetables and jars or bottles
- Lengths of colored cloth (optional)

Resource

- ■ 10-4 Charles Demuth, TRB page 161 (artist profile)

• • • • • • • • • • • • • •
TEACH

■ Motivator

Ask students to identify the kinds of subjects they think make the "best" paintings. List these on the board. Then ask if students can think of subjects that would not make an interesting painting. Direct attention to Figure 10-8. Do they think this is an interesting work? A successful work? What can be learned from this painting that features such humble subject matter?

190

Painting a Watercolor Still Life

To the average person, an eggplant and a green bell pepper are ingredients of a meal. To artist Charles Demuth, these simple vegetables were ingredients of a still life (Figure 10–8). Study this work. It helped secure Demuth's reputation as a great watercolorist. A **watercolorist** is *a painter who works in watercolor.*

In this lesson, you will create your own still life using watercolor and ink. Like the painting in Figure 10–8, yours will feature ordinary vegetables. See if you can paint them in a way that pleases even viewers who usually don't like vegetables!

Figure 10–8 What steps has the artist taken to "spice up" his ordinary subject matter?

Charles Demuth. *Eggplant and Green Pepper.* 1925. Watercolor with graphite. 45.7 × 30.2 cm (18 × 11"). The Saint Louis Art Museum, St. Louis, Missouri. Eliza McMillan Fund, 2:1948

WHAT YOU WILL LEARN

You will complete a watercolor-and-ink painting of two vegetables and a jar or bottle. Create highlights within your painting by leaving some areas of the paper unpainted. Use broken ink lines to strengthen contour lines and to create details and textures.

WHAT YOU WILL NEED

- Two different vegetables and a jar or bottle as props
- A length of colorful cloth (optional)
- Pencil
- White drawing paper, 12 x 18 inches (30 x 46 cm)
- Watercolor paint
- Large flat brush
- Mixing tray
- Paint cloth
- A wooden skewer
- Black india ink

WHAT YOU WILL DO

1. Begin by studying the watercolor in Figure 10–8. Notice that the artist has left some parts of the paper unpainted. Observe how this helps to suggest highlights, while adding a refreshing sparkle to the entire picture.

SAFETY TIP ⚠

Using Sharp Objects Always supervise students closely and carefully when they are using sharp objects like the wooden skewers called for in this Studio Lesson. At no time should students be allowed to work in the classroom without direct supervision. Establish safety rules and guidelines early on, and enforce those rules rigidly for the safety of all.

2. With several classmates, select and bring to class two ordinary vegetables and a jar or bottle. These are to be used as subjects for your still life. You may also wish to bring a colorful piece of cloth to serve as a backdrop. Place these objects on a table-top. Strive for an interesting arrangement.

3. Using light pencil lines, complete a drawing of the still life. Make sure to fill the entire sheet of drawing paper.

Figure 10–9   **Student work. Watercolor still life.**

- **Describe**   Identify all the objects in your painting.
- **Analyze**   Did you leave areas of your picture unpainted to suggest highlights and give your work a fresh look? Did you use broken ink lines to sharpen contours and add details and textures?
- **Interpret**   Would you describe your work as light and fresh-looking, or dark and somber?
- **Judge**   Do you think you succeeded in making a visually appealing painting using ordinary vegetables? Why or why not?

4. With a large flat brush, paint your still life. Work with lighter hues first and add darker hues little by little. Use a dry brush technique to apply the paint with single brush strokes. Avoid scrubbing over painted areas. As you move your dry brush over the surface of the paper, some portions will remain unpainted. Leave them this way.

5. Dip the wooden skewer into black india ink. Use this to create broken lines to emphasize contours or edges and to add details and textures.

COMPUTER OPTION

Try This!

■ Select a small Brush tool or the Pencil tool. Draw the shapes of several fruits or vegetables. Use the Selection tool to arrange the shapes to make a still life. Add a setting such as a table or cloth, and include a background. Keep in mind the mood you want to create and the surfaces you will need to communicate that mood.

Choose some hues and the Line tool to add colors and textures. Select Gradients or the Airbrush tool to add shading and emphasize the fruits and vegetables. If available, consider changing the opacity of the colors to transparent hues in order to layer colors and add shading. Title, save and print your work.

Lesson 4   *Painting a Watercolor Still Life*   **191**

Art on a Shoestring

Some watercolor rendering papers can be bought less expensively in rolls or by the foot than by the sheet or pad. A 100% rag, twenty-pound vellum is pretty tough, and you can iron the back of it to smooth it after using liquid media.

ASSESS

■ **Self-Assessment**

Have students use Examining Your Work to evaluate their art.

■ **Reteaching**

In pairs, have students identify the ways Demuth achieved texture and space in his painting.

■ **Enrichment**

Both Charles Sheeler and Charles Demuth practiced a style of art known as Precisionism. Have a student look up the definition for *precision* and read it to the class. Ask how the painting by Demuth in this lesson and the one by Sheeler in Lesson 3 conform to that definition. Ask students if they think Precisionism is a good name for the style of art both practiced.

CLOSE

Have students brainstorm a list of techniques they found effective in painting their watercolor still lifes.

TECHNIQUE TIP

Dry-Brush Technique with Watercolor and Ink
Demonstrate to students what is meant by a dry-brush technique. Point out how this technique leaves unpainted areas that add a freshness to watercolor paintings. Demonstrate how painting a given area over and over again muddies the color. Also show how a broken ink line made with a pointed stick can be used to define contours

and add detail and texture. Caution students not to use too many lines, thus adding confusion to their pictures.

For more tips on working with watercolors, see Technique Tip 14 in the Handbook, page **285.** You may also want to check out *Eyewitness Art: Watercolor* published by Dorling Kindersley (N.Y., 1993).

Art Objects

•••••••••••••••
FOCUS

☑ OBJECTIVES

After completing this lesson, students will be able to:

• Explain the function of a *vessel* and identify examples of vessels.

• Understand that applied art objects serve a dual purpose.

☑ SUPPLIES

• Pencils and sketch paper

• White drawing paper

Resource

∎ 10-5 Blankets, Bowls, and Baskets, TRB page 162 (appreciating cultural diversity)

•••••••••••••••
TEACH

∎ Motivator

Ask students to express their opinions about Figure 10-10. How many discussed it in terms of its function? How many referred to it and discussed it as a work of art? Explain that the item pictured in Figure 10-10 is an example of *applied art*, an artwork that serves a practical function yet is visually pleasing.

∎ Vocabulary

Explain that the ancient Persians typically crafted *rhytons* in the form of an animal's head or body. When the ancient Greeks invaded Persia, they were greatly influenced by Persian arts and crafts. Tell students that such *vessels* as the rhyton were eventually crafted in Greece as well.

Each of the artworks you have examined thus far in this chapter was created with a common purpose in mind. That purpose was to delight—to appeal to the viewer in terms of its subject, content, or composition. Most fine art shares this purpose. However, some art goes further, serving an everyday use as well. Such *works of art that are made to be useful as well as visually pleasing* are known as **applied art.**

In this lesson, you will examine two examples of applied art from the distant past. In the remaining lessons of the chapter, you will look at other examples of applied art.

VESSEL FROM LONG AGO

The next time you are thirsty, imagine filling the item in Figure 10–10 with water or juice. This art object is a **vessel,** *a hollow utensil made to hold something.* Vessels come in all shapes and sizes. They also serve a wide variety of purposes. The vessel pictured here was used for drinking. Pitchers and vases are other examples of vessels. What objects have you seen in other chapters that might qualify as vessels?

Look closely at Figure 10–10. This drinking vessel is called a *rhyton*. It was created about 2,500 years ago in the ancient kingdom of Persia. The object is made mostly from a single piece of gold. A gold liner at the base of the cup prevented liquid from flowing into the body of the animal. Notice the *flutings,* or bands of rings, etched into the surface of the cup. What other patterns have been used to

Figure 10–10 What animal is depicted on this object? What does that subject and the medium suggest about the person for whom the object was created?

Hamadan (Iran). *Rhyton Vessel in the Form of a Lion.* Fifth century B.C. Gold. 17 × 23 cm (6⅔ × 9″). The Metropolitan Museum of Art, New York, New York. Fletcher Fund, 1954.

192 Chapter 10 *Examining Objects*

CURRICULUM ▶ CONNECTIONS

Geography Ancient Persia was a kingdom located in an area that is now made up of Iran and Afghanistan. The Persian Empire reached its peak around 500 B.C. This expansive empire extended from North Africa and southeastern Europe in the west to India in the east, and from the Gulf of Oman in the south to the southern boundaries of what is now Kazakhstan in the north. Much of the trade between central Asia and Europe passed through the Persian Empire, especially silk, spices, pottery, textiles, and precious stones. Have students research more about the ancient Persians and their culture and draw a map of the empire at its height.

decorate this object? What do you think was the social standing of the person for whom it was crafted?

PENDANT FROM LONG AGO

An altogether different function was served by the object in Figure 10–11. That function is clear from the title of the artwork. Like the rhyton, this pendant was fashioned entirely from gold. A **pendant** is *a jewelry item worn suspended from the neck on a string or chain*. Notice its size. For a piece of jewelry that is only 2⅝″ (6.7 cm), the artist has managed to include an amazing amount of detail. Study this object. It portrays a man who projects outward in high relief. Notice the expression on the man's face and the direction of his gaze. What feeling does this portrait communicate?

Check Your Understanding

1. What is a vessel? What are some examples of vessels?
2. Could the work in Figure 10–11 be regarded as both fine art and applied art? Why or why not?

STUDIO ACTIVITY

Creating an Object Design

Look at the object in Figure 10–10. Imagine that you were a goldsmith in Persia, and you were asked to fashion a drinking vessel. Imagine, moreover, that the request was for an original design—something like no other drinking vessel seen before.

Complete a detailed pencil drawing of a cup with a handle. Make your drawing large enough to fill a 9 x 12-inch (23 x 30 cm) sheet of white drawing paper. Use shading to accent the details of your design and to emphasize its three-dimensional form.

PORTFOLIO

Write a paragraph telling how you fulfilled the challenge to create a vessel like no other drinking vessel seen before. Put it in your portfolio with your drawing.

Figure 10–11 Compare the patterns on this object with those adorning the rhyton. How many objects can you identify in this tiny piece of art?

Roman. *Chain with a Portrait Medallion.* A.D. 238–243. Gold. 6.7 cm (2⅝″) in diameter. (Detail.) The Nelson-Atkins Museum of Art, Kansas City, Missouri. Purchase, Nelson Trust.

Lesson 5   *Art Objects*   **193**

Answers to ✔ CHECK YOUR UNDERSTANDING

1. A **vessel** is a hollow utensil made to hold something. Some examples of vessels are a rhyton, a vase, and a pitcher.

2. Answers will vary. In one sense, it can be considered fine art because on its own it is pleasing to look at. However, it also serves a function as something to be worn, as part of one's costume or apparel. In that regard, it can be considered applied art.

STUDIO ACTIVITY

Creating an Object Design

Tell students to give free reign to their imaginations in order to arrive at a truly original design. Emphasize the need for originality.

■ Cooperative Learning

Divide the class into four or five groups. Pass out slips of paper that say either "for" or "against." Explain that each group is a museum committee formed to decide whether their museum should add the rhyton (illustrated in Figure 10-10) to their permanent collection. Each "committee" is to provide reasons why they are for or against the purchase of the rhyton. Tell groups to make specific references to features of the rhyton when giving their reasons.

ASSESS

■ Self-Assessment

Have students complete the Check Your Understanding questions on this page. Answers are provided below.

■ Reteaching

Ask students to brainstorm examples of vessels, explaining the function of each.

■ Enrichment

Invite students to identify ordinary objects they encounter daily that they consider to be well designed. What features set these objects apart from others?

CLOSE

Have students explain how the pendant in Figure 10-11 is an example of applied art.

193

LESSON TIME: 4 hours

• • • • • • • • • • • • • •

FOCUS

☑ OBJECTIVES

After completing this lesson, students will be able to:

• Use clay to create a musical instrument in the form of a real or imaginary animal or human.

• Describe, analyze, interpret, and judge their clay object as both musical instrument and artwork.

☑ SUPPLIES

• Pencils and sketch paper

• Two balls of water-base clay per student

• Slip (liquid clay)

• Clay modeling tools, fingernail files, or other flat instruments

• Round plastic drinking straws

Resources

■ 10-6 Art or Craft? TRB page 164 (aesthetics)

• • • • • • • • • • • • • •

TEACH

■ Motivator

Ask students to examine Figure 10-12. Discuss it as both art object and musical instrument. Tell students that in this lesson they will create a clay bird or other animal that will also serve as a musical instrument. Point out the large fish-form of the work illustrated and discuss possible forms their own musical instruments might take.

194

LESSON 6

Building a Clay Musical Instrument

Applied art objects, as you have learned, are meant to serve an everyday function. The object in Figure 10–12 goes a step further. It was designed to have *two* functions. The first, as the credit line reveals, was as a vessel. The item was, in fact, a vase. Can you guess its second function? Would it help you to know that its spout is adorned with finger holes, much like those found on a flute?

WHAT YOU WILL LEARN

In this lesson you will make your own musical wind instrument. Like the object in Figure 10–12, yours will be an example of **pottery.** This is *art, and the craft of making art, from clay.* Your instrument will not only create sound. It will also have the appearance of a real or imaginary bird, animal, fish, or person. You will use a variety of different textures to add interest to your instrument.

WHAT YOU WILL NEED

• Sketch paper and pencil
• Water-based clay
• Clay modeling tools
• A fingernail file, coffee stirrer, or other flat instrument
• A round plastic drinking straw

WHAT YOU WILL DO

1. Make several sketches of animals that might serve as the shape of your pottery object. Choose your best sketch. Set it aside.

2. Make two clay pinch pots in the shape of bowls. The pots should be the same size. (For instructions on joining clay, see Technique Tip **17** on page **285.**) With a modeling tool, *score*—make shallow lines in—the lip of each pot. Add **slip,** *clay with enough added water to give it a runny, liquid consistency.* The slip will function as a kind of glue. Join the edges together firmly.

3. Lightly tap the resulting hollow clay sphere on your work surface. Shape the ball into the form that most resembles the body of the animal you have chosen.

Figure 10–12 What words would you use to describe this object? What feeling does this object summon up?

Peru. *Spouted Vessel with Tubular Handle: Man on Fish.* 300–100 B.C. Ceramics. 18.7 × 11.4 × 22 cm (7⁵⁄₁₆ × 4½ × 8⅝″). Dallas Museum of Art, Dallas, Texas. Gift of Mrs. Nora Wise.

MEETING SPECIAL NEEDS

Manual Dexterity For some students with disabilities relating to neurological/orthopedic conditions or mental retardation, the task of making and joining the two pinch pots to create a sphere, as well as adjusting the windway and making the holes, may pose a challenge. In order for such students to more fully understand the separate steps involved in making the finished project, they might hold in their hands and examine a finished, fired clay musical instrument prior to making their own. They may need assistance in some of the more intricate steps of the project.

Notice, for example, that the fish in Figure 10–12 has a long, tapering, cylindrical body. Refer back to your sketch. Use additional clay to fashion the details for your creature.

4. Choose a body feature to serve as the *windway*. This is the tube or channel of a musical instrument through which air is blown to produce sound. A tail, leg, or mouth will make a good windway.

5. With a fingernail file or coffee stirrer, push a flat hole through the windway. The hole should extend all the way into the body cavity, or *sound chamber*.

6. Push a plastic drinking straw into the opening to create a vertical shaft. This should run perpendicular, or at a right angle, to the windway. Returning to the flat instrument, angle the vertical clay wall opposite the windway.

7. Test the instrument at this stage by blowing into the opening. You should hear a whistle-like sound. If no sound comes out, adjust the clay tip opposite the windway until you can make a sound.

8. Pierce the sound chamber with the straw several times. This will create finger holes. These may be used to raise the

EXAMINING YOUR WORK

- **Describe** Is the subject of your clay musical instrument recognizable? Does your pottery object function as a musical instrument?
- **Analyze** Did you use a variety of textures to add visual interest to your instrument?
- **Interpret** Is your creature pleasing to look at? Does the object produce sounds, and are these pleasing to the ear?
- **Judge** Is your work successful as an example of applied art?

pitch or tone. The location of these holes is not important. You will want to place them, however, where you can reach them easily with your fingers. Use the clay modeling tools to add small details and textures to the surface.

9. Allow your musical instrument to dry completely. Then, with your teacher's help, bake, or *fire,* the instrument in a **kiln**. This is *a special hot oven in which pottery objects are fired*. After firing, apply a glaze carefully. Make sure you do not cover the finger holes. Fire your object a second time.

Figure 10–13 **Student work. A musical instrument.**

Try This!

STUDIO OPTION

■ Use the same procedure—and your imagination—to create a second musical instrument. This instrument should be "from another planet."

Lesson 6 *Building a Clay Musical Instrument* **195**

more about • • •

Ceramics Pottery is any object made from clay and hardened by fire; it is also the name given to the craft of making such objects. A word for both is **ceramics**. Before becoming a finished piece of pottery, clay takes six different forms:
- Plastic clay—clay that holds its shape.
- Slip—clay with enough water added to make it runny.

- Leather-hard clay—clay that is still damp but too hard to model.
- Greenware—dry clay ready to be fired.
- Bisqueware—fired pottery.
- Glazeware—pottery with a hard, glasslike finish.
  Most ceramic objects are made hollow so they will not explode or crack during firing.

■ **Vocabulary**
Inform students that there are several terms they will learn in this lesson. *Sound chamber* refers to the air pocket in the center of their musical instrument. *Windway* is the term used to describe the opening to the sound chamber through which one blows to produce sound. *Air vents* are holes that pierce the sound chamber. Air vents are used to change the *pitch* of the *tone* produced when blowing on the instrument.

■ **Studio Skills**
Demonstrate the clay hand-building process to form the two pinch pots. For each, use an amount of clay that fits neatly into the palm of the hand. Tell students to work *slowly* using thumbs and fingers. Show them how to score the edges and add slip to join the two pinch pots together. Demonstrate how the windway and sound vent are made. Have students test the whistle, telling them that if it does not produce sound when wet, it will not work later when dry.

• • • • • • • • • • • • •
ASSESS

■ **Self-Assessment**
Have students use Examining Your Work to evaluate their art.

■ **Reteaching**
In pairs, have students explain how their musical instruments work.

■ **Enrichment**
Appoint a team of students to conduct a search for information about sound instruments representing different cultures. Have them present their findings to the class.

• • • • • • • • • • • • •
CLOSE

Have students demonstrate how their finished musical instruments make sounds.

Decorative
Arts

(pages 196–197)

Decorative Arts

The success of applied art objects is measured not only in terms of their beauty. A second yardstick is how well they do the job for which they were intended.

In this lesson you will learn about objects whose job is to *adorn*, or decorate.

JEWELRY

Some art is made to be worn. Several examples of such objects appear on these pages. Other examples may adorn your own ears, fingers, neck, or waist at this very moment. Such objects are grouped together under the label *jewelry*. **Jewelry** is *art, and the craft of making art, to be worn.* The pendant that you studied in Figure 10–11 on page **193** is an example of jewelry.

The earliest jewelry can be traced to the time of cave dwellers. These objects consisted mostly of shells or feathers strung together on woven leaves or vines. Since that time, the category of jewelry items has been expanded to include rings, earrings, necklaces, pins, and belts. Some, though not all, jewelry contains precious stones or metals.

Jewelry from the 1500s

Imagine that you are living in England during the late 1500s. You have been invited to a *masque ball*. This was a social event of the day that included dancing and a performance by actors in masks.

At such gala events, you were likely to see numerous figures dressed up like the woman in Figure 10–14. Inspect this period portrait.

Figure 10–14 Notice the carefully crafted gems set in gold on this gown. More than ninety appear on the woman's dress.

Unknown British painter. *Portrait of a Noblewoman*. Late sixteenth century. Oil on wood. 113 × 88.3 cm (44½ × 34¾″). The Metropolitan Museum of Art, New York, New York. Gift of J. Pierpont Morgan, 1911.

196 Chapter 10 *Examining Objects*

FOCUS

☑ OBJECTIVES

After completing this lesson, students will be able to:
- Define *jewelry*.
- Explain how a timepiece serves a dual purpose.

☑ SUPPLIES

- Pencils and sketch paper
- Black construction paper
- Oil pastels or metallic crayons

Resource

- 10-7 TV Talk Show, TRB page 165 (cooperative learning)

TEACH

■ Motivator

Have students look at what they and their classmates are wearing. Ask if anything they are wearing could be classified as an adornment. Encourage them to point out earrings, belt buckles, watches, and necklaces. Explain that these items are simple objects of art made to be worn. These are objects labeled as jewelry.

■ Vocabulary

Explain that *châtelaine* is a French word that originally referred to the mistress of a castle or any large household. This woman wore an ornamental chain or clasp, usually at the waist. On the chain were the keys to the manse, a watch, and sometimes a small purse.

196

---

more about • • •

Jewelry in Time Prehistoric jewelry was probably worn for religious purposes or to show rank in the group. In the Bronze Age, people began using silver, copper, and bronze to shape ornamental objects. The ancient Egyptians believed that gemstones held magical powers, so gems were used in their headdresses, pendants, rings, and bracelets. The ancient Greeks preferred fine metalwork for their jewelry. In Europe in the 1500s, it was popular to weave precious gems into one's hair or sew them on to clothing. As gem cutting became more sophisticated in the 1700s, diamonds and other rare jewels were used to make necklaces, pendants, and rings. Today most jewelry is mass produced, but finer items are still crafted by hand.

How many jewels and baubles can you find glinting and sparkling on this grand lady's person? Notice that these adornments are not limited to her splendid silk dress. Jeweled trinkets and pearls sparkle in her hair and on her ears, hands, and neck as well. How would you describe the look of this woman in all her splendor?

Jewelry from the 1700s

In Lesson 6, you learned that applied art objects serve a dual function. At least one item of jewelry shares this distinction. That item is a timepiece, or watch.

Figure 10–15 This object was worn attached to a belt. What objects are suggested in these arrangements?

German. *Watch and Chatelaine.* Eighteenth century, third quarter. Agate, gold, gemstone. 15.3 cm (6"). The Metropolitan Museum of Art, New York, New York. Collection of Giovanni P. Morosini, presented by his daughter, Giulia, 1932.

STUDIO ACTIVITY

Creating a Jewelry Design

Make several sketches for a jewelry item. Begin with a simple geometric or free-form shape. Choose three shapes and colors of gemstones to appear in your object. Arrange these, as in Figure 10–15, using a variety of shapes and sizes to create a pattern. With pencil, transfer your design to a sheet of black construction paper. Complete the object using light, bright hues of oil pastels or metallic crayons.

PORTFOLIO

Write an advertisement for your jewelry. Describe the item and the jewels and metal from which it is made. List a price for which it would sell. Put this ad in your portfolio with your artwork.

Such an object appears in Figure 10–15. It was made in Germany some two hundred years after the jewelry items shown in Figure 10–14. The timepiece is the circular item at the very bottom of the photograph. The rest of the image is given over to a popular jewelry object of the day called a *châtelaine* (shaht-eh-**len**). This châtelaine contains a key, the watch, and a seal. Notice the repeating gemstone motif. Do you think this repetition adds harmony to the art objects? How has the artist introduced variety?

Check Your Understanding

1. What does the portrait in Figure 10–14 reveal about life in the 1500s?
2. What two functions are served by wristwatches?

Answers to ✔ CHECK YOUR UNDERSTANDING

1. The portrait in Figure 10-14 reveals that there were social events that took place in the 1500s in which women wore highly ornamented dresses, as well as splendid, sparkling jewelry in their hair and on their ears, hands, and necks.

2. Wristwatches function as timepieces. They also function as works of art.

STUDIO A

Creating a Jewelry Design

To help students get ideas for their designs, bring in a number of catalogs and advertisements for jewelry. Encourage students to use the ads for ideas, but do not let them copy or reproduce designs they see.

■ **Aesthetics**

Ask students to compare the images in Figure 10-14 and Figure 10-15. In what way is the use of gems similar? In what way is it different? Does the fact that these objects are worn diminish their worth as art? Have students explain their responses.

• • • • • • • • • • • • • • •
ASSESS

■ **Self-Assessment**

Have students complete the Check Your Understanding questions on this page. Answers are provided below.

■ **Reteaching**

Ask students what current-day custom is similar to that of wearing the châtelaine shown in Figure 10-15. *(A clip of keys worn hooked over the belt.)*

■ **Enrichment**

Divide students into two groups and assign one of the works in this lesson to each. Ask both groups to investigate why the work assigned to them has historical value. Have them use a variety of resource materials as they research the time and place of each artwork. Ask students to share their findings with the class.

• • • • • • • • • • • • • • •
CLOSE

Have students name items of jewelry that serve a dual purpose.

LESSON 8

Creating a Pendant

Jewelry, like other art, varies from culture to culture. This is true not only of the specific kinds of items crafted but of their design. The three objects in Figure 10–16 are *bolo slides.* You may have seen objects like these. They are decorative jewelry made to wear with string neckties.

Study these objects. Notice the geometric shapes. These are typical of rugs, baskets, pottery, and other art objects of native cultures of the Southwest. Can you identify the simplified figures in these pieces?

WHAT YOU WILL LEARN

You will create a design for a pendant. You learned in Lesson 5 that a pendant is a jewelry item worn suspended from the neck on a string or chain. Like the bolo slides in Figure 10–16, your pendant will use geometric shapes. These will be cut from tagboard. Begin with a single simple shape. Then layer other smaller shapes on top to build a relief design. You will organize your work to create a center of interest by using contrasting geometric shapes.

Figure 10–16 These bolo slides were crafted by Native American artisans. What figures or objects do you recognize?

Bolo Slides. Left: *Trail of Tears* (Colorado). Middle: *The Eagle* (Alaska). Right: *Yee, Sun Spirit* (Arizona). Contemporary. Silver, turquoise, coral, wood. Approx. 2.5–3.8 cm (1–1½″). Private collection.

198 Chapter 10 *Examining Objects*

✏ *more about* • • •

Jewelry Design of the Southwest Jewelry in the Southwest Indian tradition used wrought, overlay, sand cast, or inlay techniques and followed traditional techniques until a few innovative artists began experimenting with gold and new methods in the 1950s. Tourist trade influenced the design of much Native American jewelry, rugs, and pottery of the Southwest.

Bolo tie designs were introduced by the Hickok Leather Company of Rochester about 1949. They were based on the South American gaucho's string ties with ornaments. The handsome bolo tie slides in Figure 10-16 are made from wood and silver inlaid with turquoise, coral, shell, and wood.

WHAT YOU WILL NEED

- Sketch paper and pencil
- Tagboard scraps in a variety of sizes, ranging from approximately 2 inches (5 cm) to ⅜ inch (1 cm) on a side.
- Scissors
- White glue
- Paper towels
- Small stiff-bristle brush
- Foil paper or aluminum foil
- Cord or yarn

WHAT YOU WILL DO

1. Create several sketches of pendant designs. Your design should consist of layered geometric shapes. (See the student work in Figure 10–17.)
2. Choose one of the largest tagboard scraps for the base. Following your design, cut the tagboard into a circle, oval, square, rectangle, or other geometric shape.
3. Layer smaller geometric shapes on top of the base. Attach the shapes with white glue. Carefully blot away any excess glue with a lightly dampened paper towel. Work little by little from larger shapes to smaller ones. Make small round shapes with a hole punch. Repeat similar shapes. Create a center of interest by using contrasting shapes or by introducing a pattern.
4. Use a stiff brush to cover the completed design with a layer of thin white glue. Carefully apply a sheet of silver or gold foil paper or aluminum foil. Using your finger, gently push the foil into the corners and creases of the design. Work quickly before the glue dries.

Try This!

COMPUTER OPTION

■ Choose from the Shape and Line tools. Use a variety of thicknesses. Draw a large geometric shape with a thick line. Add smaller geometric shapes on top to layer the design. Create a center of interest by using a contrasting shape. Use the Selection tool to arrange and duplicate shapes. Think of shiny metal surfaces. Select the Color tool and a hue to match bronze, gold, or silver metal. Choose Gradients, if available, to achieve a reflective look. Fill all the spaces with the same color. (If your program does not have a Multigon tool, use the Line tool to draw triangles and other multi-sided shapes.)

EXAMINING YOUR WORK

- **Describe**   Describe the shapes and textures in your design. Identify the purpose of the jewelry.
- **Analyze**   Explain how you organized the design to create a center of interest. What shape or patterns add contrast?
- **Interpret**   Could your pendant be worn every day, or does it appear to be better suited for special events? Why?
- **Judge**   Is your work a success? Explain why or why not.

5. Fold back any foil paper edges that extend beyond the borders of the tagboard. Glue these to the back of your ornament. Attach cord or yarn to your pendant.

Figure 10–17   Student work. Pendant.

CONNECTIONS *Music*

Everald Brown. *Instrument for Four People.* 1986. Wood and paint. 73.5 × 183 cm (29 × 72″). National Gallery of Jamaica, Kingston, Jamaica.

The Language of Music

Try to imagine a world without music. You would not be able to listen to a new CD. Commercials would have no melodies. Your favorite television show would not have a theme song. The school orchestra would not be able to play any instruments, and birds could not sing. Music may play softly in the background, or it may be the main source of entertainment. Regardless of how it is used, music is an important part of our society.

Music is as varied as the people who create and perform it and the instruments they use. All music, however, has four basic elements: melody, harmony, rhythm, and form. Melody is a logical succession of musical tones. Harmony involves tones played together, or chords, and the building of these chords. Rhythm is the combination of long and short sounds that convey a sense of movement. Form is musical design, incorporating repetition and contrast, unity and variety. Musical form should be unified yet varied enough to be interesting.

Take a look at Everald Brown's *Instrument for Four People.* Have you ever seen an instrument like this one? The artist created this unique musical instrument from his imagination.

MAKING THE CONNECTION

- ✔ What are the four basic elements of music?
- ✔ Why do you think Everald Brown chose to include birds in *Instrument for Four People?*
- ✔ Create your own musical instrument. Draw a sketch of the instrument and write a description of how it works.

INTERNET ACTIVITY

Visit Glencoe's Fine Arts Web Site for students at:

http://www.glencoe.com/sec/art/students

BUILDING VOCABULARY

Number a sheet of paper from 1 to 9. After each number, write the term from the box that best matches each description below.

applied art   pottery
jewelry   slip
kiln   vessel
pendant   watercolorist
perceive

1. Clay with enough added water to give it a runny, liquid consistency.
2. Art, and the craft of making art, to be worn.
3. A jewelry item worn suspended from the neck on a string or chain.
4. A painter who works in watercolor.
5. A hollow utensil made to hold something.
6. A special hot oven in which pottery objects are fired.
7. Works of art that are made to be useful as well as visually pleasing.
8. Art, and the craft of making art, from clay.
9. To become aware through the senses of the special nature of objects.

 REVIEWING ART FACTS

Number a sheet of paper from 10 to 13. Answer each question in a complete sentence.

10. What events during her life prompted Georgia O'Keeffe to paint objects "larger than life"?
11. When were the first still lifes in the West produced? By whom were they produced?
12. Based on the objects shown in the still life in Figure 10–7, what can we suppose to be true about the geography and culture of Japan?
13. Name two ways of judging applied art.

 THINKING ABOUT ART

On a sheet of paper, answer each question in a sentence or two.

1. **Compare and contrast.** An obvious, if minor, difference between the still lifes in Figures 10–7 and 10–8 is the set of objects in each. What are some other differences?
2. **Analyze.** Early watches, like the one in Figure 10–15, kept time poorly. They were popular nevertheless. What does this reveal about the regard of viewers and users for the two functions of applied art objects?

MAKING ART CONNECTIONS

1. **Language Arts.** Imagine that you are a poet in China during the 1700s. Your friend, Lik'an, has just completed a scroll painting of bamboo, Figure 10–3 on page **185**. Write a two-line poem that sums up the feeling expressed by the painting.

2. **Family and Consumer Sciences.** You have written a cookbook, and your publisher thinks one of the still-life paintings in this chapter would make a good cover illustration. Think about which painting you would choose. Give reasons to explain your choice.

■ Building Vocabulary

1. slip
2. jewelry
3. pendant
4. watercolorist
5. vessel
6. kiln
7. applied art
8. pottery
9. perceive

■ Reviewing Art Facts

10. During the early twentieth century, the pace of life quickened. O'Keeffe feared that people were moving too fast to notice the beauty in nature. She therefore made her paintings as large and attention-getting as the skyscrapers erected during this era.
11. They were produced as early as 2400 B.C. by the Greeks.
12. We can assume that the nation has a considerable sea coast and that shellfish play an important role in the Japanese diet.
13. Applied art is judged both on its aesthetic merits (beauty) and on its functionality, or use.

? THINKING ABOUT ART

1. Differences include the media, the cultural clues evident in the two works, and the differences in style.

2. It suggests that viewers and users sometimes value the aesthetic appeal of an applied art object over its functionality.

Recording Events

(pages 202–221)

Resources

- 11-10 Chapter Test, TRB page 183
- Transparency CC-11, *Hmong Story Cloth* by Chaing Xiong
- Transparency 11, *Building More Stately Mansions* by Aaron Douglas
- Fine Art Print 17, *The Return of Ulysses* by Romare Bearden
- 11-1 Dorothy Brett, TRB page 171 (artist profile)

Music
While studying this chapter, use Performing Arts Handbook page 323 to learn how Jester Hairston composed a song expressing his feelings of isolation and exclusion from the mainstream.

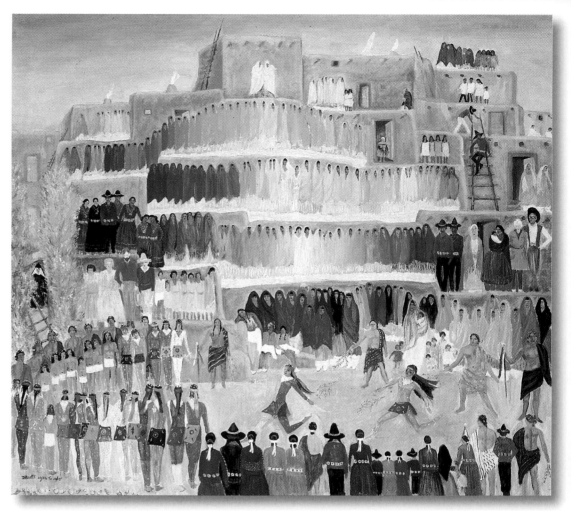

Figure 11–1 Notice the use of bright, lively colors to help capture the mood of this event. What art principles has the artist used to organize the festive scene?

Dorothy Brett. *San Geronimo Day, Taos.* 1924–1965. Oil on canvas. 122 × 137 cm (48 × 54″). In the collection of Glenna Goodacre, Santa Fe, New Mexico.

202

FEATURED ARTISTS

Dorothy Brett	Jacob Lawrence
Roger Brown	Emanuel Leutze
J. A. Holzer	Franklin McMahon
Kevin Kallaugher	Marjorie Phillips

Recording Events

Life is filled with events that impact us for better or worse. Some events—wars, floods, medical breakthroughs—affect people on a national or even global scale. Others—team championships, birthdays, moving to a new community—affect individuals or smaller groups.

In this chapter, you will learn about different ways in which artists have recorded events, both large and small. You will also come to recognize that a picture often *can* be worth a thousand words.

PORTFOLIO IDEAS

You may be asked to assess the artwork you include in your portfolio. To evaluate a project on your own, begin by asking questions such as:
- Does this artwork meet the assignment requirements?
- Does this artwork demonstrate how I have grown as an artist?
- What improvements could I make?

OBJECTIVES

After completing this chapter, you will be able to:
- Describe various art media and techniques that have been used to capture events.
- Recognize how artists of different times and cultures have recorded events.
- Define *photography* and trace the development of this art form.
- Create several works of art that record events.

WORDS YOU WILL LEARN

camcorder
caricature
frieze
gouache
mosaic
pan
photography
story board
video documentary
videographer

■ Chapter Overview

In this chapter, students will explore the efforts and techniques artists have used over time and among different cultures to record events. In addition, they will create several works of their own that capture noteworthy events and activities.

■ Chapter Motivator

Bring in several newspapers and newsmagazines and ask students to find examples of recorded events. Discuss the kinds of images that can be used to record events and tell students that in this chapter, they will be learning about a variety of media and techniques used by artists to capture events.

National Museum of Women in the Arts

You may wish to use the National Museum of Women in the Arts videodisc and/or CD-ROM. The videodisc features a bar code guide, and the interactive CD-ROM provides stimulating activities.

203

DEVELOPING A PORTFOLIO

Teacher Feedback As much as students appreciate hearing good comments from their friends and peers, positive teacher feedback can be more powerful. Keeping a portfolio of work over a period of time and monitoring one's growth is enlightening for students. Your written comments or a checklist of desired outcomes can inspire students to do so much more. Your challenge in the review process is to motivate students to pursue standards of good, thoughtful artwork. Established guidelines offer a framework for this, and the written reflections play a supporting role. Feedback can include recognition of demonstrated strengths in the portfolio, areas for future focus, and recognition of specific examples that stand out.

LESSON 1

The Media of Visual Reporting

In a way, artists who record events are like newspaper reporters. Like reporters, their goal is to get the whole story and to report the facts accurately and thoroughly. Like reporters, artists always seek out an interesting angle.

Unlike reporters, however, artists are not limited to words when capturing events. Rather, they have at their disposal a wide range of tools. In this chapter, you will learn about some of those tools. You will explore the media of visual reporting.

PHOTOGRAPHY

Open any newspaper or magazine today, and you are apt to see photographs. This wasn't always so. As an art form, **photography**—*the art of making images by exposing a chemically treated surface to light*—is in its infancy. The first photographs were produced just over 150 years ago.

Photograph of an Event

Throughout its brief life, photography has been a key tool of the visual reporter.

Figure 11–2 After Gutzon Borglum died, his son, Lincoln, took over the project. The last sculpture, of Theodore Roosevelt, remains unfinished to this day.

Workers on Mt. Rushmore. Photograph. Undated. Mt. Rushmore, South Dakota.

204 Chapter 11 *Recording Events*

TECHNOLOGY OPTIONS

National Gallery of Art Videodisc   Use the following images to show the various media used in visual reporting.

George Bellows
Tennis Tournament

Thomas Eakins
The Biglin Brothers Racing

Edouard Manet
At the Races

Search Frame 2078

Search Frame 2020

Search Frame 1248

Use Glencoe's *National Gallery of Art Correlation Bar Code Guide* to locate more artworks.

Examine the compelling photograph in Figure 11–2. Like any good reporter, the photographer has answered the "four W's" of journalism—*who, what, when,* and *where.* Look carefully at the photo. The *who* is a crew of workers under the guidance of sculptor Gutzon Borglum. The *when* is 1937, the *where,* a mountaintop in the Black Hills of South Dakota. The *what* is a giant bust of a United States President carved out of the mountain's natural granite face.

Notice that the photographer has raised a fifth question—*how* to get the most interesting "angle." His answer was to take a personal risk and position himself on a rocky ledge a mile high in the sky.

PAINTING

An event no less dramatic is recorded in the painting in Figure 11–3. The *what, when,* and *where* are noted in the credit line below

Figure 11–3 The artist has used *abstraction* to record this event. Notice how he has simplified the shapes.

Jacob Lawrence. *Study for the Munich Olympic Games Poster.* 1971. Gouache. 90 × 86.6 cm (35½ × 27"). Seattle Art Museum, Seattle, Washington. Purchased with funds from P.O.N.C.H.O.

STUDIO ACTIVITY

Composing a Photograph

Like other works of art, photographs can be judged in terms of composition— the way the parts are arranged. Practice composing and shooting still lifes. Gather three or four objects with different forms, shapes, and textures. Experiment arranging these in various ways on a table or other flat surface. Study each arrangement through your camera's *viewfinder.* This is the hole you peer through to see your subject. When you feel the objects are arranged to your satisfaction, click the shutter.

P O R T F O L I O

Put your photographs in your portfolio along with a self-assessment.

the artwork. The *who* is clear from the uniforms and batons. Study the expression on the faces of the front runners. Observe their body language. This is no ordinary relay race. It is a run for the Olympic gold medal. Each sprinter seems to be digging deep into his very being. Each is searching for that burst of energy that will propel him forward across the finish line first.

Look again at the credit line below the picture, this time at the medium. That medium, **gouache** (**gwash**), is *a form of watercolor that uses non-clear pigments.* Gouache creates flatter, more intense colors than normal watercolor paints. How do the flat areas of color in this painting help convey the intensity of the moment?

Check Your Understanding

1. In what way are artists who record events like newspaper reporters?
2. Each of the artworks on these pages captures a dramatic moment. Tell how each succeeds.

Lesson 1   *The Media of Visual Reporting*   **205**

■ **Aesthetics**

Obtain books from the library for students on the subject of photographers of the twentieth century. Note that they have many different approaches to photography and deal with many different subjects. Find photographs by Edward Weston (1886–1958), for example, whose elegant images of sand dunes, peppers, and many close-up forms of nature are considered among the classic works of photography.

■ **Art Criticism**

Have students critique their photographs for light effect and control, composition, emphasis, line, movement, and so on. Encourage continued effort to use a camera for art purposes rather than just for snapshots.

● ● ● ● ● ● ● ● ● ●
ASSESS

■ **Self-Assessment**

Have students complete the Check Your Understanding questions on this page. Answers are provided below.

■ **Reteaching**

Discuss the four W's of journalism shown in Figure 11-2.

■ **Enrichment**

Encourage student photographers to document one place, such as a gas station, a zoo, a playground, or the action of a game, framing objects carefully in their lens. Set up a display of student photographs.

● ● ● ● ● ● ● ● ● ●
CLOSE

Ask students to give examples of what they have learned about photography that will affect the way they look at photographs of events.

Answers to ✔ CHECK YOUR UNDERSTANDING

1. Artists who record events are like newspaper reporters because, like reporters, the artists try to report the facts accurately and thoroughly. Like reporters, too, they seek out an interesting angle.
2. Figure 11-2 captures a dramatic moment during the creation of Mt. Rushmore. The artwork succeeds in showing up-close the danger and scope of the task. Figure 11-3 captures a climactic moment of the Olympics in 1972. This artwork succeeds in communicating the intensity of the struggle of the runners to summon the strength and energy to win the race.

Drawing a Sporting Event in Action

Look back at the painting in Figure 11–3 on page **203**. Much of the drama can be traced to the subject matter—a foot race. Figure 11–4 records another sporting event. It, too, is filled with tense action. Study this painting. Can you identify the event without looking at the title? Notice the feeling of movement suggested by the repeated shapes of the fans dotting the grandstand. Observe the abundant use of diagonals. Even if you've never attended a baseball game, you can sense the excitement as pitcher and batter prepare to compete.

WHAT YOU WILL LEARN

In this lesson, you will create your own artwork based on a sporting event. Begin by gathering magazine or newspaper photographs of baseball, basketball, or football games. Then select a sport. You will do a gesture drawing of a model in an action pose similar to one in a photo. Add background details based on the setting in the picture. Use bright colors in the foreground, dull colors in the background. Include diagonal lines and repetition to give a sense of movement to your drawing.

Figure 11–4 How many diagonals can you count in this painting? What objects have been repeated?

Marjorie Phillips. *Night Baseball.* 1951. Oil on canvas. 61.5 × 91.4 cm (24¼ × 36"). The Phillips Collection, Washington, D.C. Acquired c. 1951.

206 Chapter 11 *Recording Events*

FOCUS

☑ OBJECTIVES

After completing this lesson, students will be able to:
• Complete a gesture drawing of a model in an action pose.
• Describe, analyze, interpret, and judge their artwork.

☑ SUPPLIES

• Magazines and newspapers with photos of sporting events
• Pencils and sketch paper
• White drawing paper
• Fine-tipped black felt marker
• Colored markers, charcoal, or colored drawing pencils

Resource

■ 11-4 The Mood Is the Message, TRB page 175 (aesthetics)

TEACH

■ Motivator

Review with students the techniques used in gesture drawing. See Chapter 3, Lesson 2, pages 44–45; or the Handbook, page 281. Analyze photographs that include a variety of men's and women's sports.

Many times the camera angle causes exaggeration of a gesture. Discuss how students can do this themselves as they draw.

206

more about •••

Jacob Lawrence Jacob Lawrence (1917–) is an African-American artist best known for his portrayal of the daily life of African-Americans, and for his paintings of the history of their struggle for liberty and justice. Lawrence tells stories and records events using flat, bold shapes, bright colors, and geometric patterns. As a Social Realist, he uses his art to express his social values and to record events as he sees them. Locate some of his series of works, such as *The Migration of the Negro* (1940–41) or the *Frederick Douglass* series (1938–39), to discuss the diverse talent of this important artist. Have students read *The Great Migration* by Lawrence (N.Y.: Harper-Collins, 1993), written for the middle school audience.

WHAT YOU WILL NEED

- Photographs of sporting events
- Pencils and sketch paper
- White drawing paper, 12 x 18 inches (30 x 46 cm)
- Fine-tipped black felt marker
- Colored markers, charcoal, or colored drawing pencils

WHAT YOU WILL DO

1. Study the photographs you have gathered. Look for examples that show exciting action. Study the gestures and other body language of the athletes. Note the appearance and fixtures of the stadium or arena pictured.
2. Take turns posing with a fellow student. Ask your model to assume a pose similar to one in the picture. In a basketball drawing, for example, your model might appear with arms raised high and legs outstretched, as though shooting a basket. On sketch paper, do several rapid gesture drawings of your model.
3. Transfer your best sketch to white drawing paper. Still using pencil, add foreground and background details. Foreground details should include a uniform for your athlete and equipment—a ball, bat, basket, and so on. Background details should include crowds of fans and features of the setting—chalk lines or foul lines and a scoreboard, for example. Include as many diagonals as you can.
4. With a fine-tipped black marker, retrace important contour lines. Use color to complete your drawing. Choose markers, colored pencils, charcoal, or drawing pencils. Consider bright colors that capture the mood of the game.

EXAMINING YOUR WORK

- **Describe** What sporting event does your work show? What moment in the event have you captured? What details of the setting have you included?
- **Analyze** Have you included diagonal lines? Have you used bright colors?
- **Interpret** Does you work communicate a sense of vivid action and movement?
- **Judge** Is your work successful? What would you do next time to increase the excitement of the sporting event?

Figure 11–5 Student work. A sporting event.

Try This! COMPUTER OPTION

■ Use the Line tool to create a slender, downward-pointing triangle with sharply slanting sides. Make and rotate slightly a copy of this shape. Fill each with a different flat, bright color. Move the two shapes together to form the legs of an abstract action figure. Create arms and a trunk in similar fashion. Switch to the Oval tool. Draw one oval for the figure's head, and a circle to represent the ball. Place this within reach of your athlete.

■ Cooperative Learning

Divide the class into groups of three or four. Distribute a variety of examples of illustration from magazines. Ask each group to compare and critique the various techniques used. Ask: Are all of the illustrations works of art? Have each group decide why or why not and take turns sharing their findings with the rest of the class.

■ Art Criticism

Bring in children's magazine illustrations and illustrated non-fiction children's books and have students compare the two kinds of illustration. How are they different from the magazine illustrations? Which techniques are most successful? Why?

ASSESS

■ Self-Assessment

Have students use Examining Your Work to evaluate their art.

■ Reteaching

Emphasize that learning how to draw figures and to create space in compositions is an ongoing process. Encourage students to use sketch books and to draw figures from poses at home with friends, animals, or family.

■ Enrichment

Ask students to research an artist known for portraying sports figures and events, such as Bernie Fuchs, a well-known, award-winning illustrator for *Sports Illustrated*. Have them bring in examples of the artist's work and share their research with the class.

CLOSE

Let students work with partners to critique their drawings. Have them evaluate the gesture drawings in terms movement.

TECHNIQUE TIP

Figure Drawing Have students keep individual portfolios of their figure sketches. Aim to make them confident and comfortable drawing from posed models. For example, encourage them to draw their family members at home. Too, they should be able to quietly ask another student to get up and pose for a quick sketch when they are drawing a scene from social studies or other subjects. Periodically, take the sketches out and do a critique. Encourage students to point out problems they see in their own drawings, seeing this not as a negative, but rather as a positive, constructive means of improving their figure drawing techniques.

LESSON 3

The Artist as Historian

☑ OBJECTIVES

After completing this lesson, students will be able to:

• Understand the role of the artist in recording historical events.

• "Read" the artist's message expressed by selection and emphasis.

☑ SUPPLIES

• Pencils and sketch paper
• Newspapers
• White drawing paper
• Colored pencils, markers, or oil pastels

Resources

■ 11-5 Art-i-FACT, TRB page 177 (studio)

■ 11-6 The Four W's, TRB page 179 (reproducible master)

■ Motivator

Discuss the role of the artist in this age of video and the immediacy of media. Lead students to find examples of the special contribution artists can make, as in the roles of courtroom and law enforcement artists.

■ Vocabulary

Discuss with students the expression "history in the making." Ask: How does one know that an event may be important enough to be considered historic? Who decides what is historic?

"Today's news," someone once noted, "is tomorrow's history." Artists have long been mindful of this bit of wisdom. For centuries, they have used their talents and various tools to record events of the past and history in the making. In this lesson, you will examine some of the events they have captured in their art.

PAST EVENTS

Before the age of photography, portraits were used to provide "visual information" about leaders and celebrities. The painting in Figure 11–6 provides another kind of historical record. Do you recognize the individual at the far left? He was a great military strategist who later went on to become our nation's first president. His name, of course, is George Washington.

In this page from history, General Washington is leading his troops across the Delaware River. The time of year is indicated by large chunks of ice around which the oar operators carefully maneuver. You might wonder why the party is venturing out under such frigid conditions. The answer is that they are planning a surprise attack on the British troops on the opposite shore. Notice that Washington stands taller than any other figure in the painting. The only object rising higher is the American flag. Observe that the diagonal lines of the oars and the flag lend movement to the scene. What do you think might have been the artist's reasons for recording the scene this way? How would you describe the future president's posture as he leads a nation-to-be to its destiny?

Figure 11–6 Notice how the artist has conveyed a sense of forward motion. How has he conveyed a sense of suspense?

Emanuel Leutze. *Washington Crossing the Delaware.* 1851. Oil on canvas. 387.5 × 644 cm (149 × 255"). The Metropolitan Museum of Art, New York, New York. Gift of John Stewart Kennedy, 1897.

208   Chapter 11   *Recording Events*

TECHNOLOGY OPTIONS

National Gallery of Art Videodisc   Use the following images to show additional works by artists who recorded historical events.

Francisco Goya	Childe Hassam	Edward Hicks
The Disasters of War: Nada	*Allies Day, May 1917*	*Penn's Treaty with the Indians*

Search Frame 3256	Search Frame 2086	Search Frame 1854

Use Glencoe's *National Gallery of Art Correlation Bar Code Guide* to locate more artworks.

RECENT EVENTS

In a sense, the event pictured in the painting in Figure 11–6 paved the way for the one in Figure 11–7. The time is two hundred years later. Do you recognize the individual projected in black and white on the giant TV monitor in the painting? He is Jimmy Carter, our thirty-ninth president. The setting is the 1980 Democratic National Convention. Despite Carter's broad smile and reassuring wave, he lost his bid for re-election to Ronald Reagan.

Inspect this busy painting. Much of it is given over to a sea of politicians. They are represented as dots of color. What other artwork have you looked at in this chapter that depicts crowds in this fashion? Balloons in the colors of the American flag float gaily from the ceiling of the vast room. How has the artist conveyed the mood of this historical event? What art principle organizes the lively work?

 Check Your Understanding

1. Which figure stands tallest in Figure 11–6? Why do you think the artist painted the scene this way?
2. What details and properties do Figures 11–6 and 11–7 have in common?

STUDIO ACTIVITY

Recording a Historical Event

With a group of students, brainstorm other events in national or local history. Possibilities include the landing of the pilgrims at Plymouth and the founding of your own town or city. Look in an encyclopedia or similar resource to learn the *who, what, where,* and *when* of the event. Sketch the event you have selected. Complete your drawing using colored pencils, colored markers, or oil pastels.

PORTFOLIO

In several paragraphs, compose a description of your event. Include the who, what, where, and when of the event, and put the description in your portfolio with your artwork.

Figure 11–7 **What three colors has the artist emphasized? Why has he emphasized these colors?**

Franklin McMahon. *1980 Democratic Convention.* 1980. Acrylic watercolors and pencil on paper. 22 × 30 cm (8⁷⁄₁₀ × 11⅘"). Courtesy of the artist.

Lesson 3 *The Artist as Historian* **209**

■ Aesthetics

Consider with your students the immediate rush of T-shirts, posters, framed photos, and so on that flood the market the moment a team wins a championship, the day a candidate announces he or she is running for an important political office, or at the release of a "hit" movie. The artist recording the event in a dramatic sketch like that of Franklin McMahon is producing a work of art. Can we identify art amid the gaudy array of products produced in the name of art? Discuss good taste, and the ways that students can make choices.

■ Art Criticism

Have students work as partners and discuss their point of emphasis and the ways they kept that focus in their drawings. Have them critique each other's use of line, shape, and direction.

· · · · · · · · · · · · · ·
ASSESS

■ Self-Assessment

Have students complete the Check Your Understanding questions on this page. Answers are provided below.

■ Reteaching

In pairs, have students read to each other their descriptions of their events. Have them evaluate whether the four W's are clearly stated.

■ Enrichment

Franklin McMahon is an internationally-known artist-reporter. His drawings of world events have appeared in magazines such as *Life, Sports Illustrated,* and the *Saturday Evening Post.* Have students find other examples of his work and discuss his talents as artist-historian.

· · · · · · · · · · · · · ·
CLOSE

Ask students to discuss ways in which artists help "capture" and interpret historical events.

Answers to ✔ CHECK YOUR UNDERSTANDING

1. George Washington stands tallest in the painting. The artist probably did this to emphasize the importance of George Washington as the leader of the troops and as the future president of a great nation.

2. They share the depiction of an emotion-filled moment, a sense of excitement, and a focus on two presidents of the United States.

• • • • • • • • • • • • • •
FOCUS

☑ OBJECTIVES

After completing this lesson, students will be able to:

• Understand the use of caricature or exaggeration to express an idea.

• Select significant features to symbolize an idea.

• Explain the Greek myth about Pandora's box.

☑ SUPPLIES

• Examples of cartoons from newspapers and magazines

• Pencils and sketch paper

• White drawing paper

• Fine-tipped black markers

• • • • • • • • • • • • • •
TEACH

■ Motivator

Ask students what they know of the two symbols (elephant and donkey) seen in Figure 11-8. Review the concept of a mascot (see Chapter 7, page 125). Ask about other mascots or symbols students are familiar with. How is this image used to symbolize the election? (Perhaps it says that either party will have trouble governing, once elected.)

■ Vocabulary

The term *cartoon* originally referred to the preparatory sketch for a fresco, a tapestry, or a stained-glass window. The use of the word as *caricature* is traced back to the nineteenth century in England, when a competition for fresco designs for Parliament was parodied in the magazine *Punch*.

210

 LESSON 4

Drawing a Cartoon

During a political campaign, newspapers are filled with *editorials*—words that try to persuade you to take a particular position. Television gives or sells time to candidates to speak about their positions. Cartoonists also use their art form to try to persuade their viewers. They use **caricature** (**kar-ih-kuh-chur**), *a humorous drawing that exaggerates features of a person to make fun of or criticize him or her.*

The cartoon in Figure 11–8 uses the elephant and the donkey to symbolize the Republican and Democratic parties respectively. The cartoonist drew them as images on an ancient Greek vase because democracy began in ancient Greece. His title, *Pandora's Ballot Box*, adds another symbol. Do you know the ancient Greek myth of Pandora's Box? She was a very curious girl who opened a forbidden box. By doing so she released troubles into our world. What does this say about the election?

WHAT YOU WILL LEARN

In this lesson, you will create your own cartoon. Think of a neighborhood problem, such as littering, noise, or pollution. You might select a school problem, such as a playground bully. You will draw your characters using exaggeration of facial features, size, and expression to give meaning to your cartoon. You will add background details that help to set the scene and emphasize the problem.

Figure 11–8 How many symbols can you identify in this cartoon?

Kevin Kallaugher. *Pandora's Ballot Box.* 1996. Ink on paper. 15.2 × 16.5 cm (6 × 6½"). Cartoonists and Writers Syndicate.

210 Chapter 11 *Recording Events*

— *more about* • • • —

Cartoons Students may be motivated to read and discover more about cartoons, cartoonists, and cartoon animation. Encourage them to explore any of the following selections:

• *The Man in the Ceiling* by Jules Feiffer (N.Y.: HarperCollins, 1993), fiction

• *Meet Jim Henson* by Louise Gilow (N.Y.: Random

House, 1993), nonfiction

• *The Man Behind the Magic: The Story of Walt Disney* by Katherine and Richard Greene (N.Y.: Viking, 1991), nonfiction

• *Funny Papers: Behind the Scenes of the Comics* by Elaine Scott (N.Y.: William Morrow, 1993) nonfiction

WHAT YOU WILL NEED

- Examples of cartoons from newspapers
- Pencils and sketch paper
- White drawing paper, 9 x 12 inches (23 x 30 cm)
- Fine-tipped black marker

WHAT YOU WILL DO

1. Study the cartoons to look for ways to use exaggeration.
2. Decide what you want your cartoon to say about the problem you want to solve. Think about ways to *symbolize* your idea. A book can symbolize study, for example.
3. Do several quick sketches, changing size and emphasizing the objects or persons to make your point. Decide whether you need any words in "balloons" or at the bottom of your cartoon.
4. Transfer your best sketch to white drawing paper. Still using pencil, draw

EXAMINING YOUR WORK

- **Describe** What are you saying in your cartoon? What persons or things have you used to make your point?
- **Analyze** How have you used caricature to exaggerate or symbol to express an idea?
- **Interpret** How well does your cartoon get its message across?
- **Judge** Ask your fellow students to decide if you have convinced them about your point.

your cartoon lightly, adding foreground and background details.

5. Use your fine-tipped black marker to go over all of your lines. Think about making some lines thicker for emphasis.

Figure 11–9   Student work. A cartoon.

Try This!

STUDIO OPTION

■ Redraw your cartoon. This time add color with watercolors or tempera paints. Use bright colors for emphasis, duller hues for less important details. Go over the outlines with a black marker, making some lines thicker than others. Decide if the color version of your cartoon conveys a stronger message than the black-and-white version.

Lesson 4   *Drawing a Cartoon*   **211**

MEETING STUDENT DIVERSITY

Less Proficient Speakers of English The study of cartoons and caricatures provides an excellent opportunity for students who are less proficient in reading or speaking English. Many of the issues depicted in cartoons created for this age group are universal in their appeal. Spats between siblings, pets who don't get along, and the trials of adolescence are all subjects of popular cartoon series. Have students bring in a favorite cartoon from a book or other source, read it, and explain it to the class. Encourage all students to use body language and words in their presentations. Students who are struggling with English can practice their presentations with more proficient speakers.

■ Aesthetics

Discuss the differences between fine art and caricature. Look at works by Honoré Daumier, George Grosz, and Francisco Goya. These artists used caricature powerfully. Have students compare some of their work with contemporary political caricatures.

■ Cultural Diversity

Discuss with students the kinds of subjects that lend themselves to caricature. Explain that celebrities and political figures are public figures whose actions and words are often targeted by the media. Emphasize that jokes and caricatures that demean a nationality, race, or religion are destructive and unacceptable.

• • • • • • • • • •
ASSESS

■ Self-Assessment

Have students use Examining Your Work to evaluate their art.

■ Reteaching

Reinforce the meaning of caricature, myth, and symbol. Ask students to find examples of cartoons in books, newspapers, and magazines.

■ Enrichment

Encourage students to list the kinds of topics and issues that cartoons address: politics, personal relationships, ecology, discrimination, violence, social problems, and so on. Extend the meaning of *cartoon* to comic strips and animated films. Ask students to give examples of some of their favorites and explain why they appeal.

• • • • • • • • •
CLOSE

Ask students to explain how their cartoons used exaggeration to express an idea.

Recording Exploration

Recording Exploration

• • • • • • • • • • • • • • •
FOCUS

☑ OBJECTIVES

After completing this lesson, students will be able to:
• Explain what a *frieze* is.
• Understand what the term *mosaic* means.
• Understand that artists create visual records of explorations.

☑ SUPPLIES

• Pencils
• Black construction paper
• Strips of colored construction paper or colored magazine pages
• White glue or glue sticks

Resource

■ 11-7 Birth of an Art Form, TRB page 180 (appreciating cultural diversity)

• • • • • • • • • • • • • • •
TEACH

■ Motivator

Engage students in a discussion of some of the explorations they have studied in social studies. Ask them how we know about those travels. Point out that artists have provided visual records to complement the written documents that tell about those events.

■ Vocabulary

Have students look up *frieze* in a dictionary. Ask a student to explain the distinction between a frieze and an architectural frieze. Have students try to identify an example of any kind of frieze they have seen and describe it to the class.

212

For as long as there have been people, there have been explorers. There have also been countless stories of the brave men and women who ventured into the unknown and forged new paths. In this lesson you will view visual records of two explorations. You will also learn about the media used to create such records.

PAST EXPLORATION

The first explorers were probably cave dwellers curious to know what lay beyond the next hill. It was not until around 1500 that exploration got under way in earnest. During this century, pioneers began embarking on journeys that would, in the end, make the world seem smaller.

Mosaic Frieze

One of these pioneering expeditions is the subject of the colorful work in Figure 11–10. This work is a **frieze** (**freez**), *a decorative band running across the upper part of a wall.* This frieze recounts the adventures of French-Canadian explorers Jacques Marquette and Louis Joliet. The two set out in the late 1600s on a quest to locate the source of the Mississippi River. Look closely at the work. All the figures and objects are made up of *small bits of colorful glass and jewels set in cement.* This art medium and the art form that results are known as **mosaic** (moh-**zay**-ik). Notice the care with which the artist mixed and matched pieces to create subtle shadings and depth. Can you find the lifelike images of the two explorers?

RECENT EXPLORATION

Since the time of Marquette and Joliet, our planet's deepest secrets have been laid open. Explorers of the second half of the twentieth century were left with only one direction in which to go. That was up. Many turned their attention to the "final frontier"—space.

Figure 11–10 Look at the detail in this mosaic. What do you think are some of the challenges facing artists working in this medium?

J.A. Holzer. *Departure of Marquette and Joliet from St. Ignace on Their First Voyage to Illinois.* 1895. 1.2 × 2.7 m (4′ × 9′). Harr, © Hedrich-Blessing.

212   Chapter 11   *Recording Events*

more about • • •

Mosaics   Mosaic art is found in cultures throughout the world. The Greeks, the Romans, and the Byzantines all used mosaics to decorate the walls, ceilings, floors, and interior walls of churches, public buildings, and exterior pavements. Muslims of India and Persia used mosaic art in their temples as did the Aztec and Mayan peoples of Central and South America.

Provide students additional opportunities to explore the history and use of mosaics. Have them read *Piece by Piece! Mosaics of the Ancient World* by Michael Avi-Yonah (Minneapolis, Minn.: Lerner, 1993).

Figure 11–11 shows an outpost in this realm of exploration. It is a photo of one of the nine worlds in our solar system. It was taken during a spacecraft "fly-by." Do you recognize this planet? Notice the vivid colors in the photo. What do they reveal about the effects of recent technology on the art of photography?

Check Your Understanding

1. What medium was used for the frieze in Figure 11–10? Describe this medium.
2. What does the photo in Figure 11–11 reveal about the changing face of exploration?

Figure 11–11 **This photograph was taken by a camera on a spacecraft. How do you suppose this view differs from ones available to scientists of past centuries?**

Jupiter. Photo by NASA.

Planning a Mosaic

Working in mosaic takes great skill and patience. You can see this for yourself by trying the following activity.

Using pencil, lightly sketch a familiar form, such as an insect, on black paper. Retrace the lines, this time applying a little more pressure. Make ½-inch (1.3-cm) strips of colored construction paper or colored magazine photos. Cut small, square "tiles" from these strips to fill the shapes you drew. Glue the squares down, leaving space between them. Suggest depth and shading by using darker values of a single hue.

P O R T F O L I O

Write an evaluation of the technique you employed to complete this work. Add any ideas you might have for improving the method you used.

STUDIO ACTIVITY

Planning a Mosaic

As an alternative to sketching an object, have students sketch a famous explorer they have studied. For example, Christopher Columbus, Ferdinand Magellan, Lewis and Clark with Sacajawea, James Cook, Mary Kingsley, Roald Amundsen, Thor Heyerdahl, Sir Edmund Hillary, Yuri Gagarin, John Glenn, Valentina Tereshkova, Neil Armstrong, Sally Ride, and Guion S. Bluford, Jr.

■ Art History

Bring in to the class several books about Greek architecture. Have students identify an example of a frieze from one of the books and compare that frieze with the one pictured in Figure 11-10. What does each of the friezes communicate?

● ● ● ● ● ● ● ● ● ● ● ●
ASSESS

■ Self-Assessment

Have students complete the Check Your Understanding questions on this page. Answers are provided below.

■ Reteaching

Have students design a frieze to decorate the classroom.

■ Enrichment

Ask volunteers to become explorers themselves and find out more about the story behind the mosaics in the Marquette Building in Chicago. Have them research the four W's of this artwork and report back to the class.

● ● ● ● ● ● ● ● ● ● ● ●
CLOSE

Have students give examples of explorations that artists have recorded in their art.

Answers to ✔ CHECK YOUR UNDERSTANDING

1. Mosaic is the art medium used in Figure 11-10. Mosaic is a medium and art form made up of small bits of colorful glass and jewels set in cement.

2. The photo in Figure 11-11 reveals that the "final frontier" is outer space.

213

LESSON TIME: 3 hours

FOCUS

☑OBJECTIVES

After completing this lesson, students will be able to:

*   Design and create a model of a living room in a space station.
*   Understand the design implications of the fact that there is no gravity in space.
*   Describe, analyze, interpret, and judge their artwork.

☑SUPPLIES

*   Pencils and sketch paper
*   Rulers
*   Shoe boxes
*   Sheets of colored construction paper
*   Scissors; white glue
*   Scraps of thick cardboard
*   Fabric scraps
*   Colored markers

TEACH

■ Motivator

Spend time imagining with students what it would be like in Roger Brown's *Homesick-Proof Space Station* (Figure 11-12). Note that in a room with no gravity, the entire space can be used. People can float anywhere in the space. Encourage dealing with the entire space and filling it with objects and people. Note the importance of measuring their box dimensions before cutting the walls they plan.

LESSON 6

Creating a Room in Outer Space

During the Age of Exploration, nations established colonies in places where their explorers landed. Someday the citizens of Earth will do the same with planet Mars. To help with this future mission, plans are already under way for an orbiting laboratory where people will work.

What will this space station look like? One artist's answer appears in Figure 11–12. Study this tongue-in-cheek painting. What reality of life far from home has the artist tapped into in his humorous solution? In what way is this space station "homesick-proof"?

WHAT YOU WILL LEARN

In this activity, you will imagine what life is like in a space station. You will construct a three-dimensional room in your family's imaginary space home, including furniture and other objects for work and play. Use a soothing color scheme for your room design and add patterns for variety. The success of your design will be measured in terms of both its usefulness and how well it pleases the eye.

Figure 11–12 In what way has the artist made this space station look like an artist's rendering? How can you tell he is not making a serious design proposal?

Roger Brown. *Homesick-Proof Space Station.* 1987. Oil on canvas. 122 × 183 cm (48 × 72″). Phyllis Kind Galleries, Chicago, Illinois.

more about • • •

Space Exploration   For more information about space travel and exploration, consider the following:

*   Teacher resource materials from NASA, including short films on zero gravity: *Zero-G* (HQ 260A), 15 minutes; *Fluids in Weightlessness* (HQ 260D), 15 minutes.
*   *Educational Horizons,* a newsletter published in April, September, and December by NASA. Write to Educational Horizons, Mail Code FE, NASA Headquarters, Washington, D.C. 20546-0001.
*   *Heroes in Space: From Gagarin to Challenger* by Peter Bond (N.Y.: Blackwell, 1987).
*   *Your Future in Space: The U. S. Space Camp Training Program* by Flip Schulke et al. (N.Y.: Crown 1986).

WHAT YOU WILL NEED

- Pencil and sketch paper
- Ruler
- Shoe box or other larger box
- Sheets of colored construction paper, 12 x 18 inches (30 x 46 cm)
- Scissors
- White glue
- Scraps of thick cardboard
- Colored markers
- Fabric scraps

WHAT YOU WILL DO

1. Sketch ideas for your space room. Try to picture a room in one of the box-like houses in Figure 11–12. What kind of furniture would you include? Remember that there is no gravity in space. Every surface has the potential to be a floor or wall.
2. With the ruler, measure the height, length, and depth of your shoe box. Note these measurements on scrap paper. With the ruler, measure and draw rectangles of corresponding size on construction paper. These are to be the walls and floor of your room. Choose a soothing color. Cut out the rectangles. Attach these to the sides and bottom of the shoe box with white glue.
3. Design chairs, tables, and other furniture. Cut these out as two-dimensional shapes from cardboard scraps. Arrange these over the inside space of the room. For variety, you might place some furniture on the "walls." Add color and detail to the objects using markers. Paste the furniture in place.

EXAMINING YOUR WORK

- **Describe** What furniture and other objects have you included in your space room?
- **Analyze** What colors did you use for the walls and floor? What patterns did you add?
- **Interpret** Is the color scheme of your space room soothing? Do the patterns you chose lend variety to the setting?
- **Judge** Is your work successful? In what way is it useful as well as pleasing to the eye?

---

4. Choose fabric scraps with interesting patterns or designs. The colors should blend with those of your walls and floor. Glue these down to the walls and floor as "throw rugs."
5. Place your room alongside those of classmates to make a space neighborhood.

Figure 11–13 **Student work. A room in outer space.**

 COMPUTER OPTION

Try This!

■ Choose the rectangle Shape and Line tools. Draw the outside view of one side of a building using a combination of geometric shapes such as squares, rectangles, and triangles. Pick the Lasso selection tool to select, copy, and paste a duplicate of this side view in front of, but slightly off to one side of, the first building shape. Use the Line tool to connect the corners and make the second side. Erase unnecessary lines. Then choose from a combination of Shape tools to add doors, windows, columns, chimneys, porches, and other details. Use the Bucket tool to fill the spaces with hues and textures. If available, use a Gradient fill to add shading with a consistent light source. Title, save, and print.

Lesson 6 *Creating a Room in Outer Space* **215**

RESOURCES BEYOND THE CLASSROOM

Local Business Tours Arrange for students to tour facilities where art-related work is produced. Examples might be a photography studio or an artist's studio, but it could also be an advertising agency, an industrial design studio, a silk screen plant, a publishing company, or even a neon sign shop. Discuss how the company uses art and artists as part of its business, and describe the range of careers available to individuals interested in art-related work. You might also arrange a career day that focuses on careers in art, and invite speakers from a variety of companies to talk about how they use art and artists to conduct business.

■ Aesthetics

Discuss with students what space exploration has added to aesthetics. We have new understandings of the universe, of the earth as seen from outer space, of color and light as the satellites have sent back incredible photographs from other planets and from space. Ask: What does the idea of zero-gravity add to the element of space in painting?

■ Art History

Have students look at medieval paintings with gold or blue backgrounds, showing no awareness of depth or space. Then have them look at Renaissance paintings with landscape often viewed through a window, and Dutch landscapes of the 1600–1700s that show an understanding of the universe and of the earth as a planet orbiting the sun. Point out that now we see space in whole new ways, as we view the earth from the moon and from outer space.

• • • • • • • • • • • • • •

ASSESS

■ Self-Assessment

Have students use Examining Your Work to evaluate their art.

■ Reteaching

Have pairs of students explain to each other how their creations are useful as well as pleasing to the eye.

■ Enrichment

Ask students to write a short story about their imaginary space home. Remind them that their stories should have a beginning, a middle, and an end.

• • • • • • • • • • • • • •

CLOSE

Have students critique each other's room designs in terms of color scheme and variety.

☑ OBJECTIVES

After completing this lesson, students will be able to:

- Understand the role of video in today's society.
- Evaluate the aesthetic quality of video programming.
- Appreciate the marvels of video technology.

☑ SUPPLIES

- Pencils
- White drawing paper

Resource

■ 11-8 That's Entertainment, TRB page 181 (art history)

■ Motivator

Discuss with students the place that film and television have in the lives of people today and how we rely on TV to get news and other information. Ask students to talk about the kinds of motion pictures and TV programs they watch and why.

■ Vocabulary

Introduce the concept of a **video documentary** by showing a short one if possible. Students may be very familiar with this type of visual record. Ask them to give examples of documentaries they have seen on television.

216

LESSON 7
Advances in Visual Reporting

Technology and art have always been partners. The invention of paint in tubes in the mid-1800s freed artists for the first time to go outdoors and paint. Advances of the past hundred years have had equal importance and impact. In this lesson you will look at some of these advances and their effect on the field of visual reporting.

MOTION PICTURES

The visual records of generations past, as you have seen, were created using a variety of media. Yet, all shared a common limitation. All, even the camera, provided "frozen" views of an action event. If a still image is worth a thousand words, how many words could be expressed by a *moving* visual record?

An answer to this question came shortly before the beginning of the twentieth century. It was delivered in the form of the

technological breakthrough pictured in Figure 11–14. This item, the *kinetoscope* (kuh-**net**-uh-skohp), was a forerunner of the modern movie projector. It was invented by the same person who gave us the electric lightbulb. His name was Thomas Edison Examine this device. Do any of the parts look familiar? Can you guess what any of them do?

THE VIDEO REVOLUTION

The kinetoscope produced moving images by rapidly stringing together still ones. This same principle is at work in today's movie and video cameras. One advance of the last several decades is the **camcorder,** *a small hand-held video camera.* Camcorders have revolutionized the recording of video events. They have managed this by reducing the cost of the technology while, at the same time, increasing the ease of use.

Figure 11–14 How has the making of motion pictures changed since the days of this device?

A moving picture machine invented by Thomas Edison. 1915. UPI/Corbis-Bettman.

216   Chapter 11   *Recording Events*

MEETING SPECIAL NEEDS

Taking Photographs   For students with neurological/orthopedic disabilities, drawing may be difficult. Photography can be a fulfilling activity and a source of pride and achievement. Investigate whether your school's Special Education service department has adapted devices that could enable students with disabilities to use a camera. Camera holders to attach a camera to a wheelchair and

touch pads for shutter release are available. Self-focusing cameras can help students with the focusing process. Always urge students, and especially those who tend to act impulsively, to carefully consider their photo compositions. For example, moving an object around to find the best lighting, clear configurations, and foreground interest will help to create high quality photographs.

The Video Documentary

The video camera and camcorder have introduced an exciting new type of visual record. This is the video documentary. A **video documentary** is *an in-depth study of a person, place, thing, or event.* Today there are many sources of excellent documentary programming. Nature videos are at the top of the list for artistry. These works have brought the viewer up close to the wonders and mysteries of nature. They have recorded the habits of the tiniest insect to the endless marvels of the vast oceans. See Figure 11–15 for an example of a video documentary crew in action.

Check Your Understanding

1. What advances in the visual reporting of events have occurred in the last hundred years?
2. What is a video documentary?

Figure 11–15 This camera crew is about to film a video documentary. What do you suppose is around the bend in the path?

Photo by Kurtis Productions, Chicago, Illinois.

STUDIO ACTIVITY

Planning a Story Board

No video documentary could exist without careful planning. One step in this planning is the creation of a **story board.** This is *a frame-by-frame plan of a video production.*

Think about a video documentary you might like to make. Consider your subject and the points of interest you might emphasize. Think about your audience as well. Then draw lines to divide a 12 x 18-inch (30 x 46-cm) sheet of drawing paper into six sections. In each section, sketch a scene in your documentary. The first frame, for example, might show a person—the narrator—speaking. Include the beginning, middle, and end of your documentary in your story board. Plan the characters, setting, situation, or problem, and solution. Write a script to accompany your images.

PORTFOLIO

Put your story board in your portfolio with your script.

■ Cultural Diversity

Many motion pictures and video documentaries provide an excellent means of learning about and understanding other cultures. Try to find a few video documentaries about other peoples and cultures and show them to the class. Ask the class to critique the videos on their artistic merit.

■ Studio Skills

Sketching ideas in a story board is good experience for students to gain confidence in expressing their ideas. Finished drawings are not necessary as long as the ideas are clear. Suggest drawing lightly. Have students use the story board as a thinking medium.

● ● ● ● ● ● ● ●
ASSESS

■ Self-Assessment

Have students complete the Check Your Understanding questions on this page. Answers are provided below.

■ Reteaching

Have students work in pairs to improve their story board designs. Ask partners to provide constructive criticism to suggest ways of clarifying ideas.

■ Enrichment

Ask students to study television program guides for one week and make a list of recommended programs. Their list should include mostly video documentaries if possible. Before they make their list, have them establish viewing goals or guidelines.

● ● ● ● ● ● ● ●
CLOSE

Ask students to discuss the importance of being selective in their viewing of TV and motion pictures.

Answers to ✔CHECK YOUR UNDERSTANDING

1. Some of the advances in visual reporting that have occurred in the last hundred years are the invention of the kinetoscope, a forerunner of the modern movie projector, the video camera and camcorder, and the video documentary.

2. A video documentary is an in-depth study of a person, place, thing, or event.

• • • • • • • • • • • • • •
FOCUS

☑ OBJECTIVES

After completing this lesson, students will be able to:

• Organize ideas into a sequential plan to design and videotape a documentary video.

• Work with composing space in a lens and zooming in for close-up views of their subject.

• Describe, analyze, interpret, and judge their work.

☑ SUPPLIES

• Writing pads and pencils
• Straight edges
• White drawing paper
• Markers
• Camcorders
• VHS videotape cassettes
• Tripods (optional)
• Television and VCR

Resource

■ 11-9 From Art to Docudrama, TRB page 182 (cooperative learning)

• • • • • • • • • • • • • •
TEACH

■ Motivator

Discuss theme and list on the board several possible themes and approaches to a documentary. When students have chosen a theme (a place or event that they can get to), have them list at least ten images that could be parts of the video.

218

Making a Video Documentary

When you watch a documentary on TV, do you imagine yourself as the **videographer**—the *person who operates a video camera?* Do you picture yourself trekking deep into the heart of Africa on a safari? Maybe you see yourself scaling a snow-capped mountain peak. In this lesson, you will have the chance to be a videographer. You will probably have to limit your travel to within your own town or city, however. Figure 11–16 shows a student your age "on location" at Chicago's Lincoln Park Zoo. Can you identify her subject?

WHAT YOU WILL LEARN

You will design and videotape your own documentary video. You will begin by choosing a subject. You will then plan and draw a story board. In it, you will identify images that will help give viewers a broad picture of the place or event. Based on your story board, you will shoot your video. You will use a variety of video techniques, including closeups, long shots, and pans. A **pan** is *a slow, steady, sideways movement of the video camera to capture details in a panorama.*

Figure 11–16 **Sixth-grader Emma Walsh on location during the taping of her video documentary.**

Student using video camera at the Lincoln Park Zoo, Chicago, Illinois.

MEETING SPECIAL NEEDS

Videos A storyboard plan for a video or movie might be made about an individual who has lived with a disability. It might show how the individual goes about the activities of daily living, relating with others with and without disabilities, and meeting his or her creative, recreational, or social goals. Think about the closeups, pans, and long shots which will best tell the story.

WHAT YOU WILL NEED

- Writing pad and pencil
- Yardstick or other long straight edge
- Sheet of white drawing paper, 18 x 24 inches (46 x 61 cm)
- Markers
- Camcorder
- VHS videotape cassette
- Tripod (optional)

WHAT YOU WILL DO

1. With a group of students, brainstorm possible events that would make good topics for a video documentary. Choose subjects and locations that are realistic. Possibilities include a race, game, or parade. Locations might include the school grounds, a park, or a zoo.
2. After choosing an event, make a list of ten or more images that are important to your subject. Note these on the writing pad. Organize your images into an outline.
3. Create a story board. With the pencil and yardstick or other straight edge, draw lines to divide a large sheet of drawing paper into sixteen sections. In each section, sketch a scene from your outline. Use markers to add color to your story board.
4. Write an introduction to your documentary. Make sure the camcorder has been loaded with a videotape cassette and that the battery is charged. Set up the camcorder on a tripod if you wish, and tape yourself reading the introduction. Alternatively, you might ask a friend to serve as your narrator.
5. Following your story board, shoot your video scene by scene. Tell what you see

as you tape to provide a running commentary. Include close-up shots, long views, and pans.

6. Plan your closing. Include a wrap-up commentary. Play your finished work for members of your class.

Figure 11–17   **Student work. A story board.**

 STUDIO OPTION

▪ Do a video interview with a member of your class or community. Prepare by making a list of questions to ask.

Focus on questions that will bring out the interests and talents of your subject. Videotape your interview.

Lesson 8   *Making a Video Documentary*   **219**

CONNECTIONS *History*

The Book of the Dead by Scribe Nebqued. c. 1400 B.C. Egyptian papyrus with hieroglyphs. Height: 30 cm (11¾"). Louvre, Paris, France. Giraudon/Art Resource, NY

How Do Societies Record Events?

Can you remember what happened on your last birthday? Do you recall how you spent the day? What presents did you receive? If you don't remember, how could you find out? Perhaps you described the day in a diary. Maybe someone took photographs or made a videotape. By keeping a record of the event, you will always be able to remember it vividly.

Throughout time, people have recorded the important events in their history. During the U.S. Civil War, for example, soldiers kept journals of their experiences. Photographers took pictures of soldiers and battlefields. Artists depicted scenes of the war in paintings.

Today, modern technology has provided us with additional ways to record events. The explosion of the space shuttle *Challenger,* for example, was recorded on live television. Through computers via the World Wide Web, we can access sound and video clips of current events, such as the most recent presidential inauguration.

Before modern technology, however, how did societies record events? In the earliest times, people drew pictures on cave walls. In *The Book of the Dead of Nebqued,* the ancient Egyptians told stories by painting them on papyrus, an early form of paper. This work is generally considered the world's first book.

┌─ **MAKING THE CONNECTION**
☑ Identify four ways in which societies record events.
☑ Create a time line of the important events in your life. Start with the day you were born and end with an event that occurred within the past year.
☑ Learn more about *The Book of the Dead of Nebqued.* What was the purpose of the book?

INTERNET ACTIVITY
Visit Glencoe's Fine Arts Web Site for students at:
http://www.glencoe.com/sec/art/students

┌─ **INTERNET ACTIVITY**

Getting Your School Connected   The technology that opened the Internet to businesses and private individuals has also increased its potential for educational use. This great potential was recognized by the president, who challenged the nation to connect every classroom in America to the Internet by the year 2000. Problems such as cost, installation of telephone lines, availability of local service providers, and acceptable use by students are all challenges that educators face. Show your school district and administrators examples from this program that guarantee the learning experience and benefits available to your students once your classroom is on-line. Find us at **http://www.glencoe.com/sec/art**

BUILDING VOCABULARY

Number a sheet of paper from 1 to 10. After each number, write the term from the box that matches each description below.

camcorder	pan
caricature	photography
frieze	story board
gouache	video documentary
mosaic	videographer

1. The art of making images by exposing a chemically treated surface to light.
2. A small hand-held video camera.
3. A form of watercolor that uses non-clear pigments.
4. An in-depth study of a person, place, thing, or event.
5. A slow, steady, sideways movement of the video camera to capture details in a panorama.
6. Person who operates a video camera.
7. Small bits of colorful glass and jewels set in cement.
8. A decorative band running across the upper part of a wall.
9. A frame-by-frame plan of a video production.
10. A humorous drawing that exaggerates features of a person to make fun of or criticize him or her.

 ## REVIEWING ART FACTS

Number a sheet of paper from 11 to 15. Answer each question in a complete sentence.

11. What are the four W's of visual reporting?
12. What personal risk was taken by the photographer of Figure 11–2 to record the event from the best angle?
13. What reasons might the painter of Figure 11–6 have had for making George Washington the tallest figure in the painting?
14. What event was recorded in the frieze in Figure 11–10?
15. When was the kinetoscope invented and by whom?

 ## THINKING ABOUT ART

On a sheet of paper, answer each question in a sentence or two.

1. **Extend.** Look back at Figure 11–6. The painting shows an event at which the artist could not have been present. What details in the painting do you think were accurate? Which might the artist have added for dramatic effect?
2. **Synthesize.** If technology continues on its present course, what developments in the video recording industry do you expect to occur in the future?

 ## MAKING ART CONNECTIONS

1. **Language Arts.** The descriptive recording of events is not limited to the visual arts. Poets are also noted for adding color and immediacy to events from history. Find a copy of the ballad "Paul Revere's Ride" by Henry Wadsworth Longfellow. Read this colorful poem aloud to appreciate its rhythm. If you can locate a copy, study Grant Wood's "visual record" of this historical event.

2. **Science.** The image in Figure 11–11 was taken by a NASA space probe. Using on-line or library resources, learn more about NASA. Begin by determining what the letters in the organization's name stand for. In addition, try to learn when NASA was founded, where it is headquartered, and what work it does. Share your findings in a report.

■ Building Vocabulary
1. photography
2. camcorder
3. gouache
4. video documentary
5. pan
6. videographer
7. mosaic
8. frieze
9. story board
10. caricature

■ Reviewing Art Facts
11. These are who, what, when, and where.
12. He placed himself on a rock ledge a mile up.
13. This may have been done to emphasize Washington's status as supreme commander of the Continental Army.
14. The event was the search by Marquette and Joliet for the source of the Mississippi River.
15. It was invented just before the turn of the century by Thomas Edison.

THINKING ABOUT ART

1. Probable accurate details include the ice floes and clothing of the period. Unlikely details include Washington's appearing in a standing position and his "noble" posture.

2. Answers will vary. Among possibilities students might note are: higher-definition videos and more lifelike three-dimensional images.

Telling a Story

(pages 222–241)

Resources

- 12-12 Chapter Test, TRB page 202
- Transparency CC-12, *I and the Village* by Marc Chagall
- Transparency 12, *Dorothea and Francesca* by Cecilia Beaux
- Fine Art Print 18, *Sundance Ceremony* by George Washakie

Theatre
While studying this chapter, use Performing Arts Handbook page 324 to understand how Nobuko Miyamoto discovered her true identity.

NATIONAL STANDARDS

This chapter addresses the following National Standards for the Visual Arts:

1. (a, b)	**4.** (a, c)
2. (a, b, c)	**5.** (a, c)
3. (a, b)	**6.** (a, b)

222

Figure 12–1 Notice the abundant use of geometric shapes. What art principle has been used to organize these shapes?

John Thomas Biggers. *Starry Crown.* 1987. Acrylic, mixed media on canvas. 155 × 124.5 cm (61 × 49″). Dallas Museum of Art, Dallas, Texas. Texas Art Fund.

222

FEATURED ARTISTS

John Thomas Biggers	L. Joe
Pieter Bruegel	Faith Ringgold
Leo and Diane Dillon	Diego Rivera
Marina Gutierrez	David Alfaro Siqueiros
Richard Haas	

Telling a Story

The art of storytelling is as old as humanity itself. Long before people could write, they were telling tales of intrigue and adventure. Some of these stories have been handed down through the ages and teach a lesson or moral. Others offer accounts of real people and events.

Examine the "story" on the facing page. Who are the characters? What is the setting? Does this story tell about people from our own culture or from some distant place?

In this chapter, you will learn how to read stories without words. You will examine works by visual storytellers from different times and places.

PORTFOLIO IDEAS

Artwork doesn't always fit into a folder or even a large portfolio. What if you worked with a group to make a three-dimensional sculpture or a mural? Photographs and drawings are one way to document the experience of working together. Another way is to write about it in detail. When describing work performed in groups, outline the goal and list each member's responsibility. Then focus on your own specific tasks for self-reflection and evaluation.

OBJECTIVES

After completing this lesson, you will be able to:

- Recognize the story that runs through some works of art.
- Explain ways in which different cultures tell stories through art.
- Identify outside factors that impact the creation of visual stories.
- Tell stories using different art media and methods.

WORDS YOU WILL LEARN

cartouche
cutaway
embroidery
font
fresco
gold leaf
Kachina
petroglyph
pictogram

■ Chapter Overview

The art of the tale can take many forms. In this chapter, students will learn that stories can be told a number of ways, even without the use of words. They will "read" the story that is to be told in some works of art. They will see that different cultures tell stories in their own unique ways.

■ Chapter Motivator

Choose a classic or contemporary wordless picture book to "read" to the class, such as *The Silver Pony* by Lynd Ward or *Free Fall* by David Weisner. Consult the school or public librarian for other suggestions. Show students each page as you present the book, allowing them time to study each picture carefully. After finishing the book, have students respond to the story. Tell them that in this chapter, they will learn about the ways artists tell stories without using words.

■ Examining the Artwork

The woman in the center of this trio represents the Dogon weaver of the word. The string running through her mouth is symbolic of the transfer of knowledge from one generation to the next through folk tales and proverbs.

National Museum of Women in the Arts

You may wish to use the National Museum of Women in the Arts videodisc and/or CD-ROM. The videodisc features a bar code guide, and the interactive CD-ROM provides stimulating activities.

223

DEVELOPING A PORTFOLIO

Group Projects When assigning group projects, discuss student responsibility and contribution to the group prior to the beginning of the project. Clear expectations of group members as well as the actual project will help students begin with a defined objective and clear focus. If there is to be an end project, consider how it can be documented in some way so that it can be included in all group members' portfolios. Group summaries of peers are often part of group projects. Rubrics provide a common point of reference for the students in completing the assignment and a clear understanding of what is expected.

Picture Languages

•••••••••••••

FOCUS

☑ **OBJECTIVES**

After completing this lesson, students will be able to:

• Know the origin of hieroglyphics.

• Explain the history and purpose of petroglyphs.

• Define what a *cartouche* is.

☑ **SUPPLIES**

• Brown butcher paper or several large brown paper bags

• Rulers, scissors

• Pencils, markers, crayons

•••••••••••••

TEACH

■ **Vocabulary**

Connect picture stories to the history and meaning of names. For example, in English, *Smith* was originally the name for the village blacksmith, *Potter* was the maker of clay pots. Such meanings are found in most language groups. Explain to students that no matter what the ethnic origin of a name, there is a story to be told. Have them find names in any language and research the story of each.

Ask people to define *story,* and most will mention "words." Few, if any, will include "pictures" in their definition. Yet, in a very real sense, all word stories *are* picture stories. If this statement is confusing, read on. On this page and the next, you will learn about and see examples of images that link the subject areas of writing and art.

EARLY PICTURE WRITING

Do you know someone who reads Korean, Chinese, or Japanese? Maybe you are able to yourself. If so, you are probably aware that these languages use not only letters but pictograms. A **pictogram** is *a small picture that stands for a word or an idea.* Early human languages were written entirely in pictograms. All alphabets today descend from collections of symbols such as these.

Egyptian Hieroglyphic

One of the earliest pictographic languages was that used by the ancient Egyptians some 3,000 years ago. As noted in Chapter 5, this language was a type of *hieroglyphic* (hy-ruh-**glif**-ik), or form of picture writing.

Figure 12–2 shows an object that was common in Egyptian hieroglyphic. That object, a **cartouche** (kar-**toosh**), is *an oval or oblong containing an important person's name.* Study the two cartouches in the picture. Can you make out any familiar shapes? If you cannot, don't be discouraged. It took scholars many hundreds of years to crack the code of this complex language.

Native American Petroglyphs

Even older than the cartouche is the image shown in Figure 12–3. This object is a

Figure 12–2 The picture writing in these ovals represents people's names. What images can you find?

Egypt. *Cartouche.*

224 Chapter 12 *Telling a Story*

MEETING SPECIAL NEEDS

Using Picture Words Pictographs are a good way to maintain students' interest in writing. Especially for students with learning disabilities such as dysgraphia and dyslexia, combining hieroglyphic symbols with their own written words adds a lot of fun and creativity to a project integrating art and writing. It is possible that some students with mental retardation or neurological/orthopedic disabilities will have difficulty figuring out measurements and doing the cutting. Assistance may be required.

petroglyph (peh-truh-glif), a *symbolic rock carving or painting.* Objects of this kind were created long ago by Native American artists. Such images have been found in 41 of the 50 states and in Canada. Many petroglyphs are thought to date as far back as 8000 B.C., nearly 10,000 years ago.

Examine the petroglyph in this picture. Can you identify the creature shown? The four pairs of legs should provide a clue to its identity. It is a spider. Note that this is no ordinary spider. Rather, it is the Spider Woman. This is a goddess-like figure common to the teachings of the Hopi and Zuni peoples of the American Southwest. The petroglyph symbolizes the story of creation. According to this tale, the Spider Woman formed all living creatures out of clay using her many slender fingers. A second figure, the Sun God Tawa, sent glowing rays to warm the creatures, thus breathing life into them. How does this creation story compare with others you may have heard? What does it reveal about the role of nature in the Hopi and Zuni system of beliefs?

STUDIO ACTIVITY

Designing a Cartouche

Design your own personal cartouche. Begin by cutting a 4 x 9-inch (10 x 23-cm) rectangle from a large brown paper bag or from a sheet of brown butcher paper. Using pencil, draw an oval that fills most of the surface area. Within the oval, sketch images that correspond to letters in your name—a cat for *Catherine*, a car for *Carl*. Alternatively, sketch objects that symbolize your interests or hobbies. Go over all lines in fairly wide-tipped dark brown, red, and black markers. Allow a few minutes to make sure the markers have dried. Crumple the paper, then carefully smooth it out. The remaining creases will give your art an aged look.

P O R T F O L I O

In self-reflection, write what you learned about symbolizing your name for a cartouche.

✔ Check Your Understanding

1. What type of language was used by the ancient Egyptians?
2. What is a cartouche?
3. How were petroglyphs made?

Figure 12–3   What type of balance has been used in this image?

Native American. Petroglyph. *Spider Woman.* Nina River, Wyoming. Photo by Andrea Bush.

Lesson 1   *Picture Languages*   **225**

Making a Visual Autobiography

LESSON TIME: 90 minutes

☑OBJECTIVES

After completing this lesson, students will be able to:

• Design and create a visual expression of who they are.

• Describe, analyze, interpret, and judge their visual autobiographies.

☑SUPPLIES

• Pencils and notebook paper

• Rulers, scissors, glue or glue sticks

• Variety of old magazines

• White or colored drawing paper

• Markers, oil pastels

■ Motivator

Discuss with students the Gutierrez self-portrait (Figure 12-4). Point out images and have students tell what they think each means. Then ask them to make a written list in three columns—persons, places, and things—that they would like to include in their visual autobiography.

■ Vocabulary

Discuss the terms *biography* and *autobiography.* Note the difference in point of view. Also, have students talk about the difference between a self-portrait and a visual autobiography.

Who am I? That question might at first seem easy for most of us to answer. Careful thought, however, reveals that each of us is a complex, one-of-a-kind individual. The person you see when you look into the mirror has a story to tell unlike anyone else's. Some writers have, in fact, written entire books about themselves and their lives. These are called *autobiographies.*

The painting in Figure 12–4 is an autobiography of sorts. In this case, the artist has answered the question *Who am I?* without using words. Study the painting. The artist has painted herself three times. What differences can you find among the three self-portraits? Notice the images—an eye, a shoe, a factory, a chicken—which the artist has placed in front of her own image. What meaning do you suppose she wants us to "read" into these?

WHAT YOU WILL LEARN

In this lesson, you will make your own "visual autobiography." Think of qualities and traits that make up the one-of-a-kind individual that is "you." Use a combination of found and original images to tell your story. You will emphasize the importance of events and objects in your picture through size and color contrast.

WHAT YOU WILL NEED

• Sheet of lined notebook paper and pencil
• Used magazines
• Scissors
• Sheet of white or colored drawing paper, 9 x 12 inches (23 x 30 cm)
• White glue
• Markers and oil pastels

Figure 12–4 **The images of hands and other objects are painted metal cutouts. They stand out in relief from the large triple self-portrait.**

Marina Gutierrez. *Biography.* 1988. Acrylic on Masonite with painted metal. 122 × 183 × 15.2 cm (48 × 72 × 6″). Courtesy of the artist.

226 Chapter 12 *Telling a Story*

WHAT YOU WILL DO

1. Divide a sheet of lined paper into two columns. In one column, list your hobbies, interests, likes, talents, and so on. Also include memories that have special meaning to you. In the second column, note images that relate to the items in the first column. If you play an instrument, for example, you might draw several musical notes in the image column.

2. Look through old magazines for photographs of about half of the images you have recorded in your second column. Choose photos in a variety of sizes. Clip these out and arrange them in an interesting fashion on the sheet of drawing paper. When you are happy with the composition, glue the images in place.

3. Fill most of the remaining space on your paper with pencil sketches of other images from your list. Make some of the images larger than others. Leave some negative space between them. Write your name in a creative way between some of the images. Use block letters, squiggly lines, connected circles, and so forth.

4. Complete your illustrations with markers and oil pastels. Use bright hues for some images, contrasting duller hues for others.

EXAMINING YOUR WORK

- **Describe** What images appear in your artwork?
- **Analyze** How have you used size and color contrast to suggest the importance of some images?
- **Interpret** What does your artwork tell about you as a person? What title would you give your work?
- **Judge** Decide whether your autobiography is effective in terms of its design. Decide whether it is effective in telling about your life.

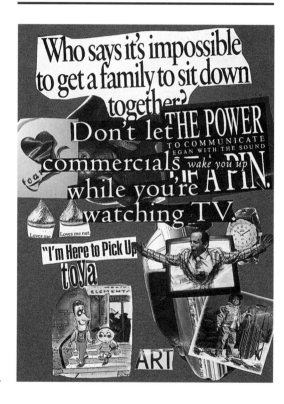

Figure 12–5 **Student work. A visual autobiography.**

COMPUTER OPTION

■ If you have access to a scanner or digital camera, scan a photograph of yourself into the computer, or have a friend capture a portrait of your face with a digital camera. Open the image in an art application. Title and save. On a new page in your application, draw six or more images and objects that reveal your interests and traits.

Select, Copy, and Paste these images, one at a time, onto the page with your portrait. While selected, resize each image and arrange around your likeness so they overlap your portrait. Consider adding images from your clip-art files. Surround your portrait with images. If available, select and apply special effects that match the mood. Title, save, and print.

Lesson 2 *Making a Visual Autobiography* **227**

CURRICULUM CONNECTIONS

Language Arts To accompany their visual autobiographies, have students write an autobiographical poem. Before they begin to write, however, draw a word-web on the board: draw one large circle in the middle of the board with the word *me* written in it. Then draw several spokes leading out to smaller, empty circles. Tell students to think of words they associate with who they are and write those words in the outer circles. They can use as many circles as they like, using appropriate descriptive words and objects. After students have their word-webs done, they can use these prewriting ideas to help them write their poems.

FOCUS

☑ OBJECTIVES

After completing this lesson, students will be able to:

• Understand the place of myth and legend in world cultures.

• Give examples of how myths and legends have appeared in visual art.

☑ SUPPLIES

• Pencils and sketch paper

• Library resources

Resources

■ 12-4 Myth and Art, TRB page 192 (art criticism)

■ 12-5 Chasers of Evil, TRB page 193 (appreciating cultural diversity)

• • • • • • • • • • • •

TEACH

■ Motivator

Discuss the many examples today of myth and legend in film and video. *Beauty and the Beast, Jurassic Park, The Hunchback of Notre Dame* are some. Find myths and legends of many cultures in your library.

■ Vocabulary

Discuss the difference between *legendary* and *real*. Dinosaurs were real. The discovery of skeletal remains shows us the actual size and characteristics of these immense creatures. Legendary creatures, like dragons, come from stories and myths. Someone or something that might have once been real, such as Daniel Boone, can take on legendary qualities over time.

228

 LESSON 3

Myths and Legends

Do you know the story of how the giraffe got its long neck? Maybe you are familiar the legend of Hercules, the mighty Greek warrior. Myths and legends like these have been passed down through generations. They have also crossed many cultural boundaries.

In this lesson, you will learn about myths and legends from around the world. You will take a quick look at visual retellings of two such legends.

LEGENDS BASED ON HUMAN TRAITS

"They all lived happily ever after." You almost certainly know these words. You probably have heard them countless times at the end of bedtime stories when you were young. These words reflect our fondness for happy endings. They also reveal our desire to overcome evil, whether it is a wicked witch or the misdeeds of real people.

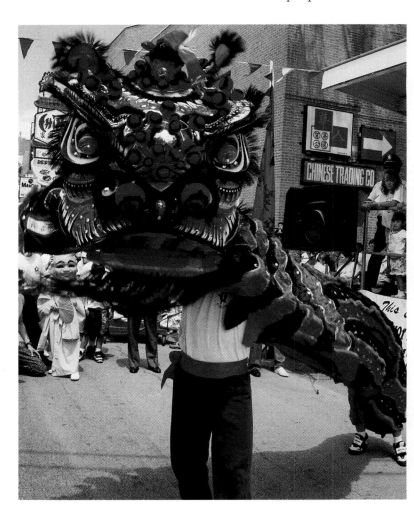

Figure 12–6 Notice how balance is used to organize this object. What role does color play?

Chinese Dragon. Photo by Brian Lee.

228   Chapter 12   *Telling a Story*

---

more about • • •

Mythology   Artists have depicted mythical creatures in their artwork since prehistoric times, but perhaps more than any other group of myths, the figures of Greek and Roman mythology have been particular favorites of Western artists. Ask students to research the system of gods and goddesses in Greek mythology. Then have them trace examples of these myths in artworks over the centuries. After students have a general understanding of *classical mythology,* as it is called, assign each student a mythological figure to identify in several different artists' works and bring copies of the works to class to show and discuss with others.

Figure 12–7 Did you recognize Ganesha as an elephant? Are you familiar with other tales or legends based on this jungle creature?

The Hindu God Ganesha and His Consorts. Early eleventh century. Cream sandstone. 41.5 cm (16⅜"). John H. and Ernestine A. Payne Fund, Helen S. Coolidge Fund, Asiatic Curator's Fund, John Ware Willard Fund, and Marshall H. Gould Fund. Courtesy of Museum of Fine Arts, Boston, Massachusetts.

Object Based on Myth

The subject of Figure 12–6 is a creature that is often used to represent evil in the legends of our own culture. Can you identify this mythical beast? It is a fire-breathing dragon. Study the menacing frown, flaring nostrils, and glowing red eyes. Don't bother looking for the brave knight you are accustomed to seeing wherever dragons lurk. In the culture of China, where this object was created, dragons are a symbol of good luck. A costume like this is typically worn by the lead figure in a parade to bring in the Chinese New Year. Can you think of other cultures you have learned about in which frightening masks are worn on happy occasions? How has the artist used the element of line to emphasize the dragon's fierceness?

 STUDIO ACTIVITY

Sketching a Mythical Beast

Another mythical beast appears in Chapter 7 on page **136.** That creature is a unicorn. Take a moment to return to that page and examine the creature. Notice ways in which it is similar and different from the mythical creatures in this lesson.

Based on your comparisons, do sketches for a mythical beast of your own invention. Decide what trait or quality your beast will represent. Decide whether it will have legs, wings, horns, a tail, scales, or feathers. Set your sketches aside in a safe place for use in the following lesson.

P O R T F O L I O

Make a list of other characteristics you might like to consider for your mythical beast. Put them with your sketches and review them before you begin Lesson 4.

Sculpture Based on Myth

The sculpture in Figure 12–7 depicts another creature meant to bring luck. The work is a product of a culture neighboring that of China. That culture is India.

This mythical figure is Ganesha, the ancient Hindu god of good fortune. Works like this once adorned the outsides of Hindu temples. People about to embark on a new undertaking would bring offerings in the form of sweets before the god's likeness. What kind of creature is Ganesha? How did the sculptor go about breathing life and energy into this mythical being?

 Check Your Understanding

1. What do the two artworks on these pages share in common?
2. What differences do you detect?

Lesson 3 *Myths and Legends* **229**

Assign small groups of students to work collaboratively and go to the library or Internet to find examples of mythological creatures from many lands and cultures. Have each group choose one culture—Chinese, Japanese, Native American, Meso-American, for example— to read about and find artworks that tell about mythological figures from that culture. Prepare a myth hall of fame to display materials students bring in to share.

■ **Art History**

Ask a few volunteers to find out about the legend of the sword in the stone from the legend of King Arthur and compare it in art and literature to the legend of Alexander the Great and the Gordian knot. Have students bring in any artworks they can identify depicting either of these two legends.

ASSESS

■ **Self-Assessment**

Have students complete the Check Your Understanding questions on this page. Answers are provided below.

■ **Reteaching**

Ask students to discuss different ways in which dragons have been portrayed in art.

■ **Enrichment**

Have students act out the legend of Ganesha and how he came to be. Invite students to research this mythical figure in Indian lore. Have them create visuals to support their skits.

CLOSE

Ask students to discuss various traits of legendary creatures.

Answers to ✔ CHECK YOUR UNDERSTANDING

1. These two artworks both depict symbolic, mythological creatures.

2. Ganesha is part imaginary animal, part real animal. The dragon is not at all real.

LESSON TIME: 90 minutes

• • • • • • • • • • • • •
FOCUS

☑ OBJECTIVES

After completing this lesson, students will be able to:
• Create a mythical creature that exhibits formal balance and rhythm based on color and pattern.
• Understand the significance of Kachinas in Hopi culture.
• Describe, analyze, interpret, and judge their artwork.

☑ SUPPLIES

• Cardboard tubes from paper towels, 3 per student
• Colored construction paper
• Tape, scissors or wire snips
• Work gloves (optional)
• Tempera paints, brushes
• Found objects such as fabric, raffia, and feathers; small boxes
• Stapler or white glue

Resource

○ ■ 12-6 Native American
○   Report, TRB page 194
○   (cooperative learning)

• • • • • • • • • • • • •
TEACH

■ Motivator

Find many examples of Kachina dolls and have students read to learn about their meaning and the way that the Hopi culture is continued through these dolls.

230

LESSON 4
Creating a Mythical Creature

In the previous lesson, you learned about two mythical creatures. Figure 12–8 shows an object based on another. This object is a **Kachina** (kuh-**chee**-nuh), a *hand-crafted statuette that represents spirits in Pueblo rituals.* Kachinas are used to teach Native American children about the traditions of their people. Such figures were long believed to embody Kachina, spirits who once dwelled among the Pueblo. Examine this object closely. What features of the bird in the object's title are represented in this statuette? How would you describe the use of color?

WHAT YOU WILL LEARN

You will use the sketches you made in the previous lesson as a jumping-off point for creating your own Kachina. Everyday found objects will be used to construct your Kachina. Your finished object, like the one in Figure 12–8, will exhibit formal balance and rhythm based on color and pattern.

WHAT YOU WILL NEED

• Three cardboard tubes from paper towels
• Colored construction paper
• Transparent tape
• Wrapping paper
• Scissors
• Work gloves (optional)
• Tempera paints, brushes
• Found objects such as fabric scraps, raffia, and feathers
• Stapler or white glue
• Jewelry boxes or other small boxes

WHAT YOU WILL DO

1. Begin construction by cutting one of the cardboard tubes in half lengthwise. The two narrow half-cylinders that result are to be the creature's legs. Wrap a scrap of brightly colored construction paper around the left leg. Secure it with transparent tape. Use a scrap of wrapping paper in a busy pattern to cover the right leg.

Figure 12–8 How would you describe the figure's stance? What principle of art has been used to organize this object?

L. Joe. *Eagle Kachina.* 1990. Wood, leather, feathers, yarn, and fur. 30 cm (12"). Private collection.

230   Chapter 12   *Telling a Story*

— more about • • • —

The Hopi   The Hopi are one of the Pueblo tribes. Their towns in the arid mesa lands of northeast Arizona are some of the oldest continuously inhabited villages in the United States. The Hopi are a small, friendly group, tied together by their religious beliefs. Other tribes attribute great healing powers to Hopi doctors.

The driving force of the Hopi religion is the need for water. The rain ritual, the planting ritual, and the corn-growing rituals are very important ceremonies. When clouds hang over the mountains, it is the rain-bringing Kachinas that are present. The Hopi do not worship these Kachinas but treat them as friends or partners.

2. Follow a similar procedure with a second tube to form the arms. This time, begin by cutting away about three inches of the tube. Then cut the remaining part in half lengthwise. Again, attach colored paper and wrapping paper, this time to the opposite limbs. Attach arms to body with tape.

3. Cut two slits into the top of each leg. Slide the upper body down into the slits.

4. Create the Kachina's head by painting the top of the body tube. Use a medium brush to apply the base paint for the head. Add facial features—eyes, nose, mouth—with contrasting hues. Use a fine brush for this task. The features and other decorations should be highly geometric, as in Figure 12–8.

5. Look back at the sketches you made for the Studio Activity on page 229. Choose your best sketch. Identify your mythical beast's most interesting parts and features. These might include wings, scales, a tail, or another such part. Use found objects such as fabric scraps, raffia, and feathers to create these features. Add the features to your Kachina with a stapler or white glue.

6. Use jewelry boxes or other small boxes for the Kachina's feet. Notch the bottoms of the legs and glue them to the boxes. Paint the feet.

EXAMINING YOUR WORK

- **Describe** Point out the arms, legs, and body of your figure. Identify wings, scales, or other such features.
- **Analyze** Does your Kachina exhibit formal balance and rhythm based on color and pattern?
- **Interpret** What feeling or mood is communicated by your Kachina?
- **Judge** What are the best features of your figure? What would you do differently if you were to repeat the lesson?

Figure 12–9 **Student work. Kachina.**

STUDIO OPTION

■ Make a soft-sculpture doll to represent a legend you know. Draw your design on paper. Place the paper over a length of fabric and cut out the shape. Repeat this step so that you have two identical shapes. Place the fabric shapes with right sides together. Sew the pieces together, leaving a section unsewn. Clip seams with scissors up to stitching. Turn inside out. Fill with fiberfill, then finish sewing the open section. Use markers and add beads, trims, and buttons to complete your doll.

Lesson 4 *Creating a Mythical Creature* **231**

Art Stories Larger than Life

Some storytellers create *short* stories. These tell about an event or experience so specific that it may be recounted in just a few pages. Other stories are told on a much grander scale. These stories focus on events that are more complex or of great importance. They require hundreds and sometimes thousands of pages.

Visual stories, too, may be told on a large or small scale. In this and the following lesson, you will look at stories that are larger than life.

FRESCOES

When you were little, you may have been scolded for drawing on the wall. Some professional artists make a living doing just that. They create frescoes (**fres**-kohz). A **fresco** is *a painting created when pigment is applied to a section of wall spread with fresh plaster.* The word *fresco* is Italian for "fresh." The technique of fresco painting got its start in Italy during the late Middle Ages.

Frescoes that Tell a Story

The fresco in Figure 12–10 was painted closer to our own time. Observe the work's

• • • • • • • • • • • • •

FOCUS

☑**OBJECTIVES**

After completing this lesson, students will be able to:

• Understand the meaning and origin of the word *fresco*.
• Understand that frescoes and murals can both tell a story.

☑**SUPPLIES**

• Cotton fabric pieces, 12 × 12 inches
• Embroidery hoops (if possible)
• Embroidery needles with medium large eyes
• Colored embroidery cotton thread
• Scissors, pencils

Resource

■ 12-7 Mural or Fresco TRB page 196 (reproducible master)

• • • • • • • • • • • • •

TEACH

■ **Motivator**

Introduce the idea of large scale stories. Ask students to talk about some of their favorite books and movies. Explain that art, too, can tell a grand story on a large scale. Direct students' attention to the Rivera fresco in Figure 12-10. Ask students to identify some of the "characters" in the Rivera fresco in Figure 12-10.

Figure 12–10 Notice that the figures in the room at the viewer's lower right are wearing lab coats. What service do you think they provide to city dwellers?

Diego Rivera. *The Making of a Fresco Showing the Building of a City.* 1931. Fresco. 6.9 × 9 m (22′ 7″ × 29′ 9″). Located at the San Francisco Art Institute, San Francisco, California.

232   Chapter 12   *Telling a Story*

— *more about* • • • —

Diego Rivera   Most of Rivera's murals and frescoes deal with Mexican culture and history. A native of Guanajuato, Mexico, Rivera (1886–1957) studied art in Mexico City and in Europe. He and artists like David Alfaro Siqueiros experimented extensively with fresco painting. Rivera was commissioned by the Mexican government to paint many murals and frescoes; some of his best are in the National Palace in Mexico City. He also painted a number of murals in the United States during the 1930s. Rivera was considered controversial because of his political views. His wife, Frida Kahlo, was also a famous artist. Have students read *Diego Rivera: Artist of the People* by Anne E. Neimark (N.Y.: HarperCollins, 1992).

Figure 12–11 This building, which was completed the year the artist died, bears his name. The mural shown covers 274 square meters.

David Alfaro Siqueiros. *Poliforum.* 1974. Acrylic enamel on asbestos-cement and steel. 15 m (49′ 2½″). Mexico City, Mexico. Mexican Government Tourism Office, New York.

physical dimensions. The figures and objects in it have been painted life-size. You may have been struck by the painting's unusual shape. The artist has provided a **cutaway** of a house under construction. This is *a view in which an outside wall has been removed to reveal the scene within.* Most of the details in this painting are activities you would expect to find in such a scene. There are workers in coveralls laying foundations. In the center room on the ground floor, men in business suits—the architects, maybe—review plans.

The story seems straightforward enough. Yet, there is more to this painting than meets the eye. Notice the title. The fresco depicts not the building of a house but of a city. People from all classes and walks of life work cooperatively toward a common goal. What is that goal? In what way is a house a fitting symbol of a city?

STUDIO ACTIVITY

Experimenting with Embroidery

Another larger-than-life story is the focus of the artwork in Figure 7–14 on page **136.** Turn to this work. It is an example of **embroidery.** This is *the art of making ornamental designs with needle and thread.*

Experiment with embroidery yourself. Start with a needle and colored cotton embroidery thread. Try doing a running stitch, one that goes simply in and out. Go back over the line you made, filling in the blank parts. Practice "drawing" with your needle and thread to make a picture.

 P O R T F O L I O

Write an explanation of your results for your portfolio. Tell what you learned in this activity.

MURALS

The artist who painted the fresco in Figure 12–10, Diego Rivera, was a notable Mexican artist. So was the individual responsible for the work in Figure 12–11. His name was David Alfaro Siqueiros (ahl-**far**-oh see-**cay**-rohs). This gigantic work is a *mural,* a type of public art done on a wall. The mural shown here graces the outside of an arts center in Mexico City. There are twelve such works, one for each of the sides of this oddly shaped building. Each mural addresses a different theme. Examine this giant artwork. What story does it tell? How would you describe its composition?

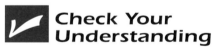

Check Your Understanding

1. What is a fresco? What is the origin of the word?
2. In what ways are the works on these pages similar? How are the two different?

STUDIO ACTIVITY

Experimenting with Embroidery

Have a piece of wax or a bar of soap handy to use on the thread ends before students thread the needles. It will keep the two threads together and stiffen the thread end. Advise students to keep the thread from knotting by not letting it twist.

■ **Cultural Diversity**

Invite students to bring in examples from home of embroidery done by family members. If possible, have a display of many forms of stitchery characteristic of different cultures. Make sure students have permission from parents to bring in any personal items.

• • • • • • • • • •
ASSESS

■ **Self-Assessment**

Have students complete the Check Your Understanding questions on this page. Answers are provided below.

■ **Reteaching**

In pairs, have students identify the differences between a fresco and a mural, finding examples of each in the book.

■ **Enrichment**

The Hmong are a peaceful people, whose women do remarkable fabric designs in stitchery and appliqué. Have several students find out more about the Hmong and their art and share their information with the class, bringing in pictures if possible.

• • • • • • • • • •
CLOSE

Have students apply the four art-criticism questions to one of the artworks presented in this lesson.

Answers to ✔ CHECK YOUR UNDERSTANDING

1. A fresco is a painting created when pigment is applied to a section of wall spread with fresh plaster. The word *fresco* is Italian for "fresh."
2. They are similar in that they both are large and are public art. Their differences involve media and surface: Rivera's is a fresco painted on a wall; Siqueiros's is a mural painted on the outside of a building.

LESSON TIME: 4 days

• • • • • • • • • • • •
FOCUS

☑ OBJECTIVES

After completing this lesson, students will be able to:
• Plan and work together to design and paint a mural.
• Describe, analyze, interpret, and judge their murals.

☑ SUPPLIES

• Pencils and sketch paper
• Butcher or plain wrapping paper, 36 inches by 6 feet
• Old newspapers, masking tape
• Tempera paints, brushes of various sizes, water and trays

• • • • • • • • • • • •
TEACH

■ Motivator

Have students study the Richard Haas mural in Figure 12-12. Explain that not all murals are done in the *trompe-l'oeil* style. Do they think this mural is a successful work of art? Why or why not?

■ Vocabulary

Have students review the qualities of color (hue, value, and intensity) in Chapter 1, Lesson 4. Recall ways to mix colors to change value and intensity. Have students also review the principles of art in Chapter 2, noting how the principles are applied in a large composition such as a mural.

234

LESSON 6

Painting a Mural About School Life

As an art form, murals date back to ancient Egyptian times. They have remained popular ever since for telling stories in a larger-than-life way. Consider the mural in Figure 12–12—that is, if you can find it. You may have trouble because the work was painted in a *trompe-l'oeil* style. As noted in Chapter 8, this is a style of painting in which objects are depicted with photographically realistic detail. Furthermore, the subject, building façades, blends in with its surroundings. This is because the mural covers the side of a building! The work pays tribute to the architects who designed the city of Chicago. You may recall learning about one of these pioneers, Louis H. Sullivan, in Chapter 9. Do you remember what Sullivan was famous for?

WHAT YOU WILL LEARN

You will work with a group of five or six classmates. Together you will plan and paint a mural for your school or classroom. Emphasize key images in your mural by making them larger and brighter in color. Introduce harmony by repeating shapes.

WHAT YOU WILL NEED

• Sketch paper and pencils
• Butcher or plain wrapping paper, 36 inches (1 m) wide by 6 feet (2 m) long
• Masking tape
• Sheets of newspaper
• Brushes of various sizes
• Tempera paints, water

WHAT YOU WILL DO

1. Brainstorm with group members for a theme for your mural. Jot down ideas for images associated with particular themes.

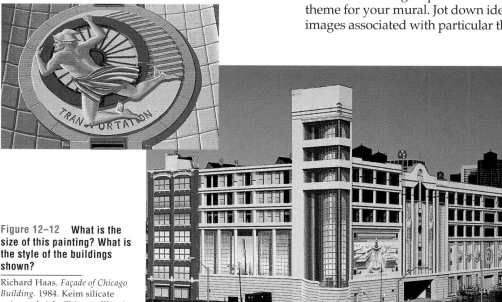

Figure 12–12 What is the size of this painting? What is the style of the buildings shown?

Richard Haas. *Façade of Chicago Building.* 1984. Keim silicate paint on brick. Chicago, Illinois. © 1988 Richard Haas/Licensed by VAGA, New York, New York.

234   Chapter 12 *Telling a Story*

MEETING STUDENT DIVERSITY

Small Groups Small group instruction and collaborative learning can be extremely beneficial to students who may learn at a slower pace. Assign groups so that there is a heterogeneous mix of abilities and personalities. Make sure each group has students who can offer direction, students who provide organization and order, students who risk ideas, and students who are willing contributors. Stress to the class that in group projects, each individual is important to the success of the group as a whole.

2. Plan the creation of the mural so that each group member works on a separate section. Begin by working individually on sketches of background objects and details. Stop from time to time to share and compare your work with that of other group members. Strive for a single, consistent style.

3. Concentrate next on any images of people that might be pictured. Again, pause and compare your efforts with those of group members. Emphasize important people and images by making them larger.

4. Lay out all of the sketches on a large work surface. Working as a team, decide which images to include and where to place them.

5. Complete a finished sketch of your portion of the mural. Use the method outlined in Technique Tip **5** on page **281** to impose a grid over your sketch. Still working in pencil, re-create your grid on the butcher or wrapping paper. Transfer the enlarged image to the butcher paper using the grid.

6. Use the masking tape to connect sheets of newspaper. These are to protect the

EXAMINING YOUR WORK

- **Describe**   What images did you include in your mural?
- **Analyze**   Did you emphasize important images by making them larger and brighter? Did you add harmony by repeating shapes throughout?
- **Interpret**   What theme does your mural express? Which objects help convey this theme?
- **Judge**   How effectively did you and your fellow group members work together? Did you succeed in your goal as a group?

surface on which you will work during the painting stage.

7. Using a fairly large brush loaded with tempera paint, begin coloring in background objects, such as sky. Switch to a finer brush for small details. Use bright hues for important images, duller hues for less important ones.

8. When the mural has dried completely, hang your mural on a wall by affixing loops of tape along the back.

Figure 12–13   **Student work. A mural about school life.**

Try This!

STUDIO OPTION

■ With several classmates, design and create a mural made up of abstract shapes. Transfer your image to a long strip of cloth. Use colored markers to complete the mural. What idea or mood does your mural communicate?

Lesson 6   *Painting a Mural About School Life*   **235**

TECHNIQUE TIP ▼

Making a Mural   In addition to the Technique Tip 5 on page **281,** you may find the following suggestions helpful while guiding students through the planning stages for a mural.

On the large mural paper, have students plot a composition and divide the space for the number of parts the mural will have. Then assign parts to students. Have them use sketch paper for their preliminary designs. When they have transferred their sketches to the mural paper, have the group stand back to see the mural as a whole and discuss ways to achieve a single, consistent style.

■ **Aesthetics**
Discuss with students the importance of murals in beautifying cities. Find additional examples of urban murals. They are often done in highly used or depressed areas of the city to give support to everyday people.

■ **Cultural Diversity**
Many of the city murals found in large cities of the United States are done by individuals who represent a large variety of ethnic groups. Find some examples (or ask students to find some) of these ethnic works in your own city or community. If possible, contact the muralists and arrange for them to visit the class. Remind students that a muralist must have permission from authorities before painting on any public structure.

• • • • • • • • • • • • • • • •
ASSESS

■ **Self-Assessment**
Have students use Examining Your Work to evaluate their art.

■ **Reteaching**
Ask students to explain why it may have been difficult to find the mural in Figure 12-12.

■ **Enrichment**
Contact the local municipal authorities to find out whether and how a student mural could be commissioned for your city. If you can acquire the proper permission, arrange for your class to paint a city mural based on the town's history.

• • • • • • • • • • • • • • • •
CLOSE

Ask students to look back on the group's efforts and critique the group's ability to work together to create a colorful, harmonious mural.

LESSON 7

Book Illustration

• • • • • • • • • • • • • • •

F O C U S

☑ OBJECTIVES

After completing this lesson, students will be able to:

- Understand the functions of book illuminations and the purpose of missals.
- Understand the functions of book illustrations.
- Recognize the differences in producing handmade and printed books.

☑ SUPPLIES

- Pencils and sketch paper
- White drawing paper
- Rulers, compasses (optional)
- Scissors
- Colored markers or watercolors
- Gold and silver crayons

Resource

- 12-9 Book Illustration Questionnaire, TRB page 198 (aesthetics)

• • • • • • • • • • • • • • •

T E A C H

■ Motivator

Explain that the printing press made it possible to produce books faster and in greater quantities. As a result, the role of books changed. Today, book illustrations still go beyond mere decoration. They serve to work with the text to communicate what the writer has to say.

■ Vocabulary

Have students recall terms introduced earlier: *illuminations*, *woodcuts*, *miniatures*.

236

As has been noted, some stories are told in words, others in pictures. In this lesson, you will look at picture stories that co-exist successfully side by side with the printed word. Pictures of this kind appear scattered throughout the book you are holding at this moment. They are called *book illustrations*.

MANUSCRIPT ILLUMINATION

The practice of illustrating books goes back some eleven hundred years. The earliest such illustrations were tiny paintings known as *illuminations*. They were so called because their job was to illuminate—or shed light on—the words on the page. Illuminations were common in Europe at a time when most people could not read. These illustrations thus served a function that went beyond mere decoration. Do you recall the name for art of this type?

The object in Figure 12–14 is an illuminated page from a book produced around the turn of the fifteenth century. This book was called a *missal* (**mis**-uhl). Its purpose was to teach. The bulk of the instruction was provided by miniature framed images of the sort appearing at the top of the page shown. Notice the richly colored border of fanciful plants and creatures. Each of these objects was individually hand-painted. What kind of lessons do you think missals taught? Do you know the story narrated by the framed picture on this missal page?

BOOK ILLUSTRATION OF TODAY

The invention of the printing press in the 1400s changed for all time the way books were made and illustrated. At first, all illustrations were done as woodcuts. The printing plates for such illustrations

Figure 12–14 In what ways is this book page similar to others you have seen? How is it different?

Artist unknown. Missal. 1389–1404. Tempera colors, gold leaf and gold paint on vellum in a medieval, blind-stamped binding. 33 × 24 cm (13 × 9⁷⁄₁₆″). The J. Paul Getty Museum, Los Angeles, California.

TECHNOLOGY OPTIONS

National Gallery of Art Videodisc   Use the following images to show additional works that tell a story.

Albrecht Dürer	Bartolomé Esteban Murillo	Peter Paul Rubens
Apocalypse: The Four Horsemen	*The Return of the Prodigal Son*	*Daniel in the Lions' Den*
Search Frame 3119	Search Frame 549	Search Frame 776

Use Glencoe's *National Gallery of Art Correlation Bar Code Guide* to locate more artworks.

Figure 12–15 The artists have used the art element of line to suggest action. What role does proportion play in this book illustration?

Leo and Diane Dillon. *Marie and Redfish.* Illustration by Leo and Diane Dillon from *Her Stories: African American Folktales, Fairy Tales and True Tales* by Virginia Hamilton. Illustrations copyright © 1995 by Leo and Diane Dillon. Reprinted by permission of Scholastic, Inc.

could be arranged conveniently alongside the type.

In time, changes brought about through advances in technology simplified this process. Artists today are free to create book illustrations in any medium they choose. One recent illustration appears in Figure 12–15. Examine this artwork. It was created to accompany a story titled "Marie and Redfish." The story tells of a teenager whose path crosses that of a prince. Find the "prince" in the picture. In what ways does this creature remind you of the mythical beasts you learned about in Lesson 3? In what ways does this illustration help the story come alive in the same way as the missal illustrations did?

STUDIO ACTIVITY

Designing a Letter

Look back at the book illumination in Figure 12–14. Note, in particular, the care that has gone into crafting simple capital letters. Each is a miniature artwork unto itself. The shimmering gold effect here and elsewhere is the result of **gold leaf.** This is *a very thin layer of gold glued to a surface for decoration.*

Choose a letter of the alphabet and decorate it in the manner of early illuminated manuscripts. Lightly draw the capital letter at least six inches high and one inch wide. Follow the graceful lines of the capitals in the missal, or create your own design. Add flowers or other decorations in and around the letter shape. You may want to set the letter in a rectangle. Use fine-tipped colored markers to capture details. Use gold or silver crayons to create rich effects.

 P O R T F O L I O

Write a short paragraph describing how you used the elements and principles of art in your illumination. Keep the paragraph and the drawing together in your portfolio.

✔ Check Your Understanding

1. What is an illumination? What is a missal?
2. How have book illustrations changed since the Middle Ages?

Lesson 7 *Book Illustration* **237**

Designing a Letter

After making a sketch for their letter, students will need to transfer it to their white drawing paper. By rubbing the pencil on the back of their sketch, they can make a carbon copy to use for transferring. Or, students may carefully cut out the sketched letter and draw around it on the white drawing paper.

Art in Everyday Life

Point out that illustrations can be found in most textbooks, newspapers, and magazines. Ask students to evaluate illustrations to determine whether they help communicate ideas.

• • • • • • • • • •
ASSESS

■ Self-Assessment

Have students complete the Check Your Understanding questions on this page. Answers are provided below.

■ Reteaching

Ask students to evaluate a map, poster, or drawing they created for a class. How was the visual effective?

■ Enrichment

Help students become aware of the numerous awards that exist for literature in children's book publishing.

• • • • • • • • • •
CLOSE

Have students choose a book that they think is beautifully and effectively illustrated. Have them explain why they chose that book.

LESSON 8

Creating a Book Cover

Despite what you may have heard, you *can* tell a book by its cover. For proof, examine the center portion of the quilt in Figure 12–16. It was used for a book cover. The group is having a "picnic" on the tar roof— the "tar beach"—of an apartment building in a big city. Notice how the illustration draws you right into the story. Do you think this art makes a good book cover?

WHAT YOU WILL LEARN

In this lesson, you will design a book cover of your own. Begin by finding a story or making one up. Then plan a cover design that will invite readers to pick up your book and read it. You will create the title and author's name in a type style that suits the story theme or topic. The colors used for the title and the author's name should contrast with the colors of the illustration. Complete a picture to fit your chosen theme or topic.

WHAT YOU WILL NEED

- Sketch paper and pencil
- Sheet of white drawing paper, 9 x 12 inches (23 x 30 cm)
- Sheet of colored construction paper
- Colored markers, crayons, or tempera paints and brushes
- Ruler

Figure 12–16 How would you describe the style of this artwork? How does the artist draw your attention to the figures?

Faith Ringgold. *Tar Beach.* 1988. Pieced and printed fabric. 188 × 175.3 cm (74 × 69"). Faith Ringgold, Inc. © Solomon Guggenheim Collection.

238 Chapter 12 *Telling a Story*

• • • • • • • • • • • • • •

FOCUS

☑ OBJECTIVES

After completing this lesson, students will be able to:
- Plan and design a book cover.
- Describe, analyze, interpret, and judge their book cover designs.

☑ SUPPLIES

- Pencils and sketch paper
- White drawing paper
- Colored construction paper
- Markers, crayons, or tempera paints and brushes
- Rulers, compasses
- Scissors, white glue

Resources

- 12-10 Faith Ringgold, TRB page 199 (artist profile)
- 12-11 For the Record, TRB page 200 (studio)

• • • • • • • • • • • • • •

TEACH

■ Motivator

Bring a copy of Faith Ringgold's book *Tar Beach* to class along with a selection of other books. Then ask students to choose at least one book that seems to invite them to read. Have students explain their choices.

■ Vocabulary

Reinforce the vocabulary introduced in this lesson. Ask students to point out different type *fonts* within this textbook. Have them bring in and point out additional fonts they find in other textbooks.

238

— *more about* • • • —

Book Illustration Bring in a large selection of illustrated books. Include children's picture books, intermediate story books, and books for older readers. Have students go through the books to critique each artist's style and evaluate how successfully the illustrations and text work together. Here are some suggested illustrators to look for:

Misumasa Anno
Molly Bang
Eric Carle
Tomie de Paola
Leo and Diane Dillon
Richard Eglieski
Lois Ehlert

Patricia Polacco
Jerry Pinkney
James Ransome
Uri Shulevitz
William Steig
John Steptoe
Chris Van Allsburgelinsky

- Compass
- Scissors
- White glue

WHAT YOU WILL DO

1. In the school library, examine several books. Notice the covers or book jackets. Pay attention to the cover illustration and to the **font**, or *typeface*. In what way does the font add to the impact of the illustration?
2. Choose a book that you like. The book may be a made-up story, like *Tar Beach*, or it may be a book about science or some other subject. If you prefer, you may make up a story and title.
3. Think of a picture that will attract readers to your book. Decide how large your picture will be. Will it fill the cover, as in *Tar Beach*, or will it fit into a smaller space? Make several sketches. Transfer your best sketch to a sheet of white drawing paper. Complete your illustration using markers, crayons, or tempera paints.
4. Think next about lettering styles for the title. Look through books for fonts that fit in with your story. If the story is humorous, you might choose rounded letters. A frightening story might call for tall, pointed letters.
5. Imitating the font you have chosen, carefully letter your title on colored construction paper. Choose a color that will stand out against your illustration. To control the height, measure and cut a strip from the construction paper about one inch wide. Draw the title on this strip. Use a ruler for the straight edges on letters such as *m* or *t*. Make the round parts of *p* and other letters by using a compass. Draw letters for the author's name in a similar fashion. These should be smaller than the title. Cut a half-inch-wide strip of construction paper to help

- **Describe**   What part of the story did you choose for the cover picture? What images appear in this illustration? What kind of font did you choose?
- **Analyze**   Does color of the lettering in your title stand out vividly against colors of the illustration? Is the author's name smaller than the title?
- **Interpret**   Does the font you chose fit the theme or message of your story? Is the message clear?
- **Judge**   Tell whether your book cover would draw readers in and why.

guide you. With scissors, cut out the letters when you have finished.
6. Organize the design of your book cover. Experiment placing the words in relation to the illustration. When you are satisfied, glue the words in place.

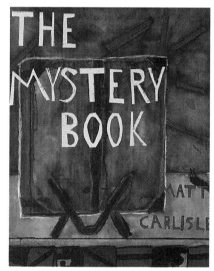

Figure 12–17   **Student work. A book cover.**

Lesson 8   *Creating a Book Cover*   **239**

Try This! COMPUTER OPTION

■ Select the Text tool in your program. Experiment with creating titles in different fonts and sizes. Choose different fill and outline colors for your wording. If your program has special effect filters, such as an Extrude command, try applying a filter.

MEETING SPECIAL NEEDS

Using the Computer   Students with disabilities in reading and writing will enjoy and may greatly benefit from using the computer to create special lettering effects. They can use different fonts in a variety of sizes and fill letters with colors and textures. The fusion of visual and verbal communication can have a powerful learning effect. Acquaint students who have visual disabilities with the computer's zoom function so they can see their work enlarged.

■ Studio Skills

Work on letter design by helping students measure and cut a 1 to 2-inch strip of paper, so the height of the letters will be uniform. Students can use rulers and compasses to achieve the straight and curved lines and shapes of the letters. Students can draw their illustration on a separate piece of paper and glue it in place, or they may draw directly on the cover paper. As students develop and execute their designs, remind them to keep the total composition of the page in mind.

■ Art Criticism

Have students study magazines, textbooks, and picture books for the format used. Have them look for the good use of space, margins, and placement of visuals. Tell them that good design applies to all text material, whether printed or on a computer screen.

• • • • • • • • • ASSESS

■ Self-Assessment
Have students use Examining Your Work to evaluate their art.

■ Reteaching
Ask students to evaluate their math and science or other textbook covers.

■ Enrichment
Bring library books to class that have received the Caldecott award for good design. Ask students to discuss what qualities in these books contributed to their award-winning design.

• • • • • • • • • CLOSE

Have students discuss how their study of book design may affect their reading choices in the future. Are they now more aware of different formats and styles? Will they look for well-designed books?

OBJECTIVES

After completing the feature, students will be able to:

- Describe how allegories are told in literature.
- Explain how allegories are presented in artwork.

Teaching the Connection

- Have students read the feature on this page.
- Ask volunteers to share what they know about allegories. What are some other life lessons that you learned in childhood? *(Answers will vary.)* What other symbolic literary forms are you familiar with? *(Fairy tale, fable, parable.)* What secondary allegory might Bruegel have intended by making Icarus' fall go unnoticed by the people in this painting? *(People are unaware of the world around them.)*
- Tell students that the legend of Icarus is a story from Greek mythology. Myths are narratives that explain how certain elements of a culture came into being. For example, a myth may describe the creation of humans and animals, the origins of the world, or the beginning of certain customs or activities.

Answers to Making the Connection

- Bruegel conveyed the tragedy of the story by showing only Icarus' legs in the water after he had fallen from the sky.
- Answers may include listen to your elders, don't be too ambitious, don't think that you know more than everyone else, don't think that you are invincible.
- Student examples will vary.

Pieter Bruegel. *Fall of Icarus.* c. 1555. Oil on canvas. 73.5 × 112 cm (29 × 44"). Musees Royaux des Beaux Arts de Belgique/The Bridgman Art Library, London.

What Is an Allegory?

When you were a child, your mother or father taught you many essential life lessons. "Look both ways before you cross the street," "Respect your elders," and "Don't talk to strangers." You also learned many other important truths in the stories you read.

In literature, these truths are often presented as allegories. An allegory is a narrative that conveys a symbolic meaning. This meaning is in addition to the literal meaning of the story. On the surface, for example, *Beauty and the Beast* is a love story. The underlying truth, however, could be summarized by the saying "You can't judge a book by its cover."

Allegories are also told in artwork. In *The Fall of Icarus,* Pieter Bruegel presented a classic myth. Look carefully and you will see the legend of Icarus. In this story, Icarus escaped from jail using wings made of wax. Although his father told him not to fly too close to the sun, Icarus ignored the warning. When Icarus flew near the sun, his wings melted and he fell to his death.

MAKING THE CONNECTION

- Describe how Bruegel conveyed the story of Icarus in this painting.
- What do you think is the lesson to be learned from the legend of Icarus?
- Find another example of allegory in literature or art. Describe the literal and symbolic meanings of the story.

INTERNET ACTIVITY

Visit Glencoe's Fine Arts Web Site for students at:

http://www.glencoe.com/sec/art/students

INTERNET ACTIVITY

Classrooms On-Line...   Experience working together and learning with other teachers and classrooms who use the Glencoe Fine Arts programs. Escape the walls of your classroom and connect with many teachers who are doing the same projects and who want to share their thoughts. Let us hear about your best ideas and share with others your successes. Promote the art and accomplishments of your own students. Find this connection within the *Teacher Resources* area of Glencoe's Fine Arts Site. Find links to kindred classrooms in this section of Glencoe's site to expand students' learning experiences. Find us at **http://www.glencoe.com/sec/art**

BUILDING VOCABULARY

Number a sheet of paper from 1 to 9. After each number, write the term from the box that matches each description below.

cartouche	gold leaf
cutaway	Kachina
embroidery	petroglyph
font	pictogram
fresco	

1. A very thin layer of gold glued to a surface for decoration.
2. A view in which an outside wall has been removed to reveal the scene within.
3. Typeface.
4. A symbolic rock carving or painting.
5. A painting created when pigment is applied to a section of wall spread with fresh plaster.
6. The art of making ornamental designs with needle and thread.
7. A hand-crafted statuette that represents spirits in Pueblo rituals.
8. An oval or oblong containing an important person's name.
9. A small picture that stands for a word or an idea.

REVIEWING ART FACTS

Number a sheet of paper from 10 to 15. Answer each question in one or two complete sentences.

10. What is a hieroglyphic? When did ancient Egyptian hieroglyphic come into being?
11. How old are Native American petroglyphs?
12. How is the dragon viewed in the culture of the Chinese?
13. What are Kachinas believed to represent?
14. From what language does the word *fresco* come? What does it mean in that language?
15. Why were illuminations common in the Middle Ages?

THINKING ABOUT ART

On a sheet of paper, answer each question in a sentence or two.

1. **Compare and contrast.** The cartouche in Figure 12–2 and the petroglyph in Figure 12–3 have many similarities. Yet, in many ways, the objects are different. What are some of these ways?
2. **Synthesize.** How has the art of visual storytelling changed from earliest times through the present?

MAKING ART CONNECTIONS

1. **Language Arts.** With the school librarian's help, find the poem "Ganesha, Ganesh" by Myra Cohn Livingston, "Dragon" by Karla Kuskin, or another such poem. Compare the poem's subject and meaning with what you learned in the chapter about such mythical creatures. Share your findings with the class, along with a reading of the poem you chose.

2. **Technology.** Computers have had an impact not only on book production but on book illustration as well. Speak with a teacher in your school's computer department or, if possible, with a local computer artist. Find out from this expert about advances in book illustration. Share the information with classmates, along with any tips you pick up.

Chapter 12 Review **241**

ANSWERS TO CHAPTER 12 REVIEW

■ Building Vocabulary

1. gold leaf
2. cutaway
3. font
4. petroglyph
5. fresco
6. embroidery
7. Kachina
8. cartouche
9. pictogram

■ Reviewing Art Facts

10. A hieroglyphic is a form of picture writing. The ancient Egyptians perfected their hieroglyphics about 3,000 years ago.
11. Many are thought to be about 10,000 years old.
12. It is seen as an object of good luck.
13. They are thought to embody spirits who once dwelled among the Pueblo.
14. The word is Italian for "fresh."
15. This was a time when many people were unable to read. The illuminated books served as a source of information to these people.

? THINKING ABOUT ART

1. The two are products of different ancient cultures. The petroglyph is significantly older. The petroglyph is almost entirely pictorial, whereas the hieroglyph borders on alphabetic characters.

2. Answers will vary. Students might mention the influences of technology and changes in styles of art. They might also identify different uses for storytelling pictures, such as the use of such works as book illustrations.

Celebrations

(pages 242–261)

Resources

- **13-11 Chapter Test,** TRB page 221
- **Transparency CC-13** *Music in the Plaza* by John Sloan
- **Transparency 13** *Luncheon of the Boating Party* by Auguste Renoir
- **Fine Art Print 19** *In Celebration* by Sam Gilliam

Music

While studying this chapter, use Performing Arts Handbook page 325 to understand how people use the arts as a powerful way to honor an event.

NATIONAL STANDARDS

This chapter addresses the following National Standards for the Visual Arts:

1. (a, b)　　**4.** (a, b, c)
2. (a, b, c)　**5.** (a, b, c)
3. (a, b)　　**6.** (a, b)

242

Figure 13–1 **Notice the title of this painting. Do you know when and for what a maypole was used?**

William Glakens. *May Day, Central Park.* c. 1905. Oil on canvas. 63.8 × 76.8 cm (25⅛ × 30¼″). The Fine Arts Museums of San Francisco, California. Gift of the Charles E. Merrill Trust with matching funds from The de Young Museum Society.

FEATURED ARTISTS

Thomas Hart Benton
Everald Brown
Bing Davis
Carmen Lomas Garza
William Glackens
Alfred Cornelius Howland

Fred Kabotie
Rie Muñoz
James Phillips
Faith Ringgold
Antonio M. Ruiz

CHAPTER 13

Celebrations

What do you think of when you hear the word *celebration*? If you are like most people, you probably picture festive food, smiling faces, and lively activity. Songs and dances may be part of the image as well.

The painting on the facing page reveals that some of these features were common in celebrations a century ago. Examine this painting. What is being celebrated? Where is the celebration taking place? What is the mood? How are the participants dressed?

In this chapter, you will learn about the ways in which artists have recorded celebrations through the ages. You will glimpse visual celebrations of many cultures.

PORTFOLIO IDEAS

A portfolio can serve a number of purposes. The work you include will demonstrate what you have done and how you did it. Written self-reflections and evaluations help you define goals and recognize achievements. A teacher may use your portfolio to evaluate your progress too. In any case, a portfolio is evidence of your participation, understanding, and growth as an artist.

OBJECTIVES

After completing this chapter, you will be able to:

- Identify media and methods artists have used to capture celebrations.
- Describe how artists of different periods and places have depicted celebrations.
- Create several works of art that focus on celebrations.

WORDS YOU WILL LEARN

adenla
kinetic art
pueblo
seal
shadow puppet
tricolor

DEVELOPING A PORTFOLIO

Rubrics for Assessment When using a rubric to assess assignments or a portfolio, it is meaningful to have more than one reviewer. If you have two or three people review the work independently, then come together to determine what student work looks like at each level of the rubric, you have set *benchmarks*. Benchmarks for specific assignments or portfolios offer concrete examples for students at each level of the rubric. You need a large pool of student work to make this effective. For more information on the use of rubrics for portfolios, refer to the separate booklet, *Portfolio and Assessment Techniques* that accompanies the *Introducing Art* program.

Holiday Celebrations

• • • • • • • • • • • • •

FOCUS

☑ OBJECTIVES

After completing this lesson, students will be able to:

• Recognize that artists depict holiday celebrations to capture the emotions and the setting of the event.
• Create a flag for a group or event using simple repeated colors and shapes.

☑ SUPPLIES

• Pencils
• White paper
• Assorted sizes and colors of construction paper
• Scissors, white glue
• Markers

Resources

• ■ 13-1 Happy Holiday!, TRB page 207 (appreciating cultural diversity)
• ■ 13-2 Critique of a Celebration, TRB page 209 (art criticism)

• • • • • • • • • • • • •

TEACH

■ Motivator

Ask students to identify their favorite holiday. Ask if there are any months that do not have a patriotic, religious, or seasonal event celebrated by different groups of people. Direct student attention to the two artworks. Both are Independence Day pictures. Ask: What similarities and differences are apparent?

Every culture around the world celebrates holidays. Some holiday celebrations are joyous occasions. They are marked by parades, decorations, and possibly the exchange of gifts. Other holidays are times of solemn remembrance.

One common link among all holiday celebrations is the frequency with which they have turned up through the centuries as art subjects. In this lesson, you will examine two such artworks. Both celebrate a single holiday as it is observed in two different cultures.

HOLIDAY ART

If you look up *celebrate* in a dictionary, you discover that the word has many meanings. One of these is "to give thanks for." The painting that opened this chapter depicts a holiday event that is all but forgotten in our own country. That event is the giving of thanks for the coming of spring. The holiday is May Day.

Art Celebrating American Independence

A "thanksgiving" of a different sort is pictured in Figure 13–2. The subject is obvious from the title. The setting is a small New England town. Even without glancing at the credit line, you can probably guess the year this work was done. The clothing styles and presence of horse-drawn vehicles offer clues.

Take a moment to study this painting. Notice how the artist has used lighter color values to focus the viewer's attention on the parade. A careful inspection reveals that this is no well-disciplined, uniformed marching band. Rather, it is a random gathering of

Figure 13–2   What colorful associations do you have with the holiday shown in this painting? Would you describe this work as realistic?

Alfred C. Howland. *The Fourth of July*. 1886. Oil on canvas. 60.8 × 91.6 cm (24 × 36⅛"). High Museum of Art, Atlanta, Georgia. Gift of Life Insurance Company of Georgia in celebration of the Nation's Bicentennial.

244   Chapter 13   *Celebrations*

more about • • •

Ruiz's *School Children on Parade*   The setting of this painting is the town of Tepetlaoxtoc, whose name appears on the flag with the portrait of Miguel Hidalgo Costilla, the priest who first declared Mexican independence from Spain in 1810. A gazebo repeats the same light colors of the parade and of the buildings in the background. This emphasizes the main feature of the event—the parade. Ruiz loves to include contrasts. Notice the European dress of the boy on the bike on the right and the blue dress of the woman on the left.

townspeople. They are simply bound to-gether by their patriotic spirit and the steady boom of the bass drums. What mood or feel-ing does this work bring to mind?

Art Celebrating Mexican Independence

Compare the style and subject matter of Figure 13–2 with those of the picture on this page. This work, too, celebrates Independence Day—in this case, Mexico's. Like the painting at the left, the centerpiece of this one is a pa-rade. Unlike Figure 13–2, the marchers in this work are schoolchildren. All are dressed in white, and each carries a miniature Mexican **tricolor** (try-kuhl-uhr). This is *a flag with three broad bands of color.* In stark contrast to the chil-dren's costumes is the black suit worn by the man leading the procession. Who do you sup-pose he is? Note the serious expressions on the people's faces. What do these suggest about the tone or mood of the celebration?

Check Your Understanding

1. How does the artist of Figure 13–2 draw your attention to the parade?
2. What difference in mood do you detect be-tween the paintings in Figures 13–2 and 13–3?

STUDIO ACTIVITY

Making a Tricolor

Design a tricolor to represent your class, school, or community. Choose colors with symbolic value. Use red, for example, for courage, blue for loyalty. Begin with a 9 x 12-inch (23 x 30-cm) sheet of paper. Divide it into three geo-metric shapes—squares, circles, rec-tangles, triangles, or a combination. Measure and cut from colored construc-tion paper the three shapes in the colors of your choice. Using white glue, attach these so as to fill the sheet of drawing paper. Complete your flag by creating an official **seal**—a *symbolic image or emblem*—on a sheet of white paper. Color the seal with markers. Cut it out and glue it to the center of your tricolor.

PORTFOLIO

Write a short paragraph describ-ing what your tricolor symbolizes and what each color stands for. Put the paragraph in your portfolio along with the tricolor.

Figure 13–3 What art principle is used to organize this painting? What art elements does it control?

Antonio M. Ruiz. *School Children on Parade.* 1936. Oil on canvas. 24 × 33.8 cm (9½ × 13¼"). The Metropolitan Museum of Art. Secretaria de Hacienda y Credito Publico, Mexico City, Mexico.

Lesson 1 *Holiday Celebrations* **245**

LESSON 2

Creating an "Event" Quilt

(pages 246–247)

LESSON TIME: 10 hours

• • • • • • • • • • • • • •
FOCUS

☑ OBJECTIVES

After completing this lesson, students will be able to:

• Create a quilt square and border from fabric, then work together with classmates to assemble the quilt.

• Describe, analyze, interpret, and judge their artwork.

☑ SUPPLIES

• Pencils and sketch paper
• Assorted scraps of fabric
• Fabric squares
• Fabric glue or hot glue gun
• Needles and thread
• Fabric paint
• Assorted colors of felt

Resource

■ 13-3 Mix and Match, TRB page 210 (aesthetics/art criticism)

• • • • • • • • • • • • • •
TEACH

■ Motivator

Ask students to describe what they know about quilts: how they are made, what they are used for, what kind of art they represent. Ask them to tell what a quilting bee is. Explain that quilts were traditionally created as bedcoverings, but many have evolved into outstanding examples of folk art.

■ Vocabulary

Ask students if they can think of another kind of "bee" other than the kind that buzz *(spelling bee)*.

246

Creating an "Event" Quilt

The painting you looked at in Figure 13–2 celebrates a milestone in the growth of our nation. The work in Figure 13–4 celebrates *eight* such milestones. On the surface, the painting shows a simple and distinctly American pastime—a quilting bee. Eight women appear seated around the quilt they have sewn. A deeper meaning begins to form when the viewer learns the identities of these individuals. The figure in the blue suit at the center is Harriet Tubman. The person in the polka-dot dress to her left is Rosa Parks. What personal sacrifices did these women make? What did they fight for?

WHAT YOU WILL LEARN

A quilt is a fitting symbol for the contributions of people who are working together in a group effort. With classmates, you will make a quilt that celebrates an important group effort you or others in your community have made. Working alone, each of you will create a quilt square from fabric scraps and paint. This will help introduce variety. All the pieces will then be glued or sewn together. You will complete your quilt by creating a large frame or border that adds harmony and unifies the work, as in Figure 13–4.

Figure 13–4 How has the artist added harmony to this busy painting? How has she introduced variety? Can you appreciate why this scene is an impossible one?

Faith Ringgold. #4 *The Sunflowers Quilting Bee at Arles.* 1991. Acrylic on canvas, pieced fabric border. 188 × 203.2 cm (74 × 80″). Faith Ringgold Inc., © Oprah Winfrey Collection.

246   Chapter 13   *Celebrations*

— *more about* • • • —

Ringgold's Quilting Bee   Ask students to study Figure 13-4 in detail. Ringgold comments on the way many male artists work alone, while women quilters work together as a team. Prominent women in black history are portrayed: (left to right) Madame Walker, Sojourner Truth, Ida B. Wells, Fannie Lou Hamer, Harriet Tubman, Rosa Parks, Mary McLeod Bethune, Ella Baker, and standing alone in the field—Vincent van Gogh. Have volunteers choose one of the women pictured and report on her role in black history.

WHAT YOU WILL NEED

- Sketch paper and pencil
- Assorted scraps of fabric
- Fabric pieces (to be the basis for the quilt)
- Fabric glue or fusible webbing
- Needle and thread
- Fabric paint

WHAT YOU WILL DO

1. With group members, brainstorm an event to celebrate. Possibilities include a successful school fund-raising drive, a cleanup campaign, or an effort to save a local park.

2. After choosing an event, select colors and materials that reflect the theme and help create the mood. For example, you might choose green and blue for a Save the Earth campaign.

3. Working by yourself, make several pencil sketches for a quilt square. Look through the fabric pieces to see if any of the designs suggest ideas. Decide whether you will cut out figures and objects or use shapes and symbols to tell about the theme.

4. Using your best sketch as a guide, cut out shapes from a variety of fabrics. Arrange and overlap these on a piece of fabric. Attach the shapes using either fabric glue, fusible webbing, or needle and thread.

5. Decide if a title will be part of the entire quilt design. Letters may be cut from felt or fabric. The letters could be accented with hand sewn stitches or fabric paint.

6. Stitch all the quilt squares together. Make an overall border for the entire quilt out of fabric scraps.

EXAMINING YOUR WORK

- **Describe** Identify the objects and figures in your quilt square. Identify the event the quilt celebrates.
- **Analyze** Explain how you organized the art elements in your quilt to create harmony, variety, and unity.
- **Interpret** Explain how your square helps capture the event. Describe the mood and idea your square communicates.
- **Judge** Were you successful in creating a quilt that celebrates an event?

Figure 13–5 Student work. Quilt: Four seasons in Western New York.

 STUDIO OPTION

■ Make a paper quilt that tells a story. Choose a favorite story or historical event. Choose colors and textures to emphasize the idea and mood. Use a variety of paper media, including construction paper, butcher paper, foil, tissue, and wallpaper. Cut out and layer shapes, symbols, or objects that relate to your story. Imitate cross-stitches by drawing parallel diagonal lines or X's with pen or paint.

SAFETY TIP

Using a Glue Gun If you choose to use a glue gun for this Studio Lesson, be certain to caution students about the safe use of this appliance. Supervise the location and use of the hot glue and make sure students understand that they must be extremely careful or risk burning themselves. Follow the manufacturer's directions carefully. If using fusible interfacing, show students how to place it between two layers of fabric and use the iron to fuse the fabrics.

■ Art History

Have students research the history of quilts in this country, and find out what styles and designs were common. Have them discover which are considered important artworks and why.

■ Studio Skills

Have students brainstorm ideas for a commemorative quilt. Help students decide on the size of the overall quilt and compute the size of the individual sections and the width of border needed.

Art on a Shoestring

Contact local fabric stores or clothes manufacturers for possible donations of fabric remnants. If possible, invite a local quilter in to give students some practical advice.

•••••••••••••••
ASSESS

■ Self-Assessment

Have students use Examining Your Work to evaluate their art.

■ Reteaching

Ask students to identify the objects and figures in each other's quilt sections.

■ Enrichment

Bring in books from the library that show some of the many quilting patterns that exist. Have students choose a geometric pattern and reproduce one quilting square using a medium of their choice. Display the squares as individual wall hangings.

•••••••••••••••
CLOSE

Have students write a brief summary of what they think the group's quilt communicates.

• • • • • • • • • • • • • •
FOCUS

☑ OBJECTIVES

After completing this lesson, students will be able to:

• Recognize the role of dance and artistic interpretations of dances in important celebrations.

• Draw a gesture drawing of a group of dancers.

☑ SUPPLIES

• Pencils and sketch paper
• Tape or CD player
• Tapes or CD's
• Percussion instruments or found objects to create sound (optional)

Resource

■ 13-4 Shall We Dance?
TRB page 211 (appreciating cultural diversity)

• • • • • • • • • • • • • •
TEACH

■ Motivator

Engage students in a discussion of current dance styles. What kinds of dances do they like to do? Explain that in some cultures, dances are featured in important rituals and celebrations. Direct students' attention to Figure 13-6. Ask: What kind of music do you think the people hear? Compare this dance to that shown in Figure 13-7. How does Brown represent rhythm in this painting? *(Through use of lines, shapes, and color.)*

LESSON 3

Celebration Dances in Art

Does your school sponsor dances? Maybe a youth or social club in your community does. With few exceptions, such events in our society are leisure-time activities. Yet, in some cultures, dance plays a featured role in important celebrations.

In this lesson, you will explore two such celebrations. You will view artistic interpretations of dances that are part of these events.

A NATURE DANCE

Most of our dances are recreational. A few, however, have some special meaning. The opposite is true for the Hopi people of the American Southwest. In their culture, only a small number of dances are considered social events. The majority occupy an important place in rituals celebrating their people's oneness with nature.

One of these, the Green Corn Dance, is pictured in Figure 13–6. Examine this painting. Did you find your eye drawn to the sweeping curve formed by the ceremonial procession on the right side? The people in this line are the dancers. They are dressed in traditional clothing. Within the semi-circle is a second, smaller group that includes a drummer. Notice the dancers' upright posture. What does their body language suggest or tell about the *tempo,* or speed, of the music? Find the figure in the feathered headdress standing atop the **pueblo** (**pweh**-bloh), or *dried-clay dwelling.* Who do you think this person is?

A VICTORY DANCE

Some dances, like the one in Figure 13–6, are calm and dignified. Others are fast-paced and frenzied. How would you characterize

Figure 13–6 What do you think is the purpose of this dance? What role do the repetition of colors and forms and the use of vertical lines play in creating the painting's mood?

Fred Kaboti. *Pueblo Green Corn Dance, Hopi.* 1947. Oil on canvas. 75 × 64.8 cm (29½ × 25½"). The Thomas Gilcrease Institute of American History and Art, Tulsa, Oklahoma.

248   Chapter 13   *Celebrations*

MEETING SPECIAL NEEDS

Dance Gestures   When having students pose in dancing positions in front of the class, be sure to include as models students in wheelchairs or those with other disabilities such as vision or hearing problems. Urge students to show feelings of joy through their body positions and facial expressions. Dancing is an activity in which everyone should have the opportunity to participate; it does not necessarily have to be limited to those who have full use of their bodies.

the dance pictured in Figure 13–7? Without looking at the title, you can probably sense the joyous mood and high energy level of the dancers. The painting captures a part of a victory celebration in the artist's native island of Jamaica. Can you think of a dance or "ball" with a similar purpose in our own country?

Look closely at this painting. It is divided into three main sections. The top and bottom thirds of the picture plane are given over to musicians in brightly colored costumes. At the center are the dancers, framed against a field of vivid orange. Observe how the angled lines of their arms, legs, and bodies help convey a strong sense of urgent movement. Notice the array of bold colors that make up the buildings and plant life. What art principle has the artist used to control the many colors and shapes in this action-filled painting?

Check Your Understanding

1. What do most Hopi dances celebrate?
2. What event is the focus of the painting in Figure 13–7?

STUDIO ACTIVITY

Dance Gesture Drawing

Work with a group of about six classmates to learn and perform a popular dance step. The group is to repeat the same movements over and over. While they perform, the remainder of the class is to make individual gesture drawings of the event. Sketching rapidly in pencil, the students should try to capture the sense of movement, paying close attention to the angles of arms and legs. After completing their sketches, a second group of volunteers should perform the same step to allow the dancers to do their own gesture drawings.

portfolio

Write an evaluation of your gesture drawings. Did they capture movement? Were they in proportion? Put your critique in your portfolio with your drawings.

Figure 13–7 Would you describe this treatment as realistic? Has the artist used linear perspective or any of the other space-giving techniques described in Chapter 1?

Everald Brown. *Victory Dance.* 1976. Oil on canvas. 83.8 × 124.5 cm (33 × 49"). Organization of American States Museum, Washington, D.C. Collection of the Art Museum of the Americas.

Aesthetics

Both paintings shown in this lesson are about dances and celebrations, but each is different. Ask students which painting they would buy and where they would hang it. Have them explain their choices.

Art History

The *Pueblo Green Corn Dance* shows a traditional Hopi dance. Have students research other dance rituals and celebrations of Native American groups, such as the *Buffalo Dance, Rain Dance, War Dance,* and the *Hoop Dance.* Then have students investigate the dances of Jamaica and share what they find out.

Cooperative Learning

Have students work in groups of 5 or 6 so that they can share resources and ideas. Have students create a mood for the celebration they enact—using music, instruments, and found objects to create sound and rhythm—and share their dance with the class.

• • • • • • • • • • • • • •
ASSESS

Self-Assessment

Have students complete the Check Your Understanding questions on this page. Answers are provided below.

Reteaching

Have students find examples of movement in either of the paintings in the lesson.

Enrichment

Encourage students to research dance and music celebrations of other cultures.

Lesson 3 *Celebration Dances in Art* **249**

• • • • • • • • • • • • • •
CLOSE

Have students explain the role of dance as an art form and as a means of celebration.

Answers to ✔ CHECK YOUR UNDERSTANDING

1. Most Hopi dances celebrate their people's sense of "oneness" with nature.

2. The focus of the painting in Figure 13-7 is a victory celebration on the artist's native island of Jamaica.

• • • • • • • • • • • • • • •
FOCUS

☑ OBJECTIVES

After completing this lesson, students will be able to:

• Design and create a piece of kinetic art for a festival.

• Describe, analyze, interpret, and judge their artwork.

☑ SUPPLIES

• Pencils and sketch paper
• Tagboard
• Pens, watercolors, or markers
• Brushes
• Scissors
• Hole punch, book brads
• String or thin wooden dowels

Resource

☐ 13-5 A Celebration!, TRB page 213 (cooperative learning)

• • • • • • • • • • • • • • •
TEACH

■ Motivator

Have students make a list on the board of festivals they know about or have studied. Ask students to share their experiences with festivals. Ask students to examine the fish in Figure 13-8. Have them imagine the festival associated with such a colorful creature.

Creating Kinetic "Festival" Art

The Pueblo Green Corn Dance in Figure 13–6 is an ingredient in a Hopi *festival*. Festivals are colorful events that include food, music, dancing, and other forms of entertainment. They are celebrated in every culture. The purpose of some festivals is to usher in a new year. Others are meant to ensure a bountiful harvest.

No festival would be complete without live performances. The "performer" in Figure 13–8 is a **shadow puppet.** This is *an art object in the shape of an animal or human attached to a wand or stick.* Shadow puppets are popular throughout much of Asia, where they are featured in special events known as *shadow dances.* In these events, the puppets are made to sway gracefully to and fro behind a screen on which a bright light has been trained. Each figure appears to be dancing with its shadowy partner. Can you guess the type of festival to which this art object relates?

WHAT YOU WILL LEARN

Shadow puppets are an example of **kinetic** (kuh-**net**-ik) **art.** This is *an art style in which parts of a work are set into motion by a form of energy.* In this lesson, you will design and create your own piece of kinetic art for a festival. You will begin by deciding what form your art object will take. Then you will create the object out of tagboard. You will add visual texture to emphasize a specific part. You will repeat lines or shapes to create rhythm, as in Figure 13–8.

Figure 13–8 What kind of balance is exhibited by the fish's head? Where in this object has the artist used the principle of repetition?

China. *Fish Shadow Puppet.* c. 1900. Leather with color. 13.5 × 30.5 cm (5⅜ × 12"). Museum of International Folk Art, a unit of The Museum of New Mexico, Santa Fe, New Mexico. The Girard Foundation Collection.

250   Chapter 13   *Celebrations*

CURRICULUM CONNECTIONS

Social Studies   All across the United States, there are thousands of festivals held throughout the year. Many such festivals feature arts and crafts, ethnic celebrations, harvest days, food fests, music and dance performances, puppetry, and plays. Some regional festivals feature food, music, arts, and crafts that are unique to that area.

Encourage students to research some of the many festivals that contribute to the fabric of the country and to locate on a map where they are held. One source they might use is *Festivals U.S.A.* by Kathleen Thompson Hill (N.Y.: John Wiley & Sons, 1988).

WHAT YOU WILL NEED
- Sketch paper and pencil
- Sheet of tagboard, 14 x 22 inches (35.6 x 56 cm)
- Pens, watercolors, or markers
- Brushes
- Scissors
- Hole punch, book brads
- String or wooden dowel ¼ inch (6 mm) or less in diameter

WHAT YOU WILL DO
1. With classmates, brainstorm a list of joyous festivals. Exchange information on animal shapes and other images associated with these festivals.
2. Working alone, choose a festival. Make several sketches of an image connected with it. The image should be one that has potential for a kinetic art project. This might be a shadow puppet, a kite, or a lantern. Your object should have at least two parts, such as a body and tail (see Figure 13–8). Arms, legs, and a head are other possibilities.
3. Transfer your best sketch to tagboard. Draw outline shapes for all of the parts of your object. Fill as much of the surface as possible. Add details and color with pens, watercolors, or markers. Cover the entire surface of each part with color. Repeat lines and shapes to create a rhythmic pattern. Emphasize one part by introducing visual texture.
4. With scissors, carefully cut all parts out of the tagboard. Use a hole punch to make holes at the points where the parts will be joined. Use book brads to attach the parts. Make an additional hole in either the top

EXAMINING YOUR WORK
- **Describe** Identify the type of kinetic art you have created. Indicate the energy source—the wind or muscle power, for example.
- **Analyze** Tell whether you repeated lines and shapes to create a rhythmic pattern. Point to a part you emphasized by adding visual texture.
- **Interpret** Explain how the art object will be used. State whether it expresses the joyous mood of the festival.
- **Judge** Explain whether your artwork is successful. Tell whether the parts move freely.

or bottom of your creation. Tie string through this hole if your object is to be hung. Insert a wooden dowel as support if your object is a shadow puppet.
5. Share your work with classmates. Can they identify the festival you have chosen?

Figure 13–9 **Student work. Shadow puppet.**

Try This! COMPUTER OPTION

■ Use the Rectangle and Oval tools in your program to create outline shapes for body parts of a fish or other creature. Fill each shape with a bright, festive hue. If your software offers gradient fills, use these to create shading. Place the parts in their proper locations with respect to one another. In a free area of the screen, create a small shape in a contrasting color. Using the Duplicate or Copy and Paste commands, create many copies of the shape. Arrange these in a pattern. Group or select all the shapes and place them over the body of your creature.

Lesson 4 *Creating Kinetic "Festival" Art* **251**

• • • • • • • • • • • • • •
FOCUS

☑ OBJECTIVES

After completing this lesson, students will be able to:

* Recognize that rites of passage are celebrations of special achievements or honors.
* Understand the purpose of headdresses used in coming-of-age rituals.

☑ SUPPLIES

* Assorted construction paper or tagboard
* Construction paper scraps
* Beads, trims, lace, yarn, and small found objects
* Scissors, white glue

Resources

* ■ 13-6 Custom of the Country, TRB page 214 (art history)
* ■ 13-7 Art for a Special Occasion, TRB page 216 (reproducible master)

• • • • • • • • • • • • • •
TEACH

■ Motivator

Ask students what age they would like to be if they could be older. What additional privileges would they have at that age? Explain that the Chinese Coming of Age Hat is simply earned by growing older. The *adenla*, on the other hand, can only be worn by someone born into a royal family.

252

 LESSON 5

Celebrating Rites of Passage

Of all the events you celebrate, probably none is more special to you than the anniversary of the day you were born. On your birthday, *you* are the "celebrity." Friends and loved ones gather around you. Bearing presents and good wishes, they help you celebrate your passage into another year of life.

The special quality of birthdays and other "passages" is not lost on artists. In this lesson, you will look at two art objects celebrating rites, or ceremonies, of passage.

RITE OF PASSAGE ART

What do you plan to be when you grow up? This is a question you probably have been asked many times. You may have asked it of yourself as well. Growing into adulthood is a big step. With it comes more privileges and more responsibilities. Many cultures observe this "coming of age" with a special celebration. Graduating, obtaining a driver's license, and being able to vote are examples of coming of age that bring a feeling of excitement and a desire to celebrate.

Chinese Rite of Passage Object

In some cultures, rites of passage include the wearing of special articles of clothing. One such article appears in Figure 13–10. Did you recognize this colorful creation as a hat? In China, it is a tradition—and an honor—to wear a hat like this on the birthday marking one's passage into adulthood. You may be reminded of the paper hats you wore at birthday parties when you were younger.

Figure 13–10 Color helps create visual interest in this object. What other art elements contribute?

China. *Coming of Age Hat.* Mixed media, embroidery. 31 × 38 cm (12 × 15″). Private collection.

252 Chapter 13 *Celebrations*

― *more about* • • • ―

Birthday Hats Many cultures celebrate the age of puberty, about twelve or thirteen years old, as the "coming-of-age" period of time for young people. This is the time when they pass from childhood to adulthood, learning to accept the responsibilities that face adults.

In the Chinese hat in Figure 13-10, point out the elaborate stitchery and symbols used, including good luck charms and wishes. Ask students to compare this hat with birthday or other customs from their own ethnic or religious background.

Figure 13–11 What kinds of shapes appear throughout this object? How would you describe the colors that have been used? What steps has the artist taken to achieve harmony?

Africa. Yoruba. *King's Crown (adenla).* c. 1930. Bamboo framework, beads, cloth, leather. H: 50.8 cm plus 58.4 cm beaded fringe (20″ plus 23″ fringe). Diameter: 31 cm (12″). The Saint Louis Museum of Art, St. Louis, Missouri. Purchase: Museum Shop Fund.

Examine this festive object. It has been richly embroidered with beads. Notice the attention to detail. Who do you suppose the human figures toward the base of the hat might be?

African Rite of Passage Object

The custom of wearing a birthday hat in China is widespread. The "hat" in Figure 13–11, by contrast, is worn by a chosen few. This object is an adenla (uh-**den**-luh), or

STUDIO ACTIVITY

Making a Hat

Design a hat or headdress for a special event in your own life. Begin by cutting a circle from construction paper and then cutting a slit from the outer edge to the center. Pull together the "flaps" on either side of the cut to make a cone. Fasten with staples or transparent tape. Decorate your hat with beads, lace, and other found objects that convey the theme and mood of your chosen event.

 PORTFOLIO

In a written paragraph, evaluate how well your hat or headdress reflects the theme and mood of the event. Add the paragraph and a photograph of the hat to your portfolio.

"King's Crown." It was created by an artist of the Yoruba people of West Africa. An **adenla** is *a sculpted ceremonial headdress used in rites of passage.* The privilege of wearing an adenla is reserved for royalty.

As you study this object, take note of the bird-like figure at the top. Many Yoruban adenla are decorated with woodpeckers. These are symbolic of the class structure— the "pecking order"—in this West African society. The long beaded threads extending from the brim form a *veil* of sorts. The purpose is not to protect the new king from curious glances. Rather, it is to force his own gaze inward, to remind him of his obligation to serve his people well.

Check Your Understanding

1. Identify similarities and differences between Figures 13–10 and 13–11.
2. What is an adenla?

Lesson 5 *Celebrating Rites of Passage* **253**

■ Vocabulary

Have students look up the word *rite* in a dictionary and give examples of rites they are familiar with in their daily lives.

■ Aesthetics

Both hats pictured in this lesson took time and skill to make and were made for important ceremonies. Ask students if they think these hats would be as valuable if they were made for everyday wear instead. Have them explain why or why not.

• • • • • • • • • • • •
ASSESS

■ Self-Assessment

Have students complete the Check Your Understanding questions on this page. Answers are provided below.

■ Reteaching

Have students brainstorm rituals that celebrate or honor other achievements.

■ Enrichment

Headdresses are part of many different rituals and ceremonies in many cultures. Have students research the role and significance of the headdress in a different ritual, such as weddings, or in another rite of passage ritual. Have them choose a ritual from a culture they may be unfamiliar with.

• • • • • • • • • • • •
CLOSE

Ask students to explain the significance of an *adenla* to a young person in Nigeria.

Answers to ✔ CHECK YOUR UNDERSTANDING

1. The two headdresses are similar in that they both are worn on the head during a special ceremony. They are different in the media used, design, and in that one is worn by many, the other is worn by only a chosen few.

2. An *adenla* is a special, sculpted ceremonial headdress used in rites of passage. The privilege of wearing an adenla is reserved for royalty.

• • • • • • • • • • • • •
FOCUS

☑ OBJECTIVES

After completing this lesson, students will be able to:

• Make a collage that celebrates a special family gathering.

• Describe, analyze, interpret, and judge their collages.

☑ SUPPLIES

• Sturdy cardboard or tagboard sheets

• Photographs and assorted found objects

• White drawing paper

• Colored construction paper

• White glue or glue sticks, scissors

• Colored, felt-tip markers

Resources

▪ 13-8 Carmen Lomas Garza, TRB page 217 (artist profile)

▪ 13-9 In the Swing, TRB page 218 (studio)

• • • • • • • • • • • • •
TEACH

▪ Motivator

Ask students to describe what is going on in the painting in Figure 13-12. Discuss how students celebrate birthdays in their families. Ask them to think of other family gatherings that are memorable to them.

 LESSON 6

Collage of a Family Gathering

Study the painting in Figure 13–12. You don't have to speak Spanish to know that *cumpleaños*, the first word in the title, means "birthday." The frosted, decorated cakes and festively wrapped presents on the table are dead giveaways. Notice the blindfolded child in the pink party dress waving a stick. Do you know what game she and the other children are playing? Can you guess what treasures await inside the blue fish piñata suspended from a tree branch?

Like the birthday parties you may have attended, this one is a family gathering.

Notice the grownups and children who form a circle around the center of attention. Even the family dog is on hand to take part in the celebration.

WHAT YOU WILL LEARN

You will make a collage that celebrates a special family gathering. Your collage will use a variety of objects and materials. These will include items that help recall and identify the gathering, such as photographs and souvenirs. You will use size and color contrast to add variety to your composition.

Figure 13–12 **What reason may the artist have had for placing the figures at this celebration in a circle? What symbolic meaning can you attach to this shape?**

Carmen Lomas Garza. *Cumpleanos de Lala y Tudi (Lala's and Tudi's Birthday Party)*. 1989. Oil on canvas. 91.4 × 122 cm (36 × 48"). Private collection.

 MEETING STUDENT DIVERSITY

Celebrations Around the World Students can provide a wealth of information on the beliefs and practices of other cultures by drawing on their own family experiences. Lead a class discussion on celebrations from various cultures that students participate in. Discuss the origins and cultural significance of these events. How are they similar or different from celebrations of other cultures? Suggest that students bring in photographs or other items used in these celebrations to share with the class. Interested students might research celebrations not covered in class and present their findings in an illustrated oral report.

WHAT YOU WILL NEED

- Photographs and assorted found objects
- Sheet of sturdy cardboard or tagboard, 18 x 24 inches (46 x 61 cm)
- White glue
- Colored felt-tip markers
- Sheets of white drawing paper
- Sheets of colored construction paper
- Scissors

WHAT YOU WILL DO

1. Choose a memorable family gathering as the subject of your collage. It may be a birthday celebration, as in Figure 13–12, or some other event. If you like, you may focus on an event involving your "family" at school, such as a class party.
2. Collect snapshots and other objects that help to recall the event. These might include a program from a grade-school graduation ceremony or a birthday card.
3. Arrange the materials you have gathered on a sheet of cardboard or tagboard. As a way of adding variety, try placing larger objects next to smaller ones, brighter-hued pieces next to duller ones. Leave some negative space between objects. When you are pleased with your composition, glue the objects in place.

EXAMINING YOUR WORK

- **Describe** Identify the materials you used for your collage. Point to hand-lettered words and phrases that you added.
- **Analyze** Did you place objects of contrasting sizes and colors side by side to add variety?
- **Interpret** What is the theme of your collage? Write a paragraph about the event.
- **Judge** Does your collage successfully convey that the event was a family celebration? What would you change?

4. Think of single words and short phrases that capture the theme of the event. For a graduation or confirmation, the phrase *rite of passage* might come to mind. Using colored markers, hand-letter at least three such words or phrases on white drawing paper. Experiment with different letter styles. If you prefer, you might want to outline your letters on colored construction paper.
5. With scissors, cut out the words and phrases you have created. Glue these to your collage. When the glue has dried, display the finished work.

Figure 13–13 Student work. Family celebration.

STUDIO OPTION

Try This!

■ Make an abstract clay sculpture or relief that captures the idea of a family celebration. Do not include obvious forms such as human figures. Concentrate instead on a symbolic shape or abstract form. Be inventive! With your teacher's help, fire your sculpture. Give the work a title.

Lesson 6 *Collage of a Family Gathering* **255**

■ **Aesthetics**

Have students compare Garza's work with Bruegel's painting (Chapter 12, page 240). Ask students if they think a painting is more or less successful when the artist does not portray objects realistically. Have them explain their views.

■ **Studio Skills**

Have students brainstorm family celebrations and choose an event. Have them collect objects and memorabilia that relate to the event. Make sure they have permission from home to bring in photographs and other family items.

Have them explore several arrangements including formal and informal balance. They may want to layer paper or fabric shapes. Demonstrate how overlapping and clustering objects helps to create unity. Ask students to title their finished work.

● ● ● ● ● ● ● ● ● ● ● ●
ASSESS

■ **Self-Assessment**

Have students use Examining Your Work to evaluate their art.

■ **Reteaching**

Have students describe the action and event in Figure 13-12. Then ask them to explain how the work is organized.

■ **Enrichment**

Garza recalls her Spanish, Native American, and Mexican roots in her paintings. Assign students in small groups to research information about the Aztecs, Toltecas, Apaches, Incas, or Mayans including rituals, sculpture, jewelry, language, and poetry. Have them present their findings to the class.

● ● ● ● ● ● ● ● ● ● ● ●
CLOSE

Have students write a paragraph or short story about their chosen family gathering to display with their collages.

LESSON 7

Art that Celebrates Life

☑ **OBJECTIVES**

After completing this lesson, students will be able to:

• Recognize Rie Muñoz as an Alaskan painter who uses color, shape, and form to make expressive paintings.

• Explain how James Phillips's artwork celebrates his heritage in the rhythms created by lines, shapes, and colors.

☑ **SUPPLIES**

• White paper
• Pencils
• Oil pastels, crayons, colored pencils, fine line markers

Resource

■ 13-10 Lesson on Life, TRB page 220 (cooperative learning)

• • • • • • • • • • • • •

TEACH

■ **Motivator**

Have students recall the excitement of the first celebration they remember. Ask what the people in Figure 13-14 are celebrating. How does the artist create movement in this artwork? Then have students study Phillips's painting noting the strong colors, shapes, and rhythms from his African heritage. Ask students to imagine the beat of music as they view the work.

In this chapter, the focus has been on celebrations that relate to important dates on the calendar. Not all celebrations, however, revolve around "red-letter days." Some causes for celebration are simple, everyday events—skating with friends on a perfect fall afternoon, gazing out the window at a gentle spring rain, or waking up to the first snow. Can you think of similar occasions that made you feel glad just to be alive?

Every now and then life serves up such priceless moments. These celebrations of life know no cultural boundaries. In this lesson, you will look at two artists' views of such celebrations.

INUIT SUBJECTS

The painting in Figure 13–14 captures a rare moment for both the artist and her subjects. Study the work. In it, two Inuit women

Figure 13–14 Notice how the artist uses the sun, moon, and stars to symbolize the universal nature of artistic expression. How has she symbolized day and night?

Rie Munoz. *Both the Sun and Moon Belong to Women.* 1990. Watercolor. 48.2 × 55.9 cm (19 × 22"). Rie Munoz Ltd., Juneau, Alaska.

TECHNOLOGY OPTIONS

National Gallery of Art Videodisc   Use the following images to show additional artworks that celebrate life.

Jean-Honoré Fragonard
The Happy Family

Search Frame 1071

Henri de Toulouse-Lautrec
Quadrille at the Moulin Rouge

Search Frame 1560

Jan Steen
The Dancing Couple

Search Frame 924–926

Use Glencoe's *National Gallery of Art Correlation Bar Code Guide* to locate more artworks.

Figure 13–15 Can you find objects in this painting that exhibit radial balance? What other art principles are evident in this work?

James Phillips. *Ancestral Dream.* 1991. Acrylic on paper. 120.6 × 106.7 cm (47½ × 42½"). Private collection.

appear. The similarity of their positions indicate that they are celebrating. Imagine the artist's own delight in creating this scene. She expresses her feelings by recording a celebration in a symbolic way. Notice the stylized use of shape and color.

AFRICAN AMERICAN PAINTING

Some celebrations of life do not come from how we feel. They come instead from a sense of pride in who we are. The abstract artwork in Figure 13–15 is such a "celebration." The work celebrates the artist's African roots.

As you explore this busy painting, your eye never stays in one place for long. It is forever moving, much like the pulsing colors and vibrating geometric shapes that make up the work. Pause for a moment to focus on the yellow-and-black bull's-eyes nested within the

---

STUDIO ACTIVITY

Creating an African Design

In addition to suggestions of masks, Figure 13–15 contains a number of other traditional African designs. Many are organized by means of radial balance. Make an African design of your own. Begin by folding a 12-inch (30-cm) square sheet of white drawing paper in half. Fold the resulting rectangle in half again to form a smaller square. Unfold the page. Then fold it diagonally to make a triangle. Open and fold it diagonally the other way. Unfold. Beginning in the center, draw lines or shapes to make a pattern on the fold lines or spaces in between. Turn the paper as you work to make sure your shapes and lines are repeated evenly. Continue until you have completed the pattern. Add color to your design using oil pastels, crayons, colored pencils, or colored markers.

PORTFOLIO

Write a description of your design listing the elements and principles of art you used. Put this written description in your portfolio with your artwork.

---

blue circle at the upper left. These objects may remind you of a face. If so, this is no accident. Similar arrangements throughout this painting are efforts to re-create, at least in spirit, the ritual masks of the artist's African ancestors.

✔ Check Your Understanding

1. What event is celebrated in the painting in Figure 13–14?
2. What kinds of traditional images appear in Figure 13–15?

Lesson 6 *Art that Celebrates Life* **257**

■ Art Criticism

Have students use the four steps of art criticism to evaluate and compare the two paintings in this lesson. Have them use a Venn diagram to list commonalities as well as differences. Have students decide whether each artist's intent was the same. Finally, have them determine whether each painting is a successful work of art and explain why or why not.

■ Art History

Divide the class into small groups of three or four. Assign half the groups Rie Muñoz and the other half James Phillips. Ask each group to research the world events that occurred at the time the artist's painting was made. Have them include information about other local artists and art forms in drama, writing, music, and dance. Ask groups to share their findings.

• • • • • • • • • • • ASSESS

■ Self-Assessment

Have students complete the Check Your Understanding questions on this page. Answers are provided below.

■ Reteaching

In pairs, have students explain the mood and feelings expressed in each painting in the lesson.

■ Enrichment

Have students investigate the lives and customs of the Inuit people. Have them concentrate on their art and culture, but also encourage students to discover the social history of these northern people.

• • • • • • • • • • CLOSE

Ask students to explain how simple, everyday events can be cause for celebration.

257

LESSON 8

Celebrating a Role Model

LESSON 8

Celebrating a Role Model

(pages 258–259)

LESSON TIME: 90 minutes

• • • • • • • • • • • • • • •
FOCUS

☑ OBJECTIVES

After completing this lesson, students will be able to:

• Identify the significance of rituals and artwork to honor achievements.

• Use a variety of materials to make a ritual wall hanging honoring a role model.

• Describe, analyze, interpret, and judge their work.

☑ SUPPLIES

• Pencils and sketch paper
• Photographs and old magazines
• Construction paper
• Compasses, scissors, white glue
• Tissue paper, gold or aluminum foil
• Assorted yarn, colored paper, colored markers
• Round plastic lids from coffee or ice cream containers

• • • • • • • • • • • • • • •
TEACH

■ Motivator

Ask students if they have a skill or talent they practice every day. Is there a person they admire who inspires them to work harder at their skill? Tell students that everyday rituals or routines usually lead to celebrations of larger achievements, such as an athletic award, passing grades, and a diploma. These events can in turn lead to new rituals or rehearsals to prepare us for future achievements.

258

Are there grownups whose footsteps you hope to follow in someday? Maybe your role model is a person like the one whose sculpted likeness appears at the center of the work in Figure 13–16. This man is C. J. McLin. He was the first African American to be elected to public office in the artist's home state of Ohio. The work is the artist's personal tribute to McLin. It is more than just that, however. It is also intended as a message to young people—a call to them to find heroes truly worthy of admiration. What qualities of this work reveal the artist's own admiration for a leader and pioneer?

WHAT YOU WILL LEARN

You will create a three-dimensional mixed-media tribute that honors a person whose life or work inspires you. Your design will include a variety of media. The objects you choose will connect in some way with your theme. Your design will include colored yarn or paper strips that create harmony with the rest of the media. The yarn will be woven and arranged in an interesting pattern.

WHAT YOU WILL NEED

• Photographs and old magazines
• Compass
• Sheet of construction paper, 9 x 12 inches (23 x 30 cm)
• Scissors
• White glue
• Tissue paper, gold or aluminum foil
• Assorted yarns, colored paper, or colored markers
• Plastic lid from an ice-cream or coffee container

Figure 13–16 **How does the artist emphasize the image of the figure whose achievements this work celebrates?**

Bing Davis. *Puberty Ritual Image #10.* 1992. Clay and found objects. 91.3 × 45.7 cm (36 × 18″). Private collection.

258 Chapter 13 *Celebrations*

— more about • • •

Bing Davis To capture the spirit of his heritage, Davis returned to his African roots ten times. Some of the African art forms he discovered include fabric designs, carvings, music, dance, costumes, masks, and storytelling. All forms are used in important African ceremonies and rituals.

Davis uses a wide variety of media to capture his feelings through symbols. Transforming everyday recycled objects into the meaning of his artwork is a special process for Davis. Discarded objects such as the shredded tire become the halo for the face in the center of the work. Like McLin, the tire has traveled many miles, seen many places, and experienced many emotions on the highway of life. The tire represents the journey of life and the ancient rite of passage.

WHAT YOU WILL DO

1. Select a person whom you admire. This might be a relative, a leader in your community or state, a teacher, or anyone else who inspires you.
2. Think about images that communicate information about this person's appearance and accomplishments. These might include photographs and pictures clipped from magazines that symbolize the person's importance to you. Gather an assortment of such materials.
3. Trace a circle that will fit the outside measurement of the lid on colored construction paper. Choose a color that is in keeping with your tribute. Make a second circle the same size on a thin sheet of cardboard. Cut out both circles. Glue them together.
4. Arrange the photographs and images you have gathered on the colored construction paper circle. When you are satisfied with the arrangement, glue these in place. Fill the negative spaces between and around the images with strips of tissue paper, gold foil, or colored lines. Be creative! Set this object aside to dry.
5. Gather strands of thin yarn or cut paper strips in several colors. These should blend with those of the construction paper and images, so as to create harmony. Form an interesting pattern with the yarn or paper strips and glue them to the edge of the plastic lid to make a border and add repetition to the work.
6. Glue your circle to the flat surface of the lid.

EXAMINING YOUR WORK

- **Describe** Describe the materials used in your tribute. Identify the individual you are honoring.
- **Analyze** Does your work achieve harmony through the use of color? Have you used interesting patterns in the border as an organizing principle?
- **Interpret** Explain the idea, mood, and message your work expresses about its subject.
- **Judge** How does your work compare with that in Figure 13–16? In what ways is it similar? How is it different?

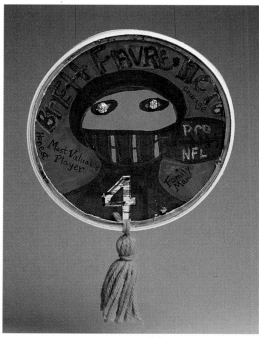

Figure 13–17   **Student work. A role model.**

 Try This!

COMPUTER OPTION

On the computer, design a certificate for a special personal achievement. Include a variety of fonts in different sizes and styles. Add graphics, either in the form of clip art or original illustrations. Complete your certificate with a decorative border that uses a repetitive pattern. Print and present copies of your certificate to deserving individuals.

Lesson 8   *Celebrating a Role Model*   **259**

Aesthetics

Ask students to explain what Bing Davis does in this artwork that is different from other artists who reflect their heritage in their message. What features are unique? Does this uniqueness make it a better or poorer design? Have students justify their opinions.

Cultural Diversity

The *Puberty Ritual Image #10* was made in 1989 in Ohio to honor a prominent African American statesman. Have students research other African Americans as well as leaders from other cultural backgrounds, male and female, who made significant contributions in the 1980s. Include science, medicine, politics, the arts, and sports.

ASSESS

Self-Assessment

Have students use Examining Your Work to evaluate their art.

Reteaching

Have pairs of students share the message they were trying to convey in their artwork.

Enrichment

Students may be familiar with Native American objects such as dream catchers. Ask volunteers to research this art form and share information with the class about its history and purpose. Invite students to create dreamcatchers of their own.

CLOSE

Have students explain the theme of Bing Davis's work.

CURRICULUM CONNECTIONS

Social Studies   Find books and magazines about celebrations, festivals, and rituals from around the globe. Discuss with students where these celebrations originated and locate these areas on a map.

The following books not only explain diverse festivals, they also provide ideas to help students experience these rituals through hands-on activities.

- *Harvest Festivals Around the World* by Judith Hoffman Corwin (N.J.: Messner, 1995).
- *Red Eggs and Dragon Boats: Celebrating Chinese Festivals* by Carol Stepanchuk (Berkeley: Pacific View, 1994).
- *Day of the Dead: A Mexican-American Celebration* by Diane Hoyt-Goldsmith (N.Y.: Holiday House, 1994).

☑ OBJECTIVES

After reading this feature, students will be able to:

- Explain how folk dancing developed.
- Describe the function of music and dance in Thomas Hart Benton's painting.

Teaching the Connections

- Have students read the feature on this page.
- Ask volunteers to share what they know about music and dance. What types of modern-day celebrations might include music and dancing? *(Examples include weddings, anniversaries, birthdays, holidays, family reunions, religious ceremonies.)* What types of dancing are you familiar with? *(Answers will vary.)* What are the sources of country music shown in Benton's painting? *(The instruments and the singers.)*
- Tell students that Thomas Hart Benton (1889–1975) was an American regionalist painter. Regionalism is art that depicts rural scenes. Benton is well known for his colorful, lively murals of the 1930s. In his art, he recorded scenes of everyday American life.

Answers to Making the Connections

- The musical instruments include a guitar, a banjo, and fiddles (violins).
- Benton used curving lines and painted the people in mid-motion. In addition, a ship and a train in the background are moving.
- Student examples will vary.

Thomas Hart Benton. *The Sources of Country Music.* 1975. Acrylic on canvas. 1.8 × 3 m (6 × 10'). The Country Music Hall of Fame and Museum, Nashville, Tennessee. ©1998 Thomas. H. Benton & Rita P. Benton Testamentary Trusts/Licensed by VAGA, New York, NY

Celebrating Music and Dance

Have you ever danced to "The Hokey Pokey" or "The Bunny Hop" at a wedding or other event? Perhaps your family does the Irish jig or the Polish polka during family celebrations. Music and dance have been a part of celebrations and rituals since ancient times.

One type of dancing—folk dancing—developed when people lived in simple, rural societies. Back then, people did not have many forms of recreation. They did not have televisions, VCRs, computer and video games, or stereos. Traveling was difficult, and most people did not know how to read.

Dancing, however, was something that almost everyone could do.

Some types of folk dancing are associated with certain cultures and traditions. The Highland Fling, for example, is a Scottish folk dance. The Hora is a Romanian and Israeli folk dance. Dancers lock their arms together or hold hands. They move counterclockwise in a circle. The dance is often performed at Jewish weddings and other celebrations. In *The Sources of Country Music,* Thomas Hart Benton depicts a celebration with music and dancing.

MAKING THE CONNECTION

- Identify some of the musical instruments shown in *The Sources of Country Music.*
- How did Benton create a sense of movement in this work?
- Find other examples of music or dancing depicted in artwork. What are the similarities and differences with Benton's piece?

INTERNET ACTIVITY

Visit Glencoe's Fine Arts Web Site for students at:

http://www.glencoe.com/sec/art/students

INTERNET ACTIVITY

Virtual Field Trips   Your students can experience and appreciate the fine art collections of countless museums and art galleries in every part of the world represented on the World Wide Web. Have your students spend a class period roaming through the collections of the de Young Museum in San Francisco, or check the current exhibits at the Solomon R. Guggenheim in New York. Work on a longer-term project as students discover art of the masters at the National Gallery in Washington, D.C. Give students a close-up view of folk art and ethnic works at regional and indigenous galleries. Locations of some sites are in the *Curriculum Links* or the *On-Line and Multimedia Resources* areas of the *Teacher Resources.* Find us at **http://www.glencoe.com/sec/art**

REVIEW

 BUILDING VOCABULARY

Number a sheet of paper from 1 to 6. After each number, write the term from the box that matches each description below.

adenla   seal
kinetic art   shadow puppet
pueblo   tricolor

1. An art style in which parts of a work are set into motion by a form of energy.
2. An art object in the shape of an animal or human attached to a wand or stick.
3. Dried-clay dwelling.
4. A sculpted ceremonial headdress used in rites of passage.
5. A flag with three broad bands of color.
6. A symbolic image or emblem.

 REVIEWING ART FACTS

Number a sheet of paper from 7 to 12. Answer each question in a complete sentence.

7. What is the purpose of May Day?

8. What do the paintings in Figures 13–2 and 13–3 "give thanks" for?
9. In what ways might Figure 13–4 be said to be an example of *impossible art*?
10. What two types of dance are featured in Hopi culture? Which type is most common?
11. Name two purposes of festivals in various cultures of the world.
12. What is a rite of passage?

 THINKING ABOUT ART

On a sheet of paper, answer each question in a sentence or two.

1. **Extend.** Which of the artworks in this chapter would you identify as having joyous subjects? Explain your choices.
2. **Analyze.** What principles of art has the artist used in Figure 13–14 on page **256** to create a feeling of celebration?

■ Building Vocabulary

1. kinetic art
2. shadow puppet
3. pueblo
4. adenla
5. tricolor
6. seal

■ Reviewing Art Facts

7. It is meant to celebrate the coming of spring.
8. Both works celebrate their nations' struggle for independence and the courage and dedication of those who participated in this struggle.
9. The work is impossible in that the figures shown represent different centuries and places.
10. The two types are social dances and dances that celebrate the oneness of people with nature. Dances of the second type are more common.
11. Some festivals celebrate the new year. Others are meant to ensure a good harvest.
12. It is a ritual that celebrates an important passage in life, such as the passage from childhood into adulthood.

MAKING ART CONNECTIONS

1. **Social Studies.** One of the historical figures celebrated in Figure 13–4 is Harriet Tubman. With several classmates, research Harriet Tubman's life. Use your findings as the basis for a multimedia presentation. Include readings from poems and stories about the Underground Railroad, such as Jim Haskins's *Railroad Songs.* You may also want to display images from artist Jacob Lawrence's narrative series on Harriet Tubman.

2. **Community Connection.** Different states and locales have their own specific holidays. Residents of Massachusetts, for example, celebrate Patriot's Day. Find out about holidays specific to your town or community, such as Founder's Day. Design and create visual materials—posters and a logo, for example—for the next celebration of this event. Share your creations with community members.

Chapter 13 Review **261**

? THINKING ABOUT ART

1. Answers will vary. Students should support their claims by noting visual details as well as the kind of event being commemorated.

2. The artist has used rhythm and movement to create a vital, celebratory feeling.

Creating Fantasy

(pages 262–277)

Resources

- 14-9 Chapter Test, TRB page 237
- Transparency CC-14 *Second Thoughts* by Yves Tanguey
- Transparency 14 *Lily and the Sparrows* by Philip Evergood
- Fine Art Print 20 *Paris Through the Window* by Marc Chagall

Theatre

While studying this chapter, use Performing Arts Handbook page 326 to celebrate our ability to create fantasy through theatre, dance, and music as a way to symbolically express the human experience.

NATIONAL STANDARDS

This chapter addresses the following National Standards for the Visual Arts:

1. (a, b)   4. (a, b)
2. (a, b, c)   5. (b)
3. (a, b)   6. (a, b)

Figure 14–1 Marc Chagall used his imagination to create this artwork. How many examples of fantasy can you find?

Marc Chagall. *Green Violinist*. 1923–24. Oil on canvas. 198.1 × 108.6 cm (78 × 42¾"). Solomon R. Guggenheim Museum, New York, New York. © 1997 Artists Rights Society (ARS), New York/ADAGP, Paris

262

FEATURED ARTISTS

Marc Chagall
James C. Christensen
Thomas Cole
M. C. Escher
René Magritte
William Rimmer

Lydia Rubio
Kay Sage
Rufino Tamayo
Pavel Tchelitchew
George Tooker

CHAPTER 14

Creating Fantasy

The imagination is a wonderful thing. When you are small, it transforms a plain box into a house or pirate ship, a stuffed animal into a living, talking friend. When you are older, it unlocks the door to creative ideas and solutions to problems.

The painting at the left is the product of an active imagination. Study the work. What mood or feeling does this unusual work arouse? In this chapter, you will look at a number of artworks that, like this one, are fueled by the power of imagination.

PORTFOLIO IDEAS

When you have completed this class, your portfolio will be the evidence of all you have learned about art. Your art portfolio shows personal achievement. Use it as a motivation to continue communicating your ideas and feelings through new artworks. As long as you continue to work, you will continue to grow as an artist.

OBJECTIVES

After competing this chapter, you will be able to:

- Define fantasy art.
- Determine what the Surrealists were trying to accomplish.
- Identify links between fantasy art of this and other cultures and times.
- Complete several fantasy artworks using different media and techniques.

WORDS YOU WILL LEARN

architectural rendering
belvedere
fantasy art
juxtapose
social protest painting
Surrealists

DEVELOPING A PORTFOLIO

Using the Rubrics Both students and teachers need to fully understand the established rubric to be used for portfolio review. Post it or give a copy to each student for reference as the portfolio is developed. Is the portfolio to show growth over time, or will it demonstrate acquired skills and accomplishments? The difference is important and directly impacts what the student chooses to include in the portfolio. The rubric provides an ongoing reference of the standards that will be used in assessing the portfolio. Remind students throughout the grading period to review the rubric as they work on their portfolio to get them into the habit of considering expectations and standards.

Dreams and Nightmares

LESSON 1

Dreams and Nightmares

(pages 264–265)

• • • • • • • • • • •

FOCUS

☑ OBJECTIVES

After completing this lesson, students will be able to:
• Define fantasy art.
• Understand the Surrealist art movement.
• Draw a nightmarish image.

☑ SUPPLIES

• Pencils and lined paper
• White drawing paper, 9 × 12 inches
• Crayons, markers, or oil pastels

Resource

■ **14-1 Moving Experience,** TRB page 225 (cooperative learning)

• • • • • • • • • • •

TEACH

■ Motivator

Ask students to share some of the images they remember from scary dreams. What do some of the images have in common? Have students examine the paintings in Figures 14-2 and 14-3. Do either of these artworks have similarly strange images? Encourage students to discuss some of the themes that reappear in nightmares and dreams. Tell them that this lesson is a reflection of the strange images that can be experienced during sleep.

Do you remember what you dreamed last night—or *if* you dreamed? Dreams are our lone connection with a world that is otherwise lost to us. This is the hidden world of sleep. It is a place where we spend eight of every twenty-four hours each day—a full third of our lives. Is it any wonder that this uncharted territory has long held fascination for artists?

In this lesson, you will look at two "dreamscapes." You will explore visual interpretations of the strange kinds of images that visit us during our slumber.

DREAM ART OF THE PAST

Depicting dreams in art is nothing new. As a branch of **fantasy art**—*art that focuses on make-believe or imaginary subjects*—dream art dates at least to the time of the ancient Greeks. During the Middle Ages, demons and other "night visitors" were frequent subjects of paintings and illustrations.

The work in Figure 14–2 is more recent. The artist, who was active during the mid-1800s, worked chiefly as a sculptor. The painting is based on a dream he actually had. In the dream *and* the painting, the figure

Figure 14–2 Look at the title and then at the painting. What principle of art has been used to heighten the suspense in this work?

William Rimmer. *Flight and Pursuit.* 1872. Oil on canvas. 46 × 66.7 cm (18 × 26½"). Museum of Fine Arts, Boston, Massachusetts. Bequest of Miss Edith Nichols.

TECHNOLOGY OPTIONS

National Gallery of Art Videodisc   Use the following images to show additional examples.

Hieronymus Bosch
Death and the Miser

Search Frame 628–33

Edvard Munch
The Scream

Search Frame 3333

Use Glencoe's *National Gallery of Art Correlation Bar Code Guide* to locate more artworks.

Figure 14–3 What properties are shared by this painting and the one opposite? How has the artist of this work suggested deep space?

Kay Sage. *No Passing*. 1954. Oil on canvas. 130.2 × 96.5 cm (51¼ × 38"). Collection of Whitney Museum of American Art, New York, New York. Purchase.

running in the foreground is the artist. That he is being chased by someone is clear not only from the title. It is equally evident from the scary shadows on the floor behind him. Who is chasing the artist? Why are they after him? Most baffling of all is the ghostlike image in parallel stride in the background. From whom is *he* running?

RECENT DREAM ART

During the first half of the twentieth century, artists struck out in many bold new directions. Some turned to their conscience for inspiration and subject matter. Others looked to their emotions. Yet others probed the inner workings of the mind. This *group of artists who explored the realm of dreams and the subconscious* called themselves **Surrealists** (suh-**ree**-uh-lists).

A Drawing in the Surrealist Style

Use your imagination to come up with an image you might expect to find in a nightmare. On a sheet of lined paper, note details of this image. Do not include people among your details. Using pencil, sketch your image lightly on a sheet of drawing paper. Imitate as much as possible the style of the painting on this page and in Figure 14–1. Use colored pencils, markers, or oil pastels to complete your work. Choose hues that help communicate a sense of fear.

PORTFOLIO

In self-reflection, write what you learned about selecting a nightmarish image and using the Surrealist style to portray the image.

The name comes from a word whose initial part, *sur-*, means "beyond or above."

The painting in Figure 14–3 was created by a Surrealist. Examine this unusual work. Beneath a sullen sky, collections of flat building-high objects (some wrapped in what looks like canvas) stretch endlessly to the horizon. Scraps of these same materials litter the ground, providing a possible clue to the work's title. Typical of Surrealist art, this "landscape" is bathed in an unnatural light that casts shadows on some of the towering structures. What is the source of this light? The answer to that question, like the meaning of the odd shapes themselves, remains a mystery.

Check Your Understanding

1. What is fantasy art? What are its roots?
2. To what did the Surrealists turn for inspiration?

■ Art Criticism

Use the following art-criticism questions to lead a discussion on Kay Sage's painting in Figure 14-3.

• What first captures your attention in this artwork? What images can you identify?
• What elements of art are most noticeable? What principles have been used to organize those elements?
• How would you describe the mood of this painting?
• Do you enjoy viewing fantasy pictures like this? Are you more attracted to pictures based on real people, objects, and events? Do you think it is possible to enjoy both fantasy and realism in art? Why or why not?

● ● ● ● ● ● ● ● ● ● ● ●
ASSESS

■ Self-Assessment

Have students complete the Check Your Understanding questions on this page. Answers are provided below.

■ Reteaching

Ask students to work in pairs to explain to each other what is dream-like about the artworks in the lesson.

■ Enrichment

Invite students to find out more about Surrealism in art and literature. Point out that Surrealism is an invented word that means "super realism." The movement began with the French poet André Breton in 1924. Students may want to investigate other Surrealists such as René Magritte, Salvador Dalí, Max Ernst, or Joan Miró, for example.

● ● ● ● ● ● ● ● ● ● ● ●
CLOSE

Ask students to explain what makes the Surrealist art movement different from other movements they have studied.

Answers to ✓CHECK YOUR UNDERSTANDING

1. Fantasy art is art that focuses on make-believe or imaginary subjects. Fantasy art dates back at least to the time of the ancient Greeks.

2. The Surrealists turned to the realm of dreams and the subconscious for their inspiration.

Creating a Fantasy Bird Collage

(pages 266–267)

LESSON TIME: 90 minutes

• • • • • • • • • • • • • •
FOCUS

☑ OBJECTIVES

After completing this lesson, students will be able to:

• Use their imaginations to create fantasy birds that arouse emotion in viewers yet exhibit some real birdlike qualities.

• Describe, analyze, interpret, and judge their artwork.

☑ SUPPLIES

• Pencils and sketch paper
• White drawing paper
• Sheets of colored tissue paper
• Scissors; white glue
• Water; brush, yarn
• Black markers or pen and black ink

Resources

■ 14-2 In the Bag, TRB page 227 (studio)
■ 14-3 Symbolic Images TRB page 229 (appreciating cultural diversity)

• • • • • • • • • • • • • •
TEACH

■ **Motivator**

Ask students whether they have ever had an experience or a feeling that they found hard to describe in words. Have them demonstrate how they might express such feelings as terror, anger, joy, or sadness without the aid of language.

266

 LESSON 2

Creating a Fantasy Bird Collage

The world of fantasy art is filled with curious creatures. Some, like the tropical plants in Figure 10–4 on page **186,** are light-hearted. Others, like the bird in this picture, are not. Study this painting. Without glancing at the title, you can still sense the girl's sheer terror. Have you ever seen a bird like this? Perhaps the artist saw it in a dream.

Figure 14–4 **Does the use of abstraction in this painting take away from the feelings the work communicates? Why or why not?**

Rufino Tamayo. *Girl Attacked by a Strange Bird.* 1947. Oil on canvas. 178 × 127.3 cm (70 × 50⅛"). The Museum of Modern Art, New York, New York. Gift of Mr. and Mrs. Charles Zadok.

WHAT YOU WILL LEARN

In this lesson you will have a chance to use your own imagination and create an image of a bird. You will use this image, along with an assortment of art media, to create a collage. Begin by discussing with classmates the various features of birds. A class member will list these features on the board. For each feature the class will brainstorm descriptive words. These will be written next to the feature. Using this list as a starting point, make several pencil sketches of birds. Transfer the best of these to drawing paper. You will use tissue paper and other materials to give your bird color and texture.

WHAT YOU WILL NEED

• Pencil and sketch paper
• White drawing paper, 12 x 18 inches (30 x 46 cm)
• Scissors
• Sheets of colored tissue paper
• White glue, water, brush
• Yarn
• Black markers or pen and black ink

WHAT YOU WILL DO

1. Working with classmates, discuss features common to birds. These might include wings, legs, claws, beak, and feathers. One class member is to write these features on the board. Space for additional words is to be left alongside each feature.

2. Still working as a class, brainstorm words to describe each feature. Let your imagination run free. For *eyes,* for example, you might mention words such as *large, narrow,* and *yellow.* The volunteer at the board should list suggested words in the space after each feature.

---

more about • • •

Rufino Tamayo   Because Tamayo was not concerned with expressing political views and preferred to create easel paintings rather than murals, he found it difficult to gain recognition in his native Mexico for a long time. However, the murals he created in 1952–53 for the Palace of Fine Arts in Mexico City changed that. Though placed alongside those of the famous muralists Rivera, Orozco, and Siqueiros, his murals more than held their own. They were widely praised, and Tamayo was added to the list of great Mexican painters. Have students research the life and career of Tamayo, and investigate how his work differed from that of Rivera and his other contemporaries.

3. Working alone, use the lists on the board to form a picture of a bird in your "mind's eye." Your bird might terrify your viewers or it may make them smile and even laugh. Make several sketches of your bird.

4. Using your best sketch as a model, redraw your bird on a sheet of drawing paper. Make sure that the drawing fills the paper. Use a firm, continuous line.

5. Cut a variety of large and small shapes from sheets of colored tissue paper. When you have enough to cover your drawing, glue these carefully in place. Use white glue thinned with water for this purpose. Then lay the tissue paper on the damp surface. Smooth it out gently with your hand. Then carefully brush a second coat of glue across the surface of the tissue. If your brush picks up any color from the wet tissue, wipe it off on a paper towel.

6. Continue in this fashion, adding layer upon layer of tissue paper. Always glue

EXAMINING YOUR WORK

- **Describe** Is your drawing easily identified as a bird? Can you point to the different features of your bird?
- **Analyze** Is your bird large and colorful? Does it contain a variety of textures?
- **Interpret** What kinds of emotions or feelings do you think your bird collage will arouse in viewers?
- **Judge** Do you think your bird is a success? Do you feel it can be described as fantasy art?

the darkest colors of tissue in place first. Add subtle shadings of color by adding pieces of lighter tissue over pieces of darker ones.

7. When all the tissue is dry, add lines to suggest feathers or other designs. Do this with lengths of colored yarn or with a black marker or pen, or with both.

Figure 14–5 **Student work. Fantasy bird collage.**

Try This! STUDIO OPTION

■ Create another imaginary bird that will stir up different feelings. If your first bird was sinister, for example, your new one might be funny. Follow the same procedures as above. This time, however, wrinkle the tissue paper before applying it to your drawing or add crumpled or three-dimensional pieces. This will add extra texture and surface interest. Compare the completed bird to your earlier one. Which one is more successful? Why?

Lesson 2 *Creating a Fantasy Bird Collage* **267**

■ **Aesthetics**

Ask students to express their opinions about Tamayo's painting. What do they find most pleasing about it? What features do they object to? Why?

Sparking Creativity

Before involving students in the studio portion of this lesson, have each student write a four-line poem that reflects the same mood as Tamayo's painting. Ask students to read their poems in class. Have them discuss how Tamayo's painting inspired them to use language creatively to express that mood.

ASSESS

■ **Self-Assessment**

Have students use Examining Your Work to evaluate their art.

■ **Reteaching**

Have students use gestures and body language to describe the feeling and mood of Figure 14-4.

■ **Enrichment**

Ask students to research some of the colorful and varied birds that are native to Central and South America. Have them bring in pictures of as many species as they can find. Ask students to discuss what features the birds have in common and point out characteristics that seem to be unique. Which birds seem least like the birds in the students' region of the country? Have students explore the "fantastic" nature of these creatures.

CLOSE

Ask students to explain how their fantasy bird collage qualifies as fantasy art.

Puzzling Paintings

☑ OBJECTIVES

After completing this lesson, students will be able to:

- Recognize that since all the images in Magritte's picture are painted, none can be accurately referred to as "real."
- Point out that both paintings in this lesson make use of a picture-within-a-picture and impossible relationships.
- Complete a picture that effectively blends a photographic image and a pencil drawing.

☑ SUPPLIES

- Pencils
- Old magazines with black and white photos and pictures of landscapes and seascapes
- Scissors; glue
- White drawing paper

Resource

- ■ 14-4 Painting Within a Painting, TRB page 231 (aesthetics)

■ Motivator

Begin this lesson by having students examine the paintings in Figure 14-6 and in Figure 14-7. Ask students why the artists may have introduced the unusual elements into their works.

You wouldn't think much of it if you saw a car go by. You might sit up and take notice, however, if the driver were an elephant! Familiar images can seem unfamiliar—even strange—when they are placed in unexpected settings. Artists sometimes surprise viewers by doing just that. They **juxtapose** (**juks**-tuh-pohz), or *place side by side*, objects that look unusual or interesting when viewed together. In this lesson, you will look at two such works.

A PUZZLING PAINTING FROM THE 1930s

Often, the images juxtaposed in an artwork have little in common. In the painting in Figure 14–6, they have *too much* in common. This work was created by a Belgian Surrealist famous for his imaginative use of juxtaposition. His name was **René Magritte** (ren-**ay** mah-**greet**).

Examine this painting. If you were asked to describe it, what would you say? Maybe you would identify its subject simply as a window opening onto a nature scene. Look more closely, however. Find the small object in the shape of an upside-down *T* juxtaposed against a cloud. It takes some viewers a moment to realize that this seemingly out-of-place object is actually part of an easel. On the easel is an unframed landscape painting that blends perfectly with the scene beyond. With your finger, trace the outline of this "painting within a painting." What statement might the artist be making? Notice the title.

Figure 14–6 **What two images are juxtaposed in this painting? Would such a juxtaposition be possible in real life?**

René Magritte. *The Human Condition.* 1934. Oil on canvas. 100 × 81 × 1.6 cm (39⅜ × 31⅞ × ⅝"). The National Gallery of Art, Washington, D.C. Gift of the Collectors Committee.

268   Chapter 14   *Creating Fantasy*

more about • • •

Magritte and Rubio   In the 1920s, the Belgian artist René Magritte abruptly abandoned his abstract painting style after seeing a painting by Giorgio de Chirico. De Chirico was an Italian painter whose work greatly influenced the Surrealist painters who followed. If possible, show students some examples of de Chirico's work.

Lydia Rubio was born in Havana, Cuba, and lived there until she was thirteen. Trained as an architect, she turned to painting in 1980. She explained her shift in careers by saying, "For me, painting is a far more personal and spiritual activity than architecture."

Maybe this artwork is a comment on the inability of some people to tell where reality begins and ends. Can you think of advances in our own time that have helped blur the line between fantasy and reality?

A PUZZLING PAINTING FROM THE 1980s

Compare the painting in Figure 14–7 with the one just analyzed. The work on this page was completed fifty years later. Yet, the two share a similar theme. Both, moreover, present "pictures within a picture."

As you study Figure 14–7, you find once again that first impressions can be deceiving. At first glance, this painting appears to be nothing more than a pleasant seascape. On closer inspection, you begin noticing details that are hard to explain. A trio of gently swaying palm trees at the left, for example, appears rooted to a wooden tabletop. On the right side is an open sketchbook propped against a mountain. As if these images weren't puzzling enough, what are we to make of the painting that floats in mid air? How about the one in the sketchbook that continues the scene behind it? Again, the title is a partial key to such mysteries. It hints at the possibility that the work is a picture album of events in the artist's life—past, present, and to come.

STUDIO ACTIVITY

Extending an Image

Study the paintings within a painting on these pages. Then look through magazines for black-and-white photographs of landscapes or seascapes that you find interesting. With scissors, trim one such photograph to measure about 3 x 5 inches (7 x 12 cm). Glue this photograph at or near the center of a 9 x 12-inch (23 x 30-cm) sheet of white drawing paper. Use pencil to "continue" the image in the photograph onto the white paper. Juxtapose unusual objects. Work as carefully as you can, adding details to the scene as you draw.

P O R T F O L I O

What did you learn from extending the photograph? What would you do differently if you did it again? Put a written evaluation and your work in your portfolio.

✔ Check Your Understanding

1. What does *juxtapose* mean?
2. Name two things that the paintings on these pages have in common.

Figure 14–7 This artwork reflects the artist's fond memories of a grandmother who introduced her to painting when she was young.

Lydia Rubio. *Ella Pintaba Paisajes (She Painted Landscapes).* 1989. Oil on canvas. 91.3 × 234 cm (36 × 92"). Private collection.

Lesson 3 *Puzzling Paintings* **269**

■ **Aesthetics**

■ **Aesthetics**

Ask students to express their initial reactions to the paintings by Magritte and Rubio. Did they find that the unusual features of these pictures caused them immediately to react in a negative manner, or did the strange features of the works arouse their curiosity and cause them to look at the works more closely?

■ **Cultural Diversity**

The Surrealist movement affected many artists in many cultures. Though this art movement started in the 1920s, it is still in evidence today in packaging art for video games, etc. Encourage students to find Surrealistic artworks from a variety of cultures and bring in examples for display.

• • • • • • • • • • • • •
A S S E S S

■ **Self-Assessment**

Have students complete the Check Your Understanding questions on this page. Answers are provided below.

■ **Reteaching**

Ask students to work in small groups to examine each painting in the lesson and identify the pictures-within-the-pictures.

■ **Enrichment**

Have students select a colored photograph and paint the surrounding scene with tempera or acrylic. Their painting could blend with the photograph or contrast with it. Contrast would involve using colors of paint that are the opposite of those found in the photograph.

• • • • • • • • • • • • •
C L O S E

Have students discuss the ways in which the works of Magritte and Rubio conform to the objectives of Surrealism. *(Both connect unrelated images in strange, dreamlike ways.)*

Creating Your Own Picture Puzzle

• • • • • • • • • •
FOCUS

☑ OBJECTIVES

After completing this lesson, students will be able to:

• Create a "picture puzzle" that targets a problem in modern society.

• Describe, analyze, interpret, and judge their artwork.

☑ SUPPLIES

• Pencils and sketch paper
• White drawing paper
• Oil pastels
• Old magazines
• Scissors; white glue

Resource

■ 14-5 I Protest!, TRB page 232 (art history)

• • • • • • • • • •
TEACH

■ Motivator

Ask students to brainstorm some of the problems that plague modern society. Write their ideas on the board. Ask students to discuss whether these problems are universal or limited to a general area or a specific group of people. Explain that social protest painting is an art style dedicated to criticizing the problems of big-city life and modern society.

Direct students' attention to Figure 14-8. Ask them to discuss some of the problems that Tooker is attacking in his painting. Ask: In what way is Tooker making a strong statement?

Some picture puzzles, as you have seen, make statements of a general nature. Others operate on a more personal plane. What sort of comment or message does the picture puzzle on this page deliver?

Before you attempt an answer, it may help to know that the work is an example of **social protest painting.** Emerging in the 1930s, this was *an art style dedicated to attacking the ills of big-city life.* A frequent target of social protest paintings are current-day problems. Look again at the thought-provoking picture in Figure 14–8. What problem of big-city life do you think this work highlights? What "surreal" or fantasy images and objects can you find?

WHAT YOU WILL LEARN

In this lesson you will create a picture puzzle of your own. Like the painting in Figure 14–8, your work will target a problem of modern life. Begin by thinking about possible themes. Make sketches that juxtapose images that relate to your theme but not ordinarily to each other. Use the best of your sketches as the basis of an oil pastel drawing.

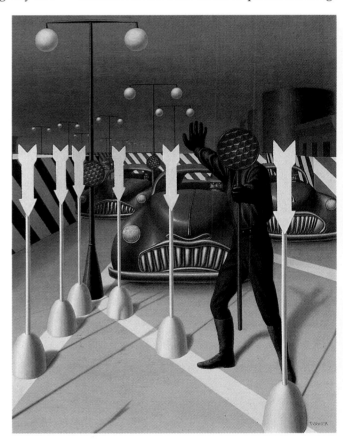

Figure 14–8 **Notice the moody sky and downward-pointing arrows. What feelings do they communicate?**

George Tooker. *Highway.* 1953. Tempera on panel. 58 × 45.4 cm (22⅞ × 17⅞"). Courtesy of Terra Museum of American Art, Chicago, Illinois. Terra Foundation for the Arts, Daniel J. Terra Collection.

CURRICULUM ⟩ CONNECTIONS

Music Just as artists have expressed strong views on social issues, so too have musicians. One such musician was the American folk singer and composer Woody Guthrie. With more than a thousand songs to his credit, Guthrie's music often expressed hope and pride in the American ideal. Yet he also composed protest songs about those who were down and out in society— migrant workers, the unemployed, and victims of the Great Depression. Guthrie was in turn a strong influence on another American singer and composer of the next generation—Bob Dylan. Dylan's early music in particular protested many social issues of the time. Bring in recordings by these musicians and discuss their music and the substance of their protests.

Add images clipped from magazines. Make one image larger than all the others to emphasize its importance.

WHAT YOU WILL NEED
- Pencil and sketch paper
- Sheet of white drawing paper, 9 x 12 inches (23 x 30 cm)
- Oil pastels
- Old magazines
- Scissors
- White glue

WHAT YOU WILL DO
1. Think of a problem you feel strongly about or have learned about. Possibilities include forms of pollution, endangered species, or homelessness. Make a list of images that might be connected with the problem. Be creative.
2. On sketch paper, experiment with juxtaposing images from your list that usually are not related but which, together, make a strong statement. On the theme of air pollution, for example, you might show a factory chimney belching smoke that forms the letters *S.O.S.* Decide on one image that is central to your theme. Draw this image the largest.
3. Transfer your best sketch to a sheet of white drawing paper. Complete your drawing using oil pastels. Choose colors that suit your theme.
4. Thumb through old magazines for additional images. Again, give free rein to your imagination. Clip four or five pictures. Experiment placing these at various points on the surface of your drawing.
5. When you are happy with your arrangement, glue the images in place. Display your finished work. Challenge classmates to solve your picture puzzle.

EXAMINING YOUR WORK
- **Describe**   List the images that appear in your work.
- **Analyze**   Did you emphasize one image by making it larger than the others? Does your picture contain an interesting juxtaposition?
- **Interpret**   What is the mood of your work? What statement does the work make?
- **Judge**   Are you pleased with your picture? Were your classmates able to identify the problem your work attacks?

Figure 14–9   Student work. Current-day problem.

Try This! | STUDIO OPTION
■ Create another picture puzzle, this time using colored pencils or markers. Include nonliving objects that have human properties, such as the scowling automobiles in Figure 14–8. Give your work a title.

Lesson 4   *Creating Your Own Picture Puzzle*   **271**

Cooperative Learning
Have students form groups of four or five and choose an area of social protest to research. Groups might choose nuclear waste, air pollution, overuse of insecticides, homelessness, or some other social issue that is often in the news. Ask each group to divide the research tasks equitably, then decide how to share their found information with the class. Hold a "social protest" session to allow groups to present their findings to the class.

ASSESS

■ Self-Assessment
Have students use Examining Your Work to evaluate their art.

■ Reteaching
Ask students to explain what it means when images are juxtaposed.

■ Enrichment
Bring in several different newspapers from various cities or regions of the country and have students identify news articles that reflect areas of social protest. Ask students to cut out the articles and mount them, then draw pictures to expand on the theme presented in the article. Hang the articles and pictures in a "hall" of social protest.

CLOSE
Ask students to discuss why they chose the problem they did and how they expressed their views.

RESOURCES BEYOND THE CLASSROOM
Local Libraries   Use the library—either the school or the public library—as a convenient source of information about the elements and principles of art, art techniques, and art history. Not only are reference books available, but so are biographies, full-color art books, art magazines, and art journals, plus museum catalogs and other relevant information, all in a variety of media. Libraries can help students research how certain techniques are done or learn more about the artistic style of any artist not discussed in the textbook. Helping students learn to use library resources will be of benefit to them beyond the art class.

☑ OBJECTIVES

After completing this lesson, students will be able to:

- Define *architectural rendering.*
- Recognize a belvedere.
- Identify strange juxtapositions in artworks by M. C. Escher and Thomas Cole.

☑ SUPPLIES

- Old magazines with photos of buildings and other structures
- Scissors; white glue
- White drawing paper
- Tempera paints, brushes, trays

Resources

- 14-6 Thomas Cole, TRB page 233 (artist profile)
- 14-7 High Profile, TRB page 234 (reproducible master)

■ Motivator

Ask students to suggest examples of optical illusions they have come across in art or elsewhere. Invite them to bring in examples if they can. Then direct students' attention to Escher's print in Figure 14-10. Ask them to describe what they see. What is "wrong" or "impossible" about this picture? Lead students to an awareness of the juxtaposition of the first and second floors of the belvedere. Explain that artists like M. C. Escher specialized in creating such thoughtful and, puzzling images.

272

Impossible Images

"Seeing," it is said, "is believing." Generally, there is much truth to this statement. Sometimes, however, our eyes play tricks on us. They cause us to see imaginary pools of water shimmering in the distance when the weather is hot. They confuse us by making images appear to shift and change no matter how long we stare at them. You have probably seen optical illusions that will not "stay still."

In this lesson, you will look at an image that, like such illusions, fools the eye. You will examine a second work that looks impossible for entirely different reasons.

AN IMPOSSIBLE BUILDING

Some of the works you have looked at in this chapter contain ghostly beings. Others show eerie, surreal landscapes. The fine art print in Figure 14–10 fits neither of these descriptions. It focuses, rather, on a perfectly straightforward subject. The work may be seen as a kind of **architectural rendering**. This is *a detailed, realistic two-dimensional representation of a proposed three-dimensional structure.* In this case, the proposal is for a **belvedere** (**bel**-vuh-deer), *a building designed to provide a view of its surroundings.* The word is a blend of the Italian roots bel, or "beautiful," and vedere, "view."

Look closely at this print. It doesn't take long before you notice that something is terribly wrong. To pinpoint the problem, locate the two figures—one on each level—gazing out at the scenery. Both stand at a railing along the narrow end on the structure's right. Yet, each faces in a different direction. The first and second floors of the belvedere have been juxtaposed at right angles! Note that a model for this impossible design is located conveniently within the print. It appears in the hands of the perplexed-looking figure seated on the bench near the bottom of the picture. Could such an object really exist in three dimensions? If you were the architect's client, would you approve this plan?

Figure 14–10 The artist was fond of such visual puzzles. Another of his prints appears in Figure 2–10 on page 34. What similarities can you find between these two works?

272   Chapter 14   *Creating Fantasy*

AN IMPOSSIBLE CITYSCAPE

In contrast to the confusing world shown in Figure 14–10, the painting on page **273** appears to promise welcome relief. The feeling

more about • • •

M. C. Escher Maurits Cornelius Escher was a Dutch graphic artist and printmaker (1898–1972). He studied at the School for Architecture and Decorative Arts in Haarlem, Holland, working with lithographs and wood engravings. Escher valued order and perfect forms. He preferred to balance definite structure with the idea of illusion. His works are thought provoking, puzzling, and masterful. If possible, find additional examples of this artist's work and bring them in to class for students to examine.

that you are on solid ground does not last for long, however.

Focus your attention on the triangular shape looming on the horizon. You have probably seen photographs of this structure before. It is one of the great pyramids of ancient Egypt. In and of itself, there is nothing strange about this landmark. It is when we look elsewhere in the painting that a sense of having left reality behind begins to emerge. Notice the building at the left with the sharply pointed steeple. Buildings of this type are not found in or near Egypt. Do you know where such structures are found? Do you know what they are called? Can you understand what makes this cityscape impossible?

Check Your Understanding

1. What is an architectural rendering?
2. What makes the image in Figure 14–10 impossible? How about the painting in Figure 14–11?

Figure 14–11 Compare the strange juxtapositions in this work with the one in Figure 14–10. Do you recognize any other landmarks in this work?

Thomas Cole. *The Architect's Dream.* 1840. Oil on canvas. 134.7 × 213.6 cm (53 × 84¹⁄₁₆″). Toledo Museum of Art, Toledo, Ohio. Gift of Florence Scott Libbey.

Lesson 5   *Impossible Images*   **273**

Answers to ✔ CHECK YOUR UNDERSTANDING

1. An architectural rendering is a detailed, realistic two-dimensional representation of a proposed three-dimensional structure.

2. The first and second floors of the belvedere have been juxtaposed at right angles. Buildings and structures from different times and locations have been juxtaposed in Cole's painting.

LESSON TIME: 2 hours

• • • • • • • • • • • •
FOCUS

☑ OBJECTIVES

After completing this lesson, students will be able to:

• Create an "etching" of an imaginary place.
• Describe, analyze, interpret, and judge their artwork.

☑ SUPPLIES

• Pencils and sketch paper
• Tagboard or white drawing paper
• Crayons
• Brush
• India ink
• Toothpicks or bamboo skewers

Resource

■ 14-8 Fantastic!,
TRB page 235
(art criticism)

• • • • • • • • • • • •
TEACH

■ Motivator

Direct students' attention to the painting in Figure 14-12. Ask volunteers to describe the image and what they see in the painting. It may be hard for some students to understand the historical context of the artwork, but they will probably fully understand the forbidding, grim mood depicted in Tchelitchew's painting. Ask students to identify details that add to the mood of this piece.

274

Creating an "Etching" of a Strange Place

Are you familiar with the game called "hide-and-seek"? Maybe you have played it. If so, it is doubtful your version looked anything like the image in Figure 14–12. Study this work. The central figure is a young barefoot girl with her back to the viewer. She gropes uncertainly through a dark, forbidding place. Can you make out the objects that surround her? Maybe this is all just a bad dream from which the girl will soon awaken. Then again, maybe it is not. Notice the year of the painting. This may help explain the subject matter and tone. Do you know the events of this era that might have prompted such a grim visual commentary?

WHAT YOU WILL LEARN

In this lesson, you will create your own vision of a strange place. You will use your imagination to picture such a place. Create sketches of what your "mind's eye" sees. Use your best sketch as the basis of a crayon drawing. This drawing will be covered in turn with black ink. Finally, you will use a bamboo skewer or other pointed object to scratch a pattern of lines into the inked surface.

WHAT YOU WILL NEED

• Pencil and sketch paper
• Sheet of tagboard or white drawing paper, 9 x 12 inches (23 x 30 cm)

Figure 14–12 Can you identify the figure who is "it" in this game of hide-and-seek? Who or what is the figure seeking?

Pavel Tchelitchew. *Hide-and-Seek.* 1940–42. Oil on canvas. 199.3 × 215.3 cm (6′ 6½″ × 7′¾″). The Museum of Modern Art, New York, New York. Mrs. Simon Guggenheim Fund.

274 Chapter 14 *Creating Fantasy*

MEETING SPECIAL NEEDS

Being Flexible with Media Processes For some students with a neurological or orthopedic disability and for some students with short attention spans, the task of heavily crayoning over a piece of paper as large as 9 × 12 inches might pose a major challenge. Using a smaller size of paper, such as one half or one fourth of a 9 × 12-inch sheet, could result in a more successful product. Also, for students who might gouge through a thinner paper when doing the "etching," a heavy paper such as oak tag, like that of a manila file folder, can be useful.

- Crayons in assorted colors
- Brush, india ink
- Ruler or other straight edge
- Round toothpick or bamboo skewer

WHAT YOU WILL DO

1. With classmates, brainstorm images of imaginary places. The images need not be gruesome, like the one in Figure 14–12. You may, for example, picture a bizarre setting in which ridiculous creatures roam wild. Make notes about the possibilities raised.
2. Choose a location for the subject of an artwork. Let your imagination run away with you. Using pencil, complete several sketches of the images that come to mind.
3. Choose colors that fit the mood of the place you picture in your mind. Fill the entire page of tagboard or paper with a thick layer of crayon. The etching technique you will be using requires a heavy application of this medium.
4. With a brush, paint over your crayon drawing using black india ink, or black tempera paint, with a few drops of detergent added. While the ink or paint is drying, design several different patterns. These should be made up of closely spaced lines.
5. Transfer your best sketch, with pencil, to the india-inked surface. With a pointed object, etch patterns onto the inked surface of your drawing. By carefully scratching through the ink, you will bring out the crayon colors underneath. Using closely spaced lines in your pattern will make it easier to see the crayon images. This will also add visual interest to your picture.

EXAMINING YOUR WORK

- **Describe**   Does your picture depict a strange location? What details have you included?
- **Analyze**   Did you use closely spaced lines to create an interesting pattern? Do these lines reveal the crayon colors beneath?
- **Interpret**   Does your subject communicate a "not-of-this-world" look? Will viewers immediately identify the mood of your picture?
- **Judge**   Are you pleased with your picture? If you were to do it again, what would you do to improve it?

Figure 14–13   **Student work. An etching.**

 Try This! ## COMPUTER OPTION

■ From the notes you made, choose another "strange" setting. With the Fill tool, flood the entire drawing space with black. Set the line width to thin. Using the Pencil or Brush tool, begin drawing outlines of shapes in your strange world. Change line thickness and color as needed. Add hatching, cross-hatching, stippling, and textures to surfaces.

MEETING SPECIAL NEEDS

Gaining Insights   For students with or without disabilities, drawings of dreams, nightmares or strange places can be a way to gain personal insights. For those who wish to, sharing thoughts about their "dream" or "nightmare" drawings with the class or a small group of peers can give a feeling that one is "OK" and not "weird." Students with disabilities, especially, may feel that they are too different to be accepted by peers, so sharing inner feelings is important.

■ Studio Skills

Remind students that their imaginary places do not have to be sinister or grim. The important thing is that they be truly imaginary, drawing on that which is unusual, impossible, or bizarre.

Caution students to handle the sharp objects very carefully. As they "etch" with the bamboo skewers or toothpicks, remind them that drawing closely spaced lines will enhance the crayon images and add visual interest.

■ Cooperative Learning

Divide the class into groups of three or four. Ask each group to research and report on some aspect of art relating to World War II. For example, some groups may choose to explore art about the Holocaust; others may choose to research the fate of museum art during the conflict. Have each group share the results of their research with the class.

ASSESS

■ Self-Assessment

Have students use Examining Your Work to evaluate their art.

■ Reteaching

Ask students to work in pairs to discuss and identify the "not of this world" aspect of each other's artwork.

■ Enrichment

Have volunteers find out more about Pavel Tchelitchew and his art. Ask them to investigate when and where he lived and the factors that influenced his artwork.

CLOSE

Have students explain the mood of their artwork. How did they communicate the mood of their strange place?

CONNECTIONS
Language Arts

☑ OBJECTIVES

After completing the feature, students will be able to:

- Compare the use of symbolism in art and literature.
- Identify the symbolism in James Christensen's painting.

Teaching the Connection

- Have students read the feature on this page.
- Ask volunteers to share what they know about symbolism. What are some other easily recognizable symbols that you see every day? *(Answers will vary.)*
- Read to students the following quote from artist James Christensen. Fine art is "a two-way, interactive process.... Certainly it is important that I communicate what I feel and see in a work of art, but what you see and feel is just as important. That's why I incorporate so many universal myths and legends into my work. I want you to think: What do you see?" Encourage students to discuss their views on this topic.

Answers to Making the Connection

- ☑ Symbols of vanity include fancy clothes, fancy hats, excessive makeup, haughty expressions, exaggerated size of the two main figures.
- ☑ Symbolism in literature uses words to convey meaning, while symbolism in artwork must rely on images and devices that viewers will recognize.
- ☑ Answers will vary, but students may suggest that the artist's message is that vanity leads to the moral decay of society.

James C. Christensen. *Vanity*. 1994. Acrylic and gold leaf. 41 × 51 cm (16 × 20"). Courtesy of The Greenwich Workshop, Inc. Shelton, Connecticut.

Symbolism in Art and Literature

When you see a red sign with eight sides, what comes to mind? You probably don't even have to see the word *stop* to recognize a stop sign. When you see golden arches, you most likely think of a popular fast-food restaurant. The red octagonal sign and the golden arches are symbols.

Symbolism is a commonly used device in literature and art. In a novel, for instance, the main character may take a journey. On the most basic level, the journey may be a trip across the country. On a secondary level, however, the journey may represent life.

In artwork, an artist cannot use words to explain this secondary level of meaning. Instead, the artist must use images and devices that viewers will recognize. An artist might use the color white, for example, to suggest purity. A dove may symbolize peace.

Look carefully at James Christensen's *Vanity* on this page. The word *vanity* means having an inflated opinion of oneself. It also means being empty or having no value. This work contains many symbols of vanity. Which ones can you find?

┌ MAKING THE CONNECTION

- ☑ Identify five symbols of vanity in this artwork.
- ☑ How does symbolism in art differ from symbolism in literature?
- ☑ What message about vanity do you think the artist is trying to convey in this piece?

INTERNET ACTIVITY

Visit Glencoe's Fine Arts Web Site for students at:

http://www.glencoe.com/sec/art/students

INTERNET ACTIVITY

Product Information Connect to the *Product Information* section to get a glimpse of the entire line of Glencoe's Secondary Fine Arts programs. Since you are using the *Introducing Art* textbook, you might want to investigate some of the excellent program components designed to accompany the Student Text and Teacher's Wraparound Edition. Find out more about the Teacher's Resource Binder, Fine Art Prints package, and the Fine Art Transparency Package, to which we have added cross-curriculum transparencies, student art, and more. You may also be interested in investigating Glencoe's entire line of art programs, which includes textbooks from middle school through high school—focusing on art media, art history, drawing, and painting. Find us at **http://www.glencoe.com/sec/art**

REVIEW

 BUILDING VOCABULARY

Number a sheet of paper from 1 to 6. After each number, write the term from the box that matches each description below.

architectural rendering	juxtapose
belvedere	social protest painting
fantasy art	Surrealists

1. A building designed to provide a view of its surroundings.
2. A detailed, realistic two-dimensional representation of a proposed three-dimensional structure.
3. Group of artists who explored the realm of dreams and the subconscious.
4. Place side by side.
5. An art style dedicated to attacking the ills of big-city life.
6. Art that focuses on make-believe or imaginary subjects.

 REVIEWING ART FACTS

Number a sheet of paper from 7 to 13. Answer each question in a complete sentence.

7. What images are juxtaposed to startle the viewer in Figure 14–1?
8. What fantasy images turned up often in art of the Middle Ages?
9. When did the Surrealists work?
10. Who was René Magritte? For what is he best noted?
11. What is the significance of the title of Figure 14–7?
12. What did social protest artists frequently criticize in their works?
13. What makes the print in Figure 14–10 "impossible"?

 THINKING ABOUT ART

On a sheet of paper, answer each question in a sentence or two.

1. **Compare and contrast.** Which of the artworks in this chapter seems to be most disturbing? Which strikes you as the least disturbing? Give reasons for your choices.
2. **Synthesize.** Choose a work from the chapter and identify the symbols used by the artist. Tell what you think they mean.

■ Building Vocabulary
1. belvedere
2. architectural rendering
3. Surrealists
4. juxtapose
5. social-protest painting
6. fantasy art

■ Reviewing Art Facts
7. The violinist floats above houses; a dog rests his paws on a rooftop; a man floats; the violinist's face is green.
8. These works depicted demons and other "night visitors."
9. Surrealists painted in the first half of the twentieth century.
10. He was a Belgian Surrealist. He is famous for his imaginative use of juxtaposition.
11. The work is an autobiographical glimpse of the painter's past and present, as well as her future.
12. They often target current-day problems.
13. The second floor of the building is arranged at a right angle to the first floor.

MAKING ART CONNECTIONS

1. **Language Arts.** Look back at Figure 14–4 on page **266**. Notice the manner in which the painting seems almost to suggest a story. Think about the story the work tells. Then write a short poem of six or eight lines that captures the action and emotions. Share your poem with classmates.
2. **Social Studies.** Use library resources to learn more about the Great Depression and its aftermath. In the course of your research, answer questions such as the following: What caused this economic disaster? Which nations were affected by it? What measures were taken in this country to recover from its effects? Share your findings in an oral report. Find images by Ben Shahn, Reginald Marsh, and other social protest painters to display during your talk.

Chapter 14 Review **277**

❓ THINKING ABOUT ART

1. Answers will vary. Students should support their claims with details of the subject and mood of works noted.
2. Answers will vary, but students should identify symbols and support their choices with reasonable explanations of the symbolic meanings.

Using the Handbook

The Handbook is a convenient reference section which offers students step-by-step procedures, additional career and artist profile information, and optional Studio Lessons. This material is designed to complement and enrich the narrative and Studio Lessons that appear earlier in the book. The Handbook is divided into the following sections:

Part 1 Technique Tips
Part 2 Artist Profiles
Part 3 Career Spotlights
Part 4 Additional Studios

The Handbook can be used in conjunction with specific chapters and lessons, or you may wish to use each section of the Handbook for independent study. For example, if you want to cover careers or art history in two separate weeks, you can use the Artist Profiles for one week and Career Spotlights for the next week. Regardless of the way you integrate the material, the Teacher's Wraparound Edition offers additional information in the outside column to help you teach, apply, and reinforce these materials.

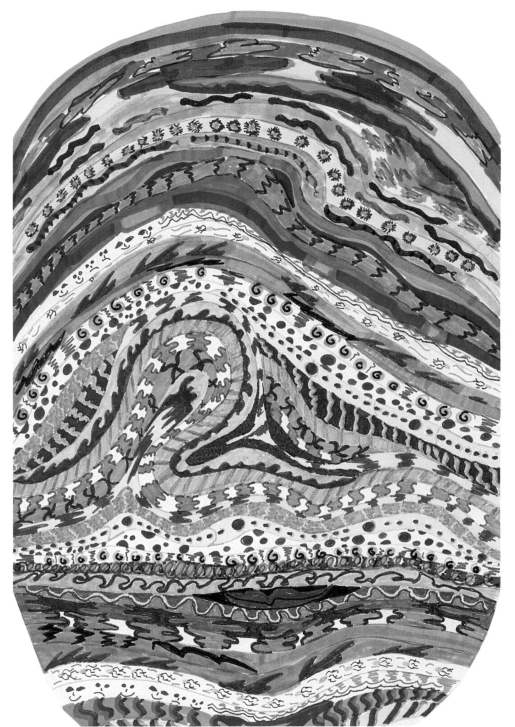

Looking at an object up close can reveal surprising details. This thumbprint was created by a student who tried the Studio Activity "Viewing Objects Up Close" on page 185.

278

HANDBOOK CONTENTS

■ PART 1: Technique Tips

This section offers students step-by-step procedures on how to do specific skills related to the areas of drawing, printmaking, painting, and sculpting. General techniques in these areas are described and, when appropriate, illustrated with the drawings. Other general skills, such as making a mat or using glue, are included in this reference section.

■ PART 2: Artist Profiles

This section provides students with background information on fourteen artists whose works appear in the text. The information gives a short biographical sketch about the artist and gives the reader an account of world events that occurred during the artist's life. The material is written in a warm, personal tone and will motivate students to seek additional information about the artist.

■ PART 3:
Career Spotlights

The information provided in this section introduces students to fourteen careers in art-related fields. Students are presented with an overview of the type of work and personal qualifications required of a person working in the featured occupation. In the Teacher's Wraparound Edition, addresses are provided so that students can research and obtain further information about the careers that interest them.

■ PART 4:
Additional Studios

The three Studio Lessons found in this section provide an extension to various chapters. These lessons can be used as independent practice for gifted and talented students, as cooperative learning projects, or as projects to culminate the objectives of specific chapters. In contrast to the lessons that appear within the text, these lessons generally take an extended period of time to complete. Each Studio Lesson has been reviewed and given an approximate time allotment that should be allowed.

TECHNIQUE TIP

Stretch Your School Budget   Check with the local art club to see if it has a benevolence fund for aid to education. Check with the local art directors' club, designers' association, or society of illustrators (in cities larger than 300,000).

Tracing vellum and some watercolor rendering papers can be bought less expensively in rolls or by the foot than by the sheet or pads. A 100% rag, twenty-pound vellum is pretty tough—and you can iron the back of it to smooth it after using liquid media.

1. Making Gesture Drawings

Gesture drawing is a way of showing movement in a sketch. Gesture drawings have no outlines or details. You are not expected to draw the figure. Instead, you are expected to draw the movement, or what the figure is doing. Follow these guidelines:

- Use the side of the drawing tool. Do not hold the medium as you would if you were writing.
- Find the lines of movement that show the direction in which the figure is bending. Draw the main line showing this movement.
- Use quickly drawn lines to build up the shape of the person.

2. Making Contour Drawings

Contour drawing is a way of capturing the feel of a subject. When doing a contour drawing, remember the following pointers:

- If you accidentally pick up your pen or pencil, don't stop working. Place your pen or pencil back where you stopped. Begin again from that point.
- If you have trouble keeping your eyes off the paper, ask a friend to hold a piece of paper between your eyes and your drawing paper. Another trick is to place your drawing paper inside a large paper bag as you work.
- Tape your paper to the table so it will not slide around. With a finger of your free hand, trace the outline of the object. Record the movement with your drawing hand.

- Contour lines show ridges and wrinkles in addition to outlines. Adding these lines gives roundness to the object.

3. Drawing with Oil Pastels

Oil pastels are sticks of pigment held together with an oily binder. The colors are brighter than wax crayon colors. If you press heavily you will make a brilliant-colored line. If you press lightly you will create a fuzzy line. You can fill in shapes with the brilliant colors. You can blend a variety of color combinations. For example, you can fill a shape with a soft layer of a hue and then color over the hue with a heavy layer of white to create a unique tint of that hue.

If you use oil pastels on colored paper, you can put a layer of white under the layer of hue to block the color of the paper.

4. Drawing Thin Lines with a Brush

Drawing thin lines with a brush can be learned with a little practice. Just follow these steps:

1. Dip your brush in the ink or paint. Wipe the brush slowly against the side, twirling it between your fingers until the bristles form a point.
2. Hold the brush at the beginning of the metal band near the tip. Hold the brush straight up and down.
3. Imagine that the brush is a pencil with a very sharp point. Pretend that pressing too hard will break the point. Now touch the paper lightly with the tip of the brush and draw a line. The line should be quite thin.

To make a thinner line still, lift up on the brush as you draw. After a while, you will be able to make lines in a variety of thicknesses.

5. Making a Grid for Enlarging

Sometimes the need arises to make a bigger version of a small drawing. An example is when you create a mural based on a small sketch. Follow these steps:

1. Using a ruler, draw evenly spaced lines across and up and down your original drawing (Figure T–1). Count

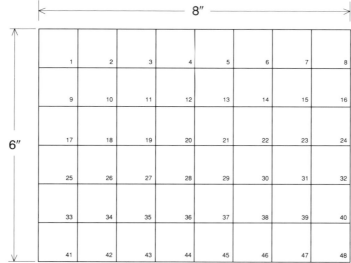

▲ Figure T–1

Using the Technique Tips

The technique tips listed on these and the following pages give students helpful hints for handling different media and tools. There are two types of technique tips. One type offers students step-by-step procedures which should be followed sequentially in order to achieve optimal results. The other type contains procedures and helpful suggestions that students may use as required by their individual studio projects.

USING THE DRAWING TIPS

TECHNIQUE TIP

Drawings Try these suggestions to help stretch your school budget:

- Some drawings look better without a mat. A backing board with a lightweight acetate covering will do the trick. If the drawing is on tracing paper or vellum, however, a piece of inexpensive white poster or tagboard needs to go between the corrugated board and the drawing. The corrugated board will discolor any drawing in a few years. Thin paper shows the corrugation ridges from the backing.

- Tracing vellum and some watercolor papers can be bought less expensively in rolls or by the foot than by the sheet or pads. A 100% rag, twenty-pound vellum can be ironed to smooth it after using liquid media.

the number of squares you made from side to side. Count the number of squares running up and down.

2. Measure the width of the surface to which the drawing is to be transferred. Divide that figure by the number of side-to-side squares. The resulting number will be the horizontal measure of each square. You may work in inches or centimeters. Using a ruler or yardstick, mark off the squares. Draw in light rules.

3. Measure the height of the surface to which the drawing is to be transferred. Divide that figure by the number of up-and-down squares. The resulting number will be the vertical measure of each square. Mark off the squares. Draw in pencil lines.

4. Starting at the upper left, number each square on the original drawing. Give the

same number to each square on the large grid. Working a square at a time, transfer your image. (See Figure T–2.)

6. Using Shading Techniques

When using shading techniques, keep in mind the following:

- Lines or dots placed close together create dark values.
- Lines or dots placed far apart, on the other hand, create light values. To show a change from light to dark, start with lines or dots far apart and little by little bring them close together.
- Use care also to follow the shape of the object when adding lines. Straight lines are used to shade an object with a flat surface. Rounded lines are used to shade an object with a curved surface.

7. Using Sighting Techniques

Sighting is a technique that will help you draw objects in proportion.

1. Face the object you plan to draw. Hold a pencil straight up and down at arm's length. Your thumb should rest against the side of the pencil and be even with the tip.

2. Close one eye. With your other eye, focus on the object.

3. Slide your thumb down the pencil until the exposed part of the pencil matches the object's height. (See Figure T–3.)

▲ Figure T–3

4. Now, without moving your thumb or bending your arm, turn the pencil sideways.

5. Focus on the width of the object. If the height is greater, figure out how many "widths" will fit in one "height." If the width is greater, figure out how many "heights" will fit in one "width."

▲ Figure T–2

TECHNIQUE TIP

Thumbnail Sketches Tell students that thumbnail sketches are small sketches drawn quickly to record ideas and information for a finished drawing. They are called thumbnail because they are almost small enough (5 × 5 inches, [13 × 13 cm]) to have been drawn on a thumbnail. They are usually done with pen and ink.

Have students think about situations in which the artist would prefer to use thumbnail sketches. For example, graphic artists and illustrators use them to record ideas and also to show ideas to other artists, art directors, and executives. Have students work in small groups and develop a series of thumbnail sketches that could be used to plan a series of paintings of animal totems or symbols of ancestry.

8. Using a Viewing Frame

Much in the way a camera is used to focus on one area of a scene, you can better zero in on an object you plan to draw by using a viewing frame (Figure T–4). To make a viewing frame do the following:

1. Cut a rectangular hole in a piece of paper about 2 inches (3 to 5 cm) in from the paper's edges.
2. Hold the paper at arm's length and look through the hole at your subject. Imagine that the hole represents your drawing paper.
3. Decide how much of the subject you want to have in your drawing.
4. By moving the frame up, down, sideways, nearer, or farther, you can change the focus of your drawing.

9. Using a Ruler

There are times when you need to draw a crisp, straight line. By using the following techniques, you will be able to do so.

1. Hold the ruler with one hand and the pencil with the other.
2. Place the ruler where you wish to draw a straight line.
3. Hold the ruler with your thumb and first two fingers. Be careful that your fingers do not stick out beyond the edge of the ruler.
4. Press heavily on the ruler so it will not slide while you're drawing.
5. Hold the pencil lightly against the ruler.
6. Pull the pencil quickly and lightly along the edge of the ruler. The object is to keep the ruler from moving while the pencil moves along its edge.

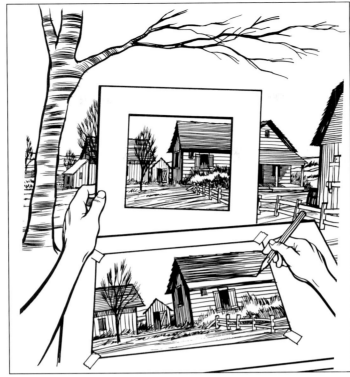

▲ Figure T–4

USING THE PAINTING TIPS

PAINTING TIPS

10. Cleaning a Paint Brush

Cleaning a paint brush properly helps it last a long time. *Always*:

1. Rinse the thick paint out of the brush under running water. Do not use hot water.
2. Gently paint the brush over a cake of mild soap, or dip it in a mild liquid detergent (Figure T–5).

▲ Figure T–5

more about • • •

Perceptual Skills Tell students that seeing the item they are drawing as a whole rather than just a collection of parts results in more successful drawings. Explain that the fact that we naturally see things as a whole was discovered in Germany in 1912 by a psychologist named Max Wertheimer. He founded a branch of psychology called Gestalt. The German word *gestalt* means pattern or form. According to Gestalt psychology, we only recognize objects by seeing total patterns or forms, not by adding up the individual parts we see. Tell students that in making most drawings, they should do the large shapes first and add the details later. Encourage them to think in terms of the Gestalt view of life.

3. Gently scrub the brush against the palm of your hand to work the soap into the brush. This removes paint you may not have realized was still in the brush.
4. Rinse the brush under running water while you continue to scrub your palm against it (Figure T–6).

▲ Figure T–6

5. Repeat steps 2, 3, and 4 as needed.
When it is thoroughly rinsed and excess water has been squeezed from the brush, shape your brush into a point with your fingers (Figure T–7). Place the brush in a container with the bristles up so that it will keep its shape as it dries.

▲ Figure T–7

11. Making Natural Earth Pigments

Anywhere there is dirt, clay, or sand, there is natural pigment. To create your own pigments, gather as many different kinds of earth colors as you can. Grind these as finely as possible. (If you can, borrow a mortar and pestle.) (See Figure T–8.) Do not worry if the pigment is slightly gritty.

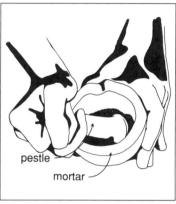

pestle

mortar

▲ Figure T–8

To make the binder, mix equal parts of white glue and water. Place a few spoonfuls of your powdered pigment into a small jar. Add a little of the binder. Experiment with different amounts of each.

When you work with natural pigments, remember always to wash the brushes before the paint in them has a chance to dry. The glue from the binder can ruin a brush. As you work, stir the paint every now and then. This will keep the grains of pigment from settling to the bottom of the jar.

Make a fresh batch each time you paint.

12. Mixing Paint to Change the Value of Color

You can better control the colors in your work when you mix your own paint. In mixing paints, treat opaque paints (for example, tempera) differently from transparent paints (for example, watercolors).

- *For light values of opaque paints.* Mix only a small amount of the hue to white. The color can always be made stronger by adding more of the hue.
- *For dark values of opaque paints.* Add a small amount of black to the hue. Never add the hue to black.
- *For light values of transparent paints.* Thin a shaded area with water (Figure T–9). This allows more of the white of the paper to show through.
- *For dark values of transparent paints.* Carefully add a small amount of black to the hue.

▲ Figure T–9

SAFETY TIP

Art Safety Resources The need to direct time and effort to safeguarding the health of students in the art studio cannot be ignored. Arts, Crafts, and Theater Safety (ACTS) is a national clearinghouse for research and information on health hazards in the arts. It publishes a newsletter which covers a range of topics including new hazards, precautions, government regulations, lawsuits, and a calendar of events. Those interested teachers can write to the following address:

Arts, Crafts, and Theater Safety (ACTS)
181 Thompson Street #23
New York, New York 10012-2586
(212) 777-0062
http://www.caseweb.com/acts/

13. Working with Poster Paints (School Tempera)

When using poster paints (school tempera) remember the following:

- Poster paints run when wet. To keep this from happening, make sure one shape is dry before painting a wet color next to it.

14. Working with Watercolors

- If you apply wet paint to damp paper, you create lines and shapes with soft edges.
- If you apply wet paint to dry paper, you create lines and shapes with sharp, clear edges.
- If you dip a dry brush into damp paint and then brush across dry paper, you achieve a fuzzy effect.
- School watercolors come in semi-moist cakes. Before you use them, place a drop of water on each cake to let the paint soften. Watercolor paints are transparent. You can see the white paper through the paint. If you want a light value of a hue, dilute the paint with a large amount of water. If you want a bright hue, you must dissolve more pigment by swirling your brush around in the cake of paint until you have dissolved a great deal of paint. The paint you apply to the paper can be as bright as the paint in the cake.

15. Making a Stamp Printing

A stamp print is an easy way to make repetitive designs. The following are a few suggestions for making a stamp and printing with it. You may develop some other ideas after reading these hints. Remember, printing reverses your design, so if you use letters, be certain to cut or carve them backwards.

- Cut a simple design into the flat surface of an eraser with a knife that has a fine, precision blade.
- Cut a potato, carrot, or turnip in half. Use a paring knife to carve a design into the flat surface of the vegetable.
- Glue yarn to a bottle cap or a jar lid.
- Glue found objects to a piece of corrugated cardboard. Make a design with paper-clips, washers, nuts, leaves, feathers, or anything else you can find. Whatever object you use should have a fairly flat surface. Make a handle for the block with masking tape.
- Cut shapes out of a piece of inner tube material. Glue the shapes to a piece of heavy cardboard.

There are several ways to apply ink or paint to a stamp:

- Roll water-based printing ink on the stamp with a soft brayer.
- Roll water-based printing ink on a plate and press the stamp into the ink.
- Apply tempera paint or school acrylic to the stamp with a bristle brush.

16. Working with Clay

To make your work with clay go smoothly, always do the following:

1. Dip one or two fingers in water.
2. Spread the moisture from your fingers over your palms.

Never dip your hands in water. Too much moisture turns clay into mud.

17. Joining Clay

If you are creating a piece of sculpture that requires joining pieces, do the following:

1. Gather the materials you will need. These include clay, slip, (a creamy mixture of clay and water), a paint brush, a scoring tool, (perhaps a kitchen fork) and clay tools.
2. Rough up or scratch the two surfaces to be joined (Figure T–10).

▲ **Figure T–10**

USING THE PRINTMAKING TIP

15. Making a Stamp Printing
Use with:
- Making a Glue-Line Print, page 130

USING THE SCULPTING TIPS

16. Working with Clay
Use with:
- Making an Animal Sculpture, page 134
- Creating a Clay Portrait, page 154
- Building a Clay Musical Instrument, page 194

SAFETY TIPS

Printing   Remind students to always wipe any remaining ink from a block and brayer after they have finished printing. If using a water-based printing ink, they can use water for cleaning. If using oil-based ink, however, they should use a solvent such as turpentine. Remember that if they use a solvent, they should be careful not to get it on their skin, or let it come in contact with their eyes.

Using Kilns   Place kilns in a separate room. If that is not possible, locate the kiln in an out-of-the-way part of the room where students are not likely to come into contact with it when it is in operation. In addition, all kilns should have local exhaust ventilation.

17. Joining Clay
Use with:
• Making an Animal
Sculpture, page 134
• Creating a Clay Portrait
page 154
• Building a Clay Musical
Instrument, page 194

3. Apply slip to one of the two surfaces using a paint brush or your fingers (Figure T–11).

▲ **Figure T–11**

4. Gently press the two surfaces together so the slip oozes out of the joining seam (Figure T–12).

▲ **Figure T–12**

5. Using clay tools and/or your fingers, smooth away the slip that has oozed out of the seam (Figure T–13). You may wish to smooth out the seam as well, or you may wish to leave it for decorative purposes.

▲ **Figure T–13**

18. Making a Clay Mold for a Plaster Relief

One of the easiest ways to make a plaster relief is with a clay mold. When making a clay mold, remember the following:
• Plaster poured into the mold will come out with the opposite image. Design details cut into the mold will appear raised on the relief. Details built up within the mold will appear indented in the relief.
• Do not make impressions in your mold that have *undercuts* (Figure T–14). Undercuts trap plaster, which will break off when the relief is removed. When cutting impressions, keep the deepest parts the narrowest.
• In carving a raised area in the mold, take care not to create a reverse undercut (Figure T–15).
If you want to change the mold simply smooth the area with your fingers.

▲ **Figure T–14**

▲ **Figure T–15**

19. Mixing Plaster

Mixing plaster requires some technique and a certain amount of caution. It can also be a very simple matter when you are prepared. Always do the following:
• Use caution when working with dry plaster. Wear a dust mask or work in a well-ventilated room.
• Cover your work space to keep the dust from spreading.
• Always use a plastic bowl and a stick for mixing. Never use silverware you will later eat from.
• Always use plaster that is fine, like sifted flour. Plaster should never be grainy when dry.
• Always add the water to the bowl first. Sift in the plaster. Stir slowly.
• Never pour unused plaster down a drain. Allow it to dry in the bowl. To remove the dried plaster, twist the bowl. Crack the loose plaster into a lined trash can.

---

more about • • •

Pottery   Before becoming finished pottery, clay takes six different forms. These are:
• *Plastic clay*—clay wet enough to be worked but dry enough to hold its shape.
• *Slip*—clay with enough water added to make it runny.
• *Leather hard clay*—clay which is still damp but too hard to model.

• *Greenware*—very dry clay that will break easily.
• *Bisqueware*—fired pottery that is hard but still not ready to use.
• *Glazeware*—pottery coated with powdered chemicals that melt during firing into a hard, glass-like finish.
Most ceramic objects are made hollow to avoid exploding or cracking during firing.

20. Working with Papier-Mâché

Papier-mâché (**pay**-puhr muh-**shay**) is a French term meaning "chewed paper." It is also the name of several sculpting methods using newspaper and liquid paste. These methods can be used to model tiny pieces of jewelry. They can also be used to create life-size creatures.

In creating papier-mâché sculptures, the paper-and-paste mixture is molded over a support. You will learn more about supports shortly. The molded newspaper dries to a hard finish. The following are three methods for working with papier-mâché:

- **Pulp Method**. Shred newspaper, paper towels, or tissue paper into tiny pieces. (Do not use glossy magazine paper; it will not soften.) Soak your paper in water overnight. Press the paper in a kitchen strainer to remove as much moisture as possible. Mix the mashed paper with commercially prepared papier-mâché paste or white glue. The mixture should have the consistency of soft clay. Add a few drops of oil of cloves to keep the mixture from spoiling. A spoonful of linseed oil makes the mixture smoother. (If needed, the mixture can be stored at this point in a plastic bag in the refrigerator.) Use the mixture to model small shapes. When your creations dry, they can be sanded. You will also be able to drill holes in them.
- **Strip Method**. Tear newspaper into strips. Either dip the strips in papier-mâché paste or rub paste on them. Apply the strips to your support (Figure T–16). If you do not want the strips to stick to your

▲ **Figure T–16**

support, first cover it with plastic wrap. Use wide strips for large shapes. Use thin strips for smaller shapes. If you plan to remove your finished creation from the support, apply five or six layers. (Change directions with each layer so you can keep track of the number.) Otherwise, two or three layers should be enough. After applying the strips to your support, rub your fingers over the surface.

As a last layer, use torn paper towels. The brown paper towels that are found in schools produce an uncomplicated surface on which to paint. Make sure no rough edges are sticking up. Store any unused paste mixture in the refrigerator to keep it from spoiling.

- **Draping Method**. Spread papier-mâché paste on newspaper. Lay a second sheet on top of the first. Smooth the layers. Add another layer of paste and another sheet of paper. Repeat until you have four or five layers of paper. Use this method for making drapery on a figure. (See Figure T–17.) If you allow the lay-

▲ **Figure T–17**

ers to dry for a day or two, they will become leathery. They can then be cut and molded as you like. Newspaper strips dipped in paste can be used to seal cracks.

Like papier-mâché, supports for papier-mâché creations can be made in several different ways. Dry newspaper may be wadded up and wrapped with string or tape (Figure T–18). Wire coat hangers may be padded with rags. For large figures, a wooden frame covered with chicken wire makes a good support.

▲ **Figure T–18**

20. Working with Papier-Mâché
Use with:
- Making a Mask with Formal Balance, page 28
- Creating a Fantasy Creature, page 138

MEETING SPECIAL NEEDS

Physical Disabilities and Safety At the beginning of each school year or new term, determine if any of your students are asthmatic, visually or hearing impaired, or on prescribed medication. Asthmatic students should not be exposed to dusts, fumes, or vapors because of breathing difficulties. Visually impaired students understandably operate very close to their artwork, and as a consequence, are more likely to inhale dusts, vapors, and fumes. Students with hearing impairments should not be exposed to activities requiring loud hammering or noisy machinery. This could aggravate their condition. If students are found to be on medication, seek a physician's advice regarding the potential harmful interaction between the prescribed medicine and art materials used in the class.

▲ Figure T–19

To create a base for your papier-mâché creations, tape together arrangements of found materials. Some materials you might combine are boxes, tubes, and bowls. (See Figure T–19.) Clay can also be modeled as a base. If clay is used, be sure there are no undercuts that would keep the papier-mâché from lifting off easily when dry. (For an explanation of undercuts, see Technique Tip **18**, *Handbook* page **276**.)

Always allow time for your papier-mâché creations to dry. The material needs extra drying time when thick layers are used or when the weather is damp. An electric fan blowing air on the material can shorten the drying time.

21. Making a Paper Sculpture

Another name for paper sculpture is origami. The process originated in Japan and means "folding paper." Paper sculpture begins with a flat piece of paper. The paper is then curved or bent to produce more than a flat

surface. Here are some ways to experiment with paper.

- **Scoring.** Place a square sheet of heavy construction paper, 12 x 12 inch (30 x 30 cm), on a flat surface. Position the ruler on the paper so that it is close to the center and parallel to the sides. Holding the ruler in place, run the point of a knife or a pair of scissors along one of the ruler's edges. Press down firmly but take care not to cut through the paper. Gently crease the paper along the line you made. Hold your paper with the crease facing upward.
- **Pleating.** Take a piece of paper and fold it one inch from the edge. Then fold the paper in the other direction. Continue folding back and forth.
- **Curling.** Hold one end of a long strip of paper with the thumb and forefinger of one hand. At a point right below where you are holding the strip, grip it lightly between the side of a pencil and the thumb of your other hand. In a quick motion, run the pencil along the strip. This will cause the strip to curl back on itself. Don't apply too much pressure, or the strip will tear. (See Figure T–20.)

▲ Figure T–20

22. Measuring Rectangles

Do you find it hard to create perfectly formed rectangles? Here is a way of getting the job done:

1. Make a light pencil dot near the long edge of a sheet of paper. With a ruler, measure the exact distance between the dot and the edge. Make three more dots the same distance in from the edge. (See Figure T–21.)

▲ Figure T–21

2. Line a ruler up along the dots. Make a light pencil line running the length of the paper.
3. Turn the paper so that a short side is facing you. Make four pencil dots equally distant from the short edge. Connect these with a light pencil rule. Stop when you reach the first line you drew. (See Figure T–22.)
4. Do the same for the remaining two sides. Erase any lines that may extend beyond the box you have made.
5. Trace over the lines with your ruler and pencil.

The box you have created will be a perfectly formed rectangle.

TECHNIQUE TIP

Classroom Demonstrations   The instructional strategy that is probably most familiar to art teachers is demonstration. This is an especially effective method of instruction when applied to studio activities. When preparing for a demonstration, always practice beforehand using the same materials students will be expected to use. Include continuous commentary with the demonstration explaining in detail what you are doing and why you are doing it this way. To be of maximum value to students, the demonstration must be amplified by a detailed explanation of every action. When this is done, students receive information by way of the eyes and ears, increasing the likelihood that this information will be understood and assimilated.

▲ Figure T–22

▲ Figure T–23

23. Making a Mat

You can add appeal to an art work by making a mat, using the following steps.

1. Gather the materials you will need. These include a metal rule, a pencil, mat board, cardboard backing, a sheet of heavy cardboard to protect your work surface, a mat knife with a sharp blade, and wide masking tape.

2. Wash your hands. Mat board should be kept very clean.

3. Measure the height and width of the work to be matted. Decide how large a border you want for your work. (A border of approximately 2½ inches on three sides with 3 inches on the bottom is aesthetically pleasing.) Your work will be behind the window you will cut.

4. Plan for the opening, or window, to be ¼ inch smaller on all sides than the size of your work. For example, if your work measures 9 by 12 inches, the mat window should measure 8½ inches (9 inches minus ¼ inch times two) by 11½ inches (12 inches minus ¼ inch times two). Using your metal rule and pencil, lightly draw your

window rectangle on the back of the board 2½ inches from the top and left edge of the mat. (See Figure T–23.) Add a 2½ inch border to the right of the window and a 3 inch border to the bottom, lightly drawing cutting guidelines.

Note: If you are working with metric measurements, the window should overlap your work by 0.5 cm (centimeters) on all sides. Therefore, if your work measures 24 by 30 cm, the mat window measures 23 cm (24 − [2 x 0.5]) by 29 cm (30 − [2 x 0.5]).

▲ Figure T–24

5. Place the sheet of heavy, protective cardboard on your work surface. Place the mat board, pencil marks up, over the cardboard. Holding the metal rule firmly in place, score the first line with your knife. Always place the metal rule so that your blade is away from the frame. (See Figure T–24.) In case you make an error you will cut into the window hole or the extra mat that is not used for the frame. Do not try to cut through the board with one stroke. By the third or fourth stroke, you should be able to cut through the board easily.

6. Working in the same fashion, score and cut through the board along all the window lines. Be careful not to go beyond the lines. Remove the window.

7. Cut a cardboard backing for your art work that is slightly smaller than the overall size of your mat. Using a piece of broad masking tape, hinge the back of the mat to the backing. (See Figure T–25.)

▲ Figure T–25

Technique Tips **289**

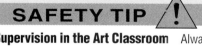

SAFETY TIP !

Supervision in the Art Classroom Always supervise students carefully. Adequate supervision of students is required for both safety and liability reasons. Safety rules should be posted and explained at the start of each term—and these rules should be rigidly enforced. At no time should students be allowed to work in the classroom without direct supervision. Teachers should also make it a rule that students not bring to class and use their own art materials. It is possible that these art materials could contain unknown hazards.

Position your art work between the backing and the mat and attach it with tape. Anchor the frame to the cardboard with a few pieces of rolled tape.

24. Mounting a Two-Dimensional Work

Mounting pictures that you make gives them a professional look. To mount a work, do the following:

1. Gather the materials you will need. These include a yardstick, a pencil, poster board, a sheet of heavy cardboard, a knife with a very sharp blade, a sheet of newspaper, and rubber cement.
2. Measure the height and width of the work to be mounted. Decide how large a border you want around the work. Plan your mount size using the work's measurements. To end up with a 3-inch (8 cm) border, for example, make your mount 6 inches (15 cm) wider and higher than your work. Record the measurements for your mount.
3. Using your yardstick and pencil, lightly draw your mount rectangle on the back of the poster board. Measure from the edges of the poster board. If you have a large paper cutter available, you may use it to cut your mount.
4. Place the sheet of heavy cardboard on your work surface. Place the poster board, pencil marks up, over the cardboard. Holding the yardstick firmly in place along one line, score the line with your knife. Do not try to cut through the board with one stroke. By the third try, you should be able to cut through the board.

▲ Figure T–26

5. Place the art work on the mount. Using the yardstick, center the work. Mark each corner with a dot. (See Figure T–26.)
6. Place the art work, face down, on a sheet of newspaper. Coat the back of the work with rubber cement. (*Safety Note:* Always use rubber cement in a room with plenty of ventilation.) *If your mount is to be permanent, skip to Step 8.*
7. Line up the corners of your work with the dots on the mounting board. Smooth the work into place. *Skip to Step 9.*
8. After coating the back of your art work, coat the poster board with rubber cement. Be careful not to add cement to the border area. Have a partner hold your art work in the air by the two top corners. Once the two glued surfaces meet, you will not be able to change the position of the work. Grasp the lower two corners. Carefully lower the work to the mounting board. Line up the two corners with the bottom dots. Little by little, lower the work into place (Figure T–27). Press it smooth.

▲ Figure T–27

9. To remove any excess cement, create a small ball of nearly dry rubber cement. Use the ball of rubber cement to pick up excess cement.

25. Making Rubbings

Rubbings make interesting textures and designs. They may also be used with other media to create mixed media art. To make a rubbing, place a sheet of thin paper on top of the surface to be rubbed. Hold the paper in place with one hand. With the other hand, rub the paper with the flat side of an unwrapped crayon. Always rub away from the hand holding the paper. Never rub back and forth, since this may cause the paper to slip.

26. Scoring Paper

The secret to creating neat, sharp folds in cardboard or paper is a technique called scoring. Here is how it is done:
1. Line up a ruler along the line you want to fold.
2. Lightly run a sharp knife or scissors along the fold line. Press down firmly enough to leave a light crease. Take care not to cut all the way through the paper (Figure T–28).

SAFETY TIP

Clean-up Routines Remind students to clean up thoroughly and often. They should make certain to clean up spills immediately to prevent accidents. If dust results, have them use a wet mop or vacuum rather than a broom. Sweeping stirs up dust that could prove harmful to some students, particularly those who are asthmatic.

▲ Figure T–28

3. Gently crease the paper along the line you made.
To score curved lines, use the same technique. Make sure your curves are wide enough to ensure a clean fold. Too tight a curve will cause the paper to wrinkle (Figure T–29).

▲ Figure T–29

27. Making a Tissue Paper Collage

For your first experience with tissue, make a free design with the tissue colors. Start with the lightest colors of tissue first and save the darkest for last. It is difficult to change the color of dark tissue by overlapping it with other colors. If one area becomes too dark, you might cut out a piece of white paper, glue it over the dark area carefully, and apply new colors over the white area.

1. Apply a coat of adhesive to the area where you wish to place the tissue.
2. Place the tissue down carefully over the wet area (Figure T–30). Don't let your fingers get wet.
3. Then add another coat of adhesive over the tissue. If your brush picks up any color from the wet tissue, rinse your brush in water and let it dry before using it again.
4. Experiment by overlapping colors. Allow the tissue to wrinkle to create textures as you apply it. Be sure that all the loose edges of tissue are glued down.

28. Working with Glue

When applying glue, always start at the center of the surface you are coating and work outward.

• When gluing papers together don't use a lot of glue, just a dot will do. Use dots in the corners and along the edges. Press the two surfaces together. Keep dots at least ½ inch (1.3 cm) in from the edge of your paper.
• Handle a glued surface carefully with only your fingertips. Make sure your hands are clean before pressing the glued surface into place.
• *Note:* The glue should be as thin as possible. Thick or beaded glue will create ridges on your work.

▲ Figure T–30

TECHNIQUE TIP

Using Spray Fixatives   To protect drawings, you can spray them with fixative to prevent smearing.

Spray fixative is sold both in aerosol cans and in small bottles with atomizers. Fixative in a bottle is applied by pumping the atomizer. Test the spray first on a piece of scrap paper marked with the same drawing medium used in the drawing. Avoid getting the spray device too close to the drawing. Hold the spray device 12 to 18 inches (30 to 46 cm) from it. Keep the sprayer moving. Several light coats are better than one heavy one. Fixative dries rapidly. Spray fixative labeled *workable* is best. This term means that after you spray an area of a drawing lightly, you can still draw on it. Always use spray fixatives outside the studio in a well-ventilated area—outdoors, if possible.

Using the
Artist Profiles

Role playing, games, and bulletin boards can be effective ways to involve students and to help them grasp information about the various artists, the time in which the artists lived, their particular art style and techniques, and their contributions to the world of art. On the following pages are teaching strategies designed to help you introduce, reinforce, and teach students about artists and their works.

▲ Artists, down through the ages, have helped us visualize what we learn about history. Art historians are responsible for much of what we know about the artists who have lived in the past.

Romare Bearden

1911–1988
American Painter, Printmaker,
Collage Artist

Saturday Morning
page 54

"Most artists take some place, and like a flower, they sink roots," Romare Bearden once said. "My roots are in North Carolina." Bearden spent his early childhood near Charlotte, North Carolina. Later, he moved to Pittsburgh, Pennsylvania, and then to New York City. These locations form the background for much of his art.

Bearden's artwork shows not only places but also the people of these areas. His paintings and collages show a rich mix of many aspects of his African-American heritage. His collages have been called quiltlike. They reflect the patchwork quilts made by African-American women in rural areas of North Carolina.

To create his collages, Bearden cut pieces of photographs from newspapers and magazines. Then he arranged them into tight compositions and pasted them on canvas. Like music and literature, Bearden's art tells stories. Some of his collages show the struggle of life in the inner city. Others reveal the joys and sorrow of African-American family life.

In addition to being an artist, Bearden was a musician. He found great inspiration in blues and jazz music. This influence can be seen in the "visual jazz" that he created in his collages.

In the art of printmaking, Katsushika Hokusai is considered the greatest artist of the Japanese style known as Ukiyo-e. The Ukiyo-e style means "pictures of the floating world." Several famous Impressionist painters, including Edgar Degas, Claude Monet, and Henri de Toulouse-Lautrec, collected Hokusai's prints. Hokusai's work had a great influence on the works of these artists.

Hokusai was born to a poor family in Edo (now Tokyo), Japan, in 1760. He studied woodcut printmaking under a Ukiyo-e master. Hokusai created a great number of color prints and book illustrations. These works reflected the lives and customs of the Japanese people. He also painted many landscapes.

Hokusai had done little of the work that has made him famous before he was 60 years old. In his lifetime, Hokusai created an estimated 30,000 pieces of art. Despite producing so much work, Hokusai was a humble man. As he neared death at the age of 89, he said, "If the gods had given me only ten more years I could have become a truly great painter."

Katsushika Hokusai

1760–1849
Japanese Printmaker, Painter

Fishing Boats at Choshi in Shoshu
page 32

A Gust of Wind at Ejiri
page 117

■ Visual Presentation

Divide the class into groups of two or three and assign different time periods to each group. Have each group research that period and report on it to the class. Encourage the students to use as many visual aids as they can, and to use the school media center and local library. Suggest that they use large prints of artworks if they are available; the library is a good source of either prints or oversize art books. The media center might have equipment with which the students can make slides from books to use in the report. Slides ensure that everyone in the class can see the works being discussed. Dressing up in costumes, role playing, or presenting a dramatization can also make a report more enjoyable and meaningful for everyone.

■ Dramatization

A good choice for a dramatization is one event from the artist's life. Dramatizations make stronger impressions than straight reports. For example, a debate focusing on style between the Impressionists and Post-Impressionists would be interesting, especially if students took on the roles of real characters, such as Monet, Renoir, Cézanne, or Van Gogh.

Artist Profiles **293**

BACKGROUND INFORMATION

Katsushika Hokusai Thanks to inexpensive woodcut prints produced by artists like Hokusai, Japanese art came to have a broader audience throughout the Western world. Hokusai produced an amazing variety and volume of scenes of everyday life. One series, called *Manga*, or *Random Sketches*, consisted of fifteen books of drawings reflecting the multifaceted culture of Japan at the time.

Though energetic and prolific, Hokusai often had to rely on showmanship to make a living, since his son and grandson kept him constantly in debt. Though his house burned to the ground when he was seventy-eight, destroying much of his work, he still left at least thirty thousand pictures.

■ Puzzles

Turn some extra prints found in magazines into puzzles. Dry mount the print on a strong backing, such as poster board or mat board. If you are going to make more than one puzzle, put each on a different color backing so that, if the pieces get mixed up, they can be separated by color. Laminate the work, if possible, to protect the surface. Then, using a sharp cutting blade, cut the print into puzzle pieces. Try to keep the puzzle pieces large to help students become familiar with the art work. Use a separate storage container for each puzzle. Puzzles can help visual learners, or you can use them to hold a puzzle speed competition. Teams of students can compete to see which team can assemble a puzzle the fastest.

Judith Leyster
1609–1660
Dutch Painter

Self-Portrait
page 80

Judith Leyster's name was hardly seen in art history books until 1893, more than 200 years after her death. At that time, workers at the Louvre made an important discovery. While cleaning a painting thought to be by Frans Hals, the workers found Judith Leyster's signature.

Leyster was born in Haarlem, Holland, in 1609. During that time, most female artists were helped by artist fathers. Because Leyster's father was not an artist, she had to rely on talent alone. Leyster also differed from other female painters in her choice of subject matter. Instead of still lifes, Leyster chose to paint *genre* paintings. These were scenes of ordinary life.

Early in her career, Leyster gained recognition. When she was 17, her name was mentioned in a book about Haarlem artists. At 24, she was elected to the painter's Guild of St. Luke. Then she taught painting for several years.

Some of Leyster's most original works are her small genre paintings of women doing household activities. These include scenes in which women are combing their children's hair or sewing by the fireside. Leyster was one of the first artists to paint subjects such as these.

René Magritte was a master of surrealism. When people view his paintings, they often look for hidden symbolism. That is not what the artist wanted, however. Magritte wrote, "People who look for symbolic meanings fail to grasp the inherent poetry and mystery of the image...."

Magritte studied art at the Académie Royale des Beaux-Arts in Brussels, Belgium. To support himself, he worked as a commercial artist for many years and even designed wallpaper.

The objects in Magritte's works are usually ordinary, and they are painted very realistically. What makes the artworks thought-provoking is the unusual placement of the objects. The artist wanted viewers to see the commonplace in a completely different way.

Magritte, however, did not think of himself as an artist. In fact, he did not even have an art studio. Instead, he painted in the living room of his home. Each week, a group of his fellow Surrealist painters came to his home. They would meet to discuss titles for Magritte's unusual paintings.

Today, Magritte's work continues to have a major influence on the world. His images have also inspired many commercial advertisements.

René Magritte
1898–1967
Belgian Painter

The Human Condition
page 268

294   *Artist Profiles*

Claude Monet

1840–1926
French Painter

Stack of Wheat
    page *12*

*Poplars on the Bank of the
    Epte River*
    page *96*

Claude Monet is considered the father of the art movement called Impressionism. He was born in 1840 in a small town in France. Although a poor student, he developed great skill in drawing.

Monet studied at the Paris Academy. To exhibit works at the academy, artists had to follow strict rules. Monet and a group of young artists did not like those rules, so they left to paint outdoors. They painted with dabs of color. When viewed from a distance, the colors blended together.

In 1874 Monet and these other artists held their own exhibit. The paintings in the show shocked the public. One of Monet's paintings in this exhibit was called *Impression: Sunrise*. An angry critic used that title to label the group *Impressionists*.

Monet was interested in the effects of light and how it changed the appearance of objects, particularly their colors. To capture these changes, he made many paintings of the same scene at different times of the day. In this way, he illustrated the changing light and how it affected color.

In 1883 Monet settled at Giverny, France. There he designed his own gardens, including a water lily pond. This pond is featured in many of Monet's paintings.

■ Time-Period Recognition Game

If you can find individual prints that are small enough, you might organize them into a time-period recognition game. For example, you might set up one deck with four Ancient Egyptian works, four Gothic, four Renaissance, four African-American, four Near East, and so forth. At the beginning of the year you can use stick-on labels that identify the periods. Later you can remove the labels. Be careful that each set of four in a deck is distinctly different from every other set in that deck.

■ Time-Style Recognition Game

For a more advanced game than the one above, organize the cards by style. In this deck you might include four Impressionist works, four Cubist works, four Surrealist works, and so forth. Again, be careful not to use two styles that might be confused, such as American Regionalist and English Landscape.

From the age of 12, Georgia O'Keeffe knew that she wanted to be an artist. She lived to be nearly 100 years old, and she painted for most of those years.

Georgia O'Keeffe was born in Sun Prairie, Wisconsin, in 1887. She studied art with several teachers, learning special techniques from each. From one teacher, she learned how to "fill space in a beautiful way." This sensitivity to space can be seen in all her work, but especially in her flower paintings. O'Keeffe painted flowers of enormous size. She did this because she wanted to surprise viewers and make them take time to see what she saw.

O'Keeffe loved the southwestern United States and lived in New Mexico for many years. She found artistic inspiration in the desert landscape. She saw beautiful form in the plants, mountains, and animals that surrounded her. Some of her paintings of the animal bones that she found in the desert shocked people. Eventually, though, they became some of O'Keeffe's most famous works.

Georgia O'Keeffe

1887–1986
American Painter

Red Cannas
    page *184*

Artist Profiles   **295**

more about • • •

Claude Monet and Georgia O'Keeffe Point out to students that although the works of Monet and O'Keeffe are very different in style, both artists had a special appreciation for flowers and nature.

Divide the class into small groups of three or four. Ask each group to choose either O'Keeffe or Monet and to choose two or three of the artist's works to examine and analyze. Then ask each group to pretend that you, the teacher, are a museum curator. Have each group select one work of art by their artist and make a case for your adding it to your collection.

■ Bulletin Boards

Divide the class into groups and have each group choose one of the artists from the Artist Profiles, Handbook pages 293–297. Set aside one small bulletin board as an "Artist of the Week" board and assign each group the responsibility of featuring their artist for one week. Set up some guidelines for the student displays and share this with the class. Some criteria for the display could be:

- catchy title and neat lettering,
- quantity and accuracy of information,
- creativity, and aesthetic quality.

The minimum information would include artist's name, country, dates of birth and death, style, and titles of works displayed, example of artist's works, information about the artist, and portrayal of the artist's style or of the time and place in which the artist lived. If appropriate, evaluate the display according to the guidelines established.

Marjorie Phillips
1894–1985
American Painter

Night Baseball
page 206

Although Marjorie Phillips was not an avid baseball fan, two of her most famous paintings feature baseball games. One of her paintings, *Night Baseball*, seemed so authentic that the Baseball Hall of Fame wanted to buy it.

Phillips studied art at the Art Students League in New York. In 1921, she married Duncan Phillips, and the couple founded the Phillips Collection, an art museum. Located in Washington, D.C., the gallery was the first museum of modern art in the United States.

In 1923, Marjorie Phillips had her first one-woman show. Many of her paintings were still lifes and landscapes in the Impressionist style. "I decided to paint the celebration of the wonder of the world," she said. "I didn't want to paint depressing pictures…. That's why my paintings are all on the cheerful side—I felt it was needed."

After her husband's death in 1966, Marjorie Phillips took over as director of the museum. Despite her busy schedule, Phillips always found time to paint. In 1977, at the age of 81, she had a one-woman show in which most of the paintings were less than ten years old.

Diego Rivera
1886–1957
Mexican Painter, Muralist

*The Making of a Fresco
Showing the Building
of a City*
page 232

Mexican painter Diego Rivera believed that art was meant for the working people. He felt that it should be available to everyone, not just people who visited museums. Rivera chose to paint huge murals on the sides of public buildings. His work adorns the walls of the Detroit Institute of Arts in Michigan as well as many buildings in Mexico.

Rivera was born in Guanajuato, Mexico, in 1886. He studied at the Academy of San Carlos in Mexico City. Between 1907 and 1921, he took two trips to Europe. There he studied the paintings of the great masters.

When Rivera returned to Mexico in 1921, he began creating large murals. These works were based on social themes, including the history, culture, and problems of Mexico. Rivera held strong political beliefs, which he sometimes included in his art. He used vivid colors in bold, simple designs.

In 1929, Rivera married Frida Kahlo. She was also a well-known Mexican painter. When he died in 1957, Rivera left his final work unfinished. It was his most ambitious project—a mural showing the history of Mexico for the National Palace in Mexico City.

296   *Artist Profiles*

BACKGROUND INFORMATION

Diego Rivera   Although Diego Rivera had dabbled in the early Cubist movement, today he is best known for his achievements as a muralist. Commissioned by the government of Mexico shortly after a revolution in the 1920s, Rivera began a series of national murals. In an effort to stir national pride, he borrowed from the style indigenous to Mexico before its colonization and conveyed the spirit of the new revolution. Combining his aesthetic ideals with social goals, Rivera's art is aimed not only at the art community, but at Mexico as a whole.

In pieces such as *The Blood of the Martyrs Enriches the Earth*, Rivera focuses on the European exploitation of native Mexicans, drawing from the symbolism of their cultures.

Jan Steen

1626–1679
Dutch Painter

The Dancing Couple
page 94

Jan Steen was as much a storyteller as he was an artist. Many of his genre paintings, or scenes of everyday life, tell humorous stories. They have entertained viewers for centuries.

During Steen's time, most artists concentrated on one type of painting, such as still life. Steen, however, did not limit himself in this way. Although he is most well known for his genre paintings, Steen's work also included still lifes, portraits, and biblical subjects.

Other artists of this time, such as Vermeer, also created genre paintings. These artists most often painted calm, quiet scenes with one or two people performing everyday tasks. Steen's works, however, were very different. He painted scenes filled with happy, loud people enjoying themselves. To create an added sense of realism, Steen often included himself and his wife and children in the paintings.

There is a Dutch expression, "a Jan Steen household," that is still used today. It refers to a home filled with happy chaos, similar to the homes depicted in Steen's paintings.

Leonardo da Vinci is probably most famous for his paintings of the *Mona Lisa* and *The Last Supper*. He was more than just an extraordinary artist, however. Leonardo was also a great scholar. He was well educated in many subjects, including anatomy, physics, geography, and architecture.

Showing talent for drawing as a young child, Leonardo trained under the artist Andrea del Verrocchio. He soon rejected both the egg tempera and fresco media that were commonly used. Instead, Leonardo turned to oil paints, which had recently been invented by the Flemish painter Jan van Eyck.

In many ways, Leonardo da Vinci was well ahead of his time. He was constantly inventing, searching, and trying new ideas. His notebooks fascinate us with ideas for ways to fly, complex machines, and studies of the human body.

Unfortunately, Leonardo's passion for experimenting did not always work out. When he painted the *The Last Supper*, Leonardo mixed oil with the fresco medium. Fresco is painted with water-base paint on freshly laid plaster. Because oil and water do not mix, the oil he added would not stick to the wall. The mural had begun to fade and flake even during Leonardo's lifetime. With continual efforts to preserve it, however, it remains one of the most well-known works of all time.

Leonardo da Vinci

1452–1519
Italian Painter

Oak Leafs and a Spray
of Greenwood
page 108

Artist Profiles **297**

■ Maps

Have world maps and globes available to help students locate cities and countries where the artists lived and worked. This helps students to visualize the geographical features that influenced the artists' work.

■ Time Line

Display a time line in the class. Have students attach sketches of the masterpieces shown in the text in the proper spot on the time line. They might even add small prints of works that are not in the text or photocopy works from books, color the photocopies, and add the name of the artist and the title of the work. If there is not enough room for all the pieces at one place in time, strings of yarn can be attached to the photocopy and pictures arranged above or below with yarn leading to the proper place on the time line.

■ Name That Artist

Place in a brown paper bag the name of each artist who appears in the Artist Profiles. Pass the bag around the room and have each student blindly select one of the cards within. Have the student list one characteristic that is associated with the artist. For example, if they pick the artist Picasso, the student may say Cubism or Spanish-born. Have them put the name back into the bag and shake it for the next student to select an artist name. If the student is able to successfully identify a characteristic that has not already been mentioned about the artist, he or she stays in the game. If not, the player sits on the sidelines until a new game begins.

BACKGROUND INFORMATION

Leonardo da Vinci In Leonardo's time, frescoes were created by the rapid application of a water-based paint to fresh patches of wall plaster; the artist could only work on the amount of wall that would remain wet for that work day. Because of this time restriction, viewers today can see ridges that define each day's worth of painting. A fresco painter began by making a drawing on the wall. Once large sheets of paper became less expensive in the mid-fifteenth century, artists could make life-size "cartoons" that helped artists efficiently plan frescoes. The cartoons were applied to the wall and pricked with colored dust to provide guide lines.

Using the Career Spotlights

On the pages that follow, you will find teaching suggestions to help you introduce students to many art-related job opportunities and careers. At the bottom of the page, you will find a list of addresses of organizations that students can write to for additional information.

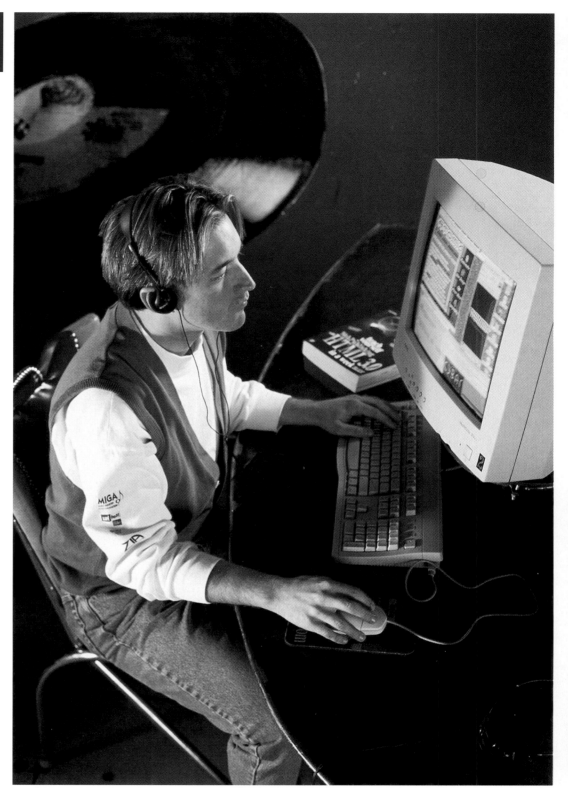

298

Advertising Artist

Advertising artists design the artwork that is used in advertisements. They usually work for an advertising agency. They may also work for a publication, such as a magazine or newspaper. Some advertising artists work in the ad department of a large corporation, such as a store or restaurant chain.

Advertising artists work as part of a design team. This team includes an art director, designers, and writers. First, the art director develops a concept, or idea, for an advertisement. The copywriters write the words that will appear in the ad. Then the artist creates a design that works with both the art director's concept and the words. Many advertising artists use computers when creating their artwork.

A career as an advertising artist usually requires a college education in art or design. Courses in computer design techniques are very valuable. Once they are hired, advertising artists may also receive on-the-job training.

Architect

An architect is an artist who designs buildings and other structures. Your home, school, and local shopping mall were all designed by architects. An architect prepares plans that show both the interior and exterior of a building. These sketches include floor plans that show the placement of rooms, hallways, doors, windows, closets, and other features. They also show the exterior walls on all sides of the building and a top-down drawing of the roof.

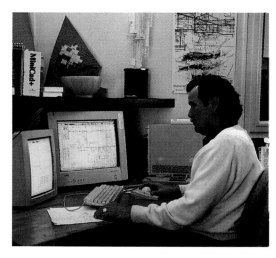

A building design must be not only visually pleasing but also functional and safe. When planning a building, architects must consider how the structure will be used. For example, the design for a home would be very different from the design for a restaurant or hospital. Architects must also keep in mind the needs of the people who will use the building. This includes such subjects as traffic patterns, living and work areas, and storage space. They must also know about heating and cooling, ventilation, and plumbing.

Architects need a college degree in architecture. They take courses in math, engineering, and drafting. In addition, they must pass an exam to become licensed.

Career Spotlights **299**

■ Analyzing Advertisements

Divide students into small groups. Select a variety of magazines from different interest areas, such as fashion, mechanics, photography, architecture, teen life, current events, health, sports, science, science fiction, television, video games, computers, and so on. Have each group compare such things as the types of advertisements and the types of advertising techniques used to capture the attention of the specific audience. Have each group present their findings to the class.

■ Appreciating Architecture

Have students each sketch a building in their neighborhood. Then, have them examine the building materials used to create the structure they have drawn. Invite an architect in, if possible, to discuss such topics as the design process, the use of computer aided design programs, and how building materials are chosen for buildings in the area.

■ Art Directors

Explain that art directors often supervise teams of artists, designers, and production people. These teams may work in the same location or may work independently in their own studios in another location, even in another state. Ask students to explore ways that art directors might communicate with "outside" design teams and direct the work of several individuals and groups. Students might mention the use of scanners, modums, e-mail, phone conferencing, fax, and overnight express delivery services as means of ongoing, fast communication. Visit a local art director at a magazine or advertising agency, if possible, to have students observe a typical day in the life of an art director.

■ Art Teacher

Invite a school counselor to speak to the class and explain the requirements for attending art and design schools. Have the counselor explain the additional requirements for becoming an art teacher in your state.

Ask students to seek out art teachers who may work in park district programs, hospitals, retirement centers, or museums. Have students interview an art teacher to find out about that person's background, training, and areas of expertise.

Art Director

Art directors are responsible for the look of the advertisements that you see in newspapers, in magazines, and on television. They are also responsible for the style and design of magazines, and of books like this one. Art directors most often work in the fields of advertising and publishing.

An art director studies the information that needs to be presented. He or she must decide how that information can be shown in a visually appealing way. The art director then works with a design team that includes artists, designers, and copywriters. The art director oversees the team's work and checks to make sure that the final printed material is satisfactory.

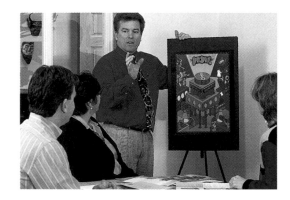

Most art directors have a college education. Courses should provide a well-rounded background in art and design. Art directors study graphic design, drafting, layout, photography, and computer design. Several years of on-the-job training are required before a person can become an art director.

Art Teacher

Art teachers instruct students in the use of various art materials and techniques. They also educate students in the theories and principles of art criticism, aesthetics, and art history. In middle schools, art teachers provide general art instruction. Art teachers in high schools may specialize in a specific area, such as painting, drawing, or crafts.

In a classroom, the art teacher helps students create their own artwork. Students are taught how to use a wide variety of media, such as pencils, charcoal, pastels, paints, and clay. The teacher encourages students to analyze their own work as well as the works of master artists.

Art teachers must have a college degree. Their educational background includes courses in both art and teaching. Many art teachers continue to study and exhibit their own artwork throughout their teaching careers. An essential part of being an art teacher is a love of art and a desire to encourage this appreciation in others.

300 *Career Spotlights*

┌─ *more about* • • •

Advertising Careers You may wish to have students write to the following for information about careers in advertising management.

American Advertising Federation
1101 Vermont Ave NW
Washington, D.C. 20005-3521

Teachers' Associations Have students contact the following organizations to learn more about teachers' unions and education-related issues:

American Federation of Teachers
555 New Jersey Avenue, NW
Washington, D.C. 20001

Artist

Artists create works of art. Their work is usually classified as either fine art or applied art. Fine art, such as a painting, is created simply to be viewed and appreciated. Applied art, such as ceramics or other crafts objects, serves a more practical purpose.

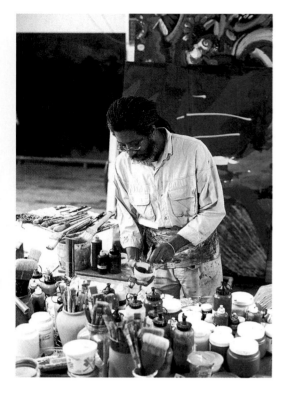

The work of an artist may involve a variety of media. The media are the materials used to create the art. A painter, for instance, might use oil, watercolor, or acrylic paint. A sculptor might create art out of stone, clay, or wood. Other artists might create jewelry, pottery, or furniture from such materials as metal, clay, or plastic.

Although not all artists have a college education, almost all have had formal art instruction. This training includes studio art classes, such as drawing, painting, and design. It also includes courses in art history. One of the most important requirements for a career as an artist is a natural talent in art.

Graphic Artist

Graphic artists design artwork for many types of products. These products might include packaging and promotional displays, brochures, advertisements, magazines, and books like the one you are reading. Graphic artists are often employed in the publishing or advertising fields. However, they may also work in other areas, such as designing the boxes that hold videos and computer games. They frequently work as a member of a design team.

Most graphic artists use computers to help in the creation of their artwork. Computer technology saves time by performing some of the tasks that artists previously had to do by hand. For example, artists can use computer graphics to easily experiment with a variety of colors, shapes, and designs.

A career in graphic art generally requires a college education and formal art training. In addition, graphic artists must have an in-depth knowledge of computer graphics. Because the computer field changes so rapidly, graphic artists must continually learn about new technology.

■ Graphic Artist

Ask a graphic artist to come in and demonstrate some of the software and multi-media programs graphic artists often use or need to be familiar with, such as Hyperstudio, Quark, or Adobe PageMaker, for example.

┌ *more about* • • •

Computer Graphics Careers Students may wish to write for more information on education and career resources in the field of computer graphics, art, and design. Have them contact the Special Interest Group on Computer Graphics (SIGGRAPH) at:

ACM SIGGRAPH
1515 Broadway, 17th floor
New York, New York 10012

■ Illustrator

Bring in examples of a variety of illustrators' work: medical illustration in journals, textbooks, and encyclopedias; technical illustration in manuals, brochures, and catalogs; and fashion illustrations appearing in catalogs and magazines. Also bring in a variety of trade books, textbooks, and children's books that are heavily illustrated. Ask students to choose one type of illustration to explore further, finding additional examples and researching the illustrators (if possible) responsible for the work.

■ Industrial Designer

Emphasize to students the broad spectrum of design included in the category of industrial design. Ask students to identify a few commonplace objects that they use every day, such as pens, backpacks, athletic shoes, bicycles, caps, doors, desks, refrigerators, and so on. Ask each student to choose an object to redesign or modify in some fashion, drawing their designs and writing a brief explanation of the purpose and appeal of their object. Have students share their designs and the process they used in their redesigns, and have them explain what improvements they think their particular design achieved.

Illustrator

The work of an illustrator revolves around drawing. Illustrators may create many different types of artwork. Most specialize in one field, such as technical illustration. Illustrators often work in the publishing and advertising industries.

A technical illustrator specializes in drawing diagrams. These might be included in instructional manuals. They help explain how to use appliances or equipment, such as a computer or VCR. A fashion illustrator draws sketches of clothing and accessories. Fashion illustrations might appear in catalogs, advertisements, or magazines.

Most illustrators have a college degree in art. Besides drawing, they learn about design, composition, and perspective. Illustrators who want to concentrate on one area must also take courses related to that subject. For example, a medical illustrator must study biology and medicine.

Industrial Designer

Have you ever wondered who designed your favorite toys and electronic games? Those are the work of industrial designers. They design manufactured products, such as computers, kitchen appliances, and cars. Industrial designers usually work for large companies, such as toy, equipment, or machine manufacturers.

Industrial designers develop new products. They also make improvements to existing products, such as adding new features or changing the design of an automobile. When developing a product, industrial designers first do research. The designers need to know who will use the product and how they will use it. Industrial designers also must evaluate similar products that are already available. Then they combine this knowledge with their artistic ability. Their goal is to create products that will work well and be popular with the consumers who purchase them.

A career in industrial design requires a college education. In addition to art courses, industrial designers study computer-aided design. Many designers use computer technology when developing products.

─ *more about* ● ● ● ─

Illustrators For information on careers in illustration have students contact:
   The Society of Illustrators
   128 East 63rd Street
   New York, New York 10021-7303

A brochure that describes careers in industrial design and lists academic programs in the field is available from the Industrial Designers Society of America. For price and ordering information write:
   Industrial Designers Society of America
   1142 Walker Road
   Great Falls, Virginia 22066-1836

Interior Designer

Interior designers plan the interior space of buildings. These buildings might include homes, offices, hotels, or restaurants. Sometimes interior designers plan upgrades to existing buildings. In addition to preparing drawings, interior designers choose furniture, carpeting, and window coverings. They also select lighting and color schemes. Interior designers must make sure that all of these individual parts work together as a whole and are aesthetically pleasing.

When planning an interior space, the interior designer must always consider the client's needs, tastes, and budget. Many designers use computer programs to create several versions of an interior plan. Using a computer also allows the designer to easily make changes to suit the client's wishes.

To be an interior designer, you need a college education. Courses include drawing, design, and art history. Interior designers also must show creativity, a flair for color, and an eye for detail.

Landscape Architect

Landscape architects combine their love of nature and the environment with their artistic ability. They design outdoor areas such as those surrounding houses or apartment complexes, shopping centers, and office buildings.

Landscape architects choose which types of trees, bushes, and flowers are best suited for the location. Then they draw sketches of how these plants should be arranged. One goal of a landscape architect is to make sure that the design is not only functional but also attractive. Another goal is to make sure that the design works well with the natural environment. As in all design fields, more and more landscape architects are using computers to complete their work more efficiently.

A career in landscape architecture requires a college education. Courses include landscape design and construction, surveying, and city and regional planning. In addition, landscape architects study science and nature and take studio art courses.

■ Interior Designer

Divide the class into small groups or pairs of students and have each group imagine that they are interior designers who have been asked to plan a student lounge for the school. Before they make their design, they should survey their classmates to see what they would like in a lounge and what they think the purpose and use of the lounge should be. Have them try to think of the lounge as a multipurpose area that could serve as space for a meeting, a party, art exhibits, and so on. What areas will they need to include? How should the spaces be furnished and decorated? Have students use their creativity. Have them make sketches for their lounge and include paint chips and wallpaper and floor covering samples to show the color scheme for the room.

■ Landscape Architect

Ask students to identify two buildings in the local area: one that has a pleasing landscape design and one that would benefit from an improved landscape plan. Ask students to analyze what they like about the first design and what is lacking in the second. Then ask students to make recommendations for an improved plan and create a small scale model of their plan using cardboard and found objects. As students work out their designs, remind them to think about color, shape, and form, and to consider what type of plants and construction materials they would use to help integrate the building with its surrounding environment.

more about • • •

Interior Designers   For information about careers in interior design, contact:
American Society of Interior Designers
200 Lexington Ave.
New York, New York 10016

■ Museum Worker

Invite a museum employee or volunteer who works at a local museum to come in and discuss what kinds of jobs exist locally. Encourage students to ask specific questions about day-to-day tasks.

If there is no museum close by, ask students to write a letter to any particular museum of their choice, anywhere in the country. Have students research different kinds of museums, with their locations and addresses. Before students write to a museum to ask about the work a museum employee does, have them draft a copy to share with the class. Encourage students to brainstorm pertinent questions to ask.

■ Photographer

Ask students to list kinds of publications in which they can observe photographs. They may mention newspapers, catalogs, magazines, fliers, books and textbooks, and encyclopedias. Have students look through such publications and notice the credit lines under the photographs. Ask them to discuss photographers whose names they see repeatedly and whether those individuals seem to specialize in one particular type of photography. Some examples of magazines students might examine for photos are *Time, Newsweek, National Geographic, American Heritage, Sports Illustrated, Audubon, Discover, Architectural Digest, Life, Photographic, Smithsonian*, and various travel magazines.

Museum Worker

Some people combine their love of art and museums to become museum employees. There are a wide variety of museums across the country. Some show artwork, such as paintings, sculpture, or photographs. Others house objects of historical value, such as antique clothing or furniture. Still others display items related to science or natural history, such as dinosaur skeletons.

People who work in museums may have several different types of jobs. A curator chooses and obtains the objects that will be displayed in the museum. An assistant curator helps the curator set up the museum exhibits. A conservator cares for and preserves the objects kept in the museum. A tour guide provides information about exhibits to the museum's visitors and answers their questions.

The degree of education required for a museum worker varies depending on the type of work. Most museum workers, however, are highly educated. Many have advanced college degrees and are considered experts in their field.

Photographer

Photographers are skilled artists who use their cameras to create artwork. Their work varies greatly depending on what type of photographs they take. For example, a catalog photographer works in a studio and takes pictures of objects such as food, clothing, or jewelry. A newspaper or magazine photographer works in the field, taking pictures of people and events in the news.

The work of photographers involves more than just taking the pictures. Photographers must first visualize the shot or set it up in an artistic way. After the pictures are taken, many photographers develop their own film in a darkroom. Then they print the slides or photographs.

A career as a photographer requires formal training in photography. Many photographers have a college degree in art. Photographers who specialize in certain areas, such as science, may need additional courses in that field. Beginning photographers sometimes receive training on the job by assisting a professional photographer.

─ *more about* • • • ─

Museum Curators   For general information about careers as a curator and schools offering courses in curatorial science, contact:

American Association of Museums
1225 I Street NW, Suite 200
Washington, D.C. 20005-3914

Textile Designer

The fabric of the clothes you are wearing was designed by a textile designer. The word *textile* refers to cloth or fabric. Textile designers create and draw patterns for fabric. The fabric may be used in clothing, furniture upholstery, draperies, or rugs. Textile designers sometimes create their own original designs. At other times, they may adapt a design or develop one based on a certain theme. Textile designers work for companies that manufacture fabric.

Like other artists, textile designers must have creativity and artistic skill. They must also understand how fabric is constructed and manufactured. In addition, they need to be aware of current fashion trends. With this knowledge, they are better able to create popular designs.

Textile designers generally need a college education. They study art, design, and textiles. Many textile designers also take courses in computer technology, including computer-aided design.

Web-Site Designer

A web site is a location on the World Wide Web, which is part of the Internet. The Internet is a network of computer systems. It allows computer users to communicate with other users around the world. Web sites may be sponsored by companies, organizations, or individuals. They are most often used to provide information, promote products, and answer questions.

Web-site designers use computer software to create and maintain these sites. The work involves laying out web pages, designing graphic elements, and creating electronic links to other sites. Web-site designers may create sites for a large company or organization. They may also work for a design firm that creates sites for many companies.

To be a web-site designer, a person must have a background in art, with an emphasis on design. A web-site designer must also have technical training in computers and computer programming. Keeping current with the latest technology is an important part of the job.

Career Spotlights **305**

■ Field Trips

Field trips contribute greatly to a course. If class field trips are not possible, individual trips that one or more students may take after school or on weekends might be arranged with the help and supervision of parents.

All trips will be more successful if you set up guidelines to help students understand the objectives. Research done prior to the trip and a follow-up evaluation will add to the value of the experience. Students should know what to look for and what to expect to gain from the experience. You might point out that the business people they visit may be possible employers some day. Appropriate conduct and dress on such trips is always in order. Students should also know what kind of follow-up will be expected, such as a written evaluation, a quiz, or class discussion.

Make the necessary arrangements for a field trip well in advance to ensure that students are welcome. Establish a time schedule and follow it carefully. While museums, organizations, and industries are usually happy to conduct tours of their facilities, the staff members usually have other responsibilities, and group tours must be prearranged in a thoughtful manner. In addition, keep the attention span and interests of your students in mind as you make such arrangements.

more about • • •

Art and Design   For a list of accredited schools of art and design, contact:

National Association of Schools of Art and Design
11250 Roger Bacon Drive, Suite 21
Reston, Virginia 22090

LESSON 1

Making A Color Wheel

LESSON 1

Making a Color Wheel

(pages 306–307)

Lesson Time: 60 minutes

☑ OBJECTIVES

After completing this lesson, students will be able to:

- Recognize Ellsworth Kelly as a Hard-Edge painter who used simple shapes and colors to make paintings.
- Identify primary, secondary, and intermediate colors. Arrange these hues in their proper order to make a color wheel.
- Describe, analyze, interpret, and judge their work.

☑ SUPPLIES

- Pencils and sketch paper
- Construction paper in primary, secondary, and intermediate hues
- Black construction paper
- Scissors; white glue or glue sticks

■ Lesson Review

Suggest that students review the following lessons before beginning this Studio Lesson:

- Chapter 1, Lesson 3, Color, pages 8–11
- Chapter 1, Lesson 4, Mixing Colors, pages 12–13

■ Motivator

Ask students whether they think about the colors of clothing they are going to buy when they go shopping. Have them discuss what influences their color choices.

Are you amazed at a rainbow's colors every time you see one? It might have been such an experience that inspired the colorful painting in Figure S–1. Examine this work. It is an example of a twentieth-century style of painting known as Hard-Edge painting. Works of this style use simple shapes and vivid colors. Like a rainbow, this painting features bands of color that change and blend. Why do you suppose the artist has included thirteen bands in all? Which color contains the extra panel?

WHAT YOU WILL LEARN

You will create a one-of-a-kind color wheel. Rather than use simple geometric shapes, as the Hard-Edge artist has done in the work on this page, you will choose a basic free-form shape. This will represent a real or imaginary plant, animal, or other object. As in Figure S–1, you will repeat the same shape. You will arrange your shapes in a circle on construction paper, placing the shapes in their correct order on the color wheel.

WHAT YOU WILL NEED

- Sketch paper and pencil
- Scissors
- Sheets of construction paper in primary, secondary, and intermediate hues, 6 x 9 inches (15 x 23 cm)
- Black construction paper, 18 x 24 inches (46 x 60 cm)
- White glue or glue stick

Figure S–1   Identify the primary, secondary, and intermediate hues. How much skill did Kelly need to paint these panels without any visible brush strokes?

Ellsworth Kelly. *Spectrum II.* (Thirteen panels). 1966–67. Oil on canvas. 203.2 x 693.4 cm (80" x 22'9"). Saint Louis Art Museum, St. Louis, Missouri.

---

more about • • •

The Hard-Edge Movement   Hard-Edge painting appeared following the Abstract Expressionism movement. While Expressionists painted with emotion by dribbling, splashing, or spilling paint on the canvas, Hard-Edge artists painted very differently. They used straight lines, geometric shapes, and few colors in their paintings, making them look very mechanical, precise, and lacking in emotion. The philosophy of these painters was summed up by Frank Stella: "What you see is what you see."

WHAT YOU WILL DO

1. With classmates, brainstorm a list of plants, animals, people, or objects that would be good subjects for a color wheel. Discuss which shapes might be the most interesting for this artwork.

2. Working by yourself, make several sketches of one of the shapes discussed. Choose your best sketch, and cut out the shape. This shape is to be a *template,* or stencil.

3. Place the template on a sheet of construction paper in one of the primary hues—blue, red, or yellow. Carefully trace around the shape using pencil. Place sheets of construction paper in the remaining two hues beneath the first. Line the sheets up. Carefully cut out the shape penciled on the first sheet. You will now have three copies of your template, one for each of the primary hues. Repeat this step, once for the secondary hues and again for the intermediate hues.

4. Note the arrangement of hues on the color wheel on page **8.** Arrange the shapes you have created in a circle in the order shown. Experiment with "flipping," or turning the shapes in different positions, being careful to maintain the color-wheel positions. When you are satisfied with your composition, glue the shapes in place.

EXAMINING YOUR WORK

- **Describe**   Identify the shape that appears in your color wheel. Tell whether it is a real, imaginary, or stylized shape.
- **Analyze**   Identify the sets of primary, secondary, and intermediate hues. Show where you have used the principle of repetition with respect to a single shape.
- **Interpret**   Explain why you chose this shape. Tell why it makes an interesting color wheel. What mood does it create?
- **Judge**   Decide whether you think your work is successful. Tell what you would do differently to improve the design.

Figure S–2   **Student work. Color wheel.**

COMPUTER OPTION

Try This!

■ Use the Pencil or Brush tool to draw the contour of your favorite shape. Choose the Lasso tool to select your shape. Make copies, and use the Rotate command to angle these. Arrange the copies in a circular fashion. Choose the Fill tool and color the shapes with the correct hues in their position on the color wheel on page **8.** Title, save, and print.

Lesson 1   *Making A Color Wheel*   **307**

■ Aesthetics

Kelly painted flat, simple shapes to represent a spectrum of color. Ask students how much skill they think is needed to make this smooth painting. Do the simple shapes, rather than more complex shapes, make the painting more or less successful? Have students give reasons for their responses.

■ Art Criticism

Have students use the four steps of art criticism to describe, analyze, interpret, and judge Kelly's painting.

■ Studio Skills

Ask students to brainstorm shapes they consider to have an interesting outline. Emphasize that the outline of the shape needs to show as much detail as possible, because they will not be able to draw additional details on the surface. Have students use sturdy paper to sketch so the cut-out drawing can be used as a stencil for the twelve color shapes. Display a color wheel to model the order of colors.

■ Self-Assessment

Have students use Examining Your Work to evaluate their art.

more about • • •

Ellsworth Kelly   Although Kelly (1923) is known as a Hard-Edge painter, he claims he is more interested in shapes than in edges. Kelly intends for viewers to see the shapes, sounds, and moods of the colors in *Spectrum II.* Art historians have credited his keen eye for color and shapes to early experiences of bird watching and to a stint in a camouflage unit during World War II. "I want to use the world rather than my own invention," Kelly has said. He exemplifies the Hard-Edge style by translating objects and forms into simple geometric shapes and colors. Brushstrokes disappear on flat surfaces. There are no lines, only implied lines as each shape of color touches the next to create an arrangement of moods, sounds, and feelings.

LESSON 2

Creating a "Clan" Robe

LESSON 2

Creating a "Clan" Robe

(pages 308–309)

Lesson Time: 90 minutes

☑ OBJECTIVES

After completing this lesson, students will be able to:

- Identify the Tlingit clan robe as an example that illustrates a family's heritage.
- Work in a group to select, create, and arrange one or more animal shapes to make a formally balanced blanket design.
- Describe, analyze, interpret, and judge their work.

☑ SUPPLIES

- Pencils and sketch paper
- Kraft paper in dark hues
- Construction paper in assorted colors
- Scissors; white glue or glue sticks

■ Lesson Review

Suggest that students review the following lessons before beginning this Studio Lesson:

- Chapter 7, Lesson 1, pages 124–25
- Chapter 7, Lesson 2, pages 126–27

■ Motivator

Ask students if they have ever attended a folk festival or event where participants wore a costume representing their family's heritage. Have students share their experiences in observing a St. Patrick's Day parade or a Bon Odori festival, for example.

Have you ever heard people with similar backgrounds or interests described as "birds of a feather"? To the Tlingit of the American Northwest, this expression was taken quite seriously. The object in Figure S–3, in fact, displays the "bird of a feather"—in this case, thunderbird—that served as a family crest to Tlingit of the Shungookeidi clan. Study this object. Notice the rich use of pattern and recurring motifs. Have you seen other Native American artifacts that made use of similar designs? What kind of balance has been used to organize this object?

WHAT YOU WILL LEARN

You will work with a group of classmates to create a blanket that represents your class. Begin by choosing an animal that symbolizes a quality you would like to emphasize. Design and cut your animal's shape from Kraft paper. Then cut and paste rounded geometric shapes, called *ovoids* and *U-forms,* to represent facial features and small details. You will add variety and contrast by alternately leaving thick and thin spaces between shapes.

Figure S–3 This Chilkat robe repeats ovoid and U-form shapes that represent the inside and outside view of an animal.

Naaxein (Tlingit) *Chilkat Woven Robe.* c. 1880. Mountain goat wool, yellow cedar bark, natural dyes. 131 x 170 cm (51¹⁵⁄₁₆ x 66¹⁵⁄₁₆"). Seattle Art Museum, Seattle, Washington.

308   Lesson 2   *Creating a "Clan" Robe*

more about • • •

Northwest Coast Art   The Northwest tribes deeply respect the earth and its inhabitants. Northwest Coast art contains a wealth of visual and verbal stories about the histories of the people, land, animals, and spirits.

The cedar tree and the salmon are two common resources that natives revere because they sustain their lives. Almost every part of the cedar tree is used to make functional as well as ceremonial objects. Many of the tales and family stories relate to the animals that are found in this region, such as the whale, salmon, eagle, raven, otter, hawk, bear, and beaver.

WHAT YOU WILL NEED

- Sketch paper and pencil
- Sheet of Kraft paper in a dark hue, approximately 30 x 45 inches (76 x 114.3 cm)
- Scissors
- Construction paper in assorted colors, 12 x 18 inches (30 x 46 cm)
- White glue or glue stick

WHAT YOU WILL DO

1. With a group of four or five classmates, brainstorm a list of animals that symbolize different qualities. Possibilities include owl (for wisdom) and lion (for bravery). From the list, choose an animal that you feel represents a quality your class as a whole exhibits.
2. Each group member is to make several large sketches of your animal. Choose the best features from several drawings. Transfer the outline of this "composite," or group, sketch to the sheet of Kraft paper. Cut out the animal's shape.
3. Transfer body parts from your design to contrasting hues of construction paper. Make parts large enough to fill the body.
4. Cut rounded shapes (ovoids)—rectangles and squares—for facial features and for smaller details. Cut U-shaped forms for ears, ribs and feathers. Since your robe is to be formally balanced, you will need to make a copy of each shape. You can easily accomplish this by cutting through two sheets of paper for each feature.
5. Arrange all features and details on the body outline before gluing any of them down. Add variety to your design by alternating the distance between features.

EXAMINING YOUR WORK

- **Describe** Tell what animal your group chose for your blanket. What features and body parts did you include?
- **Analyze** Explain how you created variety. How did you achieve contrast?
- **Interpret** How do the characteristics of your animal match the identity of your class?
- **Judge** Tell whether you think your work is successful. What part worked best?

Figure S–4 Student work. Clan robes.

Try This! COMPUTER OPTION

■ Select the Brush tool, and draw the outline of an animal shape. As you work, vary the line thickness of your brush to create contrast and variety. Fill all of the spaces within the animal shape. Use the Mirror tool, if available, to make a mirror image. Otherwise, use the copy and paste and Rotate commands for this purpose.

Lesson 2 *Creating a "Clan" Robe* **309**

■ Studio Skills

Assign students to their groups, or let them choose their teams. Remind students to consider themselves a team where everyone has a role, participates, and helps others.

After brainstorming, students should decide on their animal. Remind them that some views are symmetrical and can be made by folding the paper in half to cut out the shape. They can also cut details from two layers of paper to make identical features and to match shapes on both sides, creating balance. Tell students they can layer shapes and repeat colors and shapes to create harmony and unify their blanket design.

■ Aesthetics

Artists use the natural materials they find in their environment for artworks. While many of the art objects are used everyday, some are reserved for special occasions. Ask students whether they think everyday objects are more or less valuable than ceremonial pieces. Have them give reasons for their views.

■ Cooperative Learning

In conjunction with their blanket design, ask each group to prepare a song, dance, or story to be told or performed with the display of their clan blankets. Have groups take turns presenting their art and performance to the class.

■ Self-Assessment

Have students use Examining Your Work to evaluate their art.

LESSON 3

Contour Drawing

LESSON TIME: 90 minutes

☑ OBJECTIVES

After completing this lesson, students will be able to:

• Define the term *contour drawing*.
• Practice drawing by moving their eyes and hands together.
• Make and examine their own series of contour drawings.

☑ SUPPLIES

• Overhead projector, photograph of a person, preferably draped or in an elaborate outfit
• Fine-point felt-tipped pens; sheets of sketch paper or newsprint, a variety of objects, such as shells, pots and pans, flowerpots, driftwood, houseplants, draped fabrics, baskets, and so on
• Long pieces of yarn or string

■ Lesson Review

Suggest that students review the following lessons before beginning the contour drawings:

• Chapter 1, Lesson 2, Line, page 6
• Chapter 7, Lesson 5, Practicing Calligraphy, page 133
• Technique Tips, Making Contour Drawings, page 281

Look at Figure S–5. Notice how lifelike the subject looks for a drawing made almost totally of line. A first step toward doing work like this is learning to do contour drawing. **Contour drawing** is *drawing an object as though your drawing tool is moving along all the edges and ridges of the form.* This technique helps you become more perceptive. You are concerned with drawing shapes and curves.

In contour drawing, your eye and hand move at the same time. Imagine that the point of your pen is touching the edge of the object as your eye follows the edge. You never pick up your pen. When you move from one area to another, you leave a trail. Look at the model and not at the paper.

WHAT YOU WILL LEARN

You will make a series of contour drawings with a felt-tipped pen. First, you will draw different objects. Second, you will use your classmates as models. Finally, you will make a contour drawing of a classmate posed in a setting. (See Technique Tip **2**, *Handbook* page **281**.)

WHAT YOU WILL NEED

• Felt-tipped pen with a fine point
• Sheets of white paper, 12 x 18 inches (30 x 46 cm)
• Selected objects provided by your teacher

WHAT YOU WILL DO

1. Take one of the items from the collection on the display table. Place it on the table in front of you. Trace the lines of the object in the air on an imaginary sheet of glass. As you look at the object, you must concentrate and think. Notice every detail indicated by the direction and curves of the line.

Figure S–5 Notice how the artist gives a feeling of form by changing the thickness of the line. What ways do you know of making lines thicker and darker?

Juan Gris. *Max Jacob.* 1919. Pencil on paper. 36.5 x 27.7 cm (14⅜ x 10½"). Museum of Modern Art, New York, New York. Gift of James Thrall Soby.

⸻ *more about* • • • ⸻

Cooperative Learning   In step three of this lesson, students are asked to exchange items and to do a contour drawing of the new object. After these new drawings have been completed, ask students who have exchanged to compare their drawings of the same item. Let them notice which details of the object they have included, and which ones they have missed or handled differently. If the students have drawn the object from a different angle, let them compare the drawing with the object itself and together analyze what might have been included. Ask them to focus on detail. Give them a maximum of five minutes to compare and contrast with the goal of further developing their perceptual skills.

2. Make a contour drawing of the object on a sheet of paper using a felt-tipped pen. Do several more drawings on the same sheet of paper. Turn the object so you are looking at it from a different angle. Make another contour drawing. Keep working until your drawings begin to look like the object.

3. Next, exchange objects with your classmates. Do a contour drawing of your new object. Work large, letting the drawing fill the page. Do not worry if your efforts look awkward. Complete several drawings of different objects.

4. Work with a partner. Take turns posing for each other. Each model should sit in a comfortable pose. The first contour will look distorted. Remember, you are drawing the pose. Work large and let the drawing fill the page.

5. Finally, make a contour drawing of one person sitting in a setting. Include background details. You may stop and peek at the drawing. When you do, do not pick up the pencil. Do not take your eyes off the model while drawing.

6. Display the final drawing. Discuss how contour drawing has improved your perception.

EXAMINING YOUR WORK

- **Describe**   Show the different kinds of contour drawings you did. Identify the media you used.
- **Analyze**   Compare your first contour drawing to your last. Explain how using contour drawing has changed your perception skills.
- **Judge**   Evaluate your final contour drawing. Tell whether you feel your work succeeds. Explain your answer.

Figure S–6   Student work. This is an example of a contour drawing that shows background details.

■ Motivator
Use an overhead projector to enlarge and display a photograph of a person. Help students recognize how the edges and ridges define the image. Let students trace, either on the projector or (using a pointer) on the screen, the defining lines. Help them imagine how a drawing composed only of these lines would portray the figure.

■ Studio Skills
Students may want to use the same techniques to create a wire sculpture. See the Additional Studio Lesson 6 on page 312.

■ Self-Assessment
Have students use Examining Your Work to evaluate their contour drawings.

Try This!   STUDIO OPTIONS

■ Make a contour drawing of a chair in your classroom using colored markers or a black felt-tipped pen.

■ Use a piece of wire that bends easily and make a three-dimensional contour "drawing" of a foot or hand.

Lesson 3   *Contour Drawing*   **311**

more about ••••

Safety   Remind students that, whenever they work with long pieces of material (such as wire), they must be especially careful. Students must always be aware of others working near them. Loose ends of wire can quite easily be flipped up, possibly injuring someone's eye. Have students try to keep one foot on top of the free end of wire as they work. Also remind them to be careful in making any necessary cuts with wire snips, keeping fingers well out of the way.

Handbook Cross-Reference   Contour drawing can help students develop the feel of a subject, but making these specialized drawings may seem awkward at first. For help in developing the skill of contour drawing, refer students to Technique Tip 2, Handbook page 281.

Artsource®: Performing Arts Handbook

(pages 312–326)

■ Purpose

The 14 features in the Performing Arts Handbook are designed to enrich students' learning by correlating what they learn about the visual arts to the performing arts—dance, music, and theatre. The featured performers and groups in this handbook were specifically chosen to supplement the chapters in the student text.

■ Using the Handbook

The following categories suggest ways to use the Performing Arts Handbook.

Mini-lessons Use the features as stand-alone lessons about dance, music, and theatre.

Motivator Use the features to introduce related chapters. Listed on each chapter opening page of your Teacher's Wraparound Edition is a segment that correlates each chapter to this section. As you plan lessons, consider how you might use the Performing Arts Handbook as a way of introducing the chapter's content.

Extension Refer to the Recommended Artsource® feature found on the chapter opening page of your Teacher's Wraparound Edition, and use the appropriate feature to expand the study of that chapter. Students may volunteer for this Extension activity, or you might assign groups of students to read the feature, then complete the questions and activities on their own.

312

Performing Arts Handbook

The following pages of content were excerpted from *Artsource®: The Music Center Study Guide to the Performing Arts,* developed by the Music Center Education Division, an award-winning arts education program of the Music Center of Los Angeles County.

The following artists and groups are featured in the Performing Arts Handbook.

— *more about* • • • —

Artsource® The materials provided in this Performing Arts Handbook are excerpted from *Artsource®: The Music Center Study Guide to the Performing Arts,* a project of the Music Center Education Division. The Music Center of Los Angeles County, the largest performing arts center in the western United States, established the Music Center Education Division in 1979 to provide opportunities for life-long learning in the arts, and especially to bring the performing and visual arts into the classroom. The Education Division believes the arts enhance the quality of life for all people, but are crucial to the development of every child.

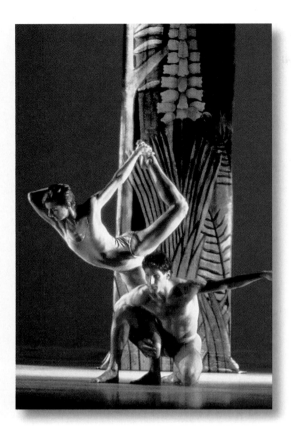

Tandy Beal is a dancer, choreographer, actress, comic, and dreamer. Born into a theatre family, she recalls her father's advice to struggling artists: "The most important thing about performing is that you must be truthful." Following his advice, her dance "Dust to Dust" explores the idea that although people look and act in ordinary ways, they can have a rich inner world of imagination. In a dramatic section of the piece, the dancers, wearing everyday clothing, tear through large sheets of paper that have projected images of themselves dressed as performers. The work ends when the dancers disappear, replaced by tall columns of sand and glitter falling lightly onto the stage.

Tandy Beal & Company. "Dust to Dust." Photo courtesy of Tandy Beal & Company.

■ DISCUSSION QUESTIONS

1. The photo on this page depicts a moment from the dance "Dust to Dust." Describe the positions of the dancers and the feelings you think they are expressing.
2. In thinking about the brief description of the dance, what do you think the choreographer was trying to show when she chose to replace the dancers with columns of sand and glitter? Discuss your ideas and give reasons to support them.
3. People can easily see the daily activities we do but cannot know what goes on in the world of our imagination. Discuss this idea and give examples from your own life.

■ CREATIVE EXPRESSION ACTIVITIES

Technology Using a camera, take close-up slides of different members of the class. Project these onto butcher paper in a darkened room and have people do simple movements, such as walking, skipping, jumping, and swaying in front of them so that the projections move back and forth from the paper to the people. Wear white for the best effect.

Language Arts Although people look ordinary and act ordinary in their daily lives, they can have a rich inner world of imagination. Write about this concept with regard to yourself.

Performing Arts Handbook **313**

Appreciating the Performing Arts

Modern Dance Tandy Beal's work ranges widely from the lyric and poetic to the theatrical and whimsical. While dance is the central medium for her performance art, theatre and music are essential elements. Ms. Beal often is inspired by a piece of music when creating a new work, though sometimes the dance evolves from ideas or images. Poetic and physical,

"Dust to Dust" was inspired by composer Jon Scoville's compelling score "Bone People." The dance begins with individual figures moving across the stage, then suddenly stopping in mid-action. This introduces the audience to Beal's exploration, on which the dance is based, of where the everyday world collides with the transformative power of art.

■ **Setting the Stage**

Direct students to read the paragraph about Tandy Beal and her dance "Dust to Dust." If you have the Artsource® selections, play them.

O P T I O N A L

Artsource®: Performing Arts Package 1, Unit 1

• VHS video segment 1–1 (Playing time 7:43)
• Audio tape segment 1–1 (Playing time 14:53)

■ Connecting the Arts

Using the Discussion Questions on this page, help students recognize that one of the roles of an artist is to express ideas from their own perspective. This can sometimes help us understand things from a different point of view. Possible responses are:

1. The woman is in a balanced position on one straight leg. One arm is holding her lifted foot. The man is crouching, balanced on one knee and one foot.
2. There is a cycle of life, from birth to death, for all living things. The sand represents the fragility of life, and the glitter is perhaps joy, magic, or mystery.
3. Example: While standing in line, I observe people, make up stories about who they are, and build scenarios for their lives.

■ Extensions

• Have students complete the Creative Expression Activities.
• Use Artsource®: Performing Arts Package 1, Unit 1, for more information about Tandy Beal & Company.

■ **Setting the Stage**

Direct students to read the paragraph about George Gershwin, then play the Artsource® selection.

OPTIONAL

Artsource®: Performing Arts Package 1, Unit 2

• Audio tape segment 1–2 (Playing time 8:10)

■ **Connecting the Arts**

Using the Discussion Questions on this page, help students recognize that theme and variation can be found in all art forms as well as in ordinary parts of life. Possible responses are:

1. Visual artists use variations in color, texture, size, design, etc; musicians use rhythm, dynamics, tempo, instrumentation, tone color, style, and so forth.

2. Variation 1: piano performs a complicated rhythm pattern while orchestra performs the melody. Variation 2: waltz time. Variation 3: melody remains with orchestra while piano imitates sounds of Chinese flutes. Variation 4: lilting strings and jazz band sounds alternate with piano in presenting melody.

■ **Extensions**

• After students have examined the photograph and, if possible, listened to the audio selection, have them complete the Creative Expression Activities.

• Use Artsource®: Performing Arts Package 1, Unit 2, for more information about George Gershwin and his composition.

314

George Gershwin. Photo courtesy of The Music Center Operating Company Archives, Otto Rothchild Collection.

Geeorge Gershwin is one of America's most celebrated composers and pianists. According to Encyclopedia Britannica, Gershwin "created a new type of urban American music." The song "I Got Rhythm" was introduced in the Broadway musical *Girl Crazy* in 1930. It is an upbeat, fun song based on a simple four-note rhythmic motif. "Variations for Piano and Orchestra: I Got Rhythm" is full of clever ideas. A lone clarinet introduces the basic theme, or melody. The piano plays a little flurry, followed by the full orchestra. The piano then states the theme in solo. All in all there are four variations and a finale, where the melody alternates between different sections of the orchestra and the piano.

■ **DISCUSSION QUESTIONS**

1. The term *variations on a theme* refers to a basic technique composers use to change a musical theme. Using creative skills and musicianship, composers change the way a melody is played. Each version introduces a variation while keeping the basic character of the melody or theme. Discuss how this is similar to the way a visual artist works.

2. Discuss the four-note rhythmic motif on which the melody "I Got Rhythm" is based. Listen to the Artsource audio cassette or other recording for the way that the simple motif is developed into different variations. Discuss the differences between the variations.

■ **CREATIVE EXPRESSION ACTIVITIES**

Music   Take a familiar, simple song like "Three Blind Mice" and see if you can create three variations in the way you sing or play it. Suggestions might include changing the tempo (speed), unison or in a round, alternating loud with soft dynamics or change of pitch.

History   Read about New York and its performing and visual arts scenes in the 1920s and 1930s. Compare the artistic movements in the visual arts, literature and poetry, drama and dance with what was happening in music during this period.

Dance   Learn a popular dance or dance step from the 1920s or 1930s (Charleston, Lindy Hop, Truckin', Suzy Q). Compare its style with a popular dance of today.

Appreciating the Performing Arts

Music   George Gershwin initially gained fame for his contributions to the musical theater, but he also composed for the orchestra, solo piano, films, and opera. He was the first American composer to successfully bridge two areas in the world of music—popular and concert. Many composers, like Gershwin, have enjoyed restating melodies (or themes) so that some features of the original remain while alterations, deletions and additions are made. The devices employed often include changes in *duration, key, meter, tempo, mood,* or *styles.* Sometimes the theme is even turned upside-down, or 'ornamented' with extra notes. The Gershwin variations on the melody "I Got Rhythm" employs some of these changes.

For over 25 years, the Ballet Folklorico de Mexico has presented authentic folk dances from different ethnic groups within Mexico. Amalia Hernández, the featured director of the dance group shown on this page, creates exciting dances based on ancient traditions. From the time of the Olmec Indians to the birth of modern Mexico, more than thirty distinct cultures have influenced Mexican culture. The dance shown in this photo is called "Los Mitos" and features the pageantry and ritual of these cultures before the arrival of the Spaniards.

Ballet Folklorico de Mexico. "Los Mitos." Amalia Hernández, artistic director.

■ **DISCUSSION QUESTIONS**

1. Compare the headdress of the dancers to the headdress on page 182 in your book. What similarities do you see in the patterns and symbols?
2. What symbolism do you see in the photo on this page that inspired ancient cultures of Mexico? What characteristics of the symbol can you name?
3. After viewing the video, describe how the dancers used geometric spatial designs.

■ **CREATIVE EXPRESSION ACTIVITIES**

Dance   Stand in an open area with 6–8 students and organize yourselves into three different geometric shapes, selecting from a circle, square, triangle, or the letter X. After your designs are organized, choose two that you like and walk or skip from one figure into another using eight counts to travel.

Language Arts   Write a personal reflection of your impressions and feelings about either the images you see in the illustration on this page or of the dance in the video.

Appreciating the Performing Arts

Dance   "Los Mitos" (the myths) is part of a suite of dances called *Los Concheros*. The suite is based on the ancient rituals of some of the indigenous cultures, such as the Toltecs and the Aztecs. These rituals connect each dancer to life and the universe. The title of the suite, *Los Concheros*, refers to the people who blow large conch shell trumpets during the ceremonial rites. Although the Concheros still enact their rituals today, the ceremonies now reflect the Spanish influence and have become a fusion of Christian and pre-Hispanic traditions.

■ **Setting the Stage**

Direct students to read the paragraph about the Ballet Folklorico de Mexico and examine the photograph of the dancers. View the *Artsource®* video if available.

OPTIONAL

Artsource®: Performing Arts Package 1, Unit 3
- VHS video segment 1–2 (Playing time 8:45)

■ **Connecting the Arts**

Using the Discussion Questions on this page, help students recognize the connections between visual and performing arts and that they are both expressions of a culture. Possible responses:
1. Elaborate decorations, patterns, design.
2. The sphere, or sun.
3. Circle, rectangles, intersecting lines.

■ **Extensions**

- After students have examined the photograph and, if possible, viewed the video, have them complete the Creative Expression Activities.
- Have students work in groups to create three sun motifs. Then choose one and make a design that shows movement using eight repetitions of the motif.
- Use Artsource®: Performing Arts Package 1, Unit 3, for more information about the Ballet Folklorico de Mexico and for additional related activities.

■ Setting the Stage

Direct students to read about AMAN and the "Danse des Balais," then play the video selection.

■ Connecting the Arts

Using the Discussion Questions, help students recognize that the dance and music of a culture capture and express the spirit of the people of that culture. Possible responses are:

1. One group has on white collared shirts and dark vests, laced shoes and woolen knee socks; the other group wears work shirts, suspenders, and soft suede boots. Movements: a knee lift with brooms touching the ground in front, torsos slightly bent forward.
2. Answers will vary.
3. Piano: keyboard, no accordion or fiddle. Guitar: electric guitar or bass. Irish drums: full percussion drum set.

■ Extensions

• Have students complete the Creative Expression Activities.
• Encourage students to share experiences and knowledge about the music and dance of cultures with which they are familiar.
• Use Artsource®: Performing Arts Package 1, Unit 4, for more information about AMAN and the "Danse des Balais."

AMAN International Folk Ensemble. "Danse des Balais" from *Suite of French Canadian Dances.* Photo courtesy of AMAN International Folk Ensemble.

The AMAN International Folk Ensemble, based in Los Angeles, is a cultural and educational organization. It is dedicated to researching, preserving, and presenting the traditional dance, music, and folklore of many ethnic groups, particularly those representing North American immigrants. Choreographers Yves Moreau and France Bourque-Moreau were asked to show a wide range of dances from the richly varied heritage of French Canadian culture. They chose to choreograph a suite of five dances to represent both rural and urban traditions. The one shown here is a broom dance called "Danse des Balais" from Chicoutimi in Quebec.

■ DISCUSSION QUESTIONS

1. Study the photo of "Danse des Balais" and describe the differences in the costumes worn by the men as well as the movement being done.
2. Imagine you were given an assignment to make a statement about today's teen culture through dance, music, and costumes in a ten-minute performance piece. What would you choose to include?
3. The names of the instruments used to play the traditional music are: piano, button accordion, fiddle, guitar, and an Irish drum called a *bodhram.* How are these instruments similar or different from those found in a popular rock band?

■ CREATIVE EXPRESSION ACTIVITIES

History   Interview your parents or grandparents to find out what folk dances they know that represent their cultural heritage. Find out what country they came from and what traditions they relate to within the culture. If possible, learn a part of the dance and teach it to the class.

Dance   Use the Artsource audio cassette or find the directions and music to the French Canadian folk dance "Les Saluts." It is a simple circle dance that is fun and gives a flavor of the traditional music and dance style.

Appreciating the Performing Arts

Dance   While these music and dance traditions belong to the people of Eastern Canada in the Province of Quebec, they have also spilled across the St. Lawrence River and are embraced by the people of the eastern United States. The principal forms of French Canadian traditional rural dance were inherited from French and British nobility. The Gigue (jig) is a solo dance influenced by Irish and English step dancing and uses a style that falls between the rigid Irish and the freer Appalachian clogging. "The Broom Dance" has a clogging pattern from the town of Chicoutimi and is related historically to the Scottish Sword Dance.

Tandy Beal and Bobby McFerrin

Tandy Beal and Bobby McFerrin

Tandy Beal, a dancer and choreographer, and Bobby McFerrin, a musician, combined their artistic talents in a creative process called improvisation. Improvisational work is very challenging. It requires a great deal of trust, alertness, and the ability of each to respond fully to the other in the present moment.

Improvisation is about playing in a serious way. Someone sets out an idea, and others who know the rules and boundaries of the improvisational process can join in the play. It is much like professional sports where the players, working within certain rules and boundaries, think and respond to the actions of each other, using great alertness and skill to achieve a goal.

Tandy Beal and Bobby McFerrin. *Voice/Dance.* Photo courtesy of Tandy Beal & Company.

■ **Setting the Stage**

Direct students to read about these artists, then view the video.

OPTIONAL

Artsource®: Performing Arts Package 1, Unit 5

• VHS video segment 1–4 (Playing time 3:00)

■ **Connecting the Arts**

Using the Discussion Questions on this page, help students recognize that when improvisation is used as a performing technique in such art forms as jazz, dance, or theatre, it is based on a highly developed skill and ability to communicate and express oneself in the moment. Possible responses are:

1. Gestures, letters, body posture, symbols, choice of car, hairstyle, dress and so on.
2. It requires that people know the point or goal of the improvisation and the agreed upon rules and boundaries.
3. Working out a puzzle, planning a party, or making up with a friend. Brainstorming and improvisation are related because they both focus on a specific goal or problem, and participants try to find all the possibilities.

■ **DISCUSSION QUESTIONS**

1. Name all the ways you can communicate without speaking in words. Demonstrate each as you identify them.
2. Discuss why artistic improvisation as described above is different from simply playing or fooling around.
3. Discuss other situations when people improvise to solve problems or create something (scientists, advertising writers, sports players, computer programmers, parents). Is brainstorming related to improvisation? If so, discuss the relationship.

■ **CREATIVE EXPRESSION ACTIVITIES**

Communication   With a partner, communicate using only vocal sounds, gestures, and body percussion. Experiment for one minute and then share your reactions to the experience. Focus on how the length of the sound or motion, rhythm, dynamics, and energy affected the improvisation. Try it again.

Technology   Selectively record sounds from the environment, such as children jumping rope, video games, a sports event, machines, and so on. Use this recording to motivate a writing assignment that uses sounds to trigger emotions and thoughts that lead to a story.

■ **Extensions**

• Have students complete the Creative Expression Activities.
• Encourage students to share experiences they may have had with improvisation.
• Use Artsource®: Performing Arts Package 1, Unit 5, for more information about these artists.

Performing Arts Handbook   **317**

Appreciating the Performing Arts

Music/Dance   Tandy Beal and Bobby McFerrin met in 1975 when he was playing piano for dance classes at the University of Utah and performing in the area. Delighting each other with their improvisational skill, they began to imagine possibilities for a joint project. The collaboration resulted in a national tour and a television special, "Voice/Dance," produced in 1987 by KQED San Francisco. Their performance was shaped through costumes, sets and lighting design. Most of McFerrin's vocals were a spontaneous response to the dancers, but some sections of the dancing were set, and there were specific guidelines for the improvisational work.

ARTSOURCE

■ Setting the Stage

Direct students to read about Paul Tracey, then play the audio selection.

OPTIONAL

Artsource®: Performing Arts Package 1, Unit 6

• Audio tape segment 1–6 (Playing time 5:00)

■ Connecting the Arts

Using the Discussion Questions on this page, help students recognize that songwriters usually write songs about things they feel, value, or have experienced. Possible responses are:

1. Pro: Everything that is created has a right to live, procreate, and fulfill its purpose. Con: A lot of creatures are just pests or are not needed, and it doesn't seem important if they become extinct. Their purpose in the balance isn't known or proven.

2. Answers will vary.

■ Extensions

• Have students complete the Creative Expression Activities.

• Encourage them to share experiences they have had with nature and to recapture specific memories connected to them. Brainstorm how these simple events can help us feel the power of nature and to better understand our responsibility in keeping nature in balance.

• Use Artsource®: Performing Arts Package 1, Unit 6, for additional related activities.

International troubadour Paul Tracey draws upon his cultural heritage to communicate ideas about life through original songs. Working on his father's farm with his father and a Swazi foreman named Simon Shabalala, he learned about farming, building, and appreciating nature. He now realizes he has been an environmentalist his whole life.

He has written a show called *Our Little Blue Planet,* which stresses the uniqueness of this planet and the delicate balance between all the species in nature. His song "Dead as a Dodo" points out that it is too late to save the dodo, for they are now extinct. However, there is still time to protect other endangered species.

Paul Tracey, minstrel. *Our Little Blue Planet.* Photo © 1995 Craig Schwartz.

■ DISCUSSION QUESTIONS

1. Make a list of endangered species, such as the condor, some species of whales, the panda, and the rhino. Select one and make a case as to why it should be preserved, or play the role of the "Devil's Advocate" and say why it should be eliminated.

2. Paul's farm in Africa has been declared a Nature Reserve. Local children and students come there to learn about nature, how to perceive its beauty, and to respect the overall balance of nature in the environment. Discuss ways that you could beautify something in your neighborhood that would also improve the environment.

■ CREATIVE EXPRESSION ACTIVITIES

Language Arts There is a saying, "Think globally and act locally." Write a jingle that incorporates this idea into a catchy tune.

Art What if the creatures who became extinct were redesigned so that they could survive. Select one extinct creature and redesign it so that it would have a better chance for survival. For example, if whales could develop armor-plated skin, they could repel harpoons.

Appreciating the Performing Arts

Music Artists draw from their personal experiences when they create a work of art. Some are good at drawing or sculpting, dancing, acting, playwriting, or puppetry. Paul and many others are best at expressing their ideas through words and music. There are many examples of songs that help us feel love or loss, and a few that are inspiring, such as patriotic or marching songs. Songwriters such as Paul feel that he can get people to think about things, such as caring for our planet, by writing songs that are both humorous and yet make a strong point. A song is so much more powerful than just saying the words or just hearing the music. When they're combined, they can reach two parts of you—your emotions and your brain.

PERFORMING ARTS

The Robert Minden Ensemble

The Robert Minden Ensemble. Drawing by Nancy Walker.

"The Boy Who Wanted to Talk to Whales" is a modern folk tale about the adventure of a boy who had a powerful desire to talk to the great whales. He meets a curious musician "playing" a carpenter's hand saw and begins a musical journey filled with possibility and discovery. Eventually, the boy gets his chance to communicate with the whales in a way he never imagined. The original score is performed without the use of synthesizers or electronically generated sounds. Instead, an odd assortment of ordinary objects are transformed into musical instruments: empty tin cans, wood, vacuum cleaner hoses, and a Slinky. Also included are conch shells and a Waterphone, which create a magical sound for his journey.

■ **DISCUSSION QUESTIONS**

1. Have you ever tried to mimic the language or song of a particular animal or bird? Can you demonstrate? Discuss the types of language and sounds made by other living creatures.
2. Have you had moments in your life when you felt truly connected to nature or all living things? Describe your experiences.
3. Study the artwork and see if you can identify the ordinary materials that are being used as instruments. Can you think of other possibilities?

■ **CREATIVE EXPRESSION ACTIVITIES**

Science Select a species of whale to study, such as the Orca, or killer, whale. Find a scientific recording of sounds made by killer whales and see if you can find recycled materials to help you imitate it.

Music Discover a new sound from an ordinary household object and bring it in to share with the class. Create an environment of sounds with all the students participating. Working with sensitivity, vary the loud and soft dynamics, rhythm and balance between the sounds in order to create something that works and sounds interesting.

Performing Arts Handbook **319**

Setting the Stage
Direct students to read about "The Boy Who Wanted to Talk with Whales." If you have the Artsource® audio tape, have students listen to it.

OPTIONAL

Artsource®: Performing Arts Package 1, Unit 7
• Audio tape segment 1–7 (Playing time 6:05)

■ Connecting the Arts
Using the Discussion Questions, help students realize that musical sound can be created from ordinary household objects. It is a matter of increased awareness and perception that makes one person hear noise and another hear musical possibilities. Possible responses are:
1. Yes. Whistling, grunting, snorting, chirping, roaring, growling, percussive vocal sounds, and hissing.
2. On a camping trip, waking up in the morning and hearing bird and frog sounds, or sitting around a camp fire at night and hearing night sounds and seeing the stars.
3. Bowls, conch shell, cardboard tubes, vacuum hoses. Other possibilities will vary.

■ Extensions
• After students have read the paragraph and listened to the tape, have them complete the Creative Expression Activities.
• Use Artsource®: Performing Arts Package 1, Unit 7, for more information about Robert Minden and his musical story "The Boy Who Wanted to Talk to Whales."

Appreciating the Performing Arts

Music The Robert Minden Ensemble was born one gray winter day through a serendipitous event. Robert Minden, a visiting professor of sociology, was musing over his afternoon lecture when a mysterious sound, sweet as honey, came drifting through his office window. He went in search of its origin and found a street musician, Thomas Jefferson Scribner, playing a carpenter's handsaw. Minden was captivated by the saw's hauntingly beautiful voice and became determined to master it. Later, he formed his ensemble, and stories and music soon evolved from their improvisations. Later, he met Richard Waters, the inventor of the Waterphone, and as he experimented with *its* sound, a simple folk tale about man and nature emerged.

Setting the Stage

Direct students to read about The Chameleons and their mime play *Life Cycle*. If you have the Artsource® video, have students view it.

OPTIONAL

Artsource®: Performing Arts Package 1, Unit 8

• VHS video segment 1–5 (Playing time 6:25)

Connecting the Arts

Using the Discussion Questions, help students recognize that there are cycles of action in many aspects of life. Possible responses are:

1. It's about the different stages of life from birth to death. Cycle means period of time when events repeat in the same order.

2. They want the audience to grasp the importance of life.

3. Sports: referees give hand signals to show the call, and athletes use hand movements to show the action or play. Gestures are a simple and direct way to communicate ideas clearly.

Extensions

• After students have read the paragraph and viewed the video, have them complete the Creative Expression Activities.

• Encourage students to share experiences and knowledge about how gestures and mime are used in various aspects of their lives.

• Use Artsource®: Performing Arts Package 1, Unit 8, for additional related activities.

320

The Chameleons: Keith Berger and Sharon Diskin. *Life Cycle.* Photo © 1990, Craig Schwartz.

*L*ife Cycle follows the relationship of two characters, one female and one male, from infancy through childhood, adolescence, courtship, marriage, parenthood, middle-age, old age, death, and finally, rebirth. On a bare stage and without costumes or props, Berger and Diskin use pantomime and mime techniques to project a variety of human emotions and enact the rituals of friendship, love, and separation. Their work began with a desire to do a story about universal relationships. They began by improvising ways to create age changes by altering their posture, expressions, and attitudes.

■ DISCUSSION QUESTIONS

1. Why do you think Keith Berger and Sharon Diskin titled their mime piece *Life Cycle*? What does the term *cycle* mean, and how does this relate to the stages of life?

2. Study the photo on this page and describe the situation and what you think is being communicated by the two mimes.

3. Identify situations where people use gestures to communicate ideas rather than words. Discuss why this is done in each of the situations.

■ CREATIVE EXPRESSION ACTIVITIES

Pantomime   Imagine that you are watching the following things, using primarily your eyes to show each idea: a tennis match, an airplane flying high, a spider crawling near your toes, and a butterfly flying around you and landing on a part of your body.

Pantomime   Show the following ideas in mime movement: fishing, writing a letter, stirring cake batter, dealing cards, getting dressed, sewing a button on a shirt, and bowling.

Playwriting   Create a mime scenario about a day in the life of a specific character. Then write an outline of the action to use as a mime script.

Appreciating the Performing Arts

Theatre   Mime is the art of dramatic representation by movement and gestures only, without words. It can also refer to a performer specializing in this art. Mime requires concentration, control of movement, and physical and emotional reaction to events. The Chameleons' performance style is characterized by strong emotions and natural characters involved in real-life dramas. They are masters of the traditional mime illusions and are acclaimed for their original mime repertoire. *Life Cycle,* a mime play, is performed to the music of Johann Pachelbel's "Canon in D Major." It was chosen as a score because it is repetitive and circular, underscoring the idea that life is a cycle with a beginning, middle, and end.

Danais and Ara Tokatlian base their personal and professional lives on the principles of universal brotherhood. They try to help people accept and understand different cultural values and styles of artistic expression. Communicating these ideas through their exciting music, they combine ethnic instruments, rhythms, and melodies from various areas of the Americas with contemporary sounds. Their composition "Peace Pipes" is drawn from the music of the Quechua and Aymara people of Peru and Bolivia.

Arco Iris: Danais and Ara Tokatlian. Photo by Deborah Allison.

■ DISCUSSION QUESTIONS

1. Think of the titles "Peace Pipes" and "Soaring Over the High Plains." What kind of musical sounds, melody, or rhythms would you create if you were able to compose music to bring these images to life?
2. Arco Iris uses instruments that are made from materials found in the environment. What instruments might you be able to create from natural objects or sources?
3. Think of three different cultures you know about. What instruments from each can you suggest that could combine to form a fusion of new sound?

■ CREATIVE EXPRESSION ACTIVITIES

Science   Explore the scientific basis for sound production of the following instruments: drums, glockenspiel (steel bars), xylophone (wood bars), and flutes.

Language Arts   Think of an instrument you find interesting. Write a paragraph, poem, or short story from the point of view of the instrument. Describe yourself in specific detail including shape and color, how you are held, treated, and produce sound to express your feelings. You might ask yourself these questions: How do I make sound? What am I made of? What kind of music do I play?

Performing Arts Handbook   **321**

Appreciating the Performing Arts

Music   Music has played an important part in the lives of people worldwide, throughout history. Ancient carvings, frescos, cave paintings, wall drawings, inscriptions, metal and clay figures, and sculptures from many cultures attest to this fact. From these sources we have discovered that musical instruments were first fashioned from materials found in the environment, such as drums from hollow logs and simple flute-type instruments from hollow reeds, bamboo, and wood. Arco Iris creates musical compositions that artfully convey ideas and evoke images and scenes through the interplay of music elements, combining the sounds of ancient folk instruments, such as the pan pipes, with modern acoustic and electronic instruments and vocal sounds.

■ Setting the Stage

Direct students to read about Arco Iris. If you have the Artsource® audio tape, have students listen to it.

O P T I O N A L

Artsource®: Performing Arts Package 1, Unit 9

• Audio tape segment 1–8 (Playing time 5:43)

■ Connecting the Arts

Using the Discussion Questions, help students recognize how new music is made by experimenting with ways to change musical sounds. Possible responses are:

1. Employing various melodic, rhythmic, and harmonic ideas and instruments to fit this mood.
2. Chimes from stones of different sizes, reeds, bamboo; ocarinas from hard or dried fruit, and so on.
3. Africa—xylophones; China—flutes; USA—synthesizer.

■ Extensions

• After students have read the paragraph and listened to the tape, have them complete the Creative Expression Activities.
• Encourage students to share experiences and knowledge connected with traditional folk music and especially music which combines traditional sounds, rhythms, and melodies with modern ones.
• Use Artsource®: Performing Arts Package 1, Unit 9, for more information about Arco Iris and their compositions.

■ **Setting the Stage**

Direct students to read about Chic Street Man and his song *Rag Man.* If you have the Artsource® audio tape, have students listen to it.

┌─────────────────────────┐
│ O P T I O N A L │
│ │
│ **Artsource®:** │
│ **Performing Arts** │
│ **Package 1, Unit 10** │
│ • Audio tape segment 1–9 │
│ (Playing time 5:34) │
└─────────────────────────┘

■ **Connecting the Arts**

Using the Discussion Questions on this page, help students recognize the role of music in telling stories and conveying the emotional impact of work, love, loss, happiness, history, and events. Possible responses are:

1. A story told in rhyming poetry and rhythm.
2. The ice cream man advertises with music on loud speakers or bells that play familiar children's songs. Food trucks advertise with a loud horn.
3. Jingles set to catchy tunes are meant to remind you of a product.

■ **Extensions**

• Have students complete the Creative Expression Activities.
• Encourage students to share experiences and knowledge about the way people tell their own stories, troubles, and relationships through music.
• Use Artsource®: Performing Arts Package 1, Unit 10, for additional related activities.

Chic Street Man. *Rag Man.* Photo by Neil Ricklen.

Chic Street Man is clever at communicating ideas through his music. He often combines storytelling in his compositions, as in *Rag Man.* He skillfully uses his guitar, his singing voice, and his speaking voice to tell the tale of a rag man, as seen through the eyes of a boy. This is a true story-song of an old man who used a horse and wagon to come into Chic's neighborhood looking for rags. The song is sung in a style derived from African cultural traditions, combining storytelling and poetry with music.

■ **DISCUSSION QUESTIONS**

1. Chic Street Man calls his *Rag Man* performance a "rap recitation." Why do you think he calls it that?
2. In *Rag Man* Chic weaves a story about a man who advertised his work by riding through the streets calling and singing to his potential customers. Do vendors still come to your neighborhood? If so, discuss what they sell and how they call to their customers.
3. Discuss how songs and music are used to advertise and sell products. Recall some songs that are memorable or are being currently used.

■ **CREATIVE EXPRESSION ACTIVITIES**

Language Arts Select three commercials using music or song that are memorable. Demonstrate and describe them, discuss the various music styles used, and suggest what type of audience the companies wish to reach.

Art/History/Culture Examine the artworks of African-American artists who, like their counterparts in music, have portrayed the historical, cultural, social, and political lives of their people. Look for the messages they convey, and describe how the artists communicated their messages through visual art.

Appreciating the Performing Arts

 Music Storytelling has become deeply enmeshed in the music and poetry of the African American culture, which is evident in blues, spirituals, gospel, jazz, jazz-rock, calypso, reggae, and rap. Chic often draws upon these musical forms to communicate his ideas. The blues evolved at the turn of the century. Its roots are found in old slave songs and spirituals. The blues in turn spawned other musical forms such as jazz, pop, and rock. As the century progressed, the basic twelve-bar structure of the blues changed, and urbanization reshaped its character. Blues writer Willie Dixon said, "The blues are basically about the facts of life. This is why they hang around."

Dr. Jester Hairston was born in 1901 and has lived through more than 90 years of history. Although he was musically trained, he didn't become interested in the music of his own people until he was an adult. He composed "Goin'Down That Lonesome Road" as a "protest song without hatred." Although a feeling of dissatisfaction is expressed in some of the lyrics, the melody, tempo, rhythm, and styling of the song convey a positive spirit. The lyrics also contain phrases that transmit a feeling of hope with a confident look to the future. This song uses a swing style that gives it an uplifting and lively mood.

Dr. Jester Hairston. "Goin' Down That Lonesome Road."
Photo courtesy of Jester Hairston.

■ DISCUSSION QUESTIONS

1. Why do you suppose a composer would choose an upbeat swing style of music when composing a protest song?
2. Think of something that you strongly protest. Discuss the ideas you would include in a song or poem to communicate your main ideas and feelings.
3. Research songs of social conscience today. What are people feeling strongly about? Do these issues vary from group to group, or are these issues universal?

■ CREATIVE EXPRESSION ACTIVITIES

Language Arts   Think of contemporary popular songs that convey similar messages or themes, for example "We Are the World," "It's a Small World," and "Teach the World To Sing." Recall and write down as many titles as you can. Then write a title for an idea you believe in and would like people to sing. Write song lyrics to go with your title.

Music   In small groups, select a simple child's story, such as "Goldilocks" or "The Three Little Pigs." Write a rap style song for one of the characters to do, or tell the basic story in rap style. Perform for each other.

Appreciating the Performing Arts

Music   During the period of slave trade in the Western Hemisphere, vast numbers of Africans were taken prisoner in their lands and transported to the Americas. Upon reaching these shores they were sold into slavery. Separated from everything familiar—family, friends, environment, customs, and language—the enslaved Africans had to find new ways to communicate and sustain hope. In their native countries, music, dance and storytelling were integral elements of their daily lives. In the United States they became resourceful in devising ways to use their art forms to communicate. The songs that the African Americans created during the period of slavery are a clever mix of their limited English, occasional exposure to Western music, and their traditional song styles.

■ Setting the Stage

Direct students to read the paragraph about Dr. Jester Hairston and his composition "Goin' Down That Lonesome Road." If you have the Artsource® video, have students view it.

> ## OPTIONAL
>
> **Artsource®: Performing Arts Package 1, Unit 11**
> - VHS video segment 1–6 (Playing time 9:22)

■ Connecting the Arts

Using the Discussion Questions on this page, help students recognize that people can write songs, poems, and stories that express emotions in a powerful and universal way. Possible responses are:

1. Contrast is an important tool for an artist or composer. In this case, the rhythm, tempo, and styling of the song convey a positive spirit in a song of protest.
2. Protest homework; needing more free time; or balancing fun and work.
3. Songs about social dislocation, teen suicide, and child abuse are usually of universal concern.

■ Extensions

- Have students complete the Creative Expressions activities.
- Encourage students to share experiences and knowledge about songs or rap music that deals with protest in a variety of ways.
- Use Artsource®: Performing Arts Package 1, Unit 11, for additional related activities.

■ Setting the Stage

Direct students to read about Noibuko Miyamoto and her piece "Joanne is My Middle Name." If you have the Artsource® tape, have students view it.

OPTIONAL

Artsource®: Performing Arts Package 1, Unit 12

- VHS video segment 1-7 (Playing time 13:25)

■ Connecting the Arts

Use the Discussion Questions to help students recognize the role of both music and storytelling in telling stories and conveying the emotional impact behind them. Possible responses are:

1. Pros: sense of fitting in to the American culture more easily; people will be more able to recognize and pronounce your name. Cons: giving up your cultural identity as well as a name you are used to being called.

2. Names distinguish us from others and are closely associated with who we are; they also connect us to our mother, father, husband, wife, and siblings.

3. A name can identify you with a specific culture, and you can feel the pride of being part of that heritage.

■ Extensions

- Have students complete the Creative Expression Activities.
- Use Artsource®: Performing Arts Package 1, Unit 12, for more information.

Nobuko Miyamoto and members of Great Leap. "Joanne Is My Middle Name" from *A Slice of Rice.*

For "Joanne Is My Middle Name," Nobuko Miyamoto went deep inside herself to dramatize the dilemma of being a third generation Japanese-American searching for a way to belong. She found the theme of trying to adapt her name and examined her trail of name changes. As a young girl, she connected with the magic of the arts through music, which in turn awakened her passion to dance and dramatically tell stories. This song/story begins with her childhood experiences of living in Japanese internment camps during World War II. It continues through her various rites of passage to the acceptance of her heritage and her name.

■ DISCUSSION QUESTIONS

1. Many immigrants who come to this country change their names in order to fit into the American culture. Discuss the pros and cons of doing this.
2. Discuss the symbolic importance of names in relationship to our identity. What do names tell about us? Where did your name come from? Were you named after a relative or famous person? What do you feel that your name tells about you?
3. Make a list of the names of people in your class and what cultural heritage they represent. What are the advantages of having a name which in some way connects you to your heritage?

■ CREATIVE EXPRESSION ACTIVITIES

Language Arts Ask your parents how your name was chosen for you, and find out any interesting background related to your name and its original history. Write down this information, and then write your feelings about your name.

Theatre Assume the role of playwright and write a monologue or solo speech about an important event in your life. There should be a beginning, middle, climax, and conclusion with a clear emotional progression. Use the script for a classroom presentation.

Appreciating the Performing Arts

Theatre Personal stories are often the basis for plays and theatre works. Families and relatives know many stories about our personal histories that are rich in culture and tradition and give us a sense of our past and an indication of our future. Immigration stories, stories of courtship and marriage, travel stories, and tales of crisis all provide a wealth of material for storytelling. When people write from the real and specific events of their own life with authentic emotional responses, they will touch the hearts and minds of others across culture, age, gender, and time. Our personal stories connect us to the universal themes that are a part of the human experience.

Paul Salamunovich, Director of the Los Angeles Master Chorale.
Photo: Robert Millard, Courtesy of the Los Angeles Master Chorale.

Paul Salamunovich is the Director of the Los Angeles Master Chorale. The job of a choral director is to guide a choir, made up of individual voices, to collectively capture the mood of each piece they sing. A choral conductor serves, in a sense, as a translator. According to Salamunovich, the conductor must understand why the composer wrote as he or she did and the effect of that historical time and place on the work. Then he works to accurately interpret the intent, meaning, and technical and aesthetic requirements of the music.

■ DISCUSSION QUESTIONS

1. Have you ever been in a choir or heard a choir perform? Discuss the things that you think a choir member must do to successfully contribute to the group effort.
2. "America" is a song of celebration of our American history. What other songs do you know that celebrate American life or the qualities of other cultures?
3. Discuss the importance of "America" as one of our country's most loved and respected patriotic songs. Name occasions when this song is sung or played.

■ CREATIVE EXPRESSION ACTIVITIES

Music Experiment in combining vocal sounds with a partner or in a small group, seeing how you can transform the isolated vocal sounds into music.

Language Arts Think of something that you would like to celebrate, and write lyrics or a poem to express your feelings of joy, pride, and honor. Think of words and images that could be metaphors for your feelings, for example, rockets burst forth from my heart; rainbows paint over this day; my thoughts take wings.

Performing Arts Handbook **325**

Appreciating the Performing Arts

Music "America" is one of our most revered, patriotic songs. Regretfully, it is often performed in a very perfunctory manner, with little thought given to its meaning or how to sing it expressively. It is the job of a choir director to study a piece of music carefully and to find an arrangement that incorporates the elements of music in such a way as to inspire and touch the emotions of an audience. Under the thoughtful and sensitive direction of Paul Salamunovich, Robert Hunter's arrangement of "America" provides a beautiful setting for this inspiring song of praise. A song may be well written, but the experience of hearing it can be greatly enhanced when it is arranged well and sung by a great choir.

PERFORMING ARTS

A R T
S ● U
R C ■
ARTSOURCE

Theatre   *The Children's Theatre Company*

■ **Setting the Stage**

Direct students to read about The Children's Theatre Company and the play, *The Story of Babar, the Little Elephant.* If you have the Artsource® video, share it with your students.

┌─────────────────────────┐
│ **O P T I O N A L**   │
│   │
│ **Artsource®:**   │
│ **Performing Arts**   │
│ **Package 1, Unit 14**   │
│ • VHS video segment 1–8 │
│   (Playing time 5:00)   │
└─────────────────────────┘

■ **Connecting the Arts**

Using the Discussion Questions on this page, help students recognize that children's books are a collaboration of text and illustrations. Possible responses are:

1. Design style, how an actor would move in the costume, breathe, and see.

2. Know the actor's dimensions. Does the character walk on all fours or two legs?

3. Make a list of scenes in the play and the characters in each one. Plan the main plot event that takes place in each scene. Then evaluate whether the existing dialogue in the book successfully achieves each scene's objective. Add additional dialogue to make each scene come alive for an audience. Think how song and movement carry the plot forward.

■ **Extensions**

• Have students complete the Creative Expression Activities.
• Use Artsource®: Performing Arts Package 1, Unit 14, for more information.

326

The Children's Theatre Company. *The Story of Babar, the Little Elephant.* 1996 Season. Courtesy of the Children's Theatre Company.

The Children's Theatre Company in Minneapolis, Minnesota is known for its ability to vividly re-create the storybook page on stage. The play featured on this page is *The Story of Babar, the Little Elephant,* based on the children's story by Jean de Brunhoff. The biggest challenge in bringing a book off the page and onto the stage lies in expanding two-dimensional art to three dimensions. In this case, it was important to create an accurate scale of the elephant characters to the human ones. The costumes for Babar and his elephant friends needed to look exactly like those in the book but be flexible enough so the actors could move and dance! The play's creative team left nothing to chance, inventing action and dances for every scene in the story.

┌───┐
│ ■ **DISCUSSION QUESTIONS**   ■ **CREATIVE EXPRESSION ACTIVITIES** │
│   │
│ 1. Select a specific animal as a character in   **Language Arts**   Read *The Story of Babar, the* │
│   a play. If you were a costume designer,   *Little Elephant,* or another book in the Babar │
│   how might you go about creating a   series such as *Travels of Babar* or *Babar the* │
│   costume that would transform a person   *King.* Divide the book up into different scenes │
│   into this animal? What would you have   that could be portrayed in a play. │
│   to consider?   │
│ 2. How might you actually construct a cos-   **Visual Arts/Theatre**   Design a basic struc- │
│   tume for your animal?   ture for the animal costume. Consider such │
│ 3. Think about how short a children's book   things as weight and frame, and the mathe- │
│   is. When you bring it from the page to the   matical proportions of the different pieces. │
│   stage, how would you go about creating   Draw to correct scale, and make suggestions │
│   additional dialogue, songs, and dances   for types of materials and fabrics to be used. │
│   for a dramatic performance?   │
└───┘

326   *Performing Arts Handbook*

┌───┐
│ **Appreciating the Performing Arts**   │
│   │
│   **Theatre**   *The Story of Babar, the Little Ele-*   fleeing from the jungle to escape the hunter who killed │
│   *phant,* is the first book in the series by   his mother. Young Babar arrives in Paris as a stranger │
│   French author/illustrator Jean de Brunhoff.   and is befriended by a rich old lady who introduces him │
│ It was inspired by a bedtime story which his wife,   to the life of a sophisticated Parisian. Babar assimilates │
│ Cecile, made up to tell their children. Jean took his wife's French culture and learns to speak the language. When │
│ simple tale, expanded it, and painted illustrations to   he returns to his jungle home, Babar is crowned the new │
│ accompany each scene. As the story unfolds, Babar is   elephant King with his Queen Celeste. │
└───┘

Artists and Their Works

Artists and Their Works

F

Fish, Janet, American, 1939–, painter
Spring Evening, 18, *Fig. 1–18*

Freckelton, Sondra, American, 1936–, painter
Winter Melon with Quilt and Basket, 27, *Fig. 2–3*

G

Gabo, Naum, American, 1890–1977, sculptor
Linear Construction No. 4, 70, *Fig. 4–7*

Garza, Carmen Lomas, American, 1948–, painter
Cumpleaños de Lala y Tudi, 254, *Fig. 13–12*
Sandia/Watermelon, 114, *Fig. 6–12*

Gentileschi, Orazio, Italian, 1563–1639, painter
Young Woman with a Violin, 93, *Fig. 5–13*

Glackens, William, American, 1870–1938, painter
Maypole, Central Park, 242, *Fig. 13–1*

Goya, Francisco, Spanish, 1746–1828, painter
The Sleep of Reason, 51, *Fig. 3–12*

Gris, Juan, Spanish, 1887–1927, painter
Max Jacob, 310, *Fig. S–5*

Grossman, Rhoda, American, 1941–, electronic art
Self-Portrait After Escher, 56, *Fig. 3–18*

Gutierrez, Marina, Puerto Rican, 1954–, painter
Biography, 226, *Fig. 12–4*

H

Haas, Richard, American, 1936–, mural painter
Chicago Building, 234, *Fig. 12–12*

Hals, Frans, Dutch, 1585–1666, painter
Portrait of an Elderly Lady, 145, *Fig. 8–3*

Hardin, Helen, Native American, 1943–1984, painter
Robed Journey of the Rainbow Clan, 9, *Fig. 1–10*

Hardouin-Mansart, Jules, French, 1646–1708, architect
The Hall of Mirrors at the Palace at Versailles, 168, *Fig. 9–6*

Harnett, William Michael, American (b. County Cork, Ireland), 1848–1892, painter
Attention, Company!, 142, *Fig. 8–1*

Heade, Martin Johnson, American, 1819–1904, painter
Cattleya Orchid and Three Brazilian Hummingbirds, 133, *Fig. 7–11*

Heem, Jan Davidsz de, Dutch, 1606–1683, painter
Vase of Flowers, 62, *Fig. 4–1*

Hicks, Edward, American, 1780–1849, painter
The Peaceable Kingdom, 140

Hockney, David, English, 1937–, painter
Mulholland Drive: The Road to the Studio, 176, *Fig. 9–15*

Hokusai, Katsushika, Japanese, 1760–1849, printmaker, painter
Fishing Boats at Choshi in Shoshu, 32, *Fig. 2–8*
A Gust of Wind at Ejiri, 117, *Fig. 6–15*

Holzer, J. A., American, mosaics in the Marquette Building, 212, *Fig. 11–10*

Homer, Winslow, American, 1836–1910, painter
Crossing the Pasture, 66, 67, 68, *Figs. 4–5, 4–6a, 4–6b*
The Gulf Stream, 177, *Fig. 9–16*

Hooch, Pieter de, Dutch, 1629–after 1684, painter
A Woman Preparing Bread and Butter for a Boy, 64, *Fig. 4–2*

Hopper, Edward, American, 1882–1967, painter
Night Hawks, 72, *Fig. 4–8*

Howland, Alfred Cornelius, American, 1838–1909, painter
The Fourth of July, 244, *Fig. 13–2*

J

Joe, L., Native American, mixed-media artist
Eagle Kachina, 230, *Fig. 12–8*

Johnston, Frank, Canadian, 1888–1949, painter
Fire-Swept Algoma, 120

Johnson, Philip, American, 1906–, architect
AT&T Building, 173, *Fig. 9–12*

K

Kabotie, Fred, Native American, 1900–1986, painter
Pueblo Green Corn Dance, Hopi, 248, *Fig. 13–6*

Kallaugher, Kevin, American, 1955–, cartoonist
Pandora's Ballot Box, 210, *Fig. 11–8*

Kelly, Ellsworth, American, 1923–, painter, sculptor
Spectrum II, 306, *Fig. S–1*

Klimt, Gustav, Austrian, 1862–1918, painter
Sleeping Boy, 42, *Fig. 3–2*

L

Lawrence, Jacob, American, 1917–, painter
Study for the Munich Olympic Games Poster, 205, *Fig. 11–3*

Leonard, Charles, American, 1944–, printmaker
Yellowfin Tuna, 130, *Fig. 7–8*

Glossary

A

Abstract   Having a recognizable subject that is shown in an unrealistic manner. (Ch. 4–6)

Adenla (uh-**den**-luh)   A sculpted ceremonial headdress used in rites of passage. (Ch. 13–5)

Aesthetics (es-**thet**-iks)   The study of the nature of beauty and art. (Ch. 4–1)

Aesthetic view   An idea or school of thought on what is most important in a work of art. (Ch. 4–1)

Ancestor figure   An image carved in wood that was used as the resting place of a spirit. (Ch. 8–5)

Applied art   Works of art made to be useful as well as visually pleasing. (Chs. 5–1, 10–5)

Appliqué (ap-lih-**kay**)   An art form in which cutout shapes are attached to a larger surface. (Ch. 7–3)

Architects   Artists who plan and create buildings. (Ch. 9–2)

Architectural rendering   A detailed, realistic two-dimensional representation of a proposed three-dimensional structure. (Ch. 14–5)

Architecture   The art of planning and creating buildings. (Ch. 5–5)

Art critic   A person whose job is studying, understanding, and judging works of art. (Ch. 4–2)

Art historians   People who study art of different ages and cultures. (Ch. 5–1)

Artist   A person who uses imagination and skill to communicate ideas in visual form. (Ch. 1–1)

Art medium   A material used to create a work of art. (Ch. 3–1)

Art movement   A trend formed when a group of artists band together. (Ch. 5–7)

Assemblage (ah-sem-**blahzh**)   A three-dimensional artwork consisting of many pieces assembled together. (Ch. 6–2)

B

Balance   A principle of art concerned with arranging the elements so that no one part of the work overpowers, or seems heavier than, any other part. (Ch. 2–1)

Belvedere (**bel**-vuh-deer)   A building designed to provide a view of its surroundings. (Ch. 14–5)

Binder   A liquid that holds together the grains of pigment. (Ch. 3–3)

Bust   A sculpture that shows a person's head, shoulders, and upper chest. (Ch. 5–1)

C

Calligraphy (kuh-**lig**-ruh-fee)   The art of beautiful writing. (Ch. 7–5)

Camcorder   A small hand-held video camera. (Ch. 11–7)

Caricature (**kar**-ih-kuh-chur)   A humorous drawing that exaggerates features of a person to make fun of or criticize him or her. (Ch. 11–4)

Cartouche (kar-**toosh**)   An oval or oblong containing an important person's name. (Ch. 12–1)

Cityscape   A drawing or painting focusing on large buildings and other objects found in cities. (Ch. 9–5)

Color   What the eye sees when light is reflected off an object. (Ch. 1–3)

Columns   Vertical posts that rise to support another structure. (Ch. 9–4)

Composition   The way the principles are used to organize the elements of art. (Ch. 4–1)

Content   The message, idea, or feeling expressed by a work of art. (Ch. 4–1)

Contour drawing   Drawing an object as though your drawing tool is moving along all the edges and ridges of the form. (Handbook)

Contours   Outlines and surface ridges. (Ch. 5–2)

Credit line   A listing of important facts about an artwork. (Ch. 4–2)

Cutaway   A view in which an outside wall has been removed to reveal the scene within. (Ch. 12–5)

D

Diorama (dy-uh-**ram**-uh)   A scenic representation in which miniature sculptures and other objects are displayed against a painted backdrop. (Ch. 5–6)

E

Eight, The   A group of American realists who worked at the beginning of the twentieth century. (Ch. 9–6)

Elements of art   The basic visual symbols an artist uses to create works of art. (Ch 1–1)

Elevation   A drawing of an outside view of a building. (Ch. 9–4)

Glossary   **331**

Glossary

Embroidery The art of making ornamental designs with needle and thread. (Ch. 12–5)

Emphasis Making an element or an object in a work stand out. (Ch. 2–3)

Environment Surroundings. (Ch. 7–1)

Façade (fuh-**sahd**) The front of a building. (Ch. 9–4)

Fantasy art Art that focuses on make-believe or imaginary subjects. (Ch. 14–1)

Figure study A drawing that focuses on the human form. (Ch. 8–3)

Fine art Art made to be enjoyed visually, not used. (Ch. 5–1)

Folk art Art made by artists who have had no formal training. (Ch. 7–8)

Font Typeface. (Ch. 12–8)

Form An element of art that refers to an object with three dimensions. (Ch. 1–5)

Fresco (**fres**-koh) A painting created when pigment is applied to a section of wall spread with fresh plaster. (Ch. 12–5)

Frieze (**freez**) A decorative band running across the upper part of a wall. (Ch. 11–5)

Gesture drawing Moving a drawing medium quickly and freely over a surface to capture the form and actions of a subject. (Ch. 3–2)

Gold leaf A very thin layer of gold glued to a surface for decoration. (Ch. 12–7)

Gouache (**gwash**) A form of watercolor that uses non-clear pigments. (Ch. 11–1)

Harmony Combining the elements of art to accent their similarities. (Ch. 2–3)

Hieroglyphic (hy-ruh-**glif**-ik) An early form of picture writing. (Ch. 5–2)

Hue A color's name. (Ch. 1–3)

Illumination Hand-painted book illustration. (Ch. 7–5)

Intaglio (in-**tahl**-yoh) A printmaking technique in which the image to be printed is cut or scratched into a surface. (Ch. 3–5)

Intensity The brightness or dullness of a hue. (Ch. 1–3)

Jewelry Art, and the craft of making art, to be worn. (Ch. 10–7)

Juxtapose (**juks**-tuh-pohz) Place side by side. (Ch. 14–3)

Kachina (kuh-**chee**-nuh) Hand-crafted statuette that represents spirits in Pueblo rituals. (Ch. 12–4)

Kiln A special hot oven in which pottery objects are fired. (Ch. 10–6)

Kinetic (kuh-**net**-ik) **art** An art style in which parts of a work are set into motion by a form of energy. (Ch. 13–4)

Landscape A drawing or painting of mountains, trees, or other natural scenery. (Ch. 6–1)

Line The path of a dot through space. (Ch. 1–2)

Line quality The unique character of any line. (Ch. 1–2)

Mascot An animal or person used by a group as a sign of luck. (Ch. 7–1)

Monoprint A print made by applying ink or paint to a plate and then transferring the image by hand-rubbing. (Ch. 6–7)

Mosaic (moh-**zay**-ik) Small bits of colored glass and jewels set in cement. (Ch. 11–5)

Movement The principle of art that leads the viewer to sense action in a work, or it can be the path the viewer's eye follows through the work. (Ch. 2–4)

Murals Large two-dimensional works painted on walls. (Ch. 8–7)

Nature study A drawing used to help artists sharpen their perception of natural objects. (Ch. 6–3)

Negative space   Empty spaces between the shapes or forms in two- and three-dimensional art. (Ch. 1–5)

Non-objective   Having no readily identifiable subjects or objects. (Ch. 4–3)

Old Stone Age   The historical period that occurred between 30,000 and 10,000 B.C. (Ch. 7–1)

Painted screen   An art object used as a wall or room divider. (Ch. 5–3)

Pan   A slow, steady, sideways movement of the video camera to capture details in a panorama. (Ch. 11–8)

Panorama   A complete view of an area in all directions. (Ch. 9–7)

Pendant   A jewelry item worn suspended from the neck on a string or chain. (Ch. 10–5)

Perception   An awareness of the elements of an environment by means of the senses. (Ch. 3–1)

Perceive   Become aware through the senses of the special nature of objects. (Ch. 10–1)

Petroglyph (**peh**-truh-glif)   Symbolic rock carving or painting. (Ch. 12–1)

Photography   The art of making images by exposing a chemically treated surface to light. (Ch. 11–1)

Pictogram   A small picture that stands for a word or an idea. (Ch. 12–1)

Picture plane   The flat surface of a painting or drawing. (Ch. 2–3)

Pigment   A finely ground powder that gives paint its color. (Ch. 3–3)

Point of view   The angle from which the viewer sees the scene in an artwork. (Ch. 4–4)

Porcelain (**por**-suh-lihn)   A fine-grained, high-quality form of pottery. (Ch. 7–3)

Portfolio   A carefully selected collection of artwork kept by students and professional artists. (Ch. 1–Opening)

Portrait   A visual representation of a person at rest. (Ch. 3–4)

Portraiture (**pohr**-tray-chur)   The art of making portraits. (Ch. 8–5)

Pottery   Art, and the craft of making art, from clay. (Ch. 10–6)

Principles of art   Guidelines that govern the way artists organize the elements of art. (Ch. 2–1)

Printmaking   Transferring an image from an inked surface to create a work of art. (Ch. 3–5)

Proportion   How parts of a work relate to each other and to the whole. (Ch. 2–3)

Public art   Art to be displayed in and enjoyed by a community. (Ch. 8–7)

Pueblo (**pweh**-bloh)   Dried-clay dwelling. (Ch. 13–3)

Renaissance (**ren**-uh-sahns)   Period of rebirth. (Ch. 5–5)

Resist   An art medium, such as crayon, that serves as a protective coating. (Ch. 6–6)

Rhythm   The repetition of an element to make a work seem active. (Ch. 2–4)

Rococo (roh-**koh**-koh)   An art style of the 1700s that emphasized graceful movement, curving lines, and delicate colors. (Ch. 9–3)

Sculpture   A three-dimensional work of art. (Ch. 3–6)

Seal   Symbolic image or emblem. (Ch. 13–1)

Seascape   A drawing or painting of the ocean and objects found on or around it. (Ch. 9–7)

Self-portrait   A painting or drawing of an artist's own image. (Ch. 8–1)

Shadow puppet   An art object in the shape of an animal or human attached to a wand or a stick. (Ch. 13–4)

Shape   An area clearly set off by one or more of the other five visual elements of art. (Ch. 1–5)

Sketchbook   A pad of drawing paper on which artists sketch, write notes, and refine ideas for their work. (Ch. 2–Opening)

Slip   Clay with enough added water to give it a runny, liquid consistency. (Ch. 10–6)

Social protest painting   An art style dedicated to attacking the ills of big-city life. (Ch. 14–4)

Solvent   A liquid used to control the thickness or thinness of the paint. (Ch. 3–3)

Glossary

Space   The distance or area between, around, above, below, and within things. (Ch. 1–5)

Staged photograph   A photographic composition that makes use of artificial images or processes. (Ch. 9–1)

Still life   A painting or drawing of nonliving objects. (Ch. 1–5)

Story board   A frame-by-frame plan of a video production. (Ch. 11–7)

Study   A drawing used to plan a painting or other large project. (Ch. 6–3)

Style   An artist's personal way of using the elements and principles of art to express feelings and ideas. (Ch. 8–1)

Stylized   Simplified or exaggerated. (Ch. 6–1)

Subject   An image viewers can easily identify. (Ch. 4–1)

Surrealists   The group of artists who explored the realm of dreams and the subconscious. (Ch. 14–1)

Symbol   An image used to stand for a quality or an idea. (Chs. 5–2, 7–7)

Tapestry   A woven wall hanging with decorative designs or colorful scenes. (Ch. 7–7)

Texture   How things feel, or look as though they might feel if touched. (Ch. 1–7)

Totem   An object that serves as an emblem or respected symbol. (Ch. 7–2)

Trait   A personal characteristic. (Ch. 7–1)

Tricolor   A flag with three broad bands of color. (Ch. 13–1)

Trompe-l'oeil (trohmp-**loy**)   A style of painting in which objects are depicted with photographically realistic detail. (Ch. 8–5)

Unity   The arrangement of elements and principles of art to create a feeling of completeness or wholeness. (Ch. 2–6)

Value   The lightness or darkness of a hue. (Ch. 1–3)

Variety   Combining one or more elements of art to create interest. (Ch. 2–3)

Vessel   A hollow utensil made to hold something. (Ch. 10–5)

Video documentary   An in-depth study of a person, place, thing, or event. (Ch. 11–7)

Videographer   Person who operates a video camera. (Ch. 11–8)

Watercolorist   A painter who works in watercolor. (Ch. 10–4)

Glosario

A

Abstract/Abstracto   Mostrar un sujeto reconocible de forma no realista. (Cap. 4–6)

Adenla/Adenla   Tocado ceremonial usado en rituales de transición. (Cap. 13–5)

Aesthetics/Estética   Estudio de la naturaleza de la belleza y el arte. (Cap. 4–1)

Aesthetic view/Punto de vista estético   Idea o escuela de pensamiento sobre qué es lo más importante en una obra de arte. (Cap. 4–1)

Ancestor figure/Figurín de un ancestro   Imagen tallada en madera que se usaba como el lugar de descanso de un espíritu. (Cap. 8–5)

Applied art/Arte aplicado   Obras de arte hechas con un fin utilitario además de ser agradables a la vista. (Caps. 5–1, 10–5)

Appliqué/Appliqué   Forma de arte en la que se adhieren recortes de material a una superficie más grande. (Cap. 7–3)

Architects/Arquitectos   Artistas que planean y crean edificios. (Cap. 9–2)

Architectural rendering/Perspectiva arquitectónica realista   Representación bidimensional realista y detallada de una estructura tridimensional propuesta. (Cap. 14–5)

Architecture/Arquitectura   Arte de planear y crear edificios. (Cap. 5–5)

Art critic/Crítico de arte   Aquel que se ocupa de estudiar, comprender y juzgar obras de arte. (Cap. 4–2)

Art historians/Historiadores del arte   Aquellos que se ocupan de estudiar el arte de las distintas épocas y culturas. (Cap. 5–1)

Artist/Artista plástico   Aquel que usa su imaginación y su habilidad para comunicar ideas de una forma visual. (Cap. 1–1)

Art medium/Medio artístico   Material utilizado en la creación de una obra de arte. (Cap. 3–1)

Art movement/Movimiento artístico   Tendencia que se manifiesta cuando se une un grupo de artistas. (Cap. 5–7)

Assemblage/Assemblage   Obra de arte tridimensional que consiste de muchas piezas ensambladas entre sí. (Cap. 6–2)

B

Balance/Equilibrio   Principio del arte que se refiere al arreglo de los elementos de manera tal que ninguna parte de la obra abrume o parezca más pesada que cualquier otra parte. (Cap. 2–1)

Belvedere/Mirador   Edificio diseñado para proveer una vista de sus alrededores. (Cap. 14–5)

Binder/Sustancia aglutinante   Líquido que une los granos de pigmento. (Cap. 3–3)

Bust/Busto   Escultura que muestra la cabeza, hombros y parte superior del pecho de una persona. (Cap. 5–1)

C

Calligraphy/Caligrafía   El arte de escribir con letra bella. (Cap. 7–5)

Camcorder/Cámara de video   Cámara de video pequeña y manuable. (Cap. 11–7)

Caricature/Caricatura   Dibujo humorístico que exagera los rasgos de una persona para ridiculizarla o criticarla. (Cap. 11–4)

Cartouche/Tarjeta   Forma oval u oblonga donde está inscripto el nombre de una persona importante. (Cap. 12–1)

Cityscape/Paisaje urbano   Dibujo o pintura que muestra grandes edificios y otros objetos que se hallan en las ciudades. (Cap. 9–5)

Color/Color   Lo que ve el ojo cuando la luz se refleja de un objeto. (Cap. 1–3)

Columns/Columnas   Postes verticales que se elevan para proveer apoyo a otra estructura. (Cap. 9–4)

Composition/Composición   Forma en que se utilizan los principios para organizar los elementos del arte. (Cap. 4–1)

Content/Contenido   Mensaje, idea o sentimiento expresado por una obra de arte. (Cap. 4–1)

Contour drawing/Dibujo de contorno   Dibujar un objeto como si el instrumento de dibujo delineara los bordes y líneas en la supersicie de la forma. (Technique Tips Handbook)

Contours/Contornos   Bordes y aristas de una superficie. (Cap. 5–2)

Credit line/Resumen de datos   Listado de información importante acerca de una obra de arte. (Cap. 4–2)

Cutaway/Sección   Vista en la que se ha quitado una pared exterior para mostrar la escena del interior. (Cap. 12–5)

Glosario

Diorama/Maqueta Representación de una escena en la que esculturas en miniatura y otros objetos se muestran contra un fondo pintado. (Cap. 5–6)

Eight, The/Los Ocho Grupo de realistas estadounidenses que trabajaron a principios del siglo veinte. (Cap. 9–6)

Elements of art/Elementos del arte Los símbolos visuales básicos que usa un artista para crear obras de arte. (Cap. 1–1)

Elevation/Alzado Dibujo de la fachada de un edificio. (Cap. 9–4)

Embroidery/Bordado Arte de realizar diseños decorativos con aguja e hilo. (Cap. 12–5)

Emphasis/Énfasis Hacer que resalte un elemento o un objeto en una obra. (Cap. 2–3)

Environment/Ambiente Lo que rodea algo. (Cap. 7–1)

Façade/Fachada El frente de un edificio. (Cap. 9–4)

Fantasy art/Arte de fantasía Arte que se enfoca en sujetos ficticios o imaginarios. (Cap. 14–1)

Figure study/Estudio de figuras Dibujo que se enfoca en la figura humana. (Cap. 8–3)

Fine art/Bellas artes Obras hechas para el disfrute visual, no para ser utilizadas. (Cap. 5–1)

Folk art/Arte folklórico Obras realizadas por artistas que no han tenido entrenamiento formal. (Cap. 7–8)

Font/Fundición Conjunto de todos los moldes o letras de un tipo para imprimir. (Cap. 12–8)

Form/Forma Elemento del arte que se refiere a un objeto con tres dimensiones. (Cap. 1–5)

Fresco/Fresco Pintura creada al aplicar pigmento a una sección de una pared revocada con yeso fresco. (Cap. 12–5)

Frieze/Friso Banda decorativa ubicada a lo largo de la parte superior de una pared. (Cap. 11–5)

Gesture drawing/Dibujo de gestos Mover un instrumento de dibujo en forma rápida y espontánea sobre una superficie para captar la forma y las acciones de un sujeto. (Cap. 3–2)

Gold leaf/Dorado a la hoja Una capa fina de oro adherida a una superficie con fines decorativos. (Cap. 12–7)

Gouache/Aguada Un tipo de acuarela que usa pigmentos no transparentes. (Cap. 11–1)

Harmony/Armonía Combinar los elementos del arte para acentuar sus similitudes. (Cap. 2–3)

Hieroglyphic/Jeroglífico Forma antigua de escritura por medio de dibujos. (Cap. 5–2)

Hue/Tono El nombre de un color. (Cap. 1–3)

Illumination/Iluminación Ilustración-a-mano de libros. (Cap. 7–5)

Intaglio/Entallar Técnica de impresión en la cual se raspa o se corta sobre una superficie la imagen que ha de imprimirse. (Cap. 3–5)

Intensity/Intensidad Luminosidad u opacidad de un matiz. (Cap. 1–3)

Jewelry/Joyería Arte y oficio de realizar obras de arte que se llevan puestas. (Cap. 10–7)

Juxtapose/Yuxtaponer Poner lado a lado. (Cap. 14–3)

Kachina/Kachina Estatuilla hecha a mano que representa a los espíritus en los ritos de la cultura Pueblo. (Cap. 12–4)

Kiln/Horno Horno especial para cocinar objetos de alfarería. (Cap. 10–6)

Kinetic art/Arte cinético Estilo artístico en el que se ponen en movimiento partes de una obra por medio de energía. (Cap. 13–4)

Landscape/Paisaje Dibujo o pintura de montañas, árboles u otra escena natural. (Cap. 6–1)

Line/Línea La trayectoria de un punto a través del espacio. (Cap. 1–2)

Line quality/Cualidad de la línea El carácter único de cualquier línea. (Cap. 1–2)

M

Mascot/Mascota   Animal o persona utilizados por un grupo como signo de buena suerte. (Cap. 7–1)

Monoprint/Monocopia   Estampa hecha al aplicar tinta o pintura sobre una plancha y luego transferir la imagen frotando con la mano. (Cap. 6–7)

Mosaic/Mosaico   Pequeños trozos de vidrio de colores y joyas asentados sobre cemento. (Cap. 11–5)

Movement/Movimiento   Principio del arte que hace que el espectador vea acción en una obra; o la trayectoria que sigue el ojo al mirar una obra. (Cap. 2–4)

Murals/Murales   Obras bidimensionales grandes pintadas sobre paredes. (Cap. 8–7)

N

Nature study/Estudio del natural   Dibujo utilizado para ayudar al artista a realzar su percepción de los objetos naturales. (Cap. 6–3)

Negative space/Espacio negativo   Espacios vacíos entre las formas o figuras de una obra bidimensional o tridimensional. (Cap. 1–5)

Non-objective/No objetivo   Que no tiene sujetos u objetos inmediatamente identificables. (Cap. 4–3)

O

Old Stone Age/Edad de Piedra   El período histórico que abarca del año 30,000 al 10,000 [A.C.] (Cap. 7–1)

P

Painted screen/Biombo   Objeto de arte utilizado como pared o para dividir una habitación. (Cap. 5–3)

Pan/Toma panorámica   Movimiento lateral lento y regular de la cámara de video para captar los detalles de un paisaje. (Cap. 11–8)

Panorama/Panorama   Vista completa de un área en todas las direcciones. (Cap. 9–7)

Pendant/Pendiente   Artículo de joyería que se lleva alrededor del cuello colgado de un hilo o cadena. (Cap. 10–5)

Perception/Percepción   Toma de conciencia de los elementos de un ambiente por medio de los sentidos. (Cap. 3–1)

Perceive/Percibir   Tomar conciencia a través de los sentidos de la naturaleza particular de los objetos. (Cap. 10–1)

Petroglyph/Petroglifo   Grabado o pintura simbólicos sobre una piedra. (Cap. 12–1)

Photography/Fotografía   Arte de hacer imágenes al exponer a la luz una superficie tratada con sustancias químicas. (Cap. 11–1)

Pictogram/Pictograma   Figura pequeña que representa una palabra o una idea. (Cap. 12–1)

Picture plane/Plano   La superficie plana de una pintura o dibujo. (Cap. 2–3)

Pigment/Pigmento   Polvo fino molido que da color a la pintura. (Cap. 3–3)

Point of view/Punto de vista   Ángulo desde el cual el espectador ve la escena de una obra de arte. (Cap. 4–4)

Porcelain/Porcelana   Forma de alfalería de grano fino y alta calidad. (Cap. 7–3)

Portfolio/Carpeta de trabajos   Colección cuidadosamente seleccionada de obras que tienen los estudiantes y artistas profesionales. (Cap. 1–Introducción)

Portrait/Retrato   Representación visual de una persona en reposo. (Cap. 3–4)

Portraiture/Pintura de retratos   El arte de hacer retratos. (Cap. 8–5)

Pottery/Alfarería   Arte y oficio de hacer objetos de arte con arcilla. (Cap. 10–6)

Principles of art/Principios del arte   Lineamientos que gobiernan el modo en que los artistas organizan los elementos del arte. (Cap. 2–1)

Printmaking/Grabado   Acción de transferir la imagen desde una superficie cubierta de tinta para crear una obra de arte. (Cap. 3–5)

Proportion/Proporción   Manera en que las partes de una obra se relacionan entre sí y con el todo. (Cap. 2–3)

Public art/Arte público   Obra de arte expuesta para el disfrute de una comunidad. (Cap. 8–7)

Pueblo/Pueblo   Vivienda de arcilla reseca. (Cap. 13–3)

R

Renaissance/Renacimiento   Period de renacimiento. (Cap. 5–5)

Resist/Capa protectora   Medio artístico que sirve como capa impermeable, como los lápices de cera o crayones. (Cap. 6–6)

Rhythm/Ritmo   Repetición de un elemento para que una obra parezca activa. (Cap. 2–4)

Glosario

Rococo/Rococó Estilo artístico del siglo dieciocho que enfatizaba la gracia del movimiento, las líneas curvas y los colores delicados. (Cap. 9–3)

S

Sculpture/Escultura Obra de arte tridimensional. (Cap. 3–6)

Seal/Sello Emblema o imagen simbólica. (Cap. 13–1)

Seascape/Paisaje marino Dibujo o pintura del océano y los objetos que se encuentran en él o a su alrededor. (Cap. 9–7)

Self-portrait/Autorretrato Dibujo o pintura de la imagen del propio artista. (Cap. 8–1)

Shadow puppet/Marioneta Objeto de arte de forma animal o humana unido al extremo de una varilla. (Cap. 13–4)

Shape/Contorno Área claramente delimitada por uno o más de los otros cinco elementos visuales del arte. (Cap. 1–5)

Sketchbook/Cuaderno de bocetos Bloc de papel de dibujo donde los artistas bosquejan, toman apuntes y pulen ideas para su trabajo. (Cap. 2–Introducción)

Slip/Arcilla blanda Arcilla con suficiente agua agregada como para darle una consistencia resbaladiza y blanda. (Cap. 10–6)

Social protest painting/Pintura de protesta social Estilo artístico dedicado a atacar los males de la vida en los grandes centros urbanos. (Cap. 14–4)

Solvent/Solvente Líquido usado para regular el espesor de la pintura. (Cap. 3–3)

Space/Espacio Distancia o área entre, alrededor, sobre, debajo y dentro de las cosas. (Cap. 1–5)

Staged photograph/Foto de estudio Composición fotográfica que usa imágenes o procesos artificiales. (Cap. 9–1)

Still life/Naturaleza muerta Dibujo o pintura de objetos no vivientes. (Cap. 1–5)

Story board/Tablero de historieta Plan toma por toma de una producción de video. (Cap. 11–7)

Study/Estudio Dibujo usado para planear una pintura u otro proyecto grande. (Cap. 6–3)

Style/Estilo Modo personal que tiene el artista de usar los elementos y principios del arte para expresar ideas y sentimientos. (Cap. 8–1)

Stylized/Estilizado Simplificado o exagerado. (Cap. 6–1)

Subject/Sujeto Imagen que el espectador puede identificar fácilmente. (Cap. 4–1)

Surrealists/Surrealistas Grupo de artistas que exploraron el mundo de los sueños y el subconsciente. (Cap. 14–1)

Symbol/Símbolo Imagen utilizada para representar una cualidad o una idea. (Caps. 5–2, 7–7)

T

Tapestry/Tapiz Paño tejido con diseños decorativos o escenas coloridas que se cuelga de la pared. (Cap. 7–7)

Texture/Textura La forma en que algo se siente al tocarlo, o como parece que se sentiría al tocarlo. (Cap. 1–7)

Totem/Tótem Un objeto que sirve como emblema o símbolo respetado. (Cap. 7–2)

Trait/Rasgo Característica personal. (Cap. 7–1)

Tricolor/Tricolor Una bandera con tres franjas anchas de color. (Cap. 13–1)

Trompe-l'oeil/Trompe-l'oeil Estilo de pintura en que se representa a los objetos detalladamente, con realismo fotográfico. (Cap. 8–5)

U

Unity/Unidad El arreglo de elementos y principios del arte para lograr una sensación de consumación y totalidad. (Cap. 2–6)

V

Value/Opacidad La claridad u oscuridad de un color. (Cap. 1–3)

Variety/Variedad Combinar uno o más elementos del arte para generar interés. (Cap. 2–3)

Vessel/Recipiente Utensilio cóncavo destinado a guardar algo. (Cap. 10–5)

Video documentary/Documental de video Estudio en profundidad de una persona, lugar, cosa o evento. (Cap. 11–7)

Videographer/Camarógrafo Persona que opera una cámara de video. (Cap. 11–8)

W

Watercolorist/Acuarelista Pintor que trabaja con acuarelas. (Cap. 10–4)

Bibliography and Resource List

The following resources provide information in various areas of art and education. The entries are organized by subject and each title is followed by a brief description to help you choose the subjects you wish to read about.

Art History

Anderson, Bjork. *Linnea in Monet's Garden.* New York: R and S Books, 1985. When Linnea visits Claude Monet's garden in Giverny, she gets to stand on the bridge over his lily pond and walk through his house. Later, when she sees his paintings in Paris, she understands what it means for a painter to be called an Impressionist. This delightful book contains photographs of Monet's paintings as well as old family snapshots.

Avi-Yonah, Michael. *Piece by Piece! Mosaics of the Ancient World.* Minneapolis, Minn.: Lerner, 1993. This book describes ancient and modern techniques as well as early Greek, Roman, and Byzantine mosaics.

Barnicoat, John. *Posters: A Concise History.* New York: Thames and Hudson, 1985. The importance of the poster, including its role in various artistic movements.

Capek, Michael. *Artistic Trickery: The Tradition of Trompe L'Oeil Art.* Minneapolis, Minn.: Lerner, 1995. From the ancient Greeks to contemporary designers, artists have long been inspired to play visual jokes. This book lets the reader in on some of the gags.

Davidson, Rosemary. *Take a Look: An Introduction to the Experience of Art.* New York: Penguin, 1993. This book introduces the history, techniques, and functions of art through discussion and reproductions of paintings, photographs, drawings, and design elements. It also includes valuable diagrams and information about seeing and looking at art.

"Introduction to the Renaissance," *Calliope: World History for Young People.* Peterborough, N.H.: Cobblestone Publishing, May/June 1994. This issue of *Calliope* deals with many aspects of the arts and sciences during the Italian Renaissance. It features articles on artists such as Michelangelo and Leonardo da Vinci, rulers such as Isabella d'Este, and composers such as Monteverdi.

Biography

Gilow, Louise. *Meet Jim Henson.* New York: Random House, 1993. The creator of the Muppets, puppet stars of television and the movies, is the subject of this biography.

Greene, Katherine, and Richard Greene. *The Man Behind the Magic: The Story of Walt Disney.* New York: Viking, 1991. This biography of Walt Disney discusses his boyhood on a Missouri farm, his struggles as a young animator, and his building of a motion picture and amusement park empire.

Heslewood, Juliet. *Introducing Picasso: Painter, Sculptor.* Boston: Little, Brown, 1993. By examining the life of the well-known modern painter and the historical and artistic influences on his work, this book gives young readers a sense of who Picasso was and how his art developed. Photographs illustrate his work and his life.

Kastner, Joseph. *John James Audubon.* New York: Harry N. Abrams, 1992. This biography chronicles the life of Audubon from his childhood in France to his adventures in the New World, and shows how he captured these adventures in his artwork.

Neimark, Ann E. *Diego Rivera: Artist of the People.* New York: HarperCollins, 1992. Diego Rivera is brought to life in this comprehensive biography. It is illustrated with reproductions of Rivera's artwork.

Newlands, Anne. *Meet Edgar Degas.* New York: Lippincott, 1988. Degas talks to the reader about 13 of his paintings, describing what it's like to be a young artist in Paris.

Careers

Gordon, Barbara. *Careers in Art: Graphic Design.* VGM Career Horizons, 1992. Provides descriptions of careers in the graphic design field including art directors, book and magazine publishers, industrial designers and production artists. Information on courses and training requirements, job opportunities, and portfolio preparation.

Kaplan, Andrew. *Careers for Artistic Types.* Brookfield, Conn.: Millbrook, 1991. The author interviews 14 people who work in careers that are of interest to young people who like art.

Bibliography and Resource List

Media and Techniques

James, Jane H. *Perspective Drawing: A Point of View.* 2d ed. Englewood Cliffs, N.J.: Prentice Hall, 1988. For students who want to learn more about perspective.

Kehoe, Michael. *A Book Takes Root: The Making of a Picture Book.* Minneapolis, Minn.: Carolrhoda, 1993. This book traces the process of making a picture book from idea to manuscript to final production. Color photographs accompany the text and make this a fun-to-read and informative book.

Lauer, David A. *Design Basics.* 2d ed. New York: Holt, Rinehart and Winston, 1985. A resource for design students.

Mayer, Ralph. *The Artist's Handbook of Materials and Techniques.* 5th ed., rev. and updated. New York: Viking-Penguin, 1991. An up-to-date reference on art materials and techniques.

Meilach, Dona Z., Jay Hinz, and Bill Hinz. *How to Create Your Own Designs: An Introduction to Color, Form and Composition.* New York: Doubleday and Co., 1975. An excellent introduction to the elements of design.

Patterson, Freeman. *Photography and the Art of Seeing.* Rev. ed. San Francisco: Sierra Club Books, 1990. This book offers good advice on creative photography and is of particular interest to the beginning photographer.

Porter, Albert W. *Expressive Watercolor Techniques.* Worcester, Mass.: Davis Publications, 1982. A useful resource with valuable information on techniques and processes.

Sheaks, Barclay. *Drawing Figures and Faces.* Worcester, Mass.: Davis Publications, 1987. A helpful resource for students who wish to expand their drawing techniques.

Weldon, Jude. *Drawing: A Young Artist's Guide.* London: Dorling Kindersley, 1994. This well-designed and beautifully illustrated book guides the young artist through a wide variety of artistic experiences. Each idea is illustrated with master drawings and paintings. Topics include light and shade, color, imagination, and storytelling.

Multimedia Resources
Laserdiscs

American Art from the National Gallery A collection of 2,600 paintings and sculpture by American artists spanning three centuries.

Louvre Compendium Includes more than 5,000 works of art and 35,000 detailed images in a three-volume series.

Videodisc Volume I: Painting and Drawings

Videodisc Volume II: Sculpture and Objets d'Art

Videodisc Volume III: Antiquities

The National Gallery of Art A guided tour of the National Gallery featuring more than 1,600 masterpieces. A printed catalog and on-screen captions identifying each work are included.

The National Gallery of Art Laserstack Use this laserstack to create your own notes or slide lists for presentations. Works may be arranged by artist, nationality, period, style, date, medium, or subject.

Regard for the Planet A resource for 50,000 photographs documenting world cultures, places, and events of the last 40 years.

CD-ROMs

Art and Music Series Focuses on art and music from medieval times to Surrealism, with text linked to 24-volume student encyclopedia and glossary. Events, challenges, and achievements of each time period are highlighted. (lab packs available) WIN & MAC

National Museum of Women in the Arts Access to 200 artworks from the collection. Available on CD-ROM or videodisc.

With Open Eyes Access to images through time line, geographical location, and close-ups. View 200 multimedia and multicultural artworks from the collection of the Art Institute of Chicago. View any object in a virtual-reality gallery to get a sense of scale. Includes games, music, poetry, and sound effects. WIN & MAC

Index

Index

Index

Credits